Liberalization, Growth and the Asian Financial Crisis

Liberalization, Growth and the Asian Financial Crisis

Lessons for Developing and Transitional Economies in Asia

Mohamed Ariff

Ahmed M. Khalid

Edward Elgar

Cheltenham, UK • Northampton, MA, USA

Published by
Edward Elgar Publishing Limited
Glensanda House
Montpellier Parade
Cheltenham
Glos GL50 1UA
UK

Edward Elgar Publishing, Inc.
136 West Street
Suite 202
Northampton
Massachusetts 01060
USA

A catalogue record for this book is available from the British Library

ISBN 1 85898 839 X

Contents

PART 5   THE LESSONS FROM LIBERALIZATION

List of figures

List of tables

Preface

The research for this book started back in 1996, a year and a half before the Asian financial crisis hit several countries included here. Major economic setbacks from the crisis created large-scale economic disorders in five of the 13 economies included in this study. The other countries, though spared the worse effects, also felt significant declines in growth at a later time, albeit not of the order experienced by the worst-hit five. In early 1999, the crisis even threatened to engulf the world. Many books appeared on the subject soon after the crisis which, incubated in July 1997 in Thailand, spread to other countries in the form of rampant speculative attacks on currencies.

Many astute comments have been made in several books by many clever persons on why the crisis hit Asian economies hitherto predicted to grow. In contrast to those books, this book offers the reader a different, long-term view which emerges from a very careful analysis of the longer-term trends in 13 Asian economies over a quarter of a century, or more in some cases. Thus the reader can differentiate this analysis from many of the popular titles on the Asian financial crisis which purport to explain what happened and, in some cases, why. But carefully documented evidence in this book points to one clear conclusion. That is, the high growth experienced by Asian economies is due to active promotion of correct economic, fiscal and financial policy responses to market demands for liberal policies. The crisis stemmed from financial excesses in those countries, creating severe financial fragility in firms and banks in the 1990s, the impacts of which pushed the economies down towards growth collapse. That is what happened in six economies. Stories of rampant corruption, connected lending, crony capitalism – perhaps *ersatz capitalism* is an apt phrase – which appeared in the popular press, while undeniably true, should not be permitted to belittle the correct things the Asian people did for many years to achieve growth at last. Recall that prosperity had eluded them in former years because of colonial exploitation and because of a general absence of peace: peace is the crucible needed for any people to initiate economic activities in the rational expectation that the fruits of their activities will improve their lot.

Those of us who can still recall the years of high growth in today's 26 developed countries will realize that this conclusion is not at all startling. High growth has occurred before, often with little or no total factor productivity gains, at some stage of economic development of today's developed economies.

High growth can happen at some growth stages, but cannot be sustained by undue reliance on short-term capital and other resource flows for too long a period, as happened in several Asian countries that are now paying a price for this excess. It is not possible to rely on external resources, it seems, when more and more economies are now increasingly adopting liberal and open-door policies. This development creates new opportunities in a globally connected world to lower production costs by constantly moving capital and other resources to where the production costs are the lowest and the rewards to capital are higher.

What is perhaps a new element in the growth formula in the Asian cases is the high dependence on non-domestic capital and (and other resource) flows, the so-called too much short-term capital argument. In some countries, such as China, Singapore and Malaysia, capital inflow (along with technology–market network) is indeed the front-running factor that ensured high growth here. But it is not so in many other economies, examples of which are Korea and Taiwan, to name just two. True, Singapore's per capita income is now 76 per cent of US per capita and China has almost tripled its GDP in 22 years. The short-term nature of these capital flows and, more importantly, as shown by us, the inadequacy of prudential central bank supervision of financial institutions against the risk of sudden withdrawals of resources have emerged as two key precipitating causes of the Asian crisis.

We provide in Chapter 2 a good deal of evidence to support these macro-economic causes of the troubles of several economies during 1997–99. The immorality of wealth concentration in Indonesia, nepotism in Thailand, cronyism in many capital cities – the reader has read about them all in the press – hastened the economic fall during a period of investment splurge in the 1990s. Exactly when the external resources were at most risk of being recalled, with declining exports, many long-serving authoritarian rulers, or rulers who organized business–government–bank connections, promoted wasteful investments, which were withdrawn rapidly when the providers of resources discovered the waste. Thus Asia's vision of continued growth dimmed for three years, and an important financial lesson was learned.

In the period before all this happened, correct responses to market demands for growth-promoting activities were the distinguishing feature of those economies that grew at high rates. Those responses were all-embracing, by which we mean that all constituents were working in the same direction. In the literature on good governance – a school of thought that sees growth as the primal cause of good governance – a *post-hoc* analysis finds growth situations *coinciding* with good governance. Therefore, such analysts miss the dynamic nature of the growth process over time, and are inclined to attribute economic success solely to wise political leadership. We have heard of great helmsmen! True, wise leadership is needed to forge collaborative and not combative neighbourliness, and to forge alliances of modernizing forces to fight the conservative vested interests seeking economic rents or unearned profits in the name of inward-looking national development.

This is where the problem begins. Unless the markets of an economy are permitted to respond in liberalized ways by creating conditions to remove entry barriers for both local and international real-sector firms, by creating conditions that foster competition and thus reduce the costs of production, and so on, no amount of wise leadership alone can ensure that an economy will grow at a sustainable rate. This message is clearly brought out in the case of Taiwan. There, multitudes of small and medium-sized enterprises respond to changing world market conditions in ways that governments are not able to do, as has been seen repeatedly in the cases of Japan's MITI in the 1990s, through the economic development boards run by bureaucrats in several countries, or through the 'big-is-better' strategy of *chaebols* in Korea. The role of good governance is to foster political amity with neighbours and a fair system of orderliness within the country while not opposing economic agents promoting open liberal policies in response to the market demands for changes in policy. The credit not only goes to the political leadership, but to a plethora of constituents who promote good neighbourliness, consensus-building among constituencies in a country, willingness of firms to respond to market demands for competition and openness, and ultimately the need to produce high-quality goods at the lowest cost demanded by the marketplace.

We see this complex meshing of decisions in a coherent whole that leads to growth and development, which brings prosperity to a country's people. We also note, in the case of those that failed to develop, a lack of consensus building to ensure peace with neighbours, a singular lack of a strong constituency for open liberal policies, and a lack of open market signals, all of which only favours interest groups seeking to preserve the *status quo* profitable to these groups. The reader will see this in Part 4 of the book in the cases of several countries covered there. The design of the Communist mode of centrally planned growth was nothing other than angry men and women with few resources and little knowledge of markets pulling resources to the central government and ordering growth to take place without the incentive of private ownership. They took no notice of the dictates of the marketplace as the invisible hand that leads to correct production decisions. The Communists have now returned to market signals but they are still adamant where it matters most – that is, to make far-reaching changes to private ownership, and institutional changes to create a market-friendly environment. Despite that, even a small dose of return to the market is beginning to pay good dividends in the transition economies: the reader can find this in Part 3.

Many important lessons are suggested by the vastly different experiences of the 13 countries with different economic approaches: six open economies, two transition economies and five less open economies are included in the book. In the case of several countries, the favourable impacts of the changes are tested to see if these effects from liberalization did in fact assist in securing growth. That is, we provide careful tests of the process of the changes in Chapter 16. The concluding Chapter 17 has more to say on the lessons learned from this study. We highlight two significant lessons. The first is that high growth in Asia has been created by promotion of market-friendly and growth-promoting responses of firms, industries, constituencies and modernizing élites that can be broadly described as favouring liberal and open policies on the one hand. On the other hand, fiscal discipline combined with strong prudential controls on the financial institutions to promote financial sturdiness appears to be associated with stability in the financial and monetary sectors. Failure to retain some degree of financial control on short-term capital flows, which is appropriate for the stage of economic growth of these economies, appears to be a differentiating factor for the severity with which the crisis affected growth trends.

Thus active pursuit of liberal open policies consistent with *long-term stability* and the imposition of necessary *discipline* on the government's and financial institutions' handling of finances of an economy are associated with stability. Inadequacies in these regimens must lead to economic instability. Readers will find this message supported by full disclosure of the ways the 13 economies managed their affairs over a long period of time, some having achieved stable growth, and some having undergone periodic crises. These two underlying causes of stability can be seen operating in those cases: ignore them, you have instability; promote them, you have stability.

We would like to take a little space to acknowledge our gratitude to many who made this study possible. This work would not have been possible but for the support of our publisher, Edward Elgar, from the outset. Edward saw a book of this kind as useful for many purposes, and we thank him and his hard-working editorial staff members for their assistance to us over almost two years. Second, but not less important, are the many persons who helped us by sharing information during our visits to all these countries, where we met bankers, professors, consultants, government officials, officers in the central banks, and so on. These people – too many to name here – have an instinct for which policies are good for their respective countries, and were not reluctant to share their views of how things could have been improved in many cases. Our research visits to these lands have led us to appreciate the attractions of these Asian countries as potential tiger economies of the future years once events come together to enable the right policies to be pursued. After all, such things happened with Deng in China, or Mahathir in Malaysia, or Rao in India, who were all responding to the market demands of their times in the single-minded pursuit of changes in the broad direction of securing growth through liberalization.

Finally, we would like to thank friends and scholars who have been very supportive of this study. First to be named is Basant Kapur, at the time Head of Economics and Statistics, who supported our joint application for research funding, which the National University of Singapore generously approved. Khalid also acknowledges with thanks the generous logistics provided at Limberg Institute of Financial Economics (LIFE), University of Maastricht, where part of the study was completed. Several research assistants helped us in the data collection and compilation: to them, our heartfelt thanks. Many scholars supported our effort. Universiti Utara Malaysia (UUM) provided generous support for the research. First and foremost, we thank the anonymous referees in the United Kingdom for useful suggestions. David Cole and Betty Slade, formerly of the Harvard Institute for International Development (HIID), encouraged this work when Ariff worked at HIID in Cambridge, Massachusetts. A word of thanks is also due to Michael Skully for the ideas on banking and John McKay for his erudition on matters relating to Korea and Japan. We are also grateful to the editorial team – Christine Boniface and Francine O'Sullivan – and the copy editor Elizabeth Teague for their meticulous and speedy processing of the manuscript. We would like to register our sincere thanks to Christine Boniface, our book editor, for her efficient services to lift the quality of the book through her careful editing of the manuscript from the outset. Lest we forget, we thank our wives and children who had to put up with our long absences in Asian countries in pursuit of a study on liberalization and growth!

Mohamed Ariff PhD, CMA, Professor of Finance,
Mt Eliza Business School, Monash University, Melbourne, Australia
(and Visiting Bank Bumiputra Commerce Chair Professor
of Banking and Finance, UUM)

Ahmed M. Khalid PhD, Assistant Professor,
National University of Singapore, Singapore

November 1999

Abbreviations

ABC	Agricultural Bank of China
ACB	Agricultural Credit Bank
ACU	Asian currency unit
ASEAN	Association of South East Asian Nations
ATMs	Automated Teller Machines
BAP	Bankers Association of the Philippines
BES	Book Entry System
BFC	Beijing Financial Centre
BIR	Bureau of Internal Revenue
BOC	Bank of China
BOK	Bank of Korea
BOP	Balance of payments
BSP	Bangko Sentral Pilipinas
CAMEL	Capital Asset Management Earnings Liquidity
CBP	Central Bank of Philippines
CFETS	China Foreign Exchange Trading System
CGT	Capital gains tax
CITIC	China International Trust and Investment Corporation
CRS	Contract Responsibility System
CSRC	China Securities Regulatory Commission
DBCC	The Development Budget Coordination Committee
DBM	Deposit money bank
EIB	Export–Import Bank
EKB	Expanded Commercial Bank
ETDZ	Economic and Technological Development Zone
FC	Finance company
FDI	Foreign direct investment
FEAC	Foreign Exchange Adjustment Centre
FEC	Foreign exchange certificates
FESM	Foreign exchange swap markets
FIR	Financial intermediation ratio
FTC	Foreign trade corporation
FX	Foreign exchange
GATT	General Agreement on Tariffs and Trade

GDP	Gross domestic product
GICS	Government Investment Corporation of Singapore
GS	Government securities
HCI	Heavy and chemical industry
IBCL	Interbank call loans
IBRD	International Bank for Reconstruction and Development
ICBC	Industrial and Commercial Bank of China
IH	Investment house
IMF	International Monetary Fund
ISI	Import substitution industrialization
KB	Regular commercial bank
LIBOR	London Inter-Bank Offered Rate
MB	Monetary board
MOFTEC	Ministry of Foreign Trade and Economic Cooperation
NBFI	Non-bank financial institution
NEITS	National Electronic Interbank Trading System
NETS	National Electronic Trading System
NFEAC	National Foreign Exchange Adjustment Centre
NG	National government
NIE	Newly industrializing economy
NSC	National Securities Committee
NSSLA	Non-Stock Savings and Loan Associations
NTS	National tax service
OECD	Organization for Economic Cooperation and Development
OEZ	Open economic zone
PBC	People's Bank of China
PCBC	People's Construction Bank of China
PCHC	Philippines Clearing House Corporation
PDDTS	Philippine Domestic Dollar Transfer System
PDS	Philippine Dealing System
PHISIX	Philippines Stock Composite Index
PNB	Philippine National Bank
PSE	Philippines Stock Exchange
PRC	People's Republic of China
RB	Rural banks
RCC	Rural credit cooperatives
RMB	renminbi
RP	Repurchase agreement
SAEC	State Administration of Exchange Control
SDB	State Development Bank
SEC	Securities and Exchange Commission
SIBOR	Singapore Inter-Bank Offered Rate

SOE	State-owned enterprise
SSAC	Securities and Supervision Administration Committee
STAQ	National Electronic Trading System
TB	Thrift banks
TIC	Trust and investment companies
UCC	Urban credit cooperatives
VAT	Value-added tax

Part I   Liberalization and the Asian Financial Crisis

The reader will find in this part an overview of the economic and financial liberalization steps undertaken by 13 Asian countries over three decades. These reforms, the reader will learn, enabled some of these countries, especially the early reforming countries, to secure high income growth of 6 to 9 per cent per year, in some cases, over 20 to 25 years. Fast-track development brought favourable social development to some countries, uplifting the social well-being of the peoples of these countries; an exception was Indonesia, with its concentration of wealth and too much belief in the trickle-down effect of growth. The source of growth in all cases is found to be pro-growth liberalization. The policy mix pursued in all these cases is based upon exposing non-financial and financial firms to more and more competition within the country as well as from outside the national borders. Such policies, one must agree, are also consistent with neoclassical development theories.

While it is true that the more liberalized economies had secured a higher standard of living, the effects of the 1997 Asian financial crisis were also felt by the very same more financially liberalized economies: see Chapter 2. Recovery from the effects of the crisis is expected to take about two to three years and will cost these countries about 20 per cent of their GDP. We find evidence to suggest that this costly crisis was not caused by liberalization *per se* but by a reluctance to enforce financial prudence rules on fiscal authorities as well as financial institutions and the absence of vigilant supervision of the capital structures of both the financial and non-financial sectors. The new reforms being implemented in the hitherto fast-growth economies are aimed at removing these persistent financial fragility factors to regain a path to sustainable high growth in Asia. Many scholars advocate some controls on short-term fund flows appropriate for the stage of economic development.

1. Asia's new-found development strategy

1. THE GREAT ASIAN EXPERIMENT

This book provides for the first time a number of significant lessons from an in-depth study of how economic prosperity was secured over a lengthy period of more than three decades by a few Asian countries, where the economic agents carefully designed and implemented pro-growth liberal economic and financial policies. The book also examines a new phenomenon, financial fragility, in the more liberalized fast-growth Asian economies. Five economies, which had a high degree of financial fragility, bore the brunt of the more damaging side-effects of the Asian financial crisis. The crisis appears to have originated in some but not all economies because of a lack of institutional prudential capacity to manage the capital structures of both the financial and the non-financial firms exposed to domestic and foreign short-term capital. Since the early 1990s, a serious mismatch had developed between the duration of investments and the short-term cash flows supporting these long-term investments in the fast-growth economies, thus making them ripe for a financial crisis. Some development lessons were learned from this episode in the closing years of the 1990s, and the crisis had a far-reaching impact on the rest of the world; it even affected the thinking of the IMF and the World Bank as no other crisis in recent memory.

The study covers 13 countries which had followed three different models of economic development even though they have now converged towards a free-market strategy: the capitalist, the mixed and command models. Some followed predominantly capitalist neoclassical policies that promoted increased competition, less regulation, withdrawal of state from production activities and more external openness. Two outstanding examples of these are Taiwan and Malaysia, the latter until September 1998, when that country introduced some illiberal policies to prevent the crisis from spreading. Others, such as India, which had unsuccessfully followed a mixed-economy, government-intervention development strategy, have recently become convinced that the road to growth must be through accelerated pursuit of liberal policies. Five such countries in the latter group are included in this study. We also study two transitional

3

economies, which had abandoned the command economy statist model in favour of making a transition to a market-economy model.[1]

Very important lessons can be learned from the understanding we provide to the reader from this extensive research on how these 13 countries with different past policy models are now converging towards a neoclassical liberal model of development strategy. We believe that the lessons from this study of the so-called Asian Miracle[2] are based on sound principles of competition, decontrol of prices, and restructuring towards a more efficient combination of resources to produce goods and services that markets demand. In short, the successful formula for development appears to be based on neoclassical principles that are consistent with (i) liberalization in the real and financial sectors as well as (ii) reduced intervention by government, while not losing sight of the need for (iii) strict standards of prudential financial management of both the real and the financial sectors.

By the early 1980s, the more developed economies in the OECD grouping had matured to become more services-dominated economies with income growth well below 4 per cent per annum. This led to a lowered capacity to fully employ available resources, in particular capital, which found its way out of these countries as foreign direct investment (FDI) in real investments and portfolio investments in the financial markets.[3] Most developing Asian countries were caught between the Communist preaching that planned growth by the state was possible and the free-market-based development thinking consistent with neoclassical economics. Amidst this debate in the 1950s, a few early reformers, such as Hong Kong, Korea, Taiwan and Singapore, put more of their unused resources to full use through liberalization. For the first time, this formula secured a respectable high rate of economic growth during the period spanning the 1960s to 1980s. The early reformers also included such countries as Malaysia, Thailand and Indonesia. Thus the six economies from this group included in this book enable us to learn lessons about Asia's liberalization and growth strategy. The experiences of these countries provide lessons on how a developing country could use free-market-based economic strategy for development.

Then there are the cases of the mixed-economy strategy of the late starters such as India, and a very large economy like that of China, which pursued state interventionist strategy unsuccessfully to build industrial and infrastructure capacities. The original vision of government intervention, strictly designed to enlarge indigenous capacity in infrastructure and to enhance industrial capacity, soon degenerated to become a scheme of financial suppression and of government interventions in the production of many other goods and services. India's state sector at one time produced almost a quarter of the GDP. Its high taxation has diverted resources to a parallel black economy reported in the popular press to be about 50 per cent of the official economy.[4]

We examine five such South Asian economies that experienced varying degrees of financial suppression and state intervention. The study of these countries enabled us to learn lessons on development failures of the mixed-economy model of development. These countries started to turn to liberalization in the late 1980s in a desperate turnaround in the face of popular displacement in national elections of hitherto well-entrenched political parties.[5] The liking for liberal reforms has grown steadily since then in these countries, even as we completed this study. But the vested interests in these economies, which had gained the most from the interventionist policies of the past, are putting roadblocks to continuing liberal reforms. Thus governments are hesitant to pursue reforms vigorously. These countries are thus again losing sight of the importance of Asia's new-found strategy of liberalization that had already been tested by them in recent years, with at least limited success in the last ten years compared with lack of success using other strategies.

With the demise of the Soviet Union and with it the abandonment of the dogma of the planned- or command-economy model, China started on the road to experimental reforms seriously in the 1980s, since then characterized as the market-economy model. We include in this study both China and Vietnam to learn lessons about how a successful transition to the market-economy model could be made by the Soviet-style economies through economic restructuring of the command economy. In the case of China, its reforms came as a result of a new regime looking for a new strategy to bring prosperity to China after Mao, China's self-proclaimed Great Helmsman, died. After Mao's death, the Gang of Four, who allegedly usurped power, were arrested.[6] Some 85 per cent of China's output was then being produced by loss-making inefficient state firms. To unshackle the moribund economy, a quick fix was sorely needed. So the Communists turned to the market to do the job after failing to make the Great Leap Forward from practising state planning.

A doctrine to legitimize the new regime was also needed in the late 1970s. A formula was found to attract capital and technology from the rest of the capitalist world – including that from Chinese migrants to more open economies that made them capital-rich – to the so-called market of 1.2 billion people. China put to use massive unused resources at the disposal of large foreign capital and also released the pent-up enthusiasm of the people by slowly granting limited private ownership of land, capital and enterprises in a still largely statist society. These two factors served as the basis of growth to date in China. It appears that China has had limited success in covering up the inefficiency of its state sector by the efficiency of the foreign and domestic private sectors. After 20 years, the proportion of GDP produced by the state sector is less than half that at the time of initiating the new strategy. It is a clever strategy. A limit to this policy pursuit is bound to be reached some time in the near future as long as the state's and financial sectors' inefficiency is not tackled.

China's initial success is so well publicized that no further discussion is needed. Including China and Vietnam in this study provides important lessons on the failure of the command-economy model and on how a transition could be made towards a market-economy model through experimental liberalization.

The remainder of the chapter is divided into four sections. The next section provides a brief overview of Asia's convergence in recent years towards a strategy of liberalization. There, we describe the process of development failures over the last 40 years, as well as the development successes in later years. The common characteristics of slow and fast growth in Asia are then identified in Section 3. The common outcomes of growth experience are described in the following section, where the reader will find the most useful characterization of the strategy that is at the root of the so-called Asian Miracle. The chapter ends with an overview of the remaining four parts of the book.

2.   ASIA DISCOVERS NEOCLASSICAL PATH TO DEVELOPMENT

To understand Asia's convergence to the contemporary liberal development strategy, one has to retrace its economic development history during the postwar years. Asia's experience in this regard is a mixed one in so far as there were well-publicized experiments with several approaches to development planning. Some approaches were dictated by a country's political doctrines while others were very much based on the experiences of others who had adopted different strategies and had secured successful social and economic development. In any case, the postwar period up to 1990 may be characterized as a period of intense rivalry among nations for three competing approaches to economic development. Some political pundits may draw parallels in such a character-ization as being equivalent to the three political doctrines of the cold war years up to 1990. Our view, however, is based on the choice of development model rather than the political window-dressing of these models.

At the background of this intense competition was the great Marxian economic experiment to create the Utopia that was thought possible based on the Marxist–Leninist command-economy model. That experiment started with the 1919 Leninist takeover of Russia, which slowly developed the Soviet model of a centrally planned economy with collectivization of individual property rights (and limitations on individual freedoms). Asia, which had not seen much development during almost two centuries of colonial domination by the West and, in the later years, by Japan, was ready to adopt any model that promised to deliver favourable outcomes. The alternative to the command model was the then existing mainstream Western economic thinking loosely characterized as a free-market economy. That suggested a model based on private-sector-owned free enterprises supplying goods and services in competitive markets made possible by an environment with little government intervention but with transparent rules firmly promoting competition, which reduced prices of goods and services to yield normal profits for producers and offered the lowest possible prices for the consumers of the goods and services.

Economists have begun in recent years to characterize this minimum interventionist market-economy model as being consistent with the neoclassical development model. Some Asian countries wanted to limit the role of government to somewhere below the level of the omnipotent state in the Soviet model and the limited government of the capitalist model. Thus was born the third strategy, which was named the mixed-economy model. This model was sold to the peoples in Asia as the socialist model for development. Even the Communists tried to use the term 'socialist' for their command-economy model. It turns out that the mixed-economy socialist model was a cop-out on the part of several Asian countries so that they could stand aloof, halfway between the superpower rivalry that promoted the command-economy model and the pure capitalist model as the only alternative worth pursuing. It was equally feasible in the 1950s to have defended the mixed model as one with market signals, not state signals, and the result would have been far better than what actually happened. None the less, that is the way the three models were sold to the public as stark choices.

Thus the superpower rivalry to win Asia's underdeveloped countries to one side of the persuasion was the driving force that led to the adoption of a given development strategy among the three. The mixed model was chosen by some countries with large populations (Brazil and India) and therefore large consumer markets as an import substitution strategy.[7] China, the other country with a large population, chose the Marxist–Leninist state planning model from 1949 while India embarked on the import substitution strategy from about the early 1950s.

In general, it was a country's relationship to the superpowers that dictated the choice of model. No systematic examination was made as to whether interventionist strategies could secure development, even though some of the approaches were not consistent with mainstream thinking in economics. China, North Korea and Vietnam adopted the command-economy model, which was consistent with their membership in the communist bloc of nations. These decisions were made more in view of the cold war *realpolitik* than because of any systematic analysis of the superiority of the strategy for development purposes. Thus development was planned by the state through collectivization of agriculture and state ownership – strictly proletarian control – of industrial enterprises. Capital had no role to play in this model. So the financial sector was reduced to one that served the circulatory function of enabling payments to factors of production and also payments needed in the process of exchange of goods and services. Financial markets were forcibly barred from playing any role in the market pricing of capital assets as resource allocation institutions. For example, the command economies had banking, but banks were 100 per cent collection and distribution agencies and not maturity transformers collecting short-term deposits and converting these at appropriate prices to long-term loans, nor delegated risk monitors of the public's savings invested as borrowed money by the firms.

The countries at the border of these communist nations were persuaded by the capitalist developed nations to follow the neoclassical model of development. Here the argument of Campos and Roots (1996) is very convincing. The countries in the Western Pacific and in the Indian Ocean served to keep communism in the Asian heartland. In that model, varying degrees of state intervention were justified in some disguised forms, in contrast with totalitarian control in the former command economies. For example, Japan had credit targeting, as did Korea and Indonesia, to favour some industries to develop more than others. Taiwan engaged in a number of forms of government assistance to grow medium-sized and small enterprises to become nimble exporters of consumer goods and consumer durables to the whole world: this country even adopted 'land to the plough' reform to privatize state ownership of land. Nevertheless these East Asian free-enterprise-based economies refrained from total government ownership of real-sector firms though ownership of financial institutions in Korea and Indonesia was favoured during the early stages of development in the 1970s.

Thus these economies – we analyse Korea, Indonesia, Malaysia, Singapore, Taiwan and Thailand – remained largely capitalist, with some degree of government intervention in the real and in the financial sectors. One characteristic they shared was greater and greater openness to the rest of the world to allow export-led growth as a feature of their development strategy. Following that growth process, these economies were able to secure a high degree of exposure in trade and capital flows, as will be documented in other parts of this book. Expressed as a percentage of GDP, these countries had a very strong trade sector, such as Korea's 16 per cent. They also attracted foreign capital flows amounting in some cases (Malaysia being one) to almost 20–30 per cent of their GDP in some years. Measured as dependence on external economy (trade and capital flows), all these countries had high exposure to the foreign sector whereas other economies had very low foreign-sector exposure.

The third model is the socialist mixed-economy model, which can be described as follows. Through some amount of government intervention in the production process – this took the form of outright rejection of private ownership in some selected segments of the economy as well as the financial institutions – the state took an active part in the production process. For example, about 200 central government enterprises in India produced many goods and services, making up anywhere from 20 to 40 per cent of GDP. This was a halfway house experiment compared with Communist China, which produced 85 per cent of its GDP through its 28 000 central-government-owned firms and many times more than that number of firms owned by the provincial governments. The Vietnamese had 78 000 firms producing practically the entire output of the economy. Before the reforms of the 1980s, Malaysia's 900-odd state firms produced almost half the GDP. With privatization in the 1980s, the number has been reduced to a manageable 150.

What differentiated a mixed economy from a totalitarian economy was the relatively larger private-sector control of the economy in the former compared with the almost total control of the economy in the latter. But government intervention was present in both the mixed and the command economies to a greater degree than would be the case in the free-market economies such as Taiwan and Thailand. The difference was one of degree, not of substance. Both, as we will document in this book, found that constraining market forces from working out efficiency gains in these economies through these interventions led to serious development failures.

As early as the mid-1970s, Asia's development strategists in government, industries and customer groupings started to realize the failures of the interventionist development programmes in both the mixed and the command economies. Meanwhile, out of necessity dictated by a general scarcity of economic resources, four Asian 'tiger' economies, namely Hong Kong, Korea, Singapore and Taiwan, were putting in place more open economic management programmes. That openness to the world secured for them a close to double-digit economic growth as soon as these economies dismantled the state interventionist programmes which they had adopted during the early 1950s. Successful development experiences of these tiger economies were quite obvious for others to see. Their success could not be ignored for too long by the followers of mixed- and command-economy models, which had not produced favourable outcomes after 30 years of experimentation. In the 1980s, a consensus started to emerge among economic agents in the mixed and the command economies to adopt a policy mix of the type followed by the tiger economies.

Thus Asia converged towards more and more openness and liberalization as the keys to securing economic growth. Acceptance of what has turned out to be a development model consistent with the mainstream neoclassical model of development took a long time. It came after its successful experimentation by the early reformers, the tiger economies as well as the potential tiger economies of Malaysia, Indonesia and Thailand.[8] After the demise in 1991 of the former Soviet Union, the mixed-economy and the command-economy model of development strategy had become discredited. Asia at last converged towards liberalization and openness as the routes to securing economic and social development. Perhaps it is apt here to refer to an earlier prescription for growth. Friedman (1958) advocated openness and said that, given more openness aimed at creating conditions for efficiency and openness in trade, resources would move to create the growth without a development bureaucracy.[9] This appears prophetic when we note that this was said 42 years ago and many nations ignored this advice preferring to interfere with the market forces which create efficiency and allocate resources much better than interventionist strategies.

3.   COMMON FEATURES OF FAST GROWTH AND SLOW GROWTH IN ASIA

It is evident from the discussion in the above two sections that the Asian economies experimented with three development approaches over a lengthy 45-year period. The result is a conviction based on actual results that growth could be secured by active pursuit of liberal policies. That it took so long a time to realize a workable policy mix is not surprising given two factors mentioned in our discussion. One was the cold war rivalry that promoted the now defunct command-economy model. To some extent, the adoption of the mixed-socialist-economy model was a knee-jerk reaction arising from a security consideration to keep a distance from the two superpowers, a sort of self-preservation using pseudo-economic arguments. The other factor was the general absence of a democratic will to pursue reforms in some countries because of several factors which do not concern us in this chapter. What concerns us is that those countries that chose a total statist interventionist model took longer to reorient their development strategies than did the countries with some democratic processes in political management. These two factors are societal-level variables that preconditioned a given economy to make the choices that they actually made under the prevalent circumstances during the postwar years.

Of greater interest to the reader is an examination of common characteristics of the three paths to development. First we examine the policy mix used by those countries pursuing the more successful liberalization and openness to which most Asian countries appeared to be converging in the 1990s. Figure 1.1 is a schematic representation of the sort of policies put into effect in some preferred sequences in the 13 economies. These reforms can be described in a simple phrase: *returning economic activities to respond to market signals wherever market failures are unlikely*. Put another way, these reforms are consistent with the mainstream neoclassical economic principles of (i) competition to promote efficiency in production, (ii) market creation to promote allocation efficiency in producing real goods and in allocating capital and other resources and (iii) reduced prices of goods and services to promote consumer sovereignty. Two

A	Real sector	• Relax barriers to entry in domestic real sector to increase competition.
		• Relax barriers to entry of foreign firms in domestic sector to increase competition.
		• Private sector is recognized as the engine of growth.
		• Laws on property rights, incorporation laws, shareholder rights to safeguard capital from trade union control, bankruptcy laws, etc.
		• Capital account openness (FDI, dividends, etc.) and investor protection.
		• Reduce the state sector and natural monopolies through privatization and/or corporatization to improve efficiency and to reduce burden on budget.
B	Fiscal sector	• Balanced budget principle promoted with limits on government borrowing.
		• Taxation reforms to create incentives for enterprise and profit-seeking.
		• Reduced corporate/income tax but diversify tax sources to increase revenue.
		• Strengthen tax and government administration via user-pay schemes.
C	Financial sector	• Remove in stages controls on interest rates to get market to price risk.
		• Relax entry barriers in financial institutions to create competition to drive down the spread in deposit and lending rates.
		• Modernize and create specialization in financial services industries to improve service standards and to reduce costs of financial services.
		• Create entities to diversify money-market transactions to provide signals about risk in base rates, T-bills, bank bills, etc., and to deepen markets.
		• Create entities to engage in securitization of corporate and government capital funds in the bond and share markets.
		• Capacity for risk management through market forces and derivative markets.
		• Prudential rules and strict implementation to remove financial fragility.
D	External sector	• Reduce tariff steadily to return firms to compete internationally to improve efficiency, market access, and even technology.
		• Relax foreign exchange controls: unify different rates for produces first; create private markets for pricing of currency rates; in steps remove exchange controls for non-producer sector; have laws to impose controls during crisis.
		• Maintain current account balance and improve the reserve support for trade.
		• If feasible, adopt at correct time truly free float of the currency.

Figure 1.1   Schematic representation of the policy mix in Asia

important further outcomes of openness to the rest of the world are (iv) increased trade and (v) capital resource flows. Let us now examine how the fast-track free-market economies differed from the slow-growth economies in taking the steps. enumerated in Figure 1.1.

Real-sector Reforms

The 13 countries that adopted three different development strategies had significantly differing approaches to each of the A, B, C and D of liberalization. Real-sector openness in the command economies was still largely absent even in the 1990s, as was the general reluctance to privatize the state sector for fear of creating unemployment.[10] While entry of foreign capital has been permitted in some sectors, which are often restricted to operating in small geographical alien production zones, these foreign firms also face barriers to trade in the domestic economy because of the high import tariffs imposed if the goods are sold to the national markets. Though the private sector is recognized implicitly as the source of growth by the political masters in these economies, private ownership incentives are largely lacking in command economies. China is making reforms to its legal and judiciary systems dealing with commercial transactions, but these are still in the early phase. Thus, in the case of command-economy model, real-sector openness is far from present.

In the case of the mixed economies, only in the late 1980s and in the 1990s were laws passed to create greater real-sector openness. For example, in India, the negative list, which restricted a large number of economic activities to be undertaken only by the state, was disbanded in 1991. This means that domestic firms may undertake any economic activity (except those few in defence and certain essential food items) in any part of the country, unlike in the command-economy countries. Even foreign firms that are producing as joint venture firms with 49 per cent share ownership with local firms have no barriers to entry in other production activities of the joint venture partners since reforms were put in place. Thus, until 1990, there was very little real-sector openness in the mixed economies, but there has been greater openness since then. Foreign firms with higher than 49 per cent share ownership are permitted to operate only in the export-processing zones with no tariffs and lower tax rates very similar to the situation in command economies. Pakistan, another mixed economy, had few barriers and low tariffs on exports but had substantial price controls on several items produced domestically. Pakistan has also slowly lifted price controls since the mid-1980s, thus exposing the real sector to competition and efficiency. Pakistan's economic problems arise from capital shortage and from a severe weakness in the fiscal sector caused by high debt servicing because of heavy defence expenditures (see Chapter 13).

In the case of the free-market economies – for example Korea – it will be observed from the information presented later in this book that the real sector was the first sector to be opened to competition. Korea relaxed controls on domestic production, as did Taiwan, Malaysia, Singapore and Hong Kong as far back as in the 1950s, thus removing barriers to entry in domestic production. Even better, capital controls for both domestic and foreign firms were lifted in the late 1950s when the parliaments passed laws in Malaya (the former name for the later expanded Malaysia) and in Singapore to attract foreign investment.[11] These laws also permitted tax holidays of up to five years to be given to certain firms that satisfied a condition called pioneer industry status. Through these and other means, the free-market economies opened their real sectors to greater and greater domestic competition as well as, in later years, to foreign competition. Unlike the situation in the command and mixed economies, the state was not the preferred producer in the real sector although some of the countries (Korea and Indonesia) had at some stages state-owned financial institutions.

In privatization, the same trend can be seen. The free-market economies generally did not encourage state ownership in the real production sector. As a result these did not have the same extent of state involvement in the real sector as did the command economies. Nevertheless, those that had state firms quickly set about disbanding them by either selling them to the private sector or corporatizing their activities. In the early 1980s, Malaysia sold most of its 900-odd state firms to the private sector, as did Singapore after adopting a privatization master plan in 1985: see Thynne and Ariff (1989). Compare this with the reluctance even after 30 years of growth in China to tame the state and military firms! China has made bold moves in 1999 to tame this shrew. In the case of the mixed economies too, privatization has not proceeded at sufficient speed to return competition and efficiency to these firms to reduce the burden they impose on government budgets in those countries.

Thus, in general, the first important step in successful liberalization appears to be a willingness to improve production efficiency through policies aimed at greater real-sector openness. The free-market economies undertook these reforms in the 1950s whereas the command and mixed economies have only taken limited reform steps to liberalize their real sectors to return government-owned firms to the private sector. Pertinent details on each country can be found in the remaining chapters of the book.

Financial Reforms

Reform of the financial sector is the next important feature of liberalization in Asia. Domestic financial firms were the targets in the initial stage of reform. Korea, for example, eased entry restrictions in the late 1960s and permitted more banks, finance companies and others, including foreign banks, to be licensed. Specialized institutions were created to cater to the more diversified economy of the 1970s. More development banks, merchant banks and investment banks were licensed, as were also agricultural and small to medium-sized enterprise banks. Similar reforms took place in Taiwan, Singapore and Hong Kong. In command economies, 100 per cent of assets were owned by the state banks, whereas in a matured typical free-market economy, the bond and the stock markets hold about 60 per cent of the assets in an economy; but very few countries fall into this category.

The last two economies, with a vision to serve as international financial centres, brought in a greater degree of modernization in the money, capital and derivative markets. Securitization was encouraged and this led to explosive growth in the money and capital markets. New listed firms increased at an annual rate of 8–12 per cent per year as a result of which the Hong Kong stock exchange emerged in the 1990s as the second largest in Asia, next to the Tokyo stock exchange. The real-sector openness was matched by substantial openness to the rest of the world in the financial sector. Hong Kong and Singapore had a very large representation of foreign financial institutions, as did also Korea. Thus the expansion of the money and the capital markets enhanced the standards of service to customers, improved mobilization of savings and offered new financial services to customers. The rest of the countries (one exception being Malaysia) in this group were quite satisfied with limited openness in the financial sectors for fear that the bigger financial institutions of the larger economies might weaken the domestic firms. This was a sort of infant-industry protection argument common in the world trade rules applied to the financial sector, which led to the growth of oligopolistic banking in most Asian countries. Oligopolistic banking has inherent weaknesses, as was found after the Asian financial crisis in 1997. A virulent type of oligopolistic banking system actually emerged, in which the government-owned or -controlled banks promoted a *quangzi* or network among the political élites, big business and the state to facilitate lending to less profitable investment activities. This has been noted by the IMF in its 1997 and 1998 reports as the crony capitalism that led to bad banking practices.

Contrast that with the experience of the command economies. In these countries, the monobanking structure peculiar to the command economies underwent great changes. In the domestic financial sector, new banks, still owned by the state, were created to provide competition in the banking sector. Specialized banks were created to cater to agricultural, industrial and in some cases provincial (Bank of Guangdong in the South) capital demands while investment trusts[12] were created to cream off the abundant savings running at 40 per cent of the GDP. In China, this happened in the 1980s; in the 1990s, it took place in Vietnam.

The reader will note that the expansion of the financial services industry took place in time to serve the expanded financial activities consistent with expanded economic activities. As will be seen later in the book, financial deepening doubled with these limited reforms over the same period. That was inevitable because a failure to take these steps would have created huge underground illegal financial structures, which would have led to economic chaos in China or Vietnam. However, the reader should note that these institutions are still state-owned and are managed by government employees with no private incentive schemes. Thus astute observers have remarked that the banking system is so poorly managed that a disaster could be waiting to happen if their inefficient management is not corrected soon.

Second, the banks still predominantly serve state firms. Vietnam has taken some appropriate steps to direct state firms to access capital needs from the banks without any more budgetary support to them: this single rule has prompted banks to supervise their loans and firms to look to profits as the norm for business. China has still not taken this or other more serious steps to improve the allocation function of the bank or the function of maturity transformation, nor the delegated monitoring functions of the banking sector.[13] Without the financial sector providing allocation efficiency and as a consequence the risk management function of monitoring real-sector investment efficiency, the banking system is still reduced largely to being the provider of the payment function, a condition no different from that under the discredited command-economy era. Thus modernization and expansion of the banking system is perhaps complete now but not the efficient management of the banking system to deliver the important function of oversight of the real-sector investments.

In the mixed economies of South Asia and the Philippines, the financial sector was turned around increasingly to serve the clever schemes of the governments. The banks were nationalized in all South Asian countries from about 1960 to 1986. This decimated private-sector banking. Government-owned banks increasingly provided improved banking services to the people in the interior of these countries, but over time the standards of services deteriorated. The banks were also directed to lend to preferred sectors – for example, cottage and heavy industries – and preferred segments of the population – for example, 'schedules castes' or the crony firms in the Philippines during the Marcos era. These directed credit schemes developed a system of widespread abuse in lending from which the financial sector has still not recovered in some of these countries.

In the late 1980s in Bangladesh and in the 1990s in other mixed economies, initial steps were taken to address the problems created by the inefficiency of the financial sector. These steps identified non-performing loans to be many times the Basle recommended level of 3 per cent of the loans outstanding after provisioning for bad loans each year. Even as far back as 1995, non-performing loans of the Indonesian state banks were 15 per cent, with a return on assets of 1 per cent: the corresponding figure for private banks was 5 per cent, with a return on assets of 4 per cent. In addition, capital adequacy, which had improved to about 8 per cent of share capital in the free-market economies by 1997, also declined. Thus, unlike the fast-track tiger economies, the mixed and command economies have still not reformed the financial sectors to serve the expanded economies so that the sector is capable of contributing if proper reforms are put in place in the financial sectors.

Fiscal Reforms

The command and mixed economies undertook very few fiscal reforms even as late as the 1990s, whereas such reforms were carefully put in place in the free-market economies as early as the 1980s. Consequently the free-market economies had achieved balanced (in some cases surplus) budgets in the late 1980s whereas the mixed and command economies had persistent budget deficits over the study period. What reforms were undertaken? The major reforms concern reducing tax rates in the fast-track economies, diversifying the tax base (in Indonesia in the 1980s, in India in 1997, and in China in 1995–96) and improving the tax-collection mechanism in all. These measures improved revenues to the governments to build capacity to sustain public-sector modernization and capacity-building programmes.

Another fiscal reform, which significantly supported growth of the real and the financial sectors, was the use of fiscal policies to attract foreign firms to locate production in these countries. In return for reduced tax or tax holidays provided by fiscal policy reforms, governments in the free-market economies favoured foreign direct investment as far back as in the 1950s to attract capital: see Asher et al. (1992). With foreign capital came market access to the developed country as well as new and modern production technology to the countries involved. For instance, manufactured export items in Malaysia constituted about 85 per cent of all exports in 1995 compared with the 1970 figure of about 20 per cent: Asian Development Bank (1997b). This was largely made possible by the discriminatory use of fiscal incentives to attract foreign direct investment. As a result, Malaysia attracted the most direct investments, amounting in 1994 to 28 per cent of its GDP, the highest in Asia.

Prudential reforms had been lacking in all Asian countries except Hong Kong and Singapore, the two financial centres, which could not function efficiently under any lack of prudential oversight of their very large financial sectors.[14] As a result, prudential reform is likely to become a major focus of reforms in the future. Especially after the Asian financial crisis has been shown to have originated in the incipient financial fragility of the financial management of these economies, such reforms became even more urgent. One could make a reasoned comment (see Chapter 2 for details) that the lack of willingness to stamp out financial fragility was a source of this crisis. Reforms are in the making in the international institutions and in the national central banks to address this urgent problem. Time will tell what steps will be taken. In February 1998, the IMF made a bid to expand its role by monitoring the banking sector. This does not portend well. Instead of submitting bad bank management to monitoring and discipline by both shareholders of the banks and the markets, bureaucratic supervision by the IMF is unlikely to be effective. Recall that the big bureaucracy, with very modern supervision of credit unions in the USA, failed to prevent their spectacular failure that cost 3.5 per cent of the GDP of the USA over 1987–91.

External-sector Reforms

The signal achievement of the early reformers, who secured fast-track development, is in the opening of their economies to the external sector to ensure more trade in merchandise and capital flows. This sets the early reformers apart from the rest of Asia. It also engendered a weakness that, in later years, was to become the Achilles heel that caused these economies to suffer severely from the 1997 Asian financial crisis. Each chapter of this book has special sections devoted to this aspect. Therefore this section provides only a broad overview.

Tariff reduction policies were the first set of reforms to be undertaken to expose domestic firms to increasing competition to improve efficiency. The world trading arrangement also favours an average tariff of under 5 per cent, though in free-trade areas – an example is the ASEAN Free Trade Area – (AFTA) – a new initiative was taken in 1999 to accelerate this for some industries. The average country tariff rate has been reduced substantially from as high as around 100 per cent in Korea and 140 per cent in India in the early years. The average tariff in the free-market economies in the 1990s is about 15 per cent, and it is planned to reduce it to zero in some free trading zones amongst the Association of South East Asian Nations (ASEAN) countries. The second aspect of this reform is the relaxation of restrictions to the entry of foreign firms to undertake domestic economic activities. Both these aspects have been commented upon in our earlier discussion on real-sector reforms.

Two remaining aspects of external sector reforms are (i) current account opening, which is the lifting of restrictions on foreign currency trade by producers and individuals, and (ii) capital account freedom. The latter is the freedom granted to producers and individuals to move capital and capital services income, such as royalties and dividends, across national boundaries. In the MacKinnon–Fry–Shaw advocacy on sequencing of financial liberalization, capital account openness is recommended only after real-sector opening is successfully completed. Similarly, current account openness is recommended after domestic real-sector reforms are completed.[15] Capital account openness, particularly to domestic individuals and producers, is only to be made available after all other reforms have been properly implemented. It has been suggested that the freeing of the current account *before* the freeing of the real sector is a reason for the Asian financial crisis that rocked six economies in Asia in 1997–99. More research is needed to investigate this assertion.

The free-market economies achieved current account openness only in the limited forms of the currency peg or basket pegging as early as the late 1970s in some cases and in the late 1980s in others. Of course the command economies of Vietnam and China have still not opened their current account, nor have they granted capital account openness to most producers and all individuals. The mixed economies have taken limited steps to free current accounts in the 1990s while also relaxing controls on capital account restrictions to most producers. Controls are still in place for individuals. Thus the fast-growth economies of Southeast Asia and Korea had adopted current and capital account openness by the late 1980s.[16] The slow-growth economies have been reluctant to adopt external openness for the very good reason that their belated real- and financial-sector reforms have not yet produced the degree of success found in the free-market economies that made the latter able to adopt external openness. Hence they are not ready to adopt the final set of reforms that needs to be put in place at the proper time to secure greater income growth than they have achieved so far with limited reforms. One exception is Taiwan. Just as in the case of Chile, Taiwan suffered a boom–bust episode in the capital market in the 1980s. This prompted Taiwan (as it did Chile) to institute some residual controls on the current accounts. This and the huge foreign currency reserves prevented the new Taiwan dollar from depreciating in the first few months of the Asian crisis.

More external openness meant that current accounts of the free-market economies became a destabilizing force of these fast-track economies. With greater external openness, economies with full current account openness (IMF Article 8 provisions) developed stronger external linkages to trade and capital flows in the 1980s and especially in the 1990s. For example, Korea's external sector is close to 70 per cent of its GDP, and Malaysia's exposure to foreign direct investment in 1994 was 28 per cent of its GDP. Compare these figures with trade exposure of about 9 per cent of GDP and capital flow of about 1 per cent of GDP in the case of India in 1995. The over-exposure to the external sector made the currency rate very sensitive to current account balances in the free-market economies. When the current account started to get into deficit first in Thailand, then in Indonesia, and so on, in the 1990s, the managed exchange rates of these countries came under severe strain. This started happening from late 1994, but the currencies were defended by the use of reserves. However, on 2 July 1997 the depreciation was a full 10 per cent, and the crisis took root on that day in Thailand. That led to the exchange rate overshooting in the second half of 1997. These countries suffered the calamitous effects of the financial crisis, which led to grave economic recessions in all these economies.

In summarizing the discussion in this section, some general observations can be made about the common experiences of the Asian economies. Liberalization – how far back and to what extent it was undertaken – appears to be the catalyst for growth in Asia. The early reformers, especially the free-market strategists, secured fast-track growth. China's success, though its reforms are still very superficial without the state sector and the banking reforms, owes to the massive mobilization of hitherto under- or unused resources by large capital inputs. Its high growth has been orchestrated very well, given its presumed access to a large market and its cheaper still abundant production resources. The late and hesitant reformers such as the Philippines and India have now begun to adopt the same path to secure economic growth as did the early reformers. Initial results in the cases of the mixed economies, as will be seen in the rest of the book, provide reason to be optimistic about their longer-term successes. These countries may be able to garner good growth in the future provided the anti-reform platform is neutralized in favour of continuing vigorous reforms.

4. COMMON DEVELOPMENT OUTCOMES

This section is concerned with the measurement of significant outcomes of liberalization over the postwar period. 'What are the highlights of liberalization and growth in Asia?' is the question we attempt to answer in this section. Key macroeconomic variables are identified in order to quantify the extent of the favourable development outcomes in Asian economies following different paths originally but now converging towards a free-market model of development. These outcomes are presented in terms of the four strategies described in the previous section as the models followed by the 13 countries. Income growth, which is an indication of economic prosperity, is one measure. Another measure is the monetary depth, which describes the growth in the monetization of these economies through diversification and depth of the money markets. The third measure included is the financial intermediation ratio as a measure of how much of the assets of an economy is held in the form of securities in the financial institutions. A fourth and important measure is the inflation experiences of these countries as a litmus test of efficient management of an economy.

Table 1.1 provides a summary of these statistics for the three groups of countries: the free-market, the mixed and the command economies. Individual country data are not given here as these can be found in the respective chapters in the book. Income growth and inflation experiences, which are two significant macroeconomic indicators of development, are found to be the most highly favoured outcomes in the free-market economies. Note that income growth rates here are about twice the income growth rates in the mixed economies. Second, the command economies, which released pent-up energies by removing Communist restrictions, were able to grow at rates very close to those of the free-market economies, after reforms (in China) since the 1980s.

Table 1.1   Three strategies and four outcomes in Asia (income growth and inflation are % rates; others are % of GDP)

Outcomes	Free-market economy	Mixed economy	Command to transition economy[a]
Income growth			
1976–80	8.08	5.05	7.71
1981–85	5.94	3.55	10.07
1986–90	8.78	5.03	6.61
1991–99	8.02	4.02	9.80
Inflation			
1976–80	10.57	8.66	2.63
1981–85	5.73	11.10	10.70
1986–90	4.25	9.49	100.00
1991–99	5.60	9.02	17.30
Money depth			
1976–80	34.72	29.03	33.00
1981–85	42.91	27.46	49.00
1986–90	60.83	29.90	73.00
1991–99	66.61	38.90	104.00
Intermediation ratio			
1976–80	33.0	33.4	46.0
1981–85	45.0	40.4	62.0
1986–90	56.0	40.0	86.0
1991–99	75.0	44.0	90.0

Notes: [a] Data to calculate financial intermediation ratio are not available for Vietnam. Hence the figure refers to China only.
We exclude the crisis years 1997 and 1998.

However, the inflation experiences of both China and Vietnam are very high compared with the mostly single-digit inflation rates of the free-market economies. The latter had experienced double-digit inflation arising from the oil-price-led inflation of the 1970s. Inflation has been well managed and kept under control in the free-market economies. Inflation rates in the mixed economies were also lower than those in the command economies. Lack of expertise about price management and a failure to prevent capital inflows from affecting money supply in the former command economies are two important reasons for the high inflation rates in these countries during the transition phase towards a market-economy model.

Income growth at about 8–9 per cent per annum over a lengthy period of growth in the free-market economies led to significant improvements in the per capita income levels of the peoples of these countries. Even Indonesia was able to improve its per capita income, thus driving down the poverty level which applied to 60 per cent of the population in 1965 to as low as 8 per cent of the population in 1996 (before the ravages of the financial crisis pushed up the poverty levels allegedly to 20 per cent). In the best case of Singapore, the per capita income level in 1995 was about 76 per cent of the US per capita level compared with 23 per cent of the US level in 1965. Korea, which was among the poorest countries in 1954, had emerged as a newly industrializing economy (NIE) by the late 1970s. In 1997, Korea became the twenty-fourth member of the exclusive club of the developed nations, the OECD.

In the case of China, which embraced reforms soon after the death of China's Communist leader, 20 years of reforms have made it possible to achieve private-sector-led growth complemented by the growth made possible by foreign capital attracted by the vast unused resources. Vietnam has also taken the same path since the early 1990s, and has managed to control its inflation only in the 1990s. Inflation in Vietnam was running at over 300 per cent in the 1980s whereas it was brought down to double digits in the mid-1990s. The initial enthusiasm for reforms in the mixed economies led to high growth in the late 1980s and early 1990s. The growth rate in India reached 6.3 per cent during 1986–90. With protectionist sentiments returning in the 1990s, which led to rolling back some reforms, the growth rates have subsided to lower levels in the South Asian economies. With major reforms put in place by the Ramos government in the 1990s, the Philippines has started to register higher growth than its past growth rates of well under 3 per cent per annum. Overall, then, the more liberal the policies pursued by an economy, the greater have been the growth rates and the lower the inflation rates.

Financial reforms also appear to have improved the securitization in and the depth of the money and capital markets. Monetary depth has doubled in both the free-market and mixed economies from about 30 per cent in the 1970s to levels closer to 70 per cent in the 1990s. In the case of China, monetary depth has trebled, especially with the high savings from high income growth in the domestic sector and with the inflow of foreign capital. We have no reliable figures for the Vietnamese economy on this measure. Improved depth (still without improved transaction rates) in the money market enables market signals to be given about the price of money-market instruments if interest rates are freed. By the mid-1990s, most countries in the sample had freed, at least in part, most of the controls on interest rates. Hence the money markets in Asia are beginning to be ready to provide economic information on the price of money in the money markets.

Financial intermediation ratios (FIRs) have also improved in all these countries. The rate has doubled in all the economies as a result of greater financial reforms put in place to enable the financial sector to service the real sector. For example, the assets held in the financial institutions of the free-market economies were about 75 per cent of their GDP in the 1990s. Compare this high rate with their initial position of 33 per cent during 1976–80. China has an FIR of 90 per cent in the 1990s compared with its ratio of 46.0 per cent in 1985. The ratio for the mixed economies was around 33 per cent of GDP during 1976–80. The FIR increased in these countries by 1996. Significant growth in the FIR actually occurred only after these countries undertook reforms in the 1986–96 period. Note that the ratio was stagnant in the earlier period at 40 per cent. After the reforms, the FIR jumped to 44 per cent of GDP in the 1990s. Therefore, financial liberalization in all these countries appears to have improved capacity in the financial sector to handle the greater volume of economic activities, and, with this, greater financial activities.

Summarizing the discussion on the outcomes of reforms will enable the reader to appreciate the beneficial effects of Asia's new-found strategy of liberalization. Economic development took place at faster rates when a liberal mix of policies supplanted interventionist strategies in the command and mixed economies. Significantly higher growth rates were experienced by the free-market economies, which started the reform process much earlier than the others. These countries made so many improvements to the relative prosperity of their peoples that it was, as noted earlier, dubbed the Asian Miracle. As we have discussed in this chapter, there is nothing miraculous about that outcome. It is the cumulative effect of sustained liberal reforms that secured the greater prosperity observed in the free-market economies compared with the late adopters of this neoclassical strategy for development. Detailed statistics on each country have been averaged to provide the information on these four desirable outcomes of the development experiences of 13 countries at various stages of development.

4.   SOURCES OF GROWTH?

There are a number of alternative approaches to studying how growth occurs in a given social network of economic relations at a point in time. Perhaps it is correct to claim that the approach taken in this book is in the tradition of mainstream economic thought. Economic development appears to take place when liberal policies are adopted to remove obstacles in the way of encouraging competition among firms and efficiency in the use of resources. The Asian countries included in this study managed to secure growth through such liberalization steps and, where the steps taken to liberalize were inadequate, economic growth has been lacklustre. Thus the approach to studying growth in this case has been to describe the process of liberal policy implementation as actually experienced by the 13 countries analysed.

The reader may very well be aware that there are alternative approaches to studying growth. A school of thought that was quite in vogue and was gaining respectability before the Asian financial crisis attempted to explain Asia's high growth as the result of good governance in several countries. This idea was given some credence in a study sponsored by the World Bank in 1994–95. While good governance is an important prerequisite for growth, this idea was often used by leaders of some countries to allege that the growth secured in their countries was purely due to the presence of good, strong, often authoritarian leadership. We know, two years after the Asian financial crisis, that the cosy relation between authoritarian rulers, banks and big businesses led to investment splurge that precipitated the crisis. We think this particular Asian representation of the idea misses the point of the proposition that good governance must precede and be present during growth phases.

Another approach often advocated is to examine growth as a consequence of modernizing élites,[17] who seek public consensus and coalition-building to pursue growth. This is patently correct as a precondition for adopting liberal policies to secure growth. However, it would require a study of the political dynamics in a society, and we leave that task to someone more qualified to do this analysis. Finally, the reader may also note that there are other schools of thoughts – let us lump them together as sociological ideas – that see growth and development as predetermined by the cultural and sociological norms of the people making up the society: an example is the Protestant work ethic as growth-promoting. The reader will note that we have refrained from such broad ideas although we are aware of their importance in explaining the success of peoples in a commercial culture, for example immigrants, which makes such groups successful in securing control of businesses.

This book therefore approaches growth broadly from the perspective of liberalization aimed at freeing the energies of economic agents, namely corporations and individuals, to engage in wealth-producing activities. Such liberalization, it will be seen throughout the book, produces growth in ways consistent with the mainstream ideas of private incentives, private ownership, managerial efficiency and factor productivity, all of which are required to produce sustainable economic growth, leading to social development of the peoples of a country.

5.   OUTLINE OF THE BOOK

It is time now to describe the structure of the book. Part 1 contains this chapter and the next chapter is on the 1997 Asian financial crisis. This chapter serves as an overview of growth through liberalization. The next chapter traces the genesis of the Asian financial crisis to events and structural weaknesses in the financial sectors of a few fast-growth economies, all of which had severe financial fragility. Part 2 is about the development experiences of six free-market economies that followed the earlier successful experiences of the tiger economies to secure growth through greater external openness to trade and capital flows. Some would say that the developments of these are like flying geese following the lead of the tigers! These are the very same economies that suffered, as we will document, from a general lack of capacity to manage the financial institutions prudentially. In the second part, the reader will find an in-depth analysis of how these six early-reforming economies managed to secure high-growth development, and had quite open external sectors that destabilized them during the crisis.

Part 3 contains two chapters, one on China and the other on Vietnam. These two Asian economies are among the six Communist countries trying to make the transition towards a market-economy model of development. Failure to develop under the command model is traced to these countries' past practices. Part 4 also describes the failures to secure sufficient growth to bring prosperity to the peoples in Bangladesh (a resource-poor country), India, Pakistan, the Philippines and Sri Lanka. The Philippines, which had greater openness to the external sector, also suffered from the ravages of the financial crisis. These countries had pursued varying degrees of financial suppression while also creating a large state sector under an earlier planned-economy model, which failed over 25 years to create the kind of growth they thought was possible. These countries adopted the reforms of the free-market economies since the late 1980s. Their collective experience is very relevant for the 126 developing countries in the world. The reader will find that their later adoption of a liberal policy mix is an interesting departure from the interventionist model being pursued in a large number of countries.

Part 5 comprises two chapters. In the penultimate chapter, we provide a careful econometric analysis of how reforms have or have not been beneficial to the countries involved. Tests on such functions as savings, investment demand functions, and so on enable us to make carefully tested observations on this topic. The reader who is not interested in a technical treatment of the subject may skip this chapter without any loss of continuity: it is addressed to the experts. The final chapter is a discussion about development lessons from this study. Relevant lessons are itemized and expanded in that chapter. The reader will find that growth is possible for any country through careful pursuit of neoclassical principles of using free markets to create competition for efficient production as well as efficient allocation of economic resources *provided that* the external openness is appropriate for the stage of economic development. If sufficient prudential structures are not strictly adhered to in the management of the financial sector of an economy, then conditions favourable for a financial crisis will emerge, as happened in the 1990s. This calls for prudential re-regulation in the financial sector while pursuing liberalization as an active policy strategy.

NOTES

1. State intervention was legitimized in Marxist economics. Around the time immediately after the Second World War, the appeal for state intervention in Asia could also be reasonably justified by the Keynesian formula of pump-priming the Western economies to absorb unused human resources. The futility of deficit-financed interventions became obvious in the 1970s after Milton Friedman showed the link between deficit budgets and high inflation. Thus these contrasting approaches to growth appeared at that time to be sound strategies in the 1950s.
2. The phrase Asian Miracle started appearing in the literature in 1993 and was popularized by several World Bank publications. We suggest liberalization as the key to how fast-track development was secured in several Asian countries. Other writers, for example Campos and Root (1996), suggest that growth was made possible by a social contract between the governed and the non-communist governments to deliver social development in return for keeping Communism out. Islam and Chowdhury (1997) attribute fast growth to good macroeconomic management.
3. According to IMF and World Bank statistics, FDI increased by the end of the 1990s to US$330 billion, while the portfolio flows are estimated to be about US$120 billion.
4. India had deferred tax reforms until the 1990s. Other Asian countries had undertaken tax reforms in the late 1970s and during the 1980s. Extensive tax reforms put in place in 1996 are expected both to increase incentives for entrepreneurial efforts as well as return the black-market economy to the mainstream.
5. We observe that those countries that have democratic platforms to express discontent with government policies were able to make the turnaround to reforms much faster than those that had no democratic platforms. Asia's Soviet bloc countries (and military dictatorships) had wallowed in poor development over very long periods, whereas those countries with democratic traditions made quick transitions to effect policy switches. Therefore the common assertion by some Asian leaders that democratic freedom and development are antithetical is not true in the long run.
6. A struggle for power that ensued after the death of Mao is at the root of the search for reforms. Deng Xiaoping, the eventual winner in the power struggle, made a surprising return to power even though he was twice incarcerated by Mao's regime as a capitalist. He was the principal person responsible for the overthrow of the so-called Gang of Four, which included Mao's wife, who, along with Huo Guo-fong, took power after announcing the death of Mao. Reforms in this country came about from a search for political legitimacy of the Communist control of this large nation.
7. The import substitution strategy was based on the assumption that by putting to use unused economic resources to produce the badly needed goods and services in poor countries, such

as India, the state would reduce poverty. Economic development would soon ensue. Initially, the plan called for building infrastructure and industrial capacity. However, politicians slowly diverted this strategy to serve their purpose of targeting investments to some sectors to attract popular support for political parties. By the 1960s, the import substitution strategy had degenerated towards credit-targeting schemes. Different shades of this were practised by many countries, including Japan, Indonesia and others. By the mid-1980s, almost all countries had abandoned these schemes as unsuitable and wasteful.

8.   This statement is not strictly true. These potential tiger economies had suffered setbacks from becoming the new tiger economies after the 1997 Asian financial crisis. It was generally suggested in the early 1990s that Malaysia and Thailand would graduate to become the new tiger economies. Since the financial crisis hit them, such discussion has disappeared from the press.

9.   Friedman (1958). For a full discussion of this point see Ariff (1998c).

10. The extent of state involvement in production both in China and Vietnam is still very high. Some estimates reported in the financial press suggest that active privatization may release millions of workers in these countries. China may experience unemployment of about 15–20 million people in the non-agricultural areas: it already has substantial unemployment in the heavy-industry belt where reforms have led to corporatization of loss-making firms. In December 1998, China's military announced that it had taken steps to refrain from producing civilian goods and services. Vietnamese state firms are now required to raise capital from banks without any protection from the state budget. Thus the inevitable taming of the state firms must come soon, with attendant problems.

11. These were the first two countries to have specific laws to attract foreign investment. The laws were included in the Economic Incentives Act, which has become a major reference point for capital account opening in Asia.

12. The largest investment trust in China failed in the second half of 1998, as in many other economies, because of lack of central bank prudential supervision of its activities. The failure of GITIC, one of 260 such investment corporations in China, led to the discovery that only 17 cents per dollar of investment could be found when the assets were put in the hands of the Courts! Before the collapse, GITIC had US$60 billion in assets. A large number of such unsupervised investment firms have been permitted to fail in China. This is evidence of the serious state of affairs in China's statist financial sector.

13. Banking theory suggests that banks perform the very useful function of collecting small deposits and then making large loans to firms: this is their maturity transformation function. Banks are presumed to be good at monitoring the firms to discover whether they are efficient at using the borrowed money. That is the delegated monitoring functions of banks, which is largely absent in command economies as well as in mixed economies, the latter because of rampant state intervention.

14. As financial centres, these sectors account for almost one sixth of the GDP of these economies. The financial sector normally contributes about 5–8 per cent to GDP in most countries.

15. More will be said on financial liberalization and sequencing of reforms. Though there is a lack of complete consensus on sequencing, there is general agreement that external openness should take place after real-sector reforms are completed. There are exceptions to this rule, as in the case of Indonesia.

16. In the case of Korea, one has to be cautious about such assertions. Korea postponed full reforms to open the economy to foreign entry to as late a date as possible. For example, capital account openness came only in mid-1996, just before its admission as the twenty-fourth member of the OECD grouping. In fact some observers have mentioned the lack of two-way openness in Korea as a glaring anomaly in Korea's commitment to liberalization.

17. This is a very old idea going back to the 1960s. The social organization skill of a small minority of modernizing élites in a society was found to be present in societies that secured modernization and economic and social growth. This idea has been used by sociologists and political scientists to examine changes in societies undergoing modernization and economic growth. An excellent introduction can be found in Deyo (1987).

2. The Asian financial crisis

1. A WORLD OF INCREASING FINANCIAL FRAGILITY

The Asian financial crisis started when the previously basket-pegged Thai currency was free-floated on the fateful Thursday, 2 July 1997.[1] We want first to make a statement of verifiable fact about Asia's growth experience before examining the genesis of the crisis. The path to growth over the last quarter-century, it will be seen throughout the remaining chapters of this book, was very assuredly liberalization, which helped Asia to secure higher growth than before. The readers may just note in passing this stylized fact that will emerge at the end of the book; this chapter examines the financial crisis. The crisis unleashed by the currency volatility in this instance in July 1997 had a historical root stretching back to 1946. The world bottled the currency volatility genie for the next 26 years through the Bretton Woods Agreement. That agreement enabled the world to rein in stable prices over that period. Through the sterling performance of the General Agreement on Tariffs and Trade (GATT) (now the World Trade Organization), the volume of trade in goods and services increased, while the traders did not have to worry about how the exchange rates would affect their sales. In 1998, the total value of trade in goods and services amounted to US$6900 billion, which is 23 per cent of the world GDP. The weaker currencies of smaller economies were given protection from volatility by the stronger currencies of the developed countries through a system of cross-fixing the vulnerable exchange rates of smaller economies to the much stronger currencies of the developed countries. Smaller economies faced greater weakness from exports of less competitive commodities and/or less aggregated goods. The more prosperous economies thereby provided exchange rate stability, maintaining the fixed exchange regime by themselves.

Of course that agreement broke down in 1971. Nixon, the American president, is famously connected to this event when he unhooked America, a key participant, from the fixed exchange system linked to the dollar peg to the price of gold. This let the exchange rate genie out of the bottle. Over the last 28 years, exchange-rate-led instability has periodically set back growth prospects mostly in those countries, such as Thailand, that used basket-peg currency management.[2] The fixed exchange rate system of the world came unstuck with that American decision, which has led to very high exchange rate volatility ever since. During the 20 years from 1971 to 1989, there were 49 cases of documented banking crises, most of which were related to weakening currencies.[3]

The costs arising from the increasingly exchange-rate-led crises have been quite high during the last 28 years. Let us add up the costs of putting the economies through a few crises since 1981. These cases are well documented in several published studies: the cost to Chile was 30 per cent of GDP during 1981–86; 20 per cent in Malaysia to redress the effects of a currency speculation and the failure of cooperatives, 1985–88; 20 per cent in Venezuela, 1990–91; and 18 per cent in Mexico for recovery from the now famous *tequila* crisis of 1994. A total of 35 banking crises have been reported over 1990–98. Almost all these had some connection with exchange rate instability.

The Asian countries under the IMF reconstruction schemes and Malaysia are expected to incur a cost equivalent to about 20 per cent of GDP or about US$25–35 billion over the next three years to regain their previous path to growth. Japan, whose economic troubles have several other causes, is expected to spend ¥60 trillion, US$440 billion at the 1998 exchange rate, to rescue Japan's banking system and make it healthy enough to resume its important role in Japan's and indeed Asia's recovery from the crisis.[4] Of the 50 top banks in the world, 14 are from the Asia Pacific region with a total asset base of US$4700 billion measured in 1995–96 exchange rates. The capital base of 11 of the Japanese top banks is 5.1 per cent of total assets in 1997. The average capital base was much higher for the other 36 banks from OECD countries in the top 50 list. Four UK banks included among the 50 had a capital-to-asset ratio of 7 per cent while the German banks had about the same ratio as the Asian banks. The US banks had the highest ratio of about 8 per cent of assets. These figures are based on book values reported in financial statements compiled according to generally accepted accounting principles.

The worldwide flow of money in search of higher returns in the money, bond and share markets has increased during the same period as well. Globalization in the sale of money as opposed to the sale of goods and services (Bhagwati, 1997) has brought opportunities to make huge gains for those doing money transmission business across national boundaries. The 1998 statistics for the total estimated value of the daily transactions in currencies is US$1400 billion.[5] It is reported in the popular press that this level of monetary exchange activities is about twelve times the currency exchange needed to support the world trade in goods and services. Thus the intensive currency trade is intrinsically connected to the flow of money to the more liberalized economies, and thereby exchange rate volatility is a serious candidate as a destabilizer of economic and social development in small nations.

With the opportunity for profits in the trade of money as opposed to profits from the trading in goods and services has come a powerful Wall Street lobby to open barriers to entry for short-term capital into the financial markets of the world. Though exact statistics are not available, there are some ball-park numbers reported in the press and on the Internet. For example, due to the persistently low real interest rates in Japan's financial markets, the Japanese investors invest large amounts in the US short-term money market. That amounts to about US$120 billion in the bills markets. Given the large size of the US market, a placement of that magnitude by the Japanese may not create severe jumps in volatility.

That is not the case when large short-term flows take place into and out of small economies.[6] For instance, the entry of investors into the then newly liberalized Korean share market in the late 1980s led to a temporary increase in share prices, which collapsed when the foreign investors withdrew short-term capital from the market. The 1993 stag attack on the emerging share markets led to huge price increases and diversification gains for international portfolio investors. Share prices collapsed after the withdrawal of foreign portfolio investments during 1994–95.[7] Flow of foreign capital, when such capital is invested as physical assets through foreign direct investment (FDI) does not cause such destabilization of the currencies of the recipient countries. Money invested in cement and machines cannot be moved suddenly.

Asia's share in the latter was consistently one third of the current US$300 billion or so FDI flows during most years from 1987 to 1996. These flows to the developing countries have been growth-promoting in that FDI also brings a network of markets for the developing countries to connect them to the world and the technology for the locals to work with, and hence, perhaps learn to operate new applied technologies. Tax incentives and, in some countries, subsidized financing incentives have been offered by many countries to attract FDI. Five of the fast-growing developing countries – China, Indonesia, Malaysia, Singapore and Thailand – alone attracted about US$70 billion of the US$300 billion worth FDI in some years during 1987–96.[8] This has been a tremendous boon to growth. Not surprisingly, after a temporary decline in this flow since the onset of the Asian financial crisis, the FDI flows were slowly increasing in late 1999: reports in the financial press such as *The Economist* suggest that this flow started to increase in 1999 in all but Indonesia, which was awaiting political resolution from a more democratic election in 1999. In November 1999, political uncertainty was resolved with the election of a moderate democratic leader (Abdurahman Wahid) who formed a national coalition government from all parties with priority on economic recovery and national integrity. Multinationals from Asia and elsewhere are beginning to buy up firms in troubled Asia because of the crisis.

The first task in our efforts to understand the Asian financial crisis is to describe the extent of liberalization that had taken place at the time of its onset. Section 2 provides a brief overview of the liberal policy experiences of selected countries. The background to the genesis of the crisis is provided in Section 3, which deals with the bigger picture of currency volatility that had become a permanent feature of the post-Bretton Woods world with more or less market-determined exchange rates. The genesis of the financial crisis is described in section 4 by reference to a table of the chronology of the events over July 1997 to December 1998. A causality test shows that the origin of the contagion of the crisis can be traced to the five currencies with the most exposure to short-term foreign capital flows. The financial fragility suggested here as the root cause of the genesis of the crisis is explored further with more statistics on this factor and its effects: see Section 5. The chapter ends with general observations of the salient points covered in this chapter.

2. A GLIMPSE OF ASIA'S FINANCIAL LIBERALIZATION

The rest of this book provides a lengthy documentation of the steps taken during a 25-year period by Asian countries to implement programmes of economic and financial liberalization. Such reforms by a group of early reformers produced very high economic growth rates of about 6 to 8.5 per cent in real economic growth in Korea, Malaysia, Singapore, Thailand and Indonesia. These five countries had together, therefore, amassed huge foreign reserves from the healthy external sectors during the mid-1980s to 1996. These reserves have been an instrument, a critical one, in helping the central banks to defend the basket peg put in place in some cases as long ago as ten or more years before the crisis. There are five chapters, one for each country, in the rest of the book that detail the liberalization programmes followed by them, and readers can get detailed statistics for these countries.

China, in many ways still a command economy, with 28 000 central government-owned inefficient state enterprises and a largely state-owned financial sector, has invited multinationals and overseas ethnic Chinese capital to its shores to generate private-sector growth. This experiment can be characterized as a major effort to overcome the inefficiency of the state enterprises by expanding the private-incentives-based private sector's capacity to generate efficiency. This strategy also helped this domestic-capital-starved country in a previous period to upgrade technology, which it could ill afford to buy at this stage of its development. China, too, built a huge foreign currency reserve estimated at end of 1998 at US$95 billion. A fixed currency exchange rate is still in force and is likely to be in force for a while now that there is good reason to defer a promised change to a managed float in 1999: a decision on this has been postponed by the State Council. China's reserves are unlikely to be needed to defend the currency immediately, but that reserve may be needed soon, as China adopts pegging or basket-pegging of its yuan in the future. Vietnam is a late-comer to this brand of so-called market economy with a socialist character. Detailed information about the progress of these two transitional and successful reformers – at least up to now without the urgent need to reform the state sector – can be found in the respective chapters of the book. This is the background of one situation at the time of the crisis.

A few other countries that did not go that far in adopting liberal policies also secured growth: Vietnam, Pakistan, the Philippines, India and Bangladesh are these reluctant or late reformers. In all these cases, too, post-liberalization growth experiences have been significantly higher than growth in the pre-reform era, but these growth rates were muted. Growth in the post-reform period has gone up by about 2 per cent per annum from the pre-reform growth rate of 3 per cent that these countries were stuck at over long periods of poor growth. These countries were not seriously affected by the financial crisis simply because they still had some degree of control on imports. They had also not built short-term capital flows in their banks or their firms to the same extent that the fast-track countries did in the 1990s. These features of these economies are discussed in a later section.

Table 2.1 provides a brief, very basic, summary of the liberalization policies already in place before the onset of the crisis. Only four countries are included in this table for the purpose of setting the general framework for analysing the crisis. A quick review of its contents provides the flavour of the reforms of the three different experiences of the 13 countries. The early reformers had undertaken extensive reforms to such an extent that they had almost full current and capital account openness. Here a private-sector-led real sector dominated the output despite some state ownership, though not to as great a degree as in the other two groups of countries. These had greater openness to the world, and so had a large foreign portfolio and direct investment as a feature of their growth, which is now known to have been a source of instability. The financial sector was also mostly under the control of private firms, though in Korea some state ownership (about 13 per cent of the assets in the banks) continued, especially in the foreign exchange banks.

India is taken as a case to illustrate the effect of long-delayed reforms being torpedoed onto this large economy during a short period of ten years. After that, the country took a major miscalculated step to explode atomic bombs, and later long-range missiles, which dissuaded the external world from taking advantage of the liberal conditions to enter the economy. Nevertheless it had, at the time of the onset of the financial crisis, a greater degree of openness without the huge short-term capital-chasing low-profit investments that the other five fast-growing countries were busy putting in place. There are four

Liberalization and the Asian financial crisis

Table 2.1   *Overview of liberal policies in force in selected countries before the crisis*

Countries	Sectors	Description of state of liberal reforms
Early reformers (Korea)	Real sector	Entry barriers to domestic sector not eased for foreign firms. Through MFN and infant-industry provisions of the GATT, tariff reforms delayed as long as possible. By 1993, tariff reduced to very low levels of about 17% for foreign goods.
	Fiscal sector	Tax reforms in 1981 broadened tax base. Many state banks.
	Financial sector	State ownership of financial institutions. 1985–86 reforms to divest share ownership. Still significant state shareholding kept. Entry barriers to foreign banks eased as Korea developed external economy in the 1970s and 1980s. Generally suppressed financial sector.
	Exchange rate	From US$ peg to managed exchange rate in 1990. Daily fix. Capital account opening only in July 1996.
	Interest rates	Slow adoption of reforms. Only long-term rate reforms in 1988.
(Malaysia)	Real sector	Real sector laid open to foreign firms with even 100% equity ownership. Tariff reduced to low levels in the late 1980s. Tax and other incentives for firm bringing FDI.
	Fiscal sector	Tax reforms in the late 1980s and early 1990s. Privatization used to divest; private-sector management of public services.
	Financial sector	Banks in private sectors. Central bank task to grow domestic institutions. Already-present foreign banks required by 1995 to be locally incorporated. Bank modernization and improved supervision.
	Exchange rate	Early removal of fixed rate: 1978. Capital accounts have been open since then as well.[*]
	Interest rates	Interest rates administered with consultation with the banks. This was changed in 1991 until no controls were placed on interest rates.
Hesitant reformers (India)	Real sector	Real sector under heavy government intervention rapidly decontrolled both domestic and foreign entry since 1991. Still not fully liberalized. Mostly 51% foreign equity; priority areas up to 100% equity. Capital controls relaxed since 1994. From a base of under US$200 million in the 1980s, FDI has grown to about US$3000 million in 1996.

Countries	Sectors	Description of state of liberal reforms
	Fiscal sector	In 1991, about 24% of the output from government-owned inefficient enterprises. Privatization plan not actively pursued yet.
	Financial sector	No tax reforms until 1996. Tax reforms announced in 1997. Banking sector has high non-performing loans; reforms not yet implemented. State-owned financial institutions still dominate the sector since reforms have been put in over 1993–94 in all subsectors.
	Exchange rate	Exchange rate liberalized in 1994. Capital account reforms extensive, except for individuals limited. Exchange rate volatility has declined since then. A form of free float offered.
	Interest rates	Heavy interest rate intervention and controls. Reforms extensive. Not yet fully effective.
Transitional economies (Vietnam)	Real sector	Transitional economy and central planning led to domination by state enterprises (about 80 000). Now limited freedoms to form private enterprises. Limited reforms to attract foreign capital to special production zones. High tariff still maintained. No capital account opening to local firms. FDI flows mainly from ASEAN have increased substantially, but not enough.
	Fiscal sector	State budget heavily subsidizes loss-making state firms. Since 1994, decentralization, and limited cut-off of financing are making the state firms turn around with some profits.
	Financial sector	Banking reforms being undertaken in 1997–98. Long way to go. New and specialized banks set up in the 1990s. Capital market reform not yet accomplished.
	Exchange rate	Moved from fixed multiple exchange rates to a unified exchange rate. Daily fixing since 1996 is a form of managed float.
	Interest rates	Interest rates still controlled. In 1997, long-term interest rates were freed from controls. Deposit rates under minimum rate controls.

Note: * Exchange and capital controls in October 1998.

Source: See the tables in each country chapter.

more countries in this hesitant reformer group. More details on India and others are contained in the relevant chapters of the book.

The transitional economies are represented by Vietnam in Table 2.1. Though China, the other case in this category, still has many structural weaknesses of the kind found in Vietnam, it managed to cover the inefficiency of the state firms in the real sector (and the financial sectors) by smothering it with the efficiency of the private sector. This has been achieved by an elaborately planned FDI-originated huge stimulation of real-sector activities driven by foreign owners of capital and local small businesses owned for the first time as private-sector enterprises. Vietnam began on the road to reform in the early 1990s. But it still has a form of exchange fixing, limited capital account opening, and poor management skills in operating financial aggregates.

This quick review of the book's central theme, liberalization, suggests one common theme. The financial sectors of the very same countries that were affected quite badly by the crisis can be described as being wide open. The exchange rate was basket-pegged; the interest rates were responding fully to world rates; there was foreign capital, especially of the short-term kind, which is now linked to the onset of the crisis, which supported huge expansion by the domestic firms investing these resources in such low-profit schemes as infrastructure, land-based tourism and property ventures. There was a greater mismatch between the average maturity of bank deposits and that of bank lending. As long as the basket-peg could keep the exchange rate as high as possible, the short-term money would keep coming as capital flows, and there would be no liquidity crunch on the financial sector. The canalization in the financial sector would go undisturbed. The acquiescing central banks from Seoul to Jakarta were not in a hurry to consider enforcing already available (for example in Malaysia) prudential norms, nor to put into effect new reforms to remove this dangerous source of banking fragility in their economies.

2. THE 1997 ASIAN FINANCIAL CRISIS

The Genesis of the Crisis

It is unlikely that a financial crisis[9] is caused by a single factor, since several factors work together and then lead to what later becomes labelled as a crisis Kindleberger (1996). The particular event that may trigger a crisis may be termed the contagion event. In that sense, the dramatic and rapid decline in the volatility of the Thai baht is the contagion event for the 1997 Asian financial crisis. Table 2.2 offers a chronological record of how the contagion spread to the rest of the world. As can be seen in that table of events, the crisis appears to have affected the immediate neighbours in Asia first, then spread to the stock markets, and then to the world at large. By the end of 1998 the Asian financial crisis began to assume a world dimension. This was particularly made worse by the political destabilization in several affected countries, notably Indonesia, and mistakes in the implementation of the IMF programme of assistance. These factors led to the crisis being dragged out to the end of 1998 and into 1999.

Table 2.2   The baht currency crisis triggers a contagion

Date	Country	What happened
1997		
July 2	Thailand	After four years of defending the weakening baht, the Bank of Thailand announced free float of the baht. Baht loses 10% of its pre-float value.
July 20	Philippines	IMF grants US$1000 million as emergency grant after peso falls outside a widened band to defend the basket peg. IMF warns Thailand to cut its spending, requests it to take a loan from the IMF.
July (undated)		The trade economist Bhagwati condemns free trade in money.
July 24	Malaysia	Malaysian ringgit comes under speculative attack. The famous Mahathir's attack on speculations such as those of George Soros begins.
August 11	Thailand	IMF, led by Japan's pressure, pledges US$16 billion to Thailand as rescue package.
	Indonesia	Indonesia's rupiah under attack. Bank Indonesia's attempt to contain the troubles proves unsuccessful.
	Asia	Asian stock markets plunge in unison: Manila 9.3%; 4.5% in Jakarta, etc.
September 4	Philippines	Philippine peso falls to the lowest level before central bank intervenes to maintain basket peg.
	Malaysia	Malaysia spends US$20 billion to prop up the share market.
October 8	Indonesia	Indonesia considers asking IMF for an emergency bailout.
October 27	USA	New York share market loses 7.2% in value.
October 23–8	Hong Kong	Hong Kong share market declines by nearly 25% in value.
November 3	Japan	Japan's Sanyo Securities files for bankruptcy. South Korean won loses 7%, biggest one-day loss.
	Korea	South Korea begins talk with IMF for tens of billions in emergency aid after Japan turns down Korean request.
November 8	Japan	Japan's third financial house to apply for closure: the seventh largest Yamaichi Securities.
November 20	Korea	Korean stock market plunges with a loss of 7.2%.
November 24	Japan	Tokyo City Bank, a regional bank, closes.
November 25	Korea	Korea agrees to IMF conditions for restructuring assistance of $55 billion.
December 3	Malaysia	Malaysia imposes tough reforms including budget cuts.
December 22	Korea	Korean won plunges further.
December 25		IMF and lender nations move to finance US$10 billion loan to Korea.

Table 2.2   continued

Date	Country	What happened
1998		
January 12	Hong Kong	Peregrine of Hong Kong files for liquidation from share market loss.
January 17	Indonesia	Indonesian president fires the central bank governor.
May 21		Indonesia's President Suharto resigns after a wave of bloody riots.
August 11–27	World	Stock markets plunge around the world in expectation of interest rate rises in the USA.
August 20	(Internet)	Paul Krugman supports temporary imposition of fixed exchange rate as the desperate Plan B for a troubled world.
September 1	Malaysia	Malaysia announces going back to a fixed rate (RM 3.8 = US$1) from October 1998. All free-market currency transactions are abolished.
September 27	Japan	A major leasing company in Japan files for bankruptcy.
October 2	USA	The Long-Term Hedge Fund is reported to have lost US$5 billion. The Federal Reserve mounts a rescue by putting together a consortium to rescue the Long-Term Hedge Fund.
October 17	USA	The Fed announces interest rate cuts, and the share market rebounds. Two more rate cuts follow by November 20.
December 1998	Asia	Most currencies that had overshot (baht, rupiah, peso. ringgit and won) recovered about halfway from their worst declines. The rupiah gained the most from its low of some Rp 20 000 to Rp 7600 = US$1.

Source: Internet publications of *Asian Economies Reports, 1997–1998*.

The highlights of the events unleashed by the baht contagion may be summarized by a few generalizations. The contagion from the baht crisis spread quickly before the end of the year to the Philippines, then to Malaysia, then to Korea, and then to Indonesia where it took on a virulent dimension because of the worsening political instability surrounding the end of authoritarian rule for 34 years. By the end of 1997, currency depreciation in US dollar terms was very severe and unprecedented in Asia. Losses relative to the June 1997 exchange rates were: Thailand lost 56 per cent; the Philippines 54 per cent; Malaysia 40 per cent; Korea 78 per cent; and Indonesia 76 per cent. Second, the contagion weakened the ability of those affected countries to sustain their then current levels of imports, which forced them to take measures to reduce imports, and then borrow to redress the damages to the financial system to meet trading commitments. This led to the third effect: Indonesia, Thailand, the Philippines and Korea came under IMF reconstruction schemes while Malaysia decided to ride the crisis with its own resources. Fourth, the share markets of the neighbouring countries, and then the world, started declining by up to half or more as interest rates were about to go up a year after the onset of the crisis. This led to a few spectacular bankruptcies of banks, large securities and leasing companies. Fifth, the contraction in regional trade brought declines in the exchange rates of several other countries. Examples are the Singapore dollar, the Australian dollar, and the yen. Towards the end of 1998 the currencies had, however, recovered from their overshot levels by about half or more. But at 1999 levels, almost all Asian currencies were a good deal cheaper than they were in June 1997.

The effect on the financial systems has been very severe indeed. The banking systems have come under strong IMF restructuring programmes in Indonesia, Korea, the Philippines and Thailand. Malaysia was raising funds in late 1998 and early 1999 to address its banking problems. The lack of prudential norms in bank lending in all these countries has been seriously exposed – so much so that there is now strong lobby to cut off the nexus of connected lending practised in all these countries. The asset markets have also felt the impacts of the crisis. Property markets in all these countries have begun to lose value, and prices have come down by 30 to 60 per cent. In a peculiar twist of events, even the heavily controlled car prices – an asset of great status value – in Singapore have come down by 20–30 per cent! All the affected economies have gone from above 5 per cent growth rates before the crisis to experience one to three-quarter per cent of declines in output growth in 1997 and 1998. Korea, Malaysia, the Philippines, Singapore, Thailand and Indonesia have gone into recession. Korea experienced a –4.6 per cent output decline in 1998; Thailand a –7.8 per cent decline. In short, the secondary effect of what started as a currency crisis has now become a full-blown economic crisis. Several years of hard-earned prosperity in all these countries is being rolled back.[10]

The Contagion and Causality

The baht contagion has been commented upon in the press and in the literature. However, it is instructive to test if the contagion actually happened as has been suggested. Tables 2.3 and 2.4 provide evidence to settle this question with the help of reliable statistical tests. Table 2.3 summarizes cointegration test results. Econometric wisdom suggests that if two time-dependent variables are moving closely together, then these variables may be described as being closely cointegrated. That is, the Thai baht and Filipino peso move together if their time series of currency prices are significantly cointegrated. A test can also be done on the direction of this movement: whether the baht or the peso, and so on caused the changes in the other currency. This question may be answered by reference to the causality test results presented in Table 2.4.

Table 2.3   Johansen–Juselius cointegration test results[11] (lags of two intervals)

Currency of	Eigenvalue	Likelihood ratio	5% critical value	1% critical value	Hypothesized no. of CE(s)[a]
Philippines	0.891672	273.0216	156.00	168.36	None * *
Thailand	0.655366	161.8922	124.24	133.57	At most 1 **
Hong Kong	0.515010	108.6286	94.15	103.18	At most 2 **
Singapore	0.398356	72.44727	68.52	76.07	At most 3 *
Korea	0 330278	47.04281	47.21	54.46	At most 4
Malaysia	0.259304	26.99818	29.68	35.65	At most 5
Indonesia	0.167355	11.98991	15.41	20.04	At most 6
Japan	0.055075	2.832495	3.76	6.65	At most 7

Notes:
[a] CE = cointegrating equation(s) found significant. Significance is denoted by * (5% probability) and ** (1% probability) of rejection of the hypothesis that there is cointegration.
L.R. or likelihood ratio test indicates 4 cointegrating equation(s) at 5% significance level.

The statistics in Table 2.3 would have us believe that in broad terms the exchange rates moved together during the test period, January to December 1997. It may be recalled that the crisis started in July: the first six months of the year had normal currency movements and the second six months experienced the familiar overshooting of currencies experiencing crisis. Contrary to popular public perception created in the financial press, currencies other than the baht appear to move together as well. The question of which currency caused which currency to change will be discussed with the statistics in Table 2.4. However, it appears that all the currencies mentioned in Table 2.3 moved together to produce the Asian financial crisis.

The figures from the next set of statistics (Table 2.4) would also have us believe that the contagion has not just a Thai origin, but a common origin from six currencies all moving together to cause the overshooting. The first set of results is for one-way causation (see column 2 under Unidirectional). These results suggest that a change in any one of the seriously affected currencies did cause significant changes in other currencies. If we only take into account the very pronounced results by restricting ourselves to the figures marked with one asterisk (*), then it appears that the Thai baht, the Singapore dollar and the Malaysian ringgit were the main currencies causing contagion. That is, any changes in those currencies led in turn to significant changes in the other two as well as in other currencies. This is as expected since these three countries had more advanced and integrated economies with more financially open conditions. Further, there were huge regional investments among these partners in ASEAN.

Table 2.4 *Causality test results for contagion (Pairwise Granger causality tests with two lags)*

Currencies tested		Unidirectional	Reverse causation
1	Thailand vs Philippines	11.12*	No
2	Hong Kong vs Philippines	2.99***	No
3	Singapore vs Philippines	6.36*	No
4	Korea vs Philippines	2.74***	No
5	Malaysia vs Philippines	5.27*	No
6	Indonesia vs Philippines	2.53***	No
7	Japan vs Philippines	No	No
8	Hong Kong vs Thailand	No	No
9	Singapore vs Thailand	5.49*	2.57***
10	Korea vs Thailand	No	No
11	Malaysia vs Thailand	3.96**	3.98**
12	Indonesia vs Thailand	No	3.65**
13	Japan vs Thailand	No	No
14	Singapore vs Hong Kong	No	2.50***
15	Singapore vs Hong Kong	No	5.77*
16	Malaysia vs Hong Kong	No	No
17	Indonesia vs Hong Kong	No	No
18	Japan vs Hong Kong	No	No
19	Korea vs Singapore	No	No
20	Malaysia vs Singapore	No	2.43 * * *
21	Indonesia vs Singapore	No	No
22	Japan vs Singapore	No	4.34**
23	Malaysia vs Korea	3.06***	No
24	Indonesia vs Korea	No	3.74**
25	Japan vs Korea	No	No
26	Indonesia vs Malaysia	No	No
27	Japan vs Malaysia	No	2.99***
28	Japan vs Indonesia	No	2.75***

Notes:
Statistical significance indicated by * (1% probability); ** (5% probability); and *** (10% probability) that the hypothesis of no causality may be rejected. Note the few currencies causing the contagion.

Changes in the Hong Kong dollar and Korean won appear to be also weakly connected in this unidirectional causation of currency instability since the F-ratios are significant at the much lower acceptance levels of 10 per cent probability. Note that the Indonesia rupiah is not found to be significantly connected to this contagion.

When reverse causation was tested, it appears that the Japanese yen, the Indonesian rupiah, the Malaysian ringgit and the Korean won are found to have reverse-caused the changes in other currencies. This finding is interesting and is also consistent with expected economic effects from the extensive trade and investment links these four economies have with all the other countries in the region. Hence, again, the common idea that the problems of Thailand's and of Indonesia's economic problems were the main factor in the financial crisis can easily be rejected. The greater integration of these countries among themselves and with others through a significantly greater degree of financial and real-goods flows is the reason for the severity of the crisis effects in all these countries.

Therefore, we may conclude that the financial crisis appears to have a multi-country origin even though it started on 2 July 1997 as contagion from Thailand. The role of the Hong Kong dollar and the Singapore dollar in the currency crisis appears to be confirmed also, since these are financial centres where the other country currencies were transacted. Finally, the greater integration of Korea and Japan with the economies of the region meant that changes in the values of their currencies would naturally affect the other currencies as well. In conclusion, the contagion appeared first in Thailand, but had several sources.

3.   FINANCIAL FRAGILITY IN ASIA REVEALED

Build-up of Foreign Currency Loans

The discussion up to this point suggests that the baht contagion had a common origin in six other currencies, all of which appear to have some role in the crisis in each other's currency volatility. These are the peso, the ringgit, the rupiah, the yen, the won and the Singapore dollar. The reader will recollect from the survey on liberalization that the central banks of these six currencies had regular interventions to defend them at some targeted levels. Next, these very same countries have been documented as practising connected bank lending, which has been shown to have led to significant non-performing loan build-up in the financial sectors. Third, it is in these six countries that a large number of financial institutions failed or large-scale banking reform efforts have been mounted within a year after the onset of the Asian financial crisis. This last factor is in a sense sufficient evidence of the serious financial fragility that had existed in these six economies. Therefore, the next task in this chapter is to analyse how financial fragility occurred.

Table 2.5   Foreign debt exposure and the financial crisis

	Bank foreign liabilities		Growth in outstanding private debt securities			
	June 1997	Dec. 1997	1992–94	1994–96	1996–97	1997–98
China	–	–	–	–	–	–
Indonesia	23.4	24.1	83	143	57	–2
Korea	90.6	78.7	29	140	31	–4
Malaysia	25.5	22.6	–11	124	17	–3
Philippines	11.4	10.1	77	209	45	0
Thailand	85.7	67.6	100	108	15	–3

Note: Figures are given as percentage change over the previous period.

Sources: Bank of International Settlements and IMF (November 1998).

 We first identify the international exposure of the banking sector in selected Asian countries: see Table 2.5. These statistics refer to the percentage changes in the domestic banking sector's foreign loans (see columns 2 and 3) and in the private sector's foreign origin loans in selected countries with data available: China is included to show that we have no data available for this country. The banking sector's exposure to foreign currency loans grew by large margins during the years 1996 to 1998. The three economies with the largest increases in foreign loans in the private sector are Thailand (108%), the Philippines (209%) and Korea (140%). Similarly, the changes in the banking sector's foreign loans in 1996 alone are very large in Korea (90.6% and 78.7% within 1997 and 1998), for example. In these countries, the value of foreign currency loans increased by a very large percentage. Banks in two countries almost doubled foreign loans: Thailand by 90.7 per cent and Indonesia by 90.6 per cent. Others too had large loan increases in both sectors. These high levels of loans were forthcoming after the liberalization of the financial sectors, which gave both the banks and the designated firms greater freedom to borrow from overseas without prudent limits tied to the capital base of the banks or to the capital structure of the firms. IMF publications released in September 1997 suggest short-term foreign loans rose in Indonesia by 160 per cent in 1995; by 85 per cent in the Philippines.

Things began to change after a year of crisis. For example, the supreme body, the Financial Reform Board of Korea, announced in November 1998 that firms were required by the end of 1999 to have a debt-to-equity ratio of no more than 200 per cent: this is reported on Internet pages. This rule means that firms could have only 2 dollars of loans for every dollar of equity, which would create a debt-to-asset ratio at most of 0.67. At the time of the crisis, Korean firms had as much as 7 dollars of loans for every dollar of equity. Press reports also suggest that Korean firms in general had 7 dollars of debt for every dollar of share capital at the height of the crisis: as will be seen later, this ratio for Malaysia and the USA was about the same at the time of the crisis, which suggests that some other variables were at work in the case of Malaysia. Some countries such as Chile had passed prudential regulations that placed a limit for banks on foreign currency loans equivalent of no more than 25 per cent of the regulatory capital. Prudential banking rules of this kind, if present *and* implemented, would not have fostered financial fragility. They would have prevented such weakness from destabilizing the economy and making it prone to financial crisis.

Another source of weakness before the crisis was the currency basket peg practised by these countries. Japan did not practise a basket peg, but in effect intervened in the market quite frequently in the 1990s as part of its policy first to synchronize its currency value to the G7 accord and second as a tool to support its trading policies. Continued interventions in the markets were made possible by this peg, bolstered by the healthy amount of reserves all these countries had built up in the period running up to the crisis. In a free-floating economy such as that of Australia, the currency adjustments are smooth as information hits the market, and slow adjustments are made. In a peg system, human intervention increases volatility in the currencies. When export growth was slowing down in a free-float regime, the currency adjusted slowly. With a basket peg, the volatility was high, and not smooth.

Exports were beginning to weaken as far back as October 1994 in Thailand. The Philippines experienced cash outflows surrounding the uncertainties of the post-Ramos government. Singapore's dominant electronic sector (46 per cent of its manufactured exports) weakened in 1995. Generally the high export growth rates either became very small or turned negative in Malaysia, Indonesia and Korea during a lengthy period of about ten quarters before the onset of the crisis.[12] The currency peg in these countries and the fixed exchange rates in many others ensured that the worsening current account statistics did not translate as lower currency values. Lower currency values have been registered with current account weaknesses in other countries with greater central bank independence: Australia, Canada and New Zealand. The Australian dollar went from close to A$1.00, yielding US$0.89 in 1993 to A$0.65 in 1996, a fall in value equal to 27 per cent. Such a smooth reaction was not possible under the managed peg.

This led to the inevitable delayed effect of cumulative bad news. The simmering current account problems and the banking fragility in Thailand were pushed to the headlines by an 18-month-long political drama in Thailand, which led the analysts to re-examine closely the economic fundamentals of the country. They began to sing a tune about Asia altogether different from those played hitherto by the World Bank, which in 1993 dubbed the Asian development experience a miracle brought about by the moving hand of good governance.[13] In July the baht devaluation occurred and its contagion spread quickly to other economies between July 1997 and March 1998. Subsequent political uncertainties in Indonesia during March to May 1998 worsened the effects of the crisis. The Indonesia rupiah went from about Rp 3500 = 1$US before the crisis to about Rp 8500 and then at the height of the political crisis to Rp 20 000 during a particular day in June 1998. The rupiah recovered to Rp 7600 = 1$US by October 1998.

Non-performing Loans

The obvious reaction to a sudden loss of control of the currency rate was a knee-jerk reaction of foreign short-term lenders to pull off or curtail further lending to the countries affected. Information in the previous subsection (in Table 2.5) reveals statistics on that reaction in all cases. Both the banking and the private-sector firms experienced sharp falls in the growth rates of foreign borrowing. There were also substantial declines in some cases. Soon the effect of the withdrawal or reductions in the further availability of loans or even dis-intermediation by depositors withdrawing their savings as a flight to safety or any combinations of these would lead to increases in bad debts. That is exactly what happened, as is shown for one country in Table 2.6.

Table 2.6 Non-performing loans as percentage of outstanding loans in Malaysia

	1988–90*	1991–93	1994–96	1997	1998
Commercial banks	24.67	14.33	5.70	3.60	3.30
Merchant banks	18.43	6.87	8.08	1.70	3.60
Finance companies	27.77	14.80	10.97	4.70	5.00

Note: * This was just after a recession during 1986–88.

Sources: Bank Negara Malaysia (1994) and press reports.

These figures for Malaysia suggest that its non-performing loans were not substantial in 1997 and 1998. The high levels of bad loans in 1988–89 are due to the economic recession that hit this economy during 1986–87. As the banks were coming out of that recession, the bad loans had still not been paid off, as happened later. The high bad loans in 1992–93 are also due to the after-effects of the Gulf War in 1991. The financial crisis does not seem to have had as severe an effect as these two previous major external shocks. Non-performing loans in the commercial banks are reported to be under 4 per cent of outstanding loans. Finance companies – there were 57 financial companies of which 8 were affiliated to major banks – had the highest levels of non-performing loans. International data sources give some further but sketchy statistics on this topic. Thailand's top banks had the following levels of bad loans: total bad loans amounted to B 4900 million in 1998. This is 20 per cent of the total loans of these banks. Before the onset of the crisis in July 1997, non-performing loans constituted 8 per cent. In Indonesia, non-performing loans were 15 per cent in state banks and 5 per cent in private banks during 1995. The next year witnessed a slight increase in these figures, but the crisis led to the closure of more than half the financial institutions when the currency, which initially went down from Rp 2500 per US dollar to Rp 3600, then depreciated severely to around Rp 12 000 in the month when the president of that country resigned on 20 May 1998!

Little or no information is available on this topic in Korea. But other information available in Korean Internet sources suggests a sudden jump in dishonoured cheques. The value of dishonoured cheques as a percentage of the value issued is as follows: under 8 per cent in 1992; 13 per cent over 1993–94; 15 per cent over 1995–98; and 23 per cent at the beginning of 1997, rising to 60 per cent by the middle of 1998. These statistics suggest the severity of the fragility of the financial sector of that country. Indonesia's dishonoured cheques must have been large as well. From about 5–10 per cent of the issued values in 1994–96, this statistic worsened to 15 per cent (in one month it went up to 19 per cent) in 1997. This has declined to the 15 per cent level in 1998.

Demand deposits in the Hong Kong banking system went down by 21 per cent following the crisis compared with the pre-crisis period. Savings deposits declined by 25 per cent during the crisis, which must have placed a huge strain on the banking sector to create credits. This and other information suggests that the monetary effect of the crisis has been a general weakening of financial strength – increased banking fragility, in other words – of the Asian countries. What is unique in the analysis is the kind of endemic non-performance, as is the case for Malaysia.

A similar effect, perhaps not of the same magnitude as in Asia, would be expected even in the developed economy's monetary sector during a financial crisis. This is not necessarily unique to Asia, though the severity may be less in more developed economies. For example, the American credit union bailout cost over US$300 billion. This amount is less than 5 per cent of GDP in the USA, but not in the Asian cases. But the important fact is that the banking sector was already having severe bad loan problems for well over two years before the crisis. The crisis could not have come at a worse time. Information released in November 1998 by the IMF suggests that the bailout in the worst cases may cost about 20 per cent of GDP.

— Non-performing loans can be seen as the consequence of imprudent lending, made worse by the crisis. The effect on the banks later weakened the situation of businesses which were unable to bear the high interest or to secure credits for normal operations. The overall effect is that the heavy reliance on foreign borrowing by the banking and the real sectors evaporated in 1998. Growth in foreign borrowing by banks declined by a quarter during the second half of 1997, at the worst point of the crisis. Even with the special reasons for borrowing abroad, it became difficult to attract such funds. The private sector, which had doubled and trebled foreign loans (for example, the Philippines) in the pre-crisis period, had negative growth in foreign outstanding loans. Other statistics available from IBRD and IMF sources in 1999 suggest that even before the crisis hit these countries, the banking sectors in all the affected countries had severe fault lines. They had too many foreign currency loans, exposure to the property sector was too high (Thailand had 28 per cent of loans to this sector), related party lending rules were not strictly followed, and foreign currency exposures were not hedged since there was a belief that the high level of reserves would be sufficient to ward off speculative attacks on the currencies.

The overall effect of the non-performing loans and the general weakness of the banking sector can be better evaluated by examining the revisions in the ratings of the financial strength of the banking system as documented from the IMF sources in Table 2.7.

Table 2.7   Financial strength rating following the crisis

	Mid-1996	End 1996	Mid-1997	End 1997	End 1998
China	D	D	D	D	D
Indonesia	D	D	D	D	E
Korea	D	D	D	D	E+
Malaysia	C+	C/C+	C/C+	D+	D
Philippines	D+	D+	D+	D+	D+
Singapore	B	B	B	C+/B	B
Thailand	C+	C+	C+	D	E+

Note: A (highest rating) to E (lowest rating) with the scale defined as the financial institutions not requiring support from shareholders, government and other institutions.

Source: Moody's Investor Services.

China's financial sector fragility has not been revealed as it was protected by its fixed exchange rate regime and was still on the export-led growth path without any significant declines at the time of the crisis.[14] All other countries had their ratings downgraded, as can be seen in the table. Even Singapore's sterling financial strength came under doubt. Its rating was downgraded in the second half of 1997. Korea's rating went down to E even though it had been admitted in 1997 to the OECD after three years of scrutiny about its suitability for membership. Malaysia was downgraded to D; the rating was moved one notch up in early 1999. Thailand has been worst hit, losing its rank from C down to grade E. Thus the crisis sapped the financial strength of these countries as never before. These ratings of the financial sectors in the affected countries reveal the financial fragility in Asia.

Impact of the Crisis on Exchange and Interest Rates

Table 2.8 contains summary statistics on the interest rate and exchange rate experiences of selected countries. We also provide data on official reserves as a percentage of GDP for various periods. It can be observed that there was significant weakening in all these factors. For example, China's reserves go down after the crisis, which suggests an external weakening, consistent with a still unreported decline in exports in China. In all the other countries, reserves have been built up during 1997 and 1998 to prevent further collapse of the ability of the economies to service imports at the increased post-crisis prices. The only exception is the Philippines, where the reserves declined substantially in 1997.

In all the countries – with the notable exception of China – exchange rates declined substantially compared to their long-term levels predicted by buoyant external conditions in 1991–96. The Thai currency went down to 39.14 compared with the pre-crisis level of B 25.2 = 1$US: a decline of 36 per cent in an economy that had the help of IMF support. The Philippine peso has depreciated to 40.00 from the pre-crisis level of 26.5 to one US dollar – a 34 per cent decline also under IMF help. For a US buyer, a dollar buys almost 49 per cent more ringgit: this is a case of no help from IMF or a case of self-help. The Korean won declined by almost 44 per cent while the Indonesian rupiah had the worst depreciation of the crisis, a 55 per cent decline for a US buyer. The mid-1999 exchange rates were much improved compared to the mid-1998 rates. Exchange rates were Rp 8500; Korea W 1200; Malaysia RM 3.80 (fixed); Philippines P 39; Singapore $1.74; Thailand B 37. It can be noted that the exchange rates have recovered (except in the case of Malaysia and Indonesia) to levels nearer to those in mid-1997 before the crisis. Currency rates are now recovering to levels reflective of more realistic levels underlying the fundamentals.

Table 2.8   Notable exchange rate declines and interest rate increases

	1981–85	1986–90	1991–96	1997	1998–99*
China					
Reserve to GDP	n.a.	n.a.	11	29	20
Interest rate	5.90	8.60	9.60	8.64	7.92
Exchange rate[a]	3.20	5.22	10.04	11.17	11.03
Indonesia					
Reserve to GDP	n.a.	6	6	15	33
Interest rate	10.40	17.22	17.60	21.82	55.95
Exchange rate	906	1744	2308	4650	7700
Korea					
Reserve to GDP	n.a.	5	4	5	15
Interest rate	10.3	10.00	9.20	21.82	7.70
Exchange rate	890	716	775	951	1395
Malaysia					
Reserve to GDP	n.a.	43	54	36	58
Interest rate	8.81	5.90	5.94	9.53	7.07
Exchange rate	2.43	2.70	2.55	3.89	3.81
Philippines					
Reserve to GDP	n.a.	1	2	0.3	0.5
Interest rate	11.54	11.40	15.06	16.28	12.56
Exchange rate	21.3	21.20	26.50	29.47	40.00
Thailand					
Reserve to GDP	n.a.	6	15	17	22
Interest rate	12.90	10.10	9.90	13.65	9.20
Exchange rate	26.70	25.30	25.20	31.64	39.14

Notes:
* Mid-year figures.
[a] Yuan per special drawing rights since it is more market-related. All other exchange rates are computed against one US dollar.

Source: IMF, *International Financial Statistics.*

The consequence of exchange rate decline was that it made subsequent inflation higher. That translated immediately as high interest rates as predicted by interest rate theories. The Thai interest rate went up to a hefty 13.65 per cent in 1997 compared with 9.90 before the crisis – a 38 per cent increase. By mid-1998, with the easing of monetary controls, interest rates have recovered to the pre-crisis levels in this country and the Philippines. That is not the case in other countries: the Indonesian interest rate for short-term borrowing is above 30 per cent! In early 1999, this came down to about 23 per cent. In other countries, interest rates have declined to a level closer to pre-crisis levels. In the still troubled Malaysia, statutory reserves were dramatically cut from 12 to 8.5 per cent in October 1998 and to under 5 per cent by mid-1999. This led to higher credit growth, which in turn has led to a fall in interest rates. That helped to expand credits and bring down the interest rate to 7.07 per cent in 1998 and 5.25 per cent in 1999, which is lower than the pre-crisis level of 5.54 per cent.

The reader has seen a substantial amount of statistics on a proposed explanation for the severity of the financial crisis in 1997. In Mexico there was merely a loss of confidence in the ability of the government to manage the economy when the native armed uprising showed signs of being successful in mounting a credible challenge to the former government. That loss of confidence led to the *tequila* crisis of 1994 in Mexico. In the case of the Asian financial crisis of 1997, the sequence of macroeconomic events appears to be as follows:

- Some economies liberalized and secured a more or less open regime with fully open external conditions for currency and capital trading.
- Absence of prudential rule enforcement on exposure to short-term loans built up quickly in the banking and in the real sector.
- The well-practised defence of basket-pegged currencies, successfully defended over 1995 to mid-1997, hid the impending problems due to weakening exports.
- Political crises partly caused by connected lending led to runs on currencies starting with the baht, then the peso, then the ringgit, then the rupiah and then the won.
- Financial fragility revealed after the normal effects of currency declines led to a large number of financial institution failures, when repayment of foreign currency borrowing and non-performing loans to the real sector worked through the banks.

The contagion theory, when tested, reveals a joint origin of the currency crisis among six currencies of the region. The primary reason for the severity of the crisis appears to be the already-present financial fragility, which emerged from failures to enforce prudential regulations in almost all the countries to address connected lending, too much lending to the property sector, non-performing loans, and so on. This theme will be taken up in the ensuing discussion in the next section.

5.　A PROVISIONAL ANSWER AND CONCLUSION

What, then, are the causes and the effects of the crisis on the countries analysed in this book? From the perspective of international economics, two main factors and a necessary condition can be identified as the factors that created the crisis. The necessary condition, which is not the same as causation, was created in Indonesia, Korea, Malaysia, the Philippines and Thailand through the greater degree of deregulation in these countries with respect to short-term cash flows into their banks and the real-sector firms. This was done as part of a greater liberalization to attract capital of any kind to sustain the high growth rates of around 8.5 per cent per annum in the 1990s precisely when the export sector, the backbone of servicing the foreign capital base, was steadily weakening.

The causal factors for the currency decline are two, namely a weakening of the export sectors in these countries and the central banks' attempts to keep the value of their exchange rates high through managed floats. The declining exports and the low profit of long-gestation investments in land- and property-based investments were inconsistent with the high exchange rates being maintained by the central bankers. More and more of the capital was being lent on the basis of connectedness of the borrowers to the government, big businesses, and often cross-border investments. In fact the idea of 'relational lending' was wrongly being encouraged as the Asian way of doing business. The world found that the quick fixes offered by this networked business facilitated by the triumvirate of the government, business and the banks – call them *quanzi* loans – flouted all the basic rules of lending. The provision of an implicit guarantee by the presence of government in the transactions (as pointed out in the Group of 22 Bankers' report to Bill Clinton, the American president, in December 1998) was at the root of the problem.

The effect of this multi-factor-led crisis can be summed up in one phrase: *increased financial fragility*. Increased financial fragility led to economic slowdown, to recession within about a year of the crisis in all the countries affected by it, and then to recoveries, after costing as much as about 20 per cent of the GDP of each of these countries. The social upheavals of these secondary effects on the economy, not to mention the political fallouts in all but Singapore, are sudden loss of employment for increased number of workers, and a general decline in the quality of life of the peoples in the near term of about one to three years.

Banking fragility, which was at the root of the severe problems after a year of the crisis, is a more dramatic symptom of financial fragility. This became a byword after the crisis. The exchange rate instability over a quarter-century of free floats of few developed-country currencies and the pegging-cum-managed floats of many developed and developing countries provided the ingredients necessary for increasing severity of this crisis. As noted in an earlier section, banking failures have become more frequent, severely threatening the sustainability of growth in the developing countries. Exchange rate instability has become stuck and speculators are trading 12 times the values of currency required to sustain the present level of world trade in merchandise (Bhagwati's *widgets*). Globalization of financial flows – especially with short-termism of portfolio funds in seeking returns within an accounting period across a global network of investments – translates in practice as endemic operational risk to the Asian banks and firms. This is especially severe when central banks fail to adopt prudential limits to external capital in the real and financial sectors.

None of the three models of banking organization has been able to cope with the adverse effects of continuing financial crises in the last ten years; the crises are bringing severe retardation to bear on normal economic activities. The American model with deposit insurance is evidently creating a moral hazard problem, leading to episodes of failure when banks make imprudent investments knowing in advance that the government or the deposit insurance will rescue them from a crisis: recall the deposit insurance failure in America in the credit union bailout in the 1980s. Unfettered competition among atomized US banks has been good to customers in the USA as the margin between deposits and lending narrowed the most under this model. Narrowed profits or bank failures from too small a margin would make more banks fail but improve services to the customers. The English model of banking, with few large banks providing the bulk of deposit management, has also led to periodic failures, in this case more from weaknesses in government policies in respect of prudential lending practices of the monopolistic large banks. The third model, the mono-banking of the Communists, is no longer a choice to be considered.

Banking fragility weakens the ability of the banks to fulfil their functions efficiently after the crisis. In both the developed and developing economies, the banking sector fulfils three key functions. These are (a) undertaking guarantees in financial transactions, an example being the letter of credit on which world trade depends heavily, (b) collecting small savings into large loans and (c) providing the framework for efficient payments among parties undertaking financial transactions. These functions cannot be taken over by the direct financial markets. In all the countries affected by the crisis, bank credits run at around 80 to 100 per cent of their GDP with direct market funds being a small portion of the total funds raised. In many other countries, the level of bank lending to the non-financial sector is below 80 per cent of GDP. Thus banking fragility becomes worse given the heavier reliance on bank credits for sustaining the very high growth rates of these developing economies.

One factor offered as an explanation for the crisis is financial liberalization. In Table 2.9, we demonstrate the beneficial effects of financial liberalization in deepening the markets to support a higher level of economic activities in a fast-growing economy. Financial deepening is seen to be a slow process that takes time. When financial liberalization was pursued vigorously, as in Malaysia and Singapore, the results were greater financial depth, as can be seen in the table. This eventually helps to create viable direct financial markets. Money-market depth in the less liberalized economies such as Korea and Indonesia is shallower, about 50 per cent of GDP, than in the more liberalized ones where this ratio is closer to 100 per cent.

Table 2.9   Greater financial depth to support economic growth

Financial depth	Korea		Indonesia		Malaysia		Singapore	
	1976–80	1999	1976–80	1999	1976–80	1999	1976–80	1999
Money-market depth (M2/GDP)	31.8	43.8	16.7	53.5	47.6	97.0	73.0	116.0
FIR (Financial intermediation ratio)	39.0	78.0	15.0	53.0	33.0	106.0	33.0	86.0
Capitalization ratio	22.0	80.0	3.0	45.0	55.0	220.0	95.0	160.0

Sources: IMF, *International Financial Statistics* and IFC publications. Figures computed by authors.

The financial intermediation ratio, FIR, which is the ratio of assets in the financial system as a proportion of GDP, shows the same pattern over time. FIR is just above 50 per cent in the less financially deep Indonesia compared with the ratio of over 100 per cent in the more developed Malaysia, for example. The capitalization ratios in these countries are also much higher than in slow-growth countries such as Vietnam or Pakistan (statistics are reported in their respective chapters). Thus, far from being the cause of disaster, financial liberalization supported the fast-growing economies to secure high output growth in the 1980s to 1996. It is financial fragility that has led to the crisis. A greater degree of financial openness, along with a subservient central bank that failed to enforce fragility-removing prudential regulations or monetary reforms (free-floating currencies), has facilitated the onset of the crisis. If the policy makers had taken steps to remove or even manage the financial fragility well, along with policies of liberalization, then the severity of the crisis would have been less pronounced.

The Internet releases on the top banks in the world provide information that suggests a strong oligopolistic banking structure in Australasia. Fourteen of the top 50 banks in the world are from Australasia. Of these, 11 are Japanese. While the decentralized American banking structure has spawned about 7898 banking institutions serving the US economy,[15] the model favoured in Asia is oligopolistic banking. The top few banks dominate the banking sector in all Asian countries and these promote very widespread feather-bedding practices of depressing deposit rates, keeping high margins, engaging in connected lending, and generally favouring easier regulatory burdens on them, and promoting oligopolistic banking, where the top four to five banks will account for the majority of deposits. Strangely, this form of banking in one country (Australia) is called the Four Pillars, when it should be named the Four Monopolistic Cousins. Compare this with the market share of 71.7 per cent of the deposits by America's 7898 banks! Even the largest 800 bank-holding companies there account for only 50.9 per cent of the deposits. In most Asian countries, a single savings bank will have more than 50 per cent of the deposits: an example is the case of the POSTBank in Singapore up to July 1998, when the POSTBank was merged with the DBSBank.

These top banks are even represented in the boards of the central banks, and thereby become privy to inside information of the regulators in some countries. Outside the boardrooms, the top bankers network with political and big business groups to facilitate anti-competitive practices in the industry. The command economies (China and Vietnam) and the socialist economies (India and so on) fail to make a distinction between responsibilities of the rule-makers and those of the rule implementors. The big businesses have thus produced a recipe for creating weak banking systems with huge non-performing loans. These latter cases are documented elsewhere in the book, and may be examples of the general weakness of people to seek monopoly rent – wealth without serious and honest effort. As long as financial intermediaries are likely to engage in a game of wresting more economic rent by seeking or working around the regulators' often flawed idealized rules (see Kane, 1999), no model will be fully proofed against manipulation.

Looking at the 1997 Asian financial crisis after it had run its course over 24 months gives a different conclusion from the one an observer might reach in the midst of the crisis. The one fact is that this crisis may cost the most in terms of the rescue efforts as well as in reduced growth it will perpetrate in the hitherto fast-growth economies during the two years surrounding the crisis. But a sobering fact is that the more we come to know of the genesis of the crisis, the more it reveals the following stylized facts:

- Pursuit of inappropriate policies by (a) relying on short-term domestic and foreign capital, (b) switching to long-gestation investment projects at the wrong time, when export growth was declining and (c) central banks failing to enforce independent monetary and prudential processes.
- The root cause of the problem that made the crisis worse was an endemic financial fragility resulting from the pursuit of the above policies.

Financial liberalization provided greater depth and resilience to sustain the greater amount of economic activities that were taking place in the crisis-hit countries. Liberalization therefore provided a necessary but not a sufficient condition for the crisis to have taken the severity it had taken in just about 24 months after the fateful Thursday 2 July 1997, when the Thai baht could not be stage-managed any longer.

NOTES

1. The Thai central bank was defending a weakening currency for a while. By mid-1997, when the Thai cabinet dithered over taking bold decisions to tackle its banking problem, a wrong signal was sent to the much more open financial markets. Confidence was shattered and the currency declined. Both authors of this book were conducting interviews in the financial sector, and witnessed these events as they travelled to these countries during May 1997 to March 1998 and met with senior officials and bankers.
2. IMF Article 8 provides the guidelines for exchange rate management. Countries may choose to free-float currencies: Australia chose this in October 1984 to solve its economic problem. A country could peg to a strong currency and maintain that peg when currency came under speculative attacks: Hong Kong did this in 1981 to escape the attack on its currency. China's final agreement with Britain led to Hong Kong currency weakening. Thailand, among others, chose to basket-peg, which is also a peg, but linked to the average currency exchange rate of the top 10–15 trading partners.
3. Widespread banking failures were observed in the late 1920s and early 1930s, followed soon after by the Great Depression of the 1930s and thereafter to a second human tragedy, the Second World War. The lessons learned from that depression and the efforts to strengthen the financial sector in the developed countries saved countries from experiencing severe bank failures in the postwar years. The Asian bankers failed to take a history lesson from that experience. The central banks did not take steps to wipe out a particularly vicious form of government–banking–big-business *quanzi*, or connected lending. Lending practices under this ignored the basic consideration of project viability, which is one reason for the high levels of non-performing loans in all Asian banking systems.
4. This figure is reported on the Internet under BankWatch report on Asia, dated 29 October 1998.
5. Trade in goods and services, as pointed out by Bhagwati (1997), is growth-promoting in that there is a limit to the demand for goods and services. He sees free trade in money as not being in the same league for the simple reason that there is no satiation in the demand for money to make an automatic break.
6. Instability could also arise from domestically driven forces without cross-border transactions. With an appreciating currency in an economy with low interest rates, savers would redirect cash holdings to obtain speculative profits by pushing up asset prices. Because the real interest rates in Singapore have been very low since the mid-1980s, people's savings were channelled into speculation in the property and other asset markets, which weakened the Singapore currency during 1997–98. With huge foreign reserves to support such currencies, exchange rates may even be maintained at high levels in such economies.
7. The build-up of huge portfolio investments in the Asian markets took place over 1988–93 as a result of many of the countries adopting new regulations easing entry and volume restrictions in the bond and share markets. For example, Malaysia liberalized its share market in 1989–91, which led to a huge increase in foreign activities. In 1993, the peak of this flow of short-term money, the Kuala Lumpur stock market yielded a 104 per cent return. The subsequent two years saw a correction by 35 per cent.
8. One study (Asher et al. 1992) found that these measures are meant to reduce the cost of capital to almost zero, and in some cases to negative cost of capital. With such incentives, any normally unprofitable investments could be turned around to become profitable.
9. Much has been said about too much debt being incurred in the name of development; in particular the banking sectors have been at the root of the problem in this respect. See Rowley (1998).
10. In the case of Malaysia, for example, per capita income has declined from close to US$6000 to about US$4000 within a year. This crisis has set back the gains of about seven years of carefully nurtured growth in that economy.

11.　The data sets were daily and weekly observations of closing exchange rates in each of the markets. The results reported in this and the next table (Table 2.4) are for weekly data.

12.　That the export sector was weakening was not widely publicized in the press. In the case of Malaysia, current account deficits were growing fast as far back as 1993, but the capital flow to the financial and real sector offset the dangers of the weakening in the trade sector, leading to a false sense of security widely given coverage by the local press and in official discussions during the 1990s.

13.　A closer examination of the miracles performed by the so-called political sages turned out to be good neoclassical macroeconomic management. Political élites across the Asia Pacific rim had to deliver economic growth to impoverished masses in the face of the attraction Asia had for the communist propaganda of 1960–89. For two interesting accounts of the transformation of the Asian economies, see Campos and Root (1996) and Islam and Chowdhury (1997): see also a review article by Ariff (1997).

14.　This was no longer true at the start of 1999, when export growth touched zero level. Worse, overproduction of all kinds of goods and services is leading to a general price decline. There is speculation that China may opt for a crawling depreciation to address the competition issue now that its neighbours with rock-bottom currencies and double-digit export growth rates are gaining export markets faster.

15.　See *Federal Reserve Bulletin* (January 1996), p. 5.

Part 2 The Early Reformers

The early reformers are the pioneers in Asia. Our analysis has to start with them as they undertook needed reforms as a means to high growth to secure social development. There were more than six countries in this group, but steps taken in these six are fully described in the six chapters on Korea, Malaysia, Singapore, Indonesia, Taiwan and Thailand. These economies gained the most from reforms observed in Asia in recent decades. Perhaps the World Bank's description of an East Asian Miracle applied more to these countries (and perhaps China included) than others. Growth in income and the resultant improvements in social well-being of these countries are described in this part. The policy unpreparedness to respond to loss of competitiveness in 1992–97 led to a serious erosion of their high growth during the closing three years of the 1990s.

The reforms, though these were adopted in different sequences, subjected the government sector and the private sector to more internal and external competition. The financial sector, which had suppressive policies, underwent changes while the trading with the world outside was liberalized to attract trade and capital flows in four countries, but not so in Taiwan and Korea. Increased capital flow was achieved by current and capital account opening. The outcome was a consistent growth path that led to economies growing at rates in the region of 7–10 per cent per year. Their collective weakness (except in Taiwan) was overdependence on short-term domestic and/or external capital to finance longer- and longer-term investments in increasingly technology-intensive projects as well as excessive infrastructure projects in the non-traded sector. Hence five of these countries suffered from the 1997 Asian financial crisis more than did the others with much less exposure. Those that did not suffer adversely (Taiwan and China) had capital controls and had also not removed all their current account controls, as had the other five economies.

3. Korea: a case of cautious capital account liberalization

1. BACKGROUND

A very significant feature of the Korean development experience is that it enjoyed continuous growth between 1960 and 1997 with only one short-lived recession in 1980. The economy grew steadily at an annual average rate of about 8.5 per cent. That aside, the Korean development experience is also unique in development literature in that this high level of continued growth was based on one-sided openness to take advantage of the postwar trade liberalization of the developed and developing countries to which Korea sent its exports. Japan had secured growth for a long time in much the same manner a short while earlier without a simultaneous easing of entry into the domestic economy. An important fact is also that the 1997–98 Asian financial crisis affected Korea's output very severely in 1998, with GDP declining by 7.8 per cent, the largest ever decline. As a result of this massive shock to the economy a year after it opened its capital account fully in 1996, which led to a 67 per cent (US$55.3 billion) increase in debt over just two years, and under the restructuring efforts of the IMF, Korea is rapidly adopting the kind of reforms that it had shunned during the high-growth period.[1] Thus, this analysis brings to the fore the need for balanced reforms as an important lesson from this case.

Korea's economic development is based on an earlier path followed by Japan, and is different from the later approaches of the potential tigers in that they relied excessively on foreign capital and technology. The strategy followed was to turn to industrial restructuring, and then develop through reaching out to the rest of the world as a newly industrializing economy, just as Hong Kong, Singapore and Taiwan were pursuing similar policies at about the same time. The results were impressive, as can be seen from the statistics in Table 3.1.

The achievement of sustained high growth had done many good things for the Korean people. The quality of life improved significantly for Koreans as a result of successful economic development. Life expectancy improved by almost 20 years since 1965. The infant mortality rate declined to 11 per 1000 births over the same period. Poverty and illiteracy have been reduced to nil in this country, while education received a large share of about 21 per cent of the government budget. Symptomatic of a developed economy, most of the

Table 3.1 Basic economic and social indicators of development in Korea, 1960–98

Indicators	1971–80	1981–90	1991–93	1994	1995	1996	1997	1998[a]
National accounts								
GDP growth (%)	8.27	9.24	6.65	8.58	8.95	7.11	5.50	–4.3
Per capita GDP (won)	846	3183	7013	8728	10 111	10 144	6320	7270
Private consumption/GDP	0.674	0.572	0.537	0.537	0.529	0.54	0.53	0.52
Gov. consumption/GDP	0.102	0.104	0.106	0.106	0.104	0.11	0.11	0.11
Financial indicators								
Gross domestic savings (% of GDP)	22.3	32.0	35.6	35.1	35.1	35.2	33.0	34.9
Gross fixed capital formation (% of GDP)	28.0	29.9	37.0	35.7	36.6	38.2	35.9	34.1
Inflation (% per year)	16.489	6.4	6.8	8.1	8.6	6.0	9.5	6.7
M2/GDP	0.318	0.359	0.403	0.435	0.438	0.457	0.445	0.390
M3/GDP	0.330	0.367	0.417	0.455	0.453	0.470	0.410	0.400
Fiscal balance/GDP	–0.017	–0.009	–0.005	0.003	0.003	–0.3	–0.5	–2.0
Current account balance/GDP	–0.056	0.006	–0.013	–0.010	–0.018	–4.8	–2.9	0.8
Trade balance/GDP	–0.063	0.004	–0.009	–0.008	–0.010	–4.0	–0.6	0.5
Discount rate (%)	13.7	6.7	6.3	5.0	5.0	5.0	12.0	5.8
Social indicators								
Unemployment rate (%)	–	3.5	2.4	2.4	2.0	2.0	2.5	7.2
Expenditure on education (% of exp.)	15.91	18.89	16.18	20.36	20.21	20.50	19.00	20.0
Expenditure on health (% of exp.)	1.26	1.72	1.34	0.69	0.67	0.65	0.61	0.60
Population growth (%)	1.69	1.18	0.92	0.89	0.89	0.89	0.89	0.89

Note: [a] A mid-1999 estimate of GDP growth for 1999 is 6%

Sources: IMF, *International Financial Statistics*, May 1997; *Asian Development Outlook 1998*; *Government Finance Statistics Yearbook, 1985–1998*; *World Development Reports*, various years.

population (84 per cent) live and work in cities and the capital city is home for one out of three Koreans.

The Republic of Korea is situated in the southern part of the Korean Peninsula, which is to the north-east of China and to the west of Japan. Korea has a population of 46 million within a small land mass, since most of the land was kept by North Korea at the time of separation of Korea in 1955. Its development efforts started in the 1960s from the basement, so to speak, as a low-income country, but graduated to middle-income status within 20 years and then to upper-middle-income status by the end of 1990.

Korea was admitted to the OECD group of developed countries in 1997 after three years of careful analysis to ensure that Korea would have the kind of institutional framework required of a member. The per capita income, which was 9 per cent of US income in 1965, improved to 48.8 per cent in 1995. This rate of improvement has not been matched by any except the city economies of Hong Kong and Singapore,[2] both of which have the revenue but not the land mass of a country to spread the expenditure, hence having a distinct advantage.

The country, caught up in the cold war politics of the 1950s, was divided, with the agriculturally productive part of the land going to North Korea, which is still aligned to the Communist bloc. With very little natural resources except a large population base, and ravaged by civil war, it can be argued that Korea's dire preconditions provided the proper environment for a government-directed development programme with an authoritarian character. Korea modernized and reformed its domestic economy but adopted a one-sided openness to the rest of the world to take advantage of the postwar opening that was occurring in all developed countries and in some early-reforming developing countries. After the careful implementation of a development strategy during the first two economic plan periods over 1961–70, Korea saw a quick transformation of the economy based on exports of light manufactured goods to the rest of the world. This strategy, based on creating competitive small to medium-sized enterprises, paid off handsomely, with the economy registering 8.4 per cent growth per annum during the 1960s. That period of growth absorbed the unemployed labour pool and importantly legitimized the development efforts directed from the top by petty authoritarian governments.

The population growth was very high – 1.69 per cent – but the growing economy absorbed the expanding workforce. With prudent government consumption at 10.2 per cent of GDP, there were large savings of 23.6 per cent.[3] The external trade terms were very good, as Korea was the second country to put faith in export-led development, and its external sector provided more funds for the expanding economy. With the import substitution policy of the earlier years came a huge foreign capital build-up. In 1962, Korea decided to rely no more on foreign direct investment and stuck to that decision till 1996.

Inflation during this period was very high, averaging 16 per cent: the rest of the world also experienced high inflation during this period.

The next decade of the 1970s saw the restructuring of the economy towards a planned reliance on heavy and chemical industries (HCI) that heralded a new era. This scheme was not exactly similar to the one in India led by the Oxford economists; the Korean case lacked the huge economic base of a large economy. Cash-rich Indonesia followed a similar policy to generate an internal capacity for production through low-interest capital support to selected industries: Indonesia was then earning huge cash from its oil exports. Investment in heavy industries was actively supported by the Korean government to produce high-value-added exports, not import substitution. Though the switch to an HCI economy required a number of liberal policies, these policies were implemented only internally and the Korean economy opened at best only modestly to the rest of the world.

Foreign banks were permitted to enter, but not foreign manufacturers. Domestic banking was expanded, but the foreign banks permitted into Korea could not expand their network because of branching limits. Some form of import protection scheme was put into effect right up to the mid-1980s, the key reason being that the infant industries nurtured under the policy loan (the term used for government directed bank loans) regime needed protection for a period of time: this was legitimate under the then GATT rules. The external balance of the economy suffered severely: the trade deficit averaged –6.3 per cent and current account declined to –5.6 per cent of GDP. Inflation shot up to 17 per cent and the interest rate for borrowers was the highest during this ten-year period at 13.7 per cent. There was over-investment in the heavy industries, and capital was redirected at the expense of the more competitive small to medium-sized enterprises. Unofficial finance enterprises sprouted up all over the country to meet the capital needs of the latter. The banks that were told to direct policy loans had not much left to give to the other more productive sectors. This laid the basis for the birth of a new entity, the non-bank financial institutions to meet credit needs. Nevertheless average economic growth was yet again 8.4 per cent during the 1970–79 period. This costly but timely switch to high-value-added production paid off later.

The next phase in the 1980s witnessed a series of reforms to redress the strains of the move to restructure the economy. It started after the 1980 economic recession, Korea's first recession since 1956. The rest of this chapter gives extensive details of the reforms undertaken in this period. The upshot of these was that the economy was put on an even keel very quickly, and reforms started to yield favourable results. This is a period when serious efforts were made to time-table a sequence of financial reforms to open the economy to the rest of the world. The average for all indicators improved. One example is the massive decline in the bank discount rate to as low as 5 per cent; another is the decline in inflation to a single digit that headed towards 5 per cent.

Soon came a different concern. The admission of Korea as a member of the OECD was expected to herald an era of development. There was a large degree of closedness in the financial sector as well as the real sector that had helped to protect domestic enterprises. These were not going to be sustained. Besides, citizens were demanding a greater share of the wealth placed in the companies under various forms of industry protection. Greater transparency in the management of the economy and the corporate sector was needed. Political transformation began to occur. The events connected with these demands led to political changes in the 1990s. During that very period of severe political strains came the Asian currency crisis, which crippled the Korean economy in 1997–98. The outcome was a series of reforms to make Korea to adopt balanced reforms to open its sectors to the external economies, now under the tutorship of the IMF team of experts.

2.   ECONOMIC AND FINANCIAL STRUCTURE

Korea, with a middle-sized population, has a very large economy essentially built on externally oriented liberalization to turn the country into an industrialized economy. To move the economy from its dependence on the export of light manufactured goods, the efforts that were made to restructure the economy towards high-value-added manufacturing ever since 1970 paid off well. Despite some serious strains, the restructuring has been a success, judged with hindsight. The share of primary produce in exports was 35.2 per cent of all exports 27 years ago compared to today's share of 8.1 per cent. Similarly, the share of the scale-intensive electronics exports increased from almost nothing to about 50 per cent of the manufactured exports over the same period. Korea's trade amounts to 67 per cent of GDP. This suggests that the extent of restructuring from light manufactured goods to high-value-added manufacturing during the last two decades has been a successful experiment. Manufacturing is the mainstay of the economy now, with services and agriculture (about 10 per cent) taking the lesser share of the economy. Almost two-thirds of the population lives in urban enclaves, working in industries.

Typical of such an externally oriented economy, private consumption declined from the high of 67.4 per cent of GDP during 1971–80 to about 50 per cent in 1997. Government consumption has been held down at about 10 per cent during the 27 years. With near fiscal balance during the same period, the trade sector provided a strong source for the expansion of the economy while at the same time the savings generated were directed to investments in the private sector. Gross domestic savings increased from 22.3 per cent over the years to

the 1995 high of 35.1 per cent.[4] This and the healthy external sources of funds – this was possible when firms were permitted to borrow from outside in the 1980s – enabled a higher rate of fixed capital formation by securing more funds than were available domestically.

The financial structure of the economy also underwent substantial changes. We discuss here the structure of the budgets and the structure of the financial sector. The financial structure was based from the beginning on the restricted model, which relied upon a limited number of financial institutions providing the basic and some specialized financial functions.

The Bank of Korea is the central bank but it was not independent of the government until it was restructured in 1997–98 following the IMF intervention. During most of the period, the government was able to influence the financial sector through its control of the BOK as well as having shareholdings in the key deposit-taking institutions. The commercial banks were mostly owned by the government and they had the most influence in the market until the reforms of the mid-1980s. There were a large number of foreign banks – about 80 in the 1990s – but they operated under restrictions on branching at least until the late 1980s. This meant that the government-owned commercial banks tended to dominate domestic financial transactions. The specialized banks were also owned by the government, and these were instrumental in targeting financing to priority areas during the economic restructuring of the country. As part of the reforms in the 1980s to create institutions to cater for the demand for funds for the small to medium-sized enterprises, the non-bank financial institutions (NBFIs) were licensed. These formed the third category of financial institutions. The capital market was reorganized and that constituted an important source of fund-raising for the larger enterprises. By the end of 1987, Korea's share market became the second largest next to that of Japan.

The economic transformation over the 1960–97 period required a series of changes to the structure of the economy as well as the financial sector. This will be examined in the next section. The impact of the reforms on the social conditions in Korea is now described. As noted earlier, Korea managed to increase its per capita income at a steady rate so that it improved dramatically to the 1997 figure relative to the USA of 50 per cent. This general improvement in the income level was also achieved with moderate inflation except in the 1970s. The benefit of this can be seen in improved socioeconomic indicators. Korea is one of the few countries with safe drinking water both in the cities and in the rural areas. It has a 99 per cent literacy rate, and the standard of education has been improved, with about one quarter of the government budget going towards education. Life expectancy improved from 49 in the 1950s to 74.9 in 1990s for females (46 and 67.3 for males). Infant mortality (per ten thousand) declined from 115 in the 1950s to the present 11. These social statistics would justify placing Korea among the top five developing countries to have achieved remarkable socioeconomic improvement through an externally oriented development strategy while also achieving a degree of domestic ownership of the means of production unparalleled in East Asia except in Japan.

3. LIBERALIZATION

Liberal policies were implemented during 1960–97 to the extent consistent with the aim of developing the economy through exports of manufactured goods and services. Korea took advantage of the external openness in the developed and some developing countries and reciprocated by opening the Korean economy as little as possible to other countries. Next, it adopted a policy of balanced government budget and reliance on internal funds as much as possible, with large external trade providing a steady injection of funds for expansion. Therefore, the main reason for reform of the financial sector was to enable the sector to cope with the greater need for funds for a fast-growth situation and to facilitate capital formation.

While domestic financial reforms gained speed steadily on account of sustained income growth, reforms to the financial sector were aimed at keeping abreast of the internationalization of the Korean economy. Thus, from 1961 on, several specialized deposit money banks (DMBs) were licensed, the first being the Industrial Bank of Korea. There were a total of six specialized DMBs, four NBFIs and six other fund-related institutions. The Korean Stock Exchange (KSE) was expanded to cater to the fast-developing economy. In 1980, there were 352 firms listed with a value of 2.421 trillion won: by 1992, the hey-day of the stock market boom, there were 688 firms with a capitalization of 84.712 trillion won. That represents a phenomenal growth of 31 per cent per annum. The bond market also was expanded, though not at the same speed. During the same period, corporate bond value increased to 32.7 trillion won from 2070 issues. The value of government bonds also increased to 32.5 trillion won. Overall, the capital market reforms made it possible for firms to take good advantage of the growth potential in the economy.

3.1 Economic Reforms

The Korean economy at the end of 1996 – before the crisis – was the second largest economy in East Asia, with a gross domestic product of 376 trillion won or US$454 billion. This also represented progress to upper-middle-income status among the nations. This level of growth was reached after a series of far-reaching reforms that successfully moved the economy from the status of a low-income country in 1960.

The four stages of reforms

Opening to the World, 1960s   Korea had become a divided and poor country
in the 1950s, largely because of the cold war conflict. To secure growth and to
move towards the status of a higher-income country, Korea adopted a strategy
of planned changes through industrialization. The security needs of the country
were taken care of by the American security umbrella. Korea marshalled its
domestic resources to manufacture consumer goods produced by labour-
intensive methods. It therefore based its expansion on exporting its light
manufactured goods all over the world, particularly to the developed markets.
Korea was the second country after Japan to do this. It paid off very well, and
led to a level of prosperity which became threatened when other countries,
notably Hong Kong and Taiwan (as well as some central American countries),
started to compete in the same export markets. When the first oil shock hit the
economy in 1973, it became clear that the country needed to move to higher-
value-added manufacturing to avoid becoming non-competitive with more
entrants into the consumer light manufacturing route to development.

Ambition towards heavy industries, 1970–79   Opening to the world led to a
slow restructuring of the economy towards reliance on heavy industries. This
was labelled the HCI policy, which required some degree of protection. So,
the tariff was increased for some sectors. An ambitious programme of reforms
in other sectors followed. Foreign financial institutions were permitted during
this period, but they were restricted to operating as single entities without
branching permits. Most of these banks came from the countries to which Korea
was exporting its manufactured goods or from which it was importing materials.
But the economic policy pursued was to enable the heavy industry firms to
become profitable as soon as possible. This was done through preferential
treatment of the national priority firms and through cheaper policy loans to
enable capital investment. As this expansion continued, the second oil shock
occurred in 1978. The after-effect of subsidizing these heavy industries began
to take a toll in other parts of the economy. The strains led to a major recession
in 1980.

Reckoning costs and reforms, 1980–1991   The next 12 years saw a gradual
phasing out of the subsidies to the heavy industries, and redressing the damages
to financial institutions and small to medium-sized businesses. First, industry-
specific incentives were phased out slowly, import restrictions on domestic
firms were lifted, and limited financial liberalization was set in motion. While
the reforms were removing protection from the heavy industries, the government
ensured that those industries that had become burdened did not get wiped out.
The government's National Investment Fund was set up using the pension fund

balances, and banks also participated. Initially, the import liberalization ratio had declined to 40 per cent, but it was permitted to go up to 57 per cent in 1980 just to sustain the protection needed for the heavy industries soon after the second oil shock.

The peg to the US dollar was abandoned and a flexible exchange rate introduced in 1980. Soon after, the interest rate came under control, wage formation was returned to wage settlement schemes and dividends were reduced. As a result, the current account deficit was cut by 60 per cent in 1982, while inflation declined from 25 per cent to 7 per cent. Tax reforms introduced in 1981 reduced the special tax treatment to the supported industries. Depreciation was permitted at 100 per cent to reduce the shock from withdrawal of financial support. The supported industries came under a three-year rationalization plan to make them efficient. When the economy began to respond by 1983, further opening to the rest of the world was effected in the form of gradual reduction of the tariff from 95 per cent in 1984 to 18 per cent by 1988 and later to 7 per cent by 1998. This introduced competition gradually, and the crisis of the type that plagued Indonesia with similar policy loan withdrawal was avoided by Korea by the end of 1998.

Move to balanced reforms, 1990s   There followed several financial reforms that will be examined later. However, the reforms of the three periods to prepare for the changeover to an industrial economy were more or less completed by 1991. What remained to be done was to bring in reforms in the financial sector and to create a balanced norm for reforms needed for a more mature economy by the end of 1990. This was accomplished in the 1990s, and led to (a) a market average exchange rate and (b) capital account opening in 1996 and (c) planned liberalization of interest rates thereafter.

Thus economic reforms of the type described in this chapter moved the largely low-income country of the 1960s to the higher-income country by 1991, which led to the admission of Korea into the OECD group in 1996.

3.2   Financial Liberalization

The postponement of extensive financial reforms by the adoption of basic reforms to support the economic restructuring in the real sector has been seen by some observers as the best way to insulate a fast-growing economy from external shocks. It is also consistent with the widely held view that financial opening must come after other reforms. It is interesting that such sentiments are now being expressed as a desirable theoretical position by some economists after 20 years of financial crises in several developing economies.[5]

Broadly, the financial reform in the 1960–79 period was extensive within the domestic economy: see Table 3.2 for a summary of reforms. The banking

Table 3.2   Major economic and financial reforms in Korea, 1960–98

Date of reforms	Liberalization policy implemented
1961	Industrial Bank of Korea to finance small and medium enterprises.
1962	Fisheries Credit Bank Cooperatives. 85% foreign investment, so reverse policy.
1963	Citizens National Bank to provide small loans to firms and households.
1967	Korea Long Term Credit Bank to finance capital for the manufacturing firms. Korea Housing Bank to finance housing loans.
1969	Export–Import Bank of Korea to finance exports and imports of Korean firms.
1974	National investment laws to develop and support heavy and chemical industries.
1976	Credit guarantee laws to help policy loan firms with inadequate collateral.
1979	Industrial restructuring through heavy industries had created over-investment, and there were imbalances in the economy. To address these concerns, a 20% devaluation of currency was made.
1980	The peg with US$ was abandoned in favour of a managed exchange rate.
1980	To fight the inflation from the unproductive policy loans, wage setting was introduced along with control on the interest rate, and reduced government budget.
1981	Tax reforms were made. Special tax treatment of key industries substantially reduced, but 100% depreciation permitted to reduce shock.
1981	Laws to assist credit and banking sector of the livestock cooperative sector. National housing policy laws to help workers to have state-built housing.
1982	Most preferential interest rates abolished or reduced. But still some interest rate control.
1984	Major change: certain financial intermediaries permitted to set interest rate lending only within a range of interest rates. So no decontrol of interest rates.

Date of reforms	Liberalization policy implemented
1983–85	Banking reforms: government divested its share in major commercial banks. Barriers to entry relaxed. Additional commercial banks, finance companies, mutual savings companies.
1986	Industrial promotion laws replaced with industrial development laws.
1984–88	For the first time, major import liberalization. Liberalization ratio improved from 80% to 95%. Average tariff on imports reduced from 24% to 18% (1998: to 7%). Capital account still controlled for fear of flight. But foreign borrowing for capital and materials liberalized.
1988 (Dec.)	Further decontrol of interest rates for long term but not short term, nor for deposit rates.
1989	Laws to control major shareholdings in companies. 12.4% individual holdings brought down to 2.25% by 1995.
1985–89	Because of the effects of the policy loans that affected the banks throughout the early 1980s, non-performing loans (NPL) shot up to 10.5% in 1985–86. To reduce this, BOK lent 1700 billion won low-interest loans to the banks and made a subsidy of 189 billion won. This led to inflation of 9% and to a real-estate boom. By 1989, NPL reduced to 5.9%.
1988–89	Further financial reforms with more commercial bank licensing, entry to NBFIs outside the capital city permitted.
1990 (March)	Major switch to 'market exchange rate' based on the previous day's average exchange rate. (August 1997 free float in the face of the Asian crisis.)
1996 (July)	Capital account freed for the first time.
1997 (Sept.)	Onset of currency crisis. IMF invited. Fully floating currency.

Sources: Mainly Bank of Korea reports; also IMF announcements in 1998 and Reuter's reports.

structure was expanded, and special banks were licensed to cater to the needs of newly emerging special situations as the economy was being restructured towards high-value-added production. Foreign banks – some 70 of them – were permitted to support the economic linkages that were occurring as trade expanded. By 1979, total trade had reached almost 35 per cent of GDP. This is also consistent with the financial institutions following trade theory in the banking literature. The creation of special banks helped to target investment to preferred industries, which built huge over-capacity on the back of capital subsidies and import protection.

The capital account was tightly controlled for fear of capital flight, since more capital was needed by the heavy industries. But the foreign exchange needs for capital and material requirements were made readily available. Between 1981 and 1983, the government started divesting its shareholdings in commercial banks. The entry barriers to the sector were eased and more banks were licensed during 1988–89 while entry barriers to NBFIs outside Seoul were scrapped. (removed, abolished)

Limited reforms to interest rates were started in 1984 for the first time, about a quarter-century after planned growth was put in motion, very unlike the situation in Indonesia. Certain financial intermediaries were permitted to set their own interest rates within a broad band. When the market gained some experience with this reform in interest rates, most banks were permitted in 1988 to set their rates for RPs (repurchase agreements). However, the short-term deposit interest rate was still fixed. That mattered significantly to depositors, whose interest rates were still fixed. Corporate trust account interest rates were decontrolled only in 1987.

These measures were meant to open the financial sector to become more efficient, and to ride the bad policy loan effects that kept dragging the economy down in the early 1980s. With a limited opening of the capital market to foreign investment, the KSE – Korea Stock Exchange – experienced a boom in 1986–89. This helped the banks to raise equity to overcome the lingering effects of their participation in the failed policy loans to heavy industries. As a result of these reforms to overcome the negative effects of the policy loans scheme, the economy recovered and registered an average growth rate of 10.4 per cent during 1985–91. These two favourable events acted as precursors to major financial reforms that would be planned for the 1990s.

With these structural reforms in place, one would imagine that Korea had a more open economy. But there were several institutional barriers that prevented the extent of opening one would have expected at each stage of economic development. This continued to be an irritant in bilateral negotiations with trading countries.

Exchange rate policies
Korea adopted a cautious policy of exchange rate reforms. The won was pegged to the US dollar right up to 1979. A switch was made in 1980 to a managed float regime. It was based on a trade-weighted management of the currency with a large weight on the US dollar because of Korea's extensive trade with the USA. This was adopted only after the 1979 devaluation of 20 per cent. The exchange

rate was fixed at 484 won per dollar during 1974–79. After the managed float, it declined to 659.9 won per dollar, which is a decline of 27 per cent. The imposition of controls on the non-corporate sector foreign transactions kept the managed float working for a while. The exchange rate worsened to 890 won per dollar by 1985, but improved thereafter following the recovery of the economy.

The first reform was the adoption of a market-average-rate system to manage foreign exchange. Recall that a managed float was put in place in 1980 after abandoning the peg to the US dollar. Under the new system the day's exchange rate was set at the average of the last day's exchange rate. This was implemented from March 1990. Korea is the only country covered in this book that moved from a basket managed float to a quasi-free float based on market average. It is reported that the volatility in the real exchange rate declined substantially after this reform. This is one reason why the currency crisis of 1997 did not stem from the exchange rate but from too much short-term loans taken out by industries. When the Asian crisis hit the exchange rate in September 1997, the exchange rate was left completely to market forces; thus it was fully floated. In the following year, the capital account was fully opened under the IMF instruction.

With the financial- and real-sector reforms in the 1980s, the economy started to perform better, registering a high growth of 7 per cent in 1981 after the 1980 recession. By the middle of the 1980s, the managed float had led to an over-valuation of the won. Pressure began to mount, especially from the USA, for more realistic exchange rates. After prolonged efforts, Korea accepted a return to a more market-determined exchange rate. This was reluctantly done only in March 1990 and the so-called market-average exchange rate management was adopted. The result was actually a decline in the exchange rate by 5 per cent in 1990. The improvements in the exchange rate over 1985–89 under the managed float were making Korea less competitive.

Under the market-average exchange rate system, the exchange with the US dollar was set within a range of the weighted average of the inter-bank rates on the previous day. That base rate was used to set the exchange rate with other currencies. This had the effect of returning the exchange rate, though still managed within a band, nearer to a market-based system. This was only abandoned in 1997 because of the Asian currency crisis. The exchange rate freedom achieved was not matched with capital account freedom. The capital account was still tightly controlled. But the exchange rate was allowed to be set freely in the market with little intervention within an ever-expanding band. At the time of writing this chapter, Korea is continuing with the free float of its currency even though there is pressure to return to some form of management of the currency.

Compared to most countries, Korea had adopted a very cautious exchange rate management right up to the time when it considered that the real sector had sorted out most of its problems and by keeping the capital account closed. Since the economy was based on the trade sector playing the more important role, it made sense to reduce exchange rate uncertainties within a band. There is merit in this cautious approach. It is difficult to fault the logic of limited reforms in the light of the heavy toll the more reformed Asian economies had to pay, while the exchange rates of the Asian economies that did not adopt exchange rate reforms did not suffer exchange rate declines. The adoption of a cautious external open condition for the real sector and the preservation of strict controls on individuals wanting foreign currencies helped traders during the light manufacturing era (1960s) and the heavy industry era after the 1970s.

The exchange rate management of Korea differed quite significantly from that adopted by the ASEAN countries. ASEAN countries moved to managed exchange rates very early in the 1970s, and also adopted full capital control opening to attract foreign direct investment. Even the non-corporate sector had free access to foreign exchange. Most ASEAN economies adopted a form of managed exchange rates. Since the trade flows in these countries are based on foreign direct investment from several countries, the trade-weighted exchange rate management was markedly different from that of Korea. Korea's trade-weight with the US was quite high – recall the pressure from the USA to free the exchange rate during the 1985 Plaza Accord – because of Korea's large trade dependence on the USA in the earlier period.

The volatility of the exchange rate declined substantially in the period 1990–96 when the rate was determined under the market exchange rate system.[6] However, when the capital account was freed in July 1996, it set in motion some powerful forces that would lead to a huge flight of funds in the fourth quarter of 1997, leading to a 75 per cent decline in the exchange rate, and a major recession in 1998. But in the period 1996–97, the fund flow into Korea had accelerated after capital account opening. When the crisis started in July 1997 in Thailand, the open capital account along with the market exchange rate system could not stem the outflow, resulting in a 75 per cent devaluation of the won within a six-month period.

Interest rates policies

The World Bank in 1989 praised Korea's liberalization as exemplary for its economic growth. But this was not exactly justified. While domestic liberalization helped to create the kind of favourable conditions to support economic expansion, the external economy had been kept under control to a large extent. Among the important controls was the control of interest rates throughout the period for depositors, and a limited lifting of interest rates for producers since 1991–92. Control on interest rates has been a binding feature of the economic management of Korea during the entire period of this study. It was with the introduction of the IMF restructuring that the interest rate was freed after the Asian crisis.

There are three features that can be identified relating to interest rate policy. First is the desire of the authorities to make capital as cheap as possible as a prop to develop real-sector capacity during the restructuring period towards a heavy-industry focus. Policy loans channelled through the largely government-owned financial institutions before 1986 ensured that the priority sectors received capital at low interest rates or that there were some forms of favourable treatment. One of these was the setting up of the promotion fund to protect the heavy industries when the policy loans were removed by 1982. Thus the interest rate had to be suppressed, and in some periods set at favourable rates as policy loans. For example, to overcome the huge increase in the non-performing loans from the policy loan era, banks were given a 1.7 trillion won loan (about 2 per cent of GDP at that time) at 3 per cent annual interest when government bonds were yielding about 13 per cent.

The second feature of interest rate management is the continued control of deposit rates for bank deposits throughout the period. Until the mid-1980s, deposit rates were not permitted to be set by market forces for the corporate sector. Corporate-sector interest rates were freed first in 1984, when the rates for RPs (repurchase agreements, thus not applicable to individual depositors) were allowed to be determined by market forces. At that same time, long-term interest rates for borrowers were also allowed to be set competitively.

The third feature of interest rate management was the suppression of interest rates in the deposit sector. For instance, the deposit rates remained fixed at 10 per cent during 1985–92. With world interest rates coming down in the late 1980s and early 1990s, the fixed interest rates were further lowered for bank deposits. Interest rate suppression has been a prevalent feature in Korea throughout different macroeconomic situations until 1997–98, when the interest rate was freed.

Monetary policy

The central bank of an economy with a more or less balanced current account, government budget, and no or limited foreign capital has very little else to manage except the credit growth to support the expansion of an economy growing at a high rate of about 8.4 per cent. Thus monetary management was reduced to the task of managing sufficient expansion of credits to meet the demands of an expanding economy. M2 grew at about three times the rate of growth of the economy. The average M2 growth rate was 22 per cent during 1971–96. In the fund-starved period of the 1960s, credit growth was an excessive 61 per cent.

This rate of growth is very large, and explains the inherent inflationary tendency in the economy except during those periods when inflation was brought down. Compared with the low-inflation East Asian economies with lower growth in monetary expansion – 15 per cent – Korea's policy of high credit expansion was consistent with the need for more funds to support a high-growth economy. This is particularly interesting since Korean firms could not access foreign funds until about 1987. Korea received official development assistance right up until 1976. The total assistance over 1955 to 1975 amounted to 403 billion won. Korea ceased getting development aid from 1976. Hence, during the period of economic restructuring towards heavy industries, sufficient credit creation was critical for sustaining the planned high growth.

Central banking

Central bank functions are carried out by the Bank of Korea. But, unlike in most other economies, the government plays a key role in guiding and controlling the way the central banking function is executed. As with the interest rate policy designed to support real-sector restructuring programmes, so it is with the central bank. The BOK functioned as the executor of government policies. Its role was to assist the policy-makers to bring about desired levels of economic activities through interventionist policies.

It is useful to examine banking policy to grasp the importance of the way policies are made conjointly with the government. There are three bodies involved in central bank-related decisions. The first is the Economic Planning Board under the Ministry of Finance, which works closely with the Korea Development Institute (a think-tank) to formulate economic policies. The policy mix is decided at the next level of the ministries of the government. The central bank's policy-making body, the Monetary Board, then considers the policy mix: as the chairperson of the board, the Minister of Finance has significant influence on the final outcome of the policy. Therefore, the final decision is in fact made by the Minister, and the BOK just executes the policy mix already formulated.

Thus the actions to be taken by the central bank are determined by the government through this three-tiered system of decision-making. The central bank, far from being independent to pursue stable economic growth with price stability, functions very differently. For example, the policy loan decision having been made in the early 1970s, it was the BOK's job to implement actions to ensure that the policy loans were made to the heavy industries in pursuit of restructuring. If a particular industry had to be saved (for example a shipping company or a bank) from bankruptcy, the BOK would make funds available to enable the industry to tide over a period of time. The central bank intervenes to aid the broader planned economy.

The Monetary Board of the BOK is a platform for making national policies. Far from being independent, the central bank is an instrument to ensure that monetary policies consistent with the national economic plan are formulated and put in place. Thus cross-policy consistency is ensured through this form of central banking organization in Korea. The nature of central banking is therefore vastly different. This explains how Korea managed to delay several norms of financial liberalization normally seen in other OECD economies as they reformed their economies. The end result was economic growth based on a restructured economy that had by 1996 become an industrialized economy with upper-middle income.

Capital markets

Capital market development was the most striking, in that the asset growth of listed companies was very high, 31 per cent per annum. The capital market reform is noteworthy also in that the reforms were directed more to the domestic economy. Reforms to open the capital market to the rest of the world were delayed as long as possible, in fact until the late 1980s. Domestic capital market reforms were aimed at achieving capital formation to reduce the high level of debt in Korean firms. This took the form of organizing the market rapidly to provide a clearing-house for the listing of good-quality firms on the exchange. These firms could then raise capital and reduce their dependence on bank debt. The second aim of developing the capital market was to ensure that, with the rise of large shareholding across other firms, the undue control of the *chaebols* of the economy could be reduced.

Table 3.3 provides a brief summary of key capital market developments during 1980 to 1998.

Table 3.3   Capital market development in Korea, 1980–98

Capital	1998	1990	1985	1980
Shares				
No of companies	682	669	342	352
% GDP of shares	12.1	46.1	8.4	6.9
Bonds				
No. of issues	–	1 603	1 213	434
Corporate bonds (billion won)	–	22 068	7 623	1 649
Treasury				
No. of issues	–	24	12	7
Face value	–	29 049	4 737	895

Source: Various capital market publications collected by authors.

The importance of the capital market may be judged by one indicator. An average of 25 per cent of the capital needs was raised through the organized capital markets. This ratio is far higher than is the case with most countries, the exception being Malaysia, where the capital market, much more open to the outside world than the KSE, provided about 45 per cent.

As is evident from the statistics in Table 3.3, more and more firms were listed on the exchange. The number of firms listed doubled in ten years. The depth of the market increased from a mere 6.9 per cent of GDP to about 35 per cent in 1996: after the collapse following the crisis, it was merely 12 per cent. As a comparison, examine the ratio in China. After 20 years of capital market development in China, the depth of China's regulated market is still under 30 per cent.

Korea also developed a viable public debt market. The corporate bond market has attained a high rate of growth. From its base of just 1.7 trillion won, the corporate bond market grew at a very high rate of 27 per cent per annum. The Treasury also grew in steps. Korea's bond market is reputed to have developed faster than most bond markets in developing Asia.

The share market was used as a tool to broaden the share-ownership structure of firms, particularly the non-*chaebols* which controlled the economy.[7] At times by forcing divestment across broader share-ownership, the government was able to bring these firms into more diversified ownership. From a high of 12.4 per cent individual ownership in the 1980s, the ratio was brought down to about 4 per cent in the 1990s. With the 1987 reforms to investment banking the cost of going public was brought down, which led to an upsurge in listing activities. The institutional impediment to issuing stocks priced higher than the par value was removed in 1986. As a result, 47 companies were listed in one year in 1987.

3.3   Financial Liberalization Effects

Macroeconomic effects

Korea's development experiment is one of cautious reforms in all sectors except the domestic sector to strengthen competition and increase productivity. In the financial and the external sector, reforms were put off as long as possible, which conforms to the scholarly advice given after the 1997–98 crisis. Reforms aimed at reaching out to the rest of the world were made in order to expand by exporting; foreign firms were not given free entry to prevent competition to the domestic firms. This paid off very well during most of the development period. The important indicators are summarized in Table 3.4.

Output growth in GDP has been phenomenal and continuous. Inflation, which was high at one period, was brought down significantly. Government revenues grew rapidly so that the government had no problem on the fiscal side. Monetary

Table 3.4 *Basic economic indicators in Korea: growth rates (% per year)*

	5-year average			Annual						
	1976–80	1981–85	1986–90	1991	1992	1993	1994	1995	1996	1997
GDP	7.492	8.411	10.030	9.133	5.065	5.751	8.579	9.023	7.110	−7.82
Inflation	17.22	7.113	5.421	9.300	6.240	4.797	6.270	4.543	5.000	9.50
Revenue	34.56	15.295	18.175	14.737	18.977	15.854	20.412	17.967	16.787	13.34
M1	26.35	14.700	16.045	36.762	13.029	18.119	11.946	19.575	1.721	−11.24
M2	31.81	17.909	19.188	21.887	14.942	16.581	18.677	14.310	20.593	22.1
Foreign direct investment (inflow only)	16.05	91.80	582.9	−47.7	−63.80	−19.10	37.60	119.50	29.90	22.3
Trade balance (US$ billion)	−60.29	32.04	29.27	−6.98	−2.15	1.86	−3.14	−4.75	−20.40	−9.90

Note: M2 = M1 + Quasi-Money.

Sources: IMF, *International Financial Statistics*, May 1999; World Bank, *World Bank Databank*, May 1999.

expansion kept pace with income growth. The trade balance was more or less restored whenever there was any misalignment. Overall, there was an orderly transformation of the economy towards the status of an upper-middle-income economy.

Exchange and interest rates

Exchange rates were pegged to the US dollar until 1980. There followed a period of managed float, which gave way to market-average exchange management in 1990. Interest rates have been fixed throughout the period for depositors. Limited interest rate reforms permitted the long-term lending rates to be determined by the market only in the 1980s. In 1987, firms were permitted to borrow from overseas through foreign-currency-denominated borrowing.

The exchange rate depreciated during the 1960s by 17 per cent per annum during the period of peg to the US dollar. In the next period of managed float, the won depreciated by only 4 per cent per annum over the 1970s although in the subsequent period until 1989, depreciation was only 3 per cent per annum. During the market-average exchange management period, the currency declined by 11 per cent per annum. The Asian crisis sent the won down by 75 per cent within a year from September 1997, before it started to recover with the assistance of the IMF. With hindsight, it appears that currency instability was prevalent both during the hard peg as well as during the market-average regimes.

The interest story is quite different. Through a dogged policy of not allowing deposit rates to be determined by market forces, Korea managed to keep bank deposit rates steady. The high interest rates in the 1970s and the 1980s were partly due to the policy loan scheme, which made debt cheap for the heavy industries, and that meant that the interest rates for the rest of the economy had to be high. Deposit rates were managed right up to 1991. But the borrowing rates for the firms were to some extent liberalized for long-term loans starting from 1984–87 in gradual steps.

Indicators of financial liberalization

Table 3.6 provides a summary of financial liberalization ratios over 1976–96. It is evident from the figures in the table that the public sector did not create an expanding claim on itself except in the middle of the policy loan period: claims against government were 24.9 per cent of GDP. Over the remaining period from 1981 to 1992, this ratio was kept very low, which permitted the private sector to access more credits. The claims on the private sector went up from 0.35 steadily to 0.74 by 1998, suggesting a heavy reliance, a doubling, on borrowing by the private sector. The financial sector had developed sufficient depth thanks to these reforms so that it managed to create a doubling of funds to the private sector. This indicates the favourable effect of financial liberalization. Without

Table 3.5 Exchange rates and interest rates (annual averages)

	5-year average			Annual average							
	1976–80	1981–85	1986–90	1991	1992	1993	1994	1995	1996	1997	1998
Exchange rate (mkt end period)	519.180	792.480	746.760	760.800	788.400	808.100	788.700	774.700	844.200	1695	1204
Interest rates (%)											
CB discount rate	14.800	6.200	7.200	7.000	7.000	5.000	5.000	5.000	5.000	5.000	3.000
Deposit rate	17.460	10.280	10.000	10.000	10.000	8.600	8.500	8.800	7.500	10.80	13.29
Govt bond yield	23.740	16.400	13.340	16.500	15.100	12.100	12.300	12.40	10.90	11.70	12.80
Money market rate	19.800	13.220	11.100	17.000	14.300	12.100	12.500	12.60	12.40	13.20	14.98
Lending rate	18.000	11.840	10.280	10.000	10.000	8.600	8.500	9.000	8.800	11.90	15.28

Notes: Exchange rate: (Market rate) = won per US$: exchange rate declined above 1700 won per dollar, and recovered to about 1175 won by mid-1999. Central Bank (CB) discount rate (end of period).

Source: IMF, *International Financial Statistics* (May 1999).

Table 3.6 Indicators of financial liberalization

| | 5-year average | | | Annual | | | | | | | |
	1976–80	1981–85	1986–90	1991	1992	1993	1994	1995	1996	1997	1998
Inter-relations ratio											
FIR (total)/GDP	0.39	0.52	0.54	0.58	0.58	0.59	0.61	0.62	0.65	0.75	0.79
FIR (public)/GDP	0.04	0.06	0.02	0.01	0.01	0.01	0.01	0.011	0.01	0.01	0.04
FIR (private)/GDP	0.35	0.46	0.52	0.57	0.57	0.58	0.60	0.61	0.64	0.74	0.74
GFCF/GDP	0.312	0.287	0.318	0.384	0.366	0.360	0.357	0.359	0.341	0.351	0.294
FDI/GDP	0.0118	−0.0106	−0.005	−0.011	−0.016	−0.024	−0.044	−0.0039	−0.0038	−0.01	n.a.

Notes: M3 = M1 + Quasi-money + Post Office savings deposit.
FIR = financial intermediation ratio – claims on public sector, claims on private sector and foreign assets.
GFCF = gross fixed capital formation.
FDI = foreign direct investment.

Sources: IMF, *International Financial Statistics*, May 1999; World Bank, *World Bank Databank*, May 1999.

these reforms, it is difficult to see how the real-sector demands for credit would have been met without rekindling a dash for credit and thus exorbitant interest rates.

On the other hand, capital formation was steadily held up except during the period of severe strain following the 1980 recession. The gross fixed capital formation was held steadily at above 31 per cent of GDP during the rest of the period. This rate of growth in capital formation was quite extraordinary for a country that had shut out foreign direct investment until 1991 and had only permitted very little borrowing in foreign currencies. Portfolio investment jumped eightfold in the period following reforms in 1991. Thus the ability of the economy to provide large injections of gross fixed capital formation throughout the period can only be accounted for as arising from a set of capital controls in place, which prevented capital outflows, and from the ability of the domestic financial sector to generate sufficient credits for a fast-growing economy.

Some observers have also suggested that the no-name bank accounts facilitated large-scale hiding of money, which then found its way out as available resources. No-name bank accounts were fostered corruption.

Capital controls were in place for individual transactions throughout the period up to the middle of 1996. Producers had limited freedom to transact in foreign currencies were for acquisition of capital and materials. But in the 1980s, limited permission was given to firms to invest overseas. This led to some amount of investment outflows from 1985; those ones by the banks have turned out to be bad as Korea has very little banking expertise to make its investments profitable. Portfolio investment into Korea was not permitted until 1991, when FDI started to multiply eightfold in the next year. In the two years 1991 and 1992, Korea received more foreign investment than in the 25 years before then, thanks to the reform that permitted limited foreign borrowing. But this was nothing compared with FDI, accounting for 82 per cent of investments in 1962, the year when Korea decided to go solo with domestic capital and prevented foreign investments from ever rising to dominant levels.

To sum up, it is fair to describe Korea's liberalization as one that did not make capital account opening a centrepiece of its reforms. Instead it delayed this aspect right up to July 1996, when both foreign and domestic firms were able to have nearly full freedom to move capital. Much of the development in the previous era was achieved with dependence on domestic capital, and very little FDI came to Korea. A year after the reforms to the capital account came the financial crisis. That crisis happened during a period of political turmoil, which started modestly as an investigation of huge ill-gotten gains by a former president, connected with bribe-giving and bribe-taking between the government and the *chaebols*. But long before the political crisis following this revelation in 1997, the banking system was in near disarray from bad loans,

Table 3.7 Korea investments (US$ million)

	5-year average		Annual							
	1976–80	1981–85	1986–90	1991	1992	1993	1994	1995	1996	1997
Direct investment (net)	43.6	–92.2	–8.2	–320	–481	–773	–1 715	–1 753	–1 747	4 449
Portfolio investment (net)	66	625	–203	2 934	5 702	10 530	6 867	16 159	27 181	10 279
Foreign direct investment (inflow)	61	117	799	1 180	727	588	809	1 776	2 308	2 844

Sources: IMF, *International Financial Statistics*, May 1999; World Bank, *World Bank Databank*, Feb. 1999.

and from the effects of too much borrowing by corporations during the 1994–97 period.[8] However, over the 1954–96 period, it was the choice of an industrial policy based on export-led growth that was responsible for the gains Korea made as described in these pages. In that sense, it is a unique development case in that, with almost no capital account opening and with interest rate reforms delayed as long as possible, Korea managed to grow at the real rate of about 8.5 per cent per annum over a lengthy period of time.

4. ASSESSMENT AND FUTURE PROSPECTS

The Korean economy absorbed excessive foreign short-term capital after the capital account reforms in 1996 removed all restrictions on foreign borrowing while at the same time lifting restrictions on domestic firms putting capital into other countries. This led to a huge build-up of borrowed capital in the banking sector, which helped the government and the private sector to continue their earlier established fast-track growth in income. This bore the seeds of its own destruction when the debt in the capital structure became too high at 7 dollars against 1 dollar of equity. When the baht crisis led to the re-examination of the financial soundness of the Asia Pacific economies, the Korean won declined dramatically, losing about 76 per cent of its value within three months. The rest is history.

The IMF was invited in to assist in restructuring the financial sector. Along with the IMF measures, monopolistic practices of the big businesses are being curtailed by the newly elected government. This process of major reforms will lead to significant changes in the structure of the economy in the future. The banking system, which was the worst hit, is also likely to undergo even greater change in structure and management. These developments are taking place at the same time that Korea is expected to experience a year of recession. A re-examination of this case a few years from now may reveal that the reforms being put in place will enable the economy to manage a growth of about 5–6 per cent in the near future. Assessing the longer-term prospects is fraught with danger since one impact of the Asian financial crisis may be more cautious business investment practices. That will depend on when and to what extent confidence will return to the economies in the region. However, after the biggest ever decline of 7.8 per cent in GDP in the last quarter of 1998, the Korean economy is again showing strong signs of recovery, and achieved positive growth of 5.2 per cent for the year 1999. That is not surprising since Korea has often shown a strong resolve to effect recoveries from near-disaster crises time after time.

NOTES

1. The main cause of Korea's trouble was the huge, steady build-up of debt over the 1990s. Debt of US$40 billion in 1991 ballooned to US$112 billion by 1997. By 1999, the debt soared to US$160 billion. That is a yearly growth of 22 per cent. As described in Chapter 2, the debt-to-equity ratio and the resultant interest services, even before the crisis hit Korea, had reached breaking point.
2. See Asian Development Bank (1997b). These city-based economies have per capita income equal to three-quarters of that of the US. Given the status of a country of city-based economies such as Luxembourg, Monaco, and so on, these states collect revenue as a country though they lack the land mass to spread the revenue as development expenditure. This makes cities inherently more efficient.
3. This very high savings rate in the 1960s is a remarkable feature of the Korean experience. From the start of planned growth, it forced the planners to rely on internal capital formation. For a number of reasons – one being the capital-rich Japan next door – Korea was not prepared to welcome foreign capital right up to 1996, just before its admission to the OECD. In subsequent years, domestic savings were insufficient to meet the higher capital needs of a more technology-intensive production. However, given Korea's reluctance to allow foreign ownership of domestic production, insufficient savings to meet the higher investment demands led to persistent high interest rates in this economy. This was a price Korea paid for keeping FDI as low as possible in the pre-1997 era.
4. Following the 1997 Asian currency crisis, this has changed dramatically, as will be discussed in a different part of the book.
5. The theme of whether broader reforms in the financial sector should be deferred to a later stage of development is taken up in Chapter 16.
6. Studies have shown that the variability in the exchange rate was lowest in the 1990–96 period. The standard deviation of the rate of change in the exchange rate declined by more than half in this market-average exchange rate period.
7. It has been reported in recent years that the top 50 *chaebols* produce 85 per cent of GDP. Of these 50, the five biggest ones have been the targets of reform by different governments depending on how a particular government felt towards a given set of *chaebol* families. Hence there is a political dimension to this policy as well.
8. The average debt ratio was running around 400 to 500 per cent of equity before the September 1997 currency crisis. With a sharp currency decline, this ballooned to as much as 700 per cent! As was discussed in Chapter 2, Korea's crisis was a disaster waiting to happen because of this excessive short-term borrowing and bad banking management.

4. Malaysia: broad-based financial liberalization stopped in its tracks

1. BACKGROUND

Malaysia can be described as a resource-rich small to medium-sized country supporting a population of 23 million within a total land area of 330 000 sq. km, 59 per cent of which is virgin forest plus 14 per cent in agriculture.[1] Like similar-sized countries such as Sri Lanka, Thailand, Taiwan and Korea, it had a reasonable level of modernization before its new path to recently achieved high growth. This favourable precondition of having pro-growth inclinations helped to attract industrial activities from more developed countries when policy changes signalled that such activities were appropriate. Situated next to two fast-growth areas, namely East Asia, with the world's second-largest economy of Japan and a rising China, and North America, this country could partake in the growth of the region by identifying itself as a resource-rich country to attract manufacturing activities. After all, the Portuguese and later other colonialists occupied this country for its most central position on the busiest sea-based trade route.

That is exactly what it did, after a period of experimentation with primary-produce-led growth in the first 20 years of its development history. Per capita income, which was 10 per cent of US income in 1957, improved to 30 per cent by 1996. While the primary produce, rubber and tin, made up 80 per cent of exports 40 years ago, the country's successful industrialization enables it to export manufactured items, which accounted for 71 per cent of all exports in the mid-1990s. These two vital statistics summarize the progress of this Southeast Asian economy with potent lessons for other developing countries in East and South Asia. Considered in the light of the 1997–98 Asian financial crisis, its return to exchange and capital controls in late 1998 also holds potential lessons for short-term stabilization policies in the face of capital account instability, which continues to beset small and medium-sized economies across the world. Its bold and controversial stand on currency speculation has sharply focused attention on one major source of instability in the post-Bretton Woods regime since 1973, during which period currency trade was far in excess of the currency needed for goods trade.

The Malaysian economy was developed as a primary producer over a century of colonial rule. In 1957, primary commodities, especially tin and rubber, formed the basis of its large external economy even at that time. Values were added to these commodities in the developed countries, which processed these items into final products. The benefit of commercializing agriculture and extracting more minerals was that it led to rural-sector reforms during the critical period 1958–76 in the formative years of this new country. This was a lucky experience because many other countries which developed fast failed to create prosperity in the rural sector. This resulted in a diversified agricultural modernization and further development of extractive industries, including petroleum and natural gas. By the beginning of 1970, primary produce constituted 95 per cent of the country's exports.[2]

With independence from British colonial rule in August 1957, the initial policy mix pursued by the newly empowered political élites in this country was designed to improve the general well-being of the rural population, which held a disproportionate voting pool of almost three-quarters. The majority of the indigenous peoples of the country, popularized since the 1970s as the *bumiputra* or the sons of the soil, lived in the rural sector. Almost 60 per cent of the population lived in rural areas in 1960 compared to 27 per cent in the 1990s. For the newly elected governments, capturing the rural vote to remain in power was a significant political strategy for survival. Rural improvement policies were also consistent with pro-growth advocacy at that time since demand for primary produce was very high right up to the mid-1970s. The international development institutions were extolling the wisdom of pursuing such policies in the less developed countries.[3] The pursuit of this twin policy of rural improvement and increasing the incomes of indigenous peoples was financed by huge public expenditure, the effect of which was only seen in the late 1970s.

This policy was unsustainable in the long run as incomes rose and the country lost its competitiveness in commodity production. It was very evident by the beginning of the 1980s, especially after the commodity boom ended for good (it appears) in 1983. Sixty-three per cent of the total 1981–85 government budget was financed by sovereign debt, roughly half foreign and half domestic. In the light of what is considered as prudent public debt, even in the developed European Union countries, anything less than half of that would be considered dangerous. The debt-service ratio – 4 per cent in the 1970s – increased to 16 per cent by 1985. That was still not dangerous because of a healthy external sector. But the exchange rate deteriorated as the demand for primary produce started to decline in the late 1970s. The exchange rate, which was RM 2.18 per US dollar, depreciated by 12 per cent during this high-debt period.

The impetus for re-examining the development policy mix came from observing the successful experiments of other economies with a different policy mix in the 1970s. Most neighbouring countries were already adopting new policies to restructure their economies along the lines of what the four tiger economies (Hong Kong, Korea, Singapore and Taiwan) had successfully inaugurated in the 1960s: to base sustainable growth on export-led, labour-intensive economic activities. After the oil price crises, Malaysia chose industrialization as a route to development. With a major transformation of the economy over the next two decades starting from 1978, manufactured output began to increase rapidly until industrial output comprised 34 per cent of GDP in the 1990s. Industrial output now makes up 71 per cent of exports, thus breaking away from the previous era of primary- and extractive-industry-based growth. This success spawned a vision and became a determination in Malaysia that it must arrive at developed status by the year 2020. In fact, tourists to this country often wonder at the wide publicity given to 'Vision 2020' in ubiquitous billboards clearly expressing the end-game of the rush to reach developed status. Considered in this light, the currency crisis can be perceived as a serious challenge, almost an affront, to the progress being made towards this vision.

Understanding how a liberal policy mix was adopted to restructure a low-value-added primary-producing economy to achieve this high degree of economic transformation enables one to see the Malaysian experiment as a successful case of a small resource-rich country adopting a liberal policy mix as appropriate for achieving sustainable growth. This is despite Malaysia's reversion to exchange and capital controls after failing over 12 months, following the contagion from the baht crisis in August 1997, to arrest the runaway depreciation of its currency, the ringgit.

This chapter documents the liberal policies put into effect during a span of 42 years to the date of reversion to controls in late 1998. The next section examines the structure of the economy with special emphasis on the process of the transformation of the economy from one based on primary produce to one based on manufacturing output. The details of the steps taken to reform the real and the financial sectors and their consequences are examined in Section 3. We describe the circumstances that warranted the policies as well as the effects of these policies. Special attention is paid to the policy impacts from financial liberalization: see Subsection 3.2. The reader will find a discussion of the experience of the Malaysian economy right up to the time the contagion of the baht crisis spread to this economy. How sequencing of reforms contributed to financial stability up to 1990 is described elsewhere in the book. Failure to arrest private-sector credit usage, both short-term and of foreign origin, directed at non-tradable investments at a time of declining demand for exports in the 1990s, led to a serious weakening of the fundamentals. The important question to which an answer is sought from this case study is what policy mix should be adopted to develop a competitive economy by implementing liberal reforms.

2.   THE STRUCTURE OF THE ECONOMY AND FINANCIAL SECTOR

Average economic growth over 40 years is reported to be 6.5 per cent per annum in the central bank literature.[4] Per capita income increased from RM 675 in 1959 to about RM 11500, which represents a continuous 7.75 per cent growth per annum in local currency. As stated earlier, per capita GDP in US dollars relative to US per capita income improved threefold. This level of general income growth in a primary-producing country could be considered unique in development circles.

It is useful to divide this development experience into two broad periods of about equal length. The first period from 1959 to 1977 may be labelled the commodity-based growth strategy and the later period from 1978 to 1997 the industrial strategy. This is not often the way most analysts examine Malaysia despite this classification being closer to actual experience. This approach is more revealing in that the first period may be considered a period of endogenous inward-looking growth when the main concern was to continue the past practices of emphasizing commercial agriculture and mining as the route to growth. If the primary products were in demand worldwide, why not do the same things on which success was built in the first phase? Giving the majority of the population, then in the rural sector, reasonable access to modern facilities with reasonable incomes prepared the rest of the country to take bolder steps for orderly change. The choice at that time was quite clear. Korea and Taiwan broke with the past after experiencing traumatic shocks in wars and dared to employ a policy mix to integrate their economies with the developed economies by following the main direction of the world economy towards manufacturing and services as the engines of growth. Malaysia went the other way. The then leaders used the country's advantage in the world commodities market – as top rubber and tin producer – to carry out a brave experiment in rural development that started in 1960 and lasted until the end of the 1970s.

Malaysia missed the opportunity to start with that industrial policy mix at the start of development in an earlier era since it had to build up its social fibre to equip the indigenous people with modern skills of education, training, housing and modernization. Instead, it adopted a policy of social equalization so that the indigenous people could join in the benefits of development at a later period without the social upheaval that could have occurred if the inequality of oppor-tunities for indigenous people in the rural sector were not addressed. The need to tackle this issue was discovered suddenly in the 1969 uprising and civil unrest that led to the realization that social cohesion had to be bought with uneven development for a period of time by improving the lot of the indigenous peoples by giving them a larger share of the expanded portion of growth. It took the economic effects of the world commodity price decline – the full effects of which were evident by the mid-1980s although it started in 1979 – to see that the pursuit of industrial policies was the only route to securing development.

Table 4.1   Basic economic and social indicators of development in Malaysia

Indicators	1971–80	1981–90	1991–93	1994	1995	1996	1997	1998[a]
National accounts								
GDP growth (%)	8.01	6.02	8.19	9.24	9.46	8.63	7.00	–5.20
Per capita GDP (US$)	977	2009	2941	3684	4173	4774	3670	4290
Private consumption/GDP	0.52	0.51	0.52	0.50	0.51	0.46	0.45	0.45
Gov. consumption/GDP	0.16	0.16	0.14	0.13	0.12	0.11	0.11	0.11
Financial indicators								
Gross domestic savings (%)	30.40	33.17	34.50	35.60	36.70	38.40	40.00	41.00
Fixed capital formation (%)	24.39	30.53	35.04	38.17	40.00	42.24	45.00	42.10
Inflation (% per year)	5.99	3.25	4.22	3.71	5.28	3.80	2.80	7.00
M2/GDP	0.44	0.64	0.79	0.89	0.93	0.91	1.06	1.03
Fiscal balance/GDP	–0.08	–0.10	–0.05	0.024	0.01	0.01	0.02	0.01
Current account/GDP	–0.004	0.08	–0.06	–0.06	–0.09	–0.01	0.04	0.03
Discount rate (%)	0.08	4.73	6.68	4.51	5.85	6.47	7.28	10.6[b]
Debt-service ratio	6.60	14.0	7.34	7.70	7.60	7.30	6.10	6.50
Social indicators								
IMF classification	Middle	Upper	Upper	Upper	Upper	Upper	Upper	Upper
Literacy rate (%)	46	70	82	83	83	73	84	84
Expenditure on education (%)	21.98	19.10	19.70	22.07	21.76	21.80	21.40	21.00
Expenditure on health (%)	6.53	4.89	5.71	5.52	5.57	5.70	5.75	5.80
Population growth	2.81	2.63	2.38	3.10	2.48	2.48	2.48	2.48

Notes: [a] One estimate of GDP growth for 1999 is 6%. [b] It declined to 7.7% in 1999.

Sources: IMF *International Financial Statistics*; World Bank, *World Development Report*; and Asian Development Bank (1999).

The overall performance of the country is described by the statistics summarized in Table 4.1. The average growth was in the order of 7.00 per cent (1970–98) while the growth rate during the primary producer stage was 8.01 per cent with 6.32 per cent growth in the industrialized era including 1998. At other periods, for example during the commodity-boom period of the 1970s and during the 1990s, growth was marginally higher. Per capita income grew at about 6 per cent per annum. As the economy developed a respectable export sector, private and government consumption went down significantly. Private consumption in the mid-1990s was 46 per cent of GDP; government consumption was 11.4 per cent.

Improvements in the financial indicators suggest that inflation was kept low throughout the period – a feat achieved through tight monetary policy – while the monetization as measured by the M2 to GDP ratio of the economy accelerated from 43.6 per cent in 1971–80 to 91 per cent in the mid-1990s. Total assets in banks in 1959 was 11 per cent, whereas in 1996 this was close to 100 per cent of GDP. These are notable achievements considering that the money and inter-bank markets were almost non-existent as late as 1963. Fiscal balance had been achieved by a moderately high tax regime with good collection experience as well as, importantly, using market-based activities to achieve many government policies including the credit targeting implemented in the late 1970s to improve the financial conditions of the indigenous people.[5]

The external account was managed well, given the competitiveness of the export sector in commodities and later in manufacturing. However, this balance was lost in the 1990s as capital imports increased substantially with the expansion of infrastructure and commercial-tourism-related property development during the first half of the 1990s, exactly at the wrong time, when the export growth, the mainstay of the restructured economy, started to decline significantly. Of course, this introduced severe limits on the viability of investments and, when the baht crisis occurred, this weakness started to unravel exchange rate stability, leading to a severe financial crisis in late 1997.

Largely continuous growth as well as income-equalizing social policies had a significant impact on the social well-being of a broad spectrum of the people. Rural-sector development has become an important component of national policy. Unlike what one very often observes in other developing countries at the same stage of development, the rural sector in this economy has good roads, water, electricity and telecommunications, as well as good transport facilities. Rural out-migration increased as urbanization improved from about 47 to 72 per cent of the population in the 1990s. The World Bank upgraded the status of the country from middle- to the upper-middle-income category. Education receives about 21 cents per dollar of government budget, almost the same as Korea, which helps it to produce a workforce relevant for the increasingly manufacturing-based economic activities. Illiteracy has declined to below 16 per cent of the population. Infant mortality declined, while life expectancy at birth increased to 73 years.

The change in the economic structure is noteworthy. From a largely rural commodity-based economy of the 1970s depending on primary-producing capacity, the change has been towards large-scale urbanization. Industrial output accounts for about 34 per cent, with services form 56 per cent of the output of the economy. The impact of these changes is seen in the rapid transformation of the financial sector as well, since financial reforms went hand in hand to achieve economic transformation.

The financial sector consists of (a) the banking institutions relevant for effective payment systems and intermediation, (b) non-bank financial intermediaries and (c) financial markets including capital markets for direct financing. These three entities are supervised by the Bank Negara Malaysia (BNM) and the Securities Commission (SC): this is not dissimilar to what one finds in a developed economy. The BNM was formed in 1959 as the central bank. The currency-producing function was transferred to the BNM later in 1967 after the Currency Board was abolished. This body was the sole authority for all financial regulations until March 1993, when the SC was formed to take over the supervision of the capital and derivative markets, including mergers and takeover management.

The banking institutions consist of about 36 commercial banks, 40 finance companies, 12 merchant banks, 30 foreign bank representative offices, under 10 off-shore banks and 6 discount houses. These institutions come under banking regulations, and so form the apex of the financial sector while the BNM uses these institutions to determine credit expansion or contraction for the orderly changes in economic activities. The non-bank financial institutions consist of very special institutions with large assets (the Employees Provident Fund Board, the National Savings Bank, the Pilgrim Fund Board) and the following specialized financing entities: 13 leasing companies, 7 development banks, about 60 property and unit trusts, 4 housing finance units and 59 insurance companies.

The SC is responsible for the orderly development of the stock, bond and futures exchanges while ensuring investors' protection in those direct capital markets. The Kuala Lumpur Stock Exchange is the sole share market, which has about 650 companies listed in two boards.[6] There are several futures markets for money, interest rates, commodity futures, and stock index futures which also come under their supervision.

In summary, it can be said that Malaysia has made progress towards its aim of becoming a developed country in the not too distant future by modernizing its infrastructure across the whole country through rural development, as well as pulling the rural sector out of poverty because of the majority position of the indigenous population in the political framework. Development in the first two decades was based on a policy mix that enabled the rural sector to be developed. Commercialization of agriculture through diversification across rubber, palm oil, copra, cocoa and other production was pursued while the development of the extractive industries in tin, bauxite, oil, gas and so on was stepped up. That was appropriate at that time, given the then commodity boom, which ended in the late 1970s. In the next 20 years, the policy mix was to switch to manufactured exports and private-sector-led growth. This meant that there was a greater need for financial reforms to build capacity for manufacturing as well as to introduce reforms in the financial sector to mobilize capital and know-how. Institution-building in the financial sector became important and liberalization policies were pursed aggressively after completion of the structural reforms to enable Malaysia to become a preferred location for multinational production and marketing. Liberalization will be examined in the next section.

3.   LIBERALIZATION

In the late 1950s, when development efforts in this newly independent country were being mooted, a civil war was being fought with the Communists, who had gone into the jungle, wanting to capture power through armed struggle. Another feature was that the newly empowered élites had to eradicate rural poverty, which was also the target of Communist propaganda, while the parliamentary democracy put in place also empowered the rural people, who constituted a large voting pool. A third feature was that the majority of the rural population were already engaging in commercial agriculture; these were also the indigenous people. These three factors led to the formulation of a policy mix aimed at rural development as a means of removing the attraction of Communism, while the same policy was seen as helping to improve the incomes of the indigenous people, the *bumiputra*, who held the voting pool.

Thus the political realities of the time determined the policy mix adopted over the next 20 years or so. This can be described as the twin policy of rural reforms with commercialization of primary output. When the commodity boom was coming to an end – this happened even in the more developed countries such as Australia and New Zealand – the inevitable choice led to a policy mix with three characteristics: continuation of the *bumiputra* preference, this time in equity participation; export-led manufacturing focus; and full-scale liberalization in the financial sector to mobilize resources needed for manufacturing-led growth. The contagion from the baht crisis revealed the weakness of financial dependence of the economy on exports, which was weakening from 1991, and the financial sector's exposure to foreign capital in the banking institutions as well as in the stock market, further weakening fundamentals. This led to the massive depreciation of the ringgit to its lowest level of RM 4.76, or 76 per cent at one stage. With the unprecedented step taken in late 1998 to fix the currency at RM 3.80 against the US dollar, while imposing controls on short-term funds, the era of liberalization in the financial sector appears to have come to an end, at least in the short run.

3.1   Economic Reforms

Primary production
A distinct character of the first set of reforms can be said to be the commercialization and diversification of the economy, using its advantage as a major producer of rubber, copra, palm oil, and so on while also improving the mining

of tin, bauxite, oil and gas. This is not subsistence farming. The focus was on diversifying primary production, which led to limited reforms in the industrial and financial sectors. The financial sector was built from scratch. As a BNM report says,

> the possibilities for effective monetary management were rather limited in the beginning [in the early 1960s] because the financial system which serves as the transmission mechanism for policy was relatively underdeveloped. (BNM, 1994a, p. 449)

Therefore the focus of economic reforms was on developing the infrastructure to enhance the capacity of the agricultural sector to produce goods, process them, and transport them to points of sale or export. This led to broad-based country-wide electrification, road-building, banking infrastructure, and so on. There were 111 bank branches in 1960 compared with 1200 in the 1990s. Mining development was part of the same process. Therefore the real sector developed a large-scale infrastructure unlike, for example, in Thailand, which was developing on the basis of manufacturing concentrated mostly near Bangkok, the capital city. Financial institution building and capacity to intermediate efficiently were the main areas of concern: this will be discussed in detail later in this section.

Industrialization

The exchange and interest rate instability, which arose from the abandonment of the fixed exchange rate system by unilateral action of the USA in August 1971, crippled the world economy at that time. That and the 1973 first oil price increase led to the world recession of 1975–76. The second oil price hike in 1978–79 soon led to a period of stagflation, low or no growth with high inflation. The commodity boom was also coming to an end, with falling demand all over the world. This led to the adoption of a new policy mix avoiding commodity reliance. The Indonesians were the first to move away from commodities to enter into manufacturing as a means of diversifying their economy. Of course, the success of the four Asian tigers could not be ignored by this country for too long: Malaysia was pushed into adopting industrialization to achieve further growth in the next 20 years.

Fortunately, Malaysia had experience with market-based reform policies, unlike the policies in East and South Asian socialist economies, where the government sectors were relied upon as the prime movers of change. Continuation of pro-growth market-based reforms could therefore easily be followed by Malaysia. The switch was less painful for this country than for the command and socialist economies.

Financial liberalization had to be far-reaching to support the move towards greater reliance on manufacturing and export-led growth. The experiences of several countries in these respects were not uniform. For example, Korea and Taiwan followed this path with few financial reforms whereas Malaysia did so with a substantial dose of liberal policies in the financial sector, as will be seen later in this section. In this regard, the desire to develop the financial markets as a major financial centre for the region was part of the reason, although the reforms opened the door for huge capital resources to flow in to support the industrialization effort. Just before the financial crisis, the share market was capitalized at 323 per cent of GDP. When foreign owners sold the scrips in ringgit and then converted the proceeds to foreign currencies, chiefly US dollars, the ringgit had to give way, although all other fundamentals were not as bad in this economy as they were in Korea, the Philippines and Thailand. By the end of 1997, the capitalization declined to a mere 136 per cent of GDP. Prices drifted further in the next year as more scrips were sold, and then converted to ringgits. It is this sort of short-term money that the capital controls of September 1998 were meant to stabilize.

The baht crisis
The baht crisis started in May 1997 soon after the weaknesses of the Thai economy were evident after two short-lived Thai governments failed to take bold steps to introduce financial reforms to address the financial fragility that had been evident in that country since 1992. Thai banks were already about to collapse from too many non-performing loans and Thai firms had borrowed heavily in short-term markets to invest in long-term land-based investment projects. No action was taken, the baht collapsed, and was then free-floated. The crisis spread to the Philippines, and then to Indonesia. The Malaysian ringgit started to lose its long-held stability. Attempts to manage the ringgit failed and, in August 1997, it was free-floated. Attempts to interfere in the market mechanism – in the capital market,[7] and in avoiding interest rate hikes at the right time – led to further loss of confidence in the currency. The currency depreciated to as low as RM 4.76 per US dollar in 1998 and all attempts to bring back Malaysian capital placed in hard-currency deposits just outside the country failed. Press reports indicated in early 1998 that a total of RM 54 billion (20 per cent of GDP) was deposited outside, but only a fraction returned, with the rest remaining in hard currencies. The prime minister announced the important cabinet decision taken in August 1998 to revert to fixing the ringgit (effective September 1998) at RM 3.80 for one unit of US currency: all ringgit trade outside was banned, and short-term deposits by foreigners were subject to a punitive exit tax. These measures helped both inflation and interest rates to subside quickly; they also led to some sort of stability for international trading to occur in an orderly manner. Subsequently, some relaxation of the rules on short-term funds was announced in February 1999: businessmen were assured that the controls would not be used to deny them access to foreign currencies

for trading. The current and capital account liberalization that had been praised as the correct policy choice for an economy on the road to developed status was stopped in its tracks.[8] Meanwhile at least one country, Brazil, that came under speculative attack copied the same sort of controls as temporary measures and took charge of its situation in January 1999. The verdict on the Mahathir experiment is eagerly awaited by many, both in Malaysia and elsewhere.

3.2 Financial Liberalization

The individual reforms to effect the financial (and economic) transformation of Malaysia are summarized in Table 4.2. The important financial reforms will be discussed under several sub-headings below. The reader will recall that an earlier section included a brief discussion on economic reforms. Financial reforms may be grouped into three distinct phases over the 42-year period. At the start, Malaysia developed private-sector-based financial institutions during the colonial period to facilitate international trade in commodity exchange and for the import of finished goods, mainly from the United Kingdom. There were no interbank markets in Malaysia, but the foreign banks, which controlled the financial system in the 1950s, used the London interbank markets to transact daily. There were also no capital markets in Malaysia. The share market was located in Singapore, serving two places, but Singapore was not part of Malaysia except during a three-year stint from 1963 to 1965.

In this period, too, there were more banks, more branches, more finance companies, more insurance companies, and so on. Another feature of this period was the development of money markets to trade short-dated securities, which revealed the market rates of interest, and so on. Discount houses were established, merchant banks introduced securitization expertise to list more companies on the exchange, longer-dated securities were introduced and a capital market was established in 1960, which became the Kuala Lumpur Stock Exchange in June 1973. In fact almost all institutions were modernised and expanded. The only exception was the delayed establishment of the Securities Commission, formed in March 1993.

Intervention and liberalization, 1973–98

The early to late 1970s were the heyday of the commodity boom. With the wealth accumulated after a period of 17 years of fairly good growth – despite the fact that this country did not follow the more successful examples of manufacturing in Korea, Taiwan and Hong Kong – there were calls to introduce interventionist policies, particularly to direct credits to certain segments. This found expression in interventions in the interest rate markets, preferential credit allocation for the *bumiputra* and other preferences. This came at the wrong time, since the 1975–76 world recession prevented these policies from being

Table 4.2   Major economic and financial reforms in Malaysia, 1958–98

Date of reforms	Liberalization policy implemented
1958	Economic Incentives Law: international capital and dividend allowed.
1959	Central bank formed with an act of parliament, Bank Negara Malaysia Act.
	(Foreign-origin banks dominated the economy. No money or capital markets.)
1960	Stock trading started in Kuala Lumpur in addition to Singapore.
1963	Establishment of discount houses from which money market and inter-bank activities could be developed through market-related signals.
	Treasury bill issued by the central bank to establish market interest rates.
1967	Currency-issuing power transferred to BNM from the regional Currency Board.
1969	Treasury bonds issued by BNM to establish the base rates from market bids.
1970	Establishment of merchant banks.
1971	Finance companies, which had a dominant position in lending, come under Banking Act; therefore central bank supervision.
	Commercial banks permitted to issue fixed deposits up to 36 months.
1972	Commercial banks permitted to issue fixed deposits up to 60 months.
	To induce institutions to lend to *bumiputra* economic activities, a Credit Guarantee Corporation of Malaysia, CGCM, set up as a private institution.
1973 (June)	Exchange rate no longer fixed. Most restrictions lifted.
	Capital market trading converted to ringgit as a genuine step to localization.
1973	Currency convertibility with Brunei and Singapore ends in May. Ringgit floated in June 1973.
1975	Selective credit line to *bumiputra* economic activities comes into force: of the increases, 20% in loans, 10% in agri-loans, 25% in manufacturing loans and 10% in housing loans.
1978 (Sept.)	Exchange rate fully liberalized. A basket peg to trade-weighted currency.
1978–79	Up to this period, BNM set the interest rates in consultation with the major institutions, that is, before 1978, the interest rate was controlled.
	First move to free interest rates: commercial banks could set interest rates for deposits, a year later also for lending.
1978	Interest controls introduced in lending and deposit markets (removed in 1991).
1979	Industrial Bank of Malaysia formed to finance loans exceeding seven years.
	Merchant banks brought under the definition of Banking Act.
1980s	Rationalization of the regulations to make the commercial banks diversify into securities and other activities as separate accounting units.
1983	Islamic banking with profit-sharing instead of fixed interest introduced.
1985	CAGAMAS bonds introduced to finance housing credit market.
1986	A number of cooperative finance companies and some banks failed. Central bank rescues them, and passes laws to bring them under banking supervision.

Date of reforms	Liberalization policy implemented
	A new banking act (BAFIA) passed to consolidate all amendments.
1985–86	Recession: easing of monetary controls to stimulate investments.
1986	Real-sector reforms to permit greater ownership by foreign companies. Tax reforms introduced to stimulate economic activities.
1987	Current account surplus RM 6.6 billion (or about 4% of GDP) results from reforms to the real economy and the pursuit of low-interest policy to stimulate the economy.
	Current account goes into deficit of RM 0.9 billion and continues to be in deficit.
1989	Mutual double listing of capital securities in Singapore and Malaysia ceased.
1990	Capital market reforms: eased entry barriers to broking; more mutual funds; foreign share-ownership limit increased to 49%. (High volatility in share market.)
	International Offshore Financial Centre in free-traded Labuan established.
Oct. 1990	Interest rate differential very high, large capital flows into Malaysia. Private-sector loans increased by 23% per annum mostly for non-traded investments.
1988–91	12 upward revisions of statutory reserve ratios to contain overlending to the private sector. But by that time the baht crisis had taken root.
1989-May 1996	Tariff reduction on further items, 600 more (AFTA initiative).
1993	Swaps were controlled by limiting this to only US$2 million per day per customer with an upper limit of US$5 million on all non-traded foreign exchange transactions.
1989–92	Money market operation by government stopped (this took liquidity down further as government placed deposits with BNM).
1990 (April)	Curbs on consumer credits for vehicles (75%-only rule) and credit cards (RM 24 000 annual income; age limit 21; and 10% minimum repayment.
1991–92	Excess funds of pension body, EPFB (in 1993 this was RM 10.9 billion) put in BNM to reduce credit expansion.
1992	Issue of BN bills to absorb further liquidity.
1993	Two-tier regulatory system inaugurated to improve soundness of banking. By end 1997, 18 (11 banks, 3 finance companies and 4 merchant banks) qualified as these had 2% higher capital adequacy. Incentives given.
1994	Defended the ringgit: Abandoned managed float.
1997 (Aug.)	Several interventions in the market to arrest the free fall in the stock market and in the ringgit. All failed.
1998 (Aug.)	Decision on currency and capital controls taken.
1998 (Sept.)	Fixed exchange rate at RM 3.80 effective Oct. 1998. Short-term foreign capital withdrawal limits announced. Ringgit banned from trading outside the country.
1999 (Aug.)	Internal trading of ringgit within free market. Stringent limits reduced on short-term foreign fund withdrawals.
2000 (Jan.)	With exports growing at 24%, all-time high foreign reserve US$36 billion.

Sources: Bank Negara Malaysia; Asian Development Bank reports; sources included in Bibliography.

pursued vigorously. By the time the 1970s came to an end, the commodity boom was over and the world was again in stagflation in the early 1980s. The recession came in 1985–86. The combined effect of these adverse events was that the interventionist policies could only be pursued vigorously for a short while over 1975–79. With the fast growth that came later, these interventionist policies were considered to be minor irritants in the light of the larger growth taking place for everyone, including the indigenous producers.

Far-reaching reforms had to be put in place to stimulate the economy to provide momentum for growth. Thus, by starting on the road to industrialization, substantial real-sector and financial-sector reforms had to be undertaken while the public sector had to be deflated through privatization of inefficient public goods providers. In short, there was a call to return to the market mechanism. Government reduced its expenditure, and privatized widely to improve efficiency. All forms of government-delivered goods were returned to the private sector – no doubt still maintaining a network of financial controls of related companies under political party controls – in roads, airlines, ports, power, water and telecommunications. Industrial land development was taken seriously to locate industries in five different parts of the country to spread development regionally. Where there was growth in a neighbouring country, attempts were made to latch on to that growth by forming growth triangles.

The financial sector also went through liberalization. June 1978 saw the removal of all forms of exchange controls except in the form of a basket-pegging management of the currency. Capital controls were no longer applied to domestic firms and individuals. The capital market was opened to foreign transactions to such an extent that this share market became the main attraction in Asia for international short-term money.

The Bank Act of 1973 was consolidated in 1986 with better prudential regulations on paper. A two-tiered system was put in place from 1994 to segregate the weaker institutions from the sound ones: 18 of around 90 major institutions qualified to become stronger and bigger (the intention of this reform was to get the public to see them as safer) banking institutions. Similar progress was made in introducing prudential regulations although, considered in the light of the post-crisis information on this aspect, then were not sufficient guarantees of safety, nor were they strictly fully implemented.

There began a persistent flow of capital into Malaysia due to the combined effect of (a) low inflation in the 1990s and therefore (b) low domestic interest rates and a large interest rate differential with many countries, and (c) the very open financial situation.[9] The central bank tried to mop up liquidity to stem credit expansion, but it was not successful. The excessive credit available found its way into the non-tradable sector with the result that the private sector was overladen with too much investment of borrowed money in longer-term infrastructure and property investments. The capital goods import requirements of these investments also raised current account deficits to an all-time high in the period 1994–96.

The high-priced share market attracted so much world attention that in 1993 the funds raised in the capital markets amounted to the same level as all the loans made available by the banking system! The capital market continued to provide 25 per cent of the funds instead of 3–10 per cent, which was the norm in most periods without the overpricing of asset markets in the 1990s. The cost of funds therefore went down for public companies, making it possible for the private-sector firms to undertake long-term projects in the non-tradable sector. This worsened the current account which, given the continued managed float of the exchange rate at about RM 2.50 to 2.60 per dollar, could not be sustained for long.

Liberalization stopped in its tracks, October 1998

The baht crisis exposed the weakness of the Philippines economy first, then the Indonesian economy as well as the Malaysian economy. During the two months June–July 1997, the steps taken by the authorities under the then acting prime minister did not lead to any amelioration of the situation. When the prime minister resumed work after two months of recuperation, the crisis had become a very serious threat, and had worsened. More and more individuals were taking their savings out of the country to place them in hard currencies, or simply keeping the ringgit outside the country! Further failure to take early decisive steps to bolster investor confidence led to further falls in the exchange rate and, consequently, the stock market collapsed, plummeting below the 900 index value, when the government's attempt to intervene in the market led to further falls after a short rebound.[10] Continued selling of shares and conversion to foreign currencies weakened the ringgit to an all-time low of RM 4.76 during the first half of 1998. Every rebound in the share market led to further sales of the shares, and soon further conversion of the ringgit into hard currencies. The fall was relentless.

While this was happening, the IMF's attempt to rescue Indonesia and Korea did not lead to any quick resolution of the currency problem. The March 1998 election to the fifth term of Indonesian President Suharto led to political unrest and riots. Parliament was seized by students in much the same manner as the Tiananmen reformists occupied the square in Beijing in 1989. The IMF, faced with the president's reluctance to accept the terms of IMF intervention, postponed corrective action amidst this turmoil, which had a telling effect on all the currencies in the region. Meanwhile, opposition to the IMF path to reform grew louder. In mid-1998, a number of influential scholars (Krugman and Bhagwati included)[11] supported exchange rate control as a last-ditch effort to stem the crisis.

The beleaguered leaders in Malaysia had only slim hope based on the new minority consensus on controls, and implemented exchange rate and capital controls, effective from September 1998. Consequently, large-scale trading in the ringgit came to a stop in Singapore and elsewhere, to the delight of the policy-makers in Kuala Lumpur. The exchange rate soon improved, at just below RM 3.90 by the end of September 1998 and interest rates began to decline below 10 per cent. Thus one of the more liberal policy regimes was stopped in its tracks by the 1997 Asian financial crisis.

There was widespread scepticism about whether controls can achieve the conditions needed for openness with the rest of the world to achieve the long-term aim of becoming a developed nation. Controls appear to be consistent with the widely publicized view of the country's leaders[12] that speculation in currency is not a necessary economic activity for development. It must be admitted that the result of their action stopped the run-away depreciation of the currency, at least for the time being. Interest rates halved to about 7 per cent within a month of the announcement. Further easing of credit is on the cards. The statutory reserve was reduced to 8.5 per cent in November 1998 from the earlier 12 per cent, with a promise of more relaxation to come: it was reduced to 4 per cent. The export sector is registering high growth and its financing needs may be satisfied now with cheaper money. That could well become the leading edge of the recovery for this country. Early estimates of 1999 GDP growth is 6 per cent.

Exchange and interest rate policies

Table 4.3 summarizes statistics on exchange and interest rates. Compared with most developing countries, the exchange rate experience of Malaysia could be said to be one that others would wish to emulate. The credit for this goes to a very conscious knee-jerk policy stand of the central bank on inflation.

Table 4.3   Exchange rates and interest rates (annual averages)

	5-year averages			Annual averages							
	1976–80	1981–85	1986–90	1991	1992	1993	1994	1995	1996	1997	1998
Exchange rate	2.304	2.351	2.643	2.72	2.61	2.70	2.56	2.54	2.53	3.89	3.80
Interest rates											
Discount rate	4.016	4.802	4.666	7.70	7.10	5.24	4.51	4.51	7.28	7.78	8.51
Money rate	3.516	7.212	4.590	7.83	8.01	6.53	6.53	5.07	6.98	7.61	5.90
Deposit rate	5.514	9.158	5.168	7.18	7.80	6.40	4.94	5.93	7.09	7.98	6.75
Lending rate	7.834	10.252	8.060	8.13	9.31	9.05	9.05	7.62	8.89	9.53	10.4

Source: IMF, *International Financial Statistics.*

Throughout the period, the BNM did not hesitate to take action to stem inflation at any sign that it was becoming a threat to growth. With inflation

under control, and enjoying good commodity prices while successfully restructuring the economy towards industrialization, the stable exchange rate for the
currency provided a steadying factor for investment capital to come to Malaysia
in large proportion for the size of the economy. From the period of liberalization in the late 1970s, this country attracted liberal doses of FDI every year right
up to 1996, just before the crisis. The average flow of foreign direct investment
amounted to US$4.5 billion per year: over 1990–96, the accumulated amount
was 35 per cent of GDP, assuming a projected recovery of capital in six years.

1959–73   With a fixed exchange rate during this period, the Malaysian
currency – then called the Malaysian dollar – was pegged to the pound sterling.
Very few changes to the rate were made in line with the parity conditions
prevailing. Just before the breakdown of the fixed rate system in mid-1971,
the currency lost value due to commodity price inflation. It went right up to 3.60
units per US dollar. The newly formed central bank increased the reserves from
3.5 per cent to 5 per cent to stem the credit expansion and to bring down
inflation. Again in 1972, the ratio was raised to 8.5 per cent (and 2.5 per cent
for finance companies). The oil price hike came in 1973. A new currency, the
ringgit, meant for only Malaysia (leaving Brunei and Singapore to keep the
dollar designation) was introduced in June 1973 with most exchange rate
controls removed.

1974–79   With the world recession in 1975–76, the combined effect of the
policies led to a reduction in inflation from a high of 12 per cent to a single digit.
Thus the first attempt to contain inflation in the late 1960s led to success in the
mid-1970s. With the second oil price shock in 1978, more financial liberalization was undertaken. A notable change was relaxing the controls on interest
rates. Controls were introduced in pursuit of lowering the interest costs during
the phase of commodity-led growth. The same policy was consistent with the
credit- and equity-targeting policies of the mid-1970s. Interest rate controls
was removed slowly over two years. This led to capital flows that gave some
advantage.

1980–89   This period was known for slow growth, which culminated in an
economic recession over 1986–87. The exchange rate was maintained at about
RM 2.35 during the slow-growth period. With the economy recovering in 1987,
there was a very large inflow of capital from outside. Along with that came the
potential for high inflation. The BNM maintained low real interest rates, which
helped to ease the exchange rate a little upward, but did not lead to inflation.
In this regard, the 1986 current account surplus was a great help. The current
account deficits in the years up to 1990 were not large, which also helped to keep

the exchange rate stable, though a shade higher than the rate in the first half of the 1980s.

1989–96 This period saw a continued high interest margin with other countries. This stimulated large capital flows into the country. The BNM revised the reserve ratios 12 times until the ratio was 12.5 per cent in 1996. Further corrective actions taken did not tighten the loose credit conditions, which led to excessive credit expansion in the private sector. For instance, lending to the private sector increased by 23 per cent over four years compared to 12 per cent in the previous period, when the lending rate remained below 10 per cent. However, this was well below the 60 per cent credit growth reported in Korea and Thailand. Economic growth was in excess of 8 per cent. This had the potential for inflation, but the credit controls and tightening of credits kept inflation below 5.7 per cent most of the time.

The interest rate was maintained at low levels throughout the study period. Except during the 1979–85 period, when the lending rate was a shade above 10 per cent, borrowing cost to firms became the lowest in the 1990s, when the lending rate was 8.3 per cent, a rate that could not be achieved in less open financial markets such as those in Korea and Indonesia. This low capital cost was the product of high domestic savings and high foreign capital flows. In the 1990s, this factor dulled the firms by encouraging them to make low-profit long-term investments at a time when the export sector was registering sustained declines from 1991 onwards. This led to further borrowing by the private sector as no one anticipated that a systemic crisis was developing in the region with (a) declining export growth, (b) too many short-term loans in banks and firms and, worse, (c) increasing non-performing loans in a relaxed supervisory regime.

Financial institutional development

At the time of forming the central bank in 1958, there were 26 commercial banks, of which 18 were foreign, with 111 branches. Total assets of the commercial banks were M\$1.1 billion, about 11 per cent of GDP. In 1996, there were 37 banks, all of which were locally incorporated, even though 16 of them had foreign affiliation. The total assets in 1996 amounted to almost 100 per cent of GDP. In the beginning, the foreign banks held most of the deposits in the country, and transacted with London inter-bank markets as the currency was fixed to the pound sterling.

All this changed dramatically over the years through financial institutional reforms and diversification to support a developing economy. Unlike what happened in the command and socialist economies in East and South Asia, the banking sector remained in the private sector. The government bought shares in some leading banks such as the Maybank, but no nationalization of the type found in other countries ever occurred. Throughout the 1960s to the mid-1970s, attention was focused on building a variety of financial institutions. Thus entry barriers were eased and more banks, finance companies (later consolidated into fewer firms), merchant banks, Islamic banks, savings banks and development banks were licensed. The number of branches also increased to about 1200, of which the local banks had the majority, accounting for 85 per cent of branches. By the mid-1990s there were thriving money markets in Malaysia along with robust capital markets helping to raise about 25 per cent of the capital needs of the economy.

Apart from structural changes, regulations governing the sector were rapidly changed and modernized. The Bank Act 1973 was meant to apply to commercial banks. Other deposit-taking institutions such as the finance companies, Islamic banks and merchant banks were brought under the purview of the banking laws in the 1970s. With a more industry-based development, three new regulations came into effect. A comprehensive act to cover deposit-taking and non-bank financial institutions was passed in 1986. In 1989, notice was given that banks would be required to incorporate under the Local Companies Act from 1994. The two-tier regulatory system was implemented in 1994, which by 1997 led to 18 sound banks, finance companies and merchant banks qualifying, with higher capital ratios than the rest.

There were savings cooperatives, which were outside the banking laws, as are still the large asset-based Industrial Bank, the pension fund (EPF), the Tabong Haji and the Savings Bank. The poor management of the cooperative savings units led to a massive bailout in the early 1980s, and also to few banking failures: now credit unions are under BNM supervision. Though most relevant institutions come under the prudential regulations of the BNM, exempting some is not seen as prudent.

Financial and capital markets

It has been remarked in an earlier section that the financial markets were developed from scratch in Malaysia. The inter-bank markets started in 1967 with the establishment of the discount houses, which traded short-dated monetary instruments after buying them wholesale at the time of issue. This led to the beginning of an active discount market. Treasury bills and bonds were introduced later. The freeing of exchange controls led to active trading of the local currency, both in the spot and forward markets.

Capital market development started in 1960 with the trading in Kuala Lumpur of the dual-listed stocks and bonds in Singapore. The real impetus came only when the ringgit was adopted in June 1973 as the Malaysian currency and Kuala Lumpur traded shares in the local currency. The dual-listing arrangement with Singapore worked both ways in the earlier period. With the development of the local market, more and more firms continued to restrict listing to the local market even though the more established firms were actively traded in both markets. With dual-listing coming to an end in 1989, and other reforms that came into force, the local market became extremely attractive to foreign portfolio investment. Liquidity surged very high and the market gained substantial growth in all respects. The total traded volume in 1993 represented the cumulative total volume of the past 20 years! The market yield in that year was a massive 104 per cent in this fourteenth largest market. This made foreign interest in the local market a very significant destabilizing force. Since the withdrawal of foreign interest in the market, starting in 1994, the market drifted down to lower levels, and was also badly affected by the currency crisis.

The structure of the capital market changed rapidly in the late 1980s and 1990s. The number of firms listed almost doubled in the period and capitalization soared with high-priced stocks: in 1999, there were 702 firms. The bond market also expanded with two rating companies providing rating services. To these were added a few derivative securities. Interest rate derivatives were added in 1995, followed by the offer of stock index futures on a 100-stock-based index in December 1995. Plans were afoot at that time to include options markets. With the crisis affecting market confidence, some of these plans have been put on hold.

Summary

The foregoing discussion, though brief, highlights the importance of financial reforms to support the real sector and the fiscal regime in a developing country. Exchange rate reforms, with the central bank consciously pursuing low-inflation targeting, appear to have become a permanent feature of the financial reforms in Malaysia. Not widely acknowledged, the accomplishment of inflation below 10 per cent achieved by this country, and more often below 5 per cent, is a feat not achieved by most developing countries, even those which grew at the middling growth rate of 5 per cent per annum: Malaysia's growth was about 8 per cent. Just compare the experience of China and Indonesia, two countries that grew at high rates, in this regard.

Credible reforms to liberalize the financial sector were also noteworthy features of development experience. Not only did the reforms help to build the financial institutional framework from scratch; they also helped to build a diversified financial structure that delivered the capital at a low interest rate to assist the development process. In the 1990s, there were too many capital flows into the country because of this very openness. Attempts by the central banks to mop the liquidity to prevent the private sector making too much imprudent investments failed. This failure at the time of a worsening current account deterioration weakened the exchange rate, which was held artificially high by the basket-pegging in place since 1978. When the policy responses did not restore the confidence of the investors, both local and short-term fund owners withdrew their funds to safer currencies, and the exchange rate went on a free fall that exhausted the ability of the country to sustain the shock. The adoption of a fixed exchange in 1998 reversed the liberal policies in the financial sector. It has nevertheless brought some stability after 12 months of instability. Would it deliver the long-term needs of an economy dependent on the external sector for development?

3.3 Financial Liberalization Effects

Macroeconomic effects

Table 4.4 includes summary statistics on the effects of liberalization on the overall economic performance over the study period.

Table 4.4   Basic economic indicators in Malaysia: growth rates (%) per year)

	5-year averages			Annual averages							
	1976–80	1981–85	1986–90	1991	1992	1993	1994	1995	1996	1997	1998
GDP	8.54	5 13	6.81	8.42	7.80	8 35	9.24	9.46	8.20	7.02	–5.2
Inflation	4.64	4.65	1.79	4.40	4.69	3.59	3.71	5.28	3.80	4.0	5.2
Gov. revenue	22.13	8.68	6.93	15.4	15.3	6.22	18.6	3.05	13.70	7.00	–2.0
Ml 1	17.54	7.89	12.45	9.93	27.3	35.3	16.8	13.2	16.65	11.67	–29.4
M2	22.37	12.26	9.40	16.9	29.2	26.6	12.7	20.0	24.28	17.38	–1.44
Trade balance	17.54	7.69	12.45	–84.5	706.0	–4.0	–48.0	–106.0	–12.5	120.0	104.0
FDI	25 10	–5.75	27.41	74.6	29.6	–12.6	–13.3	–4.30	13.07	–19.64	n.a.

Sources: IMF, *International Financial Statistics* and other sources included in the Bibliography.

The growth rates in the key financial indicators of the economy are very impressive, except in the case of the very wide variation in the trade sector in the 1990s. The economic growth rate was sustained within the long-term trend of about 8 per cent in the 1970s and 7 per cent in the 1980s despite world recessions in 1975–76 and stagflation in the first half of the 1980s. Growth has been impressive in the 1990s at above 7.8 per cent, suggesting a long-term path of 8 per cent. Growth in FDI flows was almost four times the economic growth rates, suggesting the increasing dependence of this economy on foreign capital, which was endemic to the Southeast Asian region: this has slowed down since 1995 as exports were declining. Between 1991 and 1996, a total of US$47 billion in FDI was invested. This does not include the private-sector borrowing from foreign sources and the portfolio flows to the equity and bond markets, both of which received substantial foreign investment. An important consequence, which could not be sustained in the long run, was a high investment rate in this economy. In most years over 1990–96, investment rates were close to or above 42 per cent of GDP.

These rates of growth in investment and economic activities were achieved without a substantial rise in the inflation rate or in the interest rate. As noted earlier, inflation control has been pursued by the central bank. Only in 1996 did inflation go above 5 per cent, whereas it remained below that figure throughout the 21 years covered by the data. This is no mean achievement even within Southeast Asia. The other countries in the region, with the notable exception of Singapore, had inflation twice or three times the rate in Malaysia. This aspect of financial and monetary management deserves further study as it may hold important lessons for development economics policy. The BNM has had signal success in this regard despite being faulted in others.

The fiscal health of the economy is also seen by the high growth rates in public finance. Public finance grew at its highest rate of 22.13 per cent during the commodity-boom period and during the 1990s, with an average growth rate of 11.7 per cent. This was achieved by the twin policy of privatization, which removed financing of several public goods producing functions and tax revision, which led to higher growth in revenue. This aspect also deserves further study since many newly emerging economies have to tackle the problem of how to divest loss-making public enterprises while reducing tax rates without losing a hold on public finance.

Monetary growth was running ahead of income growth in some periods, as for example during 1975–80, when government borrowing peaked as commodity prices declined and the rural development programmes were nearing their peak as well. Comments made earlier in the section on exchange rate management would suggest that this was due to the persistent high liquidity in the banking sector, a consequence of the financial liberalization that led to capital inflows. Repeated attempts to manage the liquidity kept these figures from getting out of control and from affecting the control on inflation. But monetary growth was high in the 1990s at the same time as the central bank was grappling with the task of reducing credit expansion. Its attempts led to keeping inflation down but failed to curb high capital usage in the non-traded sector. Not restricting private-sector investment into non-tradable production areas desta-bilized the fine balance achieved in managing inflation.

The financial sector

The overall impact of financial liberalization on the financial sector was very marked. Summary statistics on financial deepening are presented in Table 4.5.

Despite the central bank's concern about the need to control inflation, which meant that monetary growth was discouraged throughout the period, the ratio of M2 to GDP doubled over the period. This reflected the growth in economic activities over the years. This ratio went up from 0.48 (48 per cent) in the five years over 1976–80 to close to 0.90 during 1993–98. Money growth, as explained in an earlier section, was kept low to discourage large expansion in the private-sector demand for credits. The financial intermediation ratio (FIR) also doubled over the period, reflecting the public's willingness to hold assets in the organized financial sector. It also reflects the development of institutions that could facilitate the holding of assets in such institutions. This ratio, which was already high 20 years ago at 0.72 (72 per cent), increased to 1.08 (108 per cent). This level of intermediation is very close to the values of developed countries, and could well be a reflection of greater commercialization of economic activities over the years and the liberal policies that encouraged competition.

Table 4.5 Indicators of financial liberalization

Indicators	5-year average			Annual							
	1976–80	1981–85	1986–90	1991	1992	1993	1994	1995	1996	1997	1998
Money depth	0 48	0.59	0.59	0 69	0.78	0.90	0.89	0.93	0 91	0.96	0.94
Intermediation											
FIR (total)/GDP	0.33	0.55	0.72	0.78	0.80	0.77	0.87	0.94	1.06	1.08	1.61
FIR (public)/GDP	0.02	0.04	0.04	0.03	0.04	0.01	0.01	0.01	0.02	0.02	0.05
FIR (private)/GDP	0.31	0.51	0.68	0.75	0.76	0.76	0.86	0.93	1.04	1.06	1.56
GFCF/GDP	0.26	0.34	0.28	0.36	0.34	0.38	0.38	0.40	0.42	0.42	0.43
FDI/GDP	0.03	0.04	0.03	0.09	0.11	0.12	0.09	0.07	0.04	0.02	n.a.

Notes:
M2 = Currency + quasi-money.
FIR = financial intermediation ratio; claims on public sector (public), on private sector (private); and total (total).
GFCF = gross fixed capital formation.
FDI = foreign direct investment.

Sources: IMF, *International Financial Statistics*; World Bank, *World Bank Databank*, various issues.

The FIR for the public sector shows less growth, from 0.02 in 1976–80 remaining about the same. This intermediation ratio in the post-1994 period is a reflection of the structure of government finance as the economy was gradually slowing down, with declines in trade sector occurring from 1992. The private sector's FIR kept increasing very fast from the 1976–80 average of 0.31 to 1.06 in 1997. In fact, there was a build-up of too much debt as firms switched to land-based investment projects to offset the loss from reducing exports. In this, the encouragement of high-priced hotels, road schemes, condominiums, and resorts became fashionable in the mid-1990s. Obviously assets and/or liabilities were being built up in the private sector very quickly. That is consistent with the trends shown in other statistics. A particular statistic is the increase in the FDI flows, which must have increased intermediation in the real sector. FDI as a percentage of GDP increased fourfold in one year in this period. Growth in fixed capital formation was high in the 1990s. From the trend average suggested by the low figure in 1986–90 of 28 per cent of GDP (0.28 in Table 4.5), capital formation went up to 40 per cent in 1995. These figures are therefore consistent with 1990s growth being part of a greater private-sector-led expansion. However, these figures were to decline by a large margin once the baht crisis started affecting the economy in 1997.

Overall, the effects of financial liberalization on the financial sector have been salutary. The financial sector expanded in numbers, quality, and in the provision of new financial products. Further, financial deepening can be described as having doubled over the 20 years since concerted efforts to institute a greater degree of financial reforms were instituted since 1976.

Foreign investment

A close examination of the information in Table 4.6 indicates that there have been substantial capital inflows in the form of FDI over the years in Malaysia. On a per capita basis, FDI flow to this country is perhaps the largest in the region, with the exception of Singapore. Current and capital account opening was put in place before 1975, long before the worst effects of the commodity-price declines started to bite and also long before other Southeast Asian countries took steps to attract foreign capital. However, it was not until the mid-1980s that foreign majority ownership was permitted, and this led to the increased acceleration of investments in the manufacturing and energy sectors. The cumulative total investment in the real sector is said to have given multi-national firms a strong presence in this economy, given the easing of restrictions on ownership and openness in financial transactions.

Table 4.6   Foreign capital flows in Malaysia (US$ million)

	5-year average			Annual						
	1976–80	1981–85	1986–90	1991	1992	1993	1994	1995	1996	1997
Investment										
Portfolio	75	1090	−128	170	−1122	−709	−1649	−440	−268	−248
FDI	559	1083	1126	3998	5183	5006	4342	4132	5078	5106

Note: The table excludes total debt taken, which increased from US$17.81 billion in 1991 to US$33.90 by 1996, ahead of the crisis: debt service peaked at 40% of GDP.

Source: IMF, *International Financial Statistics*.

These statistics underscore the importance of external capital inflows as a result of financial openness from the mid-1970s. In some years FDI constituted close to 10 per cent of GDP, as in 1992 and 1993. Gross national savings running at about 33 per cent of GDP should be added to these flows, thus leading to about 40 per cent capital formation in the real sector in several good years. This rate of investment was sustainable, given the tight rein on inflation and high demand for exports. Once the exports declined, especially in the 1990s, capital flows were maintained for use in making huge investments in the non-traded sector of shopping complexes, recreational facilities, mega-infrastructure projects, all of which would only give low returns, not the kind that foreign money is after. The low returns were inconsistent with foreign capital requirements. Something had to give way once the currency started to weaken. Part of the weakness was due to the high portfolio investments in the capital markets and in the banks borrowing from abroad. These were short-term in nature, and liquidation of assets led to sale of currency, which further weakened the currency, as happened during the 12 fateful months during 1997–98. This led to a return to a fixed currency and the withdrawal of the open financial conditions that prevailed over more than two decades.

4. ASSESSMENT AND FUTURE PROSPECTS

The progress made over about 42 years of development activities in Malaysia had two important outcomes. It improved the well-being of the people of this country. A primary-producing country was successfully restructured on its way, most observers agreed in 1996, to becoming a newly industrializing economy in the not too distant future. That these aims were achieved while the country was pursuing limited credit and capital targeting to improve the social status of the majority of the population is notable when many countries (for example the USA, Fiji and Ghana), unlike Malaysia, which used market-based incentives, set up government organizations to achieve the same results. Another feature is the successful experience of containing inflation while maintaining high growth. This is a special lesson from this case study, and there are other lessons to be learned from the BNM.

With the return to a fixed exchange rate and therefore capital controls, many observers are sceptical about how this small economy can remain relevant to the powerful capital-movers, which augmented the local resources that led to the successful development and restructuring of the economy. Export competitiveness has improved as a result of the recent realignment of currencies in the region. This country has an upper-middle-income level of development, which means that the level of social and infrastructure development is more advanced than in other countries of the same size, or even larger emerging economies. Perhaps this is a competitive advantage in that investments in such a place as Malaysia are likely to be more profitable to international capitalists. We leave the future to be determined by the interplay of competitive forces, which could well be favourable to this economy even after the crisis, since it has the kind of attractions that many in the neighbourhood lack. One key actor is the purchasing power parity of the ringgit. It is an attractive 268 per cent, which goes against the dire predictions of the nominal GDP in US dollar terms.

NOTES

1. Malaysia is made up of two separated land areas of the Malay Peninsula, which forms 40 per cent of land with 80 per cent of the population, and Eastern Malaysia in the western part of Borneo, where 20 per cent of the population lives on 60 per cent of the land. Western Malaysia became part of Malaysia in 1963 when Britain pulled out of the area.
2. The sources for many of the statistics are Asian Development Bank (1997c) and Bank Negara Malaysia (1994a).
3. One country that was positioned well to gain from the commodity boom was Australia. Its growth was based on primary exports to developed countries. So it based its growth policies on that foundation over the postwar period. When the primary produce boom came to a stop in the late 1970s, it delayed putting reforms in place until the late 1980s. This led to a massive revaluation of its currency from A$1 = US$1.20 in late 1970s to A$1.00 = US$0.80 by the mid-1980s. A similar fate visited the New Zealand economy, where a big-bang reform of policy also jolted that economy in the mid-1980s.
4. See Bank Negara Malaysia (1994b), preface to fourth edition.
5. The outright advantage in the capital market was the interest rate set at about two percentage points below market rate. In the real sector, there were some advantages in the form of a discount for the bids by indigenous contractors in much the same way as Black contractors were treated in the USA. A third preference was in the allocation of new shares: 30 per cent of new shares were compulsorily allocated; indigenous population accounted for two-thirds of the total. Other schemes targeted at small farmers, small business, and so on provided an infant-industry sort of support.
6. There was another exchange, the Bumiputra Exchange, which had almost ceased operation by the 1990s.
7. There was a rescue package put up with MR 70 billion to prop up share prices when the market index sank below 900 points. This support was short-lived, and the index fell further, eventually towards the 300s after several months. Because the Malaysian economy did not show the kind of weakness found in others, it was thought at that stage that the decline was purely driven by speculative attacks on the currency after the baht was free-floated. A similar intervention was made by Hong Kong when that market declined in August 1998, with similar results. In August 1998, Paul Krugman also called for some form of control as necessary, as all other efforts to stabilize the currency had failed.
8. The events leading up to and following the changeover to a fixed rate regime have unleashed new political forces. The finance minister, who disagreed with the policy change, resigned at the critical moment, and is out of the cabinet and out of the ruling party. He was tried for corruption and other criminal charges, found guilty, and is serving a six-year prison term. This has since released new political forces of dissent.
9. The spread between deposit and lending rates of the Malaysian banks was 2.39 per cent in 1996. This compared favourably with Hong Kong's 2.46 per cent against the worst cases of Taiwan (0.48 per cent) and Korea (0.43 per cent). Even the banking sector appeared to be strong before the Asian financial crisis.
10. It is interesting to note that Hong Kong, a major financial centre, also did the same in mid-1998. The market rebounded for a while before declining further. Investor confidence in a neutral regulator was shaken badly in this case, though the Hong Kong government justified intervention in the public interest.

11. Krugman's position was widely publicized in the first week of August 1998. Earlier, Bhagwati (1997) suggested that free trade on currencies was not consistent with free trade on goods, given no satiation of demand for currency. He said that trading in widgets was not the same as trading in dollars!

12. Leading central bankers of the region had privately looked at controls as a quick way to end the crisis temporarily. This was evident in the authors' conversation with them during a field trip and during subsequent meetings. However, the public stand against controls by these same people in August 1998 did not come as a surprise to us. There is no validated experience of returning to controls. Even the limited controls on hot money in Chile led to mixed results. Only time can resolve this issue. Controls did arrest the free fall of the ringgit, and the World Bank has acknowledged the usefulness of this policy for the recovery of growth in 1999. Economic orthodoxy appears to have taken a dent in the case of this experiment.

5. Singapore: reform towards financial centre status

1. BACKGROUND

The impetus for economic and financial reforms comes from Singapore's current position as an international financial centre, which explains why its finance sector contributes a much larger share of GDP compared with a financial sector in another country. Singapore's central location along a trade route through a fast-growing region of the world and the simultaneous underdevelopment of sufficient competition to its position provide the key to understanding its success and its adoption of pro-growth reform policies during 1973–98. The city state – land mass about 650 sq. km, about two-thirds the size of Manhattan Island and population about 3.3 million – is located at the tip of the Malay Peninsula at the heart of a massive trade route through the Malacca Straits into and beyond the South China Sea towards Australia, Indo-China, China, Japan and the USA.[1] Singapore has carefully pursued economic rationalism – some may call it regional opportunism – and social controls within its borders to secure exceptionally high economic growth under very stable social conditions, resulting in a level of economic prosperity for its people second only to the oil-rich Brunei or Kuwait or the industrial giant, Japan.

A large part of the economic activities of this city state in postwar years was based on servicing the entrepôt trade that reached Singapore *en route* to other parts of the world. With the political separation in 1965 of the city state from its larger economic and land base within the Federation of Malaysia, Singapore had to find its own niche within the larger region as an international economy while constantly keeping ahead of others as a matter of survival. Its massive revenues have accumulated, but with very little land mass to apply them, it can constantly secure efficiency ahead of others burdened by a larger land mass and the need to look after countryside interests.

Much of the reforms discussed here arose from the need to make this small state a viable economy with only location advantage as a resource. Hence the political economy in 1965 dictated the drive for liberalization, to open the economy fully to the rest of the world and to make Singapore into an international financial centre. Some may draw a parallel with the resource-poor South

Korea after the traumatic 1954 Korean War and separation. It has been remarked that traumatic experiences of societies are often followed by dramatic achievements, as in the example of Sparta, Taiwan and others. In any case, such traumas appear to produce resolve to pursue good policies. The policy reforms to be examined in this chapter secured a level of prosperity that is far ahead of what has been achieved in other countries, many of which had the disadvantage of larger populations and land masses to develop without the capital and technology that came to Singapore from multinationals.

As a free port, much of the country's traditional economic activities were based on open trading with others. That is, Singapore had more open economic relations with other countries at the beginning of reforms, a factor that made further reforms easier to make and sustain. The reforms that came later, especially after 1958, took the form of fiscal incentives – limited period tax exemption at first and other incentives later – which were offered as attractions to encourage targeted manufacturing and financial activities to locate in Singapore. This policy is contrary to the targeted credits practised by Indonesia or Korea to create local expertise. These reforms attracted high-technology manufacturing–servicing firms to base their international operations in Singapore instead of, for example, in Hong Kong or Australia, or Japan or Sri Lanka or, for that matter, in Madras.[2] Financial liberalization created the right environment, and the business opportunities in the region acted as a magnet to attract international financial activities. This led to the entry of a very large number of financial institutions, about 430 at one time, during the period 1973–80 and again over 1987–94. The adequate business opportunities in the fast-growing region led to the financial sector also gaining depth as the financial institutions with international linkages started providing financial products and services similar to those offered in international financial centres. Capital market and risk management activities increased as a result, thus creating a reputation for the city state in the 1990s as a premier financial centre in Asia.

The remainder of this chapter is organized into four further sections. The economic and financial structure is described next. The extent of the reforms and their effects on the economy are described in the following section. The reader will find there a description of specific reforms and their effects, learning more about this successful case as being relevant for any country that aspires to internationalize its financial activities.[3] The chapter ends with a summary of lessons and a few pointers to future prospects: see Section 4. Overall, the reader will find that this chapter describes a case of relentless pursuit of carefully formulated strategic reform policies to attract worldwide resources to the real and financial sectors of a small local economy, which is able to cater to the demands of foreign capitalists as no others.

2. STRUCTURE OF THE ECONOMY AND THE FINANCIAL SECTOR

Singapore's economy in the 1990s is a mature economy with the services sector accounting for about two-thirds of all economic activities. This is also consistent with its status as an international manufacturing–servicing centre. The 1997 GDP of this small economy was large at S$128 000 million. Per capita income in 1996 in US dollars was about $28 000, second only to the levels in Brunei, Kuwait and Japan. With over 1.53 million workers, its labour participation rate is very high. This is partly explained by the high female participation rate and a large foreign casual labour force, which in 1996 constituted about 18 per cent of the total labour force. The unemployment rate has consistently been very low, for example 3.42 per cent during even the low-growth period decade 1981–90.

Table 5.1 provides further breakdown of the structure of the economy as it transformed through liberalization over 1973 to 1996. The economy grew at an average rate between 7.4 per cent (1981–90) and 10.1 per cent in 1994. This high level of growth was achieved through an exceptionally high investment rate in excess of 33 per cent, a low consumption rate in recent years under 43 per cent and therefore with a high international trade component. The average investment rate in the world is 19 per cent. The total value of trade in Singapore is about 280 per cent of the GDP, which makes this economy very dependent on trade, as it has been over historical times. This factor explains why the 1997 Asian currency crisis affected this otherwise well-managed economy. The trade and current accounts were mostly healthy in that these figures during most periods were in balance with positive foreign direct investment (FDI), and portfolio flows.

Some of the highlights of structural change can be seen in the financial structure of the economy. Inflation, which was high in the 1970s and also the early 1980s, declined to a very low level below 3 per cent in the ensuing years. This low level was achieved along with high economic growth which, in other economies such as China, India and Indonesia, led to persistently high inflation. Another strong characteristic of this economy is its high level of savings – in excess of 33 per cent of GDP – and high gross fixed capital formation at about 35 per cent of GDP. As is consistent with the higher level of financial development of the economy, the monetary aggregates M2 and M3 grew steadily from the low figures respectively of 61.4 and 67.6 per cent during the 1971–80 period to the figures of 84.5 and 102.9 per cent in the 1990s. These figures are not very far from those in the OECD economies. Relative to the less liberalized financial sectors in other countries covered in this book, these statistics underscore the effects of liberalization in this case.

Table 5.1 Growth in basic economic indicators in Singapore (%) per year

	5-year average			Annual average							
	1976–80	1981–85	1986–90	1991	1992	1993	1994	1995	1996	1997	1998[a]
GDP	8.563	6.190	8.403	7.340	6.221	10.439	10.051	8.755	8.0	6.8	1.5
Inflation	3.703	3.234	1.288	3.400	2.321	2.268	3.050	1.794	1.32	2.0	−0.003
Revenue	14.316	17.400	7.943	7.386	14.561	26.186	13.071	13.01	18.97	19.81	4.69
M1	12.059	7.445	11.678	7.660	12.690	23.586	2.312	8.282	6.66	4.430	−0.01
M2	14.497	11.870	17.050	12.446	8.895	8.454	14.428	8.500	9.790	6.199	30.22
Foreign direct investment (FDI)	46.85	−0.63	46.01	−12.34	−54.9	112.6	16.94	26.13	11.83	23.16	−25.66
Trade balance	12.059	7.445	11.678	−86.637	507.73	121.46	−148.49	20.28	127.64	−48.52	53.46

Notes:
[a] The real GDP growth in 1999 was 6.0%.
M2 = M1 + quasi-money.
– = data not available.

Sources: IMF, *International Financial Statistics*, May 1999; World Bank, *World Bank Databank*, Feb. 1997.

The financial sector grew rapidly as well during this period. The period 1971–80 saw the financial sector becoming increasingly internationalized when more and more licences were issued to new financial entities to operate off-shore banks and non-bank financial institutions in Singapore. Consequently the number of foreign financial institutions that entered the financial sector increased, as did also the new off-shore and non-bank financial institutions set up by the local banks. The structure of the financial sector thus began to change, with local banks, finance and insurance companies modernizing their operations to face the competition offered by the foreign entrants with better customer relations. The mix of products and services offered by domestic operators and international operators also changed. The number of firms in the financial sector increased from a base of less than 100 in the mid-1970s to close to 450 in the 1990s. The depth of the financial sector improved as specialized institutions opened for business, as did also the financial products offered to local and regional customers. Increasingly, the financial sector began to grow beyond the provision of efficient payment systems and intermediation. It undertook economic activities that added to the income generation of the economy, and thus the share of the financial sector in GDP doubled over the years.

Social development received a heavy dose of investment. Education and the development of public facilities took a major share of the budget, producing a well-educated population with skill levels that are comparable or even surpassing the levels in developed economies. Public housing schemes that were originally meant to provide a roof over the head for all has become in the 1990s a get-rich scheme of levering pension savings to live in luxurious public housing: 84 per cent of the people live in well organized public-built leased housing estates. The freehold private-sector housing which accounts for the remaining 16 per cent has gone up in value so high that it is not possible, except for the really rich, to own a piece of land. The non-traded sector in which housing is trapped was subject to the effect of price spiral. But the economy became larger, providing full employment and a standard of living that was the envy of the rest of the region, at least at the end of 1996.

3.   LIBERALIZATION

A case can be made that liberalization encompasses several aspects of economic transformation that take place when an emerging economy takes measures to secure greater growth in economic activities through market-based signals. Therefore we attempt to give a brief description of the economic reforms that preceded or came along with the financial reforms in Singapore. The important economic policies are described first, before we examine the financial reform policies, which are the main concern of this case study.

3.1 Economic Reforms

It is possible to state that the Singapore economy had a greater degree of economic openness than any others covered in this book, during the opening years of our analysis. To start with, there were strong private-ownership institutions (law, the courts and the markets) for both the means of production as well as the contractual legal framework for workers to offer their services in the labour market with capitalist incentives. Next, because of the historical free-trade status of the city state, which the other countries in the region did not have, there were no tariff barriers that had to be brought down, as was the case in other countries. The tariff barriers that existed in transactions relating to liquor and tobacco products and vehicles were still intact even in 1998 at perhaps the world's highest tariff levels: just order your wine at the start of a meal and you will notice that. But for almost all other economic activities, there were no tariff barriers.

Thus very few reforms were needed to open the economy of the 1950s and 1960s to international trade, as was the case with other countries such as Korea, which failed to bring down its high tariff to preserve its domestic market for its producers until it felt ready to lower the tariff in 1989. Singapore therefore had greater external openness from the early years, which helped it to introduce competition in the real sector without having to force open the real sector to competition, as happened in the 1980s in the emerging economies. Where it did not have openness – in land holdings and in property development, both being in the non-traded sector – there was no external competition, which drove prices of land and building to unprecedented heights and consequently the capital markets too, before these began to decline after 1997.

Development institutions and fiscal incentives
Two important economic reforms occurred very early. One was in the 1950s, and came as a response to the high unemployment rate in the 1950s that persisted well into the 1960s. The economy could not absorb the postwar baby boomers who entered the labour force at that time. Since political events were more critical then, only two reforms could reasonably be put in place by the government of the day. The law passed in 1958 empowered the government to offer incentives to attract foreign investors to locate economic activities and hence absorb unemployed labour. The other was the decision in 1959 to expand the then existing institutional framework of a central body – the Economic Development Board (EDB) – to plan and execute reforms to attract foreign investment. These institutional reforms had far-reaching effects in making the

city state the premier place to do business in the region in the next decade. These reforms were carried out at a time when the regional governments did not welcome foreign capital for fear of losing control.

The government also invited international bodies such as the World Bank, the IBRD, and others to help identify pro-growth policies that would help it to achieve satisfactory results.[4] The first Economic Plan covered a five-year period to 1965. An important feature of these reforms is the setting up of the institutional framework, the economic planning framework, at the highest level to search and formulate strategic policy changes to develop the economy. Readers will note that this is a special feature of the Singapore case, where institutionalizing reforms formed an integral part of economic management. These reforms may be said to be the start of the significant economic liberalization.

Labour relations reforms

A second set of reforms was aimed at depoliticizing the trade union movement. Until about 1963, the trade union was a partner in putting the ruling party in power. The government realized that it needed pro-capitalist policies to attract the needed foreign capital to absorb spare capacity. Thus the next set of reforms took away some of the traditional freedoms that the labour movement normally enjoys in developed countries, which were not thought to be relevant to a developing economy. As a result, a process began, aimed at building new labour relations institutions – a sole trade union movement, an arbitration court and leadership recognition of trade unions – to incorporate the labour movement as a co-partner with the ruling group. Between 1960 and 1979 a series of new laws was passed and institutions set up to make the mainly autonomous trade union movement become a partner in nation-building and development. This paved the way for pro-growth capitalist-oriented reforms to be undertaken with the consent and cooperation of the labour movement. Besides, the labour movement became de-linked from adversarial politicking.

These reforms were highly successful in that the labour chief now sits in the cabinet as a minister without portfolio while the traditional adversarial employer–employee relation has been replaced by the law requiring a cooperative relationship between labour and employer. As a result, wages are now tied to the performance of the economy, with wages rising when the economy is in upswing; wages decline during recessions. This has worked wonders for pay packets during good years, but not when things go badly. For example, involuntary wage cuts were implemented during the 1985–86 and the 1997–98 economic recessions which, it is argued, helped the recovery of the economy. This was done with the approval of the trade union, working together with the employer and the government to restore the economy to good shape.

When the excess labour pool was fully employed by the end of 1970s, with the entry of multinational firms attracted by freedom to manage their investments without interference from the union movement, the policy-makers decided to restructure the economy so as to attract higher-value-added industries into Singapore. The controlled small wage increases that had been in effect since 1973 gave way to substantial wage increases that made location in Singapore not advantageous to labour-intensive industries. The result was the popular campaign to usher in the second industrial revolution! The substantial restructuring that resulted as wages went up rapidly made Singapore the technological and testing centre for industries located in the region, as well as the financier of industrial growth, thus helping to make higher productivity possible for Singapore.

However, an undesirable consequence was the resulting high labour costs. These unsustainable wage increases coincided with a worldwide economic slowdown during 1984–86. The result was an economic recession over four quarters in 1984–85. There followed a period of belt-tightening and cost-cutting that included a general wage cut of about 5 per cent. These cost-restructuring reforms made Singapore attractive again to international investors and the economy was on the mend once more. The economic recovery in 1987 led to an unprecedented period of high growth which led to an asset bubble – asset prices trebled in four years – which lasted until the 1997 Asian currency crisis, which produced a potential long-drawn-out recession during 1997–99. Wage reductions also helped economic restructuring to take shape quickly.

Fiscal reforms
The government realized after the last economic recession that it needed to have budget surpluses in order to steer the economy in hard times and to pursue economic expansion into the region. So it pursued a policy of withdrawal from unprofitable economic activities within the country and cut down on the welfare scheme since there was no unemployment due to lack of jobs. Privatization policy that was pushed through Parliament in 1984 soon led to the corporatization and sale of government entities.[5] The government, which obtains very high revenue on a per capita basis to develop a small island nation, decided to curtail expenditure and introduced measures that reduced government expenditure. Government consumption, which was at a high of 11.2 per cent of GDP during the 1981–90 period, was slowly brought down to 8.0 per cent or thereabouts in the 1990s. At the same time, the fiscal surplus of about 3 per cent in the annual budget of the 1980s was slowly increased. The budget surplus has since reached about 10 per cent of GDP, a fourfold increase unprecedented in any economy and sustained over such a long period. How much can the small land mass be developed with an increasing revenue share of the economy? These two measures generated resources for the government to venture to become the financier in emerging countries, largely in China, Indonesia, Cambodia and India. To this end, the GICS (Government Investment

Corporation of Singapore) was set up using the reserves that were managed by the monetary authority before 1982.

Persuading these emerging economies to invest in tourism-related, housing, transportation and communication facilities was explained as 'growing an external wing'. It was explained that the opportunity to grow was limited within the domestic economy. Besides, it made good sense to let the reserves earn a higher rate of return if it could be managed. Whether the resources of the government should be disposed of in investment in other countries was never raised in any debate. However, this experiment has not had sufficient time to work, even though it started in 1982–83. In the early period until the mid-1980s, most of the investment was in real estate and capital markets of the developed countries: property investments particularly declined in value when most of the OECD countries were experiencing property slumps over the 1980s. In the subsequent period, most investments went to specific projects in emerging economies, and their present values after the currency crisis must have declined until recoveries lead to gains. The 1997 Asian currency crisis must have affected the values of these investments as all emerging economies except India and China, which were experiencing currency appreciation. This series of economic reforms to grow an external wing to the economy appears to have been set back since the mid-1990s. Only time will tell how much this reform policy has succeeded, and contributed to the well-being of the domestic economy.

Thus economic reforms undertaken since 1958 had raised the already very open Singapore economy to greater heights. They enlarged the amount of its economic activities, and helped it to overcome its size limitation. In fact, Singapore is acknowledged as a major player in the region's development activities. Regional cooperation was based on Singapore's participation in several pro-growth forums in the region. For the majority of people, reforms secured near full employment and social development unprecedented in Singapore, and also unmatched in the region. The structures established for economic growth are still in place to take the economy to possibly new heights once the current crisis management yields recovery and growth in the opening years of the new millennium.

Socioeconomic effects of reforms
The effects of economic policy reforms are examined in this section. Briefly stated, the reforms had a favourable effect on economic activities. GDP increased dramatically from its base figure under S$15 billion in 1976 to some S$128 billion in 1997. This is a high growth rate in each tested period of between 6.2 (in 1992) and 10.4 per cent (1995). Inflation that was close to 10 per cent during 1976–80 moderated to under 3.4 per cent after 1981. It is perhaps a significant achievement during a phase of high economic growth to have also

low inflation. Government revenues grew ahead of the economic growth rate: the average revenue growth was in the region of 13 per cent.

Money growth (M1) and credit creation (M2) mainly kept a little ahead of the economy's growth rate. Monetary expansion was about 12 per cent, perhaps sufficient to finance the expansion and also to cover the increased transaction demands of an affluent population. The foreign cash flows were very substantial, growing at many times the rate of the economy until 1995, when FDI declined by 100 per cent. The trade account improved throughout the period, with trade declining only during some years.

Table 5.2 provides the same figures as percentages of GDP. It can be seen that the monetary ratio (M1 and M2) remained stable throughout the period. Private consumption went down from 55.4 per cent of GDP and government consumption from 10.3 per cent of GDP over the period respectively to 40.7 and 8.5 per cent. The gross fixed capital formation held at about 33 per cent of GDP except in the early years 1973–80, when it was higher during the formative period of high investment. However, the trade account was not as stable as the other aggregates. But there was no systematic decline in those accounts either. Overall, the economy registered healthy growth and sustained itself to become a more international economy, with domestic consumption being less than half of GDP.

3.2 Financial Liberalization

Financial liberalization played a critical role, vastly different from that in any other countries, in the transformation of Singapore. Instead of just fulfilling the needs of the economy in intermediation and efficient payment systems, the financial sector became an important income generator, along with other economic activities. Reforms made it possible to make Singapore into an international financial centre. Since 1982, important risk management services started to deepen and hence this provides these services to the international financial institutions and real-sector firms doing business in the region. The thrust of financial liberalization is described by highlighting a number of key financial reforms.

Structure of the financial sector

The structure of the financial sector was designed to foster two types of financial institutions. Some are licensed to operate on a full-licence basis, which entitles them to participate in both the local and international economic activities. There are also specific financial institutions, licensed with restricted licences to operate as off-shore operators. These have binding limitations in transactions in the domestic economy though they are free to operate fully in international activities. This is a unique arrangement designed in 1971 for banks and in 1973

Table 5.2 Basic economic and social indicators in Singapore

Indicators	1971–80	1981–90	1991–93	1994	1995	1996	1997	1998[a]
National accounts								
GDP growth (%)	9.074	7.360	8.000	10.051	8.755	8.000	7.500	1.5
Per capita GDP (US$)	2 717	8 640	18 208	25 287	28 526	31 473	32 468	29 649
Private consumption/GDP	0.567	0.462	0.446	0.428	0.407	0.4224	0.5206	0.540
Gov. Consumption/GDP	0.104	0.112	0.095	0.083	0.085	0.0996	0.1228	0.0996
Financial indicators								
Gross domestic savings (% of GDP)	27.000	42.350	47.600	51.300	55.600	55.900	56.4	52.2
Gross fixed capital formation (% of GDP)	36.427	39.157	34.629	33.654	33.036	38.465	47.406	36.98
Inflation	6.714	2.286	2.663	3.050	1.794	1.32	2.0	-0.003
M2/GDP	0.614	0.770	0.910	0.868	0.845	0.8867	0.863	0.850
M3/GDP	0.676	0.946	1.124	1.054	1.029	1.083	1.161	1.260
Fiscal balance/GDP	0.011	0.031	0.122	0.160	0.144	0.144	0.095	-0.003
Current account balance/GDP	-0.130	0.001	0.105	0.161	0.177	0.1644	0.2146	0.182
Trade balance/GDP	-0.298	-0.129	-0.026	0.028	-0.003	-0.007	-0.014	0.172
Debt service ratio (% of GDP)	0.000	0.000	0.000	0.000	0.000	0.000	0.000	0.000

Social indicators

IMF classification	Middle	Upper-middle	High	High	High	High	High	High
Literacy rate	–	–	–	–	–	98	98	98
Unemployment rate	16.5	3.420	2.433	2.600	2.700	3.0	2.4	4.6
Expenditure on education (% of exp.)		19.1	23.3	22.6	23.0	23.0	23.0	23.0
Expenditure on health (% of exp.)	7.90	5.47	6.10	7.30	7.30	7.25	7.40	7.40
Population growth	1.533	1.188	1.931	2.091	2.048	1.9	1.9	1.9

Note: [a] A mid-1999 estimate of GDP growth for 1999 is 6%.

Sources: IMF, *International Financial Statistics*, May 1999; ADB, *Asian Development Outlook*, 1998; *Government Finance Statistics Yearbook, 1985–1996*.

for off-shore licences by the newly created Monetary Authority of Singapore (MAS), to attract some institutions to Singapore purely for the purpose of operating out of their location in Singapore to engage in international financial transactions. Another reason for this was the infant-industry protection argument that if financial institutions of larger economies are permitted to compete on even ground, these local institutions will lose out simply given the size constraints; so it was argued.

At the start of 2000, there were 32 full-licence commercial banks (of which 22 have headquarters in foreign countries), 18 finance companies, 57 insurance companies together with 4 insurance companies that underwrite insurance risk, 74 investment (merchant) banks, 7 wholesale money brokers,[6] 1 postal bank merging with a bank, 1 central provident fund organization for old-age pensions, 74 mutual funds (called unit trusts) and 2 regulators, namely the MAS and the Board of Commissioners of Currency.[7] The last-named is unusual; it is found in only a few other countries, and has the responsibility to print currency and mint coins to the extent supported by reserves as provided under a statute of the country. The postal bank, named the POSBank, played a significant role since, with almost half of all savings deposits in the economy, its interest rates for time deposits largely influenced the prevailing base rate for all time deposits. There are 13 restricted licence banks.

These 281 financial-sector organizations function in ways similar to those found in other economies, and they perform both domestic and foreign transactions. It was these that were most affected by financial liberalization, whereas the remaining organizations to be described later were the direct result of regulations to attract special classes of financial firms to do financial business, mostly with international financial clients situated outside Singapore. Following the effects the 1997 Asian currency crisis had on the banks, a number of banks are being merged. One such merger was between the largest commercial bank, the DBSBank, and the POSBank in July 1998. Another merger was between the Tat Lee Bank and the Keppel Bank Corporation. More such mergers were expected during 1999 to strengthen the banks seriously undermined by investment losses in the region.

As of 1997, there were 14 restricted licensed banks, which cannot accept domestic time deposits below a certain amount from residents. In earlier years, right up to about 1990, the minimum amount that a resident could place as deposits in a restricted bank was S$250 000. But this sum has been reduced to a much lower figure over the years, thus allowing more competition in the deposit market by the entry – no doubt restricted entry – of these restricted banks in domestic intermediation markets.

Singapore is also well known for the first introduction in 1968 of Asian dollar deposits (initially, the American dollar and later other currencies) which enjoyed exemption from withholding tax normally levied on interest incomes of foreign residents.[8] Today these off-shore licensed banks engage in wholesale banking with non-residents and limited banking with resident institutions and individuals. There are 155 off-shore banks operating in a market which grew to US$515 billion in 1997. Investment banks also engage in the Asian currency market.

These 155 off-shore operators and the 288 described earlier as full-licence entities are the financial sector organizations in the economy. Their activities collectively contribute to anywhere between 12 to 18 per cent of GDP. During economic boom years such as 1993, financial activities could become a significant proportion of the economy. Even in normal times, largely due to the international nature of the financial sector of the Singapore economy, the GDP share is about 10–12 per cent. In most economies, the GDP share of the financial sector activities is about 4–8 per cent. This underlines the importance of open international conditions for the operation of the financial sector of this economy. Its greater dependence on financial activities provided the impetus for the regulators to become pro-liberalization and anti-suppressive to achieve open financial conditions with which Singapore's financial sector could work for further growth. At the next stage, Singapore used its open conditions to argue in favour of openness for other countries, pointing to the benefits of such liberalization to those economies that were not open.

Table 5.3   Major financial reforms in Singapore, 1967–98

Date of reforms	Liberalization policy implemented
1967	Introduction of Asian dollar deposits in ACUs considered.
1968	Starting in 1968, withholding tax was abolished for foreign depositors.
1971	Establishment of Monetary Authority of Singapore to focus on developing a sound financial structure.
1971	Creation of restricted licence banks which could be licensed to concentrate on international business and limited to receive only large time deposits from residents. Provided competition to domestic banks.
1973	Off-shore banks licensed to operate in the growing financing activities of the region.
1973 (June)	Limited reform in exchange rate via S$ pegging to a basket of trade-weighted currencies.
	Most foreign exchange controls dismantled.
	Currency convertibility abolished.
	Interest cartel of the large banks abolished, and interest rate determined by market signals.
	More financial institutions licensed in the off-shore markets.

Table 5.3   continued

Date of reforms	Liberalization policy implemented
1978	Call options market introduced in the Stock Exchange of Singapore.
1978 (June)	Further restrictions on current and capital accounts removed: article VIII freedom.
1981–84	Reforms to the financial institutions to improve efficiency, training and expertise.
1983	Privatization policy approved in Parliament and government companies sold.
1984	Tax exemption on income derived from off-shore fund management.
1987	Derivative market started with the launching of SIMEX.
1989	Establishment of second board for small company listing in SESDAQ.
1991–99	Money market and bond markets were target of reform. Discount houses abolished, and approved market makers to bid in the treasury and bond markets introduced. Banks also permitted to enter into securities trades through subsidiaries set up as brokerage/securities firms. Each year over this period a series of reforms was introduced to establish Singapore as an international centre for financial activities. Most of the reforms offered further reductions in the taxable status of income derived from activities originating from abroad. Taxes were reduced mostly to 10% instead of 27%.
1996	Government attracted major fund management companies to locate in Singapore. The offer of managing upwards of a billion dollars in the central provident fund and other government funds was made. Rules introduced to attract foreign company listings on the local stock market.
1997 (July)	Exchange rate to free-float in the face of Asian currency crisis.
1998 (Jan.)	Prime Minister (Dy) appointed to MAS: managed float again.
1998 (Feb.)	Limited internationalization of S$ and CPF fund management.
1998 (July–Aug.)	New measures introduced to strengthen banking.
1999	Deputy prime minister becomes chairman of MAS and introduces new reforms; restructures the banking institutions.

Sources: Hanson and Neal (1986), Ariff (1996) and excerpts from annual reports of MAS.

Table 5.3 provides a summary of significant financial reforms undertaken over 1971–98. Financial sector reforms may be analysed over two distinct periods. Limited suppression existed before 1973, and this is described as being moderately regulated and suppressed in two ways. Informal interest rate controls were practised by a cartel formed by a small group of large banks with a leader who set the interest rate, and there were exchange (and limited capital) controls. In relation to the latter, the currency at that time was a common unit used in Brunei, Malaysia and Singapore, managed by an organization which would mint coins and print currency notes provided there was a set amount of foreign currency (usually the British pound) to back the expansion in money supply, M1. The convertibility of currency with Malaysia was terminated when Malaysia adopted the ringgit as its numeraire in June 1973.

The financial sector was then regulated by a division of the Ministry of Finance until a quasi-government body was formed in 1971 to take over the functions of central banking except for the printing of money and the minting of coins, which remained with a separate board. Despite the closedness of the economy (see Edwards and Khan, 1985), a major reform with longer-term effect had taken place three years earlier in 1968 which permitted the creation of Asian currency units (ACUs) to accept US dollar and other key currency deposits of non-residents. The withholding tax was removed on interest earned by foreigners from deposits in these special off-shore licensed units. This led to the introduction of a distinction between local and foreign transactions, and more and more businesses received preferential tax treatment based on the origin of future transactions.

In that sense, the 1968 innovation had a major effect in so far as it became the precursor of the segregation of the financial sector into domestic and foreign financial transactions. The entrepôt trade that had dominated the free-trade nature of Singapore for several decades before the 1960s provided a backdrop against which people and businessmen from the region used Singapore to make monetary transactions. The active promotion of Singapore as international financial centre only started in 1968. A financial centre may be defined as a central location where financial transactions of an area are coordinated and cleared. Increasingly, Singapore took the shape of a financial centre of the region, and later a centre in the international time zone.

Reform to the structure   The formation of a quasi-government organization, the MAS, to centralize supervision of the banking, insurance and central banking functions was a major reform of the financial sector. A special-purpose body was created to manage this sector. The MAS could now play a leading role in introducing further reforms. These reforms are itemized in Table 5.3. A centralized body dealt with all financial matters (except money creation). In larger economies, three different organizations are often formed to deal with banking supervision, securities exchange supervision and futures exchange matters. But for a small economy, the centralized approach appears to have worked well.

Exchange rate policies

Like most non-major countries in the world, Singapore had a fixed exchange rate regime during the postwar period until 1973. With the pound sterling and the US dollar forming the peg currencies, the Singapore dollar was a common currency of exchange in Brunei and Malaysia as well. The Ministries of Finance and the Currency Board situated in Singapore managed banking supervision and note-issue functions respectively, without the benefit of a central bank for Brunei, Malaysia and Singapore. All this changed in June 1973 when the Malaysian government decided to abolish currency convertibility by establishing its own currency – the ringgit. Singapore then undertook limited reforms by adopting an exchange rate based on a basket of major currencies. This simultaneous move to delink from a largely agriculture-based Malaysian economy and use a managed float exchange rate system was significant in creating dependence on the local economy for the exchange rate. In doing this it also gained confidence, with the oil-rich Brunei dollar joining the Singapore dollar as a convertible currency at par.

Full current account and capital account opening was the next step in reforming the financial sector. This came five years later, in June 1978. Complete openness in transactions with the outside world became possible, however, within the managed exchange rate based on a trade-weighted basket of currencies. The law included a clause that empowered the authorities to reimpose controls if deemed necessary during periods of crisis. The authorities had not resorted to this even during the 1997 crisis. In August 1997, the currency was free-floated. The managed float was reinstated in January 1998 when the deputy prime minister was appointed as head of the monetary authority. The restrictions on the use of the Singapore dollar in international transactions have been relaxed. Thus, on the one hand, there is complete openness in the current account and the use of the local currency, but it is still felt that a form of managed float gives confidence to local residents to hold the currency: see Tables 5.4 and 5.5.

Around the same time, Singapore adopted limited capital account openness so that external transactions could be carried out without the supervision of the monetary authorities. The MAS consolidated all but the money-printing function. This was a boon as no other country in the region provided the same extent of current account and capital account freedom for business operations in 1973. The result was a strengthening of the off-shore Asian dollar market that had begun to grow since 1968: at the end of 1997, the Asian dollar in Singapore

Table 5.4 Monetary aggregates, income and balance of payments (growth rates)

	5-year average			Annual average							
	1976–80	1981–85	1986–90	1991	1992	1993	1994	1995	1996	1997	1998
M1	26.7	23.4	23.6	21.8	22.9	24.3	21.6	21.0	21.4	0.276	–0.01
M2	62.5	69.4	85.4	92.3	93.5	87.1	86.8	84.5	88.7	1.161	30.3
Trade deficit/surplus	–24.8	–21.9	–2.9	–0.4	–2.6	–4.8	1.8	1.9	127.64	–48.52	–70.0
Budget deficit/surplus	1.4	02.5	6.1	8.6	12.6	15.5	16.0	14.4	18.89	–27.86	70.1
Current account balance	–8.6	–13.2	1.2	10.1	12.5	8.8	16.1	17.7	16.4	3.60	17.18
Private consumption (%) of GDP	55.4	45.5	46.6	44.3	45.0	44.6	42.8	40.7	42.2	42.4	39.12
Gov. consumption (%) of GDP	10.3	11.4	11.0	9.9	9.4	9.1	8.3	8.5	10.0	10.1	12.0
GFCF	37.0	45.7	32.4	33.3	35.6	35.0	33.7	33.0	38.5	38.7	37.5
Gov. expenditure (%) of GDP	19.9	24.3	25.1	21.2	19.6	17.4	13.9	15.9	18.73	41.29	–12.0

Notes:
M2 = M1 + quasi-money.
GFCF = gross fixed capital formation.

Source: IMF, *International Financial Statistics*, May 1997.

Table 5.5 *Exchange rates and interest rates (annual averages)*

	5-year average			Annual average							
	1976–80	1981–85	1986–90	1991	1992	1993	1994	1995	1996	1997	1998
Exchange rate (mkt)	2.242	2.113	1.952	1.631	1.645	1.608	1.461	1.414	1.400	1.468	1.674
Interest rates (%)											
Money market rate	6.716	7.924	4.882	4.760	2.740	2.500	3.680	2.560	2.93	4.35	5.00
Deposit rate	6.095	7.240	3.484	4.630	2.860	2.300	3.000	3.500	3.410	3.410	4.60
Lending rate	9.130	10.116	6.490	7.580	5.950	5.390	5.880	6.370	6.260	6.260	7.44
SIBOR	11.524	10.152	8.038	4.380	3.500	3.380	6.500	5.630	5.630	5.730	4.60

Notes:
M2 = M1 + quasi-money.
Discount rate (end of period).
Exchange rate: (market rate) = Sing. dollar per US$.
SIBOR = Singapore Inter-Bank Offered Rate.

Source: IMF, *International Financial Statistics*, May 1997.

was valued at about US$515 billion. This market was created by a reform to the withholding tax on interest incomes.

Add to these another attraction: the ability of foreign enterprises to fully own and operate their own enterprises – a novel idea at that time. Thus Singapore offered a fertile ground for the activities of international firms, be they financial- or real-sector ones. These four reforms in the financial sector – managed exchange rate, open capital accounts, tax incentives and wholly owned foreign management – enabled Singapore to attract the lion's share of foreign capital. From about the middle of the 1970s right up to 1995, Singapore attracted FDI of between 3 and 11 per cent of its GDP.

Some of the highlights of exchange rate behaviour are noted here. The exchange rate was close to S$3.00 = US$1.00 at the start of the 1970s. Ten years after the reforms, the Singapore dollar had appreciated to S$2.20 = US$1.00; at the end of another ten years, it was S$1.62 = US$1.00 in 1993. By the end of 1996, the exchange rate stood at S$1.41 = US$1.00. Thus the exchange rate appreciated by an average of about 3 per cent per annum over a 24-year period. This had both a salutary and a debilitating effect on the economy. The rising currency kept the prices of mostly imported raw materials from becoming too high. Non-traded goods became expensive, as did also labour and consumer items, on account of the higher input costs from high rent and high wage costs. Some observers have pointed out that the high exchange rate made Singapore residents feel wealthy in terms of regional currencies, but they paid a high price in terms of the cash flows needed to own some basic necessities in the city state. Following the 1997 currency crisis, the exchange rate declined to a lower level but was still around S$1.70 to 1.80 per US dollar. The decline of this currency by about 20 per cent compares as slight, compared to declines of more than 70 per cent in the case of Indonesia.

Interest rate policies
Before reforms to interest rates, interest suppression in general held, under a cartel-like banking system dominated by a very large local bank and three relatively large but smaller banks determining the interest rates for deposits. That was the state of affairs for a long time, and no one disturbed the pecking order which served the situation well in (Malaysia and) Singapore. However, the government of Singapore decided to free interest rates to respond to economic conditions then prevailing: inflation was in double digits in the 1970s and the interest rate had to be competitive to bring down inflation. Earlier in 1968, the government had formed a new bank by hiving off the investment division of the Economic Development Board (EDB). This was later corporatized as a private-sector bank, and expanded to become a very large bank with a potential to disturb the *status quo* in the banking world. More foreign banks had also established local operations for several years by 1973. There was thus the intro-

duction of enough competition in the banking sector to free interest rate setting to be replaced by market determination.

The monetary authority issued a regulation in 1972 requiring the deposit rates to be determined by market forces. Thus interest rates began to be determined in the marketplace. Deposit rates and savings deposits increased quickly in response to the competitive offerings of interest on fixed deposits. Inflation of around 7 per cent was experienced during 1971–80. However, interest rates on loans to the business sector did not rise dramatically, as enough credit was being created and there were substantial foreign funds, given the relative openness of the capital and current accounts, for the international-sector activities of foreign firms.

Another important element of the financial sector is the national savings bank which, until its amalgamation in mid-1998 with a commercial bank, played a significant role in keeping interest rates low. The Post Office Savings Bank, POSBank, was meant to inculcate a savings habit in the population, and it started in the 1970s to cater to children and home-makers. Soon it began to achieve a share of almost 60 per cent of all deposits in the economy at one time because it provided tax-free interest income, and deposits were guaranteed to S$100 000 by the government as well. Because the POSBank offered such low interest to its faithful customers, the banking system as a whole did not feel it necessary to increase its interest rate beyond a small margin above that offered by the POSBank. In July 1998, the POSBank was merged with the largest bank, the DBSBank.

This had the eventual effect of suppressing interest rates on deposits, and thereafter on all other interest rates, in Singapore. Another institution, the Central Provident Fund Board, which collects all old-age pension contributions and self-employed person's contributions, decided in 1989 to offer a rate of return on pension fund balances equal to the average deposit rate of the banks. This also acted to suppress the interest rate at a very low level. What was happening was similar to what took place in Japan, where the national savings bank effectively set the bottom interest rate for depositors, which helped to set the norms for other deposit rates.

As a result of this simple interest rate suppression – even though earlier reforms helped abolish the cartel rates in the early 1970s – deposit rates hovered around 3 per cent during most of 1987 to 1996. The average inflation rate was also very near the 3 per cent mark. This meant that there was almost no real interest earned by depositors. At the same time the minimum lending rate was hovering above 6 per cent. This meant that the banking system was securing a high level of profits in the intermediation market. Though this was not a deliberate policy goal, the international nature of the financial sector helped to attract too many funds into the sector, which tended to lower the rates for depositors. For foreign investors, it was a boon, as they would have made currency gains in addition to the low interest rates, but not so for the residents, who earned almost zero real interest. This changed slightly with the onset of the 1997 currency crisis. Interest rates rose by about 1.5 per cent, the currency was no longer appreciating, and exchange rates having fallen by about 20 per cent over the period of the crisis. With inflation remaining low, depositors began to earn some small real interest from mid-1997 but only till end-1998.

Monetary policy

Another aspect not yet discussed in this section is monetary policy management. Before the 1973 reforms to adopt open current and capital accounts, monetary management was simple. Interest rate management formed the main thrust of monetary policy, along with measures to keep inflation within a manageable range. With the open international conditions increasingly put into place from 1973, monetary management became closely tied to exchange rate management, since capital inflows had to be sterilized from affecting the money supply. For this purpose of exchange rate intervention, the MAS engages in routine direct and indirect foreign exchange interventions.

Most interventions are made indirectly (Ng, 1988) through the network of money brokers, so that these activities are not noticed or discussed, thus preventing undesirable speculation based on public discussion on intervention activities in open markets. The major banks and the money brokers are linked together by telecommunication networks operated by the Society of Worldwide Interbank Financial Telecommunication (SWIFT). The government is on record as wanting to maintain the exchange rate at high levels in order to prevent imported inflation, since a significant portion of factor inputs (about 45 per cent) are purchased in the international marketplace. Thus monetary policy hinges heavily on exchange rate policy and on maintaining reserves and capital flows to keep exchange rates high. In fact, the exchange rates against the US dollar appreciated, on average by 1–3 per cent over most years.

Therefore economic activities are macro-managed through exchange rate management. The large inflows of funds from international sources are sterilized through conversion into foreign currency holdings so that monetary expansion through this source is prevented from affecting the domestic economy.[9] There is no interest rate policy or pricing policy in the macroeconomic management. The interest rate may be indirectly affected by the exchange rate, determined via policy intervention. Unlike in most economies, the interest rate is not the main driver of monetary policy in this economy. Growth in money supply has been moderate throughout the period of exchange rate intervention, which suggests that the policy aim of preventing monetary expansion did in fact work.

This also had a salutory effect in keeping inflation down. Second, prices for all traded goods were determined in the marketplace. The appreciating currency reduced if not eliminated the price increases from outside the country.

However, an appreciating currency caused non-traded goods (rent, labour, health services, property and land) to appreciate in value. This is exactly what occurred every time the economy recovered, and the currency appreciated against the major currencies.

Central banking and note-issue function

The top four domestic banks, each with tier 1 capital in excess of US$3 billion, are now included among the top 125 banks in the world. The critical reforms that made this possible are described here. Two such reforms were put in place to create international confidence in the soundness of the financial sector. One relates to the separation of the money-printing function under a currency board system and the high standards of prudential supervision of all financial-sector entities. The other relates to the separation of the domestic financial activities from international financial activities. The first reform was the setting up of a monetary authority vested with supervision of all financial-sector entities and serving as the government's banker. This was done in 1971 with the establishment of the MAS, as pointed out earlier. Its function has been widened with the passing of laws in banking, insurance, finance companies, the stock and futures exchanges, and even informal finance organizations.

The printing of money and minting of coin are managed by a currency board which, under the laws governing it, is required to expand M1 so that specified reserve currencies are available to back the amount of expansion in the money created. This acts as a Chinese Wall to prevent the central banks from indiscriminate expansion of the base money. The counter-argument is that most of the credit created in an economy actually comes from the money-multiplier function of the commercial banks, and there is no similar discipline on the commercial banks, even under a currency board system. In fact the lion's share of money creation is effected by the commercial banks. Nevertheless, the separation of the money-printing function from bank credit creation is reputed to have introduced discipline of some sort into the banking system, and there is a general expectation that this is a good thing for posterity. We leave the argument at that.

From the start, the MAS established a reputation as a no-nonsense regulator which would assiduously prevent any financial institutions from misbehaviour not consistent with the spirit of the laws and the regulations in force. To do this effectively, MAS itself relied upon good-quality employees and technical expertise obtained from central banks of developed countries. To aid this policy, the banking laws (and corporation laws) have been amended a number of times to make them more relevant to achieving high standards of prudential supervision of the financial institutions. For example, under the related party lending rules passed in 1981 – far ahead of many other countries – the MAS prosecuted a bank that flouted this rule. Similar instances of rapid-fire actions have been recorded, for example, in a case of a bank flouting reserve ratios; in another of international dealings in the Singapore dollar, and so on. At one time, in 1983, the speculative attack on the Singapore dollar was prevented by actions not dissimilar to that taken in Hong Kong in 1998 when the HK$ peg was under attack from speculators. Speculators lost money when the MAS resisted their attacks in 1983–84.

Another important feature of reform was to permit international competition with the local banks to improve the latter's efficiency. Of the 35 full-licence banks in 1997 that operate in the domestic economy, 22 are subsidiaries of foreign banks from both developed and developing countries. The 13 locally incorporated banks responded well to the competition, and have themselves expanded. The reluctance to subject domestic banks to international competition has been a source of inefficiency in the banking systems of several developing countries. Unlike in other countries, which followed limited entry of foreign institutions, Singapore's experience shows that there are benefits from head-on competition rather than protection in the world of money.

The adoption of the currency board system and the high standards of prudential behaviour imposed on the deposit institutions contributed to the stability of intermediation throughout almost 30 years. An important feature of the sector is that only the very experienced and larger banks, finance companies – these are treated as deposit-taking institutions and thus comes under banking supervision – or financial institutions are issued with licences. This means that entry barriers are erected to allow only the safest to enter the market, and hence this contributes in large measure to the stability of the sector. A bank licence will be issued for a financial institution if it has tier 1 capital of about US$800 million and has demonstrated experience as a well-managed bank. Similar rules apply to non-banks as well. Limiting entry to the most qualified and capitalized firms is a means of creating stable intermediation. This is an important lesson for the emerging economies. The top four banks in Singapore in 1997 are among the top-ranked banks in the region with larger economic activities.

Key recent statistics of the 35 full-licence banks are given in Table 5.6.

At 176 per cent of GDP, the commercial banks' total assets indicate a very high level of financial intermediation in the economy. Assets grew by about 13 per cent, which is ahead of the 8.5 per cent growth in the economy in the 1990s. Over recent years, savings and demand deposits have grown at a slower rate than growth, at 13 per cent, in fixed deposits. An interesting feature of the table is the increase in the growth rate in maturities of loans for the category in excess of three years: at present, loans with maturities over three years constitute about half of all bank loans. During earlier decades, long-term loans with maturities of more than three years constituted about one third of all loans. High growth in fixed deposits appears to have moved ahead of the growth rate in the economy. This probably provided stability to the liability structure of banks, and enabled financial institutions to offer longer maturity loans whereas during the earlier years, with more non-fixed deposits, the banks could not have improved their maturity transformation.

Table 5.6   Key statistics on full-licence banks, 1991–96

End of	Equity/ Asset	Deposits of non-bank clients				Type of loans		
		Demand	Savings	Fixed	Others	One-year	1–3 years	Over 3 years
1991	0.07	0.14	0.17	0.69	–	0.51	0.12	0.37
1992	0.07	0.15	0.18	0.67	–	0.49	0.12	0.39
1993	0.08	0.16	0.20	0.59	0.03	0.44	0.11	0.45
1994	0.08	0.17	0.17	0.66	0.01	0.41	0.11	0.48
1995	0.08	0.18	0.22	0.62	–	0.43	0.12	0.45
1996	0.08	0.17	0.22	0.50	0.01	0.42	0.13	0.48
Growth rate (%)	13	11	13	5	–	7	13	16

Note: Total assets of 35 banks was S$240 billion (176% of GDP) in the mid-1990s.

Source: Monetary Authority of Singapore *Monthly Bulletin*, 1997.

GDP share of the finance sector   As stated earlier, one of the aims of liberalization was to increase GDP by locating international financial services activities in Singapore. In 1993, when the stock market yield went up to 54 per cent because of the then worldwide bull market condition, GDP share of financial (and business) services was almost 30 per cent: it increased from about 18 per cent in 1976 to 28 per cent in 1993. Since that year, GDP share has remained above 26 per cent: the share of the financial sector alone will be about half that figure.

Off-shore banking
A large number of new financial institutions were created to operate in international transactions in Singapore. A restricted licence means that a restricted bank (not off-shore banks) cannot accept time deposits below $250 000 per deposit from non-bank customers; they cannot operate a savings account and they may not open branches (Ariff et al., 1995). These are generally called off-shore banks, Asian dollar units, which deal with foreign currency transactions, limited-licence banks, which act as banks in transactions outside the country, and other special institutions. There are about 450 such institutions which operate

on the international side of the economy, and generate a level of income far in excess of their operations. Thus the regulation has been designed to separate domestic from international transactions, licensing them separately so as to have a greater degree of control. Hong Kong does not separate financial activities in this manner; thus it is reputed to have had greater exposure to risk in its domestic operations. There is an element of truth in that, as Hong Kong frequently had failed institutions, whereas Singapore had none over four decades.

Non-bank financial institutions
There are several classes of non-bank financial institutions. Finance companies are normally grouped under credit unions as non-bank entities. In an earlier section we noted that finance companies are treated as deposit-taking institutions, and they come under the banking supervision norms. There are several in this category: the merchant banks act as investment bankers in Singapore; next are the money brokers; the insurance companies; the POSBank until mid-1998; and the Central Provident Fund (CPF) Board. These institutions have all been modernized over the years, with impetus coming from the entry of international counterparts to do business in Singapore. In this respect, competition policy has been instrumental. Even the pension fund has now been asked to lend its balances to international firms to obtain higher returns by managing the assets internationally.

The CPF is not merely a pension fund. It has over the years become a social welfare mechanism funded by the contributor. It funds education and health expenses, and serves as a financier for public and private housing purchases. Beyond that, it also finances the government as much of the money is on loan to the government for such purposes as housing and investment. In this regard, a self-funded scheme has become an anchor for providing the usual assistance from public funds.

Capital markets
Singapore has been a traditional location for capital market activities in the Malay Peninsula. However, since the cessation of currency covertibility in 1973 and especially after Malaysia's cessation of double-listing since 1990, the capital market activities in Singapore are very much connected with the domestic economy. Before this, a significant amount of transactions in Singapore were with companies of Malaysian origin. With the development of a large capital market of its own, Malaysia required its corporations to seek listings only on the national exchange. As a consequence, the size of the capital market in Singapore declined in 1990. However, with more firms, including government-linked ones, seeking listing on the stock market, the size of the market had increased substantially by the end of 1997. At the end of that year, there were 259 listed firms on the share market capitalized at around US$170 billion. The share

market experienced intense activity: turnover per firm per year was US$565 which compared favourably with the more developed capital markets.

The debt market is less developed than the share market. The government issues Treasury securities periodically to determine the going interest rates through regular auctions of the issues each Thursday. Since the government has perennial surpluses, it is not able to make large debt issues. Corporations find that they can borrow money from banks at reasonable interest rates given the interest suppression noted earlier. Thus businesses do not have incentives to issue public debt in large amounts. As a result, the public debt market has been very small and was generally inactive over the study period. The current face value of the debt market is under 15 per cent of GDP, making Singapore one of the smallest international centres for debt issues. But official statistics include a huge listing of the Ginnae Mae (a New York stock market listed bond) on the board, and mask the fact that the debt market is in effect non-existent in this otherwise large international money centre. Nor does this comment take into account the syndicated loans that originate as private placements of debt of the region from government and the private sectors in the banking system: there is a large position in this market.

The Singapore International Monetary Exchange, SIMEX, was set up in 1982 to specialize in financial futures contracts. This market has now established itself as a very successful risk management centre for investors in the region. Two-thirds of the value of the contracts consist of some form of interest rate instruments, for example Eurodollar futures and Euro-yen futures. Seventeen instruments are traded. These and other developments made Singapore into a successful international financial centre linked to the major centres in Tokyo, New York and London. The SIMEX has merged with stock exchange in 1999.

3.3 Financial Liberalization Effects

Exchange and interest rates
It was noted in an earlier section that the exchange rate appreciated at an annual rate of about 3 per cent. In real terms, the exchange rate was US$1.00 = S$2.242 during 1976–80; it improved to US$1.00 = S$1.412 in 1996; it was hovering below S$1.80 during 1998. The overall impact of this was that the real sector enjoyed a level of protection from imported inflation. However, its effect on the domestic non-traded sector was dramatic and damaging. The prices of land, labour and housing appreciated so much that these factors are now beginning to weigh down economic activities. One redeeming feature of the management of this economy is that policy-makers are willing to permit a cut in the prices of these non-traded goods every time the country faces a recession. In that sense, a balance is managed over each period, but then it creates instability in relation to the managed exchange rate regime.

The effect on interest rates has been less salutary. With the financial sector becoming internationalized, there are large fund flows into the economy, which in itself provides for cheaper costs of business finance. A look at the SIBOR (Singapore Inter-Bank Offered Rate) suggests that the 1990s had so much funds in the economy that the market clearing rate was less than half the rate during the 1976–90 period. The mild interest rate suppression that originated from the low interest rates offered to the pension fund balances and the depositors in the POSBank had led to very low returns to depositors. In fact real interest rates had become negative in the 1990s right up to 1996. On balance, it must be stated that the wide spread between the deposit and minimum lending rate suggests a very high profit rate for intermediation: the return on equity of the banking system during recent years was about 13.5 per cent per annum after the 1987 economic recovery. Banks earned very low profits in the previous period.[10] The effects of interest rate and exchange rate reforms have been mixed, depending on which sector one belonged to.

Three specific financial services that have become very important through the reform process are foreign exchange transactions and Asian dollar and syndicated bond markets. These have developed at phenomenal growth rates, helped by the set of reforms aimed at attracting international business. About 10 per cent of the world's US$1380 billion trade in currencies in 1996 is transacted in this financial sector. Financial sector reforms coupled with the growing regional focus of the financial sector led to competitive pricing in the currency markets. The demand for currencies came from both central banks and businesses performing international activities in the region.

Table 5.7   Relative positions of spot transactions in currencies

Money centres	Daily average value traded in US$ billion		
	1995	1992	1989
London	465 (44%)	291 (40%)	184 (36%)
New York	244 (23%)	167 (23%)	115 (22%)
Tokyo	160 (15%)	128 (18%)	110 (21%)
Singapore	105 (10%)	74 (10%)	55 (11%)
Hong Kong	91 (9%)	61 (8%)	49 (10%)

Note: Relative position was the same in 1999 but total trade has gone up to an estimated value of US$1650 billion.

Source: *Financial Times*, 20 September 1995, p. 4.

The position of Singapore in relation to five major currency centres is given in Table 5.7. As can be seen in the table, the total foreign exchange trade is growing very fast as a result of the popularity of money market deposits in major financial centres and bankers' speculative positions on the currencies markets. The total transactions in currencies is growing at 11 per cent per year, much faster than growth in merchandise trade of about 5 per cent! Singapore traded US$370 million worth in currency in 1973 before the reforms prior to expansion in currency deposits. In 1996, it traded US$138 billion per day, and it has gained fourth position in the international trade of currencies. This position was gained by trading mostly in currencies other than regional, since the regional currency share of the transactions was less than 20 per cent. A large forward market in the US dollar and the yen developed in the 1990s, estimated at about US$52 billion.

There is also a huge forward market that has grown along with the growth in spot currencies. The forward market consists of currency swaps and outrights (that is, forward rate agreements). According to the MAS, the value of forward rate agreements averaged US$52 billion monthly in 1994, and is growing in importance in the face of rapid changes in interest rates since 1994. These deals are in US dollars and yen contracts, representing 50 and 36 per cent respectively. Currency futures contracts and currency options valued at US$39 billion were registered in 1994. As risk management became important after the Asian currency crisis in 1997, these contracts are expected to grow significantly.

There are also large Asian dollar deposits of about US$515 billion. The 1970 value of Asian dollar deposits was US$400 million, compared with the 1995 figure of US$478 billion, a growth of 31 per cent per year. In the last five years, the Asian dollar deposit growth has slowed to a mature 4 per cent per year as investment demands decreased after 1994. An Asian dollar bond market is also growing out of the latter: the current size of the outstanding issue is small, at only US$1260 million. Given the growing demand for infrastructure financing in energy and transportation in Asia, there is expected to be growth potential for this market when the regional governments issue bonds, perhaps after a period of adjustment to the 1997 crisis. The spread over LIBOR in this market is estimated to be around 100 basis points, which puts it in strong competition with other international centres for syndicated or line of credit debt financing by large corporations and governments in the region.

Domestic effects of liberalization   Other reforms carried out had more to do with deepening the market by offering licences to new players, originating new securities and improving liquidity as well as regulating to improve the soundness of the financial institutions. Of particular interest are the detailed regulations that govern the operations of financial institutions in Singapore. These detailed regulations are too many and far-reaching (some were shown in Table 5.3). They were aimed at setting out prudential supervision framework based on shared values for creating sound financial institutions. This has taken many forms. First is the quality of the joint stock company that indicates the financial capacity of the controlling management of a financial institution. To safeguard investor protection, the capital base for licensing a bank has been set very high at US$800 million for a bank to be licensed. Institutions with proven track records are the only ones likely to be licensed. The regulators consider that the small size of the economy dictates that about 22 foreign-origin banks from many countries can be useful for providing sufficient competition, and that no new major addition to this number is needed in the near future. A figure commonly cited is that, per 100 000 population, Singapore has more bank branches than many economies: in that sense, it is claimed to be 'over-banked'. However, Hong Kong and other money centres have many more banks under a more benign licensing environment which, the proponents of protection would point out, leads to periodic failures of the weaker institutions, as has happened in London, Hong Kong and Luxembourg.

Second, the entry of more financial institutions during the 1973–97 period in the special forms of ACUs, restricted-licence banks, off-shore licences, financial institutions providing specialized services in investment banking, money broking, risk management, insurance, and so on has helped to improve competition in the industry. The results are seen in (a) improved customer services, (b) competitive prices for financial services, (c) stable difference in deposit and lending rates, and (d) greater choice in the forms of securities available. Of particular interest are the low interest rates that have prevailed from 1984 to 1997. Interest rate reforms, competition from new entrants and improved mechanization of operations took place during the period when the MAS improved its supervision and worked together with industry to improve the soundness of all financial institutions.

Indicators of financial liberalization
The short-term deposits in the commercial banks in 1996 amounted to about 96 per cent of GDP. This shows the resilience of the economy. Table 5.8 gives the figures on four measures of financial liberalization. There are a number of favourable effects from the liberalization documented here. First and foremost is the depth of the financial sector. Money depth defined as the M3/GDP ratio suggests that this indicator improved from a base of 0.730 to somewhere above 1.05 from 1988 onwards. This improvement suggests that the credit and deposit balances increased by almost 30 per cent to 1.157 in 1992. But with the assets becoming more expensive in 1993 onwards, there was a 10 per cent decline in this ratio. We may call this the asset bubble effect, which appears to have led to a significant decline in money and deposit balances in the economy over 1993–98.

Table 5.8 Indicators of financial liberalization

	5-year average			Annual								
	1976–80	1981–85	1986–90	1991	1992	1993	1994	1995	1996	1997	1998
Money depth (M3/GDP)	0.730	0.866	1.046	1.129	1.157	1.084	1.054	1.029	1.083	1.161	–
Inter-relations ratio											
FIR (total)/GDP	0.33	0.74	0.69	0.62	0.61	0.59	0.58	0.61	0.66	0.72	0.86
FIR (private)/GDP	0.64	0.86	0.83	0.83	0.85	0.84	0.84	0.91	0.97	1.00	1.10
GFCF/GDP	0.370	0.457	0.324	0.333	0.356	0.350	0.337	0.330	0.385	0.387	0.375
FDI/GDP	0.049	0.062	0.099	0.083	0.021	0.073	0.087	0.024	0.025	0.033	n.a.

Notes:
M3 = (M1 + quasi-money + Post Office savings deposit).
FIR = financial intermediation ratio – claims on public sector, claims on private sector, and foreign assets.
GFCF = gross fixed capital formation.
FDI = foreign direct investment.

Sources: IMF, *International Financial Statistics*, May 1997; World Bank, *World Bank Databank*, Feb. 1997.

The next noticeable improvement is in the total financial inter-relations ratio. This ratio represents the claims of all parties on the financial sector. This figure was 0.33 during 1976–80 but improved to 0.86 in 1992. This suggests that the reforms of the 1970s created an expanded financial sector. The private sector that owns these assets appears not to have been so badly affected as the public sector. Gross fixed capital formation also held steady over 1988 to 1997. The high ratio in the earlier years suggests that there were intensive capital investments in building the infrastructure to attract international investment. Educational facilities, roads, airports, ports and telecommunications all received priority in the 1970s. The subsequent investment rate of about 32 per cent is also very high by international standards. Some would even argue that this level of investment rate is excessive for a growth rate of under 10 per cent. The investments were both for the productive sector and for building a level of social amenities compatible with the political norm of comfort in a crowded island state. The investment rate in Hong Kong was lower, yet it had higher growth. But the level of social comfort in the physical environment requires massive capital in the early period as well as in later periods. That accounts for the high level of investment rate.

What is not shown in Table 5.8 is the important fact that this level of growth was achieved without any public domestic or foreign debt. Housing for the population was built with their own savings in the pension funds, which they withdrew to buy their houses. The government did not borrow internationally to develop these facilities. It is perhaps because of the small size of the land to be developed that no borrowing was needed, and yet there was enough to sustain all economic activities. Perhaps the other reason is that funds to the tune of about 4 to 10 per cent of GDP were coming in regularly as FDI to finance the business expansion. This meant that there was no pressure from business to compete for funds from domestic savings. This issue is complex in this case, and cannot be dismissed by simple generalizations. In 1995, Singapore was rated as a AAA credit-worthy nation among a few in the world (Piggot, 1996). Standards poor rating has been consistently at B except in 1998.

Overall, the amount of cash flow from international sources is indicated in Table 5.9. It is evident that the FDI and portfolio funds complemented the domestic direct investment in the real sector. There is a ten-fold increase in direct investment over the 1976–97 period: from US$578 million to US$6912 billion. Portfolio investment did not play a significant role until the 1990s, when the share markets started to build a bubble as these funds grew more than 100 per cent over 1990 to 1996, only to be pulled down by half by the end of 1998. An interesting statistic after the current accounts were opened in 1978 is the faster growth in portfolio flows into the economy.

The per year average portfolio flow was about US$410 million during the 1976–85 period but this figure increased dramatically after this period to an

Table 5.9 Indicators of financial liberalization: investment flows (US$ million)

	5-year average			Annual						
	1976–80	1981–85	1986–90	1991	1992	1993	1994	1995	1996	1997
Direct investment (net)	477.2	1215.4	2648.4	4361	887	2665	2376	3006	5006	4661
Portfolio investment (net)	–9.20	–20.4	–340.20	–908	307	–4966	–7528	–7127	–8486	11419
FDI (inflow)	578.8	1349	3332.6	4887	2204	4686	8386	7386	7444	8631

Sources: IMF, *International Financial Statistics*, May 1997; World Bank, *World Bank Databank*, Feb. 1997; ADB (1998b).

annual average of US$5000 million – 12 times larger – during the next eight years before declining in 1994–95 by an annual average of US$2700 million per year. Asian currencies suffered exchange rate declines of 30 to 40 per cent over May–October 1997.[11]

Financial liberalization had largely a beneficial effect in improving the investment rate of the economy, and in creating financial depth in general. The reforms had a perverse effect on the non-traded sector, which was the source of instability. But this is due to the managed exchange rate, which tended to create the perverse effect in order to benefit the business sector in the form of cheaper loans, ready credits and low input costs. The asset bubbles appear to break each time there is a recession, but, with the managed exchange rate momentum sustained from the surplus of reserves, the same structural weakness reappears at each turning-point of the business cycle. Would a full free-float have been beneficial? This question requires further analysis.

Influence on trade and capital flows
Trade and capital flows are examined here informally in that their relative growth paths against GDP growth are examined: see Table 5.10. These figures show the growth rate in GDP alongside similar figures for growth in trade, growth in FDI inflows, and changes in exchange rates. It is assumed that, with openness shown to have existed from a financially liberalized economy, trade growth and net capital flows must grow at faster rates. If this is observed, then it can be argued, using evidence of slow growth in capital flows and trade patterns of closed financial sectors, that the faster growth in capital flows and trade is due to liberalization in the financial sector. This is not a direct demonstration of the effect: in a sense, it is weaker evidence than that produced in the earlier discussion.

The average real growth rate of the economy in this set of figures was about 8.3 per cent per annum over the 19 years of data shown in the table: data shown against each year are an average of growth rates in the previous three years. Thus, given low inflation of under 3 per cent in the test period, growth has been phenomenal when considered against the world average growth rate in the same period of about half that rate. This growth has been possible due to real- and financial-sector liberalization, as well as reforms in the management of economic activities.

Growth in trade was 14.26 per cent per year over the same period. The pattern of merchandise trade over 1978–97 showed a persistent deficit which is always made up by non-merchandise inflows, thus not weakening the trade link with the exchange rate. Further, the fiscal budget surpluses over many years also provided foreign exchange reserves to support the exchange rate. Hence it can be seen that trade growth has been ahead of real-sector growth by a margin of 6 per cent. This level of growth would not have been possible if the current and

Table 5.10   Cumulative average growth rates in trade and capital flows

Year (5-year moving average)	GDP growth rate (%)	Trade growth rate (%)	Net FDI growth rate (%)	Exchange rate (US$1)
5 years to:				
1978	6.0	15.0	60	2.456
1979	9.2	21.0	62	2.339 (5.0%)
1980	13.5	27.0	49	2.164 (8.09%)
1981	13.8	25.0	32	2.159 (−0.05%)
1982	13.3	13.0	18	2.094 (4.00%)
1983	10.1	7.0	33	2.114 (0.134%)
1984	7.9	3.0	16	2.133 (−0.01%)
1985	3.7	1.0	16	2.200 (−3.14%)
1986	1.5	−1.0	25	2.177 (1.94%)
1987	3.3	5.0	10	2.106 (3.26%)
1988	9.6	17.0	10	2.012 (4.46%)
1989	13.3	21.0	19	1.950 (6.70%)
1990	13.5	27.0	31	1.812 (7.10%)
1991	10.8	11.0	13	1.727 (4.69%)
1992	8.3	10.0	19	1.629 (5.67%)
1993	6.0	14.0	3	1.617 (0.74%)
1994	6.9	18.0	60[a]	1.442 (10.82%)
1995	8.7	21.0	29	1.417 (1.73%)
1996	8.5	16.0	17	1.413 (0.01%)
1997	1.5	4.0	−20	1.673 (−18.4%)[c]
1998	1.5	−12.0	15	1.673 (0.0%)
1999	4.5	8.0	40	1.680 (−0.5%)
Average over 1976–96	Real growth 8.34% rate	14.26% growth	29.37% growth	Appreciation of 3.02% pa[b] 1.59% pa[c]

Notes:
[a] FDI is declining from 1992 except for a big increase in 1993, which makes the moving average for 1993 onwards look good. Part of the reason for the net negative FDI growth is due to active promotion to invest outside Singapore to take a foothold in the growth of the region.
[b] Currency upvalued by 3.01% per annum to year 1996.
[c] Currency upvaluation cut by half by the huge devaluation from the effect of 1997 Asian currency crisis.

Sources: SEACEN, *Financial Statistics*, July 1996 and IFS, various years.

capital accounts had not been fully liberalized in June 1978. It can be argued that a substantial portion of the trade growth is due to the region's growth coinciding with the efforts of the planners to further internationalize the economy. Third, capital flows grew at rates twice that of output growth at least until 1994, when Singapore planners began to undertake massive FDI in emerging economies. This led to capital outflows to emerging economies. With more data available in the future on this external wing to the Singapore economy, perhaps one could learn if this reform policy was as successful as the previous ones.

4. ASSESSMENT AND FUTURE PROSPECTS

Among the economies studied in this book, Singapore may be singled out as a unique case of financial liberalization that made it possible for the city state to become a financial centre linking the major securities markets in Tokyo, New York and London. Active pursuit of policies was designed to achieve this status in competition with Hong Kong and Sydney as potential competitors. The fact that Singapore has emerged ahead of several potential competitors is due to its location and organizational advantages. The lessons learned from this case are relevant to other countries that aim to become international or regional financial centres in other time zones.

The financial crisis of 1997–98 has diminished the role of Singapore in this regard, as several of the regional economies are experiencing recession. Once growth returns to this region, Singapore will again emerge to play a significant role as the financier of the region and provider of specialized financial services. Singapore-based financial institutions have expanded into the regional financial systems during the Asian financial crisis.

NOTES

1. The jockeying for international financial centre position is so intense that more and more financial sectors are hoping to become yet another international financial centre in the vast region. Taiwan, Thailand and Korea have similar ambitions, and have incorporated plans to move their financial sectors to become regional centres. Malaysia has since 1991 taken serious steps to become a major centre, especially in the stock and bond markets as well as in Islamic financial instruments: these ambitions were clipped when the stock market plummeted by 70 per cent, and the currency by 42 per cent in 1997. The liberalization plan documents of all these countries contain an item on this idea. The continued reforms of the Australian financial system makes it a potential winner in the long run provided costs of transactions can be brought down to the levels in Hong Kong and Singapore, its finance minister said in 1999 at a seminar in Melbourne.
2. Sri Lanka was at such an advanced state of development during the 1950s to have been the natural location for many of the things that Singapore did successfully. But the region that was

growing was Southeast Asia, not South Asia. If South Asia had developed first, Sri Lanka would have been the natural choice for a centre as it had several stronger attractions, such as a larger resource base, more educated workforce, and so on.

3. An example that comes to mind is Thailand as the international capital market of the Indo-China Peninsula, and Iran as the financial centre of the central Asian countries around the Caspian Sea.

4. One estimate suggests that the number of man-years of expert help that Singapore received was very large: see Ariff (1998c). Through a system of local counterpart training, the selected persons to work with these experts received training in modern management techniques and expert knowledge in their fields. This was taken as a serious business and the government of Singapore is on record as acknowledging how this helped in the development process.

5. There were 505 government-linked firms, of which about 50 were targeted for corporatization and subsequent sale to the public as listed companies. The sales pitch was that the population would become share-owners, but these privatized entities were telecommunications, airline, printing firms that printed government publications, power companies, and so on. Only a small number of firms were privatized during 1984–98.

6. Singapore is also noted for a very liberal attitude in licensing retail money trade in foreign currencies. About a thousand licensees ply the trade of changing money so that the spread in transactions in Singapore is a fraction of the spread in major money centres. These ubiquitous money changers help to make the money market very efficient, driving transactions costs in handling money down to very low levels. Similar benefits could be obtained if these licensees could also trade in other money market instruments now protected in the halls of the banks; with these people entering inter-country transmission of small cash transactions, Singapore can make money transmission more efficient than has been possible with modern banking structures.

7. This chapter excludes a few traditional financial organizations in Singapore that have little impact on the sector.

8. The Asian dollar market started as a result of changes to the US laws to limit further outflow of capital in 1967, through changes to the US Tax Code.

9. This is a significant refocus of monetary management. It is through the sterilization of the flow of funds that large inflows are prevented from translating into high inflation. Recall that it was the failure to sterilize foreign capital flows into China that resulted in the hyperinflation in that country over 1980 to 1994.

10. The return on equity of foreign banks were slightly above this rate. The source for these statistics is an ongoing study of the performance of local and foreign financial institutions.

11. The worst hit were the Thai, Indonesian, Filipino and Malaysian currencies. Other currencies such as the Australian dollar and the Hong Kong dollar (reportedly defended heavily with spending of US$11 000 million over a month in October 1997) suffered much smaller shocks, given their dependence on the region for trade.

6. Indonesia: liberalization amidst persistent exchange rate instability

1. BACKGROUND

The Indonesian economy underwent massive changes as its structure was slowly changed from a primary producer in 1970 to one with 40 per cent non-oil exports in 1995. This dramatic change in the production structure of the economy could not have been achieved without a careful crafting and implementation of liberalization policies to improve the performance of the economy during 1967 to 1996. Indonesia, which is the fifth most populous country in the world, with a population of 198 million, managed to advance to a reasonable level of development despite two critical weaknesses. It is also a widely scattered country, with hundreds of islands with a land area of 1 905 000 sq. km. Lack of sufficiently developed infrastructure and scarcity of a trained workforce meant that productivity was low. In addition, the country needed foreign capital to sustain high economic growth. These conditions created a persistent need to devalue the currency to keep exports competitive, and to draw foreign capital to finance the move towards becoming a diversified economy. The result was a vicious circle of instability each time the economy was put on the right path through reforms. The political risk of an outgoing authoritarian regime in May 1998 made the economic crisis even worse, thus setting back 33 years of gains from guided development of modernizing élites in the employ of a mighty strong ruler.

The exchange rate exhibited the impacts of these factors very vividly. There were five episodes of large devaluations, ranging from 10 to 50 per cent during 1971 to 1986: the value of the rupiah in 1996 was one-sixth the value of the US dollar, equal to Rp 415 fixed in 1971 at the time of the rupiah's peg to the dollar. The currency lost 76 per cent of its value in August 1997 following the contagion of the baht crisis and the dramatic resignation of the president on 20 May during student unrest in 1998 when four students were shot dead. Considerably large devaluations were needed to bring the economy back to sustainable levels each time the problem assumed near-crisis proportions – in 1971, 1978, 1982 and 1986. The 1997–98 crisis brought the IMF to help restructure the economy, burdened by huge capital outflow and a bankrupt banking system.

The second factor that created instability was largely due to Indonesia's high consumption and low savings. Given its low level of capacity to mobilize savings, Indonesia depended heavily on imported capital throughout the period of progressing the economy from a primary producer to a manufactured goods producer by the end of 1989. To attract the capital inflow to achieve this status, it had to keep its real interest rates high, which partly explains why these rates were largely controlled right up to 1992.[1] A high real interest rate had to be maintained to attract capital in the face of the post-1982 substantial declines in oil-based revenues as the result of the fall in world oil prices. The decision to move away from oil dependence was made in the late 1970s (oil-related revenue provided 80 per cent of the state revenues at that time) when oil prices were still rising.

Two correct reform responses were implemented to improve the capacity to mobilize savings by liberalizing the financial sector – some say too much – with improved competition and improved fiscal health by reforming taxation policies.[2] The banking and fiscal reforms were implemented in the early 1980s, which led to improvements in savings mobilization, both local and foreign, while fiscal health also improved. The latter led to a reduction in the demand for capital from government, even though the private sector was not motivated to be prudent, given the freedom they were given in 1988 to raise foreign-currency loans in Indonesia or from overseas – a critically flawed policy since it created incentives for residents to undertake currency risk.

Despite carefully structured reforms in the real, monetary, banking and fiscal sectors, the heavy dependence by the private sector on foreign short-term capital flows and a government that financed off-budget expenses by borrowing from the Paris Club continued to create instability after each period of reforms. These were two serious flaws that brought down Indonesia (along with authoritarian rule). Private-sector borrowing started to build up especially after 1989, when domestic firms began to invest heavily in (a) infrastructure projects and (b) luxury projects such as golf courses, hotels, resorts, and others. Consequently, private-sector borrowing in foreign currencies increased substantially: this was similar to the Australian experience in the late 1980s. In 1997, this ballooned into massive amounts of loans which, combined with the already existing public-sector debt, brought Indonesia to a dangerous level of debt in 1997.[3] Total debt increased from US$66.9 billion in 1990 to US$131.4 billion in 1997 before the baht crisis of May 1997. Even with a healthy economy, debt becoming close to 70 per cent of GDP was not sustainable on any definition of affordability.

The final outcome was dramatic and predictable. The exchange rate could not be defended in the face of a massive withdrawal of funds, mostly by the locals, when the 1997 baht crisis spread to Indonesia in September 1997. Political unrest made the crisis worse in May 1998, when the election of a president to a fifth term brought demonstrators out on the streets. Soon the rupiah lost 76 per cent of its value. The IMF moved in with a restructuring and rescue plan. Carefully structured liberal reforms, often not effectively implemented in this country, could not overcome the persistent exchange rate instability, even in this interesting case. When the weakest link gave way in August 1997 and once again in May 1998, years of gains from the liberal policies of Indonesia were definitively lost within two years. The economy is estimated to have lost 15 per cent of GDP during 1998–99 and the recovery to any modest growth is not foreseen before the year 2001.

This chapter documents the liberal policies put into action during a span of 33 years to 1998. The next section examines the structure of the economy, with special emphasis on commercial banking. The details of the steps taken to stabilize this large economy and the consequences for policies are examined in Section 3. We examine the circumstances that warranted the policies, and the effects of these policies. Special attention is paid to the policy impacts from financial liberalization: see Subsection 3.3. The last section of the chapter discusses the experience of the Indonesian economy right up to the time of the baht crisis of 1997. The effect of sequencing reforms and the effects on the economy of the 1997 crisis are found elsewhere in the book.

2. THE STRUCTURE OF THE ECONOMY AND THE FINANCIAL SECTOR

The Indonesian economy grew at an average rate of between 6 and 8 per cent per annum over the last three decades since 1967. The growth was highest during 1990–96, supported of course by too much short-term debt in the banking sector, propping up long-term investments in the non-traded sector, which led to the crisis and economic decline since 1998. During this period of very good growth, per capita income grew by 4.7 per cent, which is very close to the growth in such exceptional cases as Malaysia and Singapore. Over the 1965–94 period, Indonesia's per capita income changed from a base of 5.2 per cent to 13.2 per cent of US per capita (ADB, 1998a). This is rapid progress in wealth increase. As the economy restructured as an exporter of non-oil and manufactured goods, consumption fell from its high of 70 per cent of GDP in 1967 to 55 per cent in 1996 – a progress comparable to that achieved by large export economies. During this period, government consumption was held steady at about 8–10 per cent of GDP, falling towards 8 per cent after 1994.

Fiscal balance as a percentage of GDP shows that the budget deficit was well under the 3 per cent mark widely considered as prudent even in the early phase over 1970–82. This gave way after the crisis. The fiscal balance narrowed to –1.7 per cent in the 1980s. At last the budget was in surplus over 1989–96.

Table 6.1   *Basic economic and social indicators of development in Indonesia*

Indicators	1971–80	1981–90	1991–93	1994	1995	1996	1997	1998[a]
National accounts								
GDP growth (%)	8.00	5.51	6.64	7.48	8.07	8.18	4.70	–7.20
Per capita GDP	242.95	508.71	715.26	903.97	996.03	1,080	981	263
Private consumption/GDP	0.68	0.58	0.39	0.58	0.59	0.55	0.54	0.65
Gov. consumption/GDP	0.10	0.10	0.09	0.08	0.08	0.08	0.08	0.10
Financial indicators								
Gross domestic savings/GDP	22.60	31.49	37.27	38.70	38.40	38.20	0.27	0.39
Gross fixed capital formation (% GDP)	19.78	30.31	34.87	34.27	33.84	36.08	0.35	0.33
Inflation (%)	17.49	8.61	8.88	8.52	9.43	7.99	11.6	53.4
M2/GDP	16.1	25.9	44.3	45.3	49.0	52.5	55.6	66.0
M3/GDP								
Fiscal balance (% of GDP)	–2.7	–1.7	0.2	0.9	0.4	0.8	–1.00	–3.2
Current account balance (% of GDP)	–1.2	–3.4	–2.4	–1.6	–3.4	–4.0	–3.90	9.00
Trade balance (% of GDP)	6.6	5.4	5.0	4.6	3.0	0.90	7.20	8.80
Debt service ratio (% of exports)	32.6	35.7	33.3	30.7	30.9	29.5	29.9	28.0
Social indicators								
IMF income classification	Low	Low–middle	Low–middle	Low–middle	Low–middle	Low–middle	Low–middle	Low–middle
Adult illiteracy rate	n.a.	n.a.	n.a.	n.a.	n.a.	16.0	16.0	16.0
Unemployment rate	n.a.	2.5	2.7	4.4	7.2	7.2	14.5	24.6
Expenditure on education (% of exp.)	7.44	9.23	9.83	9.77	10.4	10.5	10.5	10.5
Expenditure on health (% of exp.)	1.94	2.17	2.64	3.25	4.1	4.2	4.4	4.4
Income distribution								
Population growth	2.03	1.98	1.69	1.64	1.61	1.61	1.60	1.60

Note: [a] A mid-1999 estimate of GDP growth for 1999 is –2.4%.

Sources: IMF; IFS (CD-ROM); *World Development Report*.

The financial structure of the economy also provides interesting characteristics. The current account was persistently in the red. In the early period of restructuring, capital goods imports and dependence on imports in general weakened the current account: the country increased its imports by 2.7 per cent of GDP in the 1970s and 1.7 per cent in the 1980s.

The current account improved to a positive position in the 1990s up to 1994 but deteriorated to −3.7 and −4 per cent in 1995 and 1996 respectively. The trade structure was becoming unfavourable, along with the same patterns of weakening witnessed in the region as exports began to decline from about mid-1995. This placed heavy strains on the ability of the central bank to manage the currency on a band. The band was steadily increased to 12 per cent, indicating the weakening resolve of the Bank Indonesia with less foreign exchange resources to defend the slow devaluation that started in late 1995. The 1997 Asian crisis gave a huge push to this trend, and the managed float was abandoned in August 1997 with disastrous consequences for the current account. The exchange rate overshot hugely, and the current account problem then became a nightmare in 1998 made worse by the fall of authoritarianism. The cash flows from the IMF rescue have been maintaining the current account since August 1998.

Domestic savings were 22.6 per cent of GDP in 1971–80 against actual capital formation of 19.78 per cent. The structural change suggested by these statistics can be seen in the subsequent years. The savings rate increased continually to 38.2 per cent, as did also fixed capital formation. This growth was achieved at tremendous cost of high inflation and high interest rates to sustain a level of investment far in excess of what could be achieved without capital inflows. These inflows were courted from the first acts of liberalization by establishing the Foreign Exchange Bourse in 1967 to trade currencies and the laws passed in the same year to encourage capital and technology flows. Only the government or government-connected banks were licensed to engage in the lucrative currency trading.

The high inflation rate of 17.49 per cent in the 1970s was brought to manageable levels of single digits in subsequent periods. The Asian financial crisis reintroduced inflation, made worse by the civil disorder during 1997–99: in 1999 the rate was 54 per cent. Managing inflation at the single-digit level over such a long period, while maintaining high growth under high interest rates to attract borrowed capital, was the result of careful liberalization policies that addressed macroeconomic structural weaknesses. Lending interest rates were close to 20 per cent per annum during most of the period, which underlines the dependence of the economy on external funds flow to support both sovereign debt and private-sector investments. Following the crisis, interest rates have soared.

There was substantial restructuring in the money markets. Until 1984, there were no instruments in the money market with which the central bank could monitor market rates. As a result, the money market structure was one where there were very few instruments to trade. The broad money to GDP ratio was a mere 16.1 per cent in the 1970s. However, the structure of the money market changed dramatically after the introduction of SBIs (central bank acceptance bills) and SBPUs (commercial papers). The ratio changed to 52.5 per cent by 1996. Despite these remarkable improvements, the money market depth was not sufficient to conduct monetary policies; hence the central bank resorted largely to interventions in the banking sector to conduct its policy implementation. Interest rate controls continued to be maintained, and were decontrolled only in 1993, when the central bank adopted a system of bids for SBI based on market rates. Thus the structure of the monetary sector changed considerably in the period following 1984 and later, after 1993.

The social structure of society also changed dramatically given the spill-over effects of continued growth during 33 years. Wealth created remained at the top: the top 20 per cent of households retained 40.7 per cent of the income while the bottom 20 had a meagre 8.7 per cent. Even Bangladesh had a slightly better wealth distribution! The financial crisis pushed the bottom half of the population below the poverty line, and that was the main cause of the political unrest, as more and more of the population suffered under the collapsing economy. As can be seen in Table 6.1, the unemployment rate held – before and during the crisis in recent years – as did also population growth rates. The decline in population growth was significant, falling from 2.03 per cent in 1971–80 to 1.61 by 1996. With continued development, the government spent more money on health, which led to a higher survival rate (from 41.2 years to 63 years in 1993; infant mortality fell from 128 to 56) while education also received higher budget allocation.[4] The illiteracy rate improved to 16 per cent from the 1970 figure of close to three times that figure. More women found employment in the formal sector.

In summary, the Indonesian economic transformation is noteworthy, as is also its collapse under political unrest. A largely primary producer in the 1960s, it successfully adopted expansionary policies that helped it to emerge as a diversified economy with significant industrial capacity. A measure of the success of the policies right up to about 1993 is the manner in which each episode of instability was managed by implementation of liberal policies that helped the economy to steer back to normalcy after a short period of heightened crisis – this happened four times. The economy is currently going through its worst period of financial instability, aggravated by political uncertainty. The progress achieved during the 33 years to 1996 has often been highlighted by the reduction in poverty in this populous country. The percentage of the population living below the poverty line declined from a high of 60 per cent in 1960 to under 10 per cent in 1996 (see Nasution, 1998): this increased significantly in 1998 as a result of the crisis. As will be documented later, Indonesia's currency has experienced its worst overshooting in 1998, and it will take some three years before growth hovers above the negative region. This is the price, it appears, that the country is paying for neglecting prudential supervision of the financial sector, so that it is less than robust and the so-called deregulation that permitted capital structure of firms weaken so badly that each dollar of shareholders' funds supported about five dollars of the debt burden when the crisis hit this economy. Additionally, the exchange rate liberalization that permitted firms to borrow in foreign currency locally as well as from foreign sources provided incentives to make huge currency conversions to expatriate domestic savings in foreign capital by individuals and producers alike. This was the Achilles heel of Indonesia.

The structure of the financial sector had gone through rapid changes. In the 1960s, the structure changed slightly when foreign banks and joint venture banks were permitted to make a market in the Foreign Exchange Bourse. Otherwise, the banks were mostly private-sector-owned. Following the 1984–86 liberalization of the banking sector, that sector changed dramatically with the entry of a large number of banks and non-bank financial institutions. At this period there was also more specialization, with the licensing of specialized development and other banks. The rapid growth in banking and in non-bank financial institutions helped the economy as Indonesia extended its manufacturing and export capabilities.

The 1997 crisis seriously reduced the capacity of the financial sector as the overshooting exchange rate wiped out most of the assets of the financial institutions. It is reported that most banks would fall within the category of defaulting. Urgent restructuring was going on at the end of 1999. It is expected that the government will require the banks to renegotiate their private loans with the bilateral parties involved. Some help may come in the form of restructuring funds to domestic depositors. Beyond that, the banking sector was seriously damaged by the crisis.

3.   LIBERALIZATION

Indonesian society was recovering from a continual state of civil disorder from 1939 to 1964 as it emerged bloodied from its independence movement (1939–47), and began a period of unifying the diverse nation of 26 nationalities under one language. Then it had to grapple with the aborted communist *coup* in 1965. Thus, at the start of its reform process at the end of 1960s, Indonesia had only one strength. It had been woven into a nation by its vitriolic founders, Sukarno and his team-mate Hatta. The country was among the most poor, and the period of civil strife had left basic infrastructure destroyed or unmaintained. It was the discovery of oil that came as a saviour for Indonesia. At least it provided some foreign exchange to engineer growth through reforms. This it did during the early period when oil prices soared, giving huge revenues to the government.

The Indonesian liberalization took place in four episodes, after which the 1997 Asian crisis wiped off some of the gains of liberalization during the following years.

- 1966–70: foreign sector liberalization. The reforms were aimed at stabilizing the economy by bringing inflation (112 per cent) down and obtaining foreign capital for investment and for foreign exchange needs to support imports.
- 1970–78: directed credit to diversify the economy led to high inflation. To contain this, the central bank took over foreign exchange transactions and pegged the currency at 415 rupiah to one US dollar.
- 1978–82: with falling oil prices and therefore falling oil revenues, reforms needed to revamp the financial sector on a more competitive basis by deregulation and private-sector incentives. To address the fall in government revenues, the targeted credits were eased off slowly and tax reforms improved revenues.
- 1982–92: genuine reforms to restructure the economy on a balanced basis. Reforms improved macroeconomic stability from 1984, and led to a period of ten years of exchange rate stability after 1986 a golden age.

These reforms addressed the periodic instability that arose from the country's underdeveloped status at the start. Reasonable success was achieved in that real income grew by an average rate of about 7.5 per cent per annum despite the less-developed starting-point. The inherent instability, which arose from the need to be competitive in the face of stiff competition from other regional players, was managed periodically without getting out of control. However, the 1997 currency crisis, stemming from the baht crisis and the May 1998 political crisis, led to loss of control, and the economy has become mired since 1997 in severe instability. The IMF is reluctantly restructuring the economy amid severe instability. The details of the successful reforms are examined below.

3.1 Economic Reforms

The highlights of the economic reforms to be described later are summarized as key statistics in Table 6.2. As can be seen, the 1970s and early 1980s had some success with reforms. Much of the growth from liberalization took place from the mid-1980s to 1996. What were the bases on which Indonesia managed to diversify its economy and obtain the substantial improvements in all the variables included in the table? For this to be fully understood, one needs to examine the four sets of reforms that policy-makers put in place over the years.

Table 6.2   Major economic and financial reforms in Indonesia, 1965–98

Date of reforms	Liberalization policy implemented
Before first reform	
1952	Jakarta Stock Exchange reopened; Dutch firms nationalized.
1965	Economic stabilization to reduce inflation and ease exchange controls.
	Laws passed to encourage investments – local and foreign.
First reform, 1966–69	**Economic stabilization**
1967	Legalized private trade in foreign exchange through Foreign Exchange Bourse.
	New Bank Act permits foreign exchange by foreign banks and joint venture banks.
1969	Approved local banks permitted to trade in foreign exchange (*bank devisas*).
Second reform, 1971–78	**Non-oil-exporting capacity**
1970	Foreign investment laws to ease entry of foreign capital, technology and skill, especially for primary-sector capital-intensive activities.
1971	Peg rupiah to US dollar at 415 rupiah after a 10% devaluation; unified exchange rates to two: one for all transactions and 10% lower for essential items.
	Central bank takes over foreign exchange transactions; Foreign Exchange Bourse almost abolished.
	Major policy of directed credits to preferred firms to create industrial capacity,
1970–76	*Danareksa* established to distribute National Investment Certificate in unit trust.
1977	First local firm listed on the Jakarta Exchange.
1978	With the aim of making Indonesia competitive for non-oil-exporting, the rupiah devalued by 50% in November.
Third reform, 1978–82	**Towards non-oil-export capacity and foreign investments**
1978	Exchange liberalization; basket peg to trading partners' currency.
	Special exchange rate for foreign capital and central bank takes a swap to cover the risk.
	Directed credits over 1970–82 failure; reduced directed credits.
Fourth reform, 1982–92	**Banking and FDI reforms**
1982–83	Banking reforms introduced, easing entry of non-state banks and non-bank financial institutions to mobilize savings and expand credits to support non-oil-based expansion.

Table 6.2   continued

Date of reforms	Liberalization policy implemented
1983	Real-sector liberalization with tariff reduction, entry of foreign firms.
1984–85	Monetary policy instruments: SBI (bank bills) and SBPU (commercial papers) introduced to create money markets for monetary intervention.
	Repos and CDs introduced later to improve liquidity in money markets.
1987–88	Capital market reforms to ease listing requirements, lift price limits, entry of more brokers and ease foreign share ownership to 49%.
1986–89	Tax reforms to strengthen public finance; introduced point of production value-added tax; reduced personal tax since collection not easy.
1988	October: public-sector banks allowed to place up to 50% in commercial banks.
	Banks authorized to issue foreign exchange loans in domestic markets and individuals were permitted to deposit in any currency (at *devisas*).
Crisis after reforms	
1991	Adopted prudential regulations; restricted CAMEL and related party lending to improve quality of commercial banking
1991	To cap surge in private-sector borrowing, committee formed to control foreign borrowing by private-sector firms.
1992	Stock Exchange privatized in August; reorganized.
1993	Interest rate now determined by market forces in SBI market.
	Between 1992 and 1997, exchange rate intervention band widened to 12%.
1995	Controls on finance company lending; no new licence; borrowing to net worth restricted to 15 times (domestic) and 5 times (foreign).
1997	August: abandoned peg as Thai baht crisis spread; rupiah crisis; abandoned basket peg.
1998	Rupiah rescue with help from Australia, Japan and Singapore failed.
	Indonesia accepts IMF restructuring and rescue plan.
	Lifted controls on interest rates by letting market rates determine SBI tenders.
	IMF rescue plan after losing control of exchange rate devaluation.
1999	New government coalition. East Timor independence and other regional riots.

Sources: Bank Indonesia reports; Asian Development Bank reports; and Nasution (1998).

Reforms I

The new order government that emerged after the worst civil unrest of 1965 had to manage the economy to find jobs for the huge unemployed labour force. The exchange rate had to be managed to bring in expatriated capital from outside the country. To these ends, three reforms were put in place: a banking reform; capital account opening for foreign capital; and measures to ease inflation. The banking reforms introduced currency trading in the Foreign Exchange Bourse, in which foreign banks and joint venture banks were permitted to take part. This stabilized the black market for currencies, and encouraged repatriation of capital as well as helping to improve confidence. Indonesians were among the first to provide capital account openness to foreign capitalists in 1970, way ahead of many others. This was designed to attract skills, technology and capital to Indonesia.

These reforms had the intended effects. The exchange rate stabilized, foreign capital inflow, essentially to primary processing industries, surged. Inflation, which reached 112 per cent in 1967, abated to 8.8 per cent by 1970, while GDP, which was growing at the moribund rate of 2.25 per cent before, jumped to 6.65 per cent in 1970. Exports jumped by 64 per cent over the period. Thus, the macroeconomy was stabilized within five years of the most severe civil disorder that had gripped the country. A solid foundation was laid to experiment with more reforms.

Reforms II

The next set of reforms was more ambitious. These aimed to develop indigenous manufacturing capacity away from the heavy dependence on manufactured imports that drained foreign exchange – recall that the current account deficit was –3.7 per cent – and away from the over-dependence on oil, which provided 80 per cent of government revenues. With the high-priced oil providing the revenues, Indonesia could well afford to practise what Korea and Taiwan also practised to home-grow manufacturing capacity. One thing that was missing in Indonesia was the well-educated high-quality labour that is essential to home-grow manufacturing capacity; the immigration policy also did not encourage large-scale injection of skills. The capital provided as targeted credits to desired firms in preferred industries failed to create any viable industries after about ten years (Woo, 1996). Meanwhile, the oil prices were moderating in the closing years of the 1970s, presaging a need to review the targeted credits policy. The exchange rate was pegged to the US dollar. These reforms had one desirable effect. Inflation as a result of directed credits was brought down from 33.7 per cent at one time to 6.7 per cent. The price for that were two sharp devaluations of 10 and 50 per cent in 1971 and 1978 respectively.

Reforms III

With the failure of targeted credits to home-grow manufacturing capacity during a period of fast-declining oil prices, Indonesia had to adopt more comprehensive reforms rather than take less bold steps like the previous ones. But this was postponed in favour of the urgent need to stabilize the exchange rates. The peg to the US dollar was abandoned in favour of a less rigid management. In its place, a managed basket peg was put in place using the trading partner currency weights. This was implemented in November 1978 with a huge devaluation of 50 per cent. Malaysia and Singapore had adopted the basket peg in September of the same year, and the then favoured policy was to adopt this method of management.

The current account, now returned to a more market-determined exchange management, was supposed to redress the exchange rate instability that had built up over the years. Over-investment in the non-traded sector was curtailed. Protected industries with preferential exchange rates had to adjust to market discipline. Overall, inflation declined to 7.2 per cent by 1979 and exports surged by 50.2 per cent. Some degree of diversification began to emerge as the economy moved to diversified exports.

Reforms IV

The long-postponed comprehensive reform had to be undertaken now, as oil prices declined fast from 1982 onwards. Revenues were declining, and diversification was beginning to occur. The comprehensive reforms took four different directions: banking reforms and capital market reforms to improve mobilization of capital; reforms to encourage foreign direct investment; tax reforms to improve revenues through a point-of-production tax on producers; and strengthening monetary management of the economy. These reforms were more financial in nature, and will be described in the next subsection. The effects of these reforms were to turn the economy towards a stable path for the longest period over 1983–93. In fact there was only a small devaluation (by Indonesian standards) of 31.6 per cent in 1986. A small fiscal surplus resulted; current accounts improved; the exchange rate appreciated slightly; and foreign capital surge to Indonesia was the largest in the region excepting China.

Following the contagion from the baht crisis in May 1997, the weaknesses in the Indonesian economy and the political system began to surface. With full foreign exchange openness available to producers and individuals, the private sector began to take on too much debt. The banks were borrowing short, often in foreign currencies, and lending the money to firms that undertook land-based investments in the non-traded sector (hotels, resorts, condominiums, shopping malls, and so on). Often the borrowing was done directly with foreign banks or even foreign firms. Thus the public debt, which was under control, now had new debt multiplying quickly in the private sector. The contagion from the 1997 Asian crisis hugely destabilized the Indonesian economy. There was an attempt to control private-sector loans when a Foreign Currency Co-ordinating Committee was set up to control the private-sector bad debt problem in 1991, but the attempt did not seem to have any effect. If it did, it was temporary.

The IMF rescue plan has led to unexpected reforms to the financial sector. The exchange rate regime changed to free-float in August 1997. The central bank was given autonomy to pursue stabilization policies.[5] The weakest link in the reform process had given way, and the effect was to unravel the gains that had accrued to Indonesian society over 33 years of carefully executed reforms.

3.2 Financial Liberalization

The individual reforms to bring in the financial (and economic) transformation of this country were summarized in Table 6.2. The important financial reforms will be discussed under several sub-headings below (see also Table 6.3). The reader will recall that the earlier section included a brief discussion of the economic reforms.

Exchange rate policies

Indonesia, like other countries during the Bretton Woods period, was in a fixed exchange regime. This changed in 1971 when it switched to pegging against the US dollar. A basket peg was put in place from 1978 to July 1997. The intervention band was increased from 2 to 12 per cent during 1991–96 in the face of worsening current accounts. During the 33 years of exchange rate management, constant devaluations of exchange rates returned the economy to stability and competitiveness: in 1971 (10 per cent devaluation); in 1978 (50 per cent); in 1983 (40 per cent); in 1986 (31.6 per cent). These episodes turned the economy around each time, helping to reduce inflation and ensuring surges in exports. Indonesia had persistent exchange rate instability caused, in our opinion, by its low factor productivity, which in turn is largely dependent on the education and skills of the labour force apart from the technology employed in the secondary sector. The exports were largely composed of labour-intensive outputs of intermediate goods. In fact only 16 per cent of the 40 per cent of exports were non-labour-intensive.

However, with the more comprehensive reforms carefully put in place during 1984–88, the economy achieved a good degree of stability. Exchange rates stabilized and even appreciated a little; inflation was a modest 7–8 per cent; the government budget was in the black; and there was large capital inflow. But then the current account began to deteriorate from late 1995, along with several Southeast Asian economies, prompting more frantic attempts to counter exchange rate declines. Then came the baht crisis, which spread to the rupiah

Table 6.3 Monetary aggregates, national income aggregates and balance of payments (as % of GDP)

	5-year average			Annual							
	1976–80	1981–85	1986–90	1991	1992	1993	1994	1995	1996	1997	1998
M1	10.8	10.4	11.3	11.7	11.1	10.2	10.9	10.6	9.8	11.0	13.0
M2	16.7	19.9	33.7	43.7	45.8	43.4	45.3	49.0	52.5	55.6	66.0
Trade deficit	9.2	5.0	5.9	4.2	5.6	5.3	4.6	3.0	0.9	7.9	8.8
Budget deficit	−2.8	−1.0	−1.6	0.4	−0.4	0.6	0.9	0.4	0.5	−1.0	−3.2
Current account deficit	0.7	0.6	1.1	−3.7	−2.2	−1.3	−1.6	−3.6	−3.4	−3.9	9.0
Private consumption	62.2	59.3	56.2	55.0	5.2	55.7	57.9	58.7	55.4	62.1	65.0
Gov. consumption	10.9	10.8	9.4	9.1	9.5	9.0	8.2	8.2	7.6	6.8	10.0
GFCF	20.7	28.0	33.1	35.5	35.9	33.2	34.3	33.8	36.1	31.5	18.0
Gov. expenditure	22.3	21.2	20.6	18.2	20.1	16.7	16.3	15.0	16.3	17.3	20.3

Note: M2 = (M1 + quasi-money).

Source: IMF, *International Financial Statistics*, various issues.

in August 1997. Soon thereafter, a political crisis relating to the election to fifth term of a president increased the country risk. The result was a marked devaluation, in fact an overshooting of the currency by 75 per cent. The IMF rescue plan started in mid-1998, and growth is expected to decline until 2001 before any positive growth occurs.

Interest rate policies

If there was a macro-finance variable that was most managed, it was the interest rate. The interest rate was set administratively or by some intervention of the central bank throughout the period up to 1993. Before the serious attempt at banking reforms in 1984, the interest rate was largely determined by the government banks, which dominated the deposits accounting for about 80 per cent. Deposit interest rates were very low even though the lending rates were very high. Lending rates have always hovered above 15 per cent and the spread was huge. Even in the more stable 1990s, lending rates were in the region of 18.9 per cent (1995) to 25.2 per cent (1991). These high rates had to be maintained to sustain the huge capital flow needed to finance industrial development in the 1970s and 1980s and land-based developments in the 1990s. The main reason for the high interest rate was its control. With the abandonment in 1993 of the band within which the SBI bids had to be made, interest rates were largely market-determined. The SBI discount provided the floor for interest rates. After this reform, interest rates began to move away from around 20 per cent towards 17 per cent during 1993–96.

Another reason for the high interest rate was the expectation among foreign exchange traders that the real interest rate was low because of inflation. This reason (the International Fisher Effect) is perhaps the more important one since there were expectations of built-in devaluations periodically. A third reason for a high interest rate was the relative underdevelopment of the money markets to signal a going rate in a competitive situation. It was not until the mid-1980s that sufficient instruments were available to determine the going rates for money: the SBIs issued by the central bank and the SBPUs introduced by the private sector to raise short-term money. Later on repurchase agreements (RAs) and negotiable certificates of deposits (NCDs) were introduced. These increased the depth of the market, and base interest rates began to emerge in the late 1980s. This process has helped the central bank, which uses these instruments increasingly to conduct monetary interventions.

Monetary policy and the central bank

Monetary policy was conducted using reserve ratios and interventions in the commercial banking sector as a matter of expediency given the lack of a liquid market for monetary interventions. This was the state of affairs until the second half of the 1980s. With the advent of the SBI as the instrument of intervention,

Table 6.4   Growth rates of basic economic indicators in Indonesia

	5-year average			Annual average							
	1976–80	1981–85	1986–90	1991	1992	1993	1994	1995	1996	1997	1998
GDP	7.92	4.74	6.25	6.95	6.46	6.50	7.48	8.07	8.18	4.70	–7.20
Inflation	14.57	9.71	7.47	9.41	7.53	9.69	8.52	9.43	7.93	11.6	54.3
Revenue	35.24	14.35	14.23	7.20	19.40	11.20	23.35	15.78	0.50	–1.00	–3.20
M1	32.01	15.10	18.66	12.07	7.90	17.15	22.89	13.68	9.58	33.2	26.9
M2	31.01	24.63	29.57	17.47	19.78	20.21	19.98	27.16	27.18	25.2	63.5
FDI	–14.96	11.49	28.66	35.59	19.91	5.24	71.07	161.0	42.51	–24.50	–93.57
Trade balance	32.01	15.10	18.66	–10.30	46.26	17.22	–4.01	–44.17	–50.00	294.7	68.92

Sources: IMF sources; for latest years, Thompson BankWatch releases in Internet or in press.

things began to change slowly as the liquidity in that instrument began to build: see Table 6.4 for some supporting statistics. In addition, the central bank engaged in foreign exchange sterilization and swaps to manage exchange rates, as required during the peg with the US dollar (1971–78) and under the basket-peg regime later. There is a difference of opinion about the efficacy of interventions. One opinion is that they were ineffective as the power to demand compliance by the banking sector did not lie within the central bank. This is an extreme view, in our opinion.

The more moderate position is that the authorities had conflicting demands placed on them because of the targeted credit policies that were in effect until 1983. When these policies were abandoned, they had less conflict. Over the years, certain conglomerates which had the ear of politically connected groups could and did escape supervision, as happened in a number of cases made public in the 1990s. An example is the case of a private bank which had a related party loan exposure amounting to 60 per cent of the base capital! This sort of escape from basic norms could not happen without the complicity of the central bank. This diminished the ability to conduct unfettered prudential supervision and also damaged the ability to intervene decisively in a number of serious situations. Nevertheless, it must be stated that the quite good results that came about from major policy implementations, no doubt within constrained situations, must have been due to reasonably competent policy execution.

The central bank took the initiative first in 1970 to introduce an exchange rate clearing-house to obtain market rates for exchange rates. That was a success until the adoption of the peg to the US dollar, when foreign exchange transactions were abrogated to the central bank. With the adoption of the basket peg and later reforms to the capital accounts, foreign exchange was returned to the banking sector, with sterilization intervention within the central bank.

Prudential regulations adopted with the 1984 banking laws helped to reform the banking sector somewhat. Related party borrowing was restricted while a revised form of the CAMEL system was put in place to improve prudential regulations. Competition increased, deposit mobilization improved, and deposit rates improved. There was large-scale movement of deposits to private-sector banks. In 1983, 80 per cent of deposits were in government banks. By 1989, the private banks had 80 per cent of the banking system deposits. This was a dramatic turnaround. Service quality improved, and the network of branches extended throughout the country. So did also the proliferation of bad (Kane would call them 'zombie') banks with little expertise but licence to take in public savings and to lend.

Capital markets

The Dutch colonialists had developed a vibrant capital market for trading commodity-related capital, bonds and loans. This fell into disuse during the postwar years up to 1952, when it was revived, mostly for the purpose of nation-alizing the Dutch firms and then distributing the shares to locals. Nothing much happened until 1977, when it was revived again to distribute national certifi-cates in unit trust shares. In that year the first local company was listed – about a dozen years before China. Growth was incremental until the comprehensive reforms were introduced. The capital market was looked at favourably as the place to privatize public-sector firms and plans were put together to study its feasibility in the 1980s.

Three significant reforms in capital markets were made. Capital from abroad could be obtained after 1988. In that same year, listing requirements were eased, more brokerage licences were issued, and ownership of 49 per cent sharehold-ing by foreigners was approved. At the end of 1989, there were 57 firms listed compared with 214 in 1994 and about 255 in 1997. Capitalization improved from Rp 434 billion in 1988 to Rp 104 trillion in 1994! This brought in foreign capital. Volume improved and prices surged. More companies sought listing on the market. These improvements continued to develop the capital market as listing grew to over 200 companies. The basic premise of the reform was that a private-sector-managed bourse would do a better job than a government-managed exchange. This is a lesson still not yet learned by transition economies such as China, where the exchange is managed by bureaucrats, with most modern technology at their disposal.

The next reform was the privatization of the exchange when the government abandoned control of it, vesting it as a private limited company self-regulated by member companies. The trading system was automated in line with the regional practices in neighbouring countries. This 1992 reform was the most telling in that the Jakarta stock market significantly improved its attraction as Indonesia's major market. The total listing as at 1998 was 283. After privati-zation, traded value increased from about Rp 7 billion to about Rp 25 billion. Foreign interest in traded value dominated by a factor of 7:2. Before the currency crisis, the market was capitalized at 45 per cent of GDP compared with 3 per cent in the 1970s.

Summary

The foregoing discussion, though brief, has described the importance of financial reforms to stabilize the economy as it periodically lost competitive-ness. Exchange rate reforms and interventions appear to have become a permanent feature of financial reforms in Indonesia. Next in importance was the need to keep interest rates under control until exchange rate stability was achieved in the early 1990s. Interest rate decontrol was the last of the reforms put in place. The comprehensive package of banking, monetary, tax and exchange rate reforms during 1982–88 was noteworthy in that these reforms actually returned the economy to a level of stability not seen hitherto. However, bigger forces, particularly political forces and excessive short-term debt, financing land-based development in the 1990s, led to a massive overshoot of the currency when the baht contagion and then political unrest threatened the stability that the Indonesians thought was within their grasp. Indonesia will take all of 1998–2000 to recover from these shocks. The two weakest links in the reform process – political oligarchy and financial fragility in firms and banks – determined a terrible outcome, unexpected by any observers. Well into the year of the crisis, the administration thought that Indonesia would bounce back, as it was on such a good path to stability!

3.3 Financial Liberalization Effects

Macroeconomic effects

Table 6.5 gives summary statistics of the macroeconomic effects of liberalization over the study period. The overall impact was a rapid growth in income over the 33 years. With an average rate of growth of about 7.5 per cent during most of the period, Indonesia emerged out of its position as an impoverished nation, with 60 per cent living below the poverty line in 1970. International statistics showed the steady decline in this one key statistic until this figure went below 10 per cent in 1995.

As in the case with the Korean experience of almost 10 per cent growth, which lifted Korea from its lowly status in the 1960s, the liberal policies pursued in this case lifted the economy to become reasonably developed. Inflation, which was above 112 per cent in 1967, was brought down steadily to around 15 per cent during the 1970s and 1980s. With the more comprehensive reforms taking effect in the late 1980s, inflation was brought down to a single digit during 1990–96.

Government revenues from a diversified economy kept pace with new development needs. Revenues grew ahead of growth rates. Money-market growth rates were steady as the central bank developed incentives for the financial sector to develop new instruments. The growth was sufficient to enable some monetary interventions to be made through the market, as well as letting these new markets reveal market rates. Foreign direct investments started to flow, especially after 1986. Next to China, Indonesia attracted the most capital inflows.

Exchange and interest rates

Exchange rate policy was a crucial component of the policy mix in this case. From as early as 1967, managing the exchange rate was critical for maintaining competitiveness as well as, through a high interest rate policy, attracting inflow of capital. Part of the reason for exchange rate instability was the inclination of producers and individuals alike to take capital out and deposit it in foreign currency whenever there were hints of uncertainty. This was facilitated by

Table 6.5   Exchange rates and interest rates (annual averages)

| | 5-year average | | | Annual average | | | | | | | |
	1976–80	1981–85	1986–90	1991	1992	1993	1994	1995	1996	1997	1998
Exchange rate (mkt)	542	906	1744	1992	2062	2110	2200	2308	2383	4650	7,400
Interest Rates (%)											
Money market rate	10.96	15.13	13.81	14.91	11.99	8.66	9.74	13.64	13.96	27.82	75.32
Deposit rate	7.80	10.40	17.21	23.32	19.60	14.55	12.53	16.72	17.26	20.01	43.01
Lending rate	–	–	21.51	25.53	24.03	20.59	17.68	18.85	19.22	21.82	34.12

Note: Exchange rate: (Market rate) = rupiah per US dollar.

Source: IMF, *International Financial Statistics* (various issues).

pretty open capital and current accounts, as well as two specific actions: to let the firms borrow directly from overseas and for loans to be opened in foreign currencies *within* the country. It was as if the central bank was encouraging people to switch to and fro into foreign currencies, thus undermining the confidence in the currency of the country. The exchange rate which, under the peg to the US dollar, was fixed at Rp 415, slowly depreciated to the 1996 rate of Rp 2383. At the height of the political crisis in May–June 1998, the rupiah reached a low of 17 000 per dollar. By the start of 1999, it had recovered to around 7500 per dollar. This rapid decline was due to the need to realign the economy to gain competitiveness several times over. It can be seen that the rate of depreciation was the highest during 1981–90. The rate of decline slowed considerably in the first seven years of the 1990s.

Interest rates were maintained at very high levels throughout the period in double digits. With interest rate liberalization in 1993, the spread between the deposit and lending rate narrowed to about 3 per cent in subsequent years before the crisis, when it widened by 9 per cent. The spread was very high during the rest of the period. The lending rate was close to 20 per cent while the deposit rates were below the lending rates by a margin of about 6–8 per cent during most of the time. The money-market rate, however, was closer to 10 per cent. This created incentives for the firm to borrow at the short end of the market, as the difference between the short and long rates was very large, as can be seen from Table 6.5.

Financial development
Indonesia put in place substantial financial liberalization. This had the intended effects on the macroeconomy. In addition, it created a liquid and deeper financial sector. The statistics on this aspect are given in Table 6.6.

Money-market depth measured as a ratio of broad money to GDP increased steadily, showing the effect of greater depth in the market. Starting at 0.15 (16.7%) of GDP, this ratio improved to 0.53 by 1997. There was considerable improvement in this measure for a country at this level of development. Most money markets in the developed countries have a depth of about 1.00, and the more financially developed Malaysia has reached a ratio of 0.910. Claims on private sectors are measured by the FIR (total) ratio. This ratio was low at the starting-point and over the years. The FIR on the public sector did not grow rapidly, as indicated by the steady growth rate of FIR (public), but the FIR on the private sector grew by about 40 per cent over 1976–85. The growth in this ratio was very high from 1986 to 1992: it grew in the period 1981–85 by threefold by the end of 1992. As discussed in an earlier section, this was a primary reason that led to the unravelling of confidence in 1997–98, at the time of political and financial crises.

Gross fixed capital formation improved over the years from the low 20.7 per cent during 1976–80 to the high of 36.1 per cent of GDP in 1996: this has

Table 6.6 Indicators of financial liberalization (% of GDP)

	5-year average			Annual								
	1976–80	1981–85	1986–90	1991	1992	1993	1994	1995	1996	1997	1998
Money depth (M2/GDP) (%)	16.7	19.9	33.7	43.7	45.8	43.4	45.3	49.0	52.5	51.1	n.a.
FIR (total)/GDP (%)	0.15	0.06	0.26	0.45	0.49	0.47	0.50	0.52	0.54	0.57	0.52
FIR (private)/GDP (%)	0.19	0.15	0.32	0.51	0.49	0.49	0.52	0.55	0.56	0.61	0.51
GFCF/GDP (%)	20.7	28.0	33.1	35.5	35.9	33.2	34.3	33.8	36.1	31.6	33.0
FDI/GDP (%)	3.0	3.0	5.0	11.80	13.00	12.8	12.14	22.1	27.7	16.8	–265.6

Notes:
FIR: Financial intermediation ratio – claims on public sector, claims on private sector, and foreign assets.
GFCF: Gross fixed capital formation.
FDI: Foreign direct investment.

Source: IMF, *International Financial Statistics*, various issues.

Table 6.7 Foreign capital flows, Indonesia (US$ million)

	5-year average			Annual							
	1976–80	1981–85	1986–90	1991	1992	1993	1994	1995	1996	1997	1998
Direct investment (net)	252.9	236.4	598.8	1482	1777	1648	1500	3745	5594	4499	–312
Portfolio investment (net)	41.8	137.0	–36.8	–12.0	–88.0	1805	3877	4100	5005	–2637	–2002
FDI	252.9	236.4	598.8	1482	1777	2004	2109	4346	6194	4677	–356

Source: IMF, International Financial Statistics.

169

fallen marginally during 1997–99. This was the nexus for growth. Most of this improvement was due to the financial liberalization that attracted capital into Indonesia as the economy diversified into manufacturing over 1978–96. The FDI as percentage of GDP also shows this massive dependence on foreign capital. Just as the Korean firms began to borrow from abroad after 1996 and thus built up too much debt in the corporations, so did Indonesia, although its government managed its side of the finances more carefully.

The statistics in Table 6.7 underscore the importance of external capital inflows as a result of the mid-1980s reforms. From an average of about US$250 million to US$600 million in the early years, foreign direct investment increased fivefold during 1991–94. Since then, it doubled again during the years before the crisis. The total flow in the 1991–97 period amounts to US$23 billion injection of capital, representing an average of 15 per cent of GDP. Next to China, this is the largest flow of foreign direct investment. Portfolio investment also increased, particularly after 1992 following the privatization of the stock exchange and capital-market reforms to permit foreign entry.

Tests of financial liberalization (Ariff, 1996, p. 335) showed that the openness indicator of the economy improved to 0.681 during this period. This suggests a level of financial liberalization equivalent to that of Thailand though not as high as Malaysia, with its openness indicator of 1.00. Thus the financial reforms strengthened the financial sector to manage the high-growth economy. Firms that were over-dependent on short-term and foreign currency loans at the time of worsening trade had the potential to destabilize the economy in ways unknown to the economic managers. That was the key reason for the collapse of the economy. The reader should recall that the bottom 20 per cent of population was receiving less than 9 per cent of GDP compared with the top 20, receiving closer to 50 per cent. When the currency-induced economic decline during August 1997 to April 1998 pushed a large segment of the population below the poverty line, it created the mob riots that brought about the political demise of a pro-reform regime on 20 May 1998. The questions asked are 'Is it the financial crisis that led to Indonesian economic decline?' or 'Is it bad incomes policy?'

4.   ASSESSMENT AND FUTURE PROSPECTS

The market had assessed the value of the Indonesian economy, burdened with too much short-term debt in the 1990s. The 1997 Asian financial crisis and the May 1998 political crisis had revealed the danger of short-term money financing long-term investments. Without credible wealth distribution, the danger of a fast slide into poverty was unanticipated by the ruling élites. Also revealed was the lack of implementation of prudential regulations, which led to far too many instances of misdemeanour in the financial dealings of large conglomerates, some of which simply abused their close relationship with the political power centres. This has set back many years of well-earned gains. In fact, the years 1998–2000 have become years of decline as the economy mends its ways under the IMF rescue plan and a weak coalition cabinet is unable to take decisive political decisions even after two years of riots.

The Indonesian economy has had persistent instability during its development stage. The authorities were able to maintain control by using exchange rate management. Fundamental reforms to improve factor productivity have not been undertaken and must now be implemented starting with improved standards of general educational achievement and vocational skills. This reform can only be secured in the long run, and action must start soon. This is the key to improving labour productivity, which in turn will ease the pressure for huge devaluation to redress loss of competitiveness. High labour productivity, which would help increase the labour share of a growing economy, along with capital inputs should alleviate the persistent problems of this economy. Finally, the central banking authorities must seize the new freedom they have won to engineer an efficient intermediation market by improving prudential regulations. Much of what will happen is uncertain, as the IMF moves are very slow in the face of political events moving fast in this vast country of islands spread over the vast Indian Ocean.

NOTES

1. In this respect, Indonesia has many things in common with Korea. Korea too had a large demand for capital, but it mobilized savings locally by establishing a balanced budget at a very early phase of its economic development. Next, it lowered input costs by controlling wages for a long period of time. Other policies pursued enabled Korea to overcome its capital inadequacy right up to the early 1990s, when massive short-term borrowing, coupled with a political crisis, led to the Korean won losing 75 per cent of its value.
2. Comments in the international press in 1999 suggest that private bank licences were granted without too much care for a country with very little banking expertise. This led to too many inefficient banks making imprudent loans without the careful oversight of an independent central bank.
3. The total debt of US$131 billion consisted of about 50 per cent medium- to long-term debt. Of the 50 per cent that was short-term debt, US$49 billion was borrowed from banks: of this, US$19.7 billion had a term of one year. The total debt was about two-thirds the GDP value! The external-origin loan and local short-term debt amounted to US$34.7 billion; short-term debt in 1997 would amount to about 32 per cent of GDP (Nasution, 1998).
4. Indonesia did not spend as much as did other similarly fast-developing countries. The initial step in this direction was taken as *sekolah pondok* (literally 'school in the hut') in the 1960s, but further steps have not been taken towards the levels of modernization found, for example, in Malaysia or Korea.
5. In Ariff's meeting with the officials of Bank Indonesia in September 1998, this phenomenon was very apparent. Everyone was aware of the epochal change that had been brought on the Bank. The restructuring of the bad loan banks was pursued professionally, unlike in the earlier period, when high officials were transferred for pushing through actions consistent with prudential regulations. If this new-found freedom is cherished and improved on, it would be the financial sector that would benefit.

7. Taiwan: export-led growth and limited financial-sector openness

1. BACKGROUND

The Republic of China, more widely known as Taiwan, is a unique success story of economic growth in East Asia. The land area of Taiwan is just under 100 000 sq. km, and so it is a small island nation. It is situated just outside mainland China, which made a unilateral declaration to the world in early 1980s that China intends one day to win the so-called renegade province of Taiwan back into the motherland. Included among the only four newly industrializing economies (NIEs) in Asia, Taiwan progressed from a largely agricultural base in the 1950s to become a centre of innovative technology basing its industrial strength not on big firms but on small to medium-sized enterprises. In the days after the Second World War, Taiwan could be described as a poor country with the burden of having to support a large influx of mainlanders who escaped to this island nation to build a new economy along with the native peoples. It built its development path squarely on manufacturing consumer goods in the early phase of its development, and then progressed to making industrial goods, which in the 1980s led to the addition of some original brand names such as ACER computers to its international brands. How it achieved such success as a small land with a middle-sized population base is a case worthy of attention.

Taiwan's industrialization model is also unique in that it disavowed the big-is-good approach of Japan's *keiretsu* firms and Korea's *chaebols*. The Southeast Asian economies latched on to the foreign direct investment route to development: Southeast Asian economies had anywhere from 3 to 28 per cent of GDP in the form of FDI. Taiwan chose the medium-sized flexible firms as the best model for development; such firms could bend with the changing economic winds, much as the famed bamboo plant, which is so well recognized in Chinese culture as a symbol of strength and longevity. Study of Taiwan therefore has considerable fascination because of this unique feature – its dependence on small to medium-sized enterprises as the basis of its industrial structure. Some commentators have suggested that small and medium-sized enterprises are more resilient, being able to retool and change product lines and niche markets quickly in the face of changing international markets for real goods.

Taiwan is also a fascinating economy to study as it escaped, at least up to 1998, the full frontal effects of the 1997–98 Asian financial crisis. An important reason for this is the control it retained on foreign exchange transactions while liberalizing. All the six other economies that suffered the worst effects of the crisis dismantled all foreign exchange controls to establish the full Article 8 current account opening, as well as capital accounts. This conservative approach to the management of exchange rate risk appears to hold an important lesson for others in view of the severe impact on the other fully open economies from the failure to rein in this dangerous risk, especially at a time of high capital investment using short-term capital.[1]

Taiwan's GDP of about US$291 billion for a population of 21.9 million converts to $13 300.00 per capita. The exchange rate was in the region of NT$25.164 to NT$27.509 to the US dollar during 1991–97, which declined to NT$33.18 by March 1999. This represents a decline of about 18 per cent in 1998/9 compared with the average over the 1991–97 period. Taiwan residents enjoy a moderately high standard of living as measured by the conventional statistics given in the chapters on other countries. The literacy rate is high, private-sector-led tertiary education is well regarded in East Asia and most of their brightest men and women go to the USA for higher education. The infra-structure in terms of energy production, potable water, health services and transportation is well developed, and all these improved markedly in the 1990s when Taiwan had accumulated enough resources to embark on major extension of infrastructure. As detailed statistics are not available in the international publications, as in the cases of other economies, we are not including any social statistics to support the assertion made about social development in this country. Suffice it to say that the country has graduated from one of the low-income economies to one of the high-income economies.

If one were to characterize the development experience of Taiwan with a broad brush, an apt description would be something like the following. The country went through three phases of economic restructuring to meet the economic challenges peculiar to specific world and national conditions at different periods during the last half-century. The 1950s saw experimentation with import substitution, a policy that even very large economies with captive markets could not make stick. By the end of that decade, and quickly too, the policy was jettisoned when the government adopted 19 fiscal and economic measures to escape from import substitution and usher in more openness, especially in the real sector. From then on to the present, the economy restruc-tured continually, adopting more and more policies relevant to the demands of the time. Pre-eminent place in the reforms was given to the real sector, partic-ularly external real-sector openness to facilitate the grand strategy of growth with trade. Thus financial liberalization received much less emphasis, especially if that meant full financial openness of the type pursued at that time by Malaysia and Singapore, for example.

This over-emphasis on the real sector is not entirely unexpected, since 47 per cent of all sales value and 67 per cent of all exports were made by small and medium-sized enterprises. Again to emphasize the point, these small and medium-sized firms were interlocked in a system of subcontracting for large jobs. In times of low international demand for goods, these firms could shed the subcontracting, and thus limit the damage to themselves. The subcontractors bore the brunt of sudden downsizing of demand, but the core firms were unaffected. For this reason, this strategy has been called 'guerrilla capitalism' in contrast to the large-firm-based *chaebols* in Korea. The private sector sorted itself out after each business cycle, and the government's role since 1986 has been to ensure that these firms are supported by relevant policies in place to engage in economic activities suitable for changing times.

The period 1960–73 saw export promotion as the mainstay of economic development efforts. With several others such as Korea and Malaysia adopting similar policies, Taiwan refined its export-promotion policy by upgrading to skill-intensive exports during 1973–86. The period 1986–98 is generally described as promotion of small to medium-sized enterprises to bring in growth. This has also been strategically described as 'industrial nomadism' to signify the fact that these firms are highly mobile, and good at making changes suited to the changing international trade environment. Let us not forget that Taiwan still has its sights set on a seat in the World Trade Organization (WTO) with which it is able to make inroads into world trade. Mainland China, having got Taiwan out of all other international bodies after the 1979 agreement with the USA, is keen to join the WTO, also for trade purposes.

2.   LIBERALIZATION

2.1   Phase 1: Import Substitution

The postwar years saw a popular economic theory that appeared to promise a virtuous circle of growth by putting unused labour and land to produce outputs. The capital needed was to be provided by deficit budgets, and the income effect on the economy from the now usefully employed resources would create continual demand and thus economic development. What was missing in the equation were the consequences of deficit budget in the form of inflation and also the need for competition, necessarily global, to produce the outputs at the lowest possible prices so that there were welfare-promoting economic activities. Nevertheless, in that era, with visible signs of unemployed masses in many countries, import substitution appeared a coherent policy to pursue. China, in a subtle way, and India and Pakistan adopted this strategy.

So did Taiwan. For almost a decade, a closed system of import substitution was favoured, and policies were put in place to ensure its success. An important reform, which prepared the country to adopt free-market policies in the next phase, was introduced during this period: the 'land to the plough' system was implemented in 1953. The state-run enterprises occupied a dominant position at the time of what is termed the Restoration in 1949. With the new policy, most of the state-run businesses were transferred to private-run enterprises. This latter policy led to the foundation of small and medium-sized enterprises, which became the backbone of Taiwan's economy in later years.

The futility of an import substitution policy for a small economy with under 12 million population was quite evident. Again, the forces unleashed by the private sector as a result of the creation of a large network of private firms militated against the pursuit of the import substitution policy, whereas in nearby Japan and Korea, the economies were more geared towards export as the engine of growth. Therefore the strategy was jettisoned in favour of the more visibly successful policy of export-led growth pursued by Korea, Hong Kong and Singapore, which were joined by Malaysia a few years later. Thus the damage to the productivity of the economy from import substitution – as had happened in India for instance – was averted. The Taiwan economy did not grow very much beyond the inflation that it kindled in that period.

2.2   Phase 2: 1960–73 – Export as Engine of Growth

A new policy was ushered in by reforming the real sector and then the fiscal sector, both of which were increasingly opened to international competition. The restrictions natural to import substitution were removed after 1959. The 1960 Investment Encouragement Regulation laid the foundation for the encouragement of private-sector-led growth. The capital market was established during this period, with the sale of government-owned company shares to the public introduced in the 1960s. These two reforms entrenched the private sector further as the engine of growth. It can be noted that this was happening long before the conception of popular capitalism that emerged in the 1970s with the call to governments in many parts of the world to abandon private-sector businesses.

The real sector, especially the external sector, was free to engage in activities thought profitable by the firms, and entry and financing restrictions placed on them were slowly removed. Fiscal policy had to be in line with the new policy. Deficit budgeting was abandoned in favour of a balanced budget. The government refrained from engaging in economic activities except where there were particular benefits for the small and medium-sized enterprises. Large steel plants, car-making plants, and so on were not favoured, while large government-owned raw material producers were favoured: Taiwan Plastic is an example. There were 19 new policies mentioned in the literature but no details are available as to exactly what these policies were. In the later years, more liberalization took place to open the real sector to compete in the international marketplace.

The result was quite evident within a few years. Output growth exceeded 10 per cent per annum in this period while inflation was kept in check much better than was possible right up to the 1970s. In the 1970s, increased energy prices introduced high inflation. The favourable consequence was that by 1996 Taiwan became the thirteenth largest trading nation in the world. Taiwan's total trade in 1997 was more than two times that of its GDP! In US dollar terms, the total trade was $245 billion. This is a phenomenal success of a strategy that had been introduced some 35 years earlier. Guerrilla capitalism by the flexible small and medium-sized firms appears to be able to succeed well, with very little foreign capital injection into the economy.

With data available from 1986, we estimated that one of the keys to this high-growth situation is the high rate of investment in the economy. Between 1986 and 1990, gross fixed capital formation averaged 21 per cent per annum, a rate that was far above that of any other country except Malaysia and Singapore at that time. The average in the 1990s went up slightly to 22.5 per cent. Since there was no lumpy capital required for large-scale slow-gestation investments in such activities as steel mills, shipbuilding, and so on, the seemingly modest investment rate in small and medium-sized companies producing industrial and consumer goods secured very high productivity gains for the economy as a whole. This was particularly aided by the very early start made at improving the educational and skill levels of the population by huge investments in schools, and scholarships to bright students to study in developed countries.

2.3   Phase 3: 1973–86 – Skill-Intensive Industries and Electronics

With the arrival of several imitators of export-led growth as a fashion among several players, even as far away as Nicaragua, Taiwan became less competitive in producing only consumer goods. So it moved up the ladder of skill content in its range of products. Production of goods and services requiring higher skills was encouraged, and firms producing low-skill outputs were encouraged to move out, especially to Southeast Asian countries, where labour and other resource costs were much lower. Ten major construction projects in heavy industries were started. The favoured ones included petrochemicals, iron and steel, the ship-repair industry, and industrial equipment. Some of the key industries that were still run by government were now transferred to the private sector: these included petrol stations, cigarette manufacturing, breweries and so on. The state-owned iron and steel and chemical companies were corporatized and their shares sold to the public. Liberalization and internationalization were the themes of the changes that occurred slowly in response to the changing circumstances of the economy in the 1980s.

Taiwan also encouraged firms (in a timely fashion) to move to the electronics industry. The result was higher wages for labour. Non-tradable assets soon rose in value, as they did in similarly high-growing economies such as Singapore. The general input cost increases made it imperative for firms to move further out into China as well, especially before 1989, the year of the Tiananmen Square massacre in Mainland China. The reforms and incentives put in place in the 1974–86 period helped firms to move up the skill ladder, and avoid losing to competition that was becoming keen with the entry of so many players in consumer goods industries. Of special interest is the entry of China in 1979, which, with its very cheap input resources, was a far greater threat to competition than any other economy in recent times.

2.4 Phase 4: 1986 – Small and Medium-sized Enterprise Promotion and Easing Barriers to Entry into the Financial Sector

The period just before 1986 saw several significant events that had far-reaching effects on East Asian economies. The authoritarian rule of Chiang Kai-shek and his son ended just before 1986. This political event is significant in that it ushered in greater openness in political debate and consensus-making. It encouraged the modernizing élites to put on the national agenda policies that are considered to be growth-promoting for a country with such a large economy built on internationalization and heavy dependence on trade as a means of securing prosperity. This led to the promotion of small and medium-sized enterprises as the backbone to support continuing on the path to further development. With per capita income greater than Korea, Taiwan was unable to secure membership of the OECD (see Chapter 3 on Korea), but managed to become associated with the OECD group and in 1999 was actively pursuing admission as an observer. This is considered important to further secure its pre-eminent position as a substantial trading country. After all, the OECD, which includes about 16 per cent of the world's population, accounts for 60 per cent of world output. Taiwan's association with this body will give it access to information in the first-world economies.

The next important development in this phase was the realization that the private industrial and financial sectors needed to play a more active role in an already industrialized economy. Therefore barriers to entry into the financial sector were slowly lifted, leading to the entry of more domestic but only limited international financial institutions. This policy of introducing competition into the erstwhile public-owned financial institutions led to more efficiency and better services overall. Though a plan was drawn up to privatize the state-owned enterprises, this was not promoted very actively. Instead, the promotion of private-sector growth and competition increasingly limited the dominance of the public-sector enterprises, and brought favourable results without actively selling off all the state firms. There are altogether about 150 such enterprises at the central, provincial and city levels. In 1998 these firms accounted for just under 15 per cent of the national output, slightly higher than the average for the Western European countries of 12 per cent of output. State enterprises account for about 20 per cent of gross capital. In the 1980s, state enterprises accounted for far greater output, but their role has since diminished with the entry of private-sector enterprises during the current phase of development. Taiwan has been reluctant to privatize all these firms, and has used the strategy of private-sector growth to stifle public-sector firms.

These changes were also forced by the economic effects of the Plaza Accord among the G7 countries, aimed at appreciating the yen and thus finding a more lasting solution to the perennial trade deficit problem of the USA. With the appreciation of the yen, the Taiwan dollar also appreciated by about 20 per cent, and its exports became less competitive. This led to substantial restructuring, when low-skill and labour-intensive industries were encouraged to relocate in China, Malaysia, Indonesia and so forth. This led to a general upgrading to the industrial base of the country.

The real sector has therefore gone through continual changes in response to the unfolding new economic environment to secure the trading position of the Taiwan economy. There was no doctrinal pursuit of economic policy. Rather, policy formulation was reacting to the demands of the marketplace to pursue the aim of securing growth through trade. Thus these changes were limited in other sectors such as the financial sector. The continual changes to fiscal, monetary and competition policies were such as to ensure that the trade sector was foremost in securing the growth prospects of the economy.

2.5 Monetary and Fiscal Management

Table 7.1 highlights some indicators computed with the available data for Taiwan. A substantial credit expansion occurred in order to meet a very high-growth economy, as can be seen in the money growth variables. The figures for M1 and M2 as a percentage of GDP suggest that these have grown steadily as indicators of the growth of the underlying economy. M1 grew during 1986–90 by 14 per cent per annum while M2 (credit creation) grew at 23 per cent per annum. M1 growth is slightly above the long-run growth rate at that time. Credit growth was high to accommodate the vast changes that were taking place in the second half of the 1980s to meet the demands of a restructuring economy to upgrade to higher-value-added activities. In the 1990s, both M1 and M2 grew less rapidly at 11.5 and 14.5 per cent per annum respectively.

As is evident from the statistics on inflation, it appears that price increases have been held down successfully, with very modest inflation. This result is consistent with the kind of monetary policy followed, whereby money growth tracked economic growth, therefore not creating inflationary pressures. Besides, the savings rate in the economy was also healthy, not warranting a dash for credit that would have resulted in higher interest and also higher inflation rates.

State revenues were growing at healthy rates of around 10 per cent. This had a very desirable effect on the government budget each year. In the 1990s, when most of the restructuring had been put in place, state budgets began to go into deficit, but not by much. The deficits were about 2 per cent, as may be seen by the negative figures from 1991 to 1994. The budget has been in balance since then. In the 1990s, with a general softening of demand for Taiwan goods in the international markets, there has been some decline in government revenues, particularly since 1994.

Other statistics shown in the table suggest a number of important features of the economy. The trade account is persistently in surplus even after the flow-through effect of the Asian crisis meant that Taiwan lost some amount of competitiveness. This helps to explain the often-highlighted statistics on this country's huge foreign exchange reserves. Obviously a continuing trade surplus has helped the country to build huge trade and foreign exchange reserves to support its prominent trading position, which was ranked as thirteenth in the world. It is also evident that the trade account has started to weaken since 1994. Export growth, which used to be in double digits, has weakened since 1997: press statistics show that export growth declined in 1998 to a mere 1.4 per cent. The weakening of the trade sector has been in the making for a few years, and is also related to the relative strength of the currency when most economies in the neighbourhood experienced weakening currencies. Export competitiveness has been somewhat affected by the strong currency, and after 1999 constitutes an area of concern for the future.

A few other features can be noted. Government consumption has declined from a high of 17 to 15 per cent in the 1990s. This is a reflection of both the pursuit of private-sector promotion and the policy of balanced budgets practised over many years. Capital formation has held steady at between 21 to 24 per cent. We noted earlier that with the pursuit of small and medium-sized enterprises as the backbone of economic activities, capital requirement for output generation (the investment capital ratio) has been small. This means that less capital is needed to produce a given output increase. Therefore, with a capital formation of about 23 per cent of GDP, this economy is far more productive than several others such as Malaysia and Singapore, which use as much as 35 per cent of GDP to generate the same level of economic growth. This is a phenomenon of

Table 7.1 Monetary aggregates, national income accounts and balance of payments (as % of GDP)

	1986–90	1991	1992	1993	1994	1995	1996	1997	1998
Monetary variables									
M1 (% of GDP)	45	45	46	48	49	46	46	46	42
M2 (% of GDP)	127	154	166	174	183	183	182	172	188
Inflation rate (annual)	6	4	5	3	4	4	–1	–1	–1
Fiscal and trade variables									
Revenue growth over year	10	–9	14	10	10	5	2	–8	–11
Budget deficit (% of GDP)	2	–2	–3	–3	–1	0	–1	–1	–2
National accounts									
Current account (% of GDP)	233	250	153	114	97	22	41	31	22
Trade surplus (% of GDP)	407	327	239	197	188	196	35	27	15
Private consumption (% of GDP)	51	55	56	57	59	60	60	60	61
Gov. consumption (% of GDP)	15	17	17	16	15	15	15	15	15
Gross fixed capital formation (% of GDP)	21	22	23	24	23	23	21	21	22

Note: M2 = M1 + quasi-money.

Source: IMF, *International Financial Statistics* (November 1996).

great importance for this economy, and explains why it has done very well compared with other East Asian countries.

2.6 Financial Deepening

The M2/GDP ratio is generally taken as an indicator of the monetary deepening of an economy. As is seen in the statistics in Table 7.2, monetary depth increased steadily in the 1990s from about 154 per cent of GDP to 182 per cent. In the 1980s, the corresponding figure was about 60 per cent lower than before – at 127 per cent of GDP. Similar results have been seen for fast-developing and liberalizing countries such as Korea and Malaysia. So it is not surprising to find similar statistics for this economy. This suggests a relatively good level of financial depth on the monetary side of the sector.

Table 7.2   Indicators of financial liberalization (% of GDP)

	1986–90	1991	1992	1993	1994	1995	1996	1997	1998
Money depth (M2/GDP)	127	154	166	174	183	183	182	186	191
FIR (total)/GDP	138	343	368	391	415	419	420	424	434
FIR (public)/GDP	50	114	105	106	110	110	112	110	108
FIR (private)/GDP	135	331	352	370	390	391	395	401	408
FDI ($ mn)	–	1271	879	917	1375	1559	1864	2248	–
GFCF/GDP	21	22	23	24	23	23	21	21	22

Notes:
M2 = M1 + quasi-money.
FIR = financial intermediation ratio – claims on public sector, claims on private sector, and foreign assets.
GFCF = gross fixed capital formation.
FDI = foreign direct investment.

Sources: IMF, *International Financial Statistics* (November 1996); World Bank (Balance of Payment Capital Account) – for FDI.

More interesting are the financial intermediation ratios (FIRs) for this economy. We have already noted the dominance of the private sector. Thus that dominance in the asset composition of the financial system is not surprising. The FIR for the private sector is about four times the size of the economy, while that of the public sector is just about the same (112 per cent). This is in marked contrast with the other countries in the study, where the prevalent role of the government is still seen. This again reinforces the pro-private-sector policies pursued during the second to the fourth phases of development described earlier. Finally, fixed capital formation as a percentage of GDP has been holding steady. Much has been said on this in the last paragraph.

Some comments on foreign capital flows can be made, even though consistent statistics are unavailable. Although the economy was increasingly being opened to the rest of the world, most of the liberalization has been aimed at the real sector. To a limited extent the financial sector, too, has been opened to the rest of the world. Foreign direct investment did not constitute any significant part of the equation right up to the 1980s. Indeed, the stock market crash in 1987 actually led the regulators to discourage short-term cash flows into the capital markets: these regulations still remain. For an economy with close to almost US$300 billion in GDP, foreign direct investments of slightly more than US$2 billion (year 1997) constitute less than 1 per cent of GDP. Thus Taiwan stands out as a country that did not latch on to FDI as a source of growth. Far from it; the relocation of industries to other countries required that Taiwan actually exports capital to them. In terms of GDP, Taiwan exported capital to other countries in the 1990s at about 0.5 per cent of its GDP. This slowed in 1998 to about US$900 million, compared with the 1996 figure of US$2248 million.

During the period 1986–90, the average portfolio flow into the economy was a negative US$785 million, largely determined by the aftermath of the 1987 stock market crash, when most people withdrew portfolio investments in Taiwan. In that year, the Taiwan market reached its peak, and with the withdrawal of foreign portfolio flows, the market crashed. It has not recovered to that dizzy height of the 1980s again. (A similar bubble built in Korea and led to a market crash in 1988: however, Korea put in strict controls thereafter, only to dismantle them for portfolio flow in 1996 as a prelude to its entry into the OECD group.) The portfolio flows in the 1990s recovered somewhat and averaged about US$500 million, with a peak in 1993 of US$1070 million. With the impending onset of the 1997–98 Asian financial crisis, there was a net withdrawal of US$730 million in portfolio flows in 1996; the figure for 1997 was US$1550 million and for 1998, it was US$533 million. Thus, the huge portfolio flows that went the way of Southeast Asian economies were not experienced by Taiwan.

Outward investments from Taiwan were US$865 million per year during 1986–90. This increased as the restructuring of the economy led to more Taiwan firms relocating in other neighbouring countries. Starting at about US$580 million in 1991, this increased to US$1570 million by 1996. After that, there was a sudden decline in outward flow, which can be explained as the result of the financial crisis in many neighbouring countries. All in all, Taiwan's dependence on other developed economies for capital was meagre, whereas it provided huge capital to neighbouring countries.

Table 7.3 gives some statistics on the financial-sector variables. These figures can be used to judge the stability of the financial sector arising from the introduction of more competition in the sector, as well as from the pursuit of stable monetary policies of the type that were absent in some volatile financial sectors such as those in Indonesia and Korea.

During the measurement period, the monetary growth rate has been kept low, just slightly above the rate of growth of the economy. In the pre-1991 periods, the year-on-year growth rates in M1 and M2 were much higher, at about twice the economic growth rates in the 1990s.

The reader may recall that the pre-1991 years were the period when the Taiwan economy was being sporadically but actively restructured to overcome the effect of entry of several neighbours adopting the export-led growth strategy that Taiwan had implemented as far back as 1959. This was also a period of relatively higher inflation rates. However, in the 1990s, with much of the restructuring completed, and with exports performing pretty well right up to 1996, monetary policy was much less aggressive. M1 grew by an average of 9.6 per cent; M2, therefore, credit creation, grew at 12.7 per cent.

In an earlier discussion, we noted the low inflation rates during the 1986–96 period. Monetary control of the economy ensured a stable inflation rate compared with the inflation in other East Asian economies. Thus the cost of money as measured by the base discount rate was relatively stable over these years. The average rate over 1986–90, during the period of intense restructuring to face the Plaza Accord effects, was slightly high, at 7.8 per cent. In the subsequent period the rate kept declining steadily. The average over 1991–97 was 4.8 per cent. Thus the cost of borrowing for business activities, that is the lending rate, must have been quite low by East Asian standards. Taking a premium of about 4 per cent over discount rate for the lending risk to the firms, the lending rate must have been around 9 per cent for borrowing by firms. This is a very reasonable rate.

In summary, it can be said that the real- and financial-sector liberalization in Taiwan has been designed to suit the overall strategy of growth through external trade using the guerrilla capitalism of small and medium-sized enterprises. Domestic policies pursued were those of continual restructuring to achieve the status of an industrializing economy by the start of the 1980s. Subsequent reforms were aimed at differentiating the product range offered by the Taiwan firms towards more skill- and technology-intensive contents. The kind of financial reforms undertaken were those that provided stability in price levels (inflation), cost of money and competitive financial intermediation for improving the savings rate.

Certainly, there was a distinct lack of full openness in the financial sector, which meant that openness of the type found in Malaysia or Indonesia to satisfy the IMF Article 8 provisions was not pursued in this economy. After the stock market crash in the second half of the 1980s, regulations were put in place to keep short-term hot money from the capital markets. Finally, the policy to attract foreign direct/portfolio investment as an important source of capital was

Table 7.3 Exchange rates and interest rates (annual average increases)

	5-year average		Annual average							
	1981–85	1986–90	1991	1992	1993	1994	1995	1996	1997	1998
M1	14	21	12	12	15	12	1	8	4	1
M2	23	19	19	19	15	14	8	8	1.4	15
Market exchange rate	40.1	29.1	25.8	25.4	26.6	26.2	27.3	27.5	27.5	34.2
Interest rates										
CB discount rate	–	7.8	6.3	5.6	5.5	5.5	5.5	5.5	5.0	5.13

Notes:
M2 = (M1 + quasi-money).
Central Bank (CB) discount rate (end of period).
Exchange rate: (official rate) = national currency per US$.

Source: IMF, *International Financial Statistics* (November 1996).

not favoured by Taiwan, since this economy appears to have higher capital productivity. Recall the earlier discussion on output growth at double digits, though Taiwan's investment rate was just about 23 per cent of GDP compared with other countries – China, Malaysia, Singapore, Korea, and so on – with double-digit growth rates but with capital usage at GDP rates close to or above 28 per cent. Overall, Taiwan's liberalization policies may be characterized as cautious pursuit of conservative policies suitable to serve the small and medium-sized enterprises as the efficient producers and to capture higher skills and technology level. This policy served export-led growth admirably well.

3. THE ASIAN FINANCIAL CRISIS

This section draws attention to a feature of the Taiwan economy which in our opinion helped it to avoid the serious consequences of the 1997–98 Asian financial crisis. At the outset, we must note that the exchange rate of the New Taiwan dollar currency changed substantially both before and after the Plaza Accord. The exchange rate before 1986 was on average 40.1 Taiwan dollars to one US dollar. The effect of the Accord was a substantial appreciation of the currency on the back of the appreciating Japanese yen, the target of the Accord. The appreciation over the 1986–90 period was a huge 26 per cent. In the period after 1990, the currency held almost all the 26 per cent gain right up to the end of 1994, then lost about 5 per cent of the gain by the end of 1997. Meanwhile, the Asian financial crisis, which began in July 1997, did not affect the currency right up to the end of 1998, when the exchange rate declined to 34.2 Taiwan dollars to one US dollar, which was less than what it was in 1997 at the height of the crisis. Thus it appears that the crisis of such magnitude that destabilized neighbouring economies did not affect Taiwan at all, and led to a decline in the exchange rate much later as the weakness of the Taiwan economy became apparent in late 1998. The interesting question is why this economy had almost no fallout from the crisis. A number of possible factors are examined here.

3.1 Exchange Rates

With exceptionally healthy foreign reserves, Taiwan was capable of defending its currency much better than the countries affected. Thus the first factor appears to be that the reserves built during the good years were well known to be large, and currency speculators perhaps knew that, as in the case of Hong Kong and Singapore on previous occasions, speculative attack on such a currency would not be to their advantage. Besides, there was not the full currency convertibil-ity of the type possible in Korea, Indonesia, Thailand and Malaysia. So, given the reserve strength and residual controls on the currency convertibility, Taiwan was not the target favoured by speculators. What happened during July–September 1997 were unprecedented speculative attacks on the currencies of *fully* open economies: this recurred in August 1998 in the case of Hong Kong as the Hong Kong dollar was also very open, as it was pegged to the US dollar. While the won, ringgit, baht and peso declined rapidly by losing values of as much as 35 per cent within three months in the face of speculative attacks, the New Taiwan dollar did not experience much change during the same period. Except for Korea, the other affected economies were not as large as the Taiwan economy, which was more interlocked with developed than developing economies. For example, even Indonesia's economy was only about half the size of the Taiwan economy.

3.2   Productive Investments

As the Indonesian economist Annuar Nasution expresses it, the land-based investments in his country were fuelled by first hush-hush deals with connected persons in the region (and not just among the connected in Indonesia), with short-term money flowing in to build huge long-gestation investments in holiday resorts, golf courses, telecommunication expansions, energy projects, water treatment plants, and so on. Property investment/development often offered the most appeal, as real estate afforded the lenders tangible loan collateral and so these projects were easier to finance. These funds pushed up the prices of real estate and company shares and, as the exchange rate risk was perceived to be low with central banks defending the currency, foreign direct and portfolio investment moved into these areas as well. This gave the real-estate and related construction sector a further boost. Thus subsequent growth became more dependent on domestic factors rather than just the export engine. This kind of investment did not take place in the Taiwan economy as it was largely influenced by the production decisions of the private sector: this is especially true since political openness started in the mid-1980s.

3.3   Regulatory Policies

The failure of some national governments to allow direct foreign access into the domestic market meant that firms were forced to fund any loan expansion from off-shore because at the rate of demand for capital, national savings were insufficient to fund growth. This was not the case in Taiwan. Based on small to medium-sized corporations using capital effectively, the economy was able to grow at double digits for quite some time, with about a 23 per cent investment rate. Thus there was no scramble for foreign borrowing by firms as was the case in many crisis-affected countries. In Korea, for example, the exposure to both domestic and foreign debt in the capital structure of the firms was so large that

Korean firms could not service the loans once the currency depreciated or if export growth declined significantly. In the case of Taiwan, this did not apply, as firms were not overexposed to debt capital.

3.4 Foreign Capital

A minor factor for Taiwan but a major factor for the crisis-affected countries is the very high level of exposure of crisis-prone countries to foreign capital. Portfolio flows into Taiwan peaked in the 1980s, during which time the arrival of huge portfolio flows led to the now very common effect of creating a bubble in the share market, followed by a drastic fall when such capital leaves the country. This happened in 1987, with a large and sudden outflow of capital leading to the collapse of the share market in that year. In following years, Taiwan did not allow such short-term capital into the share and bond markets in the 1990s because of that bad experience. This was not the case with the crisis-ridden countries. In each of these, one observes rather lax rules about foreign ownership in securities: Indonesia, Malaysia and Thailand permitted upwards of 49 per cent share ownership in the 1990s, which led to 1993–94 bubbles in all these countries. In Malaysia, share prices went up by 104 per cent in 1993 (of course, with the nominee or numbered accounting system, more than the permitted 49 per cent of foreign ownership could have happened). The crisis-ridden countries had severe exposure to portfolio capital, which was destabilizing the capital markets during the first half of the 1990s. The share markets had gone up to a very high level by 1994, waiting to be corrected as soon as there was any sign of currency instability. That happened in mid-1997 in these countries.

Next, foreign direct investment in Taiwan was also discouraged more than in any other countries. Similar to Korea until it joined the OECD in 1997, Taiwan did not want too much foreign ownership of firms, and they discouraged it. This was decidedly a saving factor. While the crisis-ridden countries had very high trade exposure to the developed countries, as did also Taiwan, Taiwan had no more than 1 per cent of GDP in foreign direct investments. Unlike Malaysia and Singapore, which have respectively 12 per cent and one third of GDP produced by foreign multinational firms, Taiwan had had negligible foreign direct investments, even though it had foreign technology-sharing agreements under royalty payments. This is a marked difference. The crisis-ridden countries had foreign investments amounting to anywhere from 3 to 26 per cent of GDP. Some of these countries, like Malaysia, also had high savings (36 per cent of GDP). But the unique thing about Taiwan was that the industrial strategy pursued was to build on the small to medium-sized firms with some large government-owned technology firms. The other countries built their economic growth on multinationals supplying a large capital, technology and market network. This policy is satisfactory for city-based economies such as Hong Kong and Singapore as points of outreach for the multinationals into the region, but entirely unsuitable for building larger, more integrated economies.

Thus, a combination of factors in Taiwan's case meant that it was not affected by the Asian financial crisis. The two critical factors appear to be its non-reliance on foreign short-term (and long-term) capital and its residual controls on currency convertibility. Other contributing factors were the low level of inflation, greater reserves, and the large size of its economy. The crisis appears to have had no significant effect on the stability of the economy. The following quote from the Premier of Taiwan appears therefore to be justified: 'from the end of June 1997 to the present time, comparing the combined rates of depreciation and stock price decline, we see that Taiwan has suffered the least damage among all countries in the region' (Vincent C. Siew, 29 May 1998).

4.   PROSPECTS FOR THE FUTURE

Taiwan was lucky in that it had already experienced the problem of rising labour costs some time before. The government had already introduced a 'Go South' investment programme to send labour-intensive production to lower-cost economies. So where labour costs were important, Taiwanese companies moved offshore, and in the process their exports became dominated by capital and technological products. This decision, primarily arising as a response to the effect of the Plaza Accord, is a significant continuing effect that will determine the future of Taiwan's economy in the near term. Investment abroad had doubled in the period 1994–98 compared with the figure a few years earlier. Capital outflow in 1997 was 68 per cent of GDP compared with the 1991 figure of 42 per cent. Moreover, as many Taiwanese businesses had already diversified their production to Mainland China, they were somewhat more protected against the yuan depreciation than were Thai and Indonesian exporters. Of course some of their investment had been in these two markets, too. In 1997, Taiwan was seemingly the largest Asian foreign investor in Thailand. This investment, however, as often had an important domestic, as well as export, focus. It also meant that Taiwan's own trade was much more focused on America and Japan than on Southeast Asia.

Taiwan's economic structure continues to afford some additional protection. As small and medium-sized enterprises account for much of the economic activity, Taiwanese business is perhaps more flexible in responding to changing economic conditions. While being small is often considered a disadvantage, these companies are well networked and so gain the critical mass needed to compete with much larger overseas competitors, the so-called nomadic firms versus the godzillas. The large number of small firms in similar areas also ensures a high level of competition and hence efficiency gains of the type unseen in other neighbouring economies. Taiwan firms also make considerable use of subcontractors and outsourcing components rather than produce everything within their firms. This gives them more flexibility when downsizing is required. They are often suppliers to third parties under a range of other brands so they don't have to market the products themselves, affording yet further savings and flexibility. For example, they dominate as subcontractors for Japanese car parts.

Unlike the crony capitalism that supported large, but troubled, conglomerates in its neighbourhood, Taiwan's small businesses were allowed to fail. Businesses close daily but new ones start up as well, ensuring only the most competitive ones survive. Likewise, unlike many neighbours, Taiwan's legal system allows for speedy bankruptcy and liquidation. As *The Economist* (3 January 1998) suggests, 'this encourages investors, lenders, workers and managers to act prudently, because they know that the consequences of bad decisions may be fatal for the firm'. So there were strong incentives not to over-borrow. Thus during a healthy share market period in 1997, the corporate sector had taken advantage of the high share prices to raise equity capital (some US$15.3 billion in that year) and so reduce bank debt.

The country, too, had acted prudently given its international recognition problem arising from the accord of China with the USA. After some years of current account surpluses, it had accumulated the third largest pool of foreign exchange reserves in the world, some US$83.5 billion in 1997. The above factors meant that Taiwan did not experience the same current account problems as its neighbours.

However, there are some signs of impending problems for the economy from both the external sector and the financial sector. Export growth has slowed to about 2 per cent. Compare this with the 68 per cent growth in one year! There has been a softening in demand for exports. Only a part of this is due to the troubles of the crisis-ridden economies in the neighbourhood. The growth in exports to East Asian countries, including China, has declined dramatically. In 1998, Mainland China's export growth also declined to a mere 4 per cent over the previous year. Happily, though, the Taiwan currency depreciated in 1999 by 10 per cent, which is expected to work through the economy to help it regain its markets.

Another problem is the growing non-performing loans. While these stood at 3.8 per cent at the end of 1997, according to the Economist Intelligence Unit (2nd quarter, 1998, p. 24), they had risen to 4.2 in March 1998. Furthermore, in October 1998, Moody's Investor Services placed Taiwan banks under review due to concerns about deteriorating loan quality. Standard & Poor's retain their ratings level for Taiwan, but non-performing loans were predicted to reach 8

The early reformers

per cent in 1999. The US investment bank, Lehman, as shown in Table 7.4, thought that they already had.

Table 7.4   Non-performing loans to total loans (% of outstanding loans)

Thailand	48
Malaysia	33
Indonesia	61
South Korea	33
Philippines	17
Singapore	13
Hong Kong	10
Taiwan	8
Japan	13

Source: Rowley (1998).

These problems are continuing. In November 1998, for example, the Central Deposit Insurance Corporation had to appoint a manager to the Taichung Business Bank following its illegal lending to a troubled corporate affiliate, Tai Yu Products, and the collapse of the Kuang San Construction Company. Also in November, the government requested that the banks establish a US$8.7 million stabilization fund to be used to support failing companies. These measures were not sufficient to retain the public's full confidence: in February 1999, the Minister of Finance had to give reassurances over the financial strength of the local business bank, Bank of Pan Shin, following a run by depositors.

The regulatory system seems much in need of modernization. As one writer complained, foreign banks 'are discouraged from introducing new financial products by seemingly insurmountable bureaucratic hurdles'. If it is not approved, you can't do it, seems to be the message in Taiwan finance. Another indication, this time in 1996, was that the government felt it constituted a major financial liberalization when the Ministry of Finance (MOF) finally conceded that banks would be permitted to decide where they should place their automated teller machines (ATMs) rather than first obtain MOF approval. An overall impression is that the regulatory emphasis is more on detail than outcomes. As Shirazi (1998, p. 2) concluded, 'weak supervision of the financial sector, inadequate corporate governance and the general lack of transparency allowed the problems to grow and fester for much longer than was prudent'. Thus banking and in general financial liberalization ought to occupy the attention of the government in the near term.

In conclusion, however, the overall assessment of Taiwan appears to be more positive than negative. The critical thread appears to be that the strong private-sector anchor on the small and medium-sized enterprises to pursue export-led growth acts as the guide for all other policy considerations. As in the past, reforms and liberalization are intricately interwoven, with an eye on the resilience of the economy to respond to the reforms to make incremental improvements in performance. Thus the future will see more aggressive pursuit of liberalization in the financial sector to make it more private-sector-driven. The restructuring appears to be a continuous attempt to respond to new challenges, and that means there will be more such restructuring to revive the economy. With the neighbouring crisis-ridden countries coming out of the crisis in 1999, Taiwan has more freedom to pursue the aggressive reforms very much in demand in the new economic environment.

NOTE

1. It has been reported in World Bank pronouncements in the financial press that the cost of the crisis in Korea, Indonesia, the Philippines and Thailand will cost about 25 per cent of the GDP of these countries. It will be noted that those countries that had little foreign capital dependence (India, Pakistan), and/or had residual controls on current accounts, escaped any severe deterioration in the value of currencies. Taiwan is among this latter group of countries, and hence it holds some important lessons.

8. Thailand: quite open external sector but poorly managed financial sector

1. BACKGROUND

A story is told that Thailand came under the control of Great Britain in 1855 though Thailand's king still ruled the country. Like other places under Britain in the region at that time, Thailand is said to have adopted no control over trade and capital movements. This reflects the historical reality that this country did not vacillate, like others in this book, between episodes of extreme control and relative opennness to the rest of the world. Bangkok provided the easy passage to all sorts of traders in that tradition of openness which is still preserved. In the old order, Thailand's currency was linked to the pound sterling – later to be switched to the US dollar – while exports of rice were free of all duties and imports were subject to a mere 3 per cent duty. Some fiscal autonomy and increase in import duties was allowed in 1926 but full fiscal independence was only achieved in 1947. From the late 1930s until 1957, Thailand pursued a policy of increased protective tariffs and import substitution, but it never came near to the kind of closure found in India.

This attitude changed rapidly after the Korean War, when Thailand again opened up its economy. During the years 1957 to 1973, Thailand pursued internal- and external-sector open policies to attract increased foreign and domestic investment. Many concessions such as abolishing import duties, tax concessions, free movement of capital-cum-remittances and 100 per cent foreign ownership of business, which is one of the earliest instances of this kind, were later withdrawn in the mid-1960s. These policies helped this country to emerge as one of the rapidly growing economies in the region. Several other countries emulated the policy choices of Thailand, especially in the 1970s.

The second oil crisis resulted in recession for many countries, including all the Southeast Asian countries during some periods of the stagflation of the first half of the 1980s. Thailand was no exception, and was badly hit by this recession. During the first couple of years, inflation turned out to be the major concern as it jumped to double digits while the trade deficit breached the point of 10 per cent of GDP. To overcome recessionary pressures, Thailand accelerated its reform process and concentrated on export promotion, which helped the economy to recover as early as 1986. Since then, Thailand has enjoyed a remarkable growth, surpassed only by Korea in the region. But banking fragility in this country went on unnoticed until the country was hit in July 1997 by the worst crisis in its history: this crisis will go into the history books as the 1997 baht crisis.

This chapter covers details of financial liberalization in a country that has had a very steady liberalization process. In Section 2 we will discuss Thailand's economic and financial structure. Section 3 will provide the details of liberalization measures adopted by Thailand during the last 30 years. Finally, we assess the liberalization process in Section 4.

2. ECONOMIC AND FINANCIAL STRUCTURE

Thailand is a moderate-sized country with a population of 60 million occupying a land area of 513 000 sq. km, which is about 35 per cent larger than Malaysia. The Thai economy has experienced a remarkable growth trend during the last three decades. Hit by the two oil shocks, first in 1973 and the second time in 1978–79, the country managed to recover sooner than many other developing countries. One key feature of the quick recovery was the policy pursued towards macroeconomic stabilization. As a result, the country's main sectors of the economy, such as investment, economic activities and prices, stabilized very rapidly.

In the 1960s, per capita GDP in Thailand was slightly higher than in many other countries in South Asia and Latin America. Over a subsequent period of 30 years, per capita income relative to most developing countries has been about 10 times larger. That should be welcomed as a big achievement, a sign of development, despite the fact that income inequality was more widespread in general as well as between regions of the country.[1] One important aspect of policies implemented was diversification of the economic structure through a comprehensive reform programme. The 1980s saw a transformation from an agricultural economy towards an industrial economy in much the same way as Malaysia was changing from a rural to an industrial focus. That altered the then economic structure, and led to sustained high growth after the restructuring. This diversification reduced the contribution of agriculture from 25 per cent to 15 per cent by the 1980s. At the same time, manufacturing increased from 25 per cent of GDP to 35 per cent.

The restructuring was aimed at creating capacity for exports, and led to a boost to exports, contributing about one third of the country's GDP. The rapid growth in exports is also due to the dynamism of the less hamstrung Thai private sector, which agrees with what was said at the beginning of the chapter about the traditional approach of this country to its relations with the rest of the world. This industrial transformation, leading to export growth, forced the authorities to restructure the financial sector to augment financial efficiency. They developed new money and capital markets as well as removing capital and currency controls, though the currency's basket peg was to become the Achilles' heel a decade later, ushering in the baht crisis. These measures were needed at the early stage of industrial policy implementation to mobilize domestic funds as well as to attract foreign capital flows. However, financial reforms had been taken gradually, and some aspects of those reforms were inadequate; indeed, the omission of prudential regulation of the banking-cum-finance companies has led to a loss of growth momentum since 1997.

The economy of Thailand emerged as one of the strongest Southeast Asian economies in the region, and in the 1990s Thailand was tipped to become the fifth Asian tiger. In 1990–95, the average growth rate was the highest. Table 8.1 highlights basic economic, financial and social indicators of the economy. The average annual growth in GDP was 7 per cent in the 1970s, about 8 per cent in the 1980s and, on average, above 8 per cent in the 1990s until the baht crisis of 1997 led to massive currency overshooting and thence to a decline in growth.[2] The industrial sector was certainly the leading sector in this growth process; on average it grew by more than 15 per cent during the period of the early 1960s to the late 1980s.

Inflation has been moderate during most of this time, falling within single digits since 1981 while broad money (M2) showed a growth rate of less than 20 per cent per annum. Rapid economic growth and structural changes were accompanied by an increasing trend in the gross national investment and national savings, which rose to levels between 37 per cent and 41 per cent respectively during the first six years of the 1990s. These indicators also show that the economy had been successfully converted into a relatively more open economy in the Thai tradition. The growth in the export sector was remarkable, growing by an average of 19 per cent while imports grew by about 17 per cent during 1991–95. On its internal balance, the country experienced the same upward trend when the fiscal balance began to recover in the 1990s to positive levels from earlier deficits. The current account balance, however, deteriorated during the same period: the deficit was 8 per cent of GDP.

On social indicators, Thailand's record is very impressive. The unemployment rate remained under 2 per cent until 1996. Success in controlling population growth meant that growth was brought down to around 1 per cent. A reasonable proportion of about 22 per cent of total expenditure found its way into education while 8 per cent was spent on health: these are high levels for the region except in comparison with Malaysia.

This impressive performance reversed in just a few weeks after the 1997 baht crisis, when Thailand experienced the first recession in the previous two decades. The GDP growth shrank first to –0.40 per cent in 1997 and then to –7.8 per cent in 1998. The fiscal balance turned negative and the unemployment

Table 8.1 Basic economic and social indicators of development in Thailand

Indicators	1971–80	1981–90	1991–93	1994	1995	1996	1997	1998[a]
National accounts								
GDP growth (%)	6.8	7.9	8.1	8.8	8.8	5.5	-0.40	-7.80
Per capita GDP (US$)	403	953	1944	2442	2782	3036	2800	2450
Private consumption/GDP	0.7	0.6	0.5	0.543	0.538	0.541	0.549	0.590
Gov. consumption/GDP	0.1	0.1	0.1	0.098	0.095	0.096	0.103	0.120
Financial indicators								
Gross domestic savings (% of GDP)	21.5	24.9	35.7	34.7	33.6	33.7	35.6	35.9
Gross fixed capital formation (% of GDP)	24.2	29.8	40.3	41.0	42.8	42.5	39.5	34.5
Inflation	10.0	4.4	4.4	5.2	5.7	5.9	8.0	9.0
M2/GDP	35.1	55.8	75.6	78.7	79.5	79.7	89.9	92.0
Fiscal balance (% of GDP)	-3.3	-2.8	3.2	2.7	3.0	0.9	-0.6	-2.0
Current account balance (% of GDP)	-3.5	-4.2	-6.1	-5.4	-7.9	-7.9	-2.1	3.5
Trade balance/GDP	-3.9	-3.9	-4.4	-2.6	-4.8	-5.4	-5.1	-5.0
Discount rate	5.5	10.7	10.3	9.5	10.5	10.5	12.5	n.a.
Debt service ratio (% of exports)	–	–	16.1	11.3	11.4	12.2	-0.6	-2.0
Social indicators								
IMF classification	Middle	Lower-middle	Lower-middle	Middle	Middle	Upper-middle	Upper-middle	Middle
Unemployment rate (%)	–	2.87	1.87	1.30	1.10	2.00	3.7	7.6
Expenditure on education (% of exp.)	20.20	17.99	20.63	21.4	22.00	22.0	22.0	n.a.
Expenditure on health (% of exp.)	4.02	5.70	7.76	7.80	7.93	8.00	8.0	n.a.
Population growth	2.54	1.80	1.28	1.21	1.18	1.01	1.00	n.a.

Note: [a] A mid-1999 estimate of GDP growth for 1999 is 1.0%.

Sources: IMF, *International Financial Statistics*, various issues; *Asian Development Outlook, 1998, 1999; Government Finance Statistics Yearbook, 1985–1996*.

rate rose to 7.6 per cent in the same year. Although the recovery has started through internal and external policies, the country may take several years to reach to the pre-crisis growth pattern.

3.   LIBERALIZATION

Although reforms dated back to the 1970s, major economic and financial-sector liberalization measures were initiated only in 1989. Interest rate reforms, which had been delayed in Thailand for the longest time among the ASEAN countries, were introduced and the financial sector was reorganized during this period. A key factor in the initiation of reforms was the need to mobilize resources for use by the industrial sector to capture continued economic growth. There was also a high level of commitment to reforms. The authorities committed themselves to reform to remove exchange controls, but they chose to do so under a basket peg with a heavy reliance on the US dollar. Their commitments to the GATT and later to the WTO to open up the trade sector by reducing trade barriers were faithfully fulfilled.

3.1   Economic Liberalization

Economic reforms were initiated as early as the 1960s. However, as a result of the first oil shock, major reforms were made only after 1973 to expand public- and private-sector investment. These policies helped to accelerate growth and investment but also led to public-sector deficits. At the same time, current account deficits rose to 7 per cent of GDP in the early 1980s while external indebtedness increased from 15 per cent of GDP in the 1970s to 35 per cent during the same period: this was not as bad as the indebtedness of Thailand's neighbour, Malaysia, nor of that of Pakistan. The situation further deteriorated after the second oil shock in 1978–79 and with the onset of world recession.

After the first oil shock, Thailand embarked on extensive reforms conducive to greater industrialization and export expansion. This required major changes and restructuring in various sectors of the economy. Besides the financial-sector reforms, which are the focus of this study, the government undertook some bold measures to restructure its fiscal sector and the trade sector, implementing policies to reform the pricing structure in the industrial sector. We devote the discussion in the rest of this section to these items only, and then move to the financial-sector reforms.

Fiscal-sector reforms

The mechanism under which the fiscal sector operates in Thailand involves four agencies, namely, the Ministry of Finance (MOF), the National Economic

Table 8.2 Monetary aggregates, national income accounts and balance of payments (% of GDP)

	5-year average			Annual							
	1976–80	1981–85	1986–90	1991	1992	1993	1994	1995	1996	1997	1998
M1	11.2	8.9	9.4	8.8	8.8	9.4	9.6	9.3	8.9	8.9	9.2
M2	37.2	48.9	64.3	72.7	74.9	79.2	78.7	79.5	79.7	89.9	92.0
Trade deficit	-4.4	-4.8	-3.7	-6.0	-3.8	-3.5	-2.6	-4.8	-5.4	-5.1	-5.0
Budget deficit	-4.0	-4.5	1.1	4.7	2.8	2.1	2.7	3.0	0.9	-0.6	-2.0
Current account deficit	-5.7	-5.1	-3.7	-7.6	-5.7	-5.1	-5.4	-7.9	-7.9	-2.1	3.5
Private consumption	66.0	63.9	57.4	54.9	54.9	55.0	55.1	54.7	54.9	54.9	59.0
Gov. consumption	11.5	13.1	10.3	9.3	10.0	10.0	9.7	9.7	9.3	10.3	12.0
GFCF	25.8	27.8	33.0	41.4	39.4	40.2	41.0	42.8	42.5	39.5	34.5
Government expenditure	17.1	19.8	15.6	14.4	15.0	16.0	16.4	15.8	17.8	18.1	18.3

Notes:
M2 = (M1 + quasi-money).
GFCF: Gross fixed capital formation.

Source: IMF, *International Financial Statistics*, various issues.

and Social Development Board (NESDB), the Bank of Thailand and the Budget Bureau. The agencies highlight the priority areas, outline public investment projects, estimate the costs and identify possible funding sources. The Fiscal Policy Office within the Ministry of Finance has the authority to formulate, recommend and oversee the implementation of fiscal and financial policy for the government. This structure has been recognized in some of the literature as a good model of policy coordination.[3] However, this is bureaucratic planning without a central planner to guide growth.

An important basis for fiscal management was laid down in the 1959 budgetary law, which specified that planned deficits should not exceed 20 per cent of planned expenditure. The law was later amended in 1973 to include 8 per cent of the principle repayment of the public debt still maintaining the 20 per cent restriction. This law forced governments to restrict spending. In 1960, the government put a restriction on foreign borrowing by imposing a ceiling on the debt–service ratio at 5 per cent: this restriction was not in place in the fast-track period of the 1990s that led to the crisis in 1997. At the same time, the authorities specified that the foreign debt service could not be more than 13 per cent of planned revenues. There has been a gradual revision of the debt–service ratio. As of 1996, it was supposed to be maintained at 9 per cent of planned revenues. Importantly, there were no binding restrictions on the private sector.

In general, fiscal policy was expansionary over the period 1975–80 while the reverse, a contractionary policy, was adopted during 1980–90. In the 1990s, the focus was again on fiscal expansion. But at the same time, the authorities attempted to reduce fiscal deficits arising from curtailing public spending. The reform policies in the 1990s focused on social-sector development including education, which resulted in an increase in the average share of the social service sector of 35.5 per cent.

Table 8.2 shows that the country experienced a fiscal deficit during 1970–87 and a surplus thereafter. Domestic borrowing was used as the main source of financing the deficits during this period, especially through commercial banks in order to control the inflationary effect of central bank borrowing. This worked well and since 1981 (and until the Asian crisis) inflation remained in single digits. Later on, in the 1990s, the authorities realized that the surplus was sustainable and hence retired some of the public and foreign debt and implemented measures of tax reduction. However, the currency crisis in 1997 forced the government to go for extensive foreign borrowing as part of the IMF restructuring plan.

Industrial-sector policies
The most important factor in this country's high economic growth was the transformation from an agricultural base to an industrial economy. Besides a heavy emphasis on outward-oriented and export promotion policies, the Board

of Investment (BOI) was established in 1960 with the purpose of implementing new investment actions. The BOI provided certain incentives to accelerate investment, including tax holidays and import duty exemptions for particular firms or industries. In 1962, the government implemented the Promotion of Industrial Investment Act, which gave more independence and power to the BOI. During the 1980s, focus towards export promotion linked external-sector policies to foreign exchange policies, which made the role of the BOI even more important in policy planning.

Before the mid-1950s, Thailand had a very restrictive trade regime, especially in controlling rice exports. This policy was liberalized in the late 1950s by unifying the exchange rate and removing the government's monopoly over rice exports. One important aspect of external-sector policy was the relaxation in foreign exchange controls. The first set of measures was taken in 1990, much later than many neighbouring countries, when commercial banks were also allowed to engage in foreign exchange transactions without prior approval of the BOT. In 1991, controls were further relaxed by allowing residents to open foreign currency accounts and foreigners to open Thai baht accounts. In 1994, the authorities laid the foundation for developing Bangkok as the regional financial centre for Indochina.

3.2 Financial-sector Reforms

The financial-sector reforms in Thailand were very gradual, initiated in the early 1970s and continued until the 1990s. However, the rapid growth of the economy in the 1980s necessitated upgrading its existing financial infrastructure. Table 8.3 summarizes the major financial-sector reforms in Thailand in chronological order. This subsection is devoted to a discussion of the details of the reform initiatives taken by the authorities to revamp its financial sector.

Table 8.3   Major financial-sector reforms, 1979–96

Date of reforms	Liberalization policy implemented
1979	Amendment of the first Commercial Banking Act 1962 to break the family-controlled shareholding structure in most Thai banks and to have more private participation. Under this amendment, no single shareholder can own more than 0.5% shares.
	Repurchase market established as a first step to develop money market in Thailand.
1980	The 15% limit relaxed. Under new rules, interest rate charged by financial institutions would be set by the Minister of Finance on the advice of the BOT.
1984	Amendment to the Securities Exchange of Thailand (BET) Act 1974. Thai baht is pegged to a basket of currencies.

Table 8.3   continued

Date of reforms	Liberalization policy implemented
	BOT imposed minimum margin loan requirement 25% for finance companies.
1985	BOT introduced Bangkok Interbank Offered Rate (BIBOR) as a reference for the pricing of floating-rate loans.
	Financial Institution Development Fund (FIDF) established within BOT to help the financial institution in times of tight liquidity.
1987	Deregulation of commercial banks' (CBs') and finance companies' (FCs') businesses.
1989	Ceiling of interest rate on time deposit with more than one-year maturity lifted.
	Relaxation of foreign exchange controls allowing the transfer of capital for dividend, interest and principle payment for foreign loans.
1990	Interest rate ceiling on time deposit with one-year maturity or less abolished.
	All current account transactions liberalized and restrictions on capital movement reduced.
1991	Liberalization of foreign exchange controls, including: – more liberal outward transfer of funds – Thai individuals and residents were allowed to open foreign currency accounts.
	The stock market introduced Automated System for the Stock Exchange of Thailand (ASSET), a fully computerized trading system.
	Minimum asset requirement for foreign banks increased from B 5 million to B 125 million.
1992	Ceiling on interest rate on savings deposit removed.
	Branch opening requirement for commercial banks relaxed to hold government bonds as a proportion of total deposit from 8% to 7%.
	Commercial banks' and finance companies' liberalization allowing them to operate as: – selling agents for debt instrument of government and state enterprises. – information agents, sponsoring financial advisory and custodial services.
	Foreign exchange controls further liberalized for exporters, financial institutions, and resident and non-resident individuals.
	Securities and Exchange Act enacted.
	Interest rate ceiling removed on commercial bank loans and finance and credit foncier companies' loans.
	Minimum paid-up capital for finance companies increased from B 60 million to B 100 million by July 1993 and B 150 million by July 1994.
	Minimum paid-up capital for credit foncier companies increased from B 30 million to B 50 million by July 1993, B 75 million by July 1994, and B 100 million by July 1995.

Date of reforms	Liberalization policy implemented
	CBs and FCs were allowed to issue NCD (negotiable certificates of deposits) with minimum of 3 months and a maximum of 3-year maturity with a face value of not less than B 0.5 million.
1993	BIS standard for CBs adopted. CBs were allowed to maintain 7% of capital to risk–asset ratio. Foreign bank branches were required to maintain 6% of tier 1 capital to risk–asset ratio.
	46 CBs were allowed to operate international banking business known as BIBF or IBF.
	The first credit-rating agency, The Thai Rating and Information Service (TRIS), established.
	Export–Import Bank of Thailand (EXIM) Act promulgated to be effective from 7 September 1993 and established in 1994.
	CBs capital to risk asset ratio increased to no less than 7.5%, with the first-tier capital fund to risk–asset rate to no less than 5% by 1 April 1994 (8% and 5.5%, respectively by 1 January 1995). Foreign Bank branches' capital fund to risk–asset ratio increased to no less than 6.5% by I April 1994 and 6.75% by 1 January 1995.
	Adoption of BIS standard for FCs whereby FCs were required to maintain 7% of capital–risk asset ratio (5% first tier capital–risk asset ratio), effective 1 July 1995.
	Setting up of Bond Dealers' Club (BDC) to function as a secondary market for debt instruments.
1995	BOT issued short-term bond worth B 10 billion on weekly basis with 1 month's, 3 months' and 6 months' maturity
1996	BOT issued long-term bonds with 1 and 2 years' maturity. Government Savings Bank and Financial Institutions Development Fund to participate in the auction.
	FCs and FRCSs required to maintain liquidity reserves at the BOT at 7% of non-resident baht borrowing or deposit with maturity of less than one year, including the issuance of P/N, B/E, or NCDs.
	CBs, FCs, FRCSs and BIBFs required to have cash reserves of 7% of total short-term borrowing and deposits from abroad.
	Electronic Clearing System (ECS) starts operation.
	Financial Institutions Development Fund bonds (FIDF) issued.
	Capital to risk asset ratio increased to 8.5% for CBs and 8% to FCs.
	Foreign bank branches allowed to hold debenture, bond or debt instrument issued by FIDF as liquid asset.

Monetary policies

In pursuance of its monetary policy, the BOT makes use of the monetary base, which is manipulated by net foreign assets and the BOT's credit to government and financial institutions. Since the country enjoyed a balance of payments surplus over most of the first half of the 1990s, the volume of net foreign assets increased remarkably. The monetary base and the money stock had to be

controlled by reducing the net claims on the government and the financial institutions to offset the positive effect of net foreign assets. Moreover, these capital
flows did not have any adverse effects due to a surplus in the fiscal budget.

Because of the increased foreign borrowing of commercial banks and the
increasing spread between the minimum lending rate and the foreign interest
rate, the authorities were careful to take measures to avoid any adverse effects
of huge short-term lending. The BOT, therefore, introduced the maximum
credit deposit ratio and credit growth ceiling on commercial banks to control
the volume of such loans. In 1979, the authorities established the repurchase
market to provide liquidity to the financial institutions. Under this arrangement,
the bond repurchase market helped the BOT to conduct open-market operations
for government bonds. The BOT did not issue new bonds after 1991; rather it
authorized the state enterprises to do so. However, as a result of financial liberalization and also because of the availability of alternative sources of internal
and external loans for commercial banks, the scope of open-market operations
began to decline in importance. The selling volume of BOT bonds in the market
significantly declined after 1987, while commercial bank borrowing from
abroad substantially increased.[4] This, as in the other economies examined in
earlier chapters, was the source of the trouble that ballooned as financial fragility
of corporations and banks by 1997.

In June 1991, the BOT replaced the reserve requirement ratio by the liquidity
requirement ratio, which allowed commercial banks more flexibility to invest
the minimum required percentage of deposits in other selected debt instruments
issued by state institutions. In 1993, the government abolished another reserve
requirement, which was imposed on banks wishing to open new branches.
Under this requirement, each new branch was bound to keep a specified
percentage of total deposits in government bonds. This regulation was initially
introduced to finance the budgetary deficits before 1980, when 16 per cent of
the total deposits were required to be in government bonds. This was later
reduced to 5.5 per cent in 1992, when budget surpluses eliminated the need to
issue government bonds. Eventually, the requirement was completely abolished
in 1993.

Central bank reforms

The Bank of Thailand (BOT) was established in 1942 under the BOT Act.
With an initial capital of 20 million baht and another 13.5 million baht
transferred from the Thai National Banking Bureau, the BOT started as the
central bank of Thailand. The BOT consisted of ten members, with the Governor
and Deputy Governor as ex-officio Chairman and Deputy Chairman, respectively, appointed by the King, with no fixed term of office. The BOT's
operations are supervised by the Minister of Finance, who must approve any
major policy decision.

The main functions of the BOT are to act as the banker to the government and financial institutions and as the agent of the government in dealing with international organizations such as the IMF. Price stability is given as the main objective of the BOT. Besides designing and implementing monetary policy to achieve its goal, the BOT is also authorized to manage public debt and international reserves and exchange rates. In 1962, it was empowered to supervise commercial banking under the Commercial Banking Act. In 1979, the BOT's supervision also included other institutions such as finance companies, finance and securities companies, and credit foncier companies. This did not result in effective control of the finance companies, 58 of which had to be closed down during the first stage of the 1997 crisis.

The monetary policy of the BOT is based on three main objectives, namely, liquidity management, prudential regulations and moral suasion, which are achieved using two policy instruments, the repurchase market and the loan window. The repurchase market for government and enterprise bonds is one of the important components of the money market and has been crucial for liquidity management. The loan window serves the purpose of lender of last resort, which is similar in all other banks. Originally, it was open only to commercial banks, but in 1994 this was extended to finance companies. The bank rate charged on such loans is adjusted from time to time and thus serves as an important indicator to signal the future direction of interest rates in the market.

To monitor the baht exchange rates, the BOT uses the Exchange Equalization Fund as a mechanism through which the basket-pegged exchange policy is implemented. This policy, which was abandoned in August 1997, allowed a fluctuation of ± 0.02 baht per US dollar.

Reforms in the banking sector

Since the 1970s, the banking industry has gone through many changes with the establishment of both foreign and domestic branches. At June 1995, Thailand had 15 domestic commercial banks with 3289 branches, 49 overseas branches, 14 foreign bank branches and 44 foreign bank representative offices. According to an old statistic, commercial banks accounted for 65 per cent of the total assets of financial institutions in the mid-1990s. The largest 9 among the 15 commercial banks represented 82 per cent of total commercial bank assets and about 94 per cent of net profits.

The businesses of commercial banks are regulated by the BOT under the Commercial Banking Act of 1962. During the reform process initiated in the 1970s, the Act was twice amended, first in 1979 and again in 1992. These amendments helped the domestic banking industry to expand its businesses away from traditional banking to more sophisticated service industries.

Off-shore banking is an important component of the commercial banking industry. In 1993, the government established the Bangkok International

Banking facilities to further promote off-shore banking facilities. Accordingly, 46 licences were issued to 15 Thai banks, 11 foreign banks operating in Thailand, and 20 new foreign banks. To further expand off-shore banking activities, the authorities granted 37 licences for Provincial Banking Facilities (PBF) to operate in areas outside Bangkok. The Bangkok International Bank Facility (BIBF) is involved in taking deposits or borrowing in foreign currencies from abroad, lending in foreign currencies in Thailand (note the similarity with Indonesia) and abroad, foreign exchange transactions, trade-related financial transactions, and loan arrangements through foreign sources and fund managers. To encourage and facilitate financial institutions operating under the BIBF, the authorities give them some tax concessions, such as reduction in corporate income tax, exemption from special business tax, withholding tax on interest income and stamp duties.

Reforms in non-banking financial institutions (NBFIs)

Thailand's financial market offers a variety of non-bank financial institutions and the financial-sector reforms initiated in the 1970s helped to develop this subsector. Some of the important NBFIs are: finance companies and finance and securities companies, securities companies, credit foncier companies, mutual fund management companies, the Government Savings Bank, the Government Housing Bank, the Bank of Agriculture and Agricultural Cooperatives, the Industrial Finance Corporation of Thailand, the Small Industry Finance Corporation, the Export–Import Bank of Thailand, the Small Industry Credit Guarantee Corporation, agricultural cooperatives, savings cooperatives and life insurance companies.

Finance companies and finance and securities companies (FCFSCs)

In terms of assets, this category holds the largest share of financial-sector assets after commercial banks: about 19 per cent of the total assets at the end of 1994 were held in 91 such firms. The finance companies are regulated under the Act on the Undertaking of Finance Business, Securities Business and Credit Foncier Business implemented first in 1979 and amended in 1992. Under the 1992 Securities and Exchange Act, the supervision of securities companies is transferred to the Securities and Exchange Commission (SEC) from the BOT.

Issuance of promissory notes and borrowings from commercial banks are the main sources of funds, along with bills of exchange and certificates of deposits, while the funds are used for short-term lending to commerce as well as medium- and long-term lending to industries, agriculture, commerce, housing and consumers. The main source of income of securities companies is brokerage fees, fixed by the Stock Exchange of Thailand (SET) at 0.5 per cent of the value of transaction for common stock and 0.3 per cent for mutual funds and from margin loans. Foreigners can hold up to 49 per cent of equity in each security company. This relaxation or similar rules in the capital market are found in Korea, Indonesia, Malaysia and Thailand, all of which thus attracted very short-term funds. In 1995, the government designed the Financial System Master Plan to improve the efficiency of these institutions, allowing them to expand their business to include foreign exchange business.

Credit foncier companies (CFCs)

CFCs are primarily involved in extending loans for housing and the real-estate sector using the mortgage method. At the end of 1994, the value of their assets was estimated at only 1 per cent of the total assets of the financial sector with 13 CFCs operating. They are governed under provisions of the Act on the Undertaking of Finance Business, Securities Business and Credit Foncier Business initially implemented in 1979 and amended in 1992: these operate under the supervision of the BOT.

CFCs generate funds through the issuance of promissory notes of no less than one year with a minimum amount of 1000 baht. The reform process led to an expansion of their activities, which now includes services such as arranging, underwriting and dealing in debt securities, custodial service, loan-servicing agency, and insurance advice for real-estate and property services.

Mutual fund management companies (MFMCs)

MFMCs are supervised by SEC under the Security and Exchange Act of 1992 and constituted about 2.8 per cent of the total assets in 1994. The MFMCs issue unit trusts to generate funds and use the proceeds to buy securities approved by the SEC. Until 1993, there was only one mutual fund company; this increased to eight companies in 1996. The number of funds has also increased, from 27 in 1992 to 91 in 1994, with 84 equity funds, 4 fixed income funds and 3 balanced funds.

The Government Savings Bank (GSB)

The GSB was established in 1947 under the GSB Act of 1946. Using 1994 statistics, this is the third major player in terms of total assets (3 per cent of total assets of financial institutions) and had 538 branches throughout the country. Its main function is to mobilize funds and to finance the government's fiscal deficits; hence its importance as a major intermediation agency. The GSB provides services similar to commercial banks and mobilizes funds through savings and fixed deposits as well as sale of premium savings bonds. During the period of huge fiscal deficits, the bulk of GSB funds were redirected to be invested in government securities. With the improvement in the government's fiscal position since 1988, the GSB is authorized to extend more credits to state enterprises and the private sector, though the proportion is still under 20 per cent.

Other institutions

The Government Housing Board (GHB) was established in 1953 under the GHB Act, completely owned by the government and supervised by the Ministry of Finance. The main function of the GHB was to extend housing finance to middle- and low-income groups, as well as housing and land purchases under long-term instalments. The GHB Act of 1953 was amended in 1973, transferring some of the GHB's assets and liabilities to the National Housing Authority. Moreover, under the amendment, the GHB was allowed to accept deposits of any type and maturity from the public.

The Bank of Agriculture and Agricultural Cooperatives (BAAC) was established in 1966 under the BAAC Act with the sole purpose of providing credit to farmers and farming groups at low interest rates. Most of the loans are short- and medium-term loans. As part of the reforms, the functions of the BAAC were expanded in 1977 to provide technology and technical assistance to farmers under various agricultural development projects. Further liberalization permitted them to extend credit to undertakings related to agriculture, particularly cottage industries.

The Industrial Finance Corporation of Thailand (IFCT) was established in 1959 under the IFCT Act. The government owns about 13 per cent of the shares, while the remaining shares are held by the private sector, mainly the domestic commercial banks. These shares are listed and traded on the exchange. The main function of IFCT is to finance fixed assets through extending medium- and long-term loans, mainly to private industries. The IFCT, through an amendment in 1972, is allowed to undertake certain operations related to the development of capital markets in Thailand. The Small Industry Finance Corporation (SIFC) was established in May 1992 with the objective to develop domestic industries. The SIFC extends financial support to small industries for the establishment and improvement of production capacity and efficiency.

The Exim Bank was established under the Export–Import Bank of Thailand Act in 1993 to promote exports and investment overseas by extending direct loans, loan guarantee, export insurance and other financial services. It started its operations in February 1994 under the supervision of the MOF, while the governor of the BOT is the Chairman of the Board of Directors. Since its establishment, the operations of export refinancing have been transferred to the Exim Bank from the BOT.

The Small Industry Credit Guarantee Corporation (SICGC) was established in February 1992. Since then, the credit extension from financial institutions to small industries has been transferred from the Industrial Finance Corporation of Thailand to SICGC. SICGC operates under the MOF and extends credit guarantee to small industry that may lack sufficient collateral to obtain credits on their own. The agricultural cooperatives (ACs) and savings cooperatives (SCs) operate under the Cooperatives Act of 1968 but are regulated by the

Department of Cooperatives' Promotion and the Department of Cooperative Auditing, both under the Ministry of Agriculture and Cooperatives. ACs are the largest in number: by the end of 1994 there were 2474. They are organized by farmers to cooperate in farming activities and extend credits to members at low interest rates. The funds are generated through borrowings from the Bank of Agriculture, agricultural cooperatives and capital accounts. SCs are the second largest cooperatives, basically organized by public-sector employees. The funds are generated through paid-up share capital (members' own contributions) and are used to extend loans to members for a variety of unexpected needs. Long-term credit may also be provided for purposes such as house purchase or financing secondary occupational activities.

Life insurance companies operate under the Life Insurance Act of 1967, amended in 1993 and supervised by the Ministry of Commerce. At the end of 1994, there were 12 life insurance companies operating in Thailand, while one was registered abroad. According to the above Act, life insurance companies are required to be public companies and should make a security deposit of 2 million baht as well as maintain minimum capital funds of 50 million baht and deposit a minimum portion of its insurance reserves with the official insurance registrar. The amendment introduced in 1993 allowed life insurance companies to invest in promissory notes, lease assets, sell land and real estate, manage provident funds and invest in foreign stocks and debentures. The authorities also established a new company in 1993, 'Saha Life Insurance Company', to provide insurance services to members of agricultural cooperatives.

Financial-market development
The Stock Exchange of Thailand (SET) was established in 1974. The authorities enacted the Securities and Exchange Act under an amendment by which the Securities and Exchange Commission (SEC) was established in 1992, a year ahead of Malaysia. Between 1986 and 1995, the number of listed companies increased from 98 to 416, while the market capitalization increased from US$2.9 billion to US$141.5 billion. The main objective of establishing the SEC was to supervise and regulate the securities industry and the proposed derivatives market, as well as to promote the development of the domestic capital market to trade new financial instruments. The SEC is responsible for the issuance of securities (public offering and private placement), securities trading on the exchange and in the over-the-counter market, securities business (securities companies and mutual fund management companies), and information disclosure and prevention of unfair trading practices. This set of reforms boosted growth in the capital market. Financial markets in Thailand comprise three major markets: the money market, the capital market and the foreign exchange market.

In 1992, Thailand established the Bangkok International Banking Facilities (BIBF) with the objective of developing Thailand as the regional financial centre for Indochina. It was expected to provide services for trade, investment and financing. The other objective of the BIBF was to improve the efficiency of the domestic financial sector by increasing its exposure to other more advanced financial markets in the region. The government provided certain privileges such as reduced corporate income tax of 10 per cent compared to the usual 30 per cent, exemption from withholding tax, business tax and stamp duties. These policies enhanced the importance and share of the BIBF in net capital inflows.

As a result of the above policies, the SET has become one of the most dynamic emerging markets in the past few years, with total market value having grown at an average rate of 56.6 per cent over the period 1988–96. Market capitalization increased from US$1.94 billion in 1985 to US$24 billion in 1990 and US$142 billion in 1995, which gives an average growth rate of 7209 per cent during 1985–95 and 491 per cent during 1990–95. This has been one of the highest growths in the region.

The money market   The instruments of the money market include the repurchase market, the loan window (both operated by the BOT), interbank loans, overdrafts, NCDs, and commercial bills such as promissory notes, bills of exchange (B/E), and post-dated checks. Commercial banks and finance companies are the major players; while commercial bills have a maturity of less than one year, most have maturity between three and six months.

The development of the money market has been very gradual. The interbank market is the oldest of the markets and was established in the 1930s. It is a market for short-term loans, mostly ranging from overnight to two weeks in duration, traded between commercial banks, finance and security companies and other institutions. Due to the high volatility of interest rates in the market, the authorities in May 1985 introduced the Bangkok Inter-Bank Offered Rate (BIBOR), the average at which prime banks lend to each other. However, only selected banks and finance companies were allowed to use BIBOR. The Singapore Inter-Bank Offered Rate (SIBOR) is the most commonly used rate for the pricing of foreign-exchange-denominated transactions. One major problem with the market is the lack of money brokers, which makes it less competitive relative to the markets in Malaysia and Singapore. Measures including the establishment of money brokers, more participants and use of computerized transactions are expected to enhance the importance of money markets.

The Treasury bill (TB) market was established in 1944 and became operative in 1945. Besides the BOT, commercial banks have been the main purchaser of TBs. One important reason for this was the stipulation that the banks, in meeting part of the cash reserve requirement, could use such TBs. In 1979, the BOT established the government bond repurchase (RP) market as part of the money-market development process. Until 1986, the interest on bonds was tax-exempted. Banks can borrow from the BOT using their government bonds as collateral. At one time, the bond market was very active. However, with the growing budgetary surplus, the market has been completely phased out and the amount of outstanding bonds is also declining, except the small amounts held by the CBs and FCs as part of liquid asset requirements (legal reserves) imposed by the BOT.

Besides the above, the other instruments of the money market include the commercial bills market, the commercial paper market, and the transferable bills of exchange market. As a result of financial liberalization and internationalization of the financial markets, the money market became closely linked to the foreign exchange market. The BOT also made certain amendments in the rules governing the operations of financial institutions in 1992 allowing the CBs and FCs to issue NCDs. The regulations require that the minimum denomination of NCD must not be less than 500 000 baht and the maturity must be between three and 36 months.

The capital market   The capital market has a short history. After Thailand's transformation from an agriculture-based economy to an industrial economy during the 1950s, the first capital market with private incentives was organized in 1962. In July of the same year, an organized stock exchange was formed. In 1963, this changed into a limited company, named the Bangkok Stock Exchange, and started trading in equities and debentures. The market was inactive and eventually ceased operations in 1970 due to lack of investors and government support. In 1974, the government enacted the Stock Exchange of Thailand Act and a formal securities market was established in April 1975 when the SET had 16 securities quoted from nine companies. The activities in the market were slow to pick up until 1984, when the Act was amended enabling the listed companies to offer new shares and control of insider trading. In 1992, the Securities Exchange Act (SEA) was implemented which provided more transparency, efficient and effective enforcement and better supervision of the securities industry by strengthened investor protection. The supervision was then unified under the Securities Exchange Commission.

Capital markets experienced rapid development during the 1990s up to 1997, mainly as a result of the liberalization process. The establishment of legal structure, which included establishment of the SEC and a credit-rating agency, Thailand Rating and Information Services (TRIS) in 1993, a Bond Dealers' Club (BDC) in 1994, and an Over-the-Counter (OTC) market in 1995, all helped. The TRIS is responsible for information to the investors on the quality of the bonds and the issuers. The BDC was established to promote trade in secondary debt, while the OTC facilitates trade in unlisted companies. The BOT also introduced a new electronic clearing system for the transfer of cheques and funds.

The primary market for equity comprises common stocks, preferred stocks and unit trusts. During the years 1992 to 1996, both common stocks and unit trusts have enjoyed very high growth rates. The authorities have taken drastic measures to develop the secondary market for equity. These include setting up an 'alien' board for foreign investors in 1987, installing the ASSET computer system for trading securities, relaxing entry requirements for provincial companies for listing on the SET in 1993, establishing a maintenance margin system for margin loans in 1993, and extending trading hours in 1994. As a result, by the end of 1994, the capitalization of equities market was 3.3 trillion baht with the SET index reaching 1360.9. During the same period, there were 389 listed companies and 91 mutual funds with net asset value of B 179.6 billion. The market took a big correction by 75 per cent following the Asian crisis that started with the 1997 July baht depreciation.

The non-equity market comprises government and state enterprise bonds, debentures, floating-rate notes, and leasing. The market for government bonds has declined due to consistent fiscal surpluses, which increased the importance of state enterprise bonds. As a result, the amount of the latter increased from B 6.7 million in 1990 to B 57.1 million by the mid-1990s. Most debentures are traded in the unorganized OTC market, with mutual funds and insurance companies forming the major players. Since 1991, the amount of debentures issued in the domestic and overseas market has increased from B 6.3 million to B 133.2 million in 1994. Floating-rate notes (FRN) have also increased over time and many institutions have issued them abroad, mostly in US dollars. Leasing emerged in Thailand in 1987 but did not develop much until 1991. Since then the leasing business has grown rapidly, and is now a competitive alternative to hire-purchase financing. The Asian financial crisis led to a decline in the capitalization of 77 per cent by the end of 1998.

Exchange rate management   The foreign exchange market reforms focused in particular on removing foreign exchange controls. Let us look first at the measures to remove controls on foreign exchange transactions. The process of reform was initiated in 1990 when commercial banks were allowed to conduct foreign exchange transactions for customers without BOT approval. The second phase of liberalization measures was implemented in 1991 when the authorities allowed residents to open foreign currency accounts while non-residents were allowed to open local currency accounts. Exporters were also allowed to make payments from and receive into these accounts foreign currencies for trade purposes. The third phase of reforms came in 1994, facilitating trade and investment in the region.

The design and implementation of exchange rate policy in Thailand rests with the BOT. However, major decisions such as devaluation must be approved by the Minister of Finance. Thailand adopted the fixed exchange rate regime by pegging the baht to the US dollar between 1960 and 1980. Therefore, the main objective of the BOT in exchange rate policy was to maintain the stability of the currency, which in return would minimize the risk for traders and foreign investors. Hence these would provide a favourable environment for expansion in trade and foreign investment. The argument was that using the stability of the US dollar and pegging the baht would help create stability in the domestic currency. However, because of the US dollar appreciation against the yen in the 1990s, and the mark as well as the pound sterling in the early 1990s, this system overvalued the baht in terms of these currencies, thereby adversely effecting the trade balance, with sharp declines in Thai exports to these countries. Further, the level of international reserves in 1984 declined from the level of the last ten years from seven months of imports to just US$2.3 billion or an equivalent of three months of imports.

To keep the country's competitiveness intact and to correct the balance of payments deficit, the authorities decided to devalue the currency, first in April 1981 by 1.7 per cent, then in July 1981 by 8.7 per cent and finally in 1984 by 14.8 per cent.[5] However, the authorities took some other measures such as imposing a temporary ceiling on the price of some commodities to reduce the possibility of price increase through inflationary expectations. The authorities also replaced the system of pegging the baht to the US dollar with a basket of currencies in 1984. The basket includes a heavy reliance on the US dollar, the yen, the mark, the pound sterling, the Hong Kong dollar, the Singapore dollar, and the Malaysian ringgit, with the US dollar having the maximum weight of 85 per cent (65 per cent in 1985).[6] The exchange rate is announced every morning by the BOT.

These measures helped to restore the stability of the Thai baht, and the country enjoyed balance of payments surpluses since 1985. Moreover, the level of international reserves increased to US$39.4 billion in 1995, and the debt-service ratio was reduced to 11.7 per cent as compared to 27.5 per cent in 1985. Since 1985, the baht has appreciated against the US dollar at a rate of 0.8 per cent per annum, while it had depreciated at the rate of 3.7 per cent during 1978–85.[7]

However, in an effort to maintain the stability of the exchange rate, the BOT lost control over the money supply, where the money supply would react to the balance of payment conditions. The continuous interventions of the BOT in the foreign exchange market to keep the currency stable increased the gap between foreign interest rates and domestic interest over time, which led to an increase in short-term capital flows. To prevent any adverse effect of these flows on inflation and the current account deficit, the BOT in 1995 imposed certain restrictions on capital. These measures included: (i) imposing reserve requirement for the BIBF's out–in business, (ii) the minimum amount of loans made through BIBF was raised from 500 000 baht to 2 million baht, and subsequently 5 million baht, (iii) cash reserve requirements for a non-residence baht account were raised from 2 per cent to 7 per cent, and (iv) imposing a 7 per cent reserve requirement for foreign borrowing of financial institutions. In 1996, the BOT also intervened in the swap market for some Asian currencies (the Singapore dollar and the Hong Kong dollar) to prevent speculative attacks on the baht based on the rumours of expected devaluation. These bold steps helped to restore the stability of the baht at a huge cost until the currency crisis on 2 July 1997 led to a free float of the currency.[8]

3.3   Financial Liberalization Effects

Macroeconomic effects

Thailand has pursued a quite open external sector policy. The reforms started as early as 1970 and were implemented very gradually. Some important ones were implemented only in the 1990s. This is consistent with policies adopted by some other Asian early reformers such as Korea and Singapore, and the advice being given after the Asian crisis. The reforms had a positive effect on the overall economy, as evidenced by the figures provided in Table 8.4. GDP growth showed a remarkable improvement in the late 1980s and until the baht crisis hit the economy in 1997, when Thailand experienced its worst recession in decades.

Inflation has been kept within single digits during most of the last three decades. Fiscal-sector reforms helped government revenues to grow rapidly and they reached a peak in 1995, at an annual growth rate of 16.4 per cent. Policies of domestic financial- and external-sector reforms significantly increased the inflow of capital and foreign direct investment increased by more than 50 per cent during 1996. The country later on paid the price for this huge short-term capital inflow and lack of an adequate monitoring system.

Exchange and interest rates

Similar to the overall reform process, the interest rate reforms were also gradual; they constituted one of the most delayed reforms. All ceilings on the interest rate were abolished only in the mid-1990s. The first step towards interest rate liberalization was taken in 1989 when the government abolished the ceiling on time deposits with maturity of over one year. About ten years earlier Malaysia had adopted this same reform. This policy was aimed at helping to increase domestic saving and long-term capital investment. The remaining ceilings on time deposits, saving deposits and loans were abolished in 1992 for both commercial banks and finance companies. In an effort to improve transparency, the authorities imposed certain restrictions on commercial banks requiring them to announce their minimum lending and retail rates charged to prime customers and retail customers respectively.

Table 8.4   Growth rates of basic economic indicators

| | 5-year average | | | Annual average | | | | | | | |
	1976–80	1981–85	1986–90	1991	1992	1993	1994	1995	1996	1997	1998
GDP	7.9	5.4	10.4	8.4	7.8	8.3	8.8	8.6	6.7	–0.4	–7.8
Inflation	9.7	4.9	3.9	5.7	4.1	3.4	5.2	5.7	5.9	8.0	9.0
Revenue	20.1	11.4	19.9	18.7	5.8	12.1	17.2	16.4	9.8	–0.6	–2.0
M1	15.5	3.7	17.9	13.8	12.3	18.6	17.0	12.1	9.1	1.5	15.0
M2	19.5	18.7	20.8	19.8	15.6	18.4	12.9	17.0	12.6	16.4	9.6
FDI	44.5	11.4	81.5	–17.6	4.9	–14.6	–24.3	51.4	12.96	60.4	n.a.
Trade balance	15.5	3.7	17.9	–11.3	–30.5	3.13	–13.7	–114.3	–19.1	5.5	–22.1

Note: M2 = (M1 + quasi-money).

Sources: IMF, *International Financial Statistics*, various issues; World Bank, *World Bank Databank*, Feb. 1997; ADB, *Asian Development Outlook, 1998. 1999.*

Table 8.5 Exchange rates and interest rates (annual averages)

	5-year average			Annual average								
	1976–80	1981–85	1986–90	1991	1992	1993	1994	1995	1996	1997	1998
Exchange rate (mkt)	20.4	24.6	25.5	25.3	25.5	25.5	25.1	25.2	25.6	47.2	36.7
Interest rates											
CB discount rate	11.0	12.6	8.8	11.0	11.0	9.0	9.5	10.5	10.5	12.5	12.5
Money market rate	11.65	14.28	9.04	10.58	7.06	6.49	7.17	10.28	9.16	14.59	13.02
Deposit rate	9.1	12.9	10.1	13.7	8.9	8.6	8.5	11.6	10.33	10.52	10.65
Gov. bond yield	10.6	12.5	8.6	10.8	10.8	10.8	10.8	10.8	10.8	10.8	10.8
Lending rate	15.75	18.68	15.71	19.00	17.54	15.60	14.38	13.25	13.40	13.65	14.42

Notes:
M2 = (M1 + quasi-money).
Central Bank (CB) discount rate (end of period).
Exchange rate: (Official rate) = Thai baht per US$.

Source: IMF, *International Financial Statistics*, various issues.

However, due to a history of low inflation, this country always enjoyed positive real interest rates even at times when interest rates were subject to ceilings and reforms in this sector had not been introduced. The magnitude of real positive interest rates has further increased as a result of certain reform measures and controls on inflation. Tables 8.1 and 8.5 show that, since 1985, Thailand has experienced significantly positive real interest rates for both lending and deposits. This has attracted higher financial savings, as can be seen in Table 8.1 in terms of the increasing M2/GDP ratio, which is an indicator of financial deepening. As compared to an average of 0.372 in 1970s, this ratio increased to as high as 0.795 in 1995, a shade lower than in Malaysia. Table 8.5 shows that the exchange rate was maintained (probably artificially) at a lower rate against the US dollar and remained stable from 1981 to 1997 (pre-crisis). The Asian crisis badly hit the exchange rate, which initially lost about 85 per cent of its value. Later on, restructuring of the domestic banking sector and bailout by the IMF helped to restore some confidence and the currency gained some value against the US dollar. At the end of 1999, the baht has recovered two-thirds of its lost value.

Indicators of financial liberalization
Table 8.6 provides a summary of financial liberalization ratios. The positive effect is visible by the depth of M2/GDP which went from about 50 per cent in the mid-1980s to about 90 per cent in 1997. The reforms increased private-sector participation in the market as the claims to the government went from a low level in 1976–80 to 70 per cent in 1998, while claims to the private sector increased from 29 per cent of GDP to 121 per cent over the same ten years.

Gross domestic capital formation remained low until 1990 and picked up later. It remained stable at around 42 per cent of GDP until 1997. The significant impact of capital flows to Thailand is evident from the last row of Table 8.6: on average capital flows account for about 1.5 per cent of GDP during 1986–96. More details of the portfolio and foreign direct investment are provided in Table 8.7.

The government has traditionally adopted a liberal attitude towards FDI. Initiatives to attract it date back to the 1960s when new laws were passed and old ones amended to eliminate any distinction between domestic and foreign investment except in land ownership and volume of skilled manpower permitted to work in Thailand. Even these restrictions may be set aside if the firm receives BOI promotion. The firms were allowed to have 100 per cent ownership during much of the 1960s and 1970s, which was reduced to a maximum of 50 per cent in 1983. These policies led to a surge of FDI into Thailand and by 1997 the magnitude of FDI reached around US$3.8 billion per year.

During most of the 1990s, net portfolio investment remained very strong, reaching a peak of US$5.5 billion. Short-term capital flows into the banking

Table 8.6 Indicators of financial liberalization (% of GDP)

| | 5-year average | | | Annual | | | | | | | |
	1976–80	1981–85	1986–90	1991	1992	1993	1994	1995	1996	1997	1998
Money depth (M2/GDP)	37.2	48.9	64.3	72.7	74.9	79.2	78.7	79.5	79.7	89.9	92.0
Inter-relations											
FIR (total)/GDP	40	54	62	66	69	76	87	92	93	113	115
FIR (private)/GDP	29	39	53	67	72	80	92	98	100	119	121
GFCF/GDP	25.8	27.8	33.0	41.4	39.4	40.2	41.0	42.8	42.5	39.5	34.0
FDI/GDP	0.4	0.7	1.8	2.02	1.90	1.45	0.95	1.27	1.28	3.67	5.53

Notes:
M2 = (M1 + quasi-money).
FIR = Financial intermediation ratio – claims on public sector, claims on private sector, and foreign assets.
GFCF = gross fixed capital formation.
FDI = foreign direct investment.

Sources: IMF, International Financial Statistics, various issues; World Bank (Balance of Payment Capital Account) – for foreign direct investments.

Table 8.7   Investments in Thailand (US$ million)

	5-year average			Annual							
	1976–80	1981–85	1986–90	1991	1992	1993	1994	1995	1996	1997
Direct investment (net)	95	278	1111	1847	1969	1571	873	1182	1405	3386
Portfolio investment (net)	70.2	254.0	459.0	–81.0	927	5455	2481	4083	3544	4352
FDI (inflow)	97.2	279.2	1188	2014	2113	1804	1366	2068	2336	3746

Sources: IMF, *International Financial Statistics*, various issues; World Bank, *World Bank Databank*, Feb. 1997; ADB, *Asian Development Bank, 1998, 1999.*

sector and from thereon to the finance companies were the primary cause of the weakness in the economy during 1994–97. Short-term capital flows swamped the country, with most of the money going into non-profitable or slow profit-making ventures. Elsewhere, this has been pointed out as the reason why the baht came under attack in June 1997.

4.   ASSESSMENT OF FUTURE PROSPECTS

The consistently recurring theme in the development history of Thailand is that it remains a more open country, with conditions favourable for development to occur. Growth has been secured by the dynamism of the private sector, which dominates almost all economic activities. Though the real sector was very much open to competition, both within the country and from the entry of foreign firms, there has been greater reluctance compared to other countries such as Malaysia to relax controls on the financial and monetary variables. Periodic interruptions to sustained growth have also come from external shocks – an example is the oil price shocks – and domestic instability created by weak coalition governments and/or military interventions.

Despite these recurrent problems, a growth rate of about 8 per cent per annum during 1980–96 is a strong sign of the possibility for future growth. Taking steps to reform the political process in this free-for-all democracy has become a paramount challenge, and continues to be one when recovery takes place after the growth-retarding effects of the 1997 Asian financial crisis. Now that the IMF reconstruction scheme has put in place substantial financial reforms, one source of persistent weakness has been removed. The central bank has been strengthened to pursue pro-growth policies, with urgently needed increased independence. Economic recovery was expected to take place in the later part of 1999, much earlier than in Indonesia, where the political process also desta-bilized a long period of growth. Sustainable growth in Thailand also depends on how the constraints on concentrated growth in the region around the city of Bangkok are removed in the future.

NOTES

1. An aspect that keeps cropping up in our analysis is the high degree of income inequality in all the countries – one exception being Taiwan – covered in this book. Thailand's bottom 20 per cent of households had only 5.6 per cent of GDP (top 20 per cent had 52.7 per cent), a situation worse than in Indonesia. This is recognized as a source of instability today, following the work of the Nobel Laureate A.K. Sen. Uneven distribution encourages income capture by capital owners who, after a period of growth as in Thailand (and Indonesia), engage in speculative spending in the non-productive sector. Could this be the real cause of financial instability in

developing countries? This aspect deserves to be studied as it needs aggregate-level ineffi-ciencies to trace the fault lines that have destabilized many economies in the 1990s.

2. This chapter covers events up to 1996. The impacts of the financial crisis in Thailand are discussed in Chapters 2 and 17.
3. See United Nations (1997b).
4. Bank borrowing from abroad as a percentage of total borrowing increased from 56 per cent in 1985 to 90 per cent in 1995 (Nidhiprabha, 1997, p. l5).
5. It may be interesting to note here that the Governor of the BOT lost his office by opposing the Minister of Finance in a decision to devalue the baht. This simply shows the limited indepen-dence the central bank enjoys in implementing major policy decisions.
6. The weight of each currency in the basket is undisclosed and depends on the relative importance of that currency in Thai trade flows.
7. Most of this appreciation of the Thai baht was considered as artificial and analysts have indicated that the Thai baht was overvalued by about 30–40 per cent. These views suggest that part of the depreciation of the value of the baht during the currency crisis was, therefore, a correction.
8. The causes and effects of the Asian currency crisis are discussed separately in Chapter 2.

Part 3 Communists Return to Market Forces

China's recent outstanding economic development, when it gave its people choices and had the second largest amount of foreign capital inflow, amounting in some years to about US$42 billion, is perhaps at the root of the euphoria about the East Asian Miracle, which was doused by the Asian financial crisis. In Part 3 we examine the extensive reforms China and, at a later date, the limited reforms Vietnam put in place to achieve prosperity. Both China and Vietnam – if you like, add North Korea and Laos – copied the central planning model of the now dead Soviet bloc, and thus missed out on prosperity. China adopted experimental reforms with cautious opening, while continuing to incur the deadweight losses of state enterprises, which in hindsight appears to be a clever strategy to mask the inefficiency of the state sector with private-sector growth. The release of the entrepreneurial energy of its people from the switchover was astounding: per capita income almost trebled. The high inflation, which eroded years of gains up to about 1993, has since been brought down, which can be emulated by transition economies such as Cuba and North Korea. Vietnam, the reader will find, started on the path of meaningful reforms only in the late 1980s, achieving only limited success.

Political consequences arising from successful reforms are now seen as potentially destabilizing, and enthusiasm for further reforms is waning. The 1997–98 Asian financial crisis did not encourage admiration for more openness either. In the closing years of the 1990s, there was a sense of reluctance to continue with more reforms in these transition economies, particularly in financial matters. That is indeed deplorable, since both China and Vietnam gained prosperity through the very openness of bold reforms. Examples of what openness can achieve glare at them from countries that secured prosperity through openness despite the effect of the Asian crisis.

9. China: a command economy responding well to market signals for the time being

1. BACKGROUND

The economy of traditional China was based squarely on rural economic activities completely dependent on agriculture carried on by individual peasant families. The agriculture sector was dependent on traditional technology comprising human effort, animal power and natural fertilizer. It was only at the beginning of the last century that China realized the need for modern technology and allowed domestic and foreign investments in industrial and commercial enterprises. After the Communists drove the Nationalists to Taiwan in a bloody civil war, the People's Republic of China (PRC) was established in 1949 and the Chinese Communist Party decided to rely heavily on the Soviet model of economic structures and development strategies. The end result of adopting a centralization model was the transformation of the pattern of ownership from private sector to public sector, a weakness that has led to an inefficient state sector over 50 years from which the country is still trying to extricate itself in the twenty-first century. By 1956, almost all the assets, including foreign ones, were transferred to the public sector in one way or another. A mono-banking system was established as the circulatory system for domestic payments with the heart of the system being the State Council – certainly not the will of the marketplace – while the Bank of China with its overseas offices became the sole repository of foreign transactions.

These measures of collectivization of agriculture and nationalization of industry somewhat legitimized the political regime to govern the Chinese economy as a system of mandatory central planning orders. The Party assumed full control over the economy and its policies by the dictates of the People's Congress that met once in three years to rubber-stamp the decision put to them by an entrenched ruling bureaucracy. Those members of the central bureaucracy, who live a sheltered life in the protected grounds of Beijing, were supposed to execute the will of the Party so expressed at the meeting. This was in reality central planning, where, after the decision by the Congress, the state exercised its planning function primarily through mandatory procurements and allocation of key agricultural and industrial products by maintaining rigid price controls on major goods. There was no place for market prices, nor for the will of economic agents to be expressed through market prices. To ensure that economic agents had no freedom, the means of production were taken in trust by the state itself. How could economic agents express their choices if they could not own the very means that could give them the choices!?

This system created huge public enterprises with the highest level of inefficiency. The international press often reports on 28 000 central-government-owned enterprises together with another 300 000 provincial and city-government-owned firms controlling this vast economy: this excludes the military-owned firms. Most of the government resources were allocated to finance these enterprises. The government realized the inefficiencies associated with the Soviet model but made only cosmetic changes without giving up controls over the economy till the passing away of the founder of Communist China, Mao Tse-tung. The only visible change that occurred during a short space of time over 1971–75 was a slight increase of state investment on agriculture inputs such as machinery and fertilizer, with heavy industry still being the major recipient of state investment. The result was a closed economy, which hoped to grow from internal demand with minimal external openness. The sharp contrast of this with the economies described as open ones in the previous six chapters is obvious.

Lest readers have a biased view of the state sector, it must be stated that the speed of reforms to this sector has picked up since Zao Ziyang became the premier, and especially since the days of the great flood in 1998–99.[1] About 1000 very large enterprises consisting of 878 industrial enterprises and 122 service-sector firms are destined to be developed into future large firms. The official line is that these firms are needed to compete with foreign firms when China eventually adopts full reforms. The remaining small and medium-sized enterprises are to be reformed as follows. A huge number of third-category firms will be sold off in outright privatization. The promising ones with prof-itability will be permitted to become joint venture non-state enterprises, and sold off. Firms that could be established as public corporations owned by employees with state majority ownership will become shareholder cooperatives. Some progress has been made in this regard, as can be judged by the burgeoning stock-exchange-listed firms since 1987. Thus a future is envisaged still with three classes of state-owned firms in the non-public goods production sectors: the number of firms will be small, but their significance will still be potent. By any means this scheme, even if it works to improve efficiency at the restruc-turing stage, will leave the most significant part of the economy in the ownership of the state. Korea needed only 36 *chaebols* (not state-owned but with great influence on the state) to bring the great Korean economy to its knees in 1992–97 through their profligate behaviour in capital resource allocation (see

Chapters 2 and 3) and a state–*chaebol* clandestine relationship. Efforts are being made to reduce the manning levels of state enterprises to raise efficiency. To alleviate total loss of income, redundant workers are given half-pay and sent home on leave. We proceed now to give a snapshot of the reforms.

Chow (1987) split the pre-reform periods into five sub-periods. The years 1949–52 are seen as a period of recovery from civil war. No major economic change took place during this period except land reforms, whereby the land was distributed from the rich landowners to the farmers; this right was soon taken away by the establishment of collective farms. The second period covered 1953–57, when the government introduced its first five-year plan, *à la* Soviet model, as stated earlier. The years 1958–61 were the period of the Great Leap Forward, when Mao and his planners wanted to create an accelerated economic growth to unattainable levels, by public exhortation. These policies, without a set of incentives for economic agents, eventually resulted in a great failure, and economic activities declined. The fourth period, 1962–65, witnessed economic readjustment through the introduction of more liberal economic policies, which led to some recovery. Finally, the well-publicized Cultural Revolution of 1965–75 led to economic disaster. The country was effectively taken over by the near-religious zeal of the young, wanting to purge the super-stitions – as they called them – of the old China and purge the capitalist opportunists. Until Deng Xiaoping overthrew the presumed successors to Mao,[2] and initiated limited farm ownership in the late 1970s, nothing significant happened.

The factors that led to economic reforms in China were not related to the economic crisis to the same degree as in some Central European countries. Even with the negative effects of policies such as the Great Leap Forward and the Cultural Revolution, which led to depression and famine in China, the country managed to maintain an average growth rate of about 6 per cent per annum between 1958 and 1970. Price controls in place ensured relatively low inflation, and virtually no external debt was incurred. Macroeconomic instability was not the reason for initiating reforms in China. The impetus for reforms was the growing discontent with the system, which had spread to the rural areas, the power base of the Party. The televized pictures of a prosperous West following the opening to the West in 1976 created yearnings for reform. Even the neighbours, long considered as less elevated than China, seemed to have some of the prosperity which was absent in the sterile planned economy.

The other major reasons for policy change towards gradual economic reforms and liberalization were the higher growth performance of East Asia during 1965–79 relative to China's declining growth over the same period, the decline of the Soviet Union's political supremacy in Asia, meagre progress in techno-logical development and somewhat reduced tension between China and the USA, which was pursuing a policy of vigorous opposition to Russia. Although the reform process was slower and more gradual – this is why we label it 'cautious' – than in some other countries in East Asia and Eastern Europe, the result was more encouraging.

Relative to some Eastern European countries, reforms in China were more successful. The estimated growth registered was about 10 per cent during the Sixth Plan, 1981–85, with both agriculture and industries registering double-digit growth, largely attributed to the introduction of private incentives to farmers to produce and sell for their own account. The overall sectoral relationship between consumer goods and producer goods and between agriculture and industrial goods improved. The standard of living and real incomes increased compared to the pre-reform period, 1949–77. The initial reforms were of a short-term nature, basically to tackle the problems of the economic crisis of 1975–76, but the authorities recognized the potential of longer-term reforms to strengthen Communist control, even as Communism was disappearing along with the statues and walls coming down in Europe. Reform would bring major changes to existing infrastructure and planning, but would create prosperity for the masses.

This chapter therefore examines an interesting case of great relevance to the 20-odd transition economies. It is relevant to North Korea and Vietnam, for example, in the Asian region. We examine the economic and financial structure of the country in the next section. Both sectors are still burdened within the public ownership mode, but the structural reforms within the public ownership scheme have created private-sector-based competition in small and medium-sized enterprises as well as the wholesale importation of multinational involvements, mostly in the trade sector in cosmetically free trade zones. Section 3 provides details on the reforms undertaken. The impacts of these reforms are measured in the following Section 4, before we conclude the chapter with a short discussion on future prospects.

2.　ECONOMIC AND FINANCIAL STRUCTURE

After gaining control of the mainland in 1949 and up till 1975, the Communists pursued a policy of socialist economic development – correctly described – by using a system of political commands to manage the economy. Given China's lack of capital and technology, the push for prosperity had to be based on self-reliance and complete control of central planners. During the initial trial reform during 1977–80, a policy of opening up trade and investment was put in place. Since then, the leadership and policy-makers have made efforts gradually to relax central planning by decentralizing economic decision-making, and eliminating or at least reducing the gap between the two-tiered pricing systems. These steps stabilized exchange rates, eliminated the black market for foreign exchange and reduced slightly the dependence of state enterprises on government subsidies as well as on the financial sector. A detailed analysis of these reforms is given later in the chapter. None the less, the overall success of these reforms relative to some other Central and Eastern European countries is quite obvious, and is often used to illustrate that China's grip on one-party rule was the root cause of this success. Of course, that is not the case. Why did other one-party statist models come to naught? GDP grew at an annual rate of 6.9 per cent during the period 1971–80, compared with an earlier growth rate of between 3 and 6 per cent. But growth went into double digits for most of the years when more reforms, especially overseas capital and, later, technology, came China's way during 1983–97 (see Table 9.1).

Similar to the economies described in Part 2, China developed a huge dependence on the external sector for capital and technology but eschewed domestic real-sector, foreign-exchange and financial-sector openness, all three of which, along with fiscal reforms, were postponed. Table 9.2 shows statistics on socioeconomic improvements during the last 28 years.

Since the Tiananmen event[3] right up to 1997, China continued to enjoy high economic growth averaging above 9 per cent, though there were signs of slowing down after 1996 onward, with 1999 growth forecast to be no more than 5 per cent. It appears that miraculous growth rates are coming down to normal levels of 5–7 per cent. High performance is partly due to high growth in the export sector, which grew by 24.9 per cent in 1995 but declined to 17.9 per cent in 1997. It improved again later in 1997, with 20 per cent growth, according to official figures, but declined to a mere 0.5 per cent in 1998. Under China's accounting system, output is counted as sold once inventoried: high levels of inventories have built up with the slow-down in the traded sector, but the unsold inventories are giving false high-growth statistics. During the same period, merchandise imports experienced a growth of 15.5 per cent, then 19.5 per cent. In 1998 and 1999, this slowed down dramatically, which is the main cause of Hong Kong's slow-down and the decline in economic activities in Taiwan, which placed so much production in the Southeastern province. Although the civil service and state enterprises were being downsized, government expenditure increased by 18 per cent and the budget deficit remains unchanged at 0.8 per cent of GDP. Due to a tight monetary policy pursued in 1997, money supply (M2) growth declined to 17.3 per cent from 29.5 per cent in 1995. With domestic demand having abated, the government is pursuing a Keynesian-type expansion by printing money and investing in upgrading infrastructure to keep unemployment down, as well as to absorb the potential laid-off workers from state enterprises. During 1995–97 a total of 3 million workers were laid off in the state sector.

The country is very successful in attracting foreign direct investment (FDI). It received US$45 billion during 1997. This makes China the second largest

Table 9.1 Economic and social indicators of development in China

Indicators	Averages								
	1971–80	1981–90	1991–93	1994	1995	1996	1997	1998[a]
National accounts								
Gross Domestic Product								
Growth (%)	6.9	9.0	11.7	12.6	10.5	9.6	8.8	7.8
Per Capita GDP (US$)	n.a.	291	417	464	584	671	860	765
Private Consumption/GDP	0.616	0.561	0.510	0.485	0.452	0.507	0.475	0.47
Gov. Consumption/GDP	0.078	0.083	0.125	0.137	0.120	0.134	0.114	0.12
Financial indicators								
Gross Domestic Savings (% of GDP)	32.5	34.4	39.7	42.2	41.9	41.4	41.5	41.5
Gross Fixed Capital Formation (% of GDP)	30.2	35.7	35.1	40.9	40.2	39.6	38.2	39.0
Inflation	1.4	7.5	10.2	24.2	17.1	8.4	2.8	-0.8
M2/GDP (%)	n.a.	60	100	101	104	112	121	132
Fiscal Balance (% of GDP)	n.a.	-0.5	-0.9	-1.2	-1.0	-0.8	-0.7	-1.2
Current Account Balance (% of GDP)	n.a.	-0.1	0.1	1.3	0.2	0.9	3.2	2.5
Trade Balance/GDP (% of GDP)	n.a.	-0.8	0.5	1.4	2.6	2.0	6.1	4.2
Debt Service ratio (% of Exports)	n.a.	n.a.	11.6	8.9	9.9	10.1	9.8	n.a.

Social indicators

IMF classification	Low	Low	Low	Low	Low	Low	Low	Low
Literacy rate (%)	n.a.	65*	n.a.	n.a.	n.a.	82	n.a.	n.a.
Unemployment rate (%)	n.a.	2.4	2.4	2.8	2.9	3.0	3.0	8.5
Expenditure on education (% of exp.)	n.a.	2.1	2.6	n.a.	1.8	n.a.	n.a.	n.a.
Expenditure on health (% of exp.)	n.a.	0.4	0.4	n.a.	0.3	n.a.	n.a.	n.a.
Population growth	1.7	1.5	1.2	1.0	1.1	1.05	1.10	1.20

Notes:
[a] A mid-1999 estimate of GDP growth for 1999 is 7%.
* 1983 figures.

Sources: IMF, *International Financial Statistics*, various issues; Asian Development Outlook, 1998, 1999; Government Finance Statistics Yearbook, 1985–1996; ADB, *Key Indicators of Developing Asian and Pacific Countries*.

Table 9.2 Growth rates of basic economic indicators

| | 5-year average | | Annual average | | | | | | | |
	1976–80	1981–85	1986–90	1991	1992	1993	1994	1995	1996	1997	1998
GDP	7.71	10.07	7.77	8.00	13.19	13.82	12.60	10.50	9.60	8.7	7.80
Inflation	2.63	4.11	10.65	5.10	8.56	17.00	24.10	17.10	8.30	2.80	−0.80
Revenue	7.46	11.45	12.16	9.01	15.02	22.51	2.55	19.63	18.01	16.78	11.94
M1	25.58	21.30	18.36	28.22	30.34	43.08	28.51	18.84	19.79	25.05	28.0
M2	24.86	23.88	24.67	26.68	30.80	42.80	35.06	29.46	25.27	20.73	35.0
FDI		67.70	16.69	25.21	155.52	146.64	22.79	6.10	13.81	11.03	−0.88
Trade balance		21.30	18.36	−4.60	−40.72	−305.56	−168.43	147.60	8.23	136.60	8.45

Note: M2 = (M1 + quasi-money).

Sources: IMF, *International Financial Statistics*, various issues; World Bank, *World Bank Databank*, Feb. 1997; ADB, *Asian Development Outlook*, 1998, 1999.

recipient of FDI among all countries, and first among the 126 developing countries.

3. LIBERALIZATION

This experience of adopting gradual economic liberalization can be studied according to several phases. The first phase covered the period 1978–84, during which reforms were oriented to recover from the 1975–76 crisis of leadership and the accumulated effects of the cultural revolution. The policies designed and implemented in this phase were of short-term nature, emphasizing trials to test new incentive system for agricultural production, allowing market-based operations in price determination and relaxing restrictions imposed on individual decision-making in both the agricultural and the industrial sector. Another interesting and rather bold measure in this phase was the decision to end isolation from the world. The government established special economic zones as a means of attracting foreign investment and technology: private-sector incentives were permitted to operate in these areas but not in the domestic sector.

The second phase spanned 1984–88, with the focus on the urban industrial sector. Policies implemented were about reforms to the pricing, taxation and wage systems in urban areas. An important aspect was the establishment of a central bank. This led to reforms to depository institutions, and important financial-sector reforms implemented to mop up the increased savings from the real sector returning to market-oriented economic activities. The third phase started in the middle of 1988 and continued to 1991, and focused on correcting the negative impacts of certain policies implemented in the first two phases. As a result, the authorities were able to stabilize price volatility.

The fourth phase started in 1992 with the intention of accelerating the reform process and opening up to the world. Broader policies were designed and implemented, leading to more reforms in the financial sector, introducing a more appropriate legal framework, and restructuring the role and the functions of government and social-sector reforms.

3.1 Economic Liberalization

Fiscal-sector reforms

In the pre-reform era, fiscal policy had no role in macroeconomic management. In a centralized system, the main objective remained administering allocation of scarce resources by central planners. The tax system was of little use in the absence of individual and enterprise income tax, with all enterprise profits to be transferred to the state. The reform process has brought major changes in the tax system; for example, the mid-1980s saw the introduction of enterprise taxation through the Contract Responsibility System (CRS). The CRS required tax payment according to a negotiated tax contract rather than a standardized tax schedule. Under this system, the authorities decided to tax various forms of enterprises differently, on the basis of their economic importance and social desirability. Later in 1991, with the objective of unifying the taxation of all foreign-funded and domestic enterprises, it was decided to levy tax on all foreign enterprises and joint venture firms, both subject to the same tax. Further tax reforms were implemented in 1994, including a unified corporation tax of 33 per cent, a new value-added tax (VAT) on production, a reduction in income tax (ranging from a low of 5 per cent to a high of 45 per cent), a new and complex capital gains tax (CGT), applied to both property and stock transactions, a consumption tax on luxury items such as alcohol, tobacco and cars, and a business tax for services ranging from 3 to 20 per cent.[4]

The second important fiscal reform aims to curtail public spending. The experience of most transitional economies shows that they end up spending a large portion of their budget as subsidies, which includes subsidies to the loss-making public enterprises. Reforms were now directed at these subsidies. Efforts were made to reduce this spending with the hope of eventually eliminating subsidies to the agricultural sector and all products. This was not to be achieved quickly. An element of subsidy is expected to remain on the books until retail prices are adjusted to cover all costs of production: the root cause of this problem is price maintenance. At the same time, the reform has made progress in reducing the subsidy to state enterprises. These policies will be discussed in detail later in this chapter.

The third aspect of creating fiscal discipline is in the proper allocation and distribution of resources between the centre and the provinces. Starting in 1988, China introduced a combination of tax-separation and revenue-sharing approaches. The government implemented a fiscal contract system whereby the central government was able to redistribute part of the fiscal resources from surplus to deficit provinces.

While most of these policies have been directed towards revenues collected from enterprises, the non-state sector and foreign-funded enterprises were neglected until recently. While China was encouraging more autonomy in the public sector and intending to provide more incentives/opportunities to private and foreign investment, neglecting the foreign sector resulted in huge revenue losses. As a remedy, the government launched a comprehensive reform package in 1994. The new package focused, simultaneously, on the tax system, tax administration, public-sector spending, intergovernmental fiscal relations, budgetary procedures and the government administrative and personnel system. Later this system was abolished and replaced by one of uniform income tax on domestic enterprises. The new tax has a single, standard rate of 33 per cent on state enterprises, collectives and private enterprises. The government also replaced the previously individual income taxes on Chinese and foreigners by a new personal income tax which applies to both residents and foreigners. Similar changes were made to the indirect tax system.

To improve the efficiency of tax collection and distribution between the centre and the provinces, the government abolished the contract-based inter-governmental revenue system. It established in its place the National Tax Service (NTS) to collect all central and shared taxes. The government introduced this system in 1992, on an experimental basis, whereby nine provinces and municipalities were authorized to collect their own taxes. This trial helped to clarify the taxes to be collected by the centre, or by provinces, or to be shared. As a result, the provinces will depend less on the centre and will have more incentive to improve their system of tax collection. Measures such as the implementation of Budget Law in 1994 have also been used to improve budgetary procedures and government administration.

State-owned enterprise reforms

The state-owned enterprises in China had no autonomy until the reforms were initiated. All major decisions on production, pricing and investment were within government control. Surplus funds had to be transferred to the state budget and losses and investment were dependent on subsidies and funding from the state budget. Hence, one of the main concerns of these reforms was to give greater autonomy to the state-owned enterprises, SOEs. These enterprises also lacked management capability and had little accountability, which is a prerequisite for autonomy. An important step in this direction was the issuance of new rules, the Provisional Regulations on the Enlargement of Autonomy of State Industrial Enterprises, in 1994.

Other reforms in this context were further measures of taxation, as discussed earlier, as well as the introduction of two important laws, the Bankruptcy Law 1988 and the Enterprise Law 1988. The main purpose of these laws was to make SOEs accountable, as well as to create gradual autonomy in decision-making, which it is hoped will reduce reliance on the state budget. In 1992, provisional regulations were also issued to establish two types of shareholding, namely, the limited liability companies and the joint stock companies (or limited liability stock companies). To provide proper legal coverage for these experiments, China established the China Securities Regulatory Commission (CSRC) in 1992 and introduced the Company Law 1993. These measures are aimed at giving maximum legal support, introducing incentives to public ownership and also attracting foreign investment.

On the employment side, a labour contract system was authorized in 1986 for all new workers, giving both the employees and the employers a free hand to terminate the employment contract at any time. The 'iron rice bowl' promise of Communism no longer holds, at least for these new workers. The progress made in implementing this system is slow: until 1992, only 21 per cent of the total labour force were employed under this contract system. The authorities introduced an unemployment insurance scheme, which provided some cash relief and training, along with some assistance if the unemployed wished to establish businesses. Policies have also been implemented on a limited and experimental basis to provide some housing benefits to employees.

Besides weaknesses in the design and formulation of policy that failed to cover the overall systematic framework within which the enterprise economy should operate, especially during the early stage of the reform process, one cannot ignore the improvement in the efficiency of SOEs that has contributed to rapid economic growth. The government also took some bold measures to reform other sectors of the economy which are directly or indirectly linked to the operation and performance of state enterprises. For example, the price controls on certain essential items until 1991 resulted in huge state enterprise losses. Price liberalization that took place as early as 1992 has had positive impacts on the performance of SOEs. Thus our analysis suggests that China has made a good deal of progress in enterprise reforms, though a lot more is needed to convert the system into a completely market-based economy.

Price reforms
This transitional economy has been very successful in transforming a completely controlled pricing system into a market-based pricing system. Though much progress has been made, we should not expect the system to become free from all kinds of rigidities. The government has been able to reduce the subsidies to individuals and enterprises, but was not able to eliminate them completely. The reforms are also tied to removing controls over prices of many commodities. By 1992, the number of producer goods under mandatory controls was reduced from 737 to 89.

External-sector policies
The major objectives of external-sector reforms were to break the isolation the country imposed on itself and to open the economy to the rest of the world to boost foreign trade and investment: in other words, to integrate the domestic economy with that of the world. To achieve these goals, the authorities started with the transfer of improved technology to China and introduced measures to boost exports, which helped to reduce reliance on foreign borrowing. It may be interesting to note here that China's 'open to the world' policy started in early 1970, much earlier than the actual economic reforms were initiated. At the initial stage, China was only interested in trade relations without any foreign investment. With the package of overall economic reforms in 1978, the government encouraged foreign enterprises to invest in China both for export

Table 9.3 Investments in China (US$ million)

	5-year average		Annual						
	1981–85	1986–90	1991	1992	1993	1994	1995	1996	1997
Direct investment (net)	616.6	2141.6	3 453	7 156	23 115	31 787	33 849	38 066	41 673
Portfolio investment (net)	157.8	614.8	235	–57	3049	3543	789	1 744	6 804
FDI (inflow)	996	2 853	4 366	11 156	27 515	33 787	35 849	40 180	44 236

Sources: IMF, *International Financial Statistics*, various issues; World Bank, *World Bank Databank*, Feb. 1997; ADB, *Asian Development Outlook*, 1998, 1999.

goods and for new technology. Efforts have also been made to provide protection to foreign investors by invoking a proper legal framework. Passing many laws in this regard helped: for example, the Joint Venture Law and the Foreign Enterprise Law of 1979. The rights and interests of foreign investors were also protected by the 1982 revision to the constitution.

A major step in this regard was the designation of open economic zones (OEZs) that promoted trade and foreign investment in these designated areas but restricted access to the interior of the country. The government adopted new regulations in 1980 to establish three special zones in Guangdong (Shantou and Shenzhen) and Fujian (Zhuhai and Xiamen) provinces. A special economic zone (SEZ) administration was also established to manage these zones. This administration was authorized to draw up development plans, organize their implementation, examine and approve investment projects, deal with the registration of such enterprises, issue licences and land-use permits, coordinate working relations among the different ministries to reduce the bureaucratic bottlenecks for them, and provide legal protection for the investors. Certain tax and other benefits were also provided to attract foreign investors. Another related development aimed at accelerating foreign investment was the establishment of economic and technological development zones (ETDZs) in 14

Table 9.4 *Performance of special export zones*

	Year	Shenzhen	Zhuhai	Shantou	Xiamen	Hainan
Number of signed contracts	1980	142	–	–	–	–
for FDI	1985	605	117	109	–	–
	1990	602	386	174	–	–
	1994	2221	516	547	692	802
Contracted volume of FDI	1980	218.8	–	–	–	–
(million US$)	1985	974.9	130.5	16.7	–	–
	1990	516.0	282.9	147.9	–	–
	1994	2831.3	1022.9	1311.7	1864.9	1224.7
Actualized foreign	1980	2.7	–	–	–	–
investment (million US$)	1985	32.4	7.3	0.8	–	–
	1990	47.7	9.6	8.4	–	–
	1994	1729.6	762.9	773.9	1241.5	1289.0
Export trade	1980	–	–	–	–	–
(million US$)	1984	265.0	11.0	4.5	–	–
	1990	2572.7	456.3	419.5	–	–
	1994	–	1487.8	2202.4	5650.9	987.0

Source: Chan (1998).

coastal cities, which included Tianjin, Shanghai and Guangzhou, all of which offered economic incentives to foreign investors similar to those of SEZs. These two sets of incentives were the reasons for the large-scale movement of foreign capital to China. Of course, the much-advertised market of a billion people was not there, given the low incomes and the absence of a sizeable middle class. One report estimated that the middle class consisted of about 70 million compared with another poor country, India, with a corresponding 220 million.

These policies worked well to substantially improve the growth of commodity trade and foreign investment in China (see Table 9.4).[5] As of 1998, China is the eleventh largest exporting economy and second largest host country for foreign investment.

3.2 Financial Liberalization

The pace of financial liberalization was slow, experimental and only taken gradually, in some instances not covering the whole country. The liberalization process that started as early as 1978 has not given sufficient coverage to financial-sector needs and remains somewhat incomplete. Many new developments took place. The establishment of and central direction by the newly formed central bank has been very important to set the operations of commercial banks on the right track. Measures have been taken to give more autonomy to specialized commercial banks to improve the payment system, to develop securities markets and to adopt reform policies relating to the non-bank financial institutions. These issues are discussed in this sub-section.

Monetary policy

In the pre-reform period, the main instrument of monetary policy was a credit plan and a cash plan. Due to price rigidities, the demand for currency was highly correlated with cash incomes, with excess supply of money having no impact on prices or balance of payments. Under a mono-banking system, the credit plan was the only instrument to achieve its monetary target and it served as a loanable fund plan. After 1978, the credit plan alone was not enough to achieve the target, due to increasing financial transactions within an increased number of financial and non-financial institutions in the economy. It was this delinking that led to the mushrooming of illegal money dealing and credit groups that lay at the root of the reforms to the financial system. Had the Communists ignored this development, these unlicensed activities would have generated huge illegal holdings, as is happening in Russia. The credit plan also became separated from the loanable fund plan. The reform process brought gradual openness in monetary policy, by allowing other instruments such as bank lending, reserve requirements and interest rates to be used while controlling money supply. As a result, the reforms helped to change the monetary policy mechanism from direct to a mixture of direct and indirect controls.

The credit plan sets targets for assets and liabilities of the financial institutions, the central bank's monetary base and for lending. The plan has a bottom-up approach, where targets for next year's deposits and lending are planned at the branch level of the People's Bank of China, the mono-bank. The head office of the PBC will then announce the national credit plan after taking into consideration the prevailing economic environment and future movement of basic macroeconomic variables. The ceilings for total lending and investment lending set at the national level are then disaggregated for each branch.

The loanable funds are controlled by other instruments. One of the main post-reform policy instruments was PBC lending to specialized banks. This instrument helped these specialized banks to manage their overall liquidity through short-term credits to meet their credit targets in case of shortage of deposits. Annual lending has one- to two-year maturity, which basically helped to meet the planned credit targets. The maturity of short-term lending ranges from two to four months to 10 to 20 days. This helps to cover seasonal withdrawals of deposits. The PBC also makes available rediscounting of commercial paper with six-month maturity.

The reserve requirement is the second most important tool of monetary policy. Banks are required to have 13 per cent of their domestic currency deposits as reserves with the PBC; this rate is among the highest in the world. Demand and time deposits of specialized banks, universal banks, rural credit cooperatives, urban credit cooperatives and trust and investment companies are subject to this regulation, while deposits of fiscal and interbank transfers are exempted. Interest rate is another policy instrument used by the authorities.[6]

The possibility of authority-initiated open market operations as a policy instrument became available with the development of money markets. However, the PBC lacked knowledge and experience of dealing with a money market that still did not function well. It will take some time for the domestic bond market to develop to full scale to support open-market operations. With the opening up of the financial sector, the interest rate has also been used recently to provide a supporting role in controlling money supply. But the rate is not completely determined by market forces, and may not yet serve the purpose at this point. Only continued reform will help to resolve these issues. However, the most fundamental problem, which needs immediate attention of the authorities, is the question of central bank independence. Even with a separate role for the PBC, the major policy decisions are still taken at the state council level and by the Ministry of Finance. Moreover, the deposit and lending targets are still fixed in view of the needs of loss-making SOEs. Finally, the PBC provides resources to finance fiscal deficits. Unless deficits are reduced to a reasonable level and the domestic bond market is fully developed, this function of the PBC will and must continue. Until then, the PBC will not be able to function as a monetary authority, a role assigned to it as the central bank in a

Table 9.5 Monetary aggregates, income and balance of payments (% of GDP)

	5-year average			Annual							
	1976–80	1981–85	1986–90	1991	1992	1993	1994	1995	1996	1997	1998
M1	22.00	32.00	39.00	42.00	44.00	48.00	46.00	44.00	45.00	50.40	55.0
M2	33.00	49.00	73.00	86.00	91.00	100.00	101.00	104.00	112.00	120.76	126.0
Budget balance	–2.00	0.00	–1.00	–1.00	–1.00	–1.00	–1.00	–1.00	–1.00	–0.7	2.5
Current account balance		0.00	0.00	3.00	1.00	–2.00	1.00	0.23	0.87	3.23	47.0
Private consumption	60.00	59.00	53.00	48.00	47.00	45.00	46.00	48.00	48.00	47.48	46.24
Gov. consumption	8.00	8.00	8.00	13.00	13.00	13.00	13.00	11.00	11.10	11.37	12.0
GFCF	32.00	33.00	39.00	27.00	31.46	37.62	35.78	34.17	33.64	33.78	39.0
Government expenditure	29.00	22.00	20.00	18.00	14.47	13.46	12.30	11.49	11.44	12.14	13.49

Notes:
M2 = (M1 + quasi-money).
GFCF – Gross Fixed Capital Formation.

Sources: IMF, *International Financial Statistics*, various issues; ADB, *Asian Development Outlook, 1998, 1999*.

function as a monetary authority, a role assigned to it as the central bank in a future market economy.

The last but not the least important argument of monetary policy is the regulatory framework governing the financial institutions. China introduced Bank Laws in 1994. In the absence of the Bank Laws, the authorities had regulations. The regulations provided two broad categories of rules which define the functions, structure and duties of financial institutions and specify regulations on their services in dealing with cash, credit, foreign exchange and interest rates. In the post-reform period, the financial institutions are subject to two types of supervision, off-site and on-site. Until 1995 and even after the implementation of the Bank Laws, it remained true that the main purpose of the regulations was to implement the credit plan. The prudential regulations were implemented only in 1995, requiring banks to observe the capital adequacy ratio, liquidity ratio and limitations to exposure to risk.

The banking sector

Since the Communists took over China and until 1978, the banking system followed the Soviet model. The People's Bank of China as the single financial institution had the sole responsibility to provide credit to public enterprises. After the establishment of the PBC, all private banks inherited from the previous system were gradually merged into the PBS. The PBC operated directly under the State Council. Hence it emerged as the mono-bank in 1955, with an extensive nationwide branch network. Under this system the head office would receive deposits of all branches and then issue compulsory plan targets of loans to the branches, which they were obliged to pursue. The main drawback of the system was that most funds were controlled or used by the state budget, leaving limited scope for credit expansion. Therefore, the PBC served as a supplier of funds to the SOEs, with prices not playing any role, nor the demand for funds playing any role in determining credit.

Table 9.6 lists the dates and substance of financial-sector reforms.

Table 9.6   Financial reforms

Date of reforms	Liberalization policies implemented
1980	Enterprises allowed to issue corporate bonds.
	Foreign exchange certificates issued.
1981	State Council approves issue of government bonds.
1984	People's Bank of China (PBC) established as the central bank of China.
	Specialized banks established to engage in commercial banking activities.
	Government issues security trading regulations.

Date of reforms	Liberalization policies implemented
1985	Regulations Governing Foreign Banks and Joint Chinese Foreign Banks in SEZ announced.
	Shenzhen Foreign Exchange Swap Centre opened.
1986	Commercial banks established at the provincial level.
	All banks allowed to engage in foreign exchange transactions.
	Shanghai Foreign Exchange Swap Centre opened.
	ICBC Shanghai creates the secondary over-the-counter market.
1987	Two universal banks established and permitted to compete with existing banks in all forms of businesses.
	RCC and UCC established under the supervision of ICBC and ABC.
1988	State Council approves secondary market for government bonds in 61 cities.
1989	Commercial banks expand their foreign exchange operations.
1990	Shanghai and Shenzhen stock exchanges started.
1991	PBC starts using security companies as underwriters.
1992	Foreign banks allowed to open more branches in Guangzhou, Dalian, and Tianjin, and the SEZs.
	MOF and SCRES issue new accounting system for shareholding enterprises.
	State Council open 28 inland cities and 14 coastal cities to foreign trade and investment. These cities are granted preferential policies.
	Authorities announce the rules and regulations governing joint stock companies.
	MOF issue new accounting system for foreign-funded projects.
	Bank of China announced the flotation of foreign currency bonds in the domestic market.
	PBC appointed 7 accounting firms in Hong Kong to audit accounts of 35 enterprises that have applied for listing in Shenzhen and Shanghai markets.
	The authorities opened the National Foreign Exchange Adjustment Centre (NFEAC) in Beijing. The centre is fully computerized and has participants from 42 local swap centres.
	NSC established to formulate rules and regulations governing the securities markets in PRC.
	Securities and Supervision Administration Committee (SSAC) established to supervise and regulate the securities industry.
1993	PBC issued 16 provisions to regulate activities in interbank markets.
	Chinese residents are allowed to take Y 6000 abroad.
	The authorities imposed a cap on swap market rates.
	The Beijing Financial Market is replaced with the newly established Beijing Financial centre.
	The authorities implemented regulations on transaction in foreign exchange swap markets.
	State Administration for Exchange Control allowed trading of foreign currencies by local individuals in Guangzhou and Shenzhen provinces.

Table 9.6   continued

Date of reforms	Liberalization policies implemented
	The authorities issued Provisional Regulations on the management of Stock Issuance and Trade.
	Provisional Regulations on the Registration and Management of Futures Market are issued by State Administration of Industry and Commerce.
	Fully computerized NETS for trading of stocks and bonds became operational.
	Interest rates increases on:
	– 1.8% on term deposits
	– 0.8% on working capital loans
	– From 11% to 14.06% for 5-year T-bonds
	– From 10% to 12.52% on 3-year T-bonds.
	The authorities removed the cap on swap market rate.
	New Accounting System implemented.
1994	The authorities implemented a new exchange system unifying the exchange rate determined in the interbank market.
	NEITS became operational linking 12 major cities and planned to be expanded to 8 more cities.
	Foreign Exchange Trading System (FETS) starts operation.
	Three Policy Banks established, namely, State Development Bank, Export-Import Bank, and Agricultural Credit Bank to take over policy lending.
1996	New Foreign Exchange Control Ordinance promulgated which allowed RMB to be convertible for trade related account transactions and lifted restriction on repatriation of profits and dividends by foreign investors.
1997–9	State-sector reforms. New tax codes and administrative reforms. New codes of commercial laws enacted. Serious efforts being taken to reduce the state-owned enterprises with three aims. Some of them will be developed to become very large profitable enterprises to face the competition from international firms; some will be corporatised and listed, and owned by workers and the state. The rest will be privatized.

Sources: Goldie-Scott (1995); Tseng et al. (1994); Bell et al. (1993); Ho (1998).

The first phase of reforms in the depository institutions was initiated in 1978, and continued until 1984. The authorities reinstated the status of the Agriculture Bank of China, and the Bank of China in 1979. The People's Construction Bank of China was turned into an independent financial institution, still under government ownership! Further reforms were initiated during the period 1978–84: the State Administration Bureau of Foreign Exchange was set up to administer foreign exchange; commercial banking businesses went to the Industrial and Commercial Bank of China. By 1984, the PBC was transformed to become the central bank. Commercial banking activities were transferred to the newly established specialized banks mentioned above. Specialized banks for rural development agriculture, for imports, exports, and foreign exchange, for fixed investment, and for industrial and commercial activities emerged, still belonging to the government! These measures were implemented to meet the increased demand for credits as a result of privatization and decentralization, which led to growth, which in turn created demand for credit and securities from the residents.

The second phase of banking-sector reforms took place during the period 1984–94. At the very early stage of liberalization, the authorities realized that the four specialized banks might not be able to cope with the diversified needs for financial services. The private-sector demand for credit increased substantially due to increased wealth now created by 15 years of more open economic activities. Therefore, the authorities decided to increase the number of banks and expand the activities of financial institutions. Besides the existing large specialized banks, the authorities approved some small banks such as the Bank of Communications, China Everbright Bank, the Shenzhen Development Bank and the Shenzhen Merchant Bank, all of which still belonged to the government! They also encouraged the establishment of finance companies and units for rural and urban credit operations. The period also witnessed the opening of branches and representative offices of foreign institutions, securities markets and securities companies. The other important development in the banking sector was the interbank market that operates at the municipal and provincial levels. In 1997, the first privately owned bank was given a licence to operate from one branch in a major city.

The third phase of reform was initiated in 1994 and still continues. The government has established three policy banks, namely, the State Development Bank of China, the Agricultural Development Bank of China and the Export–Import Bank of China. These policy banks are given responsibility to make loans according to government policy, a function that was given to the specialized banks. This move, it was claimed, was to help specialized banks to operate on a purely commercial basis, since commercial lending is now separated from policy lending, which the PBC still does although it is not consistent with its function as an independent regulator.

As of 1993, the PBC had 2550 branches in China with Y 1017 billion of assets. The four specialized banks, namely, the Industrial and Commercial Bank of China, the Agricultural Development Bank of China, the Bank of China, and the People's Construction Bank of China (PCBC) had 123 161 branches and Y 4457 billion of assets. Besides these banks, the banking system has six universal banks, three development banks (China Investment Bank, Guangdong Development Bank and Shenzhen Development Bank) and three housing saving banks. The country also has 52 763 branches of rural credit cooperatives and 4011 branches of urban credit cooperatives, which collect deposits and extend credit to rural and urban households and enterprises, respectively. The system also comprises 69 foreign-deposit-taking banks and four foreign joint venture banks and finance companies.[7]

As regards the functions of specialized banks, the Agricultural Bank is in charge of loans to communes, state farms and individual peasants, as well as supervising rural cooperative units. The PCBC is responsible for payments and supervision of the state budgetary appropriations for investment in all sectors of the economy excluding agriculture, and the supervision of investment from enterprise funds. The PCBC also extends loans to state enterprises for fixed capital investment. Foreign exchange transactions are managed by the Bank of China with over 200 overseas branches. This bank is solely responsible for handling trade-related foreign exchange and international settlements and remittances from overseas Chinese. It has offices in many foreign countries in Europe and Southeast Asia. Thus ownership has not changed, but specialization is taking place.

Foreign banks were also allowed to open branches in China as part of the open-door policy initiated in 1979. The authorities adopted a restricted provision whereby the only banks allowed in were those from industrialized countries with international banking experience. Moreover, the reciprocity principle followed in international banking, as is clear from this gesture, would also give the PRC access to overseas operations. In 1979, Export–Import Bank of Japan became the first bank to establish a representative office in Beijing. In April 1985, the PBC announced Regulations Governing Foreign Banks and Joint Chinese–Foreign Banks in SEZs. Accordingly, foreign banks were allowed to operate in certain SEZs, and to deal with foreign exchange districts. The State Council allowed foreign banks and joint venture companies to operate in SEZs.[8] By the end of 1990, China had 209 representative offices in 14 coastal cities with 88 representative offices (42 per cent of the total) from Japan alone, reflecting the huge investments Japan had made in China. By the end of 1991, China had 37 financial institutions, of which 32 were foreign banks and 5 were non-banking enterprises (see Table 9.7).

Although the reform process is slow and gradual, and the central bank still has a dominant role in allocating and transferring funds between provinces, the commercial banks have emerged from a mono-bank to a more diversified and presumably competing banking system. As regards the administrative set-up in the reformed system, the specialized banks are given independence to supervise their branches. However, this administration is weak due to lacklustre supervision, with insufficient resources, frequent intervention from local governments and the regulation of the local PBC branches (Huang, 1998). The reforms allow banks to retain part of their profits for development and staff benefits. With a system of relatively fixed interest rates and without responsi-

Table 9.7   Structure of the financial system[a]

	No. of branches[b]	Assets (in billions of yuan)
Banking system		
PBC	2 550	1 016.8
Specialized banks		
ICBC	31 495	1 430.0
ABC	56 417	789.0
BOC (domestic and foreign)	7 110	1 422.0
PCBC	28 139	816.0
Universal banks		
Bank of Communications	547	106.1
China International Trust and Investment Corporation Industrial Bank	6	26.3
China Everbright Bank (established 1993)	–	1.5
Hua Xia Bank (established 1993)	–	1.7
China Merchants Bank	9	8.9
Fujian Industrial Bank	7	5.7
Development banks		
China Investment Bank	30	24.1
Guangdong Development Bank	11	15.6
Shenzhen Development Bank	–	6.0
Other banks		
Yantai Housing Saving Bank	5	0.4[c]
Bengbu Housing Saving Bank	–	–
Shenyang Cooperative Bank	34	–
Chengdu Huitong City Cooperative Bank	7[c]	0.1[c]
Cooperatives		
RCCs	52 763	245.4
UCCs	4 011	110.5
Other deposit-takers		
Foreign deposit-taking banks	69	5.5[d]
Foreign joint venture banks and finance companies	4	22.6[c]
Non-bank financial institutions		
TICs and ITICs	386	224.5
People's Insurance Company of China (domestic and foreign)	4 237	48.0
Finance companies	29	18.3
Financial leasing companies	12	0.7[c]
Security companies (Ministry of Finance)	63[c]	–
Security companies (PBC)	87	–
Foreign insurance companies	2	–

Notes:

[a] In the past two years, many new financial institutions have been established. This table does not fully capture the diversification of the financial sector.

[b] Includes all branches and saving deposit offices and business offices.

[c] Figure for 1990.

[d] In billions of US dollars.

Sources: China Statistical Yearbook, 1993; Almanac of China Finance and Banking, 1993; and People's Bank of China Annual Report, 1992.

bility for bad loans, banks seem to be engaged in attracting loans by taking high risks. This was evident in 1999 with the collapse of about 40 investment houses, of which the most notable was that of the Guandong Industrial Trust Investment Corporation (GITIC), which lost US$60 billion, as reported in Internet publications.[9]

Reforms in Non-Bank: Financial Institutions (NBFI)

The liberalization of the NBFIs started as early as 1978 with the establishment of trust and investment companies (TICs), rural credit cooperatives (RCCs) and other institutions engaged in leasing, insurance and securities transactions. China International Trust and Investment Corporation (CITIC) started operations in 1979. It engages in raising funds from foreign sources to finance foreign-funded enterprises through loans and equity participation. CITIC is a holding company with diverse interests in production, technology, finance, trade and services.

The basic function of RCCs, which work under the supervision of the Agricultural Bank, is to collect idle funds in rural areas and extend loans as well as provide advisory services to rural businesses and residents with financial problems. Similarly, urban credit cooperatives (UCCs) operate under the supervision of the PBC and are independent legal entities. They provide services to collectives and private industrial and commercial enterprises by taking deposits, extending loans, and undertaking settlement and remittances. The total assets of RCCs increased from Y 95.57 billion in 1985 to Y 299.95 billion in 1990, a 21 per cent growth. Similarly, total assets of UCCs increased from Y 3.19 billion in 1987 to Y 28.42 billion in 1990. Total assets of TICs improved from Y 23.89 billion in 1986 to Y 77.44 billion in 1989. The CITIC enjoyed an increase in its assets from an estimated Y 8.03 billion in 1986 to Y 33.78 billion in 1990. There were about 260 CITICs before the 1999 collapse of about 40 of them, one of which, GITIC, was among the biggest.[10]

Interest rate reforms

During the central planning era, interest rate on deposits was considered as a kind of exploitation and hence was never given any importance. With the 'iron rice bowl' of Maoist rule, little needed to be saved, and none would have to live in retirement on interest income, a scourge of the decadent capitalist system. So the story-line about exploitation was most fitting. In the post-reform period, this attitude towards interest rates changed gradually and some importance is now being placed on interest rates and related policies. It was realized when inflation was rampant after reforms that the real interest was not enough to attract deposits. Although the interest rate on a one-year fixed savings deposit was raised from 3.24 per cent in 1978 to 13.14 in 1990, there were several episodes of real negative interest rates during a span of 12 years. Similarly, in the pre-

Table 9.8 Exchange rates and interest rates (annual averages)

	5-year average			Annual average							
	1976–80	1981–85	1986–90	1991	1992	1993	1994	1995	1996	1997	1998
Exchange rate (market)	1.64	2.33	4.22	5.43	5.75	5.80	8.45	8.32	8.30	8.28	8.28
Interest rates (%)											
Deposit rate	5.40	5.98	8.60	7.56	7.56	10.98	10.98	10.98	7.47	5.67	3.78
Bank rate	–	–	7.92	7.20	7.20	10.08	10.08	10.44	9.00	8.55	4.59
Lending rate	5.04	6.88	8.96	8.64	8.64	10.98	10.98	12.06	10.08	8.64	6.39

Notes:
M2 = (M1 + quasi-money).
Deposit rate (end of period).
Exchange rate: (principal rate) = yuan per US dollar.

Source: IMF, *International Financial Statistics* (various issues).

reform period, interest rates on short-term loans used to be higher than those on medium- and short-term loans! So much for the market economy of capital. Interest rate reforms brought cost, term and risk considerations. When setting up interest rates and rates for medium- and long-term loans, these were set higher than short-term loans. After 1996 the financial institutions were allowed to set their own interest rates within a 30 per cent band around a base rate set by the authorities. Another major development was that the specialized banks adopted different interest rates for different enterprises, depending on these enterprises' demand for credit and speed of capital turnover, which is the beginning of risk consideration for lending activities.

Stock market development

The primary market for securities started in 1981 with the first issue of Treasury bonds sold by the government to enterprises and individuals. During 1988–90, the authorities developed a secondary market for securities. During the same period, the government established the National Electronic Trading System (STAQ) in Beijing. In 1991, the Ministry of Finance changed administrative placement of bond system to marketing sale of bonds through underwriting by financial institutions.

The basic reason for establishing the securities market was the change of focus from inflationary financing to bond financing. In the past, the government had adopted the policy of printing money (and unsterilized currency inflows) to finance consistent fiscal deficits, which had resulted in rising inflation. From the early 1990s, the focus changed to financing the deficits through bond financing. Accordingly, it was decided to take measures to develop money and capital markets to sell short- and long-term Treasury bonds. In 1990, the government initiated the issuance of such bonds, underwritten by financial institutions.

Securities exchanges were initiated in 1990–91 in Shanghai and Shenzhen, with the establishment of these stock exchanges that allowed trading in government and enterprise bonds and shares of joint stock companies. This was only done after about four years of experimental trading with decadent Western instruments such as shares and bonds in two cities, Shenzen and Shanghai. In 1992, the policies were further relaxed to allow foreigners to participate in this trading, which led to the creation of A- and B-class instruments. To further boost investor confidence, the authorities established two regulatory bodies in 1992 to supervise the development of the securities industry. The National Security Law was implemented. These measures helped to boost the stock market and, as a result, the number of shares listed rose from 15 to 113 by mid-1993 with combined capitalization estimated at under 10 per cent of GDP. In 1998, these two exchanges had almost 350 stocks traded. The authorities were able to sell bonds worth Y 100 billion by 1994.

Initially, the authorities opened category 'A' shares, which were denominated in local currency and were open to Chinese investors only. By 1994, the authorities had permitted 42 'B' shares, denominated in renminbi or yuan but open to foreigners in the New York, Hong Kong and Singapore markets in foreign currency. During the same year, 11 'H' shares were placed in the Hong Kong Exchange.

Another important institution is the interbank market. This is one of the most important sources of lending and borrowing among banks and other financial institutions. Before the reforms, China had a system of vertical allocation of credit from the State Council through the central bank. Under this arrangement, banks with surplus funds would hold on to them while banks with shortages were not given access to credit. Though some efforts were made to ease credit allocation as early as 1979, it was only during 1983–85 that this system was transformed to a horizontal circulation of funds across banks and industrial sectors. In 1986, the PBC issued a notice on Provisional Regulation on Management of Banks in the PRC under which the interbank market was formally established and all financial institutions were given the right to handle interbank borrowing and lending. Branches with a temporary excess of funds would lend to those branches in need of them. In 1990, the PBC issued Provisional Measures on the Management of Interbank Business. These markets were established in economically and financially advanced cities, with the restriction of one market in each of these cities. The PBC supervises the activities and operations of these markets.

The foreign exchange market

The Bank of China is responsible for any external foreign transactions including foreign exchange and international settlements of trade-related transactions and remittances from overseas Chinese businesses. China experienced various reform arrangements in the foreign exchange market. Before reforms were initiated, it was normal for several exchange rates to operate in trade transactions between foreign trade corporations (FTCs) and domestic enterprises. The authorities established a single exchange rate in 1981 for international settlement of trade transactions that were done below the official exchange rate. The official exchange rate was devalued in later years and eventually the exchange rate was unified in 1984. But capital and current account controls are still in place so that the system is still a fixed one.

A dual exchange rate system re-emerged in 1986 and was maintained until 1993. Under this system, there was an official exchange rate that was subject to periodic adjustments and a local market-determined rate set in the foreign exchange adjustment centres (FEACs) or swap centres. A third rate was a parallel market (or black market) rate determined by the usual demand for foreign exchange. The official exchange rate was pegged to the US dollar. The yuan was devalued by 21 per cent in 1989 and 9 per cent in 1990. The second rate was set at a relatively depreciated level as compared to the official rate. This system required the domestic enterprises and FTCs to surrender their export receipts at the official exchange rate and receive retention quotas against them. These enterprises were then permitted to trade these retention quotas at the swap centres. Initially, the scheme was restricted to foreign-funded projects only, but later in 1988 all enterprises with foreign exchange retention quotas were allowed to trade in the swap centres. Gradual liberalization removed controls on the determination of the swap market exchange rate and by 1991, all residents were allowed to sell foreign exchange at the swap rate at designated branches of banks. However, the purchase of exchange was subject to approval by the State Administration of Exchange Control (SAEC).

As regards individual earnings, earnings of individuals working abroad were required to be repatriated but were allowed to be maintained in foreign currency accounts within domestic banks. The same rule applied to remittances. Foreigners were issued with foreign exchange certificates, denominated in yuan, against any foreign currency brought in and could be used for domestic transactions. Up to 50 per cent could be reconverted at the official exchange rate. For capital transactions, SAEC had the responsibility to monitor country's external borrowing. All medium- and long-term commercial borrowings were subject to SAEC approval. Foreign direct investments were subject to approval by the Ministry of Foreign Trade and Economic Cooperation.

In 1994, the government again unified the exchange rate set at the prevailing swap market rate and abolished the retention system. It was decided that renminbi, also known as yuan, should be the only legal tender in China effective at 1 January 1994. According to the new rules, domestic residents were required to sell their foreign exchange receipts from abroad to designated financial institutions. However, most of the categories included foreign flows and these were allowed to be kept in foreign exchange banks.

The new system also abolished the prior approval for the purchase of foreign exchange for trade and trade-related transactions. Businesses involved in trade and holding relevant documents were allowed to purchase foreign exchange from any designated financial institution.

The unified exchange rate is determined at the interbank market and is a managed float system with a ±3 per cent movement in renminbi allowed against the US dollar. Another major reform was the establishment of the China Foreign Exchange Trading System (CFETS) in Shanghai, effective from 1 April 1994. This is an electronic system for foreign exchange trading. An institution, to trade in foreign exchange, is required to be a member of CFETS. These measures helped to stabilize the currency. From 1994 to 1998, the currency has been managed in a very stable range of 8.7–8.3 per US dollar. With the economy weakening and domestic demand waning in 1999, the rate has come

Table 9.9   Indicators of financial liberalization (% of GDP)

	5-year average			Annual						
	1976–80	1981–85	1986–90	1991	1992	1993	1994	1995	1996	1997
Money Depth (M2/GDP)	32.8	49.4	72.7	86.0	91.3	100.3	100.6	104.3	112.2	120.8
Inter-relations ratio										
FIR (total)/GDP	0.46	0.62	0.86	0.99	1.02	1.11	0.98	0.92	0.96	1.05
FIR (public)/GDP	−0.07	0.0	0.02	0.03	0.04	0.04	0.03	0.03	0.03	0.03
FIR (private)/GDP	0.52	0.62	0.84	0.96	0.98	1.07	0.95	0.89	0.93	1.01
GFCF/GDP	n.a.	28.5	28.8	27.5	31.2	37.5	36.0	34.7	35.6	33.78
FDI/GDP	n.a.	0.3	0.8	1.1	2.3	4.6	6.2	5.1	4.8	4.81

Notes:
M2 = (M1 + quasi-money).
FIR = Financial intermediation ratio – claims on public sector, claims on private sector, and foreign assets.
GFCF = gross fixed capital formation.
FDI = foreign direct investment.

Sources: IMF, *International Financial Statistics*, various issues; World Bank, *World Bank Databank*, Feb. 1997; ADB, *Asian Development Outlook, 1998, 1999.*

down below 8.00, and there were speculations in mid-1999 about a possible future depreciation of the yuan to regain economic competitiveness with the much more depreciated currencies in the neighbourhood.

These efforts have helped to reduce the gap between the official and parallel exchange rates. However, the currency is still not fully convertible and more policy changes need to be implemented to transform this sector into a completely market-determined one. At the time of writing, it seems that the promise of a fully open currency regime by the end of 1999 may not happen in view of the jitters about the likely instability of such a move, as happened in many Asian countries following the 1997–98 crisis.

4. CONCLUSION AND FUTURE PROSPECTS

China initiated major economic liberalization policies only from 1979. It did this in two clever ways: by experimentation and by retaining the command structures at the top without real decentralization. This is in direct contrast with the big-bang approach advocated by Ivy League scholars and tried in Eastern Europe's transitional economies with serious disruptions. China's reform process was gradual but consistent, with learning from small-scale applications and gradual extensions.[11] Given the political, economic and social environments that prevailed for many years before 1979 and the subsequent economic chaos of the type unleashed by big-bang reform approaches in Russia, for instance, the achievements of China are commendable despite criticisms in some quarters that China's reforms are not widespread.[12] However, it is not clear if such a slow process of reform could have worked in other emerging economies in Eastern Europe, where the economies had greater social development and higher industrial development.

The progress China made up to 1999 and the current strength of the Chinese economy are visible, with continuing interest of domestic and foreign investors. The international banks are still lending, though the country has built up huge loans at state level from multilateral lending and international development assistance: see Ariff (1998c). China has recorded very high growth rates simply because of pent-up demand and the release of the entrepreneurial energy of its people. At the close of the century, there were unsold inventories of goods waiting for customers, which have brought economic deflation, and a trend towards lowered growth rates since 1997. China is now the world's tenth largest trading nation in terms of value traded, although its share of world trade is not large (see Chapter 17). It is still a recipient of the largest foreign direct investment among developing countries because it is also the largest country, with seemingly potential markets for the multinationals from countries with near-saturated demand for goods and services. These multinationals are still waiting for the emergence of a reasonably sized middle class, the important structure needed before the kind of goods that multinationals are good at producing is demanded. That too if China permits them to enter the domestic markets in ways another giant economy, India, has made possible. If Indian political uncertainty can be reduced, India is equally attractive to the multinationals since it has a larger middle class.

During the 1997–98 financial crisis that affected most Asian economies, China managed its current and capital accounts ably to avoid major setbacks from the contagion effect. That was possible because of the fences still in place in the form of controls on capital and currencies, not because of its innate economic efficiency. Many in 1999 were speculating that China would eventually bow to the pressure and devalue the yuan in the year 2000. However, up to the time of writing, it has resisted the temptation to devalue, and greater persuasion may be needed to restrain it in the future, as more new cheap production points become available for international capital. If that happens, it will destabilize not just China, but all those who have a big stake in the country. Readers will be aware that several countries have invested too much in China. Another devaluation is bound to lead to another round of realignment of the competitive pecking order, bringing with it a huge cost to the world economy.

China has not become fully unshackled from a mind-set of central planning even though it pretends otherwise, as stated in official meetings and press briefings that such a rebirth is taking place. The sudden release of energies of the people, given choices for the first time in 1977–79 after 30 years of repressed central planning, led to enthusiastic independent economic actions not supervised by the central planners. That released the energies of a hard-working people as never before. This cannot last forever without serious reforms to bring in real competition by changing ownership rules and allowing freedom of entry into economic activities. There is also the need for development software in the form of legal rights, an independent judiciary, central banks, a professional civil service, military, police, and so on for a real return to market-economy model. China hopes to achieve all this in an experimental fashion while keeping Party control on the country. Only time will tell if this is a compatible or volatile mixture of aims.

NOTES

1. The financial press stated in late 1998 that China's mass media widely reported the anger of the premier as he witnessed the melting away of concrete dams, built to withstand flood water, as the river levels rose in several places. It appears that the contractors and provincial cadres in charge of building dams were lax in enforcing strict standards of dam construction. It took a flood to reveal to the rulers in Beijing the extent of corruption that had permeated

state-directed activities. Strident moves to reform the state sector are being taken since the new premier took control.

2. This episode is well documented in the literature on the Gang of Four, one of whom was the widow of Mao himself, who was tried and imprisoned to be executed, only to die of cancer.

3. The Tiananmen event, as it is euphemistically referred to by the world, refers to the events of the night of 4 June 1989, when a student uprising was violently put down by the PLA: Deng was then the Chairman of the committee in charge of the PLA. Students had taken control of Tiananmen Square, and they had some limited support of the clandestine workers' movement. China's cabinet took a decision after an emergency meeting of the Council on the eve of the crackdown, when the Premier Li Peng gave a speech stating that the student uprising was against the state and would be brought to an end at any cost. During the next few months, all those who took part were tried, some executed, and others imprisoned. There is no consensus on how many died, and China treats the event as a closed matter.

4. For more details on these taxes, see EIU (1995), p. 16.

5. Despite these efforts, 1986 witnessed a sharp decline in foreign investment in China, basically due to declining profits. Some explanations for this decline include low productivity, lack of motivation in the workforce, rapidly rising costs, especially for office space and accommodation, excessive bureaucratic bottlenecks and, most importantly, foreign exchange controls. Some measures were taken to improve the situation in 1986 under the 'Twenty-two Articles' reform package.

6. Interest rate reforms have been discussed in a separate section, see page 246.

7. The figures were obtained from Tseng et al. (1994), table 3, p. 13.

8. Initially, these banks were allowed to take deposits and make loans in local currency. However, the PBC later withdrew this allowance to protect the domestic banking industry from competition.

9. A May 1999 report in the *South China Post* describes the judicial finding that assets to the equivalent of 17 cents in a dollar of assets have been recovered.

10. See Dipchand (1994, ch. 5) for these figures.

11. For example, the establishment of stock exchanges preceded experimentation in two cities over several years on how to trade on the capitalist mode. Only after a period of learning was the bond and stock exchange established.

12. Gorbachev, the architect of reforms in the Soviet Union was asked about the failed Russian reforms in a television interview broadcast by SBC network in May 1999 in Australia. He said that he, when he was then the equivalent of a president, was planning for a slow reform over about 15 years, with large and painful changes. Only such a route, he said, would have been successful. Perhaps he was right in this regard.

10. Vietnam: hesitant transition from command to market economy

1. BACKGROUND

Vietnam straddles the eastern coast of mainland Southeast Asia from east of Cambodia to south of China and covers an area of 332 000 sq. km with a population of 73.5 million.[1] Much of Vietnam is rugged mountainous country and is densely forested. Agriculture, the main sector, absorbs about 72 per cent of the labour force, contributing about 32 per cent of GDP. Vietnam has reasonable mineral resources, and coal is an important export item as well as the main source of energy. Political unification of the divided Vietnam occurred in 1976 after the fall of a South Vietnam government supported heavily by armed support of the USA.

Economic liberalization over the ten years from the mid-1980s brought about fundamental changes to the structure of the economy. Vietnam has claimed to be in a reformist mould since its reunification with the south in 1976, when it announced an economic model for the Democratic Republic of Vietnam (DRV). Because of the mixed characteristics – market-oriented economy in the south and central planning in the north – the reforms failed to produce any tangible results over 1976–79. Having had a bad experience with this so-called first reform, and after noting the success of Deng's initial reforms in China during 1977–79, Vietnam moved away from a command-economy model towards a market-economy model after 1979 by adopting several new measures followed right up to 1988. But it was not until the year 1989, some ten years later, that Vietnam made efforts to implement major economic reorganization by shifting its policy stance from the command-economy model to become the boldest reformer at that time among the transition economies. Private initiatives were to be the basis of the changed focus thereafter, and reforms have taken on a bolder character especially after Vietnam's admission to the ASEAN economic grouping.

This led to dramatic increases in harvests; rice exports became possible and the industrial sector responded with mild growth. However, the country still suffered supply shortages, had low export capacity, had very little managerial capacity and lacked capital and foreign investment. Energy was in short supply, as were raw materials and spare parts. The result was that Vietnam experienced a serious balance of payments deficit in the early 1990s. There was also a decline in remittances from nationals working in Eastern Europe and in the Middle East. A huge reduction in aid and subsidies from the former Soviet Union made the situation worse. Recovery occurred in the mid-1990s. The resulting economic achievements since 1996 could be considered the most successful for a transition economy.

The next section summarizes the financial and economic structure of Vietnam – Southeast Asia's second largest country. It is noticeable that the structure is vastly different from that of the other ASEAN countries covered in Parts 2 and 4 of this book. Section 3 provides the main focus of this chapter in that it describes the liberalization steps taken to achieve a measure of development that was not possible in a command-economy model. The final section discusses the future prospects for sustaining economic growth.

2.   ECONOMIC AND FINANCIAL STRUCTURE

Before the implementation of the actual economic reforms in 1981, an observer of this economy could describe the situation as a planned economy mired in under-development. State-owned enterprises dominated the industrial and agricultural sectors: the latter, which was the mainstay of employment and production, was organized as cooperatives, the classical tool of the Communists to bring about proletarian equity. Another typical symptom was that there was near zero domestic savings. The only foreign investment was from the countries of the former Soviet Union.

The failure of DRV-originated reforms during the years 1976 to 1980 ensured that post-unified Vietnam also did not improve much. Improvements were to come later as a result of market-based reforms that were implemented in the mid-1980s, which began to extract a little growth out of an economy still taking time to restart and retool. Several factors contributed to this trend. These include continuous emphasis on subsidizing the inefficient state-owned enterprises, misalignment of policies, and the rapidly changing political conditions in the region, particularly the war with Cambodia, its neighbour. Protection and continuous financial support to the loss-making state enterprises also contributed to huge fiscal deficits, which increased from 5.5 per cent of GDP in 1987 to 11.4 per cent in 1989. Having only limited external resources also forced the authorities to resort to domestic credit expansion by printing money. Money in circulation increased from 12.3 billion dong in 1985 to 83.3 billion dong in 1988, which was a massive 89 per cent growth per year. Average inflation in 1986 reached a record high of 800 per cent as a consequence of the failure in monetary management.

Meanwhile, the external economy also worsened. Current account deficits remained in double digits until 1989. The country slid into slow growth in exports and imports. Exports could not generate the targeted income to finance the much-needed imports for technological upgrading in the industrial sector, the sector that might be a saviour. External debt remained high, in the range of US$15 billion. Despite efforts made by the government, both domestic investment and saving were very low compared with those in several countries in the region. In fact, domestic saving during the period 1987–89 was negative, a sign of lack of confidence in the financial structure of the country. This unenviable economic situation prevailed during much of the first five-year economic planning period from 1986. This plan also coincided with major political and economic changes in the region, particularly those in the major donor countries of Vietnam, which dashed any hope of relying on them to assist in the plan's objective of achieving the targeted outputs.

A series of reform measures became necessary. These were introduced as a result of the failure of the first plan. The second plan period covered 1991 to 1995 and this time the economy responded to market-based structural reforms. Major recovery could be seen. GDP gained an average increase of 8.2 per cent while industrial production increased by an unprecedented average rate of 13.5 per cent per annum. Another major achievement was a reduction in inflation, which declined from 800 per cent in 1986 to around 9 per cent in 1995. This was a feat not achieved by very many of the 20-odd transition economies.

The industrial sector depended on old machinery and equipment and outdated technology. Consequently, efficiency was low and maintenance costs were high.[2] During the more recent transformation period, when dependence on government for improving the infrastructure in state enterprises was rapidly declining, the upgrading of technology has taken priority. Securing adequate funds for capital investment is the core problem. According to the 1995 statistics, investment in capital accounted for 20 per cent of GDP. This is a reasonable figure for a transition economy, but is still quite low compared to capital investment of 30–40 per cent of GDP in the fast-track countries such as South Korea and Thailand. This scarcity of capital, coupled with inefficiencies and leakages in capital usage, poses a big threat to sustaining growth. The major task is still the mobilization of domestic capital and the creation of conditions for foreign capital to be attracted to the country. Given the poor infrastructure and the absence of legal institutions relating to private ownership, attracting foreign capital will be a difficult task.

2.1 The Current Economic Environment

Table 10.1 shows statistics[3] which suggest that this county achieved an economic growth level of 9.5 per cent in 1995 which later dropped to 4 per cent due to the regional crisis. The year 1994 seems to be the peak year for both exports and imports, which increased by 35.8 per cent and 48.5 per cent respectively. This trend also slowed down later, and exports recorded a mere 3.9 per cent increase in 1998 while imports registered a decline of 2.3 per cent during the same year. Industrial growth recorded a 12.1 per cent rise in 1998 while investment increased by less than 5 per cent only. Foreign capital is a major contributing factor to the high industrial growth. Agricultural output increased by 3.6 per cent during 1998. Due to the high budget deficit of 5.5 per cent of GDP, money supply still continued to increase by 22.6 per cent in 1995. Inflation, which reached its lowest level in 1993, increased to 12.7 per cent in 1995 and then started to slow down.

According to the 1997 statistics, the share of the agricultural sector is 26 per cent while that of the industrial and services sectors contributed 31 and 43 per cent respectively. Per capita income in 1999 was US$280, which would place Vietnam among the poorest of the poor countries. Labour participation is 51 per cent and agriculture absorbs 72 per cent of the labour force while the state sector absorbs a massive 24 per cent. Vietnam has a high literacy rate of 89 per cent, despite the fact that expenditure on social services including health and education is still very low.[4] Foreign debt of US$26.5 billion exceeded the GDP of US$22.5 billion in 1998.

On the basis of these figures, it can be said that this transition economy has at last begun to make reasonable progress during the last decade. The economy is returning to limited levels of achievement on many fronts from market-friendly policy mix, which is the source of the higher growth rates being registered since 1995. This is also acknowledged by the developed countries in the ASEAN. These more developed countries admitted Vietnam as a member of ASEAN in recognition of this progress. However, the country is just beginning on the road to the level of affluence already achieved by the more developed market economies in the region. Consistent efforts to continue the reform process are needed to make gains in order to catch up with the region's level of development.

The government is learning a great deal from the successful experiences of the other ASEAN countries, which consistently followed a remarkably market-friendly policy mix as a path to development.[5] All the same, the Vietnamese policy-makers should be mindful of the wrong or hasty policies of the ASEAN countries, which lifted residual controls needed on current accounts and led to the recent problems following the 1997 baht contagion. However, before assessing the policies to be adopted by Vietnam, we shall document the steps that have been taken in Vietnam since 1989, the year when reforms began to take effect. Most of the remaining part of this chapter is devoted to this topic.

Table 10.1   Basic economic indicators of development in Vietnam

Indicators	1987	1988	1989	1990	1991	1992	1993	1994	1995	1996	1997	1998
GDP (% change)	4.0	5.2	8.0	5.1	6.0	8.3	8.0	8.80	9.5	9.3	8.2	4.0
Growth rate of GDP (per capita)	1.7	3.0	6.4	0.2	3.6	6.1	5.6	6.6	7.4	7.3	6.2	2.3
Inflation rate	301.0	308.2	95.8	67.5	67.4	17.6	5.3	14.4	12.7	4.5	3.6	9.2
GDI (% of GDP)	10.9	14.4	11.6	12.6	15.0	17.6	23.6	25.5	27.1	28.1	28.3	28.7
GDS (% of GDP)	-2.1	-0.2	-0.2	2.92	10.1	13.8	16.5	17.5	16.1	17.8	21.5	24.6
Budget deficit (% of GDP)	-5.5	-8.3	-11.4	-8.0	-3.7	-3.7	-5.2	-2.3	-1.5	-1.3	-1.7	-1.5
Current account balance (% of GDP)	-9.2	-16.9	-10.4	-4.2	-1.9	-0.1	-7.1	-8.0	-11.0	-10.3	-6.8	-4.1
External debt (US$ billion)	13.0	14.0	14.6	22.1	22.3	23.8	24.4	25.1	26.8	n.a.	n.a.	26.5
Changes in money supply (M2; %)	466.9	252.5	121.1	59.5	78.8	33.7	18.9	27.8	22.6	22.7	26.1	22.0
Growth rate of merchandise exports	8.2	21.6	87.4	31.1	18.0	21.2	20.6	35.8	28.2	41.0	22.2	3.9
Growth rate of merchandise imports	13.9	12.3	-6.9	6.1	18.8	20.4	39.3	48.5	43.8	38.9	-1.6	-2.3

Source: Asian Development Bank (1998a, 1999).

3. LIBERALIZATION

Vietnam went through three significant reform steps: a failed attempt to reform during 1976–80; a crippling monetary crisis as a result of inflation during the first plan covering the years 1986 to 1990; and recovery over 1991–96 under the reforms of the second plan. Soviet-style socialist economic reforms adopted in the 1976–80 period turned out to be a disaster as they were inappropriate policies for a transition economy. This led to two currency reforms, which destroyed public confidence in the government's ability to manage finances, with savings turning negative. The other major factor in the failure of this first phase of reforms was a shift in focus to heavy industries. Heavy industry development was inappropriate to an agrarian economy, especially when the ability of the sector to be efficient had been curtailed by lack of proper technology and capital needed to upgrade it. This was soon realized and the focus was shifted to agriculture. This important reform was termed *bung San xuat*, meaning 'production burst'. These policies were not very successful and the economy suffered major setbacks. These failed reform episodes put pressure on the government to restructure the whole reform process on a new foundation.

The Sixth Congress of the Communist Party in December 1986 tackled this issue and a new beginning was made. The resulting *doi moi* (renovation) reforms instituted a shift away from the Marxist–Leninist Soviet model and recognized private ownership as the foundation for stimulating economic activity. It was recognized that Vietnam faced many problems, including misallocation of resources, high population growth rate, low productivity, dual pricing structure, and so on because of the wrong foundation for stimulating economic activity. This was a lesson learned more than ten years earlier in China. Having an inefficient system of taxation and the dead weight of loss-making state enterprises were seen as the causes of huge growing budget deficits. Money supply expanded to pay for subsidies and salaries within the mono-banking monetary system, which resulted in high inflation at times. Moreover, poorly understood managerial reforms, coupled with the bureaucratic resistance to change in the early phase, also led to unenthusiastic implementation, and to serious supply and distribution problems during 1981–89.

Vietnam soon suffered severe misallocation of resources and workers had no incentive to be efficient. Therefore, the basic objective of *doi moi* policies was to make resources available on the basis of efficiency, shifting resources from the low productive to the high productive sectors. A contract system in the agricultural sector was put in place while the state-owned enterprises were allowed to swap and sell goods privately, giving an incentive to use these proceeds to buy inputs and pay for services. The *doi moi* reform process was accelerated in 1989. The later years saw reforms in four basic areas: macro-economic stabilization; decentralization; liberalization, shifting economic management from a command economy under the state firms to a multi-sector commodity-producing economy; and the integration of the economy with the regional and global economies, which created an external economy, so that the much-needed foreign capital and technology could now be obtained.

3.1 Economic Liberalization

Fiscal-sector reforms

The analysis so far suggests that the root cause of most of the pre-existing problems was the huge and still-growing budget deficit in 1989. This deficit was due to expenditure on the state firms, in much the same way as was discussed in the previous chapter on China. Reform efforts to curtail fiscal deficit was the first priority in achieving macroeconomic stabilization. The authorities pledged to finance the fiscal deficit by domestic borrowing and foreign loans and grants, thus severing the state sector from government support and returning the state firms to the market-based model using both forms of financing (Table 10.2). Meanwhile, efforts were also made to improve the tax collection system and to reduce public expenditure: these were aimed at creating a balanced budget.

Table 10.2   Fiscal budget and financing deficits (in billions of dong)

Indicators	1987	1988	1989	1990	1991	1992	1993
Revenue	379	1 740	3 899	6 153	10 353	18 970	25 380
Expenditure	515	2 840	6 105	9 186	12 081	22 815	34 410
Fiscal deficits	136	1 100	2 772	3 033	1 728	3 845	9 030
Domestic financing	92	730	1 700	1 473	393	1 000	1 500
Foreign loans and grants	43	3 689	1 072	1 860	1 335	2 845	7 530

Source: Asian Development Bank (1998a, 1999).

Until 1990, Vietnam experienced huge budget deficits, running at an average of about 8 per cent of GDP. Major policy changes helped to abolish almost all budgetary subsidies, reducing public-sector employment and wage freeze. With less reliance on the central bank to finance the deficits, the bulk was financed through foreign loans and grants. The domestic bond market is still not developed so that it can not be effectively used for mobilizing domestic capital investment, not to mention increase the capacity of the central bank to conduct open-market operations to manage the economy. This will take a long time and more market-based reforms.

The other important factors that contributed to a reduction in the growing deficits were tax and state enterprise reforms. Tax reform policies had two objectives: to improve tax classification by introducing new taxes, and to improve tax administration by reorganizing the collection system. The lessons learned from such tax reforms have been very important to transition and developing economies. For example, Indonesia spruced up its tax system before embarking on financial and other reforms in 1986–89. The failure to put in place, in the absence of external capital resources, a healthy revenue base for government appears to be a handicap in pursuing other reforms effectively. Examples are Indonesia in the early 1980s and Russia in the late 1990s. Until 1990, the only national tax applied was on agriculture. Taxes on other sectors, such as trade and industry state firms, were based on government regulations, which led to several tax exemptions. Since 1991, the authorities have introduced new taxes and made improvements in the existing taxes, including the intro-duction of a progressive personal income tax code, corporate income tax, property tax, agricultural land tax, excise tax, turnover tax, profit tax, royalty, tariff and import and export duties.

On tax administration, measures taken also included reorganization of the management of the central and local tax offices, revision of the national accounting system, establishment of public auditing companies and central-ization of tax collection. The Ministry of Finance implemented a decree on accounting and statistics, under which state firms were required to submit doc-umentation, audited financial reports and to make tax declarations. As a result of these policies, central government revenues increased from about 6 trillion dong in 1990 to about 25 trillion dong in 1993, which is an average increase of 63 per cent per annum. Revenue collection increased by 24 per cent in 1995. However, this increase is still below expectation and is not enough to put the account in balance. Vietnam's bold steps taken in this regard explain why it did not take the same route as Russia, reforming at about the same time, to collect adequate tax revenues to be able to pay its employees.

State-owned enterprises were targeted for reform. These firms employed about a quarter of the labour force and formed a large part of the public sector. Such firms in a command economy enjoyed soft credits, even if they were inefficient and made losses. In a market economy, publicly held firms are owned by private shareholders, who have a number of methods to put pressure on management to create profits for the firm. The reform process had two direct effects here. The financial-sector reforms would make it almost impossible for an inefficient state firm to have soft credit facilities through commercial banks. Privatization of such firms was part of the reform process. These policies are difficult to implement. A major problem is to decide which firms are to be privatized. The strategy should be to first privatize the loss-making ones, as was done in the former East Germany and Malaysia.[6] Market conditions, for example, would not allow such actions, as the demand for buying such units was non-existent. Increase in unemployment from closure of these firms, even if a buyer could be found, is another problem that could emerge since such firms are generally over-staffed.

In 1991, Vietnam had about 12 000 such firms under central and local administration. The first line of reform policy was to reduce and eliminate subsidies and then reduce their access to bank credit. Other reform measures provided more incentives to the private sector to compete with them, providing a legal framework to support their operations and increase trade liberalization or even foreign competition.

Table 10.3   Composition of state and non-state enterprises (in units and percentages)

Categories	1987	1988	1989	1990	1991	1992	1993
Number of state enterprises	3 032	3 101	3 020	2 762	2 599	2 268	2 030
By sector (% of total):							
Heavy Industry	53	47	48	50	46	44	42
Light Industry	47	53	52	50	54	56	58
By type of management (% of total):							
Central	24	22	22	21	21	24	26
Local	76	78	78	79	79	76	74
Number of non-state enterprises	n.a.	350 909	356 522	390 786	456 559	374 837	461 475
By sector (% of total):							
Cooperative	n.a.	9.1	6.1	3.3	1.9	1.5	1.1
Private	n.a.	0.1	0.4	0.2	0.2	0.3	0.7
Households	n.a.	90.8	93.5	96.5	97.9	98.2	98.1

Source: Dodsworth et al. (1996), p. 45.

This is evident from Table 10.3. The number of such firms has dropped significantly after three years, thus showing that the worst cases have been closed down or sold at very low cost. Table 10.4 shows that the state sector received subsidies of about 10 per cent of GDP in 1988. But in 1994, the state sector became a significant contributor to GDP: it contributed 9.2 per cent. These figures reflect significant changes in these firms' reliance on the state budget and the commercial bank lending facilities.

Another major step to improve the state sector was taken in 1993, when Vietnam began to introduce equitization, that is, converting state firms to some form of share capital formation, on a trial basis. By the end of 1996, five state enterprises were operating under the new Company Law instituted in this reform. However, due to the reasons stated above, the process is very slow and the results are below expectation.

Table 10.4   Budget support to state enterprises (as % of GDP)

Categories	1987	1988	1989	1990	1991	1992	1993	1994
Transfers to the budget	10.8	7.9	8.4	8.6	8.1	10.8	11.8	12.1
Transfers from the budget	7.9	8.5	4.8	2.6	1.0	0.9	0.6	0.5
Net transfers to the budget	3.0	–0.6	3.6	6.0	7.0	9.9	11.2	11.6
Growth in bank credit to SOE	9.6	9.2	7.1	4.1	5.0	3.0	2.2	2.4
Net bank and budget support of SOE	6.6	9.7	3.5	–2.0	–2.0	–6.9	–8.9	–9.2

Pricing reforms

Accelerating inflation is a major problem in any economy undergoing price reforms. This is especially so in socialist economies during transition towards a market economy. The advantages of allowing market forces to determine prices are not questionable and have merits for reforming the economy on a sustainable path. Countries like China and those from the former Soviet Union and Eastern Europe experienced hyper-inflation as a result of price liberalization. Price liberalization gave rise to chronic excess demand leading to shortages and then to price increases. Vietnam could be considered exceptional in that price liberalization did not raise inflation. Rather inflation was controlled during the last few years, soon after the important agricultural and industrial sectors came under market discipline for financing.

Inflation became a major issue in 1990. Prices increased at a rate of about 90 per cent in 1990 and monthly inflation was estimated at between 7 and 9 per cent at that time. Later, the reform policies unified the dual-reform price system to a single price system, where official and free market prices were approximately in line with the adoption of freedom to own foreign currency. However, prices of some public utilities such as electricity, water, transport, fuel, postage and telecommunication continued under administrative regulations, thus avoiding mismatch of income and expenditure unleashed by such reform in other countries (for example Pakistan, Uruguay and Egypt). These reforms reduced inflation from a level of about 300–500 per cent during 1984–89 to a moderate level of 70–100 per cent in 1989. In 1997, it was estimated to be 3.7

per cent; in 1999 it had gone up to 9.2 per cent. The price reforms also improved the overall supply and demand structure of the economy when state enterprises moved to produce the commodities needed to fulfil increased demand.

External-sector policies

Export value was 45 per cent of GDP in 1999, which is a tremendous achievement over a short span of 12 years. In the external sector, Vietnam faced three major challenges. The first was to reduce the huge external capital; the second to lift the low rate of growth in exports; and the third was to continue reforms to overcome problems associated with command economies and hence to eliminate isolation from other economies. Therefore, external-sector policies were aimed at achieving three goals: policies geared towards export promotion; measures to attract foreign direct investment; and integration with other relatively more developed countries in the region and in the world.

As is evident from the statistics given in Table 10.5, there are budget and current account deficits. In 1995, the trade deficit was US$1.1 billion, while the current account deficit was recorded at US$1.7 billion. The 1999 current account deficit still stands at about US$1.8 billion or 8.8 per cent of GDP. External debt amounts to a huge US$7.8 billion in 1995 and US$16.5 billion in 1999, while the country had a very low level of international reserves, just enough to service about 2.5 months of exports against the norm of about six months. There is a general belief among economists and policy-makers that the successful experience of rapid growth in East Asia was basically due to export-led growth. In other words, it is believed that export of manufactured products can promote efficiency of investment and contribute to rapid growth. There is a need, therefore, to accelerate the rate of growth in exports, increase imports of modern technology to improve productivity in the industrial sector, and at the same time attract both domestic and foreign investment to reduce reliance on consumable imports. Achieving these goals requires major macroeconomic reforms. It is also difficult to isolate these policies from others. Here, we focus on some specific issues.

Foreign direct investment   FDI plays an important role in the rapid growth of a transition economy, as has been shown to be the case in China and Eastern Europe in the 1990s. The successful experience of ASEAN countries and the Asian tigers also supports this argument. Therefore, since the beginning of the reform process, a central focus of policies was to attract increased FDI. These measures started with the implementation of the Foreign Investment Law, passed in December 1987. The progress in attracting FDI was slow at first: until 1990 only US$120 million was disbursed against a commitment of US$784 million, a realization ratio of 15 per cent. By 1994, the actual disbursement increased to US$650 million with commitment standing at US$3.8 billion.[7]

The slow progress was attributed mainly to the bureaucratic bottlenecks in the approval of projects. Licensing of joint ventures, some reports say, may take about one year while approval for a 100 per cent foreign ownership may take about two years. The speed of approvals improved at the end of 1995. In that year, Vietnam had approved a total of 1351 projects worth US$19.35 billion of registered capital.[8]

Table 10.5   External balances

Categories	1987	1988	1989	1990	1991	1992	1993	1994	1995
Growth rate of merchandise exports	8.2	21.6	87.4	31.1	18.0	21.2	15.2	26.3	45.0
Growth rate of merchandise imports	13.9	12.3	−6.9	6.1	18.8	20.4	38.3	28.4	58.3
Trade balance (US$ mn)	n.a.	−1588	−350	−41	−63	−60	−655	−900	−1905
Current account balance (US$ mn)	n.a.	−474	−584	−259	−133	−8	−867	−966	−1729
External debt (US$ bn)	13	14	14.6	22.1	22.3	23.8	24.4	25.1	26.8
Debt-service ratio (% of exports)	n.a.	n.a.	18.9	9.3	9.1	15.4	13.6	6.1	10.5
FDI (US$ mn)	n.a.	347	536	784	1318	2290	3144	3843	3985

Source: *Asian Development Outlook*, various issues.

According to some estimates by Dodsworth et al. (1996), FDI in 1988–94 may have accounted for about 10 per cent of the aggregate economic activities. The inflow of FDI has increased with the lifting of the American embargo, with the exchange of ambassadors in 1997 and the entry of Vietnam into the regional ASEAN bloc.[9]

Regional integration   Vietnam's external policy to expand its relationship with the rest of the world is an important reform agenda. ASEAN has acknowledged the efforts in this regard. In recognition of the positive future prospects of the economy, the Vietnamese achieved full membership of ASEAN in 1995. The country is looking forward to playing an active role in other regional cooperations, such as in the APEC and AFTA groups. However, there are a number of challenges for the policy-makers to make this process smooth and effective. Measures needed are improved institutional changes in the legal framework, better-quality information disclosure, private ownership laws and so on.

3.2   Financial Liberalization

The banking reforms of 1988 altered the nature, functions and the structure of the banking system to a greater extent than any other reforms. However, these reforms have not changed the monetary management process at the central bank. In general, monetary policy reforms came as a package. It is difficult to differentiate monetary reforms from banking sector reforms, pricing reforms, interest rate reforms and exchange rate reforms. We shall, however, look at some of the important aspects of the monetary management policies designed and implemented as a result of the overall economic reform package.

Interest rate reforms

Interest rate repression is a well-known, frequently occurring set of rigidities in the banking systems in both command and mixed economies. This is supported by both theory and evidence. The low rates create waste and inefficiency in the state enterprises of command economies as well as in mixed economies. The fundamental question is whether the existing banking system of a country is capable of determining the level and structure of interest rates on its own. The implementation of a market-determined interest rate is also closely linked to the availability of alternative financial assets and fixed income securities. Here the development of money, bond and stock markets does play an important role. Complete liberalization of interest rates will depend on whether there is a reasonable level of macroeconomic stability. If past experience is any guide in this direction, there is no substitute for positive and even high real interest rates.

Major reforms to restructure interest rates took place in April 1989.[10] Interest rates are to be applied uniformly to various economic sectors and adjusted according to price changes.

- Banks have to pay interest for all capital resources mobilized as loans and must receive interest for all credits made. This is revolutionary for Communist Vietnam.
- The difference between the lending interest rate and the deposit interest rate will be a minimum of 0.5 per cent monthly.
- The interest rate must consist of both the basic and inflation rate. This ensures that the banks cannot pass on their inefficiency by creating negative real interest rates.

These reforms unified official interest rates and raised the rates on savings to positive levels. Positive interest rates continued until 1990, and led to a sharp increase in deposits in the banking system. However, high interest rates discouraged investors and thus had an adverse effect on production, resulting in a 3 per cent decline in gross industrial output in later years.

An important aspect of monetary reforms in Vietnam is the decision to change the interest rate policy. As a result, interest rates on deposits were raised to levels higher than inflation rates. After 1989, efforts were made to raise the real interest rate into the positive region, which is the key for mobilizing domestic saving. Financial reform also made it possible to make more state investment available to non-state sectors such as agricultural, consumer and export goods. Sixty per cent of state investment was spent in 1990 on these sectors, compared to 35 per cent in 1982. Furthermore, private investment increased to 30 per cent of total investment in 1990.

These efforts, however, did not work well in later years and even after the adjustment, real interest rates became negative for a while. For example, in 1990 depositors were being offered rates of 4 per cent on three-month deposits when the inflation rate was 7–9 per cent per month. This trend changed in the later years as control on inflation was gained. The rates reported in Table 10.6 show that, after 1992, real three-month saving deposit rates were positive.[11]

Table 10.6   Real and nominal interest rate spreads (% per month at year end)

	1989	1990	1991	1992	1993	1994	1995	1996	1997	1998
Interest rate spread[a]	–3.3	–1.3	–0.5	0.7	0.7	0.7	0.7	0.8	0.7	0.7
Inflation[b]	2.7	7.7	4.8	1.1	0.3	1.0	0.3	0.45	0.6	0.7
Real three-month savings deposits (households)[c]	4.3	–3.7	–1.3	0.9	1.1	0.4	–	0.8	0.6	0.7

Notes:
[a] Difference between interest rates on lending to industry and households' three-month savings deposits.
[b] Average monthly inflation during the quarter, not seasonally adjusted.
[c] Measured with respect to nominal interest rates at the end of each quarter and average monthly inflation during that quarter.

Sources: Dodsworth et al. (1996), p. 7; State Bank of Vietnam, *Annual Report*, 1995.

Although there is some improvement in later years, interest rates are still very high, around 10–12 per cent, relatively much higher than in other countries in the region. These higher interest rates and low inflation in the increasingly stable foreign exchange market have posed problems. This has created an incentive for overseas Vietnamese and foreigners to transfer foreign currencies into Vietnam as deposits in commercial banks or to buy equity of commercial banks.

Without much prudential supervision and a less regulated foreign exchange market, Vietnam might experience more macroeconomic imbalances. Thus there is a need for revision and further improvement in the policies governing the structure and operation of interest rate determination. The authorities need to provide more autonomy to the still state-owned commercial banks in deciding what interest rate should be charged on lending and borrowing operations, though some ceiling can be fixed. At the same time, authorities should devise

Table 10.7   Real and nominal interest rates (% per month; end of each period)

	1989		1990		1991		1994		1995	
	June	Dec.	June	Dec.	June	Sept.	Sept.	Dec.	June	Sept.[a]
Deposit rates:										
Demand deposits										
Households	9.0	5.0	2.4	2.4	2.4	2.1	0.7	0.7	0.7	0.7
Economic units	4.0	1.8	0.9	0.9	0.9	0.9	0.1	0.1	0.5	0.7
Three-month savings										
Households	7.0	7.0	4.0	4.0	4.0	4.0	1.4	1.4	1.4	1.4
Economic units	3.0	3.0	1.8	1.8	1.8	1.8	0.8	0.8	0.8	0.8
Six-month savings										
Households	n.a.	n.a.	n.a.	n.a.	n.a.	n.a.	1.7	1.7	1.7	1.7
Economic units	n.a.	n.a.	n.a.	n.a.	n.a.	n.a.	1.0	1.0	1.0	1.0
One-year savings										
Households	n.a.	n.a.	n.a.	n.a.	n.a.	n.a.	2.0	2.0	2.0	2.0
Lending rates:										
Agriculture	3.7	3.7	2.4	2.4	2.4	2.4	n.a.	n.a.	n.a.	n.a.
Industry and transport	3.8	3.8	2.7	2.7	2.7	2.7	n.a.	n.a.	n.a.	n.a.
Commerce and tourism	3.9	3.9	2.9	2.9	2.9	2.9	n.a.	n.a.	n.a.	n.a.

Note: [a] Rate as of 15 September 1995.

Sources: IMF (1991), p. 25; State Bank of Vietnam, *Annual Report*, 1995.

prudential regulatory laws and improve expertise to achieve a more efficient supervision of financial institutions. Reforms to return interest rates to determination by market forces are critical and are preferred over paramount interventions by the government, which create distortions in the long run in the economy.

Monetary policies (see Table 10.8)

Until 1990, financial activities were controlled by a mono-banking system. The main function of a central bank then was to receive funds from state firms and extend loans to them through the state budget. As noted earlier, this had resulted in huge fiscal deficits financed by inflationary financing due to the non-availability of other resources. Therefore, the important task for monetary policy-makers was to reduce this dependence of state firms on the state budget. As a result of some strict government regulations introduced, the financing requirements of the state firms have indeed declined sharply. Bank credit expansion fell from almost 450 per cent in 1988 to less than 50 per cent – a rate of growth still far in excess of underlying economic activities in 1990. Some major steps were taken to reform the banks in 1990 with the introduction of a Ordinance of the State Bank of Vietnam.

In 1991, capital spending of public enterprises was transferred to the banking system, which helped to increase the domestic financing needs of the state enterprises while also forcing the latter to enter into normal borrowing and lending activities without the support of the government budget for state enterprises. Consequently, to extend credit to the state-owned commercial banks, the State Bank of Vietnam reduced the reserve requirement to a uniform rate of 10 per cent. Furthermore, allowing commercial banks to draw down their excess reserves resulted in a reduction from 46 to 30 per cent of total deposits in 1991. Increasing the responsibility of commercial banks to finance state enterprises is also visible in the State Bank's decision in 1991 making commercial banks responsible for almost 50 per cent of the credit expansion.

Table 10.8   Financial-sector reforms

Date of reforms	Liberalization policy implemented
1981	Decentralization of foreign trade sector.
1985	Currency reforms: dong devalued.
1987	Devaluation of exchange rate.
	Liberal foreign investment law introduced.
	Restructuring of banking system.
1998	
18 October	Regulations on foreign exchange control.
1989	Positive real exchange rate policy devised.
1990	
23 May	Ordinance on the State Bank of Vietnam (SBV). The ordinance became operational on 10 October 1990.
	Under this law, SBV empowered to:
	– issue currency
	– formulate monetary policy
	– formulate and enforce banking laws and regulations
	– organize credit and banking transactions
	– Stabilize exchange rate (dong)
	– issue licences to overseas credit institutions
	– act as the commercial banks' bank
	– provide discount loans.
	Ordinance on Banks, Credit Cooperatives and Finance Companies.
	Under this law, SBV has to design legal framework governing the statutory mechanism and the licences issued to each credit institution and specify the activities these institutions may be involved in.
1991	
20 October	Guidelines for the Implementation of Decree No 330/CT.
8 January	Regulations on short-term credits extended to economic organizations.
6 May	Implementation of the regulations on short-term credit.

Date of reforms	Liberalization policy implemented
15 June	Regulations of foreign bank branches and joint venture banks operating in Vietnam.
16 August	Regulation on organization and operations of the foreign exchange trading centre.
5 October	Implementation of the regulations on foreign bank branches and joint venture banks operating in Vietnam.
25 October 1992	Temporary measures on the control of foreign currency.
20 January 1993	Circular No. 01-TT-NH7 on foreign exchange control implemented.
16 April	Regulations on foreign investment in Vietnam.
30 August	Promulgation of the statute governing the borrowing and repayment of foreign debts.
1994	
2 February	Regulations of savings for housing construction.
21 February	Statute on guarantee and re-guarantee of external debts.
5 March	Guidelines for the management and utilization of the government's borrowed foreign funds.
4 August	Adding and amending a number of stipulations on foreign exchange control under new circumstances.
5 September	Providing guidance for the implementation of Decision No. 396/TTG.
1997	Reduction in personal income tax for foreigners.
	Turnover tax is replaced by a value-added-tax (VAT).
	State bank takes control of about 50 joint stock banks.

Source: State Bank of Vietnam, *Annual Report* (various issues).

The financial sector experienced a major crisis in early 1990, when dozens of poorly regulated mutual funds collapsed. Another loss the commercial banks faced was in setting the borrowing rates below the deposit rates for state enterprises. The sharp increase in deposit rates increased the real broad money balances, which expanded by 83.5 per cent in 1991. The government adopted a tight monetary policy later and the broad money supply responded by a 17.4 per cent increase. However, this trend could not continue in later years and the money supply increased thereafter by 34 per cent in 1995.

In 1993, the country fixed a target of 15 per cent for money supply growth, just in line with inflationary expectations. In setting this target, no allowance was made for any increase in output or increased demand for dong from holders of foreign exchange, and hence banks faced serious cash shortages after 1997. To overcome these problems, the central bank instructed the Agricultural Bank and Industrial and Commercial Bank (i) to place 25–40 per cent of their cash deposits with the central bank, and (ii) initiated issuance of high-denomination negotiable cheques. These measures, however, proved insufficient.

Eventually, the central bank had to convert some of its gold into cash and issue new 5000-dong notes to help ease the continuing shortage in 1997–98.

Central bank reforms

In the early phase of transition in the banking industry, high priority is usually given to a strong programme of bank supervision and bank prudential legislation. This area has been fairly neglected in most of the command economies as well as the more open economies in Asia as a whole (see Chapters 2 and 17). Lack of prudential management of bank lending led to the collapse of the banking system in the face of the Asian financial crisis. The central bank's important role of promoting judicious legislation and prudential supervision in restructuring banks and in solving the technical difficulties during the transition period has now emerged in the twenty-first century as a key to international stabilization programmes. These steps can help to build and maintain confidence in the stability of the banking and financial system by providing liquidity needs as well as lender of last resort facilities.

After 1988, greater emphasis was given to restructuring the financial system of the country. The main focus of such restructuring was liberalization and decentralization of the banking system, which included reorganizing the central bank, creating functional commercial banks, specialized credit institutions and complementary capital markets. In June 1989, the Chairman of the Council of Ministers announced certain principles for banking operations in the country. These were aimed at easing the borrowing and lending activities of banks, increasing their effectiveness and eliminating the officialism in the industry, setting interest rates in a flexible and realistic manner, and enforcing the legal requirements for commercial banks to keep required reserves and excess reserves. Although the first banking reforms were initiated in 1988, formal legislation was issued only in 1990, the Decree Law on Banks, Credit Cooperatives and Finance Companies. This law provides conditions and procedures for establishing commercial banking and financial institutions in Vietnam. The main features of this legislation are:

- The State Bank now plays the role of a central bank to the four newly established commercial banks, which cover commerce, foreign trade, agriculture and investment.
- The new banks are autonomous and separate legal entities. There is a catch here!
- The banks are allowed to operate in any sector consistent with their functions and to handle direct external transactions.
- Foreign banks as representative offices, branches or joint ventures are now permitted.

- The new regulations allow for the establishment of shareholder banks by having prior authorization from the State Bank and meeting the minimum reserve levels. Thus shareholder controlled banks can be licensed; herein lies Vietnam's salvation.

However, lender of last resort intervention is only suggested to offset temporary liquidity shortfalls, and is not supposed to support large budgetary deficits. As the structure of commercial banks and rules for their supervision are established, additional central banking reforms are needed. These include full flexibility in interest rates, sophisticated market-based instruments and a deepening of the capital markets, which has not started yet, although announced to begin in 1999.

The Ordinance on the State Bank of Vietnam took effect in October 1990 and brought major changes to the operations of the banking system. This legislation converted the banking system to a two-tier system, the SBV as the central bank acting as the monetary authority. The SBV became the sole authority to issue currency, formulate monetary policy, design and implement banking laws and regulations, organize banking and credit transactions, monitor and manage exchange rates and interest rates, and conduct the function as lender of last resort. The ordinance also empowered the SBV to formulate and implement policies governing the operations of credit institutions, grant licences to commercial banks, financial institutions and foreign bank branches and work as an agent of the state treasury to issue securities, set reserve ratios and liquid-asset requirements for commercial banks and other financial institutions and organize a clearing-house.

Reforms in depository institutions
The four new specialized banks are Vietcombank (Bank of Foreign Trade), Agricultural Bank, Industrial Commercial Bank, and Vietnam Investment and Development Bank. The first three are considered commercial banks while the last one is a development bank providing loans to government-supported projects for state enterprises. These newly established banks have assumed various commercial banking responsibilities of the state bank. They are also allowed to operate in all sectors of the economy and were encouraged to commercialize and diversify their operations. Although, in theory, these four state-owned commercial banks are supposed to offer a complete range of banking services, in practice they are still operating in different segments of the financial markets. In 1997, most of their credit was extended to state enterprises, and the reform has not yet taken root.

The collapse of the largest of 5000 of the 7000 credit cooperatives in 1990 led to huge losses, and increased uncertainty. The reasons behind this large-scale collapse are several: the key ones are lack of sufficient knowledge or expertise and lack of sufficient regulations governing the operations of credit coopera-tives. With no regulation to enforce prudence, the reforms gave incentives to certain groups to take advantage of the free-market economy to make quick profits via fraud. The government has taken measures to provide appropriate regulations to prevent recurrence of this.

The depository institutions in Vietnam have gone through major changes during the last five to seven years. All the differently structured financial insti-tutions are now more independent, but are subject to policy control by the state bank. There is a catch here! They are still owned by the state. The state bank is supposed to form the core of the banking system, and has the power to regulate monetary, credit and banking activities. But where is its independence as a central bank? In the future, the central bank's role will be broadened to include supervision of the money and stock markets, which have already been announced to be formed in or after 1999. Press reports in 1999 suggested that a decision had been taken to defer the creation of such entities as stock markets.

The regulation on foreign bank branches and joint venture banks was issued in June 1991. The Bank of America – a first from America – was granted a licence to open a representative office in March 1992. The ANZ and Credit Lyonnais also opened branches. The joint venture banks were also licensed with shares from the Vietnam Foreign Trade Bank (50 per cent), Korean First Bank (40 per cent), and Daewoo (Korean) Securities (10 per cent). Commercial banking has experienced major developments during the last ten years. Compared to the four state-owned commercial banks a decade ago, Vietnam now has 25 branches of foreign banks, 4 joint venture banks and 55 foreign bank representative offices (Economist Intelligence Unit, *Country Report*, 1998). Dong deposits at the foreign banks increased to 28 per cent of the total deposits in 1998, while the loans extended by foreign banks rose to 9.2 per cent.

A joint venture bank is required to have a minimum capital of US$10 million while the requirement for a foreign bank branch is US$15 million. They are restricted to foreign currency transactions. They are, however, allowed to undertake activities in dong equivalent of up to 10 per cent of their registered capital. Seventy representative offices from 20 countries were granted licences as of end 1996.

Cooperation and coordination within the baking system in developed economies are considered important means of developing domestic banking and creating positive competition. Allowing entry of foreign banks will not only put pressure on the domestic banks to improve their services and acquire new technology, it will also help them to acquire expertise and share experience on how to deal with difficult situations such as unanticipated liquidity demands. Evidence shows that a liberalized licensing mechanism for foreign banks in Singapore and Hong Kong made an important contribution to the rapid development of the domestic banking industry in the two economies. The

Vietnam Bankers' Association, formed in May 1994, is an important step. One of its objectives is to cooperate and coordinate with the regional banking groups through dialogue and exchange of views on the issues relating to monetary policy, money and capital markets, and foreign exchange market developments. To further expand its activities, the association became an official member of the ASEAN Bankers' Association.

Stock market development

Every former socialist economy is striving to increase savings for greater capital formation. The development of a commercial banking system provides access to the working capital needs of the economy, while stock and bond markets will provide long-term capital finance at lower costs. The development of efficient financial intermediaries is essential for mobilizing resources and even for facilitating the monetary policy process. To increase the efficiency of the financial sector, it is also necessary to develop long-term capital markets. Setting up a stock market invariably requires economic and political stability. It also requires the concept of private property rights. Investors will only be willing to invest their money if they trust that they have no reason to fear abuse or fraud on the ownership issue.

The state treasury has the sole authority to issue Treasury bills; a secondary market for these bills does not exist. As a result, commercial banks find it very difficult to resell bills to meet their liquidity needs. Moreover, without a proper money market, it is very difficult to work out the returns and maturity of the T-bills even if investors are interested in buying securities from commercial banks in the resale market. To help the commercial banks to meet their liquidity needs, the state bank has to buy these bills but then loses its control over the money supply. Unless and until the operation of the T-bills market improves, the establishment of a stock market in Vietnam is difficult. Perhaps this is a major reason for the decision in late 1998 not to introduce the share market in 1999.

Although a legal stock market does not exist, there is an underground market where securities are exchanged between relatives and friends. This is similar to systems of non-institutional credit prevailing in many developing countries. Any formation of a formal stock market will provide a legal status for these transactions, which will automatically eliminate the illegal stock market activities.

In a move to establish an interbank market in Vietnam, the SBV announced and implemented regulations in September 1994.[12] This decision helped establish rules for trading in the interbank market by commercial banks, investment and development banks, shareholding banks, and foreign banks with branches in Vietnam, and foreign investment banks.

It is for these reasons that the authorities claim that the establishment of a stock market in Vietnam will be gradual and pursued in stages. In the first stage, during 1992–96, they decided to formulate the necessary legislation and devise a registration system and share index, while in the second stage, during 1996–2000, they planned primary stock markets to be introduced in Hanoi and Ho Chi Minh City. Some recent developments show that the stock market may not start operation before the year 2000.

Foreign exchange market

Financial-sector reforms also encompassed exchange rate reforms. The foreign exchange control system is still highly regulated and under a continuous reform process. Despite the tight regulation of the foreign exchange market, the fundamental factors of supply and demand have set the train in motion. The government has partially adjusted the exchange rate. Efficient allocation of foreign exchange to its best uses requires that the exchange rate be unified.

The government unified all exchange rates for the dong in term of convertible currencies to a single official exchange rate from March 1989. As early as 1990, the authorities devised ways to reduce the spread between the official and black market exchange rates. In May 1990, the black market exchange rate fell from 4200 dong per US dollar to 7100. The rate fell from 14 000 dong per US dollar in December 1991. The exchange rate in 1999 has been hovering around 13 900 dong per US dollar.

The foreign exchange trading floor, called the Foreign Currency Transaction Centre (FCTC) at the state bank branch of Ho Chi Minh (HCM) City, was set up in August 1991. This spot auction market operates on a marginal price basis and is held twice a week. The market deals in US dollars. Commercial banks, foreign trade organizations, and gold import and remittance companies participate in the trading. Having a legal centre for foreign exchange trans-actions helped to depreciate the dong further and to reduce the spread between the parallel market. In May 1991, the government introduced foreign currency savings accounts for households to mobilize foreign exchange. Vietcombank in Ho Chi Minh City is the only commercial bank involved in foreign exchange intervention, along with the central bank. The reader will recall the unification of parallel exchange rates in China in 1995. To expand further its active role in foreign currency trading, Vietcombank established a dealing room in 1993.

The central bank has also enhanced its supervision of the foreign exchange trade of commercial banks and has instructed commercial banks to have a foreign exchange rate fluctuating between ±1 per cent from the rate it announces daily. However, the actual fluctuation recorded in 1997 was ±5 per cent. Besides all these efforts, the actual market conditions suggest that the parallel market for the local currency and other major currencies still exists and the gap between the official and black market exchange rate is quite wide.[13]

4. ASSESSMENT OF FUTURE PROSPECTS

The discussion so far suggests that gradual and partial reforms adopted by Vietnam have been relatively successful in bringing economic stability to this transition economy within a short period of a dozen years. The policy mix contained fewer pitfalls, compared with what happened in other economies in similar situations, as is commonly noted in the literature in reference to the reform policy mix used by former Soviet Union or East European economies. The key factor in the success is that Vietnamese leaders have shown better insight into the institutional requirements of a socialist market economy. They have carefully constructed sequences of economic and financial liberalization by building the necessary institutions. In this process, they have avoided the spiral of hyper-inflation and lack of supply of goods, as has been the case in other former centrally planned economies. The keys to this were (a) delinking state enterprises from fiscal support while making credits to them through a reformed banking system; (b) making the commercial banks responsible for their lending and borrowing decisions; and (c) taking pre-emptive actions to reform the tax system to keep the fiscal balance from getting worse. These factors were missing in many transition economies.

However, not all is well with the still largely Communist-controlled statist model of development. Property rights, ownership of stocks of firms by the public and freedom of entry into any economic activities without the need for approval are still not in place for a market-economy model. To improve the efficiency of credit allocation, the monetary authority should increasingly rely on a more flexible interest rate structure to reflect market conditions, and real interest rates should be made positive, as already has been mentioned. There is a clear need to move to indirect methods of monetary control, away from the bank-specific credit quotas, by introducing effective reserve requirements in the form of statutory and liquidity reserves. So long as the mounting debts of the state enterprises and increasing dependence on bank credits continue, it will result in an unexpected increase in the state budgetary deficits. This problem may become even more severe as financial liberalization picks up speed in the opening years of the new century.

An important observation from the above analysis of the Vietnam experience is that money is still an accounting instrument of aggregation and control. Capital and investment are centrally allocated in real terms, while financing of those projects is mostly provided automatically from the state budget. The emergence of a hybrid marketized sector reflects a fundamental structural change that is still in progress. Because of the increased pressure from state enterprises for finance, more credits and currency have been issued than is desirable. Friedman's dictum that credit growth not too far in excess of growth in economic activities and money in circulation is the key for any country wishing to bring down inflation and create sustainable growth. This is not the case here, with credits growing at close to 50 per cent!

Vietnam's economic- and financial-sector reforms still face enormous challenges. Feeding the state sector through state loans and ignoring banking reserve requirements has resulted in financial and fiscal instability in the past. The price system and adjustment mechanism are still underdeveloped. Distortions such as supply bottlenecks, monopolistic pricing and an inefficient capital structure still exist in the economy and there is a need to improve the system by reducing them. There is also a need to improve the infrastructure and to privatize more state-owned enterprises. Furthermore, the country needs to increase domestic resource mobilization and develop a legal and regulatory environment ahead of creating an efficient financial system. The achievement of some degree of macroeconomic stability, while providing finance for the social sector and infrastructure, is basically dependent on the availability of external resources. The policy-makers in the country should focus on these issues if the economy is to achieve sustained and rapid growth over the next few years.

Certain priority areas are identified below for special attention in the future.

- The state budget should be strictly and carefully managed. Efforts should be made to increase revenues and curtail expenditures to reduce budget deficits. More reliance should be placed on domestic financing of budget deficits rather than external financing, which results in a heavy external debt of US$26.5 billion, which is 120 per cent of GDP.
- The state bank's capacity to manage and control the money supply should be enhanced. The payment clearing system should be improved and interest rate determination increasingly left to market conditions. This would raise the banking deposits and create an environment for the private sector to effectively participate in building and restructuring the economy.
- The exchange rate mechanism needs further improvement and more legislation to curb the black market. The government should also devise policies to make the dong the only medium of exchange in the domestic goods market, a move that China has already taken, but Vietnam has not.
- The stock market is the least reformed sector in the whole liberalization process in Vietnam. Its prompt development will help bring in changes to the ownership structure of production assets.

Although certain policies have been devised in the past, not much progress has been made either to establish the market or to formulate a legal framework to make such a market efficiently operative. Information about the operation of the financial market is not only lacking to the investors but also to the managers of commercial banks and supervisors of these markets. There is a need to enhance the capabilities of these managers and supervisors through frequent training programmes.

These reforms will come in in the near future to build on the limited success this former command economy has achieved during the 12 closing years of the old century by returning to a market economy. What we said of China is equally applicable to Vietnam. The market-economy model so well popularized by the Communists to legitimize themselves in these two countries is not at all the market economy of open economies. The Communists shouldn't kid themselves. With ownership of productive assets still largely in the hands of the state, and without the independence of the central bank, the judiciary, the military and the police from the political rule-makers, the changes to date are merely cosmetic. They have helped to preserve control by the Party of the significant means of production, and they have used the resources from gains made from a tremendous release of people's energy after years of control. The achievements speak volumes in support of continuing genuine changes to create for posterity a vibrant free-market-based society if conservative policies are abandoned early in the new century.

Fundamental changes of greater importance must be made as Vietnam begins to learn this lesson in the classrooms of the more developed ASEAN countries, to which the economic administrators/managers are now being sent for training. The enthusiasm for reform, particularly in the financial sector, began to wane after Vietnam witnessed the melt-downs of more powerful economies when speculative attacks on neighbours' currencies exposed the stark weaknesses in the financial management of these fast-track economies in East and Southeast Asia. Vietnam should by now have realized that a realignment of currency rates was long overdue in those countries when in fact its own entry and that of China realigned the competitive equilibrium in favour of these countries (and Pakistan and India) for the production of low-value-added goods and services for world markets. The currency realignment would have to come first but, given the banking mismanagement in those countries, realignment also led to banking collapse and declines in growth rates over three years. After the financial storm did its worst by mid-1999, all but Indonesia were still mired in loss of vigour due to political rather than economic weakness. Therefore, the lesson that emerges is that more genuine liberalization is the proper route to growth and prosperity for the Vietnamese people.

NOTES

1. This is based on an old estimate. Since the population has grown further, the current estimate would be closer to about 78 million. After Indonesia, this country is the second largest in the ASEAN group.

2. During our visit in 1997 to a textile factory in Hanoi, we noticed that this was indeed the case. Reliance on very outdated and less efficient production was obvious in several other sectors, for example, hotels, roads and public transportation. Former French civil servants' mansions have become hotels, and roads are in bad shape, as are the vehicles travelling on them. Upgrading the basic infrastructure is another core problem.

3. Availability of data, even on major economic indicators, is a big constraint in Vietnam. There is a usual lag of three years in obtaining statistics on such variables. We have tried our best, in this chapter, to provide the latest figures available. As of June 1999, statistics on variables in the fiscal and financial sectors were not available beyond 1996. Some of the figures are taken from Economist Intelligence Unit's county profile for Vietnam.

4. Total expenditure on social services, education and health was 2.2, 2.8 and 4.2 per cent of GDP during 1987–89, respectively.

5. The more developed ASEAN countries hold regular consultations with several levels of the Vietnamese civil service and the political groups. Through this continuous learning process, ASEAN hopes to lift the Vietnamese capacity to introduce more reforms. The Institute of South East Asian Studies (ISEAS) holds regular classes for Vietnamese.

6. The privatization programmes of Germany in absorbing a Vietnam-like inefficient public sector into the German economy and Malaysia's jettisoning of some 700 loss-making firms since the economy switched to industrialization in 1984 are two excellent examples of how privatization programmes can be planned and executed successfully.

7. Information on FDI is obtained from Dodsworth et al. (1996) and United Nations (1995).

8. *Vietnam Economic Review* (1996), p. 8.

9. This statement is based on some newspaper reports. No statistics are available to verify this.

10. The Communists in Vietnam code their changes. For example, these changes are known as Directive No. 39/HDBT.

11. Due to non-availability of data, we are unable to report the impact of this on bank deposits.

12. Decision No. 203/QD-NH13.

13. In a meeting with SBV officials in June 1997, we were told that the black market is almost non-existent. Our personal observation during our visit to Hanoi was, however, different. The official exchange rate quoted by the SBV at that time was 1US$ = 10 500 VN$. However, we were able to bargain openly in the market and converted US dollars at 1US$ = 14 000 VN$.

Part 4 The Hesitant Reformers

While the early reformers such as Korea, Malaysia and Taiwan were securing levels of prosperity unseen in recent history in Asian countries, there was bound to be a re-examination sooner rather than later of the failed development policies pursued by South Asian countries. We selected Bangladesh, India, Pakistan, Sri Lanka and the Philippines as representatives of the countries with liberalization and growth problems. India, for example, could provide lessons that are relevant for similarly placed larger economies such as Brazil and Egypt which, like India, closed their economies at one time in order to develop inward-growth-promoting capacity. They failed of course to develop without the external openness of the type put in place by the early reformers to get access to resources, markets, capital and technology, all of which were less abundant in the small, poorer economies of these early reformers.

Bangladesh is an example of a country with very few resources, as are Korea and Taiwan, two who suddenly became separated countries, just as Bangladesh did. While those two secured prosperity, Bangladesh, a South Asian economy, is still not out of the poor category. We find that the South Asian economies and the Philippines, though they were late reformers, had a greater degree of willingness to reform in the 1990s than in any earlier periods. With only a small dose of a liberal mix of policies, these hesitant reformers have secured growth rates of 5–7 per cent in the 1990s compared with the South Asian historical growth rates of 2 and 4 per cent over 40 years. The Philippines, labelled the sick man of Asia, now has a reputation as a sustainable high-growth economy with a good banking system. Hence adoption of a liberal mix of policies seems to be a route to success after experiencing failure through wrong development routes such as the mixed-economy model, import substitution or even the authoritarian model that failed to improve conditions. Hesitancy about reform is now the only stumbling-block to prosperity for these countries.

11. Bangladesh: restructuring and liberalization did help

1. BACKGROUND

Bangladesh is included among the eight least developed economies[1] in the Asia Pacific region. Bangladeshis found themselves in a new independent country after a bloody civil war in 1975. The country received the first blow to its newly established democracy and possible economic stability when the new government, headed by the founder of this country, was overthrown. Even his family members were assassinated in a macabre event more reminiscent of the Middle Ages than the twentieth century.[2] Practically, military or authoritarian rule continued until the early 1990s. It was in this respect a continuation of the bad habits of Bangladesh's erstwhile master, Pakistan, which has a history of military rule and military intervention. Bangladesh fought a war of secession from Pakistan, which ruled it from 1947 to 1975 as part of a new country carved out of the Indian subcontinent for self-rule by the Muslims. However, the imposition of Pakistan's Urdu language on the Bengali-speaking people, it is commonly believed, led to revolt and a civil war, which the might of India's military assistance helped to lead to separation.

Bangladesh is continuing with a confrontationist political process, still prevailing after 25 years of founding this new nation. This has hindered consensus-building among the élites needed to undertake the kind of long-range policy choices that are commonplace in the more successful transforming economies in East and Southeast Asia. The large population of about 128 million living in a tiny land of 144 000 sq. km (half the size of Malaysia but with six times the people) is still growing at a high rate.[3] High population growth negates any social improvement for the people unless a higher economic growth in the 5–8 per cent range is sustained over a decade. In addition, a robust external sector is needed to help bring in outside resources through the trade sector for serious development to occur since the country is very poorly endowed with resources, and consequently has a savings rate of about 7 per cent. These are stylized facts of this economy, which have to be realized by the country's élites and development institutions in understanding how fragile the growth prospects are for this economy as well for those few others in a similar position.

The first 15 years since the founding of the country have been a roller-coaster ride in politics, ranging from initial anarchy to military rule, leading to experimentation in the last ten years with a still fragile democratic process. Similar to what Pakistan had to endure from having to start development from square one in 1947, Bangladesh built up all forms of institutions needed to manage the economy amidst the initial anarchy and rule by military men. Poverty alleviation and crisis management took top priority. The country's élites failed to pause and develop the kind of far-sighted long-range strategy adopted by some other similarly placed but better-endowed countries (for example Singapore and Taiwan), two other cases of countries that involuntarily became separated countries.[4]

There is nothing of significance to examine in terms of liberalization in the period from 1975 to 1988. If anything, institution-building took most of the reform efforts. In that process markets were closed to competition and governments created enterprises that failed to solve the problems for which they were designed. The policy pursued arose from the instinct to protect the people from starvation, which had increased during the anarchy that prevailed for some years soon after independence, and to provide enterprises with resources at cheaper prices to encourage them to engage in economic activities. These were no liberal reforms, but desperate actions to introduce controls to create order out of anarchy and to establish the rule of government. Forget about the reforms of the type examined in this book, which could not be considered at that time.

This state of affairs soon changed. Substantial growth was occurring in the East and Southeast Asian countries in the 1980s as these countries were restructuring their economies. Invigorated by the resultant capital and technology flows, which enabled many Asian countries to garner higher growth than in this country, the spill-over effect could not be ruled out for too long. There is also a continuing vibrant out-migration of the élites and unskilled labour into these high-growth countries. No longer could the modernizing élites ignore the need for liberal reforms. Desire to emulate the growth path of the growing economies acted as an incentive when the political élites decided in the late 1980s to restructure the economy by relaxing price controls and introducing limited reforms under the direction of the IMF and the Asian Development Bank (ADB).[5] At the time of writing this chapter, the per capita income of Bangladesh is just US$283, about the same as for Vietnam. Its social statistics suggest that it is among the poorest countries in the world and the recent gains from limited reforms are seen as the spark that might herald a brighter future.

This chapter provides a detailed account of what occurred with the adoption of limited reforms conceived in 1987–88 and implemented over 1989–99. A discussion of the experience over the earlier period before this episode and a description of the extent of restructuring in the economy are included in the next section. Section 3 details the reforms, especially in the 1989–97 period. The prospect of sustaining the newly established growth trend just above 5 per cent is discussed in the last section. We also note the urgent need for fundamental reforms in the banking sector, which has a festering bad loans problems. A table lists the reforms. The lesson that emerges is one of caution in that this poorly endowed populous country could develop if it adopts belt-tightening measures to increase savings, to attract trade growth in line with growth in the 1990s, and, importantly, if it removes banking fragility, which is at the root of the financial-sector problems. We advocate a phased decontrol of the capital account for individuals in the light of the 1997 Asian crisis. Bangladesh, which had only a small external economy and was not linked by large trade with the countries that were affected by the currency problems, was not affected by the Asian financial crisis.

2. ECONOMIC AND FINANCIAL STRUCTURES

The Bangladesh economy is dominated by agricultural activities within a highly protected pricing system justified during the 1970s to create order and encourage production in a period of civil disorder. Only 23 per cent of the population live in the urban areas, with rudimentary infrastructure, so agricultural output is the mainstay for almost 100 million people. GDP growth was under 6 per cent in the 1970s, fell to an average of 3.9 per cent in the 1980s and, after limited reforms in the 1990s, expanded closer and closer to 5 per cent until it reached 5.5 per cent in 1997. The most important sector, agriculture, grows at about 2 per cent, and this despite wrongly motivated incentives and price controls favouring this sector.[6] The industrial and services sectors are growing at higher rates. With the favourable effects of reforms, industrial output increased to about 8 per cent in the 1990s, while manufacturing, now under a more liberalized regime, is growing at 13 per cent. Manufacturing has potential for bringing in higher growth, and is a competitive sector with small and medium-sized enterprises working under such constraints as low productivity and constant power shortages. Progress in generating a power supply is being made with the entry of the private sector in this area and power-sharing agreements with India.

Summary statistics are given in Table 11.1 on other structural features of the economy. A significant change has begun in the economy's structure. The average tariff has been reduced from a rate above 25 per cent in the pre-reform period to the 1996–97 average of 16 per cent. This is a substantial reduction, which introduced the most important element of liberalization, competition, leading to greater efficiency in the domestic production sector. Consumption came down in 1996 to below 80 per cent of GDP, which had a beneficial impact on savings, which began to edge towards 10 per cent after 1993. This is a significant achievement as it comes after four years of financial reforms that have improved savings mobilization[7] and after the favourable effects of high growth in the trade sector. With interest rate reforms, the real interest rate improved, and a genuine increase in mobilization began. Exports grew at an average of over 20 per cent in the 1990s, achieving a 37 per cent growth rate in 1995. Import growth has been held below 15 per cent. This led to the most significant result of the reform, the build-up of respectable reserves of over US$4 billion by 1996. This is equivalent to seven months of exports, a healthy level at which to establish a stable real exchange rate. Reserves declined to under US$2.0 billion in 1999, when exports amounted to 14 per cent of GDP, which is still not as high as Vietnam's 45 per cent, also achieved within a short period of about 12 years of reforms. In our opinion, Bangladesh has tremendous potential for producing low-technology consumer items for a huge population in the neighbourhood, if only it recognizes that that will entail creating a larger external sector. Importantly, Bangladesh must build good neighbourliness at the grass-roots level to be able to reach out to the larger, more prosperous neighbouring countries instead of fostering confrontation with neighbouring India.

Financial restructuring will be examined in detail in a later section. Important changes in this regard are the institutional reforms in banking, unfortunately not well implemented, steady decontrol of interest rates and exchange rates, and finally capital market reforms. The interest rate reforms have had the most beneficial effect from their impact on the overall economy. Multiple and controlled interest rates that had been in place since 1975 were reduced to wider bands in 1989, and then completely freed in 1993. One control that is still in effect is a floor below which banks cannot reduce the deposit rate. Structurally, there is control on the deposit rate floor, which is periodically set at the level of inflation to ensure that the real interest rate is not negative.[8] With the curtailment of government expenditure in recent years and projected into the future, and with reductions in subsidies when price supports are removed, much of the impact will accrue as a higher savings rate. This will be a significant factor in the future for improving investments and thus growth prospects.

The structure of the fiscal sector leaves much to be desired. There is a persistent deficit in this sector. The average deficit in the government budget was still negative in the 1990s. One study (United Nations, 1997b) traces this to a weakness in the budget control process. Control on planned expenditures is so weak that five-year plans have exceeded the budget allocation by a margin of some 6 to 8 per cent. Discipline in accounting and auditing appears to be lacking. This suggests poor management expertise at all levels of government and lack of professional institutional development.

A structural reason for the deficit is the high subsidies to the two remaining sectors, the large agricultural and the small cottage-industry sectors, both of

Table 11.1 Basic economic and social indicators of development in Bangladesh

Indicators	Average over period			1994	1995	1996	1997	1998
	1971–80	1981–90	1991–93					
National accounts								
GDP growth (%)	5.92	3.99	4.04	4.22	4.45	5.32	5.90	5.70
Per capita GDP (US$)	n.a.	154	209	223	246	260	278	286
Private consumption/GDP	0.93	0.89	0.81	0.78	0.79	0.79	0.79	0.78
Gov. consumption/GDP	0.05	0.08	0.14	0.14	0.14	0.14	0.13	0.14
Financial indicators								
Savings (% of GDP)	22.30	2.89	5.47	13.4	12.8	7.5	8.0	7.0
Fixed capital formation (% of GDP)	8.77	10.79	12.63	18.1	19.1	17.0	17.3	15.3
Inflation	20.65	10.73	3.83	1.80	5.80	6.6	2.6	7.0
M2/GDP (%)	18.1	27.4	33.2	38.1	37.7	37.5	41.4	28.7
Fiscal balance (% of GDP)	0.18	–0.30	n.a.	–6.2	–6.8	–5.9	–5.6	–5.4
Current account balance (% of GDP)	–4.37	–3.51	n.a.	–1.2	–2.87	–5.2	–3.4	–1.0
Trade balance (% of GDP)	–8.84	–10.05	–5.73	–5.60	–8.09	–9.39	–7.8	–5.7
Discount rate	7.350	10.600	7.917	5.50	6.00	7.00	8.00	8.00
Debt service ratio (% of exports)	n.a.	n.a.	n.a.	11.6	10.3	12.1	11.4	11.7
Social indicators								
IMF classification	Low	Low	Low	Low	Low	Low	Low	Low
Adult literacy rate	n.a.	n.a.	n.a.	62	62	62	60	60
Expenditure on education (% of exp.)	11.55	5.66	10.70	13.2	14.5	16.5	17.0	18.0
Expenditure on health (% of exp.)	5.35	3.04	6.4	7.8	8.1	7.5	7.0	7.0
Population growth	2.54	2.07	2.12	2.61	1.70	1.60	1.60	1.60

Sources: IMF, *International Financial Statistics*, various issues; *Asian Development Outlook 1998, 1999*; *Government Finance Statistics Yearbook, 1985–1996*.

which receive subsidies in the form of price supports and controls. Deficits as a percentage of GDP in the 1990s ranged from a high of –6.8 per cent in 1991 to a low of –5.0 per cent of GDP in 1992: see United Nations (1996b; 1997c). This is explained in part by the increasing debt in 1996 of US$19.8 billion (US$16.4 billion in 1999), which requires servicing. Over 10 per cent of the income generated by the export of goods and services is used for debt servicing. Privatization is expected to provide the resources to reduce the subsidy to the government enterprises and to provide the capital sum needed to reduce part of the debt. Unless this problem is tackled as was done by Malaysia in 1982–87, the limited resources of Bangladesh will become a severe constraint to growth, as has been shown in Indonesia, Pakistan and Vietnam, all with huge debt-servicing problems.

Improvements in social factors are also taking place, despite improvements in per capita income being at such low levels, making the country among the least developed in 1999. Officially, Bangladesh is considered to have so little development that it still falls within the low-income category after 23 years. Korea, which emerged from a devastating civil war, as did Bangladesh, became a quarrelsome group of people, but took bold steps in 1957 and drew up an agenda of national reforms to emerge by 1980 (23 years later) as a middle-income country. This has eluded Bangladesh because, as we remarked earlier, of a lack of national consensus on a vision for change to prosperity. Over the years, it has made remarkable improvements in basic conditions, if the social statistics are reliable indicators. Health expenditure, which was a very meagre part of the budget, is now almost 7 per cent, the level of the highest-growth countries on this item. Infant mortality, in a flood-prone country with lethal effects on infants, has been reduced from almost 100 in 1990 to 76 per 1000 live births in 1997. Compare this with the very low figure of under 20 for most other faster-developing Asian countries. Education is receiving more funds. This item has returned to the 1970s level of about 11 per cent of the budget after falling below 6 per cent in the hard times. The educational budget has increased from about 5.4 per cent in 1980–81 to the present 8.6 per cent of the state budget. This is still far below the levels in the high-growth economies, where it is double this level, for example in Thailand. Birth rates are falling at last with massive education about the need for small families: the present population growth rate of 2.18 is tending to decline compared with the 2.53 per cent level in 1974.

In summary, it is reasonable to say that the liberal reforms over 1989–98 are beginning to create favourable macroeconomic outcomes – so much so that there is a good chance of lifting this economy from the low level of growth of the 20 years before reform. The significant outcome is breaching the critical barrier of 5 per cent growth, which fuels a hope that more reforms in the future, aimed at creating a larger external sector, will help the country to reach growth above this level. Higher growth is needed if the country is to begin to achieve development. With consumption declining to 79 per cent of GDP, along with an expansion in the external sector, it is perhaps possible to move the economy towards the level needed to make a change from the least-developed status in which the country has been trapped for the past 23 years.

3. LIBERALIZATION

3.1 Economic Liberalization

Before examining the details on liberalization policies adopted in each sector, we examine the overall growth rates in the more important sectors of this economy. Summary statistics for this purpose are given in Tables 11.2 and 11.3. GDP growth, as noted in the previous section, has been insufficient in that a growth trend in excess of 6 per cent is required to lift this economy and to spread the benefits of development because of the high population growth rate. With reforms, growth is edging towards the 6 per cent level. The inflation rate has been brought under control from double digits to well below 7 per cent. This rate is the direct result of the net effect of the expanded traded sector creating reserves and the effect of declines in the interest rate.

Monetary management skill has been learned and inflation has at last been brought under control. Huge credit expansions in the region of 20 per cent were brought down to a single digit only in 1996. Total domestic credit (see UN, 1997c) created did not suffer, as it has increased from the low levels of between 10.1 per cent and 4.9 per cent in 1994 to the 1995–96 level of 17 per cent while inflation has been held down.

The external sector constraints have been somewhat relaxed, with exports going up while imports were going down, which led to improvement in the trade balance in 1996. There were marked increases in FDI flows, which now exceed US$130 million – the amount may be small for a large economy; this variable has been a single digit or at best went up to US$75 million sometime in the 1980s. More hope is being placed in this resource, which, if properly managed, could hold the key to improved investments needed in the export as well as the domestic sectors. Bangladesh, like Korea and Taiwan, experienced stock market bubbles with an easy-money policy: in Bangladesh this occurred in 1997. Capital-market reforms that encourage too much portfolio investment must be discouraged if Bangladesh is to avoid shocks from capital markets undoing the gains in the real sector. The price and interest rate reforms undertaken during 1989–97 are believed to have made improvements in this variable.

Table 11.2   *Growth rates of basic economic indicators*

	5-year average			Annual average						
	1976–80	1981–85	1986–90	1991	1992	1993	1994	1995	1996	1997
GDP	5.12	3.81	4.13	3.40	4.23	4.48	4.22	4.44	5.32	7.76
Inflation	7.99	11.84	9.59	7.22	4.29	1.3	1.8	5.2	6.6	2.6
Revenue	20.02	11.75	14.3	25.4	18.9	16.4	8.5	11.1	13.3	14.0
M1	19.48	17.90	7.42	7.71	13.61	15.96	24.32	16.71	4.67	80.5
M2	22.33	23.13	15.43	13.44	12.18	10.49	19.31	12.18	10.73	9.6
FDI	n.a.	n.a.	20.11	–33.33	140	–44.4	–20.7	–82.9	600.0	935.7
Trade balance (deficit)	19.48	17.90	7.42	–12.68	–9.37	–11.4	2.72	64.1	–2.1	–24.8

Note: M2 = (M1 + quasi-money).

Sources: IMF, *International Financial Statistics*, various issues; World Bank, *World Bank Databank*, Feb. 1997.

Table 11.3 Monetary aggregates, national income accounts and balance of payments (% of GDP)

| | 5-year average | | | Annual | | | | | | | |
	1976–80	1981–85	1986–90	1991	1992	1993	1994	1995	1996	1997	1998
M1	10.1	10.8	9.3	8.5	8.9	9.8	11.3	11.6	10.9	10.9	12.0
M2	19.2	25.2	30.6	31.8	32.9	34.7	38.1	37.7	37.5	41.4	28.7
Trade deficit	–9.1	–11.4	–8.5	–6.4	–5.4	–5.4	–5.6	–8.1	–9.4	–7.8	–5.39
Current account deficit	–3.6	–7.8	–3.6	0.3	0.8	1.5	–0.3	–2.9	–4.1	–1.7	–1.0
Private consumption	89.6	91.0	86.5	82.1	80.4	78.9	78.3	78.5	78.8	78.3	78.0
Gov. consumption	5.5	5.6	10.7	13.8	13.8	14.2	14.3	13.7	13.7	14.1	14.0
Gross fixed capital formation	9.9	9.7	12.3	11.5	12.1	14.3	13.8	16.1	17.2	17.3	15.3
Gov. expenditure	11.2	12.2	8.9	8.7	8.6	17.8	18.1	18.9	17.8	17.8	17.8

Note: M2 = (M1 + quasi-money).

Source: IMF, *International Financial Statistics*, various issues.

Fiscal-sector reforms

The state of the fiscal sector may be judged from two statistics. In the mid-1980s, the budget deficit as a ratio of GDP was –9 per cent and the revenue was a mere 10 per cent of GDP in 1990–91. These two vital statistics have changed for the better. Deficits declined to –6 per cent by 1993–94 and revenue in 1996 improved to about 14 per cent of GDP. These were the consequences of reforms in the fiscal sector. Fiscal-sector reforms were introduced in 1991 to (a) impose value-added tax at the point of manufacture along with expansion of the tax base for direct taxes and a lowering of income tax rates, (b) rationalize the tax structure and (c) harmonize revenue collection to budget targets. In the 1980–85 period, the tax base of 12 per cent of GDP was about the same as that of the South Asian countries, but well below the 17 per cent rate in the East Asian economies. With the tax reforms, the share of tax revenue in the budget increased from 18 per cent to 24 per cent in the early 1990s. Corporate tax collection represented 60 per cent and income tax 40 per cent of tax revenues: these direct taxes provide 25 cents in a dollar of government revenue. With only 1 per cent of the population paying tax and most firms avoiding tax, there is room for substantial improvement in future revenue growth.

Indirect taxes are more important as these form three-quarters of the government's income, not counting international aid flows. Indirect taxes amounted to 56 per cent of taxes in the 1970s. These are from taxes on domestic goods and services as well as taxes on international trade. The introduction of VAT saw the withdrawal of sales taxes on domestic goods and services, at around the 25 per cent rate. VAT-based taxes, which are designed on the same basis as in Indonesia, are becoming the single most important tax base. Revenue share of VAT taxes was 28 per cent in 1994, increasing to 30 per cent the next year, and is presently reported to be a third of government revenues. Incidentally, VAT on imported items provides a disproportionate 63 per cent of all VAT-related revenues for the government. This over-dependence of the fiscal sector on imports introduces uncertainty since imports are volatile, and may decline substantially in periods of recession.

The persistent budget deficits, which were about –5 per cent in the late 1990s, have been financed by domestic issues of government and agency bonds (and international loans). Unlike in the fast-developing countries, government expenditure has doubled over the last 12 years in this country. Expenditure used to be well under 10 per cent until 1980, whereas it is now above 14 per cent of GDP. Public-sector reforms in the next stage will restructure this sector, and substantial improvements can be expected in the future if privatization is completed and full removal of subsidies is achieved.

Budget deficits were sustained in the 1990s in order to maintain price subsidies to keep the prices of basic items low enough while structural reforms were undertaken. The deficits have been large: as indicated in UN (1997c), budget deficits reached a high of –6.8 per cent of GDP in 1991, which has since come down for the first time, with the public-sector net credit expansion having gone negative (UN, 1996b, p. 73). Since the founding of the country, the public sector has also entered into the production and distribution of goods and services, especially during the period of anarchy and rule by the military. The share of expenditure by the public sector in 1985 and 1994 increased from about 13 per cent to 19 per cent in 1996. Also, growth in government capital expenditure has been positive, at 2.9 per cent of GDP during 1984–89 compared with 8.6 per cent during 1990–94. Compare this with a decline of –11 per cent over 1984–89 and –1.5 per cent over 1990–94 in the private sector's capital formation. Happily, the private sector is beginning to get more credits, growing at the rate of 7.7 per cent in 1993 to 23.6 per cent in 1995. This will reverse the trend in the future.

Privatization has been pursued as a tool to reduce the government's presence in the private sector, and to reduce revenue loss through subsidies. The Privatization Board was formed in March 1993 with a clear mandate to reduce the presence of the public sector so that future growth will come from private-sector activities. There are as yet no clear-cut rules for the divestment process, and this is not helping the efforts to reduce the bad loans these firms are incurring, which results in a very high non-performing loan of close to 40 per cent of the value of loans made to public enterprises.[9] The number of state-owned companies has been dramatically reduced from over 600 to a small number still to be privatized: detailed data are not available to make further comments.

External-sector policies
The single most important structural change, which augurs well for future growth, is the expansion in this sector: see Table 11.4. With the (a) establishment of export processing zones where there are incentives given to foreign investors to produce, and (b) limited reforms of the economy, conditions favourable for competition and for expanding the traded sector were obtained. Exports are growing at an average trend rate higher than imports. This has led to an expanding traded sector, and has brought foreign investments and competition to the local producers.

In the field of industrial policy, investment-sanctioning regulations were relaxed to let in more investors. The areas reserved for the public sector were reduced, but not to the bold level of India, which went on to create the negative list, thereby making it possible in India to invest in almost all areas. With the Foreign Private Investment Act 1980 providing protection against nationalization, more foreign investment was attracted. One hundred per cent ownership and full repatriation of cash flows were permitted for the first time under these laws and reforms. There is also an urgent need for reform to speed up duty exemption for production in the bonded warehouses. This is being pursued.

Table 11.4   Growth of the external sector

Variables	1993	1994	1995	1996	1997	1998	1999
Exports							
Value (US$ bn)	2.40	2.50	3.50	3.90	4.60	4.70	4.80
Percentage change over previous year	19.6	6.3	37.1	12	18	2.5	2.5
Imports							
Value (US$ bn)	4.10	4.20	5.80	7.00	8.50	7.54	n.a.
Percentage change over previous year	17.5	2.9	39.2	20	22	12.3	10.0
Debt	14.90	16.60	17.50	19.00	19.80	n.a.	n.a.
Debt-service ratio	14.6	15.2	13	13	13	11.7	12.0

Note: Debt-service ratio refers to percentage of budget.

Source: United Nations (1997), *Overcoming Institutional Constraints to Implementing Macro-economic Policies*, New York.

There is also the ballooning of foreign debt over the years. With improvements in the reserves and also in foreign exchange earnings from exports and remittances from nationals working in foreign countries, the debt servicing ratio has come down to 13 per cent. This augurs well, but further improvements are needed to bring this figure down to levels below 5 per cent in the long run. This is where the sale of public firms could provide resources. Further improvements in exports are expected, which will also help. As regards the trade and current account balances, comments have made elsewhere about the still continuing instability in these items.

3.2   Financial Liberalization

The real-sector reforms were based on tariff reductions, on establishment of incentives for the entry of foreign enterprises in the bonded warehousing areas and on permission to participate with 100 or less per cent ownership. The resulting competition and efficiency gains led to overall gains. These reforms were undertaken along with reforms in the financial sector to support the real-sector reforms. It is worth remembering that the huge agricultural and cottage-industry sectors in the rural areas – about 77 per cent of the people live there – were not subjected to price decontrols. Hence the efficiency improvements are in the urban-based industrial and service activities. The financial reforms were also designed so as not to affect the rural sectors.

Monetary policies

We start with the monetary regime. As may be recalled from an earlier discussion, monetary expansion has been too high for a growth in economic activities of about 5.6 per cent in the 1970s and at below 4 per cent in the 1980s. The result was obvious: inflation reached double-digit level, 20.65 per cent in the 1970s and close to 11 per cent in the 1980s, even with a 4 per cent growth. Monetary expansion as measured by the M2/GDP ratio was running at 18 to 37 per cent. However, the high growth rate in M2 in the 1970–80 period was brought down to a manageable level of 12.3 per cent in 1990. Since then, its growth rate has increased to about 16 per cent in 1996: see UN (1997c).

Because of the retarded development of the money and interbank markets in the economy, the instruments available for executing monetary policies were limited. Interventions had to be made indirectly: these included (a) the bank rate, (b) interest rates, (c) refinance or rediscount facility of the central bank, (d) reserves and (e) limited open-market operations strictly to buy or sell government securities. The bank rate was reduced gradually from a high level of 9.8 per cent in 1990 to about 5 per cent to stimulate credit creation to boost economic activity. Interest rate easing was matched to this, as will be discussed later. The rediscount window facility was completely revamped. Separate rates applying to different sectors were unified under one central bank rate. This removed price controls at the root in one go.

To stimulate a build-up of capacity for credit expansion in the banking system, reserves were reduced. The statutory reserve was reduced from 8 to 5 per cent of deposits. Cash reserves were reduced from 23 to 20 per cent. This helped to increase credit growth in the domestic economy to as much as 17.6 per cent in 1995. Meanwhile, credit growth of the government was brought down. The rate of growth has declined since 1994, thus truly beginning the switchover to the dominance of the private sector, which is beginning to attract more credits.

With interest rate controls and a fixed exchange rate regime, the financial sector did not develop financial instruments in the money and interbank markets for use by the central bank to conduct market interventions. However, there were government bonds, which could be sold to tighten money growth or bought to inject liquidity. In 1990, the central bank introduced a three-month Treasury bill (Bangladesh Bank bill) and later also a one-month bill to create a market to reveal market interest rates as well as to use these, when the market had developed, to affect monetary conditions. These instruments were created in the mid- to late 1980s in Korea and Indonesia for exactly the same purpose. Beginning in 1995, auctions of these bills were introduced so as to create conditions that would help to reveal market rates for interest rates through competition among the financial institutions.

These developments have no doubt created new structures for the market-based system of managing financial aggregates. The capacity of the central bank to react through the markets has improved: structural and market interventions have replaced control by orders. Working through market forces prevents the aberrations that are common when the power of the central bank and not the market is used to effect changes. Orderly movements in the desired monetary and financial variables can be effected when these reforms help to build liquid interbank and money markets.

Exchange rate and interest rate reforms (Table 11.5)

Exchange rates   The exchange rate has declined continually under the fixed exchange rate regime in force over most of the 23 years. The exchange rate was about 15 taka to the US dollar in the 1976–80 period. In recent years, 1996–97, it was 45 taka to the US dollar; in 1999, 48.50 taka to the US dollar. The rate of decline of about 10 per cent per year is rapid, though not of the magnitude observed in Korea or Indonesia. The exchange value has declined to a third of its level 20 years ago. The fixed exchange rate regime was sustained with a system of multiple administered rates. These rates were unified in 1994, a year after India freed the exchange rate from controls. The secondary market in exchange rates was abolished and the rates were unified. Though Bangladesh accepts IMF Article 8 conditions, the exchange rate is determined by a system of daily fixing of the taka against the US dollar. The fix is decided on the basis of the currency's real effective exchange rate, REER, a status measured on a trade-weighted basket of currencies of 15 major trading partners. In this, it is a managed float of the type that is followed by almost all managed floaters except Australia, Japan and New Zealand before the Asian crisis. Introduction of this managed float based on the REER led to a steadying of the exchange rate. There were continuing depreciations but at half the previous rate of declines in the exchange rate in real terms, even after the 1994 change. But the exchange rate improved for a little while during October 1994 and March 1995 before resuming its decline thereafter.

Interest rates   The most significant of the reforms of the liberalization is the lifting of suppression on interest rates. Right up to April 1992, extensive interest rate controls were imposed. There was a softer form of control in that political and interest group influences were brought to bear on the nationalized banks – and sometimes the private banks as well – to lend for projects that were not viable or were made to parties who would be expected not to pay back. These loans ballooned by 1998 to 40 per cent non-performing loans in the banking sector. What this softer suppression (!) achieved was to make loans to genuine projects and clients more expensive, as the banking system had to recoup the cost of non-performance of this magnitude. This has led to the failure of the banking system to achieve efficient intermediation for which they were licensed in the first place.

Table 11.5 Exchange rates and interest rates (annual averages)

| | 5-year average | | | Annual average | | | | | | | |
	1976–80	1981–85	1986–90	1991	1992	1993	1994	1995	1996	1997	1998
Exchange rate (mkt)	15.24	25.18	32.47	38.58	39.00	39.85	40.25	40.75	42.45	45.50	48.50
Interest rates: % p.a.											
Discount rate	8.50	10.65	10.55	9.25	8.50	6.00	5.50	6.00	7.00	8.00	8.00
Deposit rate	7.20	12.00	12.00	12.05	10.47	8.18	6.40	6.04	7.28	8.11	8.46
Lending rate	11.07	12.00	15.60	15.92	15.00	15.00	14.50	14.00	14.00	14.00	14.00

Notes:
M2 = (M1 + quasi-money).
Exchange rate: (official rate) = taka per US dollar.
Discount rate (end-of-period).

Source: IMF, *International Financial Statistics*, various issues.

The hard suppression took the first form, which is a rule-based discriminatory interest rate, a widely practised sin in all Asian markets until the 1980s, to direct credits to certain perceived not-able/desired sectors or populations. An even harder form of suppression was the specification of minimum and maximum bands within which interest must be charged. This had the perverse result that the high-risk borrowers got a discount in interest rates at the sacrifice of the depositor who would receive an interest rate lower than would be the case in a free-market regime.

As part of the liberalization of the financial sector, there were only paper reforms to address the soft form of suppression. But these non-performing loans have not been reduced.[10] In an earlier period in the 1980s, banks with non-performing loans were recapitalized in the hope that the problem would not recur, but it did, with higher levels of non-performing loans in later history. Unless the prudential lending rules are imposed strictly and impartially, and the bad loans are taken off the books, a financial crisis is looming ahead for this fragile economy.

In the implementation of the reforms to remove the harder forms of suppression, there has been notable success. Put simply, a real positive interest rate emerged in the 1990s and interest rates declined from around 20 per cent to about 12 per cent with inflation under 6 per cent in 1996. Effective from April 1992, interest rate bands were abolished for all sectors except agriculture, exports and cottage industries. With a later reform meant to protect these sectors, banks subsidizing such activities will be compensated from the central bank at 3 per cent from market rates. There is no reason for the banks to pass on the cost of subsidized loans to those paying market rates. Maximum interest rate rules were also abolished. However, to prevent the banks from offering deposit rates at negative real interest rate, a floor for interest rates is still administered. The floor rate is determined by the central bank on the basis of inflation expectations in the market. Thus these several reforms have removed price controls that were affecting all segments of the economy, while preserving it for some segments. Post-1992 experience on this aspect has been very encouraging. This is a case that holds important lessons for many reforming economies.

In summary, two conclusions emerge. First, liberalizing the interest rate regime has been a signal success in removing a subtle form of price control on all aspects of the economy. The structures put in place to create money and interbank markets have now strengthened the monetary authorities institutional strength at the highest levels of the central bank and the Ministry of Finance to manage the macro-economy better. Declines in the interest rate coupled with increased savings mobilization have helped somewhat to improve the domestic savings rate while also improving credit creation for the private sector.

Foreign direct investment and capital markets

Much of the growth in the fast-track economies of East and Southeast Asia was squarely based on the injection of huge FDI and portfolio flows along with a build-up of foreign loans in the banking sector. Table 11.6 contains statistics relevant for a discussion of this aspect for the case under discussion. Bangladesh, along with South Asian economies, continued to have the rigidity not favourable for attracting FDI flows into the real sectors of these countries. The capital markets had rules prohibiting foreign capital ownership and the financial institutions were not permitted to hold any foreign assets in foreign currency. These extensive regulations kept the multinationals, from investing in these economies. In 1998, the 140 000 multinationals, mostly from the developed countries, were creating a third of the world's GDP through their multi-country network of production, distribution and sales. Countries that establish connections with FDI flows became connected to this network. Portfolio flows and rules letting banks and firms borrow in foreign currencies have been shown to create financial fragility (see Chapters 2 and 17). Therefore, while we encourage FDI flows and reforms to attract such capital, technology and market networks, caution is needed in attracting too much portfolio flow without controls in place to prevent its sudden withdrawal, leading to exchange rate shocks.

Bangladesh failed to attract these capital flows until reforms had improved the conditions of the economy after restrictive policies were removed. These reforms took four forms. First, in late 1989, approval procedures for foreign investment were simplified with the establishment of warehousing and export-processing facilities. Production activities in these special zones were to enjoy a number of benefits similar to those put in place in other countries such as China. These included tax reliefs, lower or no tariffs, and export credit at lower interest rates. To these was added permission in 1994 for 100 per cent ownership of foreign enterprises. A law was also passed in 1994 to give guarantees against nationalization of foreign assets. This set of reforms was far-reaching, and was formulated under the advice of ADB and others. There was thus endorsement of the policies.

Table 11.6   Investments in Bangladesh (US$ million)

	1981–85	1986–90	1991	1992	1993	1994	1995	1996	1997
Direct investment (net)	−0.067	2.16	1.4	3.7	14.0	11.1	1.9	13.5	136.3
Portfolio investment	−1.433	0.52	2.2	8.7	8.4	105.9	−15.2	−117.0	−9.9
FDI (inflow)	−0.067	2.16	1.4	3.7	14.0	11.1	1.9	13.5	139.4

Sources: IMF, *International Financial Statistics*, various issues; World Bank, *World Bank Databank*, Feb. 1997.

The result was a significant growth in FDI flows. As can be seen from Table 11.6, FDI flows increased substantially from a low base of about US$25 million to more than US$125 million. Before 1994, total FDI was merely US$5 million, which is not even 0.1 per cent of GDP, in some good years. In 1995, FDI increased to about 1 per cent of GDP. This level has been surpassed in recent years. Capital-market reforms were also introduced, which made share ownership and transactions by foreign owners possible. This led to a substantial appreciation in stock prices between 1994 to 1997. When portfolio investments in the market were liquidated by foreign investors, the market also suffered a huge loss, which was further complicated by speculative schemes to raise capital. The result was a capital-market crisis in March 1997 from which the market has not yet recovered.

Capital-market reforms are beginning to have a favourable impact on new issues of securities for direct trading. Domestic firms raise direct capital in the expanded capital markets, and thus can reduce capital costs substantially. Therefore the development of the capital market has been beneficial despite the adverse consequence from the flow of short-term investments of foreigners and increases in manipulative schemes of speculators.[11]

Central bank reforms and depository institutions

Many of the reforms described in the previous pages have been designed in consultation with the central bank. Thus, in a broader sense, the reforms of the economy have emanated from new thinking that has been encouraged under the IMF and the ADB collaborations. Specific reforms made to the central bank are new laws and regulations that changed the character of the central bank substantially in the 1990s. It has built capacity to macro-manage the economy. Of particular interest are the reforms on prudential regulations that the central bank adopted for the supervision of financial institutions. But these laws still badly need firm implementation, which requires political will. Without that, a time bomb is waiting to explode in the form of bank failures. This was discussed in an earlier section.

Financial deepening

We now examine the overall outcome of financial reforms by measuring the financial deepening in the sector: see Table 11.7. It was remarked in an earlier section that the development of interbank markets and money markets in the 1990s allowed monetary policy to be managed through market operation. One of the aims of the reformers was to increase credit availability to the private sector. This meant that the monetary sector's expansion had to be maintained at levels that may be considered inflationary in some situations. But that has not been the case. Further, monetary depth was very low, at 30 per cent of GDP in the 1970s and the 1980s. This has now improved as new instruments by the

Table 11.7 Indicators of financial deepening (% of GDP)

| | 5-year average | | | Annual | | | | | | | |
	1976–80	1981–85	1986–90	1991	1992	1993	1994	1995	1996	1997	1998
Money depth (M2/GDP)	19.20	25.20	30.55	31.84	32.88	34.73	38.13	37.66	37.50	38.30	39.00
Inter-relations											
FIR (total)/GDP	31.85	44.72	56.25	62.88	65.58	71.53	81.35	64.53	63.41	62.00	63.00
FIR (public)/GDP	18.19	15.96	15.11	20.71	27.22	31.08	38.58	22.50	22.00	22.50	23.00
FIR (private)/GDP	18.30	32.66	48.04	55.66	55.85	62.83	71.24	52.94	50.13	55.00	57.00
GFCF/GDP	9.93	9.68	12.26	11.50	12.12	14.28	13.85	16.08	17.21	17.3	15.3
FDI/GDP	n.a.	n.a.	0.01	0.01	0.02	0.06	0.04	0.007	0.04	0.05	0.96

Notes:
M2 = (M1 + quasi-money).
FIR: Financial intermediation ratio – claims on public sector, claims on private sector and foreign assets.

Sources: IMF, *International Financial Statistics*, various issues; World Bank, *World Bank Databank*, Feb. 1997.

301

central bank as BB bills have been introduced and the exchange market has been unified in 1992. With the reforms monetary depth as measured by the M2/GDP ratio improved to just under 40 per cent in the late 1990s. Compared with the levels of close to 90 per cent in more liberalized economies such as Malaysia and Thailand, there is much room for improvement.

Table 11.8   Limited economic and financial reforms introduced

Date of reforms	Liberalization policies implemented
1975–89	Institution-building to create economic, financial and governmental organizations needed to manage a new country after civil war.
1988	Realization that major reforms are needed to put the country on the path to development after 17 years of political instability.
1989	Agreement with IMF and ADB to initiate assistance with US$6 billion to introduce reforms to restructure the economy and to institute decontrol measures to return economic management to market signals.
Real sector	Private-sector incentives system needed for growth. Private sector recognized as source for future growth. Introduction of competition-enhancing actions. Tariff reductions from about 25% to 16% by 1996. Freeing economic activities from controls, e.g. reserved activities for public sector reduced. Entry barriers removed. Bonded warehousing and export processing zones created with tax and other incentives to promote efficiency and trade. 100% foreign ownership permitted in most economic activities.
Fiscal sector	Public-sector role to be reduced in economic activities. Privatization Board formed. About 600 public firms, mostly small ones, sold off. Major tax reforms. Sales tax abolished and VAT introduced. Corporate and individual tax rates reduced to create incentives.

Date of reforms	Liberalization policies implemented
	Tax administrative capacity improved.
	Subsidies to all but agriculture, export and cottage industries removed.
Financial sector	
Exchange rate	Article VIII conditions accepted. Multiple exchange rates unified 1994.
	Daily fixing of rate on real effective exchange rate suggested by a 15-country trading partners' exchange rates. Volatility reduced, but not depreciation.
Interest rate	No controls on holding or trading in foreign currencies.
	Interest rates suppressed right up to 1992. Multiple interest rates with minimum and maximum limits. One market rate now.
	Minimum deposit rate as suggested by inflation expectation still applies.
	Interest subsidies pervasive for targeting. Abolished and replaced with market rates and a 3% subsidy for agriculture, exports and cottage industries.
Intermediation	Entry barriers to banking, non-banking, stock trading, etc. relaxed.
	Prudential regulations introduced (but not enforced yet).
	Interest rate reforms major, based on market signals.
	Reserve requirements reduced to 8% and 20% to create credits.
Capital markets	Entry barriers in stock trading relaxed.
	Ownership restrictions on foreigners in the share market liberalized.
	Listing requirements and investor protection improved.
	Activities in capital market (bond and shares) enhanced.

Sources: Bangladesh Bank reports; United Nations (1996b; 1997c); and Centre for Policy Dialogue (in Dhaka) publications.

The financial intermediation ratio has improved from the very low level of 30 per cent in the 1970s. The current depth in this financial asset ratio to GDP is about 65 per cent. The depth in the private sector is much higher, having reached 50 per cent compared with 18 per cent in the 1970s. The asset holding of the public sector has declined after reaching a high level in 1994. This is consistent with the shift to the private sector now taking place in credit usage and growth.

4. PROSPECTS FOR THE FUTURE

The Bangladesh case has been dubbed as an interesting one in that limited reforms in the real sector supported by important interest rate reforms in the financial sector and fiscal sector brought tangible improvements, all of which offer a particularly important lesson because they happened in the worst-case scenario. The lesson is that pursuit of carefully structured reforms can help to engineer respectable growth in a populous country with very few resources. This has been borne out in our discussion: Korea is a spectacular case over 40 years. There has been a cautious step towards reforms in Bangladesh in so far as the reforms have preserved the vast majority of economic activities taking place in the rural sector. To be precise, three-quarters of all economic activities that take place in the rural sector are still protected by interest subsidy. This protection afforded to the majority of the population appears to be deliberate, perhaps cautious so that a failure of the reforms would not destabilize the fragile political climate of the country. About 100 million people in the rural sector are still enjoying price controls in production activities in agriculture and cottage industries, as is also the budding export sector, with fewer price controls but with other perks.

The reforms have reduced the average tariff rates to a low level under 16 per cent. Interest subsidies have been reduced to levels unthinkable before the changes. Only a 3 per cent direct subsidy goes to the protected sector while all forms of interest controls other than a minimum deposit rate near the inflation level have been decontrolled since 1992. This is a major price adjustment factor that has had a widespread effect. So is the move to accept a unified exchange rate, with daily fixing of rates within a range of effective real exchange rates against a basket of currencies. This has arrested the rate of depreciation in the currency to half its historic level. Simultaneous development of liquid interbank and money market instruments has provided flexibility in the management of monetary aggregates.

Much remains to be done. The level of efficiency in the economy is fairly low. A major reason for this is the extreme underdevelopment of basic infrastructure in a country with so many waterways but with a very backward transport and road system, not to mention very few bridges.[12] The main threat to continued growth is likely to come from the banking sector. The huge non-performing loan, unless tackled rapidly, is a major cause for alarm as it can lead to systemic failure. If that were to happen, most of the gains of the reforms would probably be lost in the massive adjustment process that such an event would unleash in the economy. Given the fair degree of success of the limited reforms, it is our hope that the success will inspire the planners to undertake these urgent reforms with determination. Vietnam has secured a greater degree of exports, 45 per cent of GDP, within a 12-year period. Bangladesh's neighbours, ready to buy cheaper consumer goods provide an opportunity for this country to grow a much enlarged export sector, at present valued at about 13 per cent of GDP. This may prove the way to garner more capital inflow as well as to overcome the chronic shortage of domestic capital. The time is now ripe to build a national consensus, now that the other economic and financial structures have been somewhat fine-tuned to a level of efficiency not achieved in earlier periods.

NOTES

1. GDP at market prices of this economy is estimated at US$32 billion, which works out at US$285 per capita in 1999: this is a small, poor economy. Adjusted for purchasing power of the local currency, the taka, GDP in PPP terms is equivalent to about US$160 billion, which is four and half times higher. India, its neighbour, has an adjusted GDP of US$1700 billion; it is also a low-income economy, but a larger economy with opportunities for complementarities if regional collaboration becomes not just a plan but a reality, as in several other regions.
2. By a strange coincidence, the daughter, who was not killed, was spearheading reforms in the closing years of the last century and giving hope to this most unfortunate nation, well known for natural calamities. The road to reform was laid by a president known for uprightness, but he did not live to see the fruits of the reforms, and Sheik Haseena, the daughter of the assassinated leader, is continuing the reforms.
3. Current population growth is 2.18 per cent per annum, which makes it one of the high population growth countries with an endemic low-income growth nexus. These and other statistics are from a very useful reference: see Centre for Policy Dialogue (1996). The contacts and the intellectual stimulation from the discussions with the staff of the Centre have been very useful to the authors.
4. On a visit to this country as a Ford Fellow, Ariff recognized the urgent need for change. Growth established on a long-run trend of 4 per cent since the 1980s is woefully inadequate for securing prosperity. Even with domestic reforms in the real sector, a higher growth rate in the range of at least 5–7 per cent is possible if it builds capacity for higher savings which Bangladesh, without a Vietnam-like larger external sector, cannot secure for the prosperity of its people. A major obstacle to such a change is a lack of consensus on a national agenda for reform among the political parties, similar to the one in Malaysia in 1969–70 just before that country's remarkable growth once a national consensus was achieved and pursued by three reform-minded prime ministers.
5. The IMF came with a package of assistance in 1988 under the Enhanced Structural Adjustment Facility to reform the economy. ADB also became a partner, along with others, in this effort.
6. See United Nations (1996). Some statistics are taken from this source and reported throughout the chapter.
7. Growth experience has been poor for countries with high consumption rates. India's growth in the 1950s slowed for exactly the same reason, but with import substitution policies, that country expanded consumption while also bringing it down from close to 90 per cent to well below 70 per cent. Overcoming this constraint to development has been achieved by building a robust trade sector, as did Korea and Taiwan. It is in this context that liberal reforms are needed to fast-track the external sector.

8. During periods of recession in the fast-developing East and Southeast Asian economies, real interest rates have often become negative. This has led to shifts in investment towards the supply-constrained property sector as well as the share markets. The result has been very unfavourable in that frequent building up of an asset price bubble, which wipes off savings in that sector and causes falls in share prices, weakens the very firms that need to be strengthened during recession. Pursuing a floor on the deposit rate is a prudent policy choice to avoid the other negative effects.

9. Privatization has been held back because of reluctance to lay down clear rules of sales to third parties in arm's-length transactions and to introduce sealed-bid divestment procedures. As long as these issues of sale are not properly handled, no successful divestment is likely. With no fair price for the assets sold, there could be no sizeable proceeds from sales. The bad debt problem will remain. In the light of these continuing problems, India's formula of retaining profitable firms and selling the unprofitable ones in sealed bids provides a guide to a quick resolution to the problem of managing divestment.

10. Japanese lay people have an apt description for these forms of laws. They call such laws 'water basket' laws, as nothing can be captured by such laws.

11. A system of manipulation in early 1997 wiped out more than half the value of the stock market. Since then more prudence has been exercised in the management of the capital markets. At that time, when the writer was in Dhaka, there was a ridiculous suggestion urging banks to provide bailout loans, amounting to 15 per cent of bank equity, to those who lost money!

12. The writer was amazed at the collection of tolls from all forms of vehicles on a bridge that connected the hinterland of Dhaka city to the urban enclave. Tolls would increase transport costs, but that was not the surprising thing. The bridge was built by a foreign country as a gift. The politicians decided to make it a toll road!

12. India: a decade of liberalization, a hesitant choice

1. BACKGROUND

This country experienced three decades of violence and civil disorder, despite the non-violence of the great Mohandas Gandhi, before gaining independence from Britain in August 1947. The Independence also led to further civil unrest, with millions of people moving between a partitioned India and Pakistan. In this respect, this country shared some of the vicious human tragedies that also occurred in other countries – South Korea in 1954, Taiwan in 1949 – as birth pangs. Unlike the latter two, which, because of the spirit of resolve the tragedies unleashed in their peoples, adopted significant market-opening measures to ensure long-term growth prospects through an export-led path to achieve fast-track development, India, given the large population base seen as a protected market for goods and services, followed exactly the opposite strategy by designing and aggressively pursuing an import substitution policy mix. This put reliance on home-growing industrial capacity, which later mushroomed to become a highly regulated economy with little external or investment relations with the rest of the world. This cryptic view of development is perhaps too harsh and in direct contradiction to India's half-century stand of avowed public relations about being open to the rest of the world. There are even more serious drawbacks in this country from the widespread corruption, which has pervaded all aspects of ordinary life. But why other poor countries did not have to travel this same path is the question to be asked.

As an example, take the case of Korea, whose external trade amounted to 76 per cent of its GDP in 1996, created from an outward-oriented economic vision. Yet Korea was a poorer country than India in 1954! The trade ratio for India is 19.2 per cent. This reflects clearly the extent to which India pursued a wrong policy of an inward growth strategy, thereby achieving only 3.5 per cent long-term growth while Korea harnessed a 10 per cent growth rate China is doing likewise! Korea aggressively grew an external economy to become rich enough to be the twenty-fifth member of the Organization for Economic Cooperation and Development, the OECD, and the fourteenth largest economy.[1] Things started to change for India in 1988, when, spurred by the experience of high growth in the ASEAN and East Asian economies, the political élites took significant brave steps to bring in more liberal policies. Though the pace of reforms has slowed with the coming to power of the Conservative Party in 1997 and also from the impacts of trade sanctions imposed on India for testing five atomic bombs and long range missiles, the expectations are that there is only one way for this country to go forward, that is, to continue adopting further reforms – and sooner rather than later.

Examining the contemporary development experience of India is a useful exercise for a number of reasons, given the newly found desire to adopt the critical reforms needed to move this economy to a higher growth path than in the past. Some estimate the size of this economy as potentially the fifth largest modern economy in the world.[2] By the same measure, China would be the second, and Japan the third largest economy. Adoption of a liberal policy mix by a pioneer modernizer normally leads to more or less a domino effect on others in the neighbourhood adopting changes broadly similar to the pioneer country. Think of the flying geese with the leader setting the direction, and you have the idea. For example, the excellent growth paths established in the 1960s by four of Asia's newly industrializing economies (Hong Kong, Korea, Taiwan and Singapore) led to the adoption of market-opening measures by a number of Southeast Asian countries in the 1970s. These reforming economies registered growth rates of close to 8 per cent in the 1980s. China's experimentation with liberal policies in the 1980s also influenced several East Asian economies in that some countries tried to mimic China's path of transforming command economies to respond to market signals, and thereby hope to achieve some measure of development not experienced before, as is happening in Vietnam.

In much the same way, India's adoption of liberal policies in the late 1980s has begun to nudge other countries in the neighbourhood also to consider and, in some cases such as Bangladesh, successfully adopt new policies. The long-term growth experience of the South Asian economies in the pre-reform period has been significantly below that of the world average. The very low 3–4 per cent income growth over 1970–90 in the South Asian region is inadequate to bring sufficient improvements to the quality of the life of people in the region. This is particularly so given a high population growth rate of 1.67 per cent, high youth dependency rate of around 40 per cent, and per capita income that would place the South Asian countries among the low-income countries. Countries such as Korea, Taiwan and others that started as low-income ones but moved out of that grouping by adopting relevant liberal policies achieved double the Indian rates of growth to bring prosperity to their peoples.[3]

India began the postwar age of hope with massive problems. To start with, it was a poor country unable to feed all its people. Population growth was close to 3.5 per cent immediately after the war years. India's population in 1999 was edging towards one billion, growing at a moderate rate of 1.68 per cent. Most of the population is concentrated in the northern belt, which is relatively more industrialized than the less heavily populated south, which is largely an agri-cultural belt with a mountainous interior. Its GDP of about Rs 16 700 billion[4] at current prices is the fifth largest economy in Asia. Per capita income of Rs 16 800 or US$395 puts it in the low-income category. However, per capita income has grown steadily at 3.7 per cent per year since the mid-1970s. GDP growth in the 1980s is no better, at about 3.8 per cent. Nevertheless, this growth rate is well above the current population growth rate, which provides some hope of faster development in the future: see Table 12.1.

Economic growth, on the other hand, has been more robust in the 1990s, following a good measure of financial and a limited amount of real-sector reforms undertaken since 1988. The average GDP growth of 4.5 per cent in the 1990s was well above the long-term growth rate of under 3.5 per cent. Growth after 1994 improved closer to the 8 per cent level, a level that matched that of the fast-growing ASEAN economies.

With consumption falling from a high of about 90 per cent of GDP in the 1950s to the current 60 per cent, the savings (and investment) rate increased from a mere 10 per cent of GDP in 1950 to the 1997 figure of around 26.5 per cent. Government consumption was held down at about 10–15 per cent throughout the period. This is a direct result of the failure to undertake tax reforms[5] to improve sources of revenue, with which far-reaching infrastructure investments could have been undertaken in almost all such areas as roads, rails, ports, power and telecommunication: tax reforms were announced in February 1998 effective from 1999. The poor state of the infrastructure has been a dampener on foreign capital flows into the currently more open real sector after the reforms. The country's trade with the rest of the world is also among the lowest: imports and exports as a percentage of GDP were a mere 19.2 per cent in 1997 compared with a figure of 16.6 per cent 17 years before. The corre-sponding figures for Korea are 68.4 and 68.8 per cent; for China, 12.6 and 34.8, and for Malaysia, 89.8 and 183 per cent. India has suffered and is continuing to experience persistent trade and current account deficits, which have led to serious weakening of the local currency before the 1992 exchange rate and monetary reforms. The exchange rate reforms managed to slash instability by half. The annual rate of depreciation of currency during the pre-reform period was 14 per cent! With more capital inflows, the current account may improve, but still the weakness of the trade sector is a cause for concern in this economy.

A glance at the social indicators in Table 12.1 reconfirms the lack of genuine development in this economy. The literacy rate has been improving, but not by as much as has been documented in Southeast Asian economies. Illiteracy in the 1990s is still about 40 per cent compared with the 15 per cent level in China, Indonesia and Malaysia: ADB (1997b). Education receives a low level of funding at about 2 per cent of the government budget compared with the double-

Table 12.1 Basic economic and social indicators of development in India

Indicators	1971–80	1981–90	1991–93	1994	1995	1996	1997	1998[a]
National accounts								
GDP growth (%)	3.3	5.9	4.9	6.3	5.3	5.1	4.6	5.0
Per capita GDP (US$)	167	293	294	338	341	380	386	390
Private consumption/GDP	0.7	0.7	0.6	0.6	0.6	0.59	0.58	0.59
Gov. consumption/GDP	0.10	0.10	0.11	0.11	0.11	0.11	0.12	0.12
Financial indicators								
Gross domestic savings (% of GDP)	22.3	21.9	21.1	23.0	24.4	25.6	25.7	24.6
Gross fixed capital formation (% of GDP)	17.3	21.0	22.0	24.0	26.2	27.1	28.5	25.4
Inflation	8.2	8.9	10.7	11.8	10.0	9.2	11.6	13.6
M2/GDP	32.1	43.0	47.8	50.0	47.8	37.0	39.0	43.0
M3/GDP	31.9	44.0	48.0	50.0	47.8	35.0	40.0	44.0
Fiscal balance (% of GDP)	–4.3	–7.5	–6.3	–6.1	–7.1	–7.0	–9.0	–11.4
Current account balance (% of GDP)	0.2	–1.9	–1.3	–1.2	–1.8	–1.0	–7.0	–8.5
Trade balance/GDP	–0.6	–2.4	–0.7	–2.97	–4.33	–2.66	–3.10	–3.46
Discount rate	8.2	10.0	12.0	12.0	12.0	12.0	9.0	9.0
Debt-service ratio (% of exports)	n.a.	n.a.	27.8	27.5	37.3	33.7	32.5	31.8

Social indicators

IMF classification	Low	Low	Low	Low	Low	Low	Low	Low
Adult illiteracy rate (%)	55	50	45	n.a.	n.a.	n.a.	42	42
Expenditure on education (% of exp.)	2.1	2.2	2.1	1.9	2.0	2.0	2.1	2.1
Expenditure on health (% of exp.)	1.9	2.0	1.7	1.8	1.9	1.9	1.9	1.9
Population growth	2.3	2.1	1.9	1.8	1.8	1.7	1.7	1.6

Notes:
[a] A mid-1999 estimate of GDP growth for 1999 is 7%.
Inflation in 1997 was brought down to 5.7%, but went up in 1998 and again in 1999.

Sources: IMF, *International Financial Statistics*, various issues; *Asian Development Outlook 1998, 1999*; *Government Finance Statistics Yearbook, 1985–1996.*

digit levels in Korea or Taiwan. Education-related expenditure in the ASEAN countries is closer to 20 per cent of the budget. However, Indian enrolment rates in primary schools have gone up from a low of 68 per cent of the relevant population in 1965 to the current 94 per cent. This trend, if continued, will lead to better educational statistics for this country.

Expenditure on health is also very low, at less than 2 per cent of the budget. Data available elsewhere (ADB, 1997b) suggest that the average life expectancy of 61 years compares not unfavourably with 68 years in China, or 71 years in Korea. Infant mortality in India, although it improved from a low of 150 per 1000 live births 30 years ago, is currently at 80. Comparative statistics are: Korea 11; Malaysia 13; and China 30. This is partly a reflection of lack of health infrastructure, particularly potable water, and provision of public health-enhancing facilities. There are no signs that other measures of social indicators not reported here are improving either.

From this brief background, the reader will appreciate that this chapter covers one of the important cases for a study of liberalization. India and China account for perhaps two-thirds of the Asian population. In the next section, we provide a brief review of the economic and financial structure of this large economy that has recently taken hesitant but strong steps to reform its rule-bound, relatively closed economy. The effects arising from the greater degree of financial- and real-sector reforms since 1988 are identified and explained in some detail in Section 3. The last section describes the prospects for the future. We describe very few of the import substitution policies of the 1950–87 period, which has produced some desirable outcomes despite putting the economy in a serious bind. The benefit was that it helped to build domestic industrial capacity to serve a large population. Rather, we pay more attention to recent reforms, especially in the financial sector. The reforms in the real and the financial sectors have led to some beneficial results that lift capital constraints on resources.

2.   ECONOMIC AND FINANCIAL STRUCTURE

A significant feature of the Indian economy is that it has developed a reasonably modern economy based on monetary exchange in contrast to the rural-based economy that it was some 50 years ago. The structure of the economy can be described with reference to the statistics in Table 12.2. The structure of the economy has changed significantly over the last four decades. The agriculture sector has declined to about a 31 per cent share of the economy compared with its earlier dominance of closer to a 60 per cent share. The rural population has also declined over the years as almost 30 per cent of the population now live in urban areas compared with half that figure in the 1950s. However, the agricultural sector is able to produce more, so that the country has reached grain sufficiency that it was unable to obtain right up to the end of the 1970s. In this respect India (and China) has developed its agricultural sector while achieving sufficient diversification of the economy away from agriculture. For example, the proportion of primary goods in Indian exports in 1970 was almost 60 per cent compared with the 1994 figure of about 40 per cent. That is a significant improvement, with industrial goods accounting for 60 per cent of exports. This figure is still not as high as it is for Malaysia, with more outward-looking liberal policies achieved in just 16 years. Malaysia exported primary goods making up 94 per cent of exports in 1970 compared to 29 per cent in 1995.

Table 12.2   Structure of the economy over 30 years of inward growth (% of GDP)

Period	Industry	Services	Agriculture	Exports	Investment	Savings
1960s	20	33	46	4	16	14
1990s	27	40	31	10	24	28

Sources: IMF, *International Financial Statistics*; World Bank, *World Development Reports*.

The service sector increased in size only marginally, showing a lack of development of this sector. Growth of this sector is very high – closer to 50 per cent – in other countries, which have accomplished a far greater degree of industrial activities. Industrial output has grown faster in India merely as a testament to the import substitution policies followed during the 1956–87 era. The GDP share increased to almost 30 per cent in 1998 compared with the 20 per cent 30 years ago. This is one of the great boasts of this country, in that it was able to build an industrial output capacity while having a very low savings rate, so that at the close of the twentieth century this country was among the top ten or so economies of the world in terms of industrial capacity. It is capable, given capital and higher technology, of retooling itself very quickly with its accumulation of a trained technical workforce – another boast is called for here, with the third largest technical–scientific workforce in the world – and the basic industrial structures in place.

Another significant feature is the great stride India has made to increase savings. Fifty years ago, consumption was as high as 90 per cent, so that there were hardly sufficient resources left over for investment. Over the years, and very slowly without too much dependence on external capital flows, just as in Korea, the gross investment rate in India was pushed up to the level of 23 per cent in 1996 (Korea achieved a higher rate, given its larger external sector). This is about 5 per cent higher than the world average, yet not as high as the 30–40 per cent investment rates achieved by the fast-track economies such as China, Malaysia and Thailand.

Of course, the over-dependence of the latter two countries on external capital flows destabilized them quite seriously during the 1997–98 Asian financial crisis. But India, without such a great exposure to foreign capital, remained in the late 1990s relatively unscathed by this crisis. The export sector has changed dramatically. About 58 per cent of total exports were manufactured goods in 1995, compared with their smaller proportion in earlier years. Even though it does not have as much manufactured output in exports as Korea does – 92 per cent in 1995 – India has managed to diversify its exports towards higher-value-added items. Non-textile and non-labour-intensive export items constituted two-thirds of the exports of this country in the 1990s, compared with only one third in 1965.

Great changes also took place during the same period and helped to change the structure of the financial sector as well. Financial activities in India are conducted within some 300 institutions (and 10 000 quasi-financial traditional organizations) employing almost one million workers. The financial system is rather large and complex, stretching over six central bank planning regions spread over the whole country. The bulk of financial activities are carried out in Bombay in the western region but the centres in Delhi, Gauhati, Kanpur, Calcutta, Hyderabad, Ahmedabad, Madras and Bangalore play crucial roles in the financial system of Bombay.

The banks, the share markets, the insurance sector and mutual funds (unit trusts and 'chit' funds) and the government bond markets are reasonably well developed. A start was made to create a market-based call-money market in the 1990s and also a bill-rediscounting market with repo auctions. Lack of competition restrains their growth, as there are few competitors in these markets. There is also an increasingly thriving foreign exchange market developing very fast as a result of the floating of the currency and the lifting of most exchange controls effective from June 1994. Apart from these spot markets, India has few activities in specialized futures markets (for example warrants, stock options, swaps, and so on) of any significance. A start has been made in this direction, with permission being granted to write cross-currency options. The finance minister, in his 1994–95 speech to the parliament on February 1994, said, 'The government attaches high priority to reform of the capital markets aimed at creating an efficient and competitive capital market'. This remains a continuing policy. The reforms of the 1990s reflect that sentiment. The enthusiasm for more reforms, reflected in the last ten years of liberalization, had not been evident at all in the previous 41 years.

The structure of the financial sector underwent a great many changes over the period before the 1998–99 reforms. While China was closing down all capitalist institutions in 1950 as undesirable, having driven the nationalists out of the mainland in 1949, India was pursuing a policy of nationalization that led to similar structural effects. The financial sector was put in a bind in both countries. The Communists disbanded the central bank, and set about creating a mono-banking system with the People's Bank of China subsuming all the functions of the banking sector. India started to nationalize the largely private-sector-managed banks into a few large government banks, for example the State Bank of India. The Reserve Bank of India was established to coordinate the nationalization and control plans. There were three bouts of nationalization, one immediately after independence in 1949 with the nationalization of the Imperial Bank of India, a second bout in 1969 and a third one in 1980. Fourteen banks were nationalized during the second round, and eight more in March 1980. The structural result was that banks moved from the private to the government sector. In India and China, both under government control, the banks provided the payment function but failed to develop the wherewithal to assess and price investment risks. Both countries had bad loans and failed to create a quality banking system with delegated monitors to assess and manage investment risk. Add to these connected lending practices and preferences, and the picture of an inefficient banking sector is complete.

The resulting structure was a mix of nationalized banks and a few private banks in India. Soon, there were 22 large nationalized banks owned and operated by the government, 29 domestic-origin banks owned as joint stock private companies and 24 foreign-origin banks. The nationalized banks accounted for about 55 per cent of all retail banking activities in the late 1980s (Chawala et al., 1988). These banks also had the largest network of branches, 61 per cent of the approximately 61 000 branches in the country. In short, the financial sector became structured as follows. A central bank supervised the institutions, which were (a) commercial banks, (b) specialized banks, (c) mutual credit organizations and (d) informal financing enterprises. A securities exchange body (the SEBI) was enlarged and given powers to supervise the direct capital markets and unit trusts. The insurance commission supervised the risk management enterprises.

Notable characteristics of the financial sector can now be described. The State Bank of India and its affiliates dominate the financial sector. Add to that 20 large nationalized banks and a further 12 specialized banks for long-term loans, and it can be seen that the central government effectively controls the financial sector. Take into account also the Unit Trust of India and the Insurance Corporation of India, the only two bodies permitted to operate as government-owned companies in those two areas, and the extent of the state's involvement in the financial sector can be described as rather pervasive. It is a miracle how the much less powerful 29 privately owned commercial banks and the 24 foreign-origin banks managed to retain a 40 per cent share of the market in the

1990s! The fact that the private banks existed particularly in the major urban areas perhaps provided a sort of trench-line beyond which the state-dominated banking sector would not dare move. This augured well for India as it provided a semblance of competition that preserved some degree of market influence in the financial sector even under the widespread dominance of the public-sector banks. While Indonesia's banking system was practically run by the state up to about the middle of the 1980s, the private sector lost ground and managed to account for a mere 20 per cent of the deposits. What was worse in Indonesia was that the inefficiency in managing the banks was more prevalent even in the private-sector banks until widespread banking reforms began to turn the situation around to a position such that, in 1996, 80 per cent of deposits were in the private-sector banks. Now, with state rescue of banks in trouble, it has reversed again. Not so in India.

The stock exchanges in India, altogether 23 of them, were all operated privately. These stock exchanges, the primary one being the Bombay Stock Exchange, developed on the private-sector model. Soon these developed into important institutions as sources of direct capital for major corporations. More will be said about the role of the capital market in a later section. The controls put on these financial organizations both in the private and the state sectors will be examined in detail when we describe the liberal policies put in place since 1988.

In summary, it can be said that there were severely suppressive policies in the Indian financial sector. There were very high reserve requirements (at one time as high as 45 per cent of deposits), which helped to channel deposits to the central bank. There were 20 different schedules of interest rates. By controlling the minimum and the maximum of interest rates, the regulators were able to subsidize some activities more than others in pervasive programmes of directing credits to certain economic activities. Readers will recall that this is a widespread practice in developing countries hoping to achieve fast-track growth. In all countries covered in this book, such efforts distorted market pricing of profitable investments, which led to poor investment decisions in the long run. Instead of providing fast-track growth, capital resources are wasted. Finally, there were multiple exchange rates, while capital controls were in force to prevent other than approved capital outflows. With capital outflow controls, international capital was reluctant to come in for investing even in the real sector, first because there were serious controls on the exchange rates needed for business, and second because foreigners could not, until recent reforms, own 100 per cent of a firm. Most of these controls would be steadily rolled back, starting in about 1988.

From our discussion to this point, it is perhaps accurate to describe the structure of the Indian economy as one that worked under pervasive controls designed to encourage corruption and stifle smooth economic activities. Where there are too many rules, there are opportunities to make a fast buck! As a result, the economy failed to deliver a growth in incomes sufficiently high to bring prosperity to the people. Thanks to the import substitution policies, the economy became inward-oriented. But that process produced a surprisingly perverse benefit. It led to slow but steady improvements in industrial output as domestic firms clamoured to produce goods and services to serve a huge and growing population. Hence this largely agricultural economy, with 90 per cent of the people living in the rural sector 50 years ago, slowly underwent change to become a large industrial economy though without a sufficiently developed services sector. The export sector diversified, especially in the last two decades or so, towards more value-added products. Urbanization increased to a level that means that almost three out of ten persons now live in urban areas. The financial sector has been pervasively suppressed, although the presence of 53 vibrant private-sector-owned commercial banks prevented the state from taking over the whole system. Thus the financial sector did not deteriorate to the level seen in some countries such as China and Vietnam, where any semblance of a modern financial system was removed under their Marxist–Leninist total state control.

The liberalization that started in India about 13 years ago has led to far-reaching changes, especially to the financial structures. The economic structure put in place by the import substitution policies is still holding together, and its participants are fighting to preserve the monopolistic and oligopolistic practices intact – they financed a rightist government to come to power – in order to shut out competition to earn economic rent. When the full impact of the reforms in the real sector is felt, the structure of the real sector is likely to change in the near future, as also happened in other countries.

3. LIBERALIZATION

3.1 Economic Liberalization

Pricing reforms

Consistent with received wisdom in development literature, India began with reforms in the real sector. In post-reform India, domestic and foreign investments are permitted in all sectors in any part of the country with the removal of the law that had reserved a large segment of the economy as the government's own investment domain since 1956. The first Prime Minister Nehru's enthusiasm for building industrial capacity was a way for the bureaucrats to steal the rights to run these things by themselves as part of the state. These days, after the reforms, the areas reserved for government-only investments remain only in defence, certain metals and mineral production and rail transport. The approval procedures for licences have been redesigned to bypass the corrupt bureaucracy. Conditions for automatic approvals are clearly spelt out so that the Reserve Bank of India in Bombay can approve (a) investments in 36 priority industries and also give approval for 51 per cent foreign equity ownership (b) export-oriented activities located in the export processing zones with 100 per cent foreign equity and (c) foreign technology transfer agreements valued at Rs 10 million (US$275 000) or royalties of up to 5 per cent for domestic sales and 8 per cent for exports. Other investment proposals may be made to and approvals obtained from the Indian foreign missions. The applications are then processed either by the Secretariat for Industrial Approvals or the Foreign Investment Promotion Board in Delhi. It was reported in the press in April 1994 that the time taken for approving a bank to operate in India was 69 days under the new system of approvals. To understand the extent of reforms that have been undertaken, it is necessary to look at the historical circumstances of liberalization. The genesis of controls started back in 1956 but the impetus for reforms was only evident in the late 1980s.

The 1980s witnessed a period of stagflation in the world as a whole – low growth with falling commodity and asset prices – as the more developed countries emerged weakened after the two oil price shocks of 1973 and 1979. A period of slow or no growth in the developed economies led to a sudden collapse of fast growth in the developing countries around the mid-1980s. Several such Asian economies from Japan to Indonesia introduced substantial price-reducing reforms to regain competitiveness, which led to substantial growth from about 1987 to 1996 for these reformed countries.

It was not so for India, which not only did not have the political will to challenge the entrenched protective sentiments of the industrialists running cartel-like markets, but was also experiencing insurgencies in several areas during a period of short-lived weak central government. India, under this condition of political uncertainty and still holding on to the old inward-looking policies, began to come to grips with the inadequacy of past policies to handle a worsening economic situation in the second half of the 1980s. When the short-lived government of a young leader[6] created sufficient consensus at least to think about badly needed reforms during 1985–87, a window of opportunity for reform opened. That was the situation in the late 1980s.

It is interesting to hark back to the time when India took a decision to implement controls in order to make the public sector the engine of growth. The seed for the restrictive policies is contained in a 1956 parliamentary speech made by the grandfather of that young assassinated leader urging Indians to reform: 'in a country under-developed as ours, we cannot progress except by State initiative ... by enlarging the State sector...'. This was not a speech by a Communist, but by a man of great vision and conviction of freedom. That policy was endorsed in 1956 as the now famous (or infamous!) Industrial Resolution Policy. Only 3 per cent of the state budget was allocated to public enterprises in 1956. By 1991, this had been expanded resolutely until 37.6 per cent of the state's capital expenditure was absorbed by the mostly loss-making 246 central government public enterprises. These enterprises were making no more than 2–3 per cent profit per year. The GDP share of the public sector increased from a mere 14 per cent in 1970 to almost 25 per cent in 1990. Of course there are worse examples – perhaps China or Russia. The GDP share of the public sector in China in the mid-1970s was 90 per cent!

The entry of public enterprises into the production of non-public goods was mandated through laws that reserved certain economic activities – initially covering ammunitions, basic engineering goods, machinery, telecommunications, energy, among others – to be undertaken only by public enterprises. The original list was expanded when other policy objectives, for example agricultural development, dictated other activities to be added to the restricted list. Even the so-called unrestricted items needed licences for the import of foreign inputs, be they capital or material inputs to production. This led to the rule by bureaucracy, a very corrupt bureaucracy,[7] which bred inefficiency in addition to exacting a high price in the form of corruption money given to obtain even normal approvals for licences. As the restrictive policies began to slow down economic growth, there were limited attempts to tinker at the fringes of controls without removing the restrictive list.

The number of people employed by the public enterprises increased to 2.2 million in the 246 enterprises, while the entire civil service employed only 4 million to serve a population close to a billion. In addition to these firms, there were 823 state-level enterprises, similarly making losses and forming a network of inefficient producers. The total capital expenditure in these enterprises amounted to a mere 2.9 per cent in 1951 in five enterprises: in 1990, this became 37.3 per cent of the total budget. A good measure of the entrenchment of the public sector in the non-public goods sector may be judged by the following statistics. Public enterprise shares in late 1980s GDP were 33 per cent (manufacturing), 90 per cent (utilities), 50 per cent (transport and telecommunications), 40 per cent (finance, banking and insurance) and 47 per cent (services other than administration and defence): see Rao (1995). An evaluation of the public-sector firms was made in early 1990. A decision has been made to sell off inefficient ones and to keep those that could be turned around to make profits through greater decentralization of management and corporatization. By the mid-1990s, a substantial portion of these firms has been sold as a start on a long road to divesting the public-sector enterprises.

There was an attempt in the second half of the 1980s to permit limited entry of foreign firms with promises of special approvals for higher than 49 per cent foreign ownership. This was still inadequate compared with the higher foreign ownership levels offered in the ASEAN economies. These initiatives were sporadic and did not lead to any favourable responses under the endemic political crisis years of 1986–88. The real-sector reforms began to release some energy into the domestic economy as a result of the cumulative effects of these limited reforms in the real sector. These are not examined in detail here. However, the new government that came into power in 1991 acted on a series of reports that it and the previous government had commissioned on liberalization. After the assassination of the reform-minded young leader, the new government carried out many systematic reforms in the real and the financial sectors.

The highlights of these reforms were three. First, they introduced decentralized approval powers to the foreign embassies and the central bank for most foreign investment applications while the state governments were given more power to compete for investment. Second, the restricted list was abolished (except in defence, administration and essential services), thus leaving almost the entire economy open to entry by non-government domestic *and* foreign investors. Readers will note that this openness is dramatically different from the policy of entry into only special zones in many countries. Third, a number of far-reaching financial reforms were implemented, removing most of the restrictions on financial resource flows into and out of India.

Years of pursuit of bad policies led the economy to slide slowly into a morass. The worst crisis occurred in 1991. Foreign reserves were almost depleted, the savings rate had plummeted in 1989 to 7 per cent, the current account deficit was close to danger level and the budget deficit also went to a dangerous level, close to 10 per cent of the budget. The remedy that amazingly saved the country was a 23 per cent devaluation of the currency and subsequent financial reforms put in place. The IMF lent money and provided support for this reform. These measures eased the situation slowly until the country regained a reasonable level of economic health by the end of 1992.[8] Once the economy was out of the woods, a brave set of reforms was put in place by the Rao government that paved the way for greater reforms yet to come.

External-sector policies

Further exchange rate reforms came in two stages. In the later part of 1991, restrictions on a large range of items previously not permitted as imports were removed. Among them was a restriction on the import of gold. It was feared that Indians would spend their savings on buying gold, and successive governments have imposed restrictions on the import of gold, thus making a profitable arbitrage for those who dared to bribe the customs to import gold illegally. With the removal of this restriction, there was a sudden increase in the inflow of gold imports, and the premium that was paid by Indians for gold soon disappeared when the markets equalized prices inside and outside. More restrictions on imports were removed during the years 1993–94. Finally, all restrictions for currency convertibility on producers were removed in March 1993, thus making a substantial change in the external sector. Exporters and those sending remittances to India could do so freely. For individuals wishing to go on tours and to travel for education, liberal approvals were given for foreign exchange. But for other purposes, there are still controls on the non-production sector. In July 1994, the currency became fully convertible, satisfying the IMF's Article 8. Capital accounts were liberalized. There are still controls on capital accounts of the non-exporting domestic firms.

Foreign direct investment in all industries except those on the negative list is now possible: the negative list is now reduced to a small list of seven activities. This effectively removed almost all restrictions on foreign and domestic firms' entry into the industrial sector. Automatic approvals are possible for investments with 51 per cent foreign ownership in high-priority sectors such as energy production, telecommunication and others. A Foreign Investment Promotion Board has been set up to expedite and follow up such investments.

The statistics in Table 12.3 show some improvements as well as some bad effects of the harsh policies implemented to avert a major financial crisis. One obvious bad effect was on inflation, following the current account liberaliz-ation in 1993–94. The inflation rate rose strongly as a result of the devaluation of the currency. However, by 1996 inflation had been brought to a manageable 9.2 per cent level. There were large falls in the monetary markets for the same reasons. But FDI increased by leaps and bounds. By the end of 1996, before a slowdown took place in anticipation of restrictions by the conservative government that was expected to come to power in the following year, FDI had increased from about US$100 million to close to US$3000 million. Trade deficits of about –2 per cent in 1993 declined steadily to –1 per cent by 1995 before increasing in 1996.

3.2   Financial Liberalization

Substantial financial reforms were put in place as alluded to in the previous discussion. The reforms covered wide-ranging areas and were introduced from 1989. They are still ongoing. For example, the Reserve Bank of India announced in November 1998 further easing of restrictions on domestic firms issuing securities in foreign markets. The year 1999 witnessed tax incentives coming into effect for all. In 1999, steps were taken to introduce derivatives trading.

Government finance
Because of the over-extension of financing by government to both provide capital and offset the losses incurred by public enterprises, there has been a persistent loss of control in managing the government's finances. This has been made worse by the absence of any meaningful tax reforms. The tax reforms

Table 12.3   Growth rates of basic economic indicators

| | 5-year average | | | Annual average | | | | | | | |
	1976–80	1981–85	1986–90	1991	1992	1993	1994	1995	1996	1997	1998
GDP	3.5	5.4	6.3	0.5	4.6	4.5	6.3	5.3	5.1	4.6	5.0
Inflation	3.9	9.3	8.4	13.9	11.8	6.4	11.8	10.0	9.2	11.6	14.6
Revenue	11.9	17.5	14.9	23.3	12.6	6.2	13.9	18.9	20.1	20.4	19.8
M1	10.8	15.1	15.7	22.6	7.2	18.7	27.4	11.1	12.3	12.6	10.5
M2	19.6	17.3	16.7	18.3	16.9	17.0	22.3	13.7	15.9	17.7	18.4
FDI	5.0	8.0	8.5	n.a.	276.0	99.0	146.9	120.4	20.7	26.5	10.0
Trade balance	10.8	15.1	15.7	–41.9	–28.8	7.1	–123.1	–49.4	–7.5	3.0	–1.0

Notes:
M2 = (M1 + quasi-money).
n.a. data not available.

Sources: IMF, *International Financial Statistics*, various issues; World Bank, *World Bank Databank*, Feb. 1997; *Asian Development Outlook 1998, 1999*.

Table 12.4   Government finance and deep deficit experience

Gov. budget	1983	1985	1990	1991	1992	1993	1994	1995	1996	1997	1998
Revenues	11.50	13.96	13.50	14.10	12.50	13.50	13.25	14.10	14.20	14.50	14.20
Expenses	11.30	12.50	17.00	17.50	16.80	16.10	16.13	16.20	16.10	16.20	16 30

Source: IMF, *International Financial Statistics*.

implemented since 1994 have produced some favourable results, but the real reforms came only in 1998. This is shown in Table 12.4.

The revenues always fall far short of the expenses. Part of the shortfall is offset by official development assistance from the developed countries, while the rest has to be offset by domestic or foreign borrowing. India had consistently run a 3 per cent savings to investment gap. It was filled by foreign loans (which were 4.4 per cent of the 1996 GDP, for example). Foreign loans stand at US$95.3 billion, or 24 per cent of GDP, a level much more sober than is found in many developed and developing countries. Indonesia and Vietnam each have loans worth more than a year's GDP. India has also resorted to public-sector borrowing, which has led to the ballooning of the domestic debt to about 20 per cent of GDP. In addition, the country also has international debt, taken out under multilateral lending for development.

Direct capital and money markets

The stock markets have a long history since they were developed over a long time. The share markets are presently capitalized at about 48 per cent of GDP. The stock exchanges are served and managed by around 4000 brokers and 20 000 sub-brokers, who are equivalent to the dealers in a modern market. These statistics indicate a higher level of development of the stock markets, all of which have been in the private sector. India's capital market is a very large one among the 53 emerging markets in the world. Most emerging share markets are capitalized at about 20 per cent of GDP. The stock markets are situated in several major Indian cities and are not integrated in so far as they have no integrated trading procedures and communication links similar to, for example, the associated exchanges in Australia. There are 23 separate exchanges, with Bombay Exchange accounting for two-thirds or more of the trading volume and value. A national integrated stock exchange with screen trading and automated operation is developing fast. There are some 12 000 stocks listed and traded. Of these, the exchanges in Bombay, Calcutta and Delhi account for more than 50 per cent of the listing. Trading is more intense in Bombay. The exchanges at Kanpur, Ahmedabad and Madras are also large and active.

The recent good performance of the stock exchange provides important descriptive statistics on the Bombay Stock Exchange. The total capitalization of all the world's 53 emerging markets in 1996 was about US$1900 billion. India's stock market ranks among the top ten, with a capitalization of US$150 billion. This high capitalization to GDP makes the share market a far deeper market than most of the emerging markets. The Bombay Exchange may be counted as being among the top six, following Korea, Taiwan, Mexico, Thailand and Malaysia. The value traded in Bombay is 3.5 per cent of the 30 top markets in the 1990s (IFC reports). The stock market has provided an average yield of about 38 per cent over the last 15 years. But its risk is also high, at about 40 per cent standard deviation of returns per annum. In terms of price/earnings, the Bombay market is about a third higher in risk than the average for the world. Therefore the coefficient of variation of 1.05 for India compares favourably with most developed markets (which have an average coefficient of 0.90) as well as the developing markets (which have an average coefficient of 1.7). The average price/earnings ratio in the 1990s of 25 : 33 makes the Bombay market in recent years about one third more risky than the world average (IFC reports).

India's bond market is not well developed although the government bond issues are traded within the financial institutions. There is a potentially large private market to be made with Rs 2700 billion worth of government bonds. There is also a tax-exempt bond mutual fund scheme with government securities. The capital market is still not international enough to attract foreign capital inflows. This changed in 1995–96 when much of the disinvestment in Southeast Asia led to large capital flows into the Indian markets. This is in a sense not comforting as markets such as those in Karachi and Bombay that liberalized faster went through speculative capital inflows, which, when withdrawn, destabilized the ability of these markets to provide steady streams of financing.

While the Indian companies can access foreign markets for funds, likewise foreign companies can invest in the Indian financial institutions as well, by obtaining a licence to run financial institutions. This is designed to improve efficiency while also making it much cheaper to trade in the market. An over-the-counter (OTC) market has been operational since mid-1994, and gives access to smaller firms to list their shares. Eventually, this screen-based trading system is expected to unify the exchanges. These and other reforms on capital adequacy for brokers, greater and more frequent disclosures, and so on are expected to provide opportunities for this large capital market to develop into a financial centre for that time zone in the future.

Under the planned mixed-economy model, with a large role reserved for the public sector to develop the economy, resources had to be directed towards the government sector. The state engaged in active interventions in the economy (World Bank, 1989; 1990). This meant a greater role for the government in the monetary economy of the country. From as far back as the 1950s, the central bank imposed a high liquidity requirement on the banking system. Almost 47 per cent of the deposits in the banking system ended up as reserves with the central bank in the form of bank deposits and holding of government securities. This was different from the situation in Malaysia, which followed a policy of commercializing the rural sector to improve the incomes of the rural population, and did not use reserve requirements but instead issued huge domestic debts to be bought by the financial institutions. But in most other economies this ratio was seldom above 18 per cent of deposits. In addition, the government also depended on deficit budgets for decades as a stimulus for growth, and that led to excessive money growth with high inflation.

Exchange rate policy was the leading candidate for reform when the serious crisis occurred in 1991. Reforms to the multiple exchange rates and controls on producers and individuals were lifted after a massive devaluation of the rupee by 23 per cent in 1991. Steps soon followed to unify the multiple exchange rates into one in 1992. By March 1993, further reforms were put in place to remove restrictions on producers holding foreign exchange (see Table 12.5).

Table 12.5   Exchange rate liberalization effects

Year	Exchange rate	Per cent change	Years	Exchange rate	Per cent change
1983	10.49	−8.90	1992	36.02	−16.33
1984	12.45	−11.89	1993	43.10	−19.66
1985	12.17	0.22	1994	45.81	−6.29
1986	13.12	−7.80	1995	52.30	−14.17
1987	12.88	1.80	1996	51.67	1.40
1988	14.95	−6.10	1997	52.99	−2.55
1989	17.03	−13.90	1998	43.90	20.70
1990	18.07	−6.10	1999	42.53	3.22
1991	25.84	−43.00			
Decline	10.63% per year			4.21% per year	

Source: IMF, *International Financial Statistics*.

With those significant reforms, the real sector was able to conduct foreign exchange transactions to acquire capital and technology, as well as improve trading with the rest of the world without having to obtain permission. In July 1994, all remaining controls on foreign exchange was removed, thus restoring India's external account to satisfy the stipulation of IMF Article 8. The Southeast Asian countries had reformed their exchange rate regulations by switching to a managed float of their currencies about 10–18 years earlier. Restrictions on individuals in respect of holding foreign exchange for travel and education were relaxed, while controls were maintained on other uses. Similarly, reforms to capital controls have been shelved in view of the 1997–98 Asian financial crisis.

Interest rate reforms
The banking system was designed to serve the demands of credit targeting by the government to achieve sufficient growth in outputs in the agricultural and

industrial sectors. This meant two things: first, massive redirection of deposits
to the reserve bank to make it available for the government and, second,
interest rate controls. The reserve ratios on deposits were kept high and
government ownership of banks became dominant to achieve the first
objective. To achieve the second objective, a system of maximum and
minimum interest rates was designed in order to control interest rates. Before
the interest reforms in 1992, there were 20 different schedules of interest rates:
the appendix to this chapter provides summary information on interest rates
when the 20 slabs were standardized in 1991 and again in 1993. Subsequent
deregulations removed these restrictions.

Table 12.6   Deposit and credit interest rates

Year	Minimum deposit rate (%)	Credit rate (%)	Year	Minimum deposit rate (%)	Credit rate (%)
1983	10	16.5	1992	12	18.92
1984	10	16.5	1993	12	16.25
1985	10	16.5	1994	9	14.75
1986	10	16.5	1995	9	15.46
1987	10	16.5	1996	9	15.96
1988	10	16.5	1997	9	13.83
1989	10	16.5	1998	9.0	14.00
1990	10	16.5	1999	9.5	15.40
1991	12	17.88			
Mean	10.22%	16.65%	Mean	9.83%	13.86%

Sources: IMF, *International Financial Statistics*; Internet sources.

A series of reforms to free interest rate controls was begun after 1991. The
20 slabs of interest rates (see Table 12.6) were reduced to three in 1991. The
minimum deposit rate was reduced by 3 per cent and the maximum interest rate
for bank advances was reduced by 4 per cent. Thus the market was expected
to adjust its offered rates to depositors. But there were no improvements as the
controls still continued to be binding. It was when all controls on lending rates
were removed that interest rates started to respond to market forces. In the early
phase of removing the lending restrictions, interest rates went up. Since 1993,
the lending rates have been coming down, especially with inflation falling to
the 1996 level of about 6 per cent, which is well below the double-digit inflation
in the years before the reforms. Auction of 91-day Treasury bills and

government securities began in 1993. This led to new development in that it provided broad indications of the base rates and the risk-free rates, all determined in the open market.

The credit creation of the banking system can now be examined. The high liquidity ratios dampened the money-multiplier function of the banking system since at the prevailing high reserve rate the money multiplier could be around the region of three to four times the deposit rate, unlike the nine to ten times possible with easier reserve ratios. Liberalization of the reserve requirements to the 1998 level of about 11 per cent led to greater credit creation under a market-based credit system now in force. Demand deposits have almost doubled over 1991–97, as did also time deposits, which grew at a rate of 17 per cent per annum compared with half that rate in the pre-reform period.

The growth rate in demand deposits averaged 12.6 per cent, which is also about double the rate in the pre-reform period. Interest rate reforms led to easier credit creation to support private-sector activities. In 1998, the total domestic credits in the non-financial sector amounted to about 55 per cent of GDP compared with the pre-reform ratio, which was below 50 per cent. In addition, reforms made foreign capital available to corporations and banks through more access to the international capital markets for funds. The GDP share of foreign credits to the private sector was about 8 per cent in 1998 compared with the pre-reform ratio of 1.4 per cent. Thus interest rate reforms, reductions in the bank reserve ratios and relaxation of controls on access to capital sources have all combined to make more credits available to the private sector.

It can also be noted that the bank spread of 2.88 per cent in the pre-reform period has widened a little in the post-reform period. This is as it should be, to strengthen the ability of the financial institutions to obtain higher profits at a time when more stringent capital adequacy rules are being imposed. This will have the effect of making the banks more profitable, and hence more able to modernize speedily. Reforms to bring in competition by lifting restrictions on interest rates will result in new realignments among the banks as efficiency becomes the criterion for survival, eventually leading to more mergers and takeovers.

With (a) the reforms of the financial sectors and (b) more openness in current and capital accounts, India's interest rate regime is likely to become more responsive to international forces as capital flows begin to take place both ways. Structural changes are already evident, bringing with them changes to the process of price determination in the financial system. For example, about seven new banks have been licensed in the private sector. Concentrating mostly in the metropolitan areas and therefore catering to the large industrial customers, the new banks are expected to increase competition in the more profitable market segments. With a free-floating rupee since 1994, international effects on the currency are quite evident in making it respond to economic fundamentals. This has been an important reason why the rupee did not overshoot following the Asian financial crisis during June 1997 to May 1998. Competition and creation of more liquid and varied financial intermediation will come next, to integrate India's monetary economy with the rest of the world.

Central bank and depository institutions (Table 12.7)

India's financial system at the time of independence was designed to cater to the demands of international commerce and, to a limited extent, the demands of what have come to be termed the 'big boys', the élites of society as well as the large trading and manufacturing houses (Chhipa, 1987; Sarkar, 1988). The Reserve Bank of India and the Imperial Bank of India were both nationalized in 1949. These acts were only the first of far greater interventions in the financial system to come in later years. Intervention in the financial sector was legitimized and sold to the public to usher in mass banking, with its emphasis on reaching the average citizen, which meant the rural sector where 90 per cent of the population lived. Special banks for industrial financing were formed in 1948 (Industrial Finance Corporation India), 1955 (Industrial Credit and Investment Corporation of India) and 1964 (Industrial Development Bank of India). In later years, two more specialized banks, one for agricultural financing (NABARD) and another for international trade (EXIMBANK) were set up. In September 1956, 245 life insurance companies were taken over to form the Life Insurance Corporation of India. The State Bank of India (SBI) was licensed in 1955, as a means to bring mass banking to the whole country with the aim of providing access to deposit facilities and credits to a larger base of depositors and creditors. These institutions expanded very fast, as did the banks affiliated to the SBI. Currently, the SBI and its affiliates account for about one fifth of the retail banking activities. These four and the General Insurance Corporation (GIC) formed in 1971 played critical roles in their respective financing areas. Other specialized financial institutions listed in Table 12.7 were progressively set up as demands for focused financial intermediation grew.

All financial institutions (see Table 12.7) are licensed by central government agencies, and therefore India's financial system is similar to that non-American model found in most British Commonwealth countries. Banks were divided into two groups, namely the more significant public-sector banks and the increasingly important private-sector banks. The more dominant public-sector banks number about 224, and have a large number of branches throughout the country. Of the public-sector banks, 196 are regional rural and cooperative banks, accounting for slightly more than one-seventh of the deposits.

The private-sector banks, numbering 53 (increasing fast), contribute to about one-third of banking activities. The Indian Overseas Bank and a few others have about 120 branch operations in foreign countries to facilitate international transactions. The number of branches increased from 8321 in 1969 to some

Table 12.7   Financial institutions in India

Financial institution types	Remarks
Banks	
1 Reserve bank of India (RBI)	Central bank
2 State bank of India & Affiliates (SBIA)	Largest bank
3 Nationalized banks	20 significant
4 Rural banks	Large number
5 Other scheduled commercial banks	Not nationalized
6 Foreign banks with off-shore origin	24 such banks
Specialized banks, development banks	
1 Industrial Development Bank of India	Term lending
2 EXIMBANK	Trade finance
3 NABARD	Agriculture
4 Industrial Finance Corporation India	Industrial
5 Ind. Credit & Investment Corp. of India	Industrial
6 Small Industries Development Bank	Industrial
7 Shipping Credit and Investment Company	Shipping
8 Technology Development & Information Co.	Venture capital
9 Tourism Finance Corp. of India	Tourism
10 Risk Capital & Technology Finance Corp.	Risk capital
11 National Housing Bank	Housing
12 Industrial Restructuring Bank of India	Industrial
Mutual credit organizations	
1 Cooperative rural banks	Credit cooperatives
2 Unit Trusts of India (UTI)	Small investors
3 Non-banking finance companies	Mortgage finance
Informal financing enterprises	
1 Informal finance (nidhis, chit funds)	Informal
Securities exchanges	
1 Organized securities markets	Stock exchanges
Insurance and pension enterprises	
1 Life Insurance Corporation of India	Insurance
2 General Insurance Corporation	Insurance
3 Public Provident Funds (public sector)	Not significant
4 Export Credit Guarantee Corp. of India	Export credit insurance

Sources: Reserve Bank of India and State Bank of India publications.

61 000 branches. Branches increased very fast, at an annual rate of 10.4 per cent. About 23 and 50 per cent of branches are in the rural and semi-urban areas respectively. The remaining 27 per cent are in the metropolitan areas. Branching to spread the network to the whole country has been a signal success of the plan to introduce mass banking.

In the category of specialized banks, there are 13 institutions at the national level for development, trade, agriculture, and so on. At a lower level, still in the same category, there is a network of 18 state financial corporations and 26 state industrial development corporations to finance small to medium-sized enterprises. The third category comprises non-banking financial companies, which have registered a phenomenal growth as these were new organizations that catered to a growing demand for new services. For instance, a major player in this category is the Unit Trust of India (UTI). As a ratio of gross financial savings of households, deposits in these non-banking institution amounts to 8 per cent, which is considered a large portion given the stage of development of the economy. Informal financing enterprises, the fourth category, includes traditional *Nidhis*, *chit funds* and money-lending enterprises, which are traditional informal sources of financing for commercial enterprises. Several organized exchanges for money, bills, bonds and stocks were created. This group includes potentially the fastest-growing financial institutions.

All these institutions and markets come under the central bank, the Reserve Bank of India (RBI). RBI has direct responsibility for licensing and supervising financial institutions in general, with responsibility for the smooth functioning of the entire financial system. In the pre-reform years of 1949–88, RBI played a critical role in implementing policies to support the diversion of financial resources to the central government to carry out the targeted credit programmes to home-grow industrial capacity and to expand agricultural output. These days, the RBI is more concerned about deregulating and returning the financial sector to respond to market forces, while of course being the guardian for maintaining macroeconomic stability. It has attracted some of the best and able minds in the country.[9]

The banking reforms took place during 1992–94. The aims of these reforms were to introduce greater transparency to improve investor protection, enhance efficiency and improve competition to upgrade the standard of customer services. After 25 years of targeted mobilization of savings, the country managed to bring banking services increasingly into the rural sector. Through that strategy it managed to improve the savings rate of the country from a mere 10 per cent of GDP in 1950 to about 24 per cent by the end of the 1980s. With foreign capital coming in easily, with reforms to the capital account for producers, the gross savings came close to 27 per cent in 1998. Rural residents already have access to banking services with one branch serving 21 000 rural residents in the 1990s compared to one per 425 000 in 1969!

Today there is one branch per 16 000 urban residents. Rural bank deposits have increased to 14 per cent of the total deposits from a mere 3 per cent in 1969. A targeted credit policy to improve investment in the rural areas appears to have worked. About 13 per cent of the total credit is also given to rural residents.[10] It should be pointed out, in addition, that 25 per cent of domestic savings are channelled through the commercial banks, that is the public-sector, rural and private banks of India.

All banks are now required to extend credits to priority sectors, namely agriculture, small-scale industries and small businesses, at concessionary interest rates. Up to 1990, this directive applied only to the public-sector banks but with deregulation this rule has been extended to private-sector banks as an *advisory* guideline. In addition, 1 per cent of credits is required to be made to the weaker sections – the scheduled caste persons – of the society at a concessionary interest rate.

The wide-ranging reforms of the last five years covered the entire financial sector, which has been identified as a key element in the overall restructuring of the economic system. The government-owned banking sector, which still dominates the sector, is now under pressure to improve operational efficiency, to compete with new entrants, and to come under increased scrutiny on prudential norms. More private banks are now being licensed to offer the badly needed competition to improve customer services. Some of the major reform measures undertaken are included in Table 12.8. Control on branching has been removed. Capital adequacy has been increased to 8 per cent, effective from 1996. The reserve ratio is reduced to 10 per cent. During 1997, when there was a temporary pressure on the undervalued rupee, the reserve ratio was raised by a 2 per cent margin to dampen liquidity. Restrictions on expansion and lending operations have been relaxed.

Money and exchange markets
Development of a vibrant money market was long delayed because of the controlled financial system. However, as a prelude to some degree of market-based determination of base interest rates, a money brokerage firm was licensed in 1988; a discount house was also licensed. The latter was set up by the central bank, contributing Rs 10 000 million capital. It trades in 91-day and 364-day Treasury bills, and also rediscounts commercial bills. It deals in overnight call-money instruments and also rediscounts bills of up to 14 days' maturity. The market-building activities arising from these reforms improved money-market liquidity. At the same time, this market enables the discovery of going market rates for very short-term money-market instruments. In a sense, these actions are similar to those Japan undertook in its money markets in 1984, when short-dated *Gensaki* financial instruments were approved by Japan's central bank for trading among the financial institutions, also to reveal short-term interest

Table 12.8   Economic and financial reforms

Date of reform	Liberalization policies implemented

Genesis of controls

1956 — Industrial Policy Resolution under which state sector was required to create industrial capacity by reserving a large number of activities as the reserved areas for the state to operate.

1949; 1967; 1982 — Nationalization of Reserve Bank of India and Imperial Bank of India.
Establishment of State Bank of India.
Further nationalization of more banks in the 1960s.
Nationalization of all insurance companies and establishment of a single large insurance corporation to take them over.
Establishment of specialized banks and of Unit Trust of India.

Liberalization

1980s — Limited reforms to address periodic problems in the management of the economy. No reforms taken to break out of the controls already in place.
Restrictions on certain imports relaxed to ease constraints on private sector's ability to respond to changing international

1988–89 — competitiveness.

1991–97 — Following initial success of limited reforms in 1988–89, the system of reserving certain sectors for investments by the state was dismantled.

Real-sector reforms — The reservation list was abolished, together with all entry restrictions, so that local and foreign investors can enter any sector. Only a few defence-related and certain metal manufactures and rails were still kept by the government for strategic reasons.
Export processing zones where any foreign enterprise could produce and own 100 per cent of the firms.
In other parts of India, 51% ownership permitted.
Approvals standardized; for foreigners, approvals could be obtained through the central bank and from a special investment promotion board set up for that purpose.

Banking & financial reforms — Statutory liquidity ratio reduced from high of 25% to 2.5%, total reserve reduced to 10% by 1998.
Interest rates slabs from 20 reduced to 3 by 1989–90. Further reduced to a single slab with no restriction on lending rate. Minimum deposit rate still in force.
Prudential norms improved by supervision standards for bad debt provisioning and for risk-weighting exposure to risky loans.
Capital adequacy of minimum of 4% by March 1993 and 8% by March 1996 introduced and implemented.

Date of reform	Liberalization policies implemented

	Maximum support for state-owned banks in recapitalization stipulated when state-owned banks undertook to improve efficiency. Private sector could buy up to 10% voting rights in state banks to inject slow privatization of state banks. Restrictions on branching also lifted for entry into the sector.
Capital-market reforms	Auction on Treasury bills and government securities started in 1992. Supervisory capacity of the regulator (SEBI) strengthened to reform the capital markets. Capital Issues Act repealed. SEBI relaxed issue conditions and permitted issues to be marketed after approvals. Listed companies permitted to have access to international capital markets. Monopoly by the one mutual fund company broken with entry of many more. Over-the-counter exchange established to create a screen-traded computer-assisted operation. This is expected to become the model. Foreign ownership restrictions relaxed a little.
Current & capital account reforms	India operated a fixed exchange rate regime despite most countries choosing managed floats in late 1970s and early 1980s. During this phase, India's currency depreciated at an annual rate of about 10%.
1991	Currency crisis led to a 23% devaluation of the currency.
1993	Foreign exchange controls on producers and individuals slowly relaxed.
1994	Currency free-floated, satisfying the IMF Article 8 conditions. Capital controls on producers removed substantially. Exchange controls on individuals eased for travel and education. Further easing of capital controls shelved in the face of the 1997 Asian financial crisis. Insurance sector is next to be reformed. Limited reforms being introduced in this sector by easing entry barriers.
Tax reforms 1997–99	After a period of tinkering with the tax structure and tax administration, broad-based reforms were passed into law in 1997 and 1998. This is expected to bring in widespread benefits.

Note: In a speech on the day of swearing in of ministers of his cabinet in October 1999, the re-elected Prime Minister Vajpaye promised more liberalization under his new majority government.

Sources: Reserve Bank of India publications and Ariff (1996).

rates. An important new trend with the reforms is the large increase in the issue of commercial papers, particularly by companies with good credit rating. Banks are subscribing to these papers in a large way, thus creating liquidity in short-dated risky money instruments. From October 1993, maximum maturity for such instruments was raised from six months to one year and the eligibility norms for companies issuing papers have been further liberalized.

India has followed a fixed–adjustable exchange rate regime, which, when adjusted frequently by the authorities, reflected market rates quite closely. The Indian rupee declined systematically against the US dollar over the decades except in 1985, 1987 and 1997, when it rose by small amounts. The real rate of interest was 6.5 per cent (relative to much lower real deposit rates in the USA). However, the high demand for foreign exchange on account of the deficits in funds to the tune of 3.6 per cent of GDP, the need for foreign debt servicing, and the generally lower productivity levels (figures not available) drove the rupee down over the years.

The average depreciation of the rupee against the US dollar was some 10.6 per cent per year over the decade to 1991. In ten years, the currency declined in value by half. Depreciation has halved to about 4 per cent during 1992–99. The free-float of the rupee in March 1993 sent it to its all-time low as it corrected the past misalignment with the market and partly also on account of the current account crisis just before that reform. Another often-quoted problem was the high level of monetary expansion caused by the Keynesian deficit budgeting for years under import-substituting policies. The rupee declined by some 19.66 per cent in 1993, and has since stabilized against the US dollar. Contrary to expectations before the reforms, the rupee held steady against the dollar, and on several occasions the RBI had to intervene to keep the rupee from appreci-ating in the second half of the 1990s. One report said that the RBI spent US$1000 million on protesting the rupee in the first half of 1994: see RBI reports. RBI interventions have occurred whenever inflows through portfolio investments and export receivables have surged. As part of the exchange rate reforms, authorized dealers in foreign exchange have now been permitted to write cross-currency options to provide customers a hedge on their foreign exchange exposure.

The rupee is expected to stabilize, given the open current and capital accounts, against the US dollar, and is not expected to appreciate. On the other hand, the experience of exchange rate management in other countries suggests that unless productivity improves in the economy along with a low inflation rate with high external reserves to support the currency, it is unlikely that the currency can halt the downward moves. But the depreciation of the currency since 1993 has been about 1.4 per cent, which is a vast improvement. RBI is pursuing a monetary policy based on sterilizing the inflationary effect through a foreign exchange swap operation. This is also helpful.

On the development of liquid and deep money markets, the experiment has already started with call-money markets and bills discounting, introduced in 1987. There is need for competition in this area as more players are licensed. The floating of the rupee in June 1993 and the 1994 removal of most capital controls put India on a par with the successful newly industrializing economies that introduced such reforms as far back as the late 1970s, for example Singapore and Malaysia and, in the early 1980s, Taiwan. Further impetus has been provided recently through the creation of speedy automatic approvals for investments introduced in 1994 to bypass the deadeningly slow bureaucracy. Tax incentives that will provide the pull factor needed to bring foreign investments have been put in place, which is partly the reason for the substantial increase in FDI.

Very little is known about the quantity and variety of the foreign exchange markets, the money markets, the bond and debentures market, and so on, not to mention the feasibility of the advent of futures markets. A debate is current on the introduction of financial futures. The Indian version of a forward market in shares, the *badla*, was reintroduced in 1997. Currency exposures can now be hedged via the over-the-counter option and in forward markets. Derivatives markets are being introduced to manage price risk.

3.3 Impacts of Liberalization

The 1991 financial crisis brought India to the brink of bankruptcy that would have required IMF intervention to rescue the economy. The important reform steps taken to avert that disaster were described in earlier sections. The list of significant reforms is included in Table 12.8. As readers will note, there was consistent speeding up of the reforms in the 1990s until the coming into power of a nationalist conservative Hindu party (the BJP) in 1997. Much of the impetus for reforms was still kept more or less on track by an astute new finance minister bent on bringing India to the level of openness needed for the economy to grow sufficiently. That government was still in power at the close of the century, and not much is expected to happen by way of bolder reforms.

These reforms were instrumental in slowly easing the economy out of the rut of slow growth it was stuck in for over 40 years. The reforms, very deftly implemented by a succession of three able economists and political leaders, saved the country by putting it on a path towards recovery and, it was hoped, higher growth. The detailed effects of these policy changes have been amply discussed in earlier subsections. The reforms led to a momentum for growth being achieved over 1989–99. By all indications, the economy is now being slowly returned to private-sector incentives, even though government ownership of key industries and of the financial institutions still continues. There is need for the real-sector reforms to take deeper root and stifle the still-dominant government firms, improving their efficiency levels in the process.

Financial deepening

The statistics in Table 12.9 refer to measures of financial deepening. These statistics are computed over the pre-reform and post-reform periods. Even though the financial system was generally increasingly closed, with very high levels of interest rate suppression, somehow the financial system managed to attain some depth not often seen in similarly placed economies. Part of the reason for this was the guidance that the central bank provided as it had a clear vision of what to achieve in the way of developing a financial system to accommodate the industrial and agricultural developments that were being promoted.[11]

Money-market depth was very pronounced by the standards achieved by the more open economies such as Malaysia. It improved from around 30 per cent of GDP to the current 60 per cent level. The total intermediation ratio improved from around 31 to 44 per cent. As readers will recall, the government's inter-mediation ratio grew faster than that of the private sector. This is an expected result given the far-reaching controls put in place to divert resources to the state to undertake economic activities in the real sector. A notable achievement on financial depth is the gradual improvement in the gross capital formation as a percentage of GDP. This statistic showed the greatest gain, from around 18 per cent in the mid-1970s (recall that this was a mere 10 per cent in 1950) to the current high level of 26.5 per cent. The investment rate remained fixed during the 1970s and 1980s in the region of 18–22 per cent. Since the reforms over the last seven years, the ratio has improved by a good 5 percentage points. This is largely due to the reforms, making it possible for the producer sector to secure financial resources from foreign sources. Foreign-sourced capital was 8 per cent of GDP in 1997.

Thus the fifth largest economy in the world has finally taken the needed reforms to lift the suppression that was placed on its financial sector. Meanwhile the inefficiency in the producer segment is still there because of a long period of controls as well as because of the entry of the state in several non-public goods areas. The real-sector reforms will take some time to work their way through the economy.

Impacts on foreign capital flows

Indian firms obtained private foreign sources of capital as soon as reforms permitted them to raise capital outside. The FDI and portfolio flows are given in Table 12.10.

These sources have steadily grown from about US$208 million in 1991 to the 1997 high of US$3351 million.[12] Attempts to get FDI to inject not just capital

Table 12.9 Indicators of financial liberalization (% of GDP)

	5-year average			Annual							
	1976–80	1981–85	1986–90	1991	1992	1993	1994	1995	1996	1997	1998
Money depth (M3/GDP)	36.7	41.6	46.7	47.3	47.6	49.1	50.0	47.8	58.9	55.0	63.0
Inter-relations											
FIR (total)/GDP	31	45	53	53	52	52	50	47	44	44	51
FIR (public)/GDP	14	20	26	27	25	26	24	22	21	21	21
FIR (private)/GDP	17	25	28	26	27	26	26	25	23	23	22
GFCF/GDP	18.5	19.9	22.2	22.1	22.5	21.5	22.5	24.6	26.5	28.0	29.0
FDV/GDP	n.a.	n.a.	n.a.	0.02	0.10	0.15	0.32	0.69	0.68	0.80	0.60

Notes:
M3 = (M1 + quasi-money + Post Office savings deposit).
FIR = financial intermediation ratio – claims on public sector, claims on private sector, and foreign assets.
GFCF = Gross fixed capital formation.
FDI = foreign direct investment.

Sources: IMF, *International Financial Statistics*, various issues; World Bank, *World Bank Databank, 1997*; *Asian Development Outlook 1998, 1999*.

Table 12.10 Investments in India (US$ million)

	5-year average			Annual						
	1976–80	1981–85	1986–90	1991	1992	1993	1994	1995	1996	1997
Direct investment (net)	–1.6	–	–	73.54	277	550	973	2144	2207	3242
Portfolio investment (net)	–	–	–	4.6	284	1369	5491	1590	3958	2543
FDI (inflow)	–8	–	–	n.a.	277	500	973	2144	2426	3351

Sources: IMF, *International Financial Statistics*, various issues; World Bank, *World Bank Databank 1997*; *Asian Development Outlook 1998, 1999*.

but also technology and a market network have therefore been reasonably successful. FDI has increased from about several million in the pre-reform period to a few billion in the late 1990s. It averaged about US$72 million before the reforms. It was above US$3 billion in 1998. That represents an exceptional growth not very much different from the experience of China, when it started permitting foreign-owned firms to operate in coastal areas in the 1980s.

In addition, portfolio investments have grown even more aggressively from the 1991 figure of US$8 million to the 1997 figure of US$2960 million. Obviously, foreign producers and investors are favourably disposed to investing in the large now open money and capital markets that this country represents. It is often remarked that the size of the middle class of about 220 million people in this country would make it an attractive consumer market for most of the 140 000 multinational firms from the developed countries. Meanwhile the economy's capacity to mobilize larger savings (about 26 per cent of GDP in 1998) for domestic investment would be an added attraction for the multinationals to look for potential joint venture partners.

4. FUTURE PROSPECTS

This case has been an interesting one in this study of Asian liberalization and growth. It holds relevant lessons for large economies in Asia, Africa and South America. The large economy that this case represents is interesting in that it used state resources to develop a huge industrial sector while also gearing up the agricultural sector to produce more to attain self-sufficiency in grain output to feed a huge population. The import substitution strategy for securing development was originally meant to cover a few sectors, judging from the desire of the founding father of this country. But it eventually engulfed the entire economy as those outside the restricted lists could not obtain the foreign capital, technology or the markets because of the fixed exchange rate regime adopted by the country, which also prevented the more efficient producers from accessing foreign resources. It took the simmering problems in the late 1980s and the near financial bankruptcy in 1991 to lead the élites to dismantle the controls that had grown up over the years. As was noted elsewhere in this chapter, the state sector expanded into something they were not equipped to manage, and this drained almost 40 per cent of the government budget each year to support the 246 central government enterprises and close to 823 state-owned enterprises. These enterprises are being sold off very fast and, some would claim, not fast enough, to inject cash into the state and efficiency into production. The sealed-bid auction adopted by India for this purpose is admirably transparent, worthy of emulation by others. But not worthy of praise is the behind-the-scenes manoeuvring by politicians at the time when awards were to be granted to obtain variation, and through that process, as reported in the press, to continue the corruption that engulfs the entire system. The very same corruption has created a black economy the size of the reported economy. One has only to visit shopping complexes in cities to see the purchasing power of the ordinary citizens, loaded with money suspected to come from the underground economy.

With the controls removed, particularly on most of the capital items, and all controls on the current accounts for the domestic producers, Indian firms are now free to modernize, find new markets, and to improve productivity therefrom. The real sector has proved itself very adept at this, as shown by the readiness to become more international in approach during the last ten years. Export growth responded well in double digits before the coming into power of the conservative government in 1998 with a platform to prevent greater openness to foreign capital. Despite that rhetoric, more capital resources have been secured from abroad even after this government came to power, while FDI commitments were also increasing right up until the explosion of atomic devices, then missiles and then air force and ground force actions against the Pakistani positions in Kashmir. These events have led to an economic embargo by the major powers, and the hope for good neighbourliness, for which the previous five governments strove, is put on hold by the BJP coalition government. Meanwhile, modernizing forces were holding their breath as to where the popular vote would take this country in the coming elections. In October 1999, the minority government was returned to power with a majority, won on a coalition of parties with a renamed BJP (the minority party) as a 'Democratic National Front'.

Until a resolution is achieved by both India and Pakistan, coming to terms with each other on the question of border disputes as well as coming to terms with the world's plea to stop making more nuclear bombs, prospects for fast-track development are very slim. It was the desire to catch up with the fast-growing Asia that led to the widespread reforms we have examined. Depending solely on the domestic expansion of economic activities will certainly recast India in the same slow-growth mould as before. To break away from that Indian rate of growth, the country has to grow an external economy perhaps twice the size of the current one. India needs the world, and the nationalist conservatives don't see that simple blatant truth. All the reforms that have been introduced will be to no avail if more reforms and greater openness to the rest of the world – this includes India's neighbours – are not secured quickly to build on the momentum for growth. A Humpty Dumpty that falls and breaks cannot be put together by all the king's men, so the nursery rhyme goes! Membership in the WTO alone is insufficient when a developing country like India is not likely to welcome greater trade and financial dealings with other countries. These others form the mainstream desiring to contain the spread of nuclear weapons and to develop tolerance among neighbours.

NOTES

1. Korea also started its development from a position of a low-income poor-country status. But its strategic choice of policy mix made a big difference compared with the choice made by India's modernizing élites. As a result, Korea's growth rate was close to 9 per cent while that of India was 3.6 per cent. Korea became a member of the rich OECD club in 1997. It is also quite paradoxical that Korea experienced the worst crisis in its development history precisely because of the over-exposure to too much short-term external capital that began to dominate its finances in the 1990s. India should avoid this excess to prevent a similar exposure to private-sector-led collapse from taking too much short-term foreign debt to achieve fast-track growth.

2. The World Bank (1989) ranks countries by converting GDP equivalent in purchasing power of the income levels of countries. This ranking would have us believe that India is the fifth largest economy. The Indian economy, if GDP is measured in US dollar exchange rates, may be ranked among the 14 largest economies.

3. The arithmetic of development is strikingly simple. A growth rate of 3.5 per cent will double incomes in 20 years whereas it would take only seven years to double income if the growth rate is 10 per cent per annum. Thus China almost trebled its income in half the time taken by slow-growing economies just to double their income. Of course part of the reason for China's spectacular growth over 1984–98 is also the release of people's enthusiasm, unshackled from the controls of the Maoist era. Two other reasons are the FDI flows from developed economies augmented by ethnic Chinese capital from Southeast Asia.

4. Using the 1999 exchange rate of Rs 42.5 = US$1.00, India's GDP is roughly US$390 billion in nominal terms and US$1700 billion in PPP equivalent.

5. Tax reforms have been undertaken in the mid-1990s in India with income tax reforms taking place in 1998–99. All other countries (except China and Vietnam) covered in this book made significant fiscal reforms 15 to 20 years earlier to reduce the government budget by returning some of their economic activities to the private sector or by increasing revenues through diversification of the tax base.

6. That young leader was Rajiv Gandhi, assassinated in May 1991. A new government that came to power soon after that fateful event started the path towards liberalization. Some kind of reform is still continuing. A conservative government that came to power in 1997 and then again in 1998 has not yet fulfilled the election promise to slow down the pace of reforms, but has instead increased confrontation with nuclear and missile tests.

7. On a visit to this country in 1997, an event that took place amazed the writer because of its level of corruption. A foreign Indian visiting India decided to enrich himself through night burglaries. He stole jewellery. A village vigilante force caught the man and ensured custody in a police jail. The next morning the villagers found to their dismay that the officer in charge of the police station had freed the burglar. The burglar paid a huge bribe, took his passport and left the country!

8. Much of the credit for saving India from collapse must be given to Manmohan Singh, Professor of Economics at Delhi University and a one-time World Bank executive, who worked as Finance Minister in the Rao government. How that man managed the Indian crisis is a case worth studying in detail.

9. We have met during study visits and in conference venues several very able men who are at the helm of managing the economy.

10. The disparity between rural deposits and credits in the USA was at the root of demands for state–bank licensing in that country. This led to decentralized banking whereby states were given the right to approve branching within the state. This had drastic consequences, and also led to the growth of bank-holding companies to overcome the licensing limitations. The

Glass–Steagal Act, which decentralized US banking, was amended only in 1994 to permit interstate branching.

11. Despite criticism of the Indian Civil Service as one mired in corruption, credit must be given to a core of dedicated officers. Some of them are found in key institutions such as the central bank. We had the benefit of meeting some of them. These officers have made a difference to the system by excelling in the tasks assigned them. So, it is not surprising that the financial institutions under government control had often attracted the better officers as a matter of tradition. Even outside, one finds brave efforts being made to stifle corruption by top civil servants.

12. The reporting system for FDI varies from country to country. China reports memorandum figures, that is, the promised figure signed in agreements. India reports the actual repatriated flows. As a rule, actual commitments can run as low as 15 per cent to 70 per cent of the memorandum amount. Hence the Indian figures for comparison with other countries must be multiplied by a factor of 2.5 to 7 to get the memorandum figures reported by several countries.

APPENDIX: SELECTED INTEREST RATES OF COMMERCIAL BANKS (%)

Category	As at 1 March 1993	As at 2 Sept. 1993
Bank deposits	Not exceeding	Not exceeding
Domestic term deposits	11.00	10.00
Non-resident rupee accounts	13.00	12.00[a]*
Savings deposits	6.00	5.00[a]
Bank credit (non-exports)		
Up to and including Rs 7500	11.50	12.00
Over Rs 7500 to Rs 15 000	13.50	12.00
Over Rs 1500 to Rs 25 000	13.50	12.00
Over Rs 25 000 to Rs 50 000	16.50	15.00
Over Rs 50 000 to Rs 200 000	16.50	15.00
Over Rs 200 000 (minimum)	17.00	15.00
Export credit (rupees)		
Credit on duty receivables	0	0
Pre-shipment credit 180-day	13.00	13.00
Post-shipment credit		
Demand bills	13.00	13.00
Usance bills (46–90 days)	13.00	13.00
Credit for gov. incentives	13.00	13.00
Pre-shipment (181–270 days)[b]	15.00	15.00
Post-shipment credit		
Usance bills (91–180 days)	17.00	15.00
Beyond 6-month shipment	22.00	20.00
Other export credit (min.)	17.00	15.00
Post-shipment export credit	6.50	6.50
(US$, demand bills for transit period + grace		
period of up to 6 months from shipment date)		
DRI advances		
Term loans (agriculture, SSI	4.00	4.00
and transport up to 2 vehicles)		
Over Rs 25 000 to Rs 200 000	15.00	15.00
Over Rs 200 000 (min.)	15.00	15.00

Notes:

[a] Effective date 1 July 1993.

[b] With prior approval of Reserve Bank of India.

* NRE interest rate reduced to 11% wef 12 October 1993.

  Effective 12 October 1993, structure of lending rates same for working and long-term capital.

13. Pakistan: internally suppressed economy under liberalization

1. BACKGROUND

Pakistan has experienced persistent uneven development ever since the country was established in a bloody partition from India in 1947. The first few years of this new-born country were the most difficult, given the violence and the refugee problems. Its economic performance was very poor in the first decade. The 1960s witnessed a sharp favourable turn for the better when growth approached 6 per cent. Since then the country has been experiencing fair economic growth, though with cyclical downturns (see Table 13.1).[1] The growth trend was maintained at 5–6 per cent per annum. The major reasons for cyclical growth were endemic political instability and huge defence expenditure for strategic purposes.[2] Another main obstacle to development is the high population of 131.7 million, growing at 2.7 per cent per annum, which is considered to be one of the highest growth in developing countries. Even Bangladesh has reduced its birth rate below this level.

Pakistan has been a mixed rather than a completely controlled economy, as in the cases of China and Vietnam, included in this book. Outward-oriented policies in the trade sector were not pursued vigorously in India, which adopted a policy of home-grown growth through import substitution. Pakistan, on the other hand, kept the traded sector quite open, though the domestic side had pervasive price distortions. The trade sector was relatively liberalized. The financial sector had all forms of controls to support a system of subsidies for agriculture and industry. The outcome was a lack of fiscal discipline, and the public services developed endemic inefficiencies in the process of intervening in the pricing process. Educational, social and health services were considered the least important for budgetary allocation, and political institutions, given the military rule of the country up to the late 1980s and again since 1999. After the first decade of independence, the country struggled to gain political stability as it continues to do so 52 years later in 1999.[3]

During the late 1950s to 1970, some stability was achieved although dictatorial regimes took power. Given the resource endowment of the country, a reasonable growth path of about 5–6 per cent was established. This was when it started its five-year planing strategy. The break-up of the country in 1975 –

the separation of the eastern part as an independent Bangladesh – was a major setback politically, but it helped to eliminate subsidies to the eastern provinces. The first few years after that also coincided with the oil price shocks and global inflation, which brought stagflation to the world economy up to about 1983. Due to these and some other reasons, this country, which was more open to the world economy than it ever was on the domestic front, could not make any economic progress during the period 1970 to 1990. One reason was the failure of the élites to think in terms of economic restructuring in the manner of Southeast Asian élites to make their economies relevant to the world after the end of the commodity boom and the emergence of globalization. Such a vision, based on open trading, has become the relevant win–win strategy in East Asia.

In 1990, a major package of economic reforms was unveiled. It had a wide focus on many development issues: exchange rate and payment reforms, privatization, trade deregulation and financial-sector reforms. This was a more serious attempt at reform than even the one in the 1980s. There was no political consensus built to implement these policies.

Unfortunately, political instability in the form of frequent changes of government and military interventions to make the country relevant to American defence concerns in Afghanistan ensured that no reforms could be implemented. This illustrates one of the key development dilemmas: when a country has instituted heavy doses of control, it becomes even more important to have someone in a position of power to get consensus for development polices to be implemented. The more open economies such as Taiwan do not experience this dilemma to such an extent. This was also a recurrent theme in the 1997 Asian financial crisis, when weaker governments in Thailand, Korea and Indonesia made the crisis worse.

The result was that the meagre progress made did not solve the many problems of a new, young country founded on a vision to give its people more prosperity than it thought would have been achieved in a united India. A substantial decline in foreign reserves occurred during this period and the economy reached the point of bankruptcy several times. Timely assistance from the IMF helped Pakistan to avoid the worst scenario. The revival of economic reforms was expected to take centre stage and the government focused on these reforms as its main agenda. Some drastic measures were also announced, including reforms to the tax collection system, downsizing the government and incentives to attract foreign capital both from foreigners and nationals living abroad. Despite the assurances and securities provided, investor confidence did not improve given the continued political instability. The situation at the turn of the century is no better than in 1996, when the reforms were announced.

The next section looks into the economic and financial structure of the country. Major economic- and financial-sector liberalization policies and their impact on the economy are discussed in Section 3. This section also analyses

Table 13.1   Basic economic and social indicators of development in Pakistan

Indicators	Annual average			Annual		
	1971–80	1981–90	1991–95	1996	1997	1998
National accounts						
GDP growth	6.450	6.140	5.070	5.3	4.3	3.1
Per capita GDP (US$)	170	315	372	403	490	428
Private consumption (% of GDP)	80	77	70	71	73	72.4
Gov. consumption (% of GDP)	11	13	13	12	11	11.6
Financial indicators						
Gross domestic savings (% of GDP)	13.81	13.83	14.81	11.58	11.35	15.1
Gross fixed capital formation (% of GDP)	17.97	17.49	19.33	18.27	18.38	17.4
Inflation	7.34	7.34	11.47	10.79	11.62	7.8
M2/GDP	0.418	0.412	0.423	0.455	0.436	0.455
M3/GDP	0.43	0.417	0.43	0.461	0.442	0.459
Fiscal balance (% of GDP)	–7.40	–7.00	–7.10	–6.30	–6.3	–5.4
Current account balance (% of GDP)	–5.5	–3.90	–4.50	–6.7	–5.8	–3.0
Trade balance (% of GDP)	–8.2	–8.9	–4.9	–5.7	–3.3	–2.9
Debt service ratio (% of exports)	n.a.	n.a.	30.2	33.9	38	40
Social indicators						
IMF classification	Low	Low	Low	Low	Low	Low
Literacy rate	n.a.	26.2	35.7	37.9	38.9	40.0
Unemployment rate	n.a.	3.51	5.41	5.37	5.37	5.3
Expenditure on education (% of GNP)	3.0	1.94	2.20	2.40	2.60	2.2
Expenditure on health (% of GNP)	1.42	0.68	0.68	0.80	0.70	0.7
Population growth	n.a.	3.10	3.01	2.83	2.77	2.7

Sources: IMF, *International Financial Statistics*, various issues; *Asian Development Outlook 1998, 1999*; *Government Finance Statistics Yearbook, 1985–1996*; Government of Pakistan, *Economic Survey, 1997–98*; The Economist Intelligence Unit, *Country Report: Pakistan, 1998*; Finance Minister's Budget Speech, June 1999.

the scope and function of the central bank and the instruments available to it to conduct appropriate monetary interventions. Towards the end, the section describes recent attempts to establish a viable stock market in the country. Finally, Section 4 assesses the liberalization policies and draws conclusions on future prospects.

2. ECONOMIC AND FINANCIAL STRUCTURE

Pakistan can be considered as a mixed socialist economy where the trade sector was liberalized at an early stage but the capital and current accounts were closed, and there was stringent financial suppression that distorted domestic prices made perverse by subsidies. The country did not have a capital or an industrial base at the time of its birth in 1947. Obviously, the basic focus then was on agriculture and agro-based industries. The 1960s witnessed the Green Revolution, when resources were applied to increase per capita output, but no reforms of the kind that Taiwan undertook were made to devote the land to the tillers. Shortage of natural sources, especially irrigation water, required spending huge amounts of domestic resources as well as foreign aid loans to introduce a canal irrigation system as a backbone to the agricultural output required to feed a growing population. These efforts resulted in reduced dependence on food imports, especially wheat, and increased export earnings from cash crops such as cotton, rice, jute and sugar cane.

It was only after this foundation in agriculture was laid in the 1960s that the private sector became interested in manufacturing industries such as textiles, cement, fertilizers, and so on. Meanwhile, investments were made in the services sector, to build infrastructure in banks and financial institutions, educational institutions and health facilities. The public sector, however, could not accelerate investment in these sectors as a large proportion of domestic resources were allocated for defence in a period of rule by generals. Despite that, some industrial-sector development did occur in textile- and agro-based industries.

The nationalization drive in 1972–75 reversed this process. More than that, this divisive policy and its aftermath led to a lasting impact on the future political process, which remains to this day much as in such countries as Egypt and Brazil, with very left-leaning policies having mass appeal. When the generals resumed power, they started denationalization and confidence to attract private investment which had waned. As would be expected during a period of military rule, there were doubts about political stability, and investors were not ready to take any risk or make any long-term commitment. Until 1980, distortions such as subsidized agriculture and industrial activities were the norm. By any stretch of the imagination, this was not pro-growth, nor did it allow the market mechanism to work unhindered on prices in the different sectors. During 1984–90, the authorities became desperate and could only do one thing – reduce and eventually eliminate these subsidies. In these reforms, the IMF structural stabilization programme and the USAID economic aid package did what the political élites had failed to do for a long while.[4]

The reforms prepared the economy for the main investment drive initiated in the 1990s by elected governments with a determination to open up the economy to boost the industrial sector, as had already happened first in the

Southeast Asian economies and later in East Asia, including the moribund giant, China. Although, the trade sector did not enjoy a free trade policy similar to some of these reformed economies, policies being put into effect were different in nature from those that were pursued by an inward-oriented regime, India, which at that time only made cautious moves on openness. With worldwide trade globalization and this country's involvement in some regional trade and economic blocs (SARC being one), tariff reductions had to be gradual. This is a pity because they failed to give a strong signal to the investors that there was a significant break with the past in this South Asian economy. Thus, strategy-wise, it was a bad decision to slow the process of openness in terms of the region.

2.1   Economic Outlook

Pakistan was facing tremendous economic and financial difficulties during the 1990s, mainly due to political instability. Its citizens were beginning to shake off the long years of the military's involvement in lay politics, as did people in other countries (Korea, Thailand and Indonesia in the 1990s). Some of the statistics in Table 13.2 are relevant for our discussion about the economic outlook in the late 1990s. The very high indebtedness from pursuing a twin policy of subsidies to some sectors and high defence spending brought inevitable results: debt soared and inefficiency persisted. Growth in 1997 was a mere 3.1 per cent and the prospects for growth in the next year became even gloomier. Many economic factors were responsible for this decline in growth. These include financial resource limitation, persistent fiscal imbalances, inadequate infrastructure, declining export demand, declining foreign reserves and soaring international debt. The level of foreign reserves is estimated to be equivalent to about four weeks of imports, which is a signal of a worsening situation.

Some efforts were made in early 1997 to implement reductions in income tax and tariffs to make investment attractive and to attract domestic and foreign sources. To these were added a wide range of reforms in the financial sector, which included capital markets, central bank and commercial banks. These measures, however, failed to produce any positive result, as gross domestic savings and investment continued to remain extremely low. Severe fiscal and external imbalances seem to be the root causes of economic problems in Pakistan. Fiscal deficits averaged about 6 per cent of GDP during the last three years while the debt-service ratio amounts to 4 per cent. These two factors work jointly to create a vicious circle where lack of an efficient revenue collection mechanism leaves no choice but to borrow from domestic and external sources to meet mounting government spending. The government attempted on its own and at the behest of the IMF and the World Bank to curtail public spending and improve the revenue collection mechanism. These attempts

Table 13.2   Growth rates of basic economic indicators (% growth rates)

	5-year average			Annual average							
	1976–80	1981–85	1986–90	1991	1992	1993	1994	1995	1996	1997	1998
GDP	6.43	6.29	5.79	5.57	7.71	2.27	4.54	5.24	5.3	4.3	3.1
Inflation	9.65	5.49	8.42	12.66	9.97	9.83	11.27	13.02	11.6	8.2	6.1
Revenue	20.66	14.62	13.72	4.16	26.92	12.11	20.32	23.97	18.96	4.9	8.5
M1	21.08	13.04	15.65	20.17	21.51	1.70	15.15	12.76	7.54	8.5	4.6
M2	20.82	14.55	11.78	16.30	30.30	18.00	16.90	16.60	20.10	19.9	7.3
FDI	–	40.76	15.26	5.33	30.35	3.58	20.74	52.51	27.6	–22.3	–32.1
Trade deficit	21.08	13.04	15.65	–0.001	–9.9	46.1	–38.8	26.8	46.0	–15.1	–39.7
Exports	–	33.24	11.43	–3.14	15.74	4.81	12.82	33.10	13.8	–1.8	6.2
Imports	–	8.44	22.96	29.50	23.99	2.91	15.96	20.22	8.1	–11.6	4.2

Notes:
M2 = (M1 + quasi-money).
Negative growth means decline in trade deficit.

Sources: IMF, *International Financial Statistics*, various issues; World Bank, *World Bank Databank*, Feb. 1997; Government of Pakistan, *Economic Survey*, 1997–98; Finance Minister's Budget Speech, June 1999.

included streamlining development plans and projects, a 19 per cent cut in the public-sector development outlay, restructuring the existing tax system and imposition of an agriculture income tax.

In the latter half of the 1990s, another insidious problem emerged: non-performing loans of the private sector worsened. The banking and financial sector suffered loan defaults of about 7 per cent of GDP in 1997 (*Asian Development Outlook*, 1998, p. 135). In the external sector, the country is facing three basic problems. First, remittance from nationals working abroad is declining; second, demand for exports is falling; and third, a huge allocation of funds for debt servicing must be made. Foreign debt in 1999 stood at US$29.0 billion, which is 45 per cent of GDP. Although efforts were made to enliven the export sector, this sector remained sluggish, and worsened, with a decline of 2.7 per cent in 1997. Table 13.3 provides detailed information on this single problem that remains a major obstacle to moving the economy forward.

The total debt outstanding, that is, domestic and foreign, is 88 per cent of GDP, of which 45 per cent is foreign debt. The total amounts to about US$55 billion, of which US$29 billion is external debt. In this regard, this country is facing the same dilemma that Malaysia faced after 20 years of targeting development expenditure to the rural sector. By 1980, this resulted in an amount of debt almost similar to Pakistan's debt ratio. It was this burden of debt that helped usher in the real-sector opening that Malaysia initiated in the form of industrialization based on greater openness, with outstanding results because after the reforms that country became part of the fast-growing region. The debt-service ratio to exports reached 37 per cent of the budget in 1997, the highest in Asia. With the recent political developments arising from test-firing of nuclear weapons in the region and the consequent economic sanctions being imposed on India and Pakistan, the outlook for any gains from exports is bleak in the near future.[5]

What is needed, as is true of all other cases, is a policy mix of macroeconomic and structural adjustments, within a politically stable environment, as well as a resolution of security issues. The former hinges on the latter. This is where politics may wag the tail of the economic dog. The economic reforms that were initiated first in 1991 and again in 1996 should be reformulated with firm commitments to non-reversal. These commitments must be undertaken with a clear vision of what is needed in the short- to medium- to long-term policy mix. Coalition-building across party lines and even outside interest groups must be attempted to cement commitment. Serious situations demand serious solutions and, given the debt overhang on the economy, the governing élites need to work very hard to gain consensus for an agenda of economic reforms as well as for security. In this respect, this case is very different from the rest of the eases discussed in this book.

Table 13.3 Pakistan and external debt (US$ million)

	1990–91	1991–92	1992–93	1993–94	1994–95	1995–96	1996–97
Forex reserves held by SBP	1 390	1 761	1 369	3 337	3 337	3 251	1 977
Debt outstanding[a]	15 471	17 361	19 044	20 322	22 117	22 275	23 145
Debt servicing[b]	1 316	1 513	1 648	1 746	2 042	2 136	2 265
Principle	782	921	999	1 078	1 294	1 346	1 520
Interest	534	592	649	668	748	790	745
Debt servicing as % of FEE	13.7	13.4	15.3	16.2	16.5	16.7	17.6
% of GDP							
Outstanding debt	34.0	35.6	36.8	39.0	36.3	34.5	37.5
Debt servicing	2.9	3.1	3.2	3.3	3.4	3.3	3.7
% of exports							
Outstanding debt	252.3	251.5	279.5	298.7	271.8	255.8	278.2
Debt servicing	21.5	21.9	24.2	25.7	25.1	24.5	27.2

Notes:
FEE: Foreign exchange earnings.
[a] Regular debt (payable in foreign exchange only). Medium and long term.
[b] Excluding interest on short-term borrowings and IMF charges.

Sources: Government of Pakistan, *Pakistan Economics Survey, 1997–98*; 1999 figure for foreign debt is taken from *Asia Week* regular reports in 1999.

3. LIBERALIZATION

Transitional economies such as China and Vietnam or mixed socialist economies such as India started liberalizing from a completely controlled system or a system of inward-oriented policies respectively. Pakistan did not have a completely controlled system. The trade sector was more or less open since independence, although capital and current accounts were under strong control. Even during the short-lived socialist rule of a reforming prime minister, who nationalized domestic resources, the trade sector continued to remain relatively open. This was the time when the economy produced huge capital investment directed to its export sector from workers' remittances from abroad in foreign currencies. The trade sector benefited. The liberalization and openness of the economy could be analysed in many different ways.

Further liberalization of the trade sector and wide-ranging reforms in the capital and current accounts could be pursued from the benefits that came from the capacity built into the traded sector during that short period. Our discussion on this therefore focuses on the benefits such reforms would have on certain sectors of the economy. Since the major economic reforms were designed and implemented during the period after 1991, we restrict our discussion of the liberalization process to this period.

3.1 Economic Liberalization

Major economic reforms were initiated during 1991–93. The main focus of the economic reform package was privatization to address the depletion of fiscal resources, which arose from pursuing subsidized agricultural and industrial development as well as huge defence spending. Financial-sector reforms, to be discussed in a later subsection, were meant to accelerate savings and thus investment. Infrastructure development is the third policy package in this period.

Privatization became the most important argument in the reform package. The government established the Privatization Commission in 1991 with responsibility for the design and implementation of policies on industrial projects and financial institutions. Foreign investors were also allowed to purchase divested public assets along with their local counterparts. The privatization scheme provided legal protection under the Economic Reforms Ordinance 1992. Besides affecting a large number of medium- to large-sized industrial units, it was targeted at some large public-sector institutions as well. These included the banking sector, the Telegraph and Telephone Department, and the Water and Power Development Authority: these were state-owned enterprises, SOEs.

By the end of 1997, 91 SOEs were privatized and 46 more were available for further sale in 1998. Of these, a number were sold by the end of 1999. These included non-industrial enterprises as well, two commercial banks, Pakistan

Telecommunication Company Limited (PTCL) and the National Press Trust. Even the railways are on the table for sale and negotiations are in progress. The nationalized banks are the next in line for sale. In this respect, privatization has become a way of reducing the financial overhang these inefficient organizations had brought on over decades of inefficiency, damaging government budgets; it also provided cash injection from the sales. These responses to the huge debt overhang are very similar to those undertaken by Malaysia to solve its budget problem caused by debt. The only difference was that when the latter's reforms took effect, the time was appropriate.

The aim of the policy was also to attract foreign investment by nationals living abroad, as well as by foreigners. The legal framework was modified to remove restrictions on providing protection to these outside investors. The incentives offered to the domestic and foreign investors helped to attract investment, especially in mega-projects such as motorways between big cities. As Table 13.3 shows, this pro-growth policy has attracted foreign investment during the last few years. However, this is not comparable with the broader benefits from such plans in other economies in Asia.

In July 1998, the government introduced the emergency economic package to deal with the deteriorating economic situation (and came under IMF pressure to reform some major sectors of the economy). Besides some fiscal measures, the focus of this package was to restore investor confidence, that had been shaken due to foreign exchange controls. The government therefore provided some incentives to non-resident Pakistanis to bring foreign exchange into the country. Similarly, incentives were offered to exporters and other investors. It is yet to be seen, however, how effective these measures will be in restoring such confidence.

Fiscal-sector reforms

Lack of fiscal discipline emerged as a serious management problem and it arose mainly from the wastage of resources used as targeted credits to agriculture to resolve food problems in the 1960s and 1970s and the continuation of price controls in the domestic sector. A huge excess capacity in the public sector and the inefficient system of tax collection made fiscal deficits worse than they would otherwise have been. These deficits were partly financed by domestic and foreign borrowing. Of course, the latter recourse led to inflationary financing from undisciplined monetary expansion. A number of measures were therefore taken unilaterally by the government as part of the reform process. Compliance with the IMF conditions to revamp the tax structure and collection system led to further reforms. Accordingly, the first set of reforms was implemented in 1992–93, which included vertical and horizontal expansion of the general sales tax and a self-assessment mechanism for tax returns.

The government also implemented supply-side policies with the objective of reducing tax rates while broadening the tax base. Besides measures to increase revenues, policies were also devised to reduce expenses. One of the priority areas was reduction in expenses in the services sector operated under federal or provincial governments. The authorities announced a scheme of 'golden handshakes' for those employees who would volunteer to withdraw themselves from their jobs. Another sector of special concern was reducing public-sector-enterprise reliance on budget financing. These policies were designed and implemented to meet the IMF requirement to gradually curtail worsening fiscal deficits: 4 per cent of GDP, worsening to around 7 per cent. Due to political instability, some of these policies could not achieve the objectives envisaged earlier. The civil service reduced in size substantially; however loss-making institutions – examples are Pakistan Railway, Pakistan International Airlines, and many more – are placing a continuing burden on the national exchequer.

Revenue collection also deteriorated due to tax evasion by a majority of those liable for tax. Some estimates show that, out of a population of 132 million, therefore with at least 55 million employed, only 800 000 people pay income tax.[6] During the period 1992–97, several attempts were made to impose tax on agricultural incomes. Given the concentration of ownership of land in this country – recall the lack of wider land ownership as in India or Taiwan – this reform had no chance of even being implemented. Political pressure in two of the four provinces did not allow the federal government to implement this tax. It is unfortunate not to have a tax on agricultural income in a country where agriculture sector absorbs about 70 per cent of the labour force and generates a bulk of the national income. In other South Asian countries with less ownership concentration, similar policies have been very successful. For instance, India's revenue is a healthy 20 per cent of its GDP, and a significant part comes from this sector.

Price reforms
Controlling inflation is inconsistent with large fiscal deficits, which cannot be financed through domestic resources. The limited external financing available therefore means that undue expansion in money growth would be pursued, resulting in inflationary financing, which is the result of resource constraint. Unlike the export-led economies in East and Southeast Asia, conditions for attracting external capital flows to offset budget constraints are limited.

The second important reason for the bind, noted before, is subsidies to agriculture and industry. Several episodes of consumer subsidies given for basic food items, subsidies for factor inputs in agriculture and the extension of subsidy to loss-making fertilizer industries, and so on are at the root of this problem. Due to these distortions in the price mechanism, all efforts to control inflation without tackling the root problem had no chance of success, and therefore failed. Even during the period of market reforms, inflation remained in double digits due to supply-side policies and cost-push factors. The continuous devaluation of the domestic currency further aggravated inflationary pressure and inflationary expectations. However, if the market mechanism were allowed to work without any distortions in prices[7] and a resulting fiscal discipline were attained, it would be possible to bring inflation under control in this country. Zao Ziyang of China proved this possibility, of course with the robust external resources available to him. At the end of 1999, the economy was facing an alarming depletion of foreign reserves, which was devaluing the currency further: in mid-1999, official figures indicated foreign reserves to be as low as US$700 million. With the trade sector weakening as a result of economic sanctions for nuclear tests, trade-sector weakening is expected to continue. The combined effect would be continuing worsening inflation, and a lethal blow for reforms to have any chance of the desired effects.

External-sector policies
Some of the external-sector policies are related to the exchange and payment system and will be discussed in a later paragraph. Here we describe policies designed to promote foreign investment and trade (see Table 13.4). As part of the overall reform package discussed earlier, the authorities decided to remove restrictions required on prior approvals for new investment by foreigners as well as nationals living overseas. Investors were permitted to own up to 100 per cent of equity ventures and this included purchase of equity in existing industrial companies on a repatriable basis. Central bank permission is no longer required for remittances of dividends and proceeds of sale of investment. Initially, these measures worked well, attracting foreign investment with legal guarantees provided by new laws passed by the government. With recent political and security developments, however, economic sanctions being one, confidence has been shaken. Rebuilding confidence may take a long time yet, even if there is some accommodation on security issues.

The government also introduced certain measures to boost the trade sector. Reducing import duty from a maximum of 125 per cent to 90 per cent and reducing the number of items on the restricted imports list from 118 to 87 were two key reforms. These measures proved successful: the trade deficit narrowed in the years 1993 and 1994 and the rate of decline decreased. However, the policies could not continue after 1993 due to a change in government and the deficit started to increase again when the government rolled back import restrictions.

Special export processing zones were established in 1980 in big industrial cities with the objective of attracting foreign capital, technology and modern management skills for export-oriented industries. This is a well-worn successful device used by many Asian countries. It was hoped that its success would

Table 13.4   Investments in Pakistan (US$ million)

	5-year average			Annual							
	1976–80	1981–85	1986–90	1991	1992	1993	1994	1995	1996	1997
Direct investment (net)	35.2	80.0	159.6	261.0	347.0	349.0	418.0	720.0	917.0	738.0
Portfolio investment (net)	–	23.8	88.6	92.0	371.0	292.0	1466.0	4.0	260.0	410.0
FDI (inflow)	35.2	77.4	174.8	257.0	335.0	347.0	419.0	720.0	919.0	714.0

Sources: IMF, *International Financial Statistics*, various issues; World Bank, *World Bank Databank*, Feb. 1997; *Asian Development Outlook 1998, 1999*; Government of Pakistan, *Economic Survey, 1997–98*.

provide new employment opportunities. Currently there are five EPZs operating in the country and two more have just been brought on stream. By 1997, the government had granted approval to 173 industrial units to operate in these zones while 94 were already in operation.

3.2 Financial-Sector Reforms

The financial sector plays a key supporting role in the development process of a low-income economy such as Pakistan. Not only do efficient payment services, flexibility of foreign currency transactions, development of domestic capital and money markets provide means to a lower cost of capital; a developed capital market also provides higher levels of mobilization of savings. Further, it attracts both domestic and foreign investment. The reforms in the financial sector, experts now advise, should be dovetailed after macroeconomic adjustments in the real sector are in place. We examine this aspect in some detail.

With capital and current accounts under heavy control during 1947–90, the financial sector could be described as a very inefficient one at best. It hardly developed enough to serve the open trade sector to contribute to its efficiency. Restrictive policies of all shades ranging from interest rate controls, exchange rate fixing and unbridled growth in money supply, as well as capital account closedness for most individuals and firms with no foreign-sector incomes, were the order of the economy. This level of financial-sector closedness went with fiscal indiscipline. These are perhaps the reasons why the more open traded sector failed to produce the synergies observed in other economies. In other more successful cases, the financial sector was reformed alongside or in most cases subsequent to the reforms of the trade and fiscal sectors. Pakistan failed to obtain open trade and a balanced budget first, before undertaking financial reforms. The role of the central bank was to formally implement correct policies. But in reality, it diverted resources to the public sector by all kinds of policies designed by politicians, which promoted that aim. Although the reform packages of 1991 onwards allowed market forces to work, there are still sufficient government controls over the affairs of the central bank to ensure that reforms could not lead to a great expectation of benefits.

Monetary policies

Monetary management moved from a state-controlled system to a market-oriented system during a transition period. After the nationalization of the commercial banks in 1972, the state was heavily involved in frequent interventions in the operations of financial institutions. Included in these interventions were interferences in the operations of commercial banks through directed lending and implicit guarantees for poor-quality loans. Lending on the basis of political influence by the commercial banks resulted in huge non-performing loans, which has made efficient financial management of institutions almost impossible.

The traditional instruments used in pursuit of monetary policy were not very effective in the presence of these distortions. Commercial banks were subject to the statutory reserves, only 5 per cent on demand and time deposits, and a higher liquidity ratio in the form of holding government securities. The central bank (State Bank of Pakistan), under orders from the government, found a market for government bonds. Although the bond market developed as a result of this to levels of activity higher than in most developing countries, the main objective of this was to generate funds to finance fiscal deficits.

Given the lack of confidence in any alternative investment portfolios, especially for small-scale investors, government bonds became the *de facto* best option as they are issued by the government. However, with the administered nature of interest rates, secondary markets for financial papers did not develop alongside the large bond market. Hence in central banking open-market operations, which require liquidity in the monetary sector as well as in the capital markets, there were no effective markets for monetary policy actions. The percentage of required reserves has been more or less stable over recent years, and hence cannot be taken as a very useful monetary policy instrument. Prudential regulations are also weak and poorly developed as well as poorly implemented. The important policy instrument that appears to have teeth is credit ceilings, where the central bank is required to provide credit directly or through specialized banks for high-priority sectors such as agriculture, housing, export trade, small-scale industries, and small business firms. As noted in an earlier discussion, these were the very price distortions that appear to have generated fragility of the reforms in Pakistan. Monetary policy was conducting perversely by furthering the very things that a central bank would not want to do to bring the economy on to a stable growth path. No cheers for Pakistan's central bank.

Attempts were made dating back to 1989 to convert monetary management into a market-based system. In March 1991, the authorities organized regular auctions of Treasury bills and long-term federal fund bonds. The process of privatization of new commercial banks was also under way, which would give some independence to the commercial banks in establishing their own deposit and lending rates. The immediate need was to provide full regulatory power to the central bank and adopt a hands-off policy to prevent political pressure on commercial banks to grant party-related and politically connected loans. As was examined in Chapter 2, it was these two practices in many countries (Indonesia, Malaysia, Korea and Thailand) that led to the ballooning of the currency crisis into the 1997–98 Asian financial crisis. So this is a key area of reform that this country has to succeed in putting in place for its own sake. Now that this is an open secret in capital markets from Bahrain to Beijing, no capitalists or even ordinary citizens are going to come to countries that do not have safeguards against such abuses.

The resulting problem of non-performing loans cannot be resolved until the banking sector in general and the central bank in particular are allowed to work independently of any political pressure. Privatization of the industrial sector is beginning to give relief to the banking sector by extending loans to loss-making state firms. Once the market mechanism is put to work through the pricing system and supported by prudential regulations, the management of the monetary system will be more effective. The other precondition that is still lacking for this country's effective monetary management is fiscal discipline in the form of a balanced budget. It appears that slow progress is being made in this regard with the deficit in 1999 having come down to 2.7 per cent compared with the 7 per cent a few years ago. These policies have to be coordinated between fiscal and monetary policy, with less reliance on printing money as a source of financing.

Central bank reforms
The State Bank of Pakistan (SPB) was established in 1948, just about a year after the founding of Pakistan. It was started as a jointly own body with the government and the private sector. In 1949, the government established a fully state-owned bank, the National Bank of Pakistan (NBP). The new bank was responsible for carrying out commercial banking functions and to act as the state treasury. However, SBP had complete monopoly in conducting monetary policies, working with the minister for finance. Later years saw some private-sector interest in the banking sector and a few more banks were granted charters as commercial banks.

Due to a small industrial base, an inefficient system of tax collection, loss-making state firms and the lack of a well-developed domestic bond market, the main responsibility of the SBP has been to extend credit to state firms and to find the wherewithal to support budgetary deficits. The domestic bond market gradually developed and a large proportion of the fiscal deficits were then financed through domestic borrowing. However, increasing public-sector expenditure and stagnant or low level of revenues have always put pressure on the monetary authority to print money. These episodes did not allow the authorities to design an appropriate policy. The efforts and expertise of the central bank were reduced essentially to financing fiscal deficits and to finding ways of meeting the debt-servicing requirement, given persistent low levels of foreign reserves. The central bank had independence of the worst kind: it served the dictates of the government to destroy its independent pursuit of macroeconomic stabilization through effective monetary management! There was a need to develop some coordination between the monetary and fiscal policy-makers. The inefficiency of the central bank, or rather its neglect of its prudential oversight, has now led to the so-called 'zombie' bank syndrome, signifying a disease common in many developing countries (see Kane, 1999).

The other major problem faced by the SBP is therefore the design of a nationalized banking system with built-in avoidance of prudential supervision of commercial banks and other depository and non-bank institutions. This brings us to the issue of how to manage the huge amount of non-performing loans. As a result of mismanagement, during the period 1980–90 the country saw a large number of finance institutions collapse. But the banks were not permitted to fail. Under political pressure and influence-peddling, banks were bound to extend credit to individuals and/or institutions with a history of non-performance.

As part of the reform package during 1992–97, changes were brought to bear to impose some order on this matter. The SBP now began to claim autonomy, with the sole objective of formulating and implementing monetary policy, managing the exchange rate and supervising the activities of the financial institutions. In reality, however, SBP is still functioning under directives. The Monetary and Fiscal Policies Coordination Board has been established to coordinate fiscal, monetary and exchange rate policies. The Pakistan Banking Council has been abolished and merged with the SBP. The SBP has set up a comprehensive plan to modernize and strengthen the prudential regulations as well as the supervision quality of the financial system. The reforms are therefore still not sticking, and more promises of reforms do not actually mean that reforms are in place. The banking sector is in limbo, hoping this time that there may be reforms to unshackle the fetters placed on the central bank.

Reforms in depository institutions

Commercial banking in Pakistan has experienced drastic changes over 50 years. Pakistan started its banking sector from square one. At the time of independence, out of 99 commercial banks only one, Habib Bank, had its head office located in the area that was to become the new country. The other 98 banks were located in India and were under the jurisdiction of the Reserve Bank of India. Pakistan did not have its own central bank until 1948, a year after independence.[8] From 1947 to 1974, the banking sector grew very satisfactorily. The private sector invested in establishing commercial banks with a network of branches in the country. At the same time, the authorities granted licences to some foreign banks to operate in Pakistan. The domestic banks were, however, nationalized in 1974 under the Bank Nationalization Act. The 13 commercial banks were then merged to become five nationalized commercial banks (NCBs). The deposits in the NCBs were fully insured and their activities were supervised by the Pakistan Banking Council (PCB), also established in 1974, but now abolished.[9] These NCBs enjoyed rapid expansion in terms of staff, which increased by 55 per cent, and the number of branches, by 82 per cent during 1974–78. High and increasing inflation resulted in declines in deposits (about

20 per cent). Increasing economic uncertainties following the militarization of politics brought the real deposits down by about 23 per cent.[10]

With the new martial law regime that assumed power in 1980, the process of financial reform was begun with three objectives. The first was to implement policies to gradually change the financial sector from a controlled to a market-signal-based operation. The second was to introduce Islamic banking in Pakistan.[11] The third reform sought was to create an environment for competitive banking to take root by easing entry barriers to foreign banks. To achieve these goals, the military government introduced new policies during 1979–85 for a partial deregulation of interest rates. The expansion of NCBs was slowed down while a number of foreign banks were licensed and their branches were increased from 30 to 54. However, most of these policies were implemented by the military government without a proper legal structure as is needed in the banking regulations.

In 1990, the authorities were very concerned about the poor financial position, overstaffing and inefficiencies of banks in general. Privatization, which was part of the overall economic reform agenda introduced by the newly elected government then in power, was considered to be the best option to deal with the problem. Since then these banks have been in the process of denationalization. Only three have already been privatized. At the same time, the government has encouraged the private sector to invest in the banking sector. During the last ten years, many new commercial banks have started operation in the private sector and have been very successful in attracting deposits. At the same time, provisions for keeping a foreign currency account, which offered very attractive interest rates, increased the deposits of the banking sector. Table 13.5 shows a switch from demand deposits to time deposits, where the ratio of time deposits to GDP almost doubled during 1990 to 1997 with this incentive. During the same period, the ratio of demand deposits to GNP reduced from 15.02 per cent to about 7.99 per cent. At present, resident foreign currency deposits constitute about 8 per cent of GNP.[12]

Non-performing loans are one of the major problems that severely curtail the banking system in the country. Loans extended to individuals and institutions under political pressure and on the basis of related party lending have not been paid back, amounting to billions of rupees according to some reports. As at March 1997, the outstanding balance from these defaulted loans amounted to PRs 126.15 billion.[13] Some strict measures have been formulated to deal with bank defaulters and were implemented in 1998. Recovery laws have been strengthened through the Banking Companies (Recovery of Loans, Advances, Credit and Finances) Act 1997. However, there is a need to give the bank management and operators in the finance sector more independence and powers of prosecution against political pressure. Establishing a healthy banking sector

Table 13.5   Financial assets in Pakistan (rupees)

	1990		1995		1996		1997	
	PRs billion	Per cent of GNP	PRs billion	Per cent of GNP	PRs billion	Per cent of GNP	PRs billion	Per cent of GNP
Currency in circulation	115.1	14.44	215.6	12.67	234.1	12.01	244.14	10.2
Demand deposits	119.7	15.02	201.1	11.82	205.6	10.54	192.3	7.99
Time deposits	80.2	10.06	246.2	14.47	295.8	15.17	386.8	16.1
Other deposits	2.2	0.28	5.1	0.30	6.8	0.35	7.1	0.30
Resident foreign currency deposits	n.a.	n.a.	105.1	6.18	146.0	7.49	222.9	9.3

Sources: Haque and Kardar (1995) and Government of Pakistan, *Economic Survey, 1997–98.*

is not possible when banks are forced to extend loans that they know, *a priori*, are bad.

Foreign banks provide a very competitive environment to the domestic commercial banks and have become an important part of the banking industry. Although foreign banks are not allowed to open more than four branches, they have better managerial skills and more access to international financial markets. As a result, they receive the bulk of foreign currency deposits.

Reforms in non-bank financial institutions
The need for NBFIs was realized just after the country was established. Lack of resources for term financing of industrial projects forced policy-makers to give top priority to establishing these institutions. However, in the 1950s and early 1960s, not much progress was made in this area. Long-term lending facilities for the important sectors of the economy, two examples being agriculture and housing, were almost non-existent in the public or private sector. The first progress in this regard was made in the 1960s by establishing the Industrial Development Bank of Pakistan with the objective of providing loans to small and medium-sized industrial projects. Later, other institutions, mostly in the public sector, were established to cater to the needs of some specific sectors of the economy. These included Pakistan Industrial Credit and Investment Corporation, National Investment Trust, Investment Corporation of Pakistan, Agriculture Development Bank of Pakistan, National Development Finance Corporation, Federal Bank for Cooperatives, House Building Finance Corporation, and Bankers Equity Limited. The traditional NBFIs in Pakistan have taken a new shape with the emergence of these new types of institutions, which provide new financial instruments suited to the needs of these sectors. (Domestic and foreign financial institutions are listed in Table 13.6.)

These institutions can be divided into the following sub-groups: development financial institutions; leasing companies; *modaraba* funds (short-term Islamic deposit-taking bodies); investment banks; and stock market funds.[14] These institutions were established to meet the government's long-run objectives of reforming the overall financial system. Through privatizing and deregulation, developing money- and capital-market instruments, providing more incentives to investors, reducing and eventually eliminating restrictions on foreign exchange flows and developing an Islamic system of risk-sharing in the debt market, it was thought the financial sector would be reformed. Alas, this was in reverse order, since fiscal budget discipline continued to falter, and all the reforms in the financial sector did not repair the weaknesses.

Of course these development finance institutions (DFIs) helped the SBP to concentrate more on its objective of formulating monetary and exchange rate policies by reducing the dependence of debtors and creditors on the SBP as the only source to mobilize funds and extend credit. It is expected that at some

Table 13.6   Domestic and foreign financial institutions

A. Nationalized scheduled banks
    1   First Women Bank Ltd
    2   National Bank of Pakistan
    3   Habib Bank Ltd
    4   United Bank Ltd

B. Denationalized scheduled banks
    1   Allied Bank of Pakistan Ltd
    2   Muslim Commercial Bank Ltd

C. Specialized banks
    1   Agricultural Development Bank of Pakistan
    2   Industrial Development Bank of Pakistan
    3   Punjab Provincial Cooperative Bank
    4   Federal Bank of Cooperatives

D. Private scheduled banks
    1   Askari Commercial Bank Ltd
    2   Bank Al-Habib Ltd
    3   Bolan Bank Ltd
    4   Faysal Bank Ltd
    5   Habib Credit & Exchange Bank
    6   Indus Bank Ltd
    7   Metropolitan Bank Ltd
    8   Platinum Bank Ltd
    9   Prime Commercial Bank Ltd
    10 Prudential Bank Ltd
    11 Schon Bank Ltd
    12 Soneri Bank Ltd.
    13 The Bank of Khyber
    14 The Bank of Punjab
    15 Union Bank Ltd

E. Foreign banks
    1   ABN Amro Bank N.V.
    2   Albaraka Islamic Bank BSC(EC)
    3   American Express Bank Ltd
    4   ANZ Grindlays Bank Ltd
    5   Bank of America (NT & SA)
    6   Bank of Tokyo Mitsubishi Ltd
    7   Bank of Ceylon
    8   Banque Indosuez
    9   Citibank N.A.
    10 Deutsche Bank A.G.
    11 Doha Bank Ltd
    12 Emirates Bank International Ltd P.J.S.C.
    13 Habib Bank A.G. Zurich
    14 HongKong & Shanghai Banking Corp. Ltd
    15 International Finance Investment and Commerce Bank Ltd
    16 Mashreq Bank PSC

17   Oman International Bank S.O.A.G.
18   Rupali Bank Ltd
19   Société Generale. French Int. Bank Ltd
20   Standard Chartered Bank

F.   Development financial institutions
      1   Bankers Equity Ltd
      2   Investment Corp. of Pakistan
      3   National Development Finance Corp.
      4   Pakistan Industrial Credit and Investment Corp.
      5   Pak Kuwait Investment Company
      6   Pak Libya Holding Company
      7   Regional Development Finance Corp.
      8   Saudi Pak Industrial and Agricultural Investment Corp.
      9   Small Business Finance Corp.
      10   Housing Building Finance Corp.
      11   National Investment Trust

G.   Investment banks
      1   Crescent Investment Bank
      2   First International Investment Bank
      3   Atlas BOT Investment Bank
      4   Security Investment Bank
      5   Fidelity Investment Bank
      6   Prudential Investment Bank
      7   Islamic Investment Bank
      8   Asset Investment Bank
      9   Al-Towfeek Investment Bank
      10   Al-Faysal Investment Bank
      11   City Corporation Investment Bank (Pak) Ltd
      12   Franklin Investment Bank Ltd
      13   Orix Investment Bank (Pak) Ltd
      14   Trust Investment Bank Ltd
      15   Escorts Investment Bank
      16   Al-Meezan Investment Bank Ltd

Source: Government of Pakistan, *Economic Survey, Statistical Supplement, 1997–98*.

time in the near future, DFIs will take over most of these functions and will be able to arrange credits on their own. However, this is subject to the implementation of a well-defined legal framework, without which market participants' confidence cannot be achieved. The collapse of finance companies in the 1980s destroyed investor confidence in some of these DFIs and has increased the risk factor. In an economy where the inflation rate is running in double digits and the real interest rates are consistently negative, the effectiveness of any reform measures to improve the efficiency of financial institutions on any grand scale must be taken with a pinch of salt. Market stability and guarantees against risk are also lacking.

The DFIs can further be classified into two groups. The first is the industrial development financial institutions, which are designed to meet the financing needs of industrial projects. There are also some joint ventures such as the Pak-Libya Holding Company and Saudi-Pak Industrial and Agricultural Investment Company Limited. Most of the above institutions are in the state-owned sector and the private sector has been shut out from any role they could play. The second category, the financial development financial institutions, are the mutual fund servicing companies. The National Investment Trust is an open-ended mutual fund while the Industrial Corporation of Pakistan is a closed-ended mutual fund.

Leasing companies were introduced in Pakistan a few years ago but lease financing accounts for only a small proportion of the total debt finances of commercial banks and DFIs. The leasing companies generate funds through equity, lines of credit from commercial banks and DFIs. In the early 1990s, the government allowed leasing companies to offer Certificates of Investment to the public. The main leasing activities of such companies are in financial lease, automobile lease, and leasing for industrial machinery.

A *modaraba* is similar to mutual fund management where funds from capital of investors are pooled. *Modarbas* are not allowed to borrow, having to raise their own funds through equity, are not liable to income tax if 90 per cent of their profits are distributed. They are not permitted to build up reserves. Their main uses of funds include leasing, stock trading, short-term secured lending and venture capital investment. These funds operate under a regulatory structure to monitor the performance of funds and hence have less risk as compared to other institutions. Such a form of financing can play a significant role similar to mutual funds offered in other Asian countries. There are limitations placed on the fund to participate in the market. Investment banks were allowed to operate in 1987. The objective was to fulfil one of the conditions contained in the World Bank Extended Financial Sector Adjustment Loan Agreement (see Table 13.7).

The aim of investment banks was to provide project financing and merchant banking facilities and to promote capital markets. At present, there are 15 investment banks operating. Of these, two are Islamic banks with investment from foreign Islamic banks, six are joint ventures and seven are operated by local groups. These banks have a total equity of PRs 4.99 billion and a gross income of PRs 3.16 billion as of June 1997.

Interest rate reforms

Interest rates have been suppressed over a very long period. Table 13.8 shows that rates such as the money-market rate and the central bank discount rate have not changed noticeably over the last two decades, with nominal interest rates almost constant, given high inflation, and consistent negative real interest

Table 13.7   Monetary aggregates, national income accounts and balance of payments (% of GDP)

	5-year average			Annual							
	1976–80	1981–85	1986–90	1991	1992	1993	1994	1995	1996	1997	1998
M1	27.63	26.31	28.92	29.98	30.69	28.18	27.71	26.32	24.28	29.1	26.5
M2	40.76	40.89	41.22	39.04	42.53	45.36	45.46	43.58	44.88	48.7	45.5
Trade deficit	–10.54	–11.65	–7.46	–10.00	–10.00	–4.61	–3.88	–2.69	–5.7	–3.3	–1.66
Budget deficit	–7.84	–6.24	–7.12	–8.70	–7.40	–7.90	–5.90	–5.5	–6.3	–6.3	–5.6
Current account deficit	–4.77	–7.27	–3.47	–4.77	–2.76	–7.14	–3.77	–4.07	–7.07	–6.5	–2.66
Private consumption	80.50	80.80	72.29	68.34	70.16	72.37	71.27	73.14	71.0	73.0	72.4
Gov. consumption	10.71	11.37	14.95	14.26	12.84	13.02	12.03	11.14	12.10	11.0	11.6
GFCF	17.72	16.74	17.12	17.41	18.60	19.13	17.88	17.20	18.3	18.4	17.4
Gov. expenditure	17.51	19.13	23.31	25.60	26.50	26.00	23.30	23.00	23.90	22.70	21.16

Notes:
M2 = (M1 + quasi-money).
GFCF – gross fixed capital formation.

Sources: IMF, *International Financial Statistics*, various issues; *Asian Development Outlook, 1998, 1999.*

Table 13.8   *Exchange rates and interest rates (annual averages)*

	5-year average			Annual average							
	1976–80	1981–85	1986–90	1991	1992	1993	1994	1995	1996	1997	1998
Exchange rate (mkt)	9.900	13.516	19.334	24.72	25.70	30.12	30.80	34.25	40.120	44.02	46.00
Interest rates (%)											
CB discount rate	9.800	10.00	10.00	10.00	10.00	10.00	15.00	17.00	20.00	18.00	22.0
Money market rate	9.622	8.806	6.550	7.640	7.510	11.00	8.360	11.520	11.40	12.10	10.76
Gov. bond yield	9.748	9.302	8.316	7.880	13.150	13.310	13.01	13.00	13.00	13.05	16.0

Notes:
M2 = (M1 + quasi-money).
Exchange Rate: (Market Rate) = rupees per USD.
Central Bank (CB) Discount Rate (end of period).
Central Bank (CB) Discount Rate (end of period).

Source: IMF, *International Financial Statistics*, various issues.

rates. Banks experienced a decline in deposits during this period. Another major reason for this was the emergence of finance companies that offered 2–3 per cent higher returns on deposits as compared to commercial banks. However, episodes of collapse of some of these finance companies affected public confidence in them.

The public diverted their business with banks to commercial banks for their deposits. During 1990–97, demand deposits declined from 15.02 per cent of GNP to 8.86 per cent. Also, in the same period, time deposits relative to GDP almost doubled their share (increasing from 10.06 per cent of GNP to 19.14 per cent). Reforms have not improved the situation and interest rates are still controlled by the central bank.

Stock market development

The direct financial and stock markets can easily be split into three broad categories, namely, the money market, the debt market, and the equities market. The fourth, the foreign exchange market, is discussed separately. The money market comprises instruments such as the interbank overnight funds market, ceiling trading, government short-term Treasury bills, and repo transactions. It is important to note here that despite the government's effort to develop a short-term T-bills market, commercial banks are the largest investors in T-bills. The debt market includes federal investment bonds, DFI papers, commercial papers, and other government papers – savings certificates as its instruments. Savings certificates are issued by the National Savings Centres and are a very effective source for mobilizing funds through low- and middle-income individuals as they offer tax exemption on their return. Government paper constitutes above 20 per cent of government debt. However, due to increasing inflation, financial liberalization and relaxation of currency control, people are gradually moving to other high-return portfolios.

Political instability, which led to reversals of some reform policies during the last ten years, has been the major bottleneck in the development of the stock market. The slow growth of the stock market relates to the events of the 1970s when massive nationalization left severe negative effects on the market. During the next two decades, the market was functioning without any regulatory structure and had a very poor dividend record. Individuals or a group of a few families retained most of the equity. Investors had evidence of insider trading and market manipulation. They have no incentives these days to invest in the stock market.

Some regulatory measures in 1991 were put in effect to improve the effectiveness of the stock market and to provide a better monitoring system. The government established an auction market for short-term Treasury bills and long-term federal investment bonds. The secondary market for government securities was also established during the same period. In 1992–93, the authorities set up the Securities Department within the SBP to implement the debt-management reforms. The stock market reacted positively to these policies, implemented to attract domestic and foreign capital. The Karachi Stock Exchange index reached a peak level of around 1500 at that time. This positive effect on the stock market is also evident from the statistics in Table 13.9. The pattern continued until 1993 but the political instability during the following six years resulted in a declining trend. In 1997, the newly elected government decided to pursue its reform agenda again and there were some signs of recovery up to May 1998, at a time when Pakistan decided to test a nuclear device. The country is currently facing economic sanctions and is expected to face the worst foreign exchange shortage in its history. The government has therefore imposed certain restrictions on currency mobility and has withdrawn some other foreign exchange privileges. Market sentiment is not favourable and the exchange index has gone down to a very low level below 800, a decline of more than 20 per cent.

Table 13.9   Capital-market development

	1992	1993	1994	1995	1996	1997
No. of new companies listed	178	110	112	155	90	36
Funds mobilized (by new companies, Bill. PRs)		25.93	15.28	13.48	59.72	52.39	19.5
Market capitalization (by ordinary shares, Bill. PRs)	218.4	214.4	404.6	293.3	365.2	469.1
Market capitalization (% change)	219	(1.8)	88.7	(27.5)	24.5	28.4

Sources: Government of Pakistan, *Economic Survey, 1997–98*; State Bank of Pakistan, *Annual Report, 1996–97*.

In 1998, there were three stock exchanges, in Karachi, Lahore and Islamabad. The KSE is the oldest, established in 1948, and takes care of the bulk of the country's trading. As stated earlier, the 1991–93 period saw a major increase in trading in all three stock markets. Market capitalization at KSE alone increased from PRs 38 billion in 1987–88 to PRs 200 billion in 1991–92. Similar trends were noted in the other two markets in Lahore and Islamabad. Trading activities are limited as short selling – except for *badla*, which is a variant of the futures instrument – and derivatives are not allowed. The only mutual funds traded are those issued by public-sector DFIs, such as the National Investment Trust and the Investment Corporation of Pakistan.

Foreign exchange market

During the reforms of 1991–92, the authorities announced some bold measures to eliminate the black market for domestic currency and provided incentives to attract FDI. The country moved gradually to capital and current account convertibility. The SBP also issued US-dollar-denominated bearer certificates with a rate of return of one quarter per cent over the prevailing LIBOR. Restrictions on holding foreign currency and operating foreign currency accounts were abolished. The SBP also liberalized the rules governing the private sector's foreign borrowing. SPB also authorized dealers to operate and trade in foreign currencies.

These policies worked well and the residents and non-residents opened foreign currency accounts. However, confidence was lost when the government decided to freeze all foreign currency accounts in May 1998. Most of the uncertainty created in the market was due to poor policies by the state bank (SBP). It is evident from the fact that over the period 6 June to 15 July 1998, the SBP issued 15 circulars concerning the procedure for foreign exchange transactions and foreign currency accounts by resident and non-resident Pakistanis.

Initially, the SBP fixed the exchange rate at 46 rupees per US dollar while the open-market rate reached PRs 70. This was probably the highest differential between the official and open-market rate since 1973 when the country switched to a floating-rate regime. Foreign reserves fell to their lowest level, just equivalent to two weeks of imports. This was an alarming situation in itself. During late 1998 and early 1999, the IMF agreed to extend partial loans and the reserve situation improved slightly. Recently, the government has relaxed foreign currency restrictions for exporters and travellers. At the same time, in order to discourage the black market for US dollars and to reduce the gap between the official and the open-market rate, the SBP devalued the currency and fixed it at PRs 50. The open-market rate in mid-1999 was PRs 50. Though it may be very difficult for the government to collect dollar deposits from people, at least in the near future, it is hoped that the country will be able to pull itself out of this severe foreign reserve shortage.

Financial deepening

Table 13.10 shows the impact of limited reforms undertaken by this country. M2/GDP is more or less stable over the entire period and does not reflect any changes in the behaviour of economic agents and investors. The financial intermediation ratio shows that the public sector is a major borrower in the credit market. The ratios of public- and private-sector claims are almost the same, which is very different from East Asian countries where the private sector seems to be much more active and efficient. There is no visible improvement

Table 13.10 Indicators of financial liberalization (% of GDP)

	5-year average			Annual							
	1976–80	1981–85	1986–90	1991	1992	1993	1994	1995	1996	1997	1998
Money depth (M2/GDP)	41.50	41.30	41.80	59.70	43.20	46.00	46.10	44.20	46.10	44.20	45.90
FIR (total)/GDP	46.0	49.0	54.0	51.0	56.0	55.0	51.0	50.0	53.0	52.0	51.0
FIR (public)/GDP	22.0	22.0	23.0	25.0	29.0	27.0	24.0	23.0	26.0	25.0	24.0
FIR (private)/GDP	24.0	27.0	30.0	26.0	27.0	28.0	28.0	27.0	27.0	27.0	27.0
GFCF/GDP	17.70	16.78	17.11	17.40	18.60	19.13	17.86	17.20	18.27	18.38	17.40
FDI/GDP	0.19	0.26	0.48	0.60	0.69	0.73	0.81	1.08	1.14	1.70	1.31

Notes:
M3 = (M1 + quasi-money + Post Office savings deposit).
FIR = financial intermediation ratio (32an + 32d) – claims on public sector (32an), claims on private sector (32d).
GFCF = gross fixed capital formation.
FDI = foreign direct investment.

Sources: IMF, *International Financial Statistics*, various issues; World Bank, *World Bank Databank*, Feb. 1997; Asian Development Bank 1998, 1999.

in gross capital formation. FDI improved significantly after 1993, though it is still very low as compared to some relatively developed countries in the region.

The figures do not reflect the significant impact of liberalization. This may be due to the fact that the liberalization process that was initiated in 1991 could not be continued until 1995 due to political instability.

4.   ASSESSMENT OF FUTURE PROSPECTS

The detailed analysis of the Pakistan economy shows the complexity of development problems this country is currently facing precisely because of decades of neglect in taking the right direction with respect to domestic price and financial liberalization. The country experimented with policies to boost agricultural and agri-based industrial development by the usual targeted credit practices. That was well and good, as no economic activities at tertiary level could take place without agricultural sufficiency at that time. But the later sequence of reforms was perverse, and not purposeful. Nationalization of virtually all industrial and service-sector institutions did not help when iron-clad price controls along with a heavy dependence on external capital and limited denationalization did not produce tangible results. Eventually privatization and deregulation in the 1990s had begun to show some hope of a change exactly when Pakistan (and India) exploded nuclear bombs at the worst economic moment, which failed to help recovery.

The other major problem is political instability. The country had a succession of military rulers and bureaucrat-led governments. In recent years elected governments have been dismissed by generals working behind the president. However, political instability and war-preparedness have always been two big problems. For instance, in less than a decade, the country has seen four different governments. Therefore, the main task for government now is to restore the confidence of domestic and international investors that the political state is stable and that the constitution has been changed so that the generals cannot work behind the president to dismiss governments. Recommitment to bold, sustainable reforms along with long-term guarantees are needed even if the sanctions are resolved.

One of the most pressing problems at the moment is repayment of large external debt, which will continue to rise as long as the current account deficits remain negative or the export sector is not expanded to generate enough foreign exchange. Though these problems cannot be resolved in a short period, policies and determination to get the country out of this crisis are needed urgently. Financial-sector liberalization will help to provide an efficient financial infra-structure but there is need for confidence to enable institutions to improve domestic resources as well as to attract foreign investment. The future is very grim indeed. The problems of security issues relating to nuclear policy, peace with neighbours and confidence in the political process, which are political dimensions of development, are at the root of the economic problems. To this must be added the debt overhang at a critical juncture after half a century of a mismanaged vision to create a dynamic society based on ideals. Ideals alone are not sufficient impetus without common-sense, correct policies, it appears in hindsight. If a new beginning is possible in the new century, then this will be another success story in time to come.

NOTES

1. Most other countries included in this book experienced cyclical growth, but none as frequently as this case. Hong Kong's development experience has been impeccable, with one recession in 1998. South Korea experienced one recession in 1980 and another in 1998. Pakistan holds the record as described in this chapter.

2. It is a well-known fact that this country fought three wars with India. Its strategic position to the south of Russia attracted it to the West for defence and the West's involvement with the Afghan struggle, the Mujahideen War, for freedom from the Soviet grip. Therefore, defence allocation took on a survival value, and the rulers ensured that it was not reduced, even after the end of cold war in 1991. In the closing years of the millennium, too, nuclear politics was continuing the same pattern of choice between guns or bread and butter, which is a key factor in the pattern of growth Pakistan.

3. These two countries adopted diametrically opposed development strategies. India, advised by the Oxford economists, among them the renowned Mahalanobis, opted for import substitution, as did Brazil, Egypt and even China, the last on a grander scale, by shutting off the international flow of technology and with that domestic market competition, the source of productivity. The opposite policy of openness in trade to the rest of the world was pursued by Pakistan, but, given its huge resource usage for preparedness for war, the outcome was the famous Samuelson paradigm of choice between guns or bread and butter. Both strategies failed to produce prosperity.

4. During 1982–88, Pakistan was the second largest recipient of economic aid from the United States Agency for International Development (USAID). Khalid, one of the authors of this book, worked as a project officer for several years and witnessed the development process being put in place in this country.

5. Detonation of atomic bombs by both countries in 1998, which is widely believed to have been for strategic reasons as well as for domestic popularity of governments with weak popular support, has led several Western countries to impose economic sanctions on both countries. This has put back the reform agenda for a while. With sanctions in place, kick-starting the Pakistan economy with any amount of external opening is unlikely to be successful without a major resolution of security issues behind the atomic explosions.

6. This situation is similar to the one faced by Indonesia in the 1980s. By this time, it had become clear that the fiscal balance would be seriously eroded if the tax base were not broadened. A similar problem faced by China led to its tax broadening efforts in the 1990s. However, in all these and other cases, only a small percentage of income earners are the potential targets for tax collection. Therefore, the tax base needs broadening to include sales and value-added tax and corporate taxes should be lowered to encourage more firms to pay them.

7. This was being pursued by China in the 1990s. Price decontrols on nearly 900 items have been achieved while keeping controls on less than 100 items as a way of addressing the root problem.

8. Pakistan did not have any formal stock exchange, merchant or investment bank.

9. In January 1997, the PBC was merged with the SBP.
10. See Klein (1990) for a detailed discussion on these events.
11. The intention of this particular reform was to mobilize the savings of those who would not want to participate in a secular banking system based on fixed interest rates or a profit-sharing deposit system. These were the years of the post-OPEC oil boom, which was about to come to an end, and there was hope of attracting deposits from the oil-rich region to make a market in Islamic banking: Malaysia also adopted Islamic banking at about the same time. The latter successfully permitted Islamic banks to exist side by side with modern banking because of far-reaching banking reforms in that country. The military takeover of the country was based on a return to religious orthodoxy, which, it was claimed, was not followed by the socialist regime, which the military disbanded. Hence the rationale for the vigour with which this was done.
12. In June 1998 the level of foreign reserves went down drastically due to economic sanctions imposed by the USA and other industrial countries and refusal of soft credit by the IMF. To avert the crisis, the government decided to freeze all foreign currency accounts. The holders were allowed to withdraw money in Pakistan currency at a rate fixed by the SBP, which is below the market rate. This will definitely have long-run implications on investments for resident and non-resident Pakistanis.
13. This is equivalent to US$2.66 billion, good enough to meet Pakistan's immediate need to service and pay back some 10% of the foreign loans.
14. The development of the stock market in Pakistan will be discussed in a separate section.

14. The Philippines: lost opportunities for correction of reforms

1. BACKGROUND

The Philippines faced a major task of national reconstruction following the end of its wartime occupation by Japan in 1944–46. At the time of independence after that, the economy came under the direct influence of US policies both politically and economically. This is not strange; it also happened in Japan. Even when these security-dominated agreements with the USA were lifted in later years, the remnants of that era's economic policies led to a closer link with US policies, and were not redressed until much later.[1] The reform government of the 1960s, which was able to achieve some degree of growth on the back of the commodity price boom at that time, gave way to new political forces. These forces led to authoritarian rule, setting the country on the road to ruin with the iron rule of a dictator: in the Marcos–Imelda era.

People power was needed to restore the country.[2] A popular uprising occurred in 1982, when people stopped soldiers preparing to fire at them through the simple and exceedingly brave act of offering them flowers and prayers. Seven years later no amount of flowers could stop the battalion of soldiers specially brought from the interior of China to quell another popular uprising in June 1989 in Tiananmen Square. The road to economic recovery was regained by the Filipinos much later. The groundwork laid by a short-term woman president provided sufficient improvement for the US-trained psychological warfare specialist, Fidel Ramos, as the next president to lay the political and economic foundations for sustainable growth. Thus the task of development for this economy only began in the late 1980s and is continuing under an actor turned president in 1999.

The first policy mix of the postwar economic restructuring efforts by the Philippines can be characterized as rules to foster import substitution and rules to promote commodity exports. This restructuring started in the early 1950s and continued until 1967. Industrialization through this import substitution policy mix, often described as the ISI strategy, which was implemented in the 1950s, was aimed at resolving balance of payments problems, and was later extended to preserve protectionist regulations. In this respect, the Philippines drifted in a direction very different from that of the four core members of the regional group, the ASEAN, and instead took a path similar to that prevailing in South Asia. The controls imposed on the exchange rate and on domestic trade during the 1949 balance of payments crisis continued even into later years. The ISI strategy helped the manufacturing sector to grow rapidly to serve the second most populous country in the region after Indonesia. The manufacturing sector, bolstered by import-unfriendly rules, registered a growth of 25 per cent from 8 per cent in the earlier years while the industrial growth as a whole increased from 14 to 37 per cent in some years over 1950 to 1980. Consequently, the share of the agricultural sector declined from 42 to 23 per cent. A viable industrial sector was thus born, as in India, from behind high tariff protection wall.

In later years, these same industries were unable to expand beyond a certain level, given first the limitations of domestic markets and second, competition in the external markets from several other countries such as Hong Kong, Korea, Taiwan and Singapore. The last four countries were adopting policy aimed at liberalizing a manufacturing-based export-led growth strategy. It can be observed here that the 7 per cent average annual manufacturing growth in the Philippines during the 1970s and 1980s falls short of that of its neighbouring ASEAN countries, which enjoyed growth rates of 10 per cent or more at the same time. The policy response capability of the earlier years of dismantling import controls and devaluing exchange rates to respond to the severe balance of payments crisis of some years ago, was much more muted in the later years. This led to a decline in manufacturing growth from an average growth of about 8 per cent during 1957–59 to merely 3.7 per cent during 1960–65.

The second phase spanned the period 1967–85. Two major pieces of legislation were passed and then implemented: the Investment Incentive Act 1967[3] and the Export Incentive Act 1970. Meanwhile, the authorities adopted a floating exchange rate regime in 1970; thus the Philippines was among the very few early countries to do so. These measures brought a major reversal from import substitution to export-oriented policies and encouraged some level of foreign investment through joint ventures as well as full foreign ownership in a number of priority areas. However, they were insufficient to boost economic growth or productivity since similar liberalization measures in other competing countries were much broader-based than those in this country. So the opportunity was sadly missed.

The reluctance to liberalize broadly led to serious impediments. Budget deficits increased rapidly during the years, financed through foreign borrowing. At the end of 1985, the Philippines had the lowest per capita income (806 pesos in 1950, going up to 1622 pesos in 1975 to 1987 pesos in 1984) of all the ASEAN member nations. Per capita income, which was already lower than in other countries, declined to 1644 pesos in 1985.[4] The external debt rose to a level almost equal to GNP: it was three times the value of total exports. The domestic banking system and other financial institutions were unable to function because of severe liquidity and bad debt problems while investment in the real sector declined to the lowest level. The debt-service ratio increased sharply from 21 to 38 per cent during this period. By Pakistani standards, however, this was even worse! The Latin American debt crisis at that time also meant that virtually all doors were closed to any additional foreign borrowing. This situation led first to a major political crisis, and then to a revamp of the economy. Progress started only after the then president and his wife sought exile in Hawaii following what was then called the 'people power' movement, which overthrew the corrupt Marcos regime in 1982.

The third phase of economic reforms was initiated in the mid-1980s with a structural adjustment programme focused on trade and financial-sector liberalization. Although some measures were initiated as early as during 1982, these reforms could not be continued due to political instability brought on by armed insurrections. The structural adjustment resumed in full swing in 1987. These policies helped the authorities to completely restructure the banking sector,[5] specify the functions of the central bank, deregulate the pricing system, encourage foreign investment, promote competition in the domestic banking industry by easing entry barriers to both local and foreign banks and develop domestic money and capital markets. These policies helped the country towards gaining momentum for growth, which then became impressive, in line with the already established growth path of the ASEAN economies. The final phase was ushered in in unwelcome fashion by the baht contagion, when IMF intervention was invited in September 1997 in the face of a collapsing currency.

This brief overview of how a policy mix of the liberal kind can create favourable changes is very impressive evidence in support of the need for reforms. The Philippines economy went through a roller-coaster during the last three decades largely because of an inappropriate policy mix and (readers must not forget this origin of all crises) because of the political dimension of nepotism and later insurrections. With the right political climate returning to this country in the mid-1980s, and with the adoption of liberal policies during that period, the economy stabilized again. Growth started moving upwards. During the first half of the 1990s, the Philippines experienced an incredible growth, similar to those of other ASEAN economies, only to be surprised by the baht contagion.

The next section discusses the current economic outlook of the Philippines and describes the measures taken during the last seven to nine years. The economic liberalization process is discussed in Subsection 3.1 while the details of financial-sector reforms are provided in Subsection 3.2. In the same section, we also critically evaluate the policies implemented by the Ramos government to reform the economy. Finally, we assess the policies and discuss the future prospects for the country in Section 4.

2. ECONOMIC AND FINANCIAL STRUCTURE

Similar to the experience of other Southeast Asian economies, the Philippines economy enjoyed sound macroeconomic fundamentals until the first half of 1997.[6] As can be seen from the statistics in Table 14.1, GDP recorded a high level of 5.2 per cent in 1997 but dropped to –0.5 in 1998. The industrial and service sectors registered high growth and the agricultural sector recovered from the slow-down that persisted until 1995. The industrial sector grew by 8 per cent, much above the 7.3 per cent level achieved in 1995. Gross domestic investment, which had contracted in 1995, recovered in 1996 to about 24 per cent, the level achieved in 1994, which was far higher than during the crisis years. Gross domestic savings showed a marginal increase from 15 per cent to 16 per cent in 1996.

Inflation remained high, approaching 9 per cent in 1996, but dropped to 6 per cent in 1997. The money supply growth as measured by M2 stabilized slightly at around 22 per cent after reaching a high of 28 per cent. The government continued to enjoy a surplus budget of 0.27 per cent of GDP in 1996, which was lower than the level of about 0.3 per cent in 1996 and 0.1 per cent in 1997. The expansionary monetary policy implemented after 1995 resulted in rising inflation, which also affected the interest rates. As we noted in several earlier chapters, flouting the Friedman principle by having monetary growth too far removed from the income and circulatory needs of the economy is bound to produce high inflation. This was widely known in the 1990s, and countries still flout the rules because of resource constraints, as in this case. The discount rate increased to about 11 per cent in 1995. In the external sector, the trade deficit measured relative to GDP increased from 13.7 per cent in 1996 to above 18.4 per cent in 1997. The current account deficit, which showed some improvement in 1995 (only 2.2 per cent of GDP), went back to –5.3 per cent.

However, all these impressive indicators changed as a result of the Asian financial crisis. The figures in Table 14.1 show that growth shrank by 0.5 per cent in 1998 and there is no hope for improvement in the 1999 figures (not released at the time of completing this chapter). Inflation rose to 9.7 per cent, almost double digits. The fiscal surplus changed to a deficit of 1.9 per cent of GDP. Due to huge capital outflow, the current account balance changed to positive figures and accounted for 2.0 per cent of GDP in 1998.

In the financial sector, the share market experienced a slow-down. The volatility in the financial system showed some abatement. The M3 to GDP ratio, which is an indicator of financial deepening, increased from 36.4 per cent to 38.7 per cent during this period. The exchange rates were, in general, stable until July 1997, the onset of the baht contagion.

Thanks to its earlier prosperous period, when commodities fetched high prices, the Philippines record on social indicators is quite impressive, with the

Table 14.1 Basic economic and social indicators of development in the Philippines

Indicators	1971–80	1981–90	1991–93	1994	1995	1996	1997	1998
National accounts								
GDP growth (%)	6.15	1.74	0.65	4.40	4.83	5.8	5.2	−0.5
Per capita GDP (US$)	409	598	798	1034	1063	1159	1200	8.66
Private consumption/GDP	0.66	0.69	0.75	0.74	0.74	0.73	0.73	0.74
Gov. consumption/GDP	0.09	0.09	0.10	0.11	0.11	0.11	0.13	0.13
Financial indicators								
Gross domestic savings (% of GDP)	23.40	19.52	14.77	15.40	16.00	18.50	20.3	20.0
Gross fixed capital formation (% of GDP)	21.54	21.89	21.58	23.63	22.48	23.91	23.8	19.3
Inflation	14.89	14.67	11.77	8.45	7.73	9.1	6.0	9.7
M2/GDP	21.1	28.7	37.6	45.7	50.3	54.0	61.5	60.8
Fiscal balance (% of GDP)	−1.1	−3.0	−1.6	1.1	0.5	0.3	0.1	−1.9
Current account balance (% of GDP)	−2.8	−4.1	−3.2	−4.1	−2.7	−4.7	−5.3	2.0
Trade balance/GDP	−3.7	−5.1	−9.1	−11.3	−12.3	−13.7	−18.4	−0.30
Discount rate	7.35	10.19	12.57	8.30	10.83	11.7	14.64	12.4
Debt service ratio (% of exports)	n.a.	n.a.	17.1	17.4	15.8	12.7	11.7	11.9
Social indicators								
IMF classification	Middle	Lower-middle	Lower-middle	Lower-middle	Lower-middle	Lower-middle	Lower-middle	Lower-middle
Unemployment rate (%)	n.a.	7.06	8.83	8.40	8.40	7.40	7.20	n.a.
Expenditure on education (% of exp.)	n.a.	12.5	12.23	16.17	13.98	15.51	15.60	n.a.
Expenditure on health (% of exp.)	n.a.	3.62	2.91	2.15	1.9	2.12	2.20	n.a.
Population growth	2.75	2.44	2.21	2.12	2.06	2.30	2.30	2.30

Sources: IMF, *International Financial Statistics*, various issues; *Asian Development Outlook, 1995, 1999*; *Government Finance Statistics Yearbook, 1985–1996*.

government spending an average of about 16 per cent of the budget on education; for health this ratio is 4 per cent during the period 1991–93. The country has been able to control population growth, reducing it from a level of 2.12 per cent in 1994 to 2.06 per cent in 1995. However, in the next two years the population growth rate increased to 2.3 per cent per annum. Life expectancy has improved to 67 years. This impressive achievement in a deeply religious country holds further promise of a decline in birth rates. With more affluence and education, religion has not been an obstacle to reducing birth rates. Similarly placed countries, for example in Latin America, could also achieve this if there were broad-based social and economic improvements that can only come from good income growth.

3.1 Economic Liberalization

Economic liberalization was directed at the fiscal and external trade sectors. The Development Budget Coordination Committee (DBCC) was formed and given powers as the highest body to determine fiscal policy. This is in some sense similar to the case of Thailand, which has now established an arm's-length body such as this to formulate policies unfettered by the immediate political considerations of the ruling party. These institutions in these two countries serve as the institutional link between the planning and budgeting agencies of the government to ensure consistency in the annual budget with the overall development plan. In Malaysia, there is a advisory body which works under the direction of the Planning Unit at the Prime Minister's Office to do the same thing. It appears that delinking the political control of fiscal and economic matters is a key to preventing interventions of the type familiar in the cases of China and Vietnam, as well as in some more open political systems.

The government introduced tax reforms in the mid-1980s. The main objectives of these reforms – as was the case with similar reforms in Indonesia and Malaysia – were to improve tax administration and the revenue collection mechanism. The tax burden was made more equitable by making the tax broad-based, which increased revenues while lessening the tax burden on some income levels. Another major step towards fiscal reforms was the decision to reduce the role of state enterprises by a strong dose of privatization activities. This is in some respects an emergency arrangement as there were no resources to bypass this step. Inclusion of such well-managed companies as the National Power Corporation and National Bank sweetened the process and gave the right signals of the need for prudence. At the same time, measures have been taken to reduce public spending to generate net fiscal surpluses.

Attempts were also made to bring in competition in the traded sector. Bringing in tariff reductions ensures the needed efficiency while also preparing the ground for the next set of reforms. This was done partly because policy

Table 14.2 Growth rates of basic economic indicators

	5-year average			Annual average							
	1976–80	1981–85	1986–90	1991	1992	1993	1994	1995	1996	1997	1998
GDP	5.2	−1.3	3.9	−0.5	0.3	2.1	4.4	4.8	5.8	5.2	−0.5
Inflation	13.1	17.7	11.4	12.2	11.4	11.7	8.45	7.73	9.1	6.0	9.7
Revenue	14.7	17.3	22.6	22.0	10.6	7.6	29.2	7.4	14.1	14.7	−1.7
M1	16.9	10.3	20.4	15.9	9.1	22.3	11.3	21.7	19.8	14.2	7.4
M2	21.3	23.6	18.0	17.3	13.6	27.1	24.4	24.2	23.2	26.1	8.5
FDI	−201.8	−164.7	113.3	2.6	−58.1	44.2	28.5	−8.2	4.2	−17.6	40.1
Trade balance	16.9	10.3	20.4	−20.1	46.2	32.5	26.2	13.9	25.4	−1.9	99.6

Note: M2 = (M1 + quasi-money).

Sources: IMF, *International Financial Statistics*, various issues; World Bank, *World Bank Databank*, Feb. 1997; ADB, *Asian Development Outlook, 1998, 1999.*

wisdom dictates that the real sector should be liberalized ahead of the financial sector, especially in respect of capital controls. It was also partly due to commitments made under the regional trade bloc, the AFTA decision in 1992 to usher in greater trade opening within the ASEAN grouping by the year 2010. During 1993 to 1995, several pieces of reform legislation were passed into law.

3.2 Financial-sector Reforms

The financial system comprises a wide range of institutions: commercial banks, thrift banks, specialized government banks, rural banks, investment houses, finance companies, investment companies, non-bank thrift institutions, stock brokers, offshore banking and non-banking institutions and many others. We provide a description of the financial system in this economy. By all accounts, even after the 1997–98 Asian financial crisis, observers have suggested that the financial sector in this country is far better managed than is the case with most Asian countries: see Chapter 17 for a discussion. There was more independence in the 1990s in this country's central bank. Its executives were well trained and able to put in place, given no political interference, a good set of reforms. Gone is the image of the governor taking orders to transmit money to Marcos's cronies in the 1980s. As a result, the very small but well-managed banking sector is capable of fulfilling its functions better in this country.

The central bank

The central bank reforms were initiated in July 1993 when the government re-established the Bangko Sentral Pilipinas (BSP), under the Republic Act 7653. The highest policy-making body under the BSP is the Monetary Board (MB). The governor of the BSP holds the chair and one cabinet secretary is among the two representatives from the highest-ranking officers of the government. Unlike in pre-reform Korea, where the minister for finance was the deputy chairman with powers to veto the decision of the governor of the central bank, this arrangement reduces the political influence of the government. Besides these two members, the BSP also has five full-time private representatives. All these members are appointed by the president of the country, as is common in other countries.

The BSP has two important objectives in formulating policies. These are price stability and sustained economic growth. The other role of the BSP is to attain stability of the domestic currency, the peso, by maintaining its convertibility into other currencies. This is the flawed policy that led to the adoption of a managed currency rate, in the defence of which many resources were wasted, as for example during the initial attempts to maintain the stability of the peso in the face of the baht contagion. It should also be mentioned that it was the central bank that quickly abandoned the managed float and saved a great deal of resources, unlike the banks in other crisis-ridden countries. The authorities try to achieve this objective by following a policy of a managed float, which determines the exchange rate and also holds adequate levels of international reserves to defend the currency. In order to achieve these objectives, the BSP and the MB make use of some important instruments such as open-market operations, reserve requirements and rediscounting, as well as moral suasion.

As a step towards more focus on the banking sector, especially to attain the objective of price stability, the BSP divested its fiscal agency functions steadily over a period of three phases of five years each, starting in June 1993. The fiscal function will devolve to the government. The BSP also planned to transfer its regulatory powers over finance companies and other non-bank financial institutions without banking functions to the Securities and Exchange Commission (the SEC) by 1998. Major appointments at the BSP and the MB are made by the president. The BSP cannot still be treated as having the kind of independence it needs without the specification of clear-cut targets on policy goals and without a culture that promotes independent policy pursuit even after the basis for central bank independence is enshrined in law. When one of the cabinet members is a full member of the BSP, its independence is obviously constrained.

Immediately after a year of its establishment in 1994, the BSP reported a profit of P 10.5 billion, which was its first profit in a decade. This trend continued in 1995 when the BSP reported a profit of P 9.6 billion. The move towards more policy coordination between the BSP and other government agencies also helped the policy-makers to maintain a more stable exchange rate and domestic interest rates until mid-1997. The use of open-market operations as a major monetary policy instrument was evident in the BSP's holding of Treasury bills. Similarly, the BSP has been very active in attaining goals of interest rate policy and maintaining exchange rates until it faced the Asian financial crisis.

Reforms of the depository institutions

The earlier banking-sector reforms date back to the 1970s when the liberalization process was first initiated. A second series of reforms was implemented in the latter part of the 1980s and was again strengthened in the 1990s, which we discussed in a previous sub-section. As can be seen from Table 14.3, many bold measures were taken to promote the banking and non-bank sectors. These include liberalizing the regulatory structure governing policies of minimum reserve and capital adequacy requirements. At the same time, the authorities encouraged entry of foreign banks to improve efficiency in the domestic banking industry through competition, relaxed foreign exchange controls, permission to banks to introduce new products and instruments in the markets and to remove interest rate controls.

The banking sector in the late 1990s was regulated by the provisions of the General Banking Act, while the foreign banks come under the Act Liberalizing the Entry and Scope of Operations of Foreign Banks in the Philippines. The domestic banking system is composed of commercial banks, thrift banks, rural banks, and specialized government banks. The banking sector dominates the financial sector with banks capturing about 81 per cent of the non-central bank resources of the financial system.[7] In the late 1990s, there were 69 commercial banks in the country, which included 17 branches of foreign banks and two government-owned banks. The two government-owned banks are the Land Bank of the Philippines, which is responsible for agrarian reform programmes, and the Development Bank of the Philippines, which provides long-term funds to the industrial sector. Another government-owned commercial bank, the Philippine National Bank, was privatized in 1989 as part of the reform process. About 43 per cent of its shares are in the private sector (see Lamberte and Lianto, 1993, p. 241).

Commercial banks form the largest group in the banking sector and capture almost 90 per cent of the total assets of the system. They are split into two categories: regular commercial banks or KBs and the expanded commercial banks, the EKBs. The basic objective for licensing EKBs was to provide a one-stop banking facility to clients when banks were authorized to perform securities underwriting, syndication activities, and direct equity investment in allied and non-allied undertakings (Lamberte and Lianto, 1993, p. 241). The reforms in the commercial banking sector (that is, both the KBs and the EKBs) were initiated in the mid-1980s[8] and were implemented gradually. As a first step, the central bank rationalized and simplified the rediscount window facility in 1985 by adopting market-based rates across all types of eligible papers. At the same time, the central bank also relaxed its policies on determining rediscount rates. In 1989, the central bank implemented a gradual unification of reserve requirements across banks and deposit types in order to reduce intermediation costs and improve efficiency. These liberalization policies were adopted in addition to the reserve requirements – which were set at 25 per cent of all deposits in 1992 – being reduced to only 14 per cent in 1997. Without any deposit insurance and with more flexibility in commercial banking activities, it was important to make the banks accountable for their activities by providing some safeguards to the depositors. Accordingly, the authorities established minimum capital requirements for banks and announced that there would be gradual increases in these minimum capital requirements in later years. Malaysia also worked out a similar programme announced in 1994 by segregating the banks into those in the upper tier with closer to 10 per cent share capital and those in the lower tier with lower capital adequacy requirements.

The authorities took steps towards a gradual liberalization of branching in 1989. This was further relaxed through central bank circulars in 1991, 1992 and

Table 14.3   Financial-sector reforms

Date of reforms	Liberalization policies implemented
1981	CBP deregulated all bank rates, except short-term lending rates.
1982	CBP removed the ceiling on short-term lending rates.
1985	Rationalization and simplification of CB rediscount window which included: – removal of fixed spreads – adoption of a market-based rediscount rates across all types of eligible papers Further measures were implemented during 1994–95.
1989	CBP implemented the gradual unification of reserve requirements across all banks and deposit types. 30% equity of the Philippines National Bank privatized. CBP implemented policy to relax the branching policy. These deregulation policies continued during 1991–93.
1990	The Monetary Board authorized the establishment of ATMs in off-site or off-premises areas by authorized banks.
1991	Establishment of Foreign Exchange (FX) Clearing and Settlement System in coordination with PCHS. Foreign Investment Act (FIA) implemented – allows 100% foreign equity ownership except in sectors where it is specifically restricted to 25–40% or banned. Liberalization of minimum capital requirement initiated and continued until 1996.
1992	Rural banking system strengthened. Circular issued to liberalize foreign exchange trading. Lifts restriction on off-floor forex trading among KBs with the launching of the Philippine Dealing System (PDS).
1993	Bangko Sentral ng Pilipinas (BSP) established to exercise greater flexibility and independence. Reserve requirement on deposits of banks and non-banks reduced by 3% (from 25% in December 1992 to 22% in July 1993). Further reductions announced in 1994, 1995 and 1996. The liquidity-floor requirement on government deposits/funds reduced to 50% from previous 75%. Rules and guidelines governing the operations of investment houses (IH). Rules and regulations governing the operations of finance companies (FC).
1994	Monetary Board liberalized accreditation guidelines for securities dealership of T-bills. Foreign banks allowed to operate in the Philippines under one of three modes: – establishment of branches with full banking authority – establishment of locally incorporated subsidiaries, up to 60% of which may be foreign-owned – acquisition of up to 60% ownership of domestic banks Measures to ease the operations of these banks also announced.

Date of reforms	Liberalization policies implemented
	Government lifted restriction on repatriation of investment under debt-to-equity conversion programme as well as remittance of dividends and profits which accrue thereon.
	BSP Circular no. 33 replaces the Foreign Exchange Clearing and Settlement System (FECSS) of BSP with the Philippine Domestic Dollar Transfer System (PDDTS) operated by Citibank, Manila.
	BSP Circular no. 54, allows banks' long foreign exchange (FX) position not to go beyond 25% and short FX position not to exceed 5% of unimpaired capital.
1995	Thrift Banks Act of 1995 allows thrift banks to: – accept savings and time deposits – open current or cheque accounts – act as official depository of national agencies – engage in quasi-banking and money-market operations – purchase, hold and convey real estate
	Monetary Board approved to float 3-, 5-, 7-year fixed rate T-notes.
	All expanded commercial banks required to list at least 10% of their paid-up capital at the Philippine Stock Exchange in three years.
	Expanded commercial banks, commercial banks and thrift banks allowed to increase their equity investment in commercial banks up to 49% from a previous limit of 30%.
	Banks allowed to determine their own schedule of operations according to customer needs.
	All Interbank Call Loan (IBCL) transactions to be governed by the Agreement for an IBCL Fund Transfer System executed between the BSP, BAP and the PCHC.
	Under electronic auction of government securities, the conduct of auction of government securities is returned to the Department of Finance from BSP.
	Monetary Board approved a circular that defines the scope of trading activities of banks and other financial institutions engaged in derivative securities.
1996	Islamic Bank Charter: Rules and Regulations governing the operations of Islamic Banking.
	Guidelines to implement the Rules and Regulations on Financial Derivatives such as: – currency swaps and forwards – expanded type of derivative securities
	National Commission on Savings established with the objective to accelerate capital formation through savings in banks and other financial intermediaries.
	Amendment to the Foreign Investment Act of 1991 (RA no. 7042), implemented in March.
1997	BSP Circular no. 40 increases amount of foreign exchange that foreign exchange institutions are allowed to sell to residents for any non-trade purposes without prior BSP approval, from $25 000 to $50 000.

Source: Central Bank of Philippines (Bangko Sentral Ng Philipinas).

1993. The last policy, implemented in 1993, removed all previous restrictions on this aspect and authorized the Monetary Board to approve applications for the establishment and operation of banking offices subject only to capital adequacy, liquidity, profitability and soundness of management.

In an effort to adapt banks to acquire capacity for financial innovation of the types taking place in the more developed markets, the Monetary Board allowed the establishment of automated teller machines (ATMs) in 1990. As of June 1996, the total ATMs in the network number 2210 units, of which 1913 belong to commercial banks. To provide a more competitive environment to the domestic banking industry, the government implemented a law (RA no. 7721) in May 1994 to allow the entry and operation of foreign banks. Foreign banks may enter the Philippines under any of these three categories: (a) branches with full banking authority; (b) locally incorporated subsidiaries, up to 60 per cent of which may be foreign-owned; and (c) acquisition of up to 60 per cent ownership of domestic banks. The banking sector experienced a sharp expansion during 1994–98. The number of full-service foreign banks increased from four in 1994 to 17 by 1997. Moreover, 18 foreign banks had off-shore banking licences and two foreign banks also operate a foreign currency deposit system. The result is that the share of foreign banks in the total assets of the banking system increased to 14.3 per cent in 1997. The authorities issued a circular in 1996, 'Guidelines on the Issuance of Expanded Commercial Banking Authority to Local Branches of Foreign Banks operating in the country'. The circular sets out, among other things, the minimum capital requirement for a foreign bank with expanded banking authority of P 2.5 billion, similar to the level required for domestic-owned universal banks.

Thrift banks (TBs) are the second largest category in the banking industry, holding 6 to 7 per cent of the total assets of the industry. Thrift banks consist of savings and mortgage banks, private development banks, and savings and loan associations. A major reform affecting TBs was undertaken in 1995 with the enactment of the Thrift Banks Act of 1995. This allowed thrift banks to (a) open savings and time deposits, (b) open current and cheque accounts subject to certain requirements, (c) act as official depositories of national agencies and of municipal, city or provincial funds, (d) engage in quasi-banking and money-market operations, and (e) purchase, hold and conveyance real-estate activities under the same conditions as those governing commercial banks. While reducing the reserve requirements on the commercial banks, these policies were also made applicable to non-bank institutions to reduce reserve requirements while increasing the minimum capital requirement for TBs.

Rural banks (RBs) are privately owned banks and represent the smallest group among the banks. Their number has declined over time due to failures. The rural banking system was strengthened in 1992 under the Rural Banks Act of 1992. This law allows rural banks to (a) accept and create demand deposits subject to some requirements, (b) invest in equities in allied undertakings, (c) act as official depositories of municipal, city or provincial funds, (e) be exempt from any ownership ceiling for a period of ten years, and (f) settle or liquidate arrears with the central bank through a conversion scheme or plan of investment. Policies regarding the exit/entry rules for rural banks were further liberalized in 1995. In a manner consistent with other banking categories, the authorities also undertook gradual liberalization of reserve requirements and minimum capital requirements.

In 1995, the government introduced a set of rules, the Rules on Investment in Banks, to promote the consolidation of bank resources. Specifically, EKBs, KBs and TBs are allowed to increase their equity investments in commercial banks up to 49 per cent from the previous limit of 30 per cent. The thrift banks may also own up to 100 per cent of another thrift bank or rural bank, a rule change that is an improvement on the previous maximum of 30 per cent. The liberalization policy was aimed at encouraging mergers among banks to increase efficiency and competitiveness.

The authorities also liberalized the Banking Schedule with the objective that banks would be able to serve the public more efficiently. According to these reforms, banks were allowed greater discretion in determining their schedule of operations in line with variable customer needs. They were allowed to serve longer hours during the day or transact business during more than five days a week. However, banks were still expected to comply with the minimum six-hour daily requirement for the five regular banking days.

One important development was the computerization of the payment system in the Philippines. The clearing operations of the Philippines Clearing House Corporation (PCHC) introduced bank-to-bank settlements by BSP in cooperation with the Bankers Association of the Philippines. This reduces man-hours and importantly facilitates the delivery of banking services. Furthermore, the deposit-taking transactions of most banks in current and savings accounts are computerized and operated on-line. Loan transactions, trust deposits and foreign transactions are also carried out electronically.

Reforms in non-bank financial institutions (NBFIs)

The non-bank financial institutions consist of finance companies, investment houses, investment companies, securities dealers/brokers, pawnshops, lending investors, non-stock savings and loan associations, mutual building and loan associations, venture capital corporations and insurance companies. In November 1992, the government issued a circular to relax prohibitions on the establishment of new pawnshop offices in the city of Manila. The authorities reduced the reserve requirement for non-stock savings and loan associations (NSSLAs) from 8 per cent to 6 per cent of the values respectively of savings and time deposits. The Investment House Law was approved in 1993 to establish rules and guidelines governing the investment houses, that is, mutual funds.

Finance companies In 1993 the government passed into law the Finance Company Act to establish the rules and regulations governing their operations. There are two types of finance companies, one with quasi-banking functions and one without these functions. Finance companies provide an alternative source of extending credit for consumer, agricultural, commercial and industrial enterprises. They have been regulated since 1998 by the SEC and are allowed to engage in receivable financing and lease financing.

Insurance companies Insurance companies are principally private-sector-owned companies, with the exception of five government-owned corporations. The private insurance companies are regulated by the Insurance Commission, while the government-owned insurance companies are governed by rules in their own charters. There are 127 private insurance companies in the country, including 12 foreign insurance companies.

Interest rate reforms
The CBP gradually liberalized long-suppressed interest rates in the form of rate ceilings. Beginning in mid-1981, ceilings were removed on deposits and loans except those with maturities of less than two years. Interest rate liberalization was gradual, with removal of ceilings on short-term lending rates coming into effect in 1983. The aim was to adopt an interest rate policy that would return interest rate formation to market forces to enhance overall macroeconomic stability. Accordingly, measures were taken to liberalize the interest rates and also to rationalize the rediscount rates of the CBP. Exchange rates and interest rates are shown in Table 14.4.

Stock market development
Share market performance was very poor until reforms were instituted in that sector in 1993. The two stock exchanges in Manila and Makati were merged to form the Philippines Stock Exchange (PSE). The figures reported in the BSP reports show that the turnover rate rose throughout 1993 and 1994.[9] The market price as indicated by a widely followed index rose from a low of 831.4 points in 1990 to 2868.9 in 1994, which represented an increase of 155 per cent in just one year, 1993. More companies were listed, with the scrips increasing from 161 in 1991 to 205 companies in 1995. Market capitalization increased from P 161.2 billion in 1990 to P 1544 billion in 1995 and P 2121 billion by mid-1996. The year 1993 registered a major jump in market capitalization from P 353 billion in 1992 to P 1089 billion in 1993, almost a 300 per cent increase in one year! Similar growth also took place in the money markets. More

Table 14.4 Exchange rates and interest rates (annual averages)

	5-year average			Annual average							
	1976–80	1981–85	1986–90	1991	1992	1993	1994	1995	1996	1997	1998
Exchange rate (mkt)	7.4	14.0	22.6	26.7	25.1	27.7	24.4	26.2	26.3	39.98	39.06
Interest rates (%)											
CB discount rate	6.3	9.2	11.2	14.0	14.3	9.4	8.3	10.8	11.7	14.6	12.4
Deposit rate	9.3	16.2	12.9	18.8	14.3	9.6	10.5	8.4	9.7	10.2	12.1
Lending rate	12.8	21.9	18.0	23.1	19.5	14.7	15.1	14.7	14.8	16.3	16.8
Treasury bills	11.3	19.2	16.9	21.5	16.0	12.4	12.7	11.8	12.3	12.9	15.0

Notes:
M2 = (M1 + quasi-money).
Exchange rate = (market rate) = pesos per US dollar.
Central Bank (CB) discount rate (end of period).
Deposit rate = Time (61–90 days).
Treasury bills (91 days).

Source: IMF, International Financial Statistics, various issues.

spectacular increases have also been observed in Jakarta following the reforms applied to that market in 1991–94. So this is not surprising.

With external conditions, particularly trade, becoming unfavourable since 1996, the market could not maintain the high performance, especially after the onset of the financial crisis, and the fall of Barings Bank – an event that discouraged portfolio investments in the region during 1996–97. The higher domestic interest rates in response to the depreciation of the peso initially led to relatively higher inflation. As a result the share market index, PHISIX, declined to 2594 in 1995. There was some limited up-trend in 1996 with the rise in the index to 3170.6 points. However, the number of listed companies did not increase: one new firm in 1996 and none since. There were great expectations among investors that the stock market would rebound in 1996–97 due to some international and domestic development such as a decline in international interest rates and the flotation of new public offerings. But the currency crisis due to the baht contagion from mid-1997 dashed any hope of realizing these expectations. The worst happened when the market lost more than half its value in the aftermath of the crisis. It will take a few years for the market to regain its previous peak. At end-1999, the market has recouped most of the losses, helped by a stock market boom at year end.

The money market
Major instruments of the money market are interbank call loans, government securities, promissory notes, and different corporate issues in the money markets. Aggregate transactions in the money market tripled from P 1289.5 billion in 1990 to P 4366.3 billion in 1996.[10]

Interbank call loans (IBCLs) The call loans market was first established in 1961 by eight banks on an informal basis in Manila. This transformed into a formal market by mid-1963 when the Bankers Association of the Philippines adopted a set of pro-growth rules for the market. IBCLs, representing overnight and term placements of banks with excess cash available for other banks with temporary reserve deficiencies, are the most actively traded instruments in the Philippines money market. Banks and quasi-banks are the exclusive participants of this very liquid market. The commercial banks have the most dominant position, accounting for in excess of 85 per cent. Since 1992, other banking institutions such as the thrift banks and the rural banks entered this market and thus helped to increase their share in the total volume of loans extended. Similarly, investment houses and savings banks have increased their share of their mostly lending positions. The volume of interbank loans, which accounts for more than half the total transactions in the money market, tripled in value from P 730.7 billion in 1990 to P 2761.5 billion at the end of 1996.

Beginning in the fourth quarter of 1995, all IBCL transactions come under the agreement for an IBCL fund transfer system, which is executed among the

BSP, the BAP and the PCHC. Transforming these transactions into a fully automated environment reduced the operational risk in the float of the paper-based transactions and also helped to improve the efficiency and productivity of banks. This is an example of the way the better-managed central bank was continually taking actions after the mid-1980s to fine-tune the financial system. This is in sharp contrast with what took place in Thailand and Indonesia, which helped to make their banking system very fragile and caused it to collapse when the crisis hit in 1997.

Government securities (GS)   Government securities are the second most active traded instruments in the money market. They account for nearly one-third of the total volume of transactions. The development of this market was the result of implementing the suggestions made by a consulting firm. That firm, Bancom Development Corporation, was hired to advise the central bank on the development of new money-market instruments. The bank formally issued a series of 90-day Treasury bills (TBs) worth 5 million pesos in 1966. Later, the auction was expanded to cover instruments with a longer maturity. Since then, the GS market has experienced episodes of expansion and re-establishment for certain economic reasons. For example, the TB market was suspended in 1984 during the economic and balance of payments crisis. It was subsequently revived in 1986, and is doing well.

Government securities, denominated as Treasury bills with less than one-year maturity, are issued by the central government: they account for more than 80 per cent of the total volume of transactions. Private corporations, commercial banks, trust/pension funds, and even individuals are the major investors in government securities. Since 1990, the volume of government securities traded kept pace with the growth in IBCLs, to reach P 1174 billion at the end of 1996 from P 464.8 billion at the end of 1990. This is due to the continuous liberalization process. For example, in 1994, the Monetary Board liberalized the accreditation guidelines for securities dealership to expand the dealership network. Further steps were taken in 1995 by returning the responsibility for conducting the auction to the Department of Finance. The bidding process was also computerized. The idea was to make the auction process safer, more transparent and efficient.

During the same year, the Monetary Board approved participation in the Book Entry System (BES) of insurance companies and mutual benefit associations, entitling these institutions to acquire BES-eligible government securities either from primary awards through auctions or through secondary purchase from other BES participants. This policy was pursued in order to reduce the administrative cost for both buyers and sellers.

Promissory note market   The Philippines promissory note market (PNM) is basically an unsecured promise to pay a certain sum of money at a fixed date. The note market was initiated in 1967, when the two state oil companies started issuing such notes to overcome the cash flow problems they faced. Commercial banks account for two-thirds of the total amount issued while finance and investment companies account for 20 and 10 per cent respectively. In terms of volume, the PNM is the third largest component of the money market.

Commercial paper market   Established in 1965, this market was originally dominated by the non-financial corporate firms with individuals and corporations as the major suppliers of funds. Transactions consist of commercial securities, which were issued by good quality-rated companies, maturing in less than one year. Investment houses are the most active participants in this market. The volume of transaction in the paper market increased from about 2 to 8 per cent of total transactions.

The capital market

Two broad categories of the capital market are the securities and non-securities markets. The market is regulated by the central bank's Bureau of Internal Revenue (BIR) and the Securities and Exchange Commission (SEC). The BSP monitors all foreign-origin investments. The BIR is the regulatory body for taxes on transactions. The SEC is the major body to regulate the securities market and to oversee the activities of the market participants such as stock-brokers and security dealers. Until 1993, there were two separate bourses operating in the Philippines, the Manila Stock Exchange, founded in 1927 – among the first in Asia – and the Makati Stock Exchange, formed later, in 1963, both trading the same set of stocks. The SEC, as noted earlier, moved in 1988 to merge the two exchanges. Hong Kong did the same in 1989. The merger was only formalized in early 1993. Indonesia is planning a similar merger of its two exchanges in 2000. The SEC was formalized by a directive to form the Philippines Stock Exchange, the only exchange to trade capital securities.

The authorities implemented reforms to boost liquidity in the capital market. These included the 1986 tax policy package, which eliminated double taxation on dividend income; the rules and regulations governing investment companies implemented in 1989, which revived mutual fund activities; and the rules and regulations covering foreign investment in BSP-approved securities, which transfers some of the functions of the central bank to the custodian banks. As a result of the last reform, the foreign investment in BSP-approved securities can be settled in three to four days, as compared with the four to six months needed previously.

In 1994, the flotation of fixed- and floating-rate Treasury notes was approved. The year 1995 saw the approval of trading in longer-term government securities such as three-, five-, and seven-year fixed-rate notes. The authorities also required all EKBs to list at least 10 per cent of their paid-up capital on the exchange over the next three years. These moves were aimed at making the banks more accountable to the public. Their dealings would then become more transparent through public disclosures; such moves would also deepen the financial market.

The capitalization of the stock market increased from P 170 billion in 1990 to P 1.54 trillion by the end of 1995. That represents an annual increase of about 163 per cent. The market enjoyed an annual average increase of 245 per cent in the value of turnover, which increased from P 28.7 billion in 1990 to P 378.98 billion in 1995. The turnover in volume showed an increase from P 266.8 billion to P 884.7 billion during the same period. At the end of 1995, there were 200 listed companies offering a total of 300 securities. However, as a result of the 1997 financial crisis, the market lost most of the gains made since 1994.

The derivatives market
The derivatives market is still at an early stage of development, as is common with most developing countries. However, there are good prospects for the future of these markets. Internal policies leading to foreign exchange liberalization as well as external changes, which increase the international integration of financial markets, make the prospect for hedging in the derivatives markets desirable for the economy. As a part of the reform process, the Monetary Board approved the issue of new rules in 1995. That document defines the scope of derivatives trading activities by the banks and other financial institutions. It also prescribes prudential rules to be followed by the financial institutions engaged in such activities. Under these regulations, banks and other institutions engaged in such trading are required to obtain the approval of the BSP in addition to having to comply with pre-qualification standards/requirements to ensure that the institution's capability to monitor and manage risks associated with derivatives are not compromised.

In 1996, the authorities issued additional guidelines to implement the rules and regulations on financial derivatives. These guidelines specify two types of approval/authority to engage in derivative transactions: one for the currency swaps and forwards (regular type); and another for the more extended type of transactions. As a result of these reforms, which came into force in January 1997, 44 banks and four non-banks applied for derivatives licences.

The foreign exchange market
Foreign exchange policies started with strict controls in the 1950s, liberalization in the 1960s, reimposition of controls in the 1970s to early 1980s and the eventual bold liberalization of the 1990s. Free float of the currency took place in August 1997. The 1990s reforms were aimed at deregulating controls and

at widening the coverage of the areas for liberalization. In the pre-reform period, the foreign exchange market was very much regulated and was segmented into three categories. These were the interbank market, the customer market and the parallel market. The interbank market allowed banks and the BSP to participate in on-floor trading. This trading was organized by the BAP on their floor on a daily basis between 4.30 p.m. and 5.00 p.m. on weekdays. The customer market was much larger than the interbank market. The parallel market was the informal market outside the banking system but the volume of transactions was as great as in the customer market, basically using the remittances from overseas Filipino workers. This market had a high premium of up to 20 per cent during the 1980s.[11]

The reforms in the foreign exchange markets were initiated in the year 1991 with the implementation of Circular 1300, which authorized the establishment of the foreign exchange clearing and settlement system (FECSS) with coordination by the PCHS. Bold reforms to deregulate the system were, however, only implemented beginning in 1992. Some of the major changes in foreign exchange policies involved the removal of FX surrender requirements, liberalization of access to foreign currency deposit facilities, and the lifting of quantitative restrictions on foreign investments including profit remittances. Moreover, banks were allowed to sell foreign exchange to residents for any non-trade purpose without the need of prior BSP approval and documentary requirements for amounts not exceeding US$50 000. More specifically, Circular 1318, issued in 1992, increased the limits on the amount of FX that foreign exchange institutions may sell to residents without prior CB approval. Circular 1327, issued in the same year, allows banks to keep long and short FX positions that may not exceed 25 per cent and 15 per cent, respectively, of their unimpaired capital. The Philippine dealing system, which was launched in 1992 under a new law, lifted restrictions on the off-floor FX trading among the KBs. Circular 1353, implemented in the same year, lifts all quantitative restrictions on the amounts of FX that may be purchased from banks.

In 1994, the authorities replaced the system of foreign exchange of the BSP with the Philippine domestic dollar transfer system, operated by the private-sector Citibank, Manila. In 1995, Circular 89 was issued to allow commercial banks to operate under the expanded foreign currency deposit system and to engage in foreign currency swaps. The authorities also increased the amount of domestic currency that can be brought in or taken out of the country or electronically transferred without BSP authorization up to P 10 000 under BSP Circular 98 issued in the same year. In 1997, under BSP Circular 40, the amount of FX that foreign exchange institutions are allowed to sell to residents for any non-trade purposes without prior BSP approval was further increased from $25 000 to $50 000.

Table 14.5 Monetary aggregates, national income accounts and balance of payments (% of GDP)

	5-year average			Annual							
	1976–80	1981–85	1986–90	1991	1992	1993	1994	1995	1996	1997	1998
M1	9.2	7.4	8.1	8.6	8.7	9.7	9.4	10.2	10.6	11.0	10.7
M2	21.4	27.9	30.4	34.5	36.2	42.1	45.7	50.3	54.0	61.5	60.8
Trade balance	−5.3	−5.8	−4.9	−6.9	−8.7	−11.7	−11.3	−12.3	−13.5	−18.7	−16.3
Budget balance	−1.2	−2.7	−3.1	−2.1	−1.2	−1.5	1.1	0.5	0.3	0.06	−1.9
Current account balance	−5.1	−6.1	−3.6	−2.2	−1.9	−5.5	−4.6	−2.7	−4.8	7.2	1.18
Private consumption	65.9	68.3	70.9	73.4	75.4	76.1	74.3	74.1	73.5	72.7	74.4
Gov. consumption	9.0	8.0	9.2	9.9	9.7	10.1	10.8	11.4	11.9	13.0	13.3
GFCF	25.3	23.8	19.4	20.0	20.9	23.8	23.6	22.2	23.4	24.5	21.3
Gov. expenditure	13.0	11.7	17.0	19.2	19.7	18.5	18.3	17.9	18.5	19.3	19.2

Notes:
M2 = (M1 + quasi-money).
GFCF – Gross fixed capital formation.

Source: IMF, *International Financial Statistics*, various issues.

3.3   Financial Liberalization Effects

Financial-sector reforms in the Philippines were not as consistent as in some other early reformers discussed elsewhere in this book. The reforms, however, did improve the economy and as evident from the statistics on some important indicators, the economy enjoyed high growth, budget surplus, increasing capital formation, and so on until the Asian crisis hit most countries in the East Asian region, including the Philippines. The economy is going through a recession now and complete recovery is not expected until 2001.

One area where reforms worked well was in attracting foreign and portfolio investment, which reached a peak in 1996. Again, due to the reasons mentioned earlier, this scenario could not be sustained. Lack of confidence in the market has shifted the trend and both FDI and portfolio investment have been significantly affected. Looking at the financial deepening (Table 14.7), M2/GDP has improved significantly since 1991. The ratio increased from 35 per cent in 1991 to 62 per cent in 1997. This is a remarkable increase over a short period of six years. The figures on the financial intermediation ratio suggest that the private sector has easy access to credit. FIR (private) increased from 21 per cent in 1992 to almost 68 per cent in 1996 before dropping to 48 per cent in 1998. FIR (public) also showed an increase, from 12 per cent in 1991 to 15 per cent in 1996. Public-sector borrowing has increased, however, during the last two years. Table 14.7 also shows that the reforms increased gross capital formation and FDI.

4.   ASSESSMENT OF FUTURE PROSPECTS

As one of the three populous countries within the economically more developed ASEAN regional grouping, this country has favourable prospects for fast development. The Philippines are positioned almost at the centre of the two great growth regions in East Asia and Pacific America. It is also a member of the AFTA and the APEC trade and development groups. Its prospects for development have been hampered in the past by two factors. It suffered rule by a corrupt regime over a lengthy period, during which few investment and trade flows took place while at the same time the rest of ASEAN was making substantial progress in economic and social development through liberalization. Second, there were serious insurrections in different parts of the country both during the Marcos regime, largely because of his manipulation, and in the period after his exile. It took a period of reconstruction under two later governments to put the country back to work. The new government that took power in 1999 is a populist one headed by a former movie star. There are signs

Table 14.6 *Investments in the Philippines*

	5-year average			Annual							
	1976–80	1981–85	1986–90	1991	1992	1993	1994	1995	1996	1997
Direct investment (net)	42.4	62.8	492.6	544.0	228.0	864.0	1289.0	1079.0	1335.0	1086.0
Portfolio investment (net)	4.4	2.6	62.4	110.0	40.0	–52.0	269.0	1190.0	3697.0	591.0
FDI (inflow)	53.0	62.8	492.6	544.0	228.0	1238.0	1591.0	1478.0	1517.0	1222.0

Sources: IMF, *International Financial Statistics*, various issues; World Bank, *World Bank Databank*, Feb. 1997; ADB, *Asian Development Outlook, 1998, 1999.*

Table 14.7 Indicators of financial liberalization (% of GDP)

	5-year average			Annual							
	1976–80	1981–85	1986–90	1991	1992	1993	1994	1995	1996	1997	1998
Money depth (M2/GDP)	21.4	27.9	30.4	34.5	36.2	42.1	45.7	50.3	54.0	61.5	60.8
Inter-relations											
FIR (total)/GDP	41.78	37.7	25.7	31.3	20.0	43.8	44.5	52.6	63.9	74.6	65.2
FIR (public)/GDP	9.0	4.3	7.6	11.7	–0.65	17.4	15.8	15.1	14.9	18.1	17.2
FIR (private)/GDP	37.3	30.2	19.6	28.1	20.6	26.4	29.1	37.5	66.7	56.5	48.0
GFCF/GDP	25.3	23.8	19.4	20.0	20.9	23.8	23.6	22.2	23.9	23.8	19.3
FDI/GDP	0.3	0.2	1.4	1.16	0.42	2.33	2.29	2.03	2.50	2.02	2.75

Notes:
M2 = (M1 + quasi-money).
FIR = financial intermediation ratio (32an + 32b + 32c + 32d) – claims on public sector (32an + 32b + 32c), claims on private sector (32d).
GFCF = gross fixed capital formation.
FDI = foreign direct investment.

Sources: IMF, *International Financial Statistics*, various issues; ADB, *Asian Development Outlook, 1998, 1999;* World Bank (Balance of Payment Capital Account) – for foreign direct investments.

of policy changes consistent with the populist platform on which this government was elected. One such sign is the stand on the Moro ethnic rebellion, which, under the previous government, was managed with a strong dose of foresight and fairness. If the handling of this civil war gets out of control – there are other examples, Sri Lanka and India, in this book for the Philippines – consequences for regaining the growth momentum are not likely to be favourable.

Given the more auspicious events in the period since the start of the 1990s, the Philippines is making attempts to reform the economy. The growth experience of the country from 1990 to mid-1997 was very favourable. This has established credentials for this country as one that could get its act together for development. However, the 1997 Asian financial crisis has led to pessimism, in fact severe economic recession in the period around 1998, and growth collapse. With IMF help to reconstruct the economy during 1998 and the better-managed central bank being able to take the correct measures, it was expected that this country would move to a small positive growth in 1999. Its currency regained half its lost ground by the end of 1999. The export sector is beginning to grow fast. As is normal for economic recoveries to take place after about two years of devaluation experience, there is an expectation that the Filipino economy will be back on the path to growth in the twenty-first century through domestic efficiency and an export-led stimulus expected soon, now that the strong dose of restructuring and efficiency improvements is beginning to take effect. For this, the politics of a populist leader must not wag the economic dog!

NOTES

1. The US involvement was also required due to certain strategic and security reasons that are not the concerns of this study. It has to do with forward security for USA.
2. The phrase 'people power' was coined to describe the bravery of ordinary citizens (including nuns from the Catholic Church) who confronted the soldiers who had orders to shoot peaceful demonstrators. The reason they took to the streets was the televizing of false election results by the state television when the actual results tallied at polling stations were noted by the public to be favouring the opposition candidate. People power only worked in the Philippines, and has failed in other dictatorial situations in Asia. People power was dismissed by other dictatorial regimes in the region.
3. Similar laws had been passed in Korea, Malaysia and Singapore some ten years earlier.
4. Jayasuriya (1987; Table 4.1, p. 201).
5. It was the revamping of the banking sector that helped the Philippines to absorb well some of the early shock of the Asian financial crisis in 1997.
6. Many Southeast Asian economies including the Philippines took a dip in the second half of 1997 due to the currency crisis. The Philippines currency was not hit as hard as some other currencies, such as those of Thailand and Indonesia, but the superb growth performance during the last decade was definitely affected. The causes and effects of the Asian currency crisis will be discussed in a separate chapter. This section, therefore, covers the pre-currency crisis outlook of the economy.

 7. BSP (1996a), Table 8.
 8. These reforms are summarized in Table 14.3.
 9. Latest reliable statistics on capital market activities are not available.
10. Bangko Sentral Ng Pilipinas.
11. Our conversations with some of the officials in the Philippines revealed that the market was used as the major source of currency outflow during the Marcos era. Some reports indicate that the pesos converted into US dollars in the parallel illegal exchange markets were transferred out of the country in big bags (sacks) so that there could be no account of what happened. This is one of many similar bad examples of currency outflows when the stability of the economy is no longer in the hands of the regulators.

15. Sri Lanka: a case of development regression

1. BACKGROUND

Sri Lanka, known romantically as the jewel of Asia and previously named Ceylon, became independent in 1948 by a peaceful transfer of power after it had been under Portuguese, Dutch and British colonial rule for centuries. At the time of independence, the economy was largely dependent on an export-oriented plantation sector dominated by three major crops: tea, rubber and coconuts. The physical infrastructure was just sufficient and the industrial sector comprised mainly cottage industries and services. Before independence and even in some early years after independence, the plantation helped to generate surpluses and raise government revenues. As a result, the government was able to allocate sufficient funds for social development, including education and health. At the time of independence Sri Lanka had one of the highest per capita incomes in South and Southeast Asia (Karunaratne and Fonseka, 1993, p. 193). Now, Sri Lanka has one of the highest literacy rates in Southeast Asia. With partisan politics degenerating into ethnic war, it is now sliding fast.

Sri Lanka was probably the first nation in the Asian region to obtain a right to full internal self-government (in 1931), thus making politicians responsible for people's needs and accountable for their own actions. Having this institutional arrangement was a big achievement, especially before independence and given the fact that Sri Lanka represents multi-racial, multi-lingual and multi-religious society despite its Buddhist majority. At the time of independence in 1948, an English-educated class cutting across all groups took over power and implemented certain important economic and social policies. Education and health remained an important focus of these policies. The United National Party (UNP) and the Sri Lanka Freedom Party (SLFP) are the two political parties that have ruled the country.

Although both parties were able to bring in some significant changes in the economy, their agenda and strategies were different. The UNP basically pursued market-oriented economic strategies and focused on agricultural development, promoted free enterprises and land ownership, which helped to accelerate economic growth. On the other hand, the SLFP pursued welfare-oriented strategies aimed at creating a mixed economy with a strong public enterprise and industrial development, a measure akin to that of the Northern neighbours that sowed the seeds of its destruction.

Given certain inherited benefits including a very high literacy rate, excellent health-care facilities and established political institutions which Sri Lanka had at the time of independence while other countries lacked most of these, this country could have been the first 'tiger' in the region. However, the situation started to deteriorate as early as the 1950s. High population growth and declining terms of trade worsened income inequality and increased unemployment. Political instability set in with a regime change in every parliamentary election. These economic problems meant that ethnic differences were highlighted as the source of the problems between the majority of Sinhalese and largest minority of Tamils. Karunaratne and Fonseka (1993, p. 196) note that 'Adjustments were made in regard to language, education, employment and new land settlements. Apparently these were intended to restore national resources, and economic and social opportunities to the majority Sinhalese'. The Tamil minority took this as a threat and since 1991 engage in a civil war, with which Sri Lanka is still very much occupied.[1] Discriminatory policies imposed on the minority, it is claimed, drove a small section of the minority to rebellion and then to war for independence. These developments diverted the focus from economic and social issues to internal security. Most of the resources that could have been used for continued economic development have been wasted to overcome the ethnic problems. As a result, Sri Lanka, which had the potential to excel in the Southeast and South Asian regions, has been experiencing lack of growth for a long while now. At the time when the whole region, especially the neighbouring countries, has moved to openness, Sri Lanka is bogged down in war-making and cannot undertake such policies.

2. ECONOMIC AND FINANCIAL STRUCTURE

Sri Lanka could be categorized as an inward-oriented economy during 1956–77 (Wickramanayake, 1995). During this phase, the economy experienced increasing restrictions and controls and went for import-substituting industrialization despite having such a small economy. The whole package included exchange and import controls, high duties and tariffs, quantitative restrictions, a schedule of administered interest rates and labour-market interventions. During this period, the tariff rates ranged between 10 and 300 per cent. In 1966, the government issued the White Paper on Foreign Investment, discouraging FDI by imposing restrictions on the repatriation of dividends and profits. The Companies Law of 1974 authorized the government to nationalize foreign-registered companies.

During this first phase, Sri Lanka experienced a severe form of financial repression. The Bank of Ceylon was nationalized in the 1960s and was renamed as the People's Bank. Restrictions were also imposed on foreign banks. Moreover, banks were subject to interest rate controls and credit ceilings. Later, efforts to monetize the government budget deficit resulted in increasing inflation. Restrictions on interest rates and increasing inflation produced negative real interest rates, which reduced savings and increased consumption. However, with all the controls, the social-sector policies remained untouched and the government continued its policies of food subsidy, free education and health care, with disastrous consequences on the government budget.

A new government took power in 1977 and introduced a package of economic reforms. The liberalization policies included unifying exchange rates, trade liberalization, measures to attract FDI, pricing policies, fiscal policies, policies to restructure the banking sector, and public-sector developments. As a result of implementing these measures, the economy registered an average growth rate of 6 per cent during 1978–83 compared to merely 2.9 per cent during 1971–77.

The dual exchange rate regime was transformed to a single managed float system linking the Sri Lankan currency (SR rupee) to a trade-weighted basket of currencies. This resulted in a devaluation of about 46 per cent against the US dollar, which indicated the true value of the domestic currency. The new government also abolished exchange controls and implemented limited current account convertibility. Restriction of the repatriation of profits of foreign entrepreneurs was removed, thus giving some incentives to foreign investors to invest in Sri Lanka. The government also introduced tax holidays to increase private domestic investment. Free trade zones were established to develop the domestic trade sector; this was in recognition of what was then successfully being pursued in China.

The summary indicators in Table 15.1 show the progress Sri Lanka has made during the last three decades. The table shows that the economy experienced steady but slow growth over the period 1971–96. The best performance, however, was in 1978, just after the economy was opened up, when the growth rate recorded was 8.2 per cent, the highest since 1970. The growth in the last six years has been above 5 per cent, which is reasonable given that most resources have been used for conducting the civil war. The figures on gross domestic savings and investment are very poor and show only 15 and 25 per cent of GDP respectively. The major problem seems to be the huge fiscal deficit, registered at about 9 per cent of GDP in 1996 and the very high debt-service ratio, accounting for 15 per cent of total export earnings. As stated in the last section, Sri Lanka's record on social indicators is comparable to that of relatively developed East Asian countries, with literacy rate above 90 per cent. These

Table 15.1 Basic economic and social indicators of development in Sri Lanka

Indicators	1971–80	1981–90	1991–93	1994	1995	1996	1997	1998
National accounts								
GDP (Growth)	4.4	4.3	5.0	5.6	5.5	3.8	6.4	5.3
Per capita GDP (in US$)	219	368	537	649	667	682	800	7.84
Private consumption/GDP	0.774	0.775	0.759	0.751	0.740	0.700	0.723	0.713
Gov. consumption/GDP	0.092	0.092	0.095	0.097	0.147	0.145	0.104	0.098
Financial indicators								
Gross Domestic Savings (% of GDP)	13.8	12.9	15.9	15.2	15.3	15.5	21.4	19.3
GFCF (% of GDP)	17.53	24.91	23.79	26.64	24.99	23.89	24.35	26.6
Inflation	8.91	12.36	11.77	8.45	7.67	15.9	9.6	9.4
M2/GDP (% of GDP)	24.7	30.5	31.1	33.2	34.7	33.0	32.40	31.7
Fiscal balance (% of GDP)	–9.9	–12.7	–9.1	–10.0	–9.6	–7.8	–7.9	–7.7
CAB (% of GDP)	–3.2	–6.7	–5.2	–7.9	–6.2	–5.3	–2.9	–3.1
Trade balance (% of GDP)	–3.7	–9.7	–8.1	–9.4	–7.2	–5.9	–4.3	3.79
Discount rate (bank rate)	8.1	12.5	17.0	17.0	17.0	17.0	17.0	17.0
Debt service ratio (% of exports)	18.45	22.0	16.5	13.7	14.4	13.4	13.4	12.1

Social indicators

IMF classification	Low	Low	Low	Low	Low	Low	Low	Low
Literacy rate	87.2	86.9	n.a.	90.1	n.a.	n.a.	n.a.	n.a.
Unemployment rate	17.9	15.0	14.4	13.1	12.3	11.4	11.3	n.a.
Expenditure on education (% of GDP)	3.23	2.63	2.74	3.06	2.83	2.65	n.a.	n.a.
Expenditure on health (% of GDP)	1.72	1.51	1.45	1.59	1.64	1.56	n.a.	n.a.
Population growth	1.653	1.424	1.221	1.362	1.4	1.1	1.3	1.2

Notes:
GFCF = gross fixed capital formation.
CAB = current account balance.

Sources: IMF, *International Financial Statistics*, various issues; *Asian Development Outlook 1998, 1999*; *Government Finance Statistics Yearbook, 1985–1996*; Central Bank of Sri Lanka, 1998.

statistics show that Sri Lanka has made good progress during the last ten years after abandoning the growth-retarding policies of the earlier governments since 1971. The restructuring of the financial sector will be discussed in detail in the next section.

3.   LIBERALIZATION

3.1   Economic Liberalization

First, we examine the overall growth in different sectors of the economy. Summary statistics are provided in Tables 15.2 and 15.3. The economy grew at an average rate of about 4 per cent during 1951–71 but declined to 2.9 per cent during 1971–77. Sri Lanka enjoyed very high growth of about 5.3 per cent in the post-reform period in the following years after the real and financial sectors were liberalized. However, due to sporadic civil war in later years, the growth registered sharp declines. It picked up later and, on average, the economy grew at about 5.3 per cent during the 1990s. The main contributor to this high growth in the post-liberalization period was the manufacturing sector. It appears that real-sector reforms did have a major impact on enhancing income growth despite other constraints the economy faced.[2]

This was probably the result of some successful privatization deals and improvement in domestic investment. Gross domestic capital formation increased from 17 per cent of GDP in 1971–80 to about 25 per cent in the post-liberalization period. Similarly, domestic savings increased from 13 per cent of GDP to about 16 per cent during the same period. As is evident from these figures, growth in domestic investment was much higher than in domestic savings, which means that the government had to inject funds in public-sector development projects. The official estimates[3] show that FDI accounted for 1 per cent of GDP in the post-liberalization period. This is very different from the experience of other countries, where, except in Korea and Taiwan, FDI has been anywhere from 2 to 26 per cent of GDP.

Although the economy has improved in the post-reform period, with a reasonable GDP growth of 5.5 per cent during the last few years, this growth is comparable to many other countries in the region for the same period. Also, inflation, which was brought under control up to 1995, began to soar to around 15 per cent in 1996. This was due to some unexpected natural hazards, which left adverse effects on domestic food production, worsened internal conditions and led to sharp decline in revenue collection, which might have forced the regime to use inflationary financing as a means to finance the fiscal deficit.

Table 15.2 Growth rates of basic economic indicators

	5-year average			Annual average							
	1976–80	1981–85	1986–90	1991	1992	1993	1994	1995	1996	1997	1998
GDP	5.5	5.9	3.4	4.8	4.3	6.9	5.6	5.5	3.8	6.4	5.3
Inflation	9.9	12.0	12.4	12.2	11.4	11.7	8.5	7.7	15.9	9.6	9.4
Revenue	23.6	21.9	13.4	12.5	12.2	14.8	11.7	23.8	7.4	12.7	9.5
M1	24.95	14.87	16.24	17.69	7.42	18.58	18.71	6.75	4.0	9.8	12.1
M2	34.89	18.92	12.64	22.44	16.43	23.13	19.19	19.44	10.8	13.8	13.0
FDI	213.20	–10.43	11.39	135.18	–101.6	58.6	–14.4	–97.0	114.2	2.58	n.a.
Trade balance	24.95	14.87	16.24	70.31	–11.14	3.78	46.21	–9.2	–91.9	–21.4	–11.3

Note: M2 = (M1 + quasi-money).

Sources: IMF, *International Financial Statistics*, various issues; World Bank, *World Bank Databank*, Feb. 1997; Central Bank of Sri Lanka, 1998.

Table 15.3 Monetary aggregates, national income accounts and balance of payments (as % of GDP)

| | 5-year average | | | Annual | | | | | | |
	1976–80	1981–85	1986–90	1991	1992	1993	1994	1995	1996	1997
M1	14.2	11.5	13.0	12.5	11.8	11.9	12.2	11.4	10.1	9.6
M2	28.3	30.8	30.0	30.2	30.8	32.3	33.2	34.7	32.9	32.4
Trade deficit	-6.9	-11.0	-7.6	-9.2	-7.7	-7.4	-9.4	-7.2	-6.6	-4.3
Budget deficit	-12.2	-10.2	-9.4	-9.5	-5.4	-6.4	-8.5	-7.0	-6.6	-4.5
Current account deficit	-5.3	-9.1	-6.5	-6.8	-4.9	-3.8	-6.5	-4.5	-5.0	-2.7
Private consumption	76.9	77.3	77.1	77.4	75.4	74.8	75.1	74.0	70.0	72.4
Gov. consumption	9.8	10.5	13.1	13.6	12.7	13.2	13.0	14.7	14.5	10.3
GFCF	22.9	26.8	22.4	22.6	23.5	25.2	26.6	25.0	25.7	24.4
Gov. expenditure	35.1	31.6	30.5	29.3	26.9	27.0	26.7	28.2	27.6	25.7

Notes:
M2 = (M1 + quasi-money).
GFCF = gross fixed capital formation.

Source: IMF, *International Financial Statistics*, various issues.

410

Fiscal-sector reforms

Since independence and up to the end of the 1980s, spending on public-sector development was the government's main area of concern. This improved socioeconomic status of the people – spending on education, health care and retirement benefits – received priority. It was only recently that the private sector was encouraged to become involved in these activities to help relieve some of the burden on public-sector spending. As the indicators in Table 15.3 show, government consumption is a sizeable amount (15 per cent of GDP), which is much higher than in other countries in the South Asian region. The government also has a relatively large spending figure, amounting to an average of about 30 per cent of GDP during the last ten years with an average annual increase of about 18 per cent.

Until 1977, most of the state budget was allocated to the then state-owned enterprises and nationalized units, particularly for their investment needs and to recoup their losses. The government controlled a large proportion of land under tea, rubber and coconut crops. The share of the public sector in domestic industrial production increased from 15 per cent in the 1950s to a massive 55 per cent in the 1970s. This was the time when the government was largely dependent on aid from orthodox Communist China, and the policy of state incorporation was thus not surprising. Total public-sector employment increased from 8 per cent in 1951 to 17 per cent in 1975.[4] All these factors put mounting pressure on the fiscal sector, especially as it had reduced resources to meet other obligations.

Denationalization and privatization under the new policies is naturally taking time to yield favourable results, especially when most of the state-owned enterprises are loss-making units, which makes them difficult to sell while also continuing to drain public-sector resources. Most of the emerging economies experienced this bitter fact – as was also finally recognized by China in 1998 – with a slow pace of privatization and they are still struggling. Sri Lanka is no exception. Hence, during the early stage of the post-liberalization period, the share of public spending as a percentage of GDP did not change much. The main sector of concentration was domestic industry, where the private sector's share in the value-added in manufacturing increased from 45 per cent in the 1970s to 65 per cent in the late 1980s.

Improvements, however, were realized in the 1990s when the government was able to privatize some of the large public-sector units. The government encourages the private sector to invest in domestic industry, management of agricultural resources, infrastructure development, the financial sector, and so on. Privatization efforts showed some success and by 1997, 73 state-owned enterprises were privatized, generating revenues totalling Rs 42 billion (US$750 million in 1997 exchange rates). As a result, government expenditure as a ratio of GDP declined from 35 per cent during 1975–80 to 28 per cent in 1996.

Compared with the large share of public expenditure in GDP during the 1970s, total revenues accounted for only 20 per cent, which went down to 19 per cent in 1996. The economic reform package of 1977 also introduced some measures to improve the taxation structure. These efforts were in line with the arguments of supply-side economists whereby some of the taxes and duties were removed while the tax base for others was reduced. At the time, the government introduced the goods and services tax (GST), the diesel and luxury tax on vehicles, and turnover tax on imports. Most of these measures were introduced only in 1997–98, and the outcome has yet to be seen.

Although the volume of outstanding debt increased in the post-1977 period, its relative size as a percentage of GDP declined due to availability of alternative sources of deficit financing, including foreign resources. In August 1997, the government retired Treasury bills worth Rs 10 000 million using the proceeds from privatization. This helped to reduce the interest burden on the public debt. Given moderate success in privatization efforts, debt retirement may continue and will reduce debt servicing.

External-sector policies

As stated in the first section, Sri Lanka inherited an open-economy environment at the time of independence in 1948. However, inward-oriented policies in the 1960s and up to the mid-1970s completely changed the external-sector policies. As a result of these policies, Sri Lanka's export share in the world economy declined from 0.39 per cent in 1956 to 0.07 per cent in 1977 while imports continued to grow at an average of 5.7 per cent. This changed the trade account from surplus of 3.2 per cent of GDP registered during 1948–56 to an average trade account deficit of 2.4 per cent of GDP over the period 1956–77. This deficit further rose in the post-liberalization period due to imports of capital goods needed for large projects in the public sector.

It is difficult to assess the impact of post-liberalization policies as most of the measures were introduced amidst civil unrest in the late 1980s or early 1990s. However, some signs of improvement can be seen in an increase in exports. For example, total trade as a percentage of GDP increased to 68 per cent in 1996 as compared to 35 per cent in 1977. The major policy changes in the external sector were the unification of exchange rates and the adoption of a managed float system in 1977, opening up of the current account, changes in tariff structure and quantitative restrictions, and in export-licensing requirements.

One of the important issues in external-sector policy is the mounting external debt, which increased rapidly in the post-liberalization period due to increased foreign capital. External debt, which accounted for 34 per cent of GDP in 1978 (compare that with the average of about 7 per cent for Malaysia even during the crisis), rose to 57 per cent in 1988 and moderated later to 49 per cent of GDP in 1996. As of 1996, the total external debt amounted to about US$10 billion, which is 66 per cent of GDP. The debt-service ratio as a percentage of GDP is 10.3 per cent, while as a percentage of export earnings from goods and services it is 15 per cent. This is an alarming situation given that total foreign assets in 1996 were valued at US$2.4 billion, which is only 26 per cent of the total outstanding debt whereas the same amount is equivalent to five months of import value. The need, therefore, is to introduce a combination of fiscal and monetary policies. This would require a sizeable reduction in public expenditure, probably through downsizing of the government, increasing revenues by changing the tax structure, privatizing state-owned enterprises and using the proceeds to retire some of the external debt, expanding the export sector, developing a secondary market for government bonds to reduce dependence on external borrowings and last, but not least important, improving the country's competitiveness through exchange rate management.

3.2 Financial Liberalization

At the time of independence, Sri Lanka inherited a financial system that was basically servicing the urban commercial sector and plantations. Over the following fifty years, the country has made significant progress in revamping its financial sector: in this respect, it followed policies very similar to those of its Northern neighbours. Although major reforms were only introduced in 1977, some measures in financial-sector development were also taken during the 1960–77 period of inward-oriented policies such as diversifying the banking sector and developing it to service the interior. We begin with the role of monetary policy, which is an important element in discussion on financial-sector liberalization. A summary of financial liberalization in Sri Lanka is provided below:

Monetary policy
Since the establishment of the Central Bank of Sri Lanka (CBSL) in 1950, on monetary policy aimed to achieve two objectives: stabilization and development. Among the major instruments of monetary policy, the CBSL introduced different instruments to achieve depth and liquidity in the market. Open-market operations, which are considered very effective monetary policy tools, were not used in the pre-1977 period, except over a brief period in the 1950s. They have, however, been used after liberalization policies were initiated in the post-1977 era. In the period of inward policies, the emphasis was more on direct control measures. In reality, efforts to use open-market operations as an instrument were hampered by the limited availability of a portfolio of government securities. Moreover, the underdeveloped primary financial markets and the limited existence of a secondary market for government securities acted as major impediments to an active pursuit of a more market-based monetary policy.

Table 15.4 *Financial sector reforms and regulatory changes (in chronological order)*

Date of reforms	Liberalization policies implemented
1950	Establishment of the Central Bank of Sri Lanka under the Monetary Law Act.
1961	People's Bank set up under People's Bank Act.
	Bank of Ceylon nationalized under Finance Act.
	Insurance Corporation of Ceylon established under the Insurance Corporation Act.
1972	National Savings Bank established under the National Savings Bank Act.
1975	State Mortgage and Investment Bank established under the State Mortgage and Investment Law.
1977	Deregulation of interest rates.
	Relaxation of exchange controls.
	Dual exchange rate system abolished and a unified exchange rate system adopted.
	Fixed exchange rate system replaced by floating rate system.
	Foreign banks allowed to open branches.
	New domestic private banks allowed to operate.
1978	Credit ceiling on commercial banks removed.
1979	National Development bank of Sri Lanka established.
	Banking system opened to foreign-owned and private commercial banks.
	National Insurance Corporation established through the Insurance Act.
	Sri Lanka Export Credit Insurance Corporation established under the Export Credit Insurance Act.
	Control of Finance Companies Act became effective to control and regulate non-bank financial institutions.
	Foreign currency banking units (FCBUs) established.
1981	Secondary market for Treasury bills established.
1982	Employees' Trust Fund created.
1983	Merchant banks and venture capital companies permitted to operate.
1984	Securities Council established to regulate the securities market.
	A public trading floor established by the Colombo Brokers Association.
1985	Regional Rural Development Bank established.

1987	The Securities Council Act enacted to regulate securities market.
	Insurance sector opened to local and foreign private-sector participation.
1988	Banking Act passed.
1990	Credit Information Bureau of Sri Lanka created.
	Debt Recovery Act and Recovery of Loans by Banks implemented.
	Colombo Securities Exchange (pte) Ltd changed to Colombo Stock Exchange.
1992	Foreigners allowed to buy shares of companies registered on the Colombo Stock Exchange (CSE).
1993	Sale of Treasury bills under 'repos' initiated by the central bank.
1994	Remaining restrictions on current international transactions removed.
1995	Amendment to the Credit Information Bureau Act allowing merchant banks and other institutions to have access to the Credit Information Bureau.
	Amendment to the National Savings Bank Act allowing restructuring of NSB.
	Amendment to the Banking Act enhancing regulatory and supervisory power of the central bank.
	Amendments in the following to improve government securities trading system:
	– Monetary Law Act
	– Registered Stock and Securities Ordinance (LSSO)
	– Local Treasury Bill Ordinance (LTBO).
	Commercial banks allowed to obtain foreign loans up to 5% of their capital reserves.
1996	Over-the-counter (OTC) board system introduced.
1997	Partial capital account liberalization takes effect allowing non-Board of Investment (BOI) exporters to obtain foreign currency loans through domestic and offshore units of commercial banks.
	Treasury bond auction initiated.
	CSE started fully automated screen-based trading system.

The CBSL made extensive use of the Bank rate and the statutory reserve requirement (SRR) as instruments of monetary policy. This was possible due to complete control on market forces to determine the price of market instruments. The SRR was set at 12 per cent for savings and time deposits; for demand deposits it was set at 5 per cent until 1960. In 1961, the central bank introduced a new SRR when all demand deposits with commercial banks over the level prevailing on 1 February 1961 were subject to a 38 per cent special RR. This restriction was extended to the People's Bank in 1965, requiring 40 per cent of SRR on demand deposits. These tight monetary conditions significantly reduced the profitability and competitiveness of commercial banks. These restrictions continued until 1975 and were then relaxed.

The government also used tight credit controls during 1960–77 when stringent restrictions were imposed on import financing, overdraft facilities to foreign firms and private-sector investment. Administrative controls on interest rates were retained. After the liberalization policies starting in 1977, the monetary policy focus was shifted from direct controls to market-based tools. The first positive sign was the removal of restrictions on interest rates, which were artificially set at a very low level in the pre-reform period. Policies were also implemented to gradually eliminate some of the credit controls, including the overall credit ceiling. SRRs were still a major tool of monetary policy. Though SSR on demand deposits was reduced to 16 per cent, it was still very high compared with prevailing rates in many other countries in the region. The central bank also introduced varying SRRs on different maturities of time deposits. By 1997, the SRR was reduced to 12 per cent. In 1992, the central bank imposed an SRR of 10 per cent on foreign currency deposits, which was later reduced significantly.

Another major change in post-liberalization monetary policy was the use of open-market operations (OMOs) as a major tool of monetary policy, when aggressive OMOs were used in the late 1980s and in the early 1990s. This was achieved by establishing a Treasury bill market in 1980. In 1981, the CBSL initiated the sale of T-bills and later used its own securities in market transactions. It is hoped that these policies will increase the effectiveness of monetary policy, which is essential in a liberalized economy.

Exchange rate and interest rate reforms (see Table 15.5)
Interest rates in Sri Lanka were subject to administrative controls during the pre-reform period. These controls put banks at a competitive disadvantage in financial markets. Given the high inflation rate, the real return was negative most of the time, which left no incentive for investors to circulate their funds within the banking system. These controls were relaxed in the post-liberalization period. This is evident from central banks' published statistics, which show that total assets of commercial banks increased from a mere Rs 27 billion in 1980 to Rs 132 billion in 1990 and to Rs 390 billion in 1996. This is a phenomenal growth, somewhat similar to the experience of Indonesia when the latter reformed its commercial banking system in the 1980s.

Several changes were also made to the exchange rate system. The country started with a fixed exchange rate regime in 1948, when the rupee was 100 per

Table 15.5 Exchange rates and interest rates (annual averages)

| | 5-year average | | | Annual average | | | | | | |
	1976–80	1981–85	1986–90	1991	1992	1993	1994	1995	1996	1997
Exchange rate (mkt)	14.7	24.1	34.5	42.6	46.0	49.6	50.0	54.0	56.7	61.3
Interest rates:										
CB discount rate	9.70	13.00	12.00	17.00	17.00	17.00	17.00	17.00	17.00	17.0
Money market rate	13.85	19.15	17.70	25.42	21.63	25.65	18.54	41.87	24.33	18.42
Deposit rate	10.50	18.15	14.56	18.54	18.33	18.42	15.33	16.13	16.03	14.17
Lending rate	18.33	15.31	11.99	13.83	13.00	16.43	12.96	14.68	16.27	12.0
Gov. treasury bill rate	n.a.	13.35	12.05	13.75	16.19	16.52	12.68	16.81	17.4	12.59
Gov. bond yield	n.a.	15.00	11.88	15.68	16.00	16.25	n.a.	n.a.	n.a.	n.a.

Notes:
M2 = (M1 + quasi-money).
Central Bank (CB) discount rate (end of period).
Exchange rate: (Market Rate) = rupees per USD.

Sources: IMF, *International Financial Statistics*, various issues; Central Bank of Sri Lanka, 1998.

cent pegged to the pound sterling: this was similar to the policies followed in most neighbouring countries. Until 1966, the country managed to keep rupee–sterling parity without any devaluation, although the rupee was devalued against the US dollar. This resulted in overvaluation of domestic currency and losses were visible in the trade and current account balances. The first devaluation of 20 per cent against the pound sterling took place in 1967, triggered by a widening trade deficit and declining export prices. In 1968, the government introduced the foreign exchange entitlement certificate scheme (FEECS), which meant a dual exchange rate system, with one official exchange rate applicable to essential imports and non-traditional exports while the other rate, a bit higher, was applied to trade-related transactions. This dual exchange rate system continued until 1977 when the government decided to delink the rupee from the pound sterling. Eventually, in November 1977, the exchange rate was unified with a managed float system. The US dollar was made the intervention currency and the rupee was devalued by a huge 46 per cent.

The system went through some liberalization during the following period. The controls on foreign exchange were liberalized, with commercial banks permitted to open foreign currency accounts for non-residents. By 1996, commercial banks were also allowed to obtain limited foreign loans.

Foreign direct investment

Portfolio investment and FDI are considered to be important factors in the rapid growth of Southeast and East Asian economies.[5] As evident from Table 15.6, Sri Lanka's record is very poor. This is partly due to the internal ethnic conflicts that spilled over all parts of the country and threatened the security of foreign investors and their investments. Economic liberalization, which was initiated in 1977, did not help the establishment of an efficient capital market. Direct investment and portfolio investments, which showed some upward trends immediately after liberalization, are again on the decline. Direct investment, which recorded only US$18.04 million on average during 1976–80, rose to a peak of US$194.5 million in 1993 before declining to US$63.3 million in 1995. It improved substantially to US$430 million in 1997. Similarly, portfolio investment, which touched a peak in 1993, registering US$65.2 million is on a decline. The record for FDI is extremely poor for the reasons mentioned elsewhere in this chapter.

Central bank reforms

Sri Lanka was probably the first country in the Commonwealth to replace the currency board system with a central bank. The Central Bank of Sri Lanka was established in August 1950 under the Monetary Law Act of 1949. The main responsibilities of the Central Bank were to issue currency and act as the government banker, fiscal agent and economic adviser. In this way, the Central

Table 15.6 Investments in Sri Lanka (US$ million)

	5-year average			Annual						
	1976–80	1981–85	1986–90	1991	1992	1993	1994	1995	1996	1997
Direct investment (inflow)	18.04	41.90	39.60	48.40	122.60	194.50	166.40	56	119.9	430
Portfolio investment (net)	0.20	0.00	0.00	32.10	25.70	67.2	27.00	–2.00	6.6	13.1
Foreign direct investment (net)	18.04	41.60	38.24	100.02	121	187.6	158.1	56	119.9	430

Sources: IMF, *International Financial Statistics*, various issues; World Bank, *World Bank Databank*, Feb. 1997.

Bank was brought completely under the control of the political regime. Another main function of the bank was to promote credit facilities for businesses. The Finance Act of 1963, therefore, established the medium and long-term credit fund (MLCF) to provide refinancing facilities to the credit institutions for loan repayment in the areas of agriculture, industry, trade and commerce. In order to promote exports, the Central Bank established the Sri Lanka Export Credit Insurance Corporation (SLECIC) in 1979. In 1987, the bank initiated a deposit insurance scheme to provide protection to the depositors of commercial banks, regional rural development banks and cooperative rural banks. In 1988, the government introduced a new Banking Act, authorizing the Central Bank to direct credit in priority sectors such as agriculture, fisheries and small- and medium-scale industry. Loan refinancing in priority areas was part of the social-sector policies, which the country had pursued for a long time. Another similar activity was the direct involvement of the Central Bank in rural credits and a separate department was established in 1981: the Rural Credit Advisory Board (RCAB). The objective of this board was to improve the system and operations of rural banking in Sri Lanka.

Reforms in depository institutions

In the commercial banking sector, interest rates and deposit rates were increased. At the same time, the government imposed tight reserve requirements for and controls on lending by commercial banks. In the pre-reform period, the banking system comprised foreign-owned and domestic banks. The foreign banks were of two types: the exchange banks established during British colonial rule (to facilitate foreign exchange) and the regional foreign banks (to facilitate regional trade). The domestic banks were the Bank of Ceylon and the Cooperative Federal Bank. Due to a limited number of domestic banks, foreign banks basically dominated the banking business.

Two major developments took place in 1961, with the establishment of People's Bank and the nationalization of the Bank of Ceylon. At the same time, the government decided to freeze the time deposits of domestic residents in foreign banks. Foreign banks were prevented from opening any new branches. This artificially created a monopoly for domestic banks and helped them to open new branches. As a result, the number of branches of domestic banks increased from 28 in 1960 to 554 in 1975, while the number of branches of foreign banks declined from 17 in 1960 to 8 in 1975. With the removal of some of the above restrictions in 1977, the number of foreign bank branches later increased to 22 in 1987. In May 1979, the government introduced the Foreign Currency Banking Unit (FCBU) as a move to make Colombo a financial centre in South Asia. This was a dozen years too late, when Singapore had already developed a market! Commercial banks were allowed to engage in off-shore banking transactions with non-residents and limited on-shore banking transactions with approved residents. Incentives were provided for these activities.

To encourage private-sector saving, the government in 1971 merged three institutions: the Ceylon Savings Bank (established in 1832), the Post Office Savings Bank (established in 1885), and the National Savings Movement (established in 1945) into a new state-owned institution, the National Savings Bank (NSB). The number of branches increased from 15 in 1971 to 48 in 1987 while the nominal value of time and savings deposits increased from Rs 1.6 billion to Rs 9.0 billion over the same period (Wickramanayake, 1995, p. 34). The NSB plays an important role in the country. This is obvious from the fact that above 95 per cent of the total loan and investment portfolio is invested in government securities, which means that the NSB is the main buyer of government securities.

The government also encouraged foreign banks to invest in Sri Lanka by easing barriers to entry. Between 1977 and 1996, about 20 foreign banks were granted licences. At the same time, the authorities relaxed some of the restrictions on domestic and foreign banks to open new branches and expand business. The use of information technology helped the banks to join the Society for Worldwide Interbank Financial Telecommunications (SWIFT) system in 1993. Sri Lanka Automated Clearing House (SLACH) was also established during this time. The use of ATMs was also encouraged by the commercial banks. By 1997, 1809 ATMs were operating in Sri Lanka.

Rural banks
In view of the fact that Sri Lanka is basically a rural economy, with 70 per cent of the total population living in the rural area, rural banking became one of the priority areas to attract savings, as well as to provide credits to farmers, small agri-based industries and cottage industries. During the 1950s and 1960s, the demand for credit increased substantially as a result of land and agricultural reforms and the introduction of new farming technologies. The Cooperative Federal Bank was thus established in 1958 to cater to the needs of the rural population. It later merged with the People's Bank. The People's Bank focused on rural banking and agricultural credit to cooperative societies, rural committees and individuals. Later, the government introduced further institutions to facilitate rural credits. These included the new agricultural credit scheme (NACS) in 1968 and the comprehensive credit scheme (CCS) in 1974.

It was later realized that although many institutions were providing services to the rural population, in reality, they were not very active and were not fully meeting the needs. Therefore, in 1980, after the reforms were introduced, a formal rural bank, the Regional Rural Development Bank (RRDB), was established to support the rural economy. In 1985, the government established four RRDBs and combined the operations of commercial and development banks in the rural sector. In merely two years, the number of branches of RRDBs increased from 17 to 61.

Development finance institutions

The development finance institutions (DFIs) in Sri Lanka include hire purchase finance companies (HPFCs), development finance institutions (DFIs), the Agricultural and Industrial Development Corporation (AICC), the State Mortgage and Investment Bank (SMIB), the National Development Bank of Sri Lanka (NDB), and the Housing Development Finance Corporation (HDFC).

Although the HPFCs were first established in the 1950s, they saw a rapid increase in the post-1977 period. Unfortunately, this boost to the finance companies was not accompanied with a proper regulatory framework, which led to mismanagement, and some of these companies faced liquidity problems. Finally, the government enacted the Finance Companies Act of 1988 authorizing the Central Bank to regulate and supervise these companies. It may not be necessary to discuss the detailed historical developments of all these institutions as they went through different development phases over the period 1960–95. However, we shall look at one institution, the National Development Bank (NDB), which was created in the post-1977 period with the objective to promote industrial, agricultural and commercial development of the economy, with special focus on the rural sector. The NDB was set up with equity provided by the nationalized banks and the Central Bank.

Besides the above DFIs, Sri Lanka also had some NBFIs, including insurance institutions, and pension as well as provident funds. The insurance institutions saw a major turnaround in Sri Lanka in the pre-1960 period of monopoly of foreign insurance companies, and then nationalization in 1961, giving full monopoly to state-owned companies and finally, in the post-1977 period, leading to a mixture of local and foreign firms operating in the insurance business. At present, there are four government-owned insurance companies: the Insurance Corporation of Sri Lanka (ICSL), the National Insurance Corporation (NIC), the Agricultural Insurance Board (AIB), and the Sri Lanka Export Credit Insurance Corporation (SLECIC). Among them, AIB, established in 1973, is a unique programme and provides crop insurance for paddy rice. Under the law, it was compulsory for farmers to have insurance if they wanted to have access to agricultural credits. The SLECIC was established in 1979 to provide coverage to exporters for non-payment or delayed payments by foreign buyers of goods and services.

Stock market development

Although the stock market in Sri Lanka dates back to 1896 and continued operations after independence in 1948, the real momentum to its growth was given during the reforms of the post-1977 period. The Colombo Securities Exchange was set up in 1985 and later, in 1990, was changed to the Colombo Stock Exchange (CSE). The trade volume increased significantly from a daily average of US$50 000 a day to US$750 000 a day, mainly due to the interest of foreign institutional investors. The years 1990 and 1991 were probably the best years of CSE, when it was reported to be one of the best performers in the world. The policies implemented in the post-1977 period proved to be very instrumental in this impact on the stock market. These included liberalizing foreign investment by abolishing the 100 per cent tax on profits from share purchase by foreigners.

The market has 178 listed securities and grew from US$500 million capitalization in 1990 to US$1.5 billion in 1996.

Financial deepening

We now analyse the status of financial deepening in this economy. Measures such as exchange rate unification, domestic open-market operations, and introduction of new financial instruments in the market were initiated to expand credits for the private sector. Any success arising from these measures would have been reflected in the money depth (M2/GDP) indicator provided in Table 15.7. However, it is evident that in Sri Lanka, this ratio has remained constant in the range of 30–33 per cent, which is quite low compared to other liberalized economies.

The financial intermediation ratio (FIR) has not improved: from 34 per cent in the 1970s to 32 per cent in 1997. The depth in the public sector has been around 17 per cent while the private sector improved from 18 per cent to 24 per cent in 1994. However, the indicators in the table also show a decline in private asset holding in 1996. Gross fixed capital formation (GFCF) improved slightly, from 23 per cent to 26 per cent. That rate of investment was good enough for Taiwan's double-digit economic growth. In brief, the indicators of financial deepening have remained constant in Sri Lanka except in the case of holding of assets by the private sector.

4.   PROSPECTS FOR THE FUTURE

Sri Lanka had a history of an open trading policy long before independence in 1948. It continued the same policy after independence but only until 1960. The policy made a complete reversal in 1960 when inward orientation, nationalization and public-sector developmental projects became the buzzwords in the country. As a result, the country became isolated and was not able to keep pace with the development achieved in the first few years of independence. These rigid policies continued until 1977 when the economy was eventually liberalized. Since then, based on the failure of wrong policies, new ideas have been brought into play and new policies have been implemented in various sectors of the economy. This has helped to remove or relax the controls in the trade sector, to promote domestic industries and provide incentives to domestic

Table 15.7   Indicators of financial liberalization (% of GDP)

	5-year average			Annual							
	1976–80	1981–85	1986–90	1991	1992	1993	1994	1995	1996	1997	1998
Money Depth (M2/GDP)	28.3	30.8	30.0	30.2	30.8	32.3	33.2	34.7	32.9	32.4	34.0
Inter-relations											
FIR (total)/GDP	34	42	43	40	38	34	33	36	35	32	32
FIR (public)/GDP	17	22	23	19	16	11	9	10	8	8	8.3
FIR (private)/GDP	18	20	21	21	22	23	24	27	25	24	24
GFCF/GDP	22.9	26.8	22.4	22.6	23.5	25.2	26.6	25.0	25.7	24.4	26.0
FDI/GDP	0.6	0.8	0.6	1.1	1.3	1.9	1.4	0.4	0.9	3.0	1.29

Notes: M2 = (M1 + quasi-money).
FIR = financial intermediation ratio (32an + 32ca + 32cb + 32d) – claims on public sector (32an + 32ca + 32cb), claims on private sector (32d).
GFCF = gross fixed capital formation.
FDI = foreign direct investment.

Sources: IMF, International Financial Statistics, various issues; World Bank, World Bank Databank, Feb. 1997.

and foreign investors to engage in growth-promoting investment activities. It also helped to liberalize, promote and innovate in the domestic financial sector, to improve the pricing structure determining domestic prices of goods and services, fixed income securities and, most importantly, the domestic currency. The taxation structure has been revamped to provide more revenue, and fiscal discipline has been put in place by establishing coordination between fiscal and monetary policies.

In effect, Sri Lanka became the first country in the South Asian region to prove itself willing to implement policies of openness and economic reforms in 1977, ten years ahead. The other countries that also embarked on similar themes were Pakistan in 1990 and India in 1991. The country also enjoyed an edge over the other countries in the region, with very sound social indicators. However, the country has not been able to make as much progress as the later countries due partly to the continuing domestic political problems. The resources of the government have been diverted to war efforts and away from the implementation of such policies. A sad consequence is that both domestic and foreign investors are discouraged from investment that could yield good returns with the degree of openness now in place. The situation did not change very much in the 1990s and the prospects of future economic development depends heavily on a political solution to the civil war. At one point, the Sri Lankan economy was considered to be a prospective South Asian tiger economy. Unfortunately, the tiger has still not been unleashed! Instead, a bomb attempt to kill the Prime Minister just before a national election in January 2000 has led to greater resolve to continue the war at all costs. Alas for the Jewel of Asia.

NOTES

1. There are about 5 million Tamils living in this country out of a total Tamil population estimated at 70 million, most living across the sea in an Indian state called Tamil Nadu. Assimilation of the largely multi-religious but Tamil-speaking group, after implementation of discriminatory policies, has been a major problem. Hence the civil war.
2. Any traveller to the capital city of Colombo will note the free trade zones that were buzzing with activity in the 1990s. Despite the civil war, steps have been taken to nurture this as an attractive economic enclave in the region. Exports from this sector provide the stimulus for the economy to grow at its present moderate rate.
3. Statistical report published by the Central Bank of Sri Lanka.
4. These figures are reported in Central Bank of Sri Lanka Annual Report (1998).
5. However, the current experience of these economies suggests that lack of adequate regulations and a monitoring system may lead to a financial crisis if such investments are made for a short period to make quick gains.

Part 5   The Lessons from Liberalization

It has been demonstrated in the previous four parts of the book that pursuit of a carefully crafted liberal policy mix by a modernizing economy makes a significant difference as to whether an economy makes successful transition towards economic growth and its paramount objective, which is the social development of its people. An important variable that is a necessary condition for development appears to be the absence of civil war, which has more to do with politics than economics. That economic and social development at a respectable speed is indeed possible is a general lesson from the studies in this book of Asian countries belonging to all three types of economy: capitalist, socialist and transitional. The 1997–98 Asian financial crisis occurred because of a mismatch between the long-gestation infrastructure-cum-high-technology investments undertaken in the 1990s – when exports were declining – and the shorter-term sources of investment funds, especially foreign-sourced short-term capital flows in badly managed banking systems.

In the next chapter we provide extensive tests of the macroeconomic effects of these reforms on different sectors of the economies. These econometric tests helped us to make one general observation. That is, adoption of a liberal policy mix produced favourable impacts on all macroeconomic aggregates, irrespective of the initial states of the economies. Reforms helped to secure growth, and the outcome was greater prosperity for those economies adopting liberal policies in times of good neighbourliness. The Asian financial crisis arose from special factors associated with a high degree of financial fragility in the more liberalized countries (Chapter 2), and not liberalization *per se*. The relevant lessons from this study on Asia's liberalization are presented in the last chapter, as being relevant to developing and transitional economies in Asia and beyond.

16. Macroeconomic effects of financial liberalization

1. INTRODUCTION

The McKinnon–Shaw hypothesis (McKinnon, 1989; Shaw, 1973) argues that repressive regulations in financial markets lead to financial repression, distorting incentives of savers and investors in such an economy. Regulations such as deposit interest rate ceilings, minimum/maximum lending rates, quantity restrictions on lending, and so on cause real interest rates to be negative and unstable, especially in the presence of high inflation in an economy. Regulation leads to negative impacts on the amount of domestic savings and thus capital formation, which must retard economic growth and development. Thus the policy prescription of the McKinnon–Shaw hypothesis is financial liberalization, especially deregulation of interest rate restrictions. In the formal theory of financial liberalization, writers have focused on clarifying the linkages between higher interest rates and savings as well as investment and economic growth. In a survey of the literature on this issue, Gibson and Tsakalotos (1994) have emphasized the importance of financial-sector liberalization for resource mobilization, capital accumulation and economic development. Thus the attempts to liberalize restrictions on the financial sectors in all the countries included in this study arise from the knowledge that such policy actions are growth-promoting in the long run. This was the driving force behind the financial liberalization policies in developing countries, especially in Asia, Eastern Europe and Latin America.

Empirical observation, however, shows that not all countries have benefited to the same extent from liberalization attempts. Some countries succeeded in mobilizing savings, stimulating investment and accelerating growth, but a few others experienced financial crisis with very little economic growth following the financial reforms. These differing experiences have stimulated intense research studies attempting to document the process of liberalization more fully. These types of studies have become an issue of immense importance in the wake of the recent 1997–98 Asian financial crisis and the February 1999 Brazilian crisis.

In the late 1970s and 1980s, empirical studies such as those of Fry (1978, 1988) and Giovanni (1983, 1985) focused on using pooled data across countries in an attempt to test the financial liberalization hypothesis. These cross-sectional analyses are criticized on the ground that they failed to account fully for the different economic results among countries. Hence it is difficult to generalize the results (Demetriades and Hussein, 1996). In the late 1980s and early 1990s, there was an increasing amount of empirical research focused on individual countries regarding the effects of financial liberalization on savings, investment and growth. Gupta (1984), de Melo and Tybout (1986), Rittenberg (1991) and Warman and Thirwall (1994) and Kitagawa (1995) are some examples. These studies analysed the impacts of financial liberalization on different sectors of the economies included in their studies. The results of these studies were mixed, though they mostly supported the McKinnon–Shaw hypothesis.

Most of the empirical works cited above study the experiences in Latin America. Research on Asian countries is limited. We make an attempt in this chapter to present some evidence from a sample of Asian economies, namely, Malaysia, the Philippines, Singapore, South Korea and Thailand. Our analysis in earlier chapters suggests that these countries included in our tests have pursued high interest rate policies and combated any forms of financial repression, preferring to have full openness of the financial sectors in their developmental efforts. This chapter aims to examine the effects of financial liberalization (with particular focus on interest rate deregulation) on savings, investment, economic growth and money demand to study the benefits, if any, from financial liberalization in these countries.

The remainder of the chapter is organized as follows. In Section 2 we develop an econometric model to analyse the impact of financial liberalization on different sectors of the economy. A brief discussion on the methodology and data selection is provided in Section 3. Empirical results are reported and discussed in Section 4. Finally, conclusions are presented in Section 5.

2.   ECONOMETRIC MODELS

Before moving on to the discussion of the econometric model, we first look at the theoretical predictions of financial liberalization on different sectors of the economy. These effects are on savings, investment, money demand and growth itself.

The McKinnon–Shaw hypothesis suggests that financial liberalization, which advocates reasonably high and positive real interest rates in a liberal environment, induces large financial savings. This would in turn increase credit supply to the firms and allow them to carry out positive net present value projects, which were previously constrained by credit availability in a financially repressed economy with, for example, a deposit interest rate ceiling (India and China being two good examples in the pre-1990s). An increase in capital accumulation would lead to economic growth. There is also an opposing effect on investment. The rise in the real interest rate increases the cost of borrowing and reduces investment outlays. Thus, strictly, the effect on growth may be ambiguous, depending on which effect is dominant. If economic growth is stimulated by financial liberalization due to the dominance of the credit effect, then a virtuous circle of higher savings, investment and growth would open up as savings out of current income rise when income increases.

On the money demand function, financial liberalization is expected to create a great shock to the macroeconomy. Hence the stability of the money demand function becomes a relevant issue. As liberalization would entail the opening up of financial markets to some extent, foreign variables become important in explaining the money demand function. We follow Warman and Thirwall (WT, 1994) as a basis for model specification.

2.1 The Determinants of Savings

It is important to distinguish between the effects of financial liberalization on three different types of savings, namely, total, private and financial. According to the financial liberalization hypothesis, the relevant dependent variable is private saving. However, data on private saving are not easily available and hence several authors use total savings as a proxy, based on the argument that a large proportion of total savings is private savings in non-command economies. In addition, it is argued that financial liberalization is successful if it can mobilize financial savings efficiently without increasing private or total savings. We estimate the following equation to investigate the impact of financial liberalization on savings using our sample of countries. The equation is:

$$TS_t = \alpha_0 + \alpha_1 Y_t + \alpha_2 R_t + \alpha_3 (R - Rf + e)_t + \alpha_4 P_t + \alpha_{6i} TS_{t-i} \quad (16.1)$$

where TS is total saving, Y is the level of real income, R is the real rate of interest $(R - Rf + e)$, with e defined as the expected rate of appreciation/depreciation of the domestic currency, is the capital flight variable and P is the variable measuring uncertainty associated with inflation.

According to the financial liberalization hypothesis, savings must be positively related to the real rate of interest (R) so that the deregulation of interest rates would bring about a large increase in savings for capital accumulation.[1] This positive real interest rate elasticity is especially important in the pre-liberalization period if savings are to be efficaciously mobilized by financial liberalization. After liberalization, the interest elasticity may become insignificant or decrease in magnitude as households would have already adjusted their portfolios in response to interest rate deregulation.

The level of real income (Y) is expected to have a positive effect on savings according to Keynes's absolute income hypothesis.[2] If the coefficient of the real-income variable increases in magnitude and/or is significant in the post-liberalization equation, this would support the hypothesis that financial liberalization induces growth, which in turn feeds back to increased savings. However, such a structural change may not occur in the short run, as time is needed for the transmission mechanism to feed through the economy.

The capital flight variable is shown by ($R - Rf + e$) where R is the real rate of interest in the domestic country, Rf is the level of real foreign interest rate and e is the expected appreciation/depreciation of the domestic currency against a 'basket' of foreign currencies. Changes in savings with respect to interest rate changes can be interpreted as a combination of the domestic response to interest rates and the effect of capital flows. A significant coefficient indicates a substantial capital flight to and from the country (*World Tables*, 1994, 635).

Uncertainty associated with volatile inflation is captured in the variable P, which is calculated as the standard deviation of the monthly inflation rates (quarter by quarter).[3] Before liberalization, uncertainty of the price level may have a positive effect on financial savings since nominal interest rates are fixed and the public are at least certain of this nominal return, especially when compared with the uncertainty associated with returns on other assets like curb market deposits or foreign currency holdings. After liberalization, when nominal interest rates are free to adjust, uncertainty associated with expected returns would make holdings in domestic financial assets unattractive. In general, total savings may respond negatively to uncertainty as the public prefer to spend on inflation hedges (which are consumption expenditures) rather than save their current income. An insignificant coefficient associated with P would indicate the unimportance of such uncertainty in the economy. This is usually observed in economies where inflation is relatively low and stable.

2.2   The Determinants of Investment

Following WT (1994), we now develop an equation to determine the level of gross fixed investment (I). The equation to be estimated is given by Equation (16.2).

$$\log I_t = \beta_0 + \beta_1 R_t + \beta_2 \log C_t + \sum_{i=1}^{4} \beta_{3+i} \Delta GDP_{t-1-i} + \sum_{i=1}^{4} \beta_{7+i} \log I_{t-i} \qquad (16.2)$$

The real rate of interest (R) may affect investment in two opposite directions. On the one hand, it affects investment positively through increasing financial savings and the supply of credit (C) to the investors. On the other hand, the real interest rate affects investments negatively (holding credit constant) since it is considered a proxy for the price of credit capital. To work out the net effect, the real interest rate and the credit supply are both included in the investment function in Equation (16.2).

Before financial liberalization, the coefficient of credit should be positive and significant in the investment function because credit rationing in the loan market will make the availability condition of credits binding. Once financial liberalization reduces credit rationing, the level of the real interest rate must be negative and significant. The lagged change in real income (ΔGDP_{-1}) is included as one of the explanatory variables to capture the standard accelerator effect on investments. Four lagged values of this variable are used to accommodate the adjustment process that may spread across multiple periods. In addition, four lagged dependent variables are also included to capture the adjustment process.

2.3   The Determinants of Growth

The McKinnon–Shaw hypothesis predicts that financial liberalization, which causes institutional interest rates to rise towards competitive free-market equilibrium levels, will exert a positive effect on the rate of economic growth in both the short and medium run. The deregulation of interest rates will increase savings, which in turn raises credit availability for investments stimulating growth. Hence, from such a relationship, an econometric model of growth can be constructed to test the financial liberalization hypothesis. Some studies have regressed the rate of economic growth on the real rate of interest: a positive coefficient in such regression provides support for the McKinnon–Shaw hypothesis. The positive coefficient would show up in the short and medium run, but not in the long run. Ultimately, growth in the long run depends on real factors and the competitiveness of the economy.

Based on McKinnon's virtuous circle model of growth, the equation to be estimated is of the following form:

$$g_t = \delta_0 + \delta_1 R_t + \delta_2 xg_t + \delta_3 Sgy_t + \delta_5 Sfy_t + e_t \qquad (16.3)$$

where g is the growth rate of real income, R is the real rate of interest, xg is the growth rate of real exports, Sgy is the ratio of government savings to income and Sfy is the ratio of foreign savings to income. The last term is the residual.

According to the financial liberalization hypothesis, the coefficient of R is positive and significant. Export growth, denoted by xg, is postulated to have a positive effect on economic growth.[4] This is not surprising because growth of exports is important for economic growth from both the supply side and the demand side. Exports provide foreign currency to pay for imports, which act as vital inputs to the developmental process and which may be more productive than domestic resources. Export earnings also relax the foreign exchange constraint on the other components of demand (Thirwall and Hussain, 1982). Foreign savings are important for growth especially in the early stages of development since they can fill the foreign exchange constraint as well as the savings constraint.

2.4   The Determinants of Money Demand

The money demand function is an important indicator of macroeconomic conditions. Its stability has a significant bearing on the issue of monetary control in the economy. There are many factors that affect the stability of the money demand function, and financial liberalization, which creates a great shock to the financial markets, is accorded an important place as one of the factors. Thus it is pertinent to examine the effects of financial liberalization on money demand. We use the following specification to estimate the open-economy money demand function:

$$\log\left(\frac{M}{P}\right)_t = \gamma_0 + \gamma_1 \log Y_t + \gamma_3 i_t + \gamma_3 i_t^* + \gamma_5 E_t \qquad (16.4)$$

M is given by broad money, data used are M2; Y_t is domestic real income; i_t and i_t^* are respectively the domestic and foreign nominal interest rates, and E_t is the expected depreciation of domestic currency.

It is well known that money demand is positively related to real income and inversely related to domestic interest rates. The foreign rate of interest, i^*, has a negative effect on money demand because increases in foreign rates cause residents as well as potential foreign investors to hold more bonds and reduce both domestic assets and money holdings. When there is greater expected depreciation of the domestic currency (E_t), the demand for money falls due to the following two reasons. First, both domestic and foreign residents would prefer to hold more foreign money and less domestic money. Second, as a result of expected depreciation of the domestic currency, foreign bonds (representing the preferred wealth-holding medium) become relatively more attractive than domestic bonds. Hence both foreign and domestic residents would increase their holdings of foreign bonds and reduce holdings of domestic bonds.

It is expected that financial liberalization will cause a structural change in the money demand function. In addition to institutional changes, financial liberalization entails the opening up of the financial sector to the international financial system. In periods of financial repression, the authorities not only control the domestic financial sector but must also regulate capital flows. This causes foreign factors like foreign interest rates and the exchange rate to be unimportant in influencing money demand. However, after liberalization, the foreign factors become important.

3.   DATA AND METHODOLOGY

The empirical estimation of the model requires data on total savings (*TS*), gross fixed investment (*I*), real income (*Y*), real interest rate (*R*), foreign interest rate (R_f), expected appreciation of domestic currency (*e*), inflation rate (*P*), credit (*C*), export growth (*xg*), government saving (*Sg*), foreign saving (*Sf*), nominal domestic interest rate (*i*) and nominal foreign interest rate (i^*). Savings data are mainly calculated from national account data. The level of total savings is proxied by gross domestic savings (*GDS*) for Malaysia, South Korea, Singapore and Thailand, and gross national savings (*GNS*) for the Philippines.

The three-month time deposit rate is used as a proxy for the interest rate for Philippines and Singapore; the 12-month deposit rate for Malaysia, South Korea and Thailand. In calculating the real rate of interest, we use the rate of change in the consumer price index as a proxy. Data on foreign interest rate are the weighted average of interest rates of long-term bonds in the USA, the UK and Japan. Expected rate of domestic currency appreciation/depreciation is proxied by the actual rate of change in the domestic currency value against a weighted average of foreign currencies, namely the US dollar, the pound sterling and the yen. **P** is the standard deviation of the monthly inflation rate, calculated for each quarter. Private investment is the more relevant variable to examine in the context of financial liberalization, however, quarterly data on government capital expenditure are not adequately available. Therefore, data on real investment are used to estimate the investment model, that is, the gross fixed capital formation plus changes in stocks.

Real income is proxied as real GDP. Government saving is government budget deficit/surplus while foreign saving is taken as net exports. The weights used in calculation of R^f and *e* are the relative share of an economy's GDP to total real GDP of the three industrial countries. All other data are in nominal terms. Where it is necessary to obtain data in real values, the relevant country's CPI (base year is 1990 = 100) is used to deflate the series.

All the data for Malaysia, the Philippines, South Korea and Thailand are obtained from IMF's *International Financial Statistics* (IFS) (CD-ROM, 1998) and the *Government Statistical Yearbook* (various issues). For Singapore, the national accounts and money supply data are obtained from TRENDS Database (1996) published by the Department of Statistics (Singapore). The rest of the Singapore data are obtained from the two IMF publications noted above. The sample period for this study is as follows: 1976Q1–1997Q4 for Malaysia;

1980Q4–1995Q2 for the Philippines; 1970Q1–1995Q2 for South Korea; 1978Q1–1995Q2 for Singapore; and 1976Q1–1997Q4 for Thailand.

All the above single-equation models are estimated using ordinary least squares regression. The Cochrane–Orcutt transformation (CORC) to overcome errors from serial correlation across time is used to correct for first-order serial correlation. The Chow test is used to check for structural changes in the models. Such a test of structural change in the context of financial liberalization is not undertaken in most empirical studies. Only de Melo and Tybout (1986) and Kitagawa (1995) show the changes in the model structure before and after liberalization in their empirical research.

The date for the Chow test is set at 1981–83 for most of the countries in this study. Due to the lack of sufficient data, the model is not estimated for the 1970s for the Philippines. Quarterly data are available only from 1981. However, the impact of financial liberalization in the Philippines can be studied by making a distinction between the pre-1987 and post-1987 periods. Thus the date of the Chow test is set at 1987Q1 for this country. Quarterly data for Singapore are available only from 1978 onwards, and thus the test for structural change cannot be carried out as deregulation took place in 1978.

4.   EMPIRICAL FINDINGS

4.1   Estimates for the Savings Equation

We first focus on the results of the Chow test since these statistics show the financial liberalization effects at the time of the change by verifying if there has been a structural effect. The data suggest a structural break for the savings function in South Korea and Thailand. In Malaysia and the Philippines, such evidence of a structural break is not supported, while the Chow test is not performed for Singapore for the reasons mentioned earlier.

The results of empirical estimation of the savings function are reported in Table 16.1. The results for Malaysia support the financial liberalization hypothesis as real income and capital flight variables are highly significant. The large magnitude of income variable (0.97) indicates a strong effect of liberalization on economic growth and hence gross savings. A positive capital flight parameter means capital inflow as a result of liberalization. The results for the Philippines, Singapore, South Korea and Thailand also support the financial liberalization effect on savings through increased economic growth. Again, the magnitude of income variable in the case of Thailand is very high and is equal to one. The other diagnostic tests are also satisfactory. The Chow stability test suggests a structural break in the case of South Korea. This implies that the economic system changed as a result of financial liberalization.[5]

Table 16.1   Parameter estimates of savings function

Variable	Malaysia 76Q1–96Q4	Philippines 83Q1–95Q2	Singapore 80Q2–95Q2	South Korea 71Q2–95Q2	Thailand 76Q1–96Q4
Constant	1.178	–26331	–1808	–3238	–478.34
	(0.05)	(–2.06)*	(–3.44)*	(–7.73)*	(–10.66)*
Real interest rate (R)	–189.87	26362	1445	1401	–60.95
	(–0.97)	(0.0.84)	(0.61)	(0.61)	(0.46)
Real income (Y)	0.97	0.19	0.70	0.37	1.00
	(72.71)*	(4.52)*	(6.43)*	(9.93)**	(1968)*
Capital flight	3.52*	–16497	8.14	601.2	–0.08
$(R – Rf + e)$	(3.47)	(–0.86)	(0.009)	(0.48)	(–0.17)
Uncertainty of	–28.80	–903.1	82.70	73.36	24.92
inflation (P)	(–0.02)	(–1.37)	(1.11)	(1.08)	(0.04)
$S(-1)$	0.065	0.16	–0.42	–0.08	–0.003
	(3.43)*	(1.59)	(–5.85)*	(–4.56)*	(–7.66)*
$S(-2)$	–0.02	–0.28	–0.23	–0.05	–0.002
	(–1.03)	(–2.76)*	(–4.87)*	(–3.06)*	(–3.38)*
$S(-3)$	–0.08	0.103	–0.21	–0.12	0.001
	(–3.92)*	(1.10)	(–4.55)*	(–5.80)*	(2.45)*
$S(-4)$	0.054	0.52	0.54	0.39	–0.001
	(3.90)*	(4.92)*	(6.01)*	(5.96)*	(–2.55)*
ADJ–R^2	0.99	0.99	0.96	0.99	0.999
DW	2.19	2.36	1.78	2.07	1.99
D–H	–0.91	0.16	0.16	0.16	0.043
F-statistic	1129.0	28.26	168.8	833	0.0000538
Chow test	0.59	1.64	–	2.92*	1.74

Notes: *, ** indicate parameter significance at 5% and 10% level.

4.2   Estimates for the Investment Equation

Financial liberalization may increase investment by increasing the supply of credit via the increase in financial savings, but liberalization may reduce investment by increasing the capital cost of borrowing. The investment function developed in Section 3 attempts to model these opposing effects by including both the credit supply and the real interest rate in the investment function. Financial liberalization is also expected to induce a structural change in the investment function. The coefficient of real interest rate is expected to be negative as it captures the credit/capital cost of investments. Before liberalization, with controls on nominal interest rates and high inflation, capital cost is low and hence is not significant in explaining investment. Rather, it is credit supply that constrains investments. After liberalization, the real interest rate increases and firms' investment decisions are affected by the cost of capital effect of real interest rates.

Table 16.2 presents the regression results for the investment demand function. These results suggest that the only significant determinant of investment in Malaysia is changes in GDP and the lagged investment. The results for the Philippines are similar except that the real interest rate is significant but with a positive sign. This may be a reflection of foreign investment when real returns on investment are positive. The main determinant of investment in Singapore

Table 16.2   Parameter estimates of investment function

Variable	Malaysia 75Q4–96Q4	Philippines 83Q1–95Q2	Singapore 80Q2–95Q2	South Korea 71Q2–95Q2	Thailand 76Q1–96Q4
Constant	0.59	1.10	0.77	104.4	52.56
	(0.42)	(1.11)	(1.86)**	(0.28)	(2.69)*
Real interest rate (R)	–4.97	1.04	–1.63	–7797	–245
	(–0.32)	(2.99)*	(–3.08)*	(–1.54)	(–2.78)*
Real credit (C)	0.003	–0.05	0.005	0.15	–4.17
	(1.57)	(–0.79)	(0.09)	(6.78)*	(–2.63)*
$\Delta GDP(-1)$	0.002	0.0001	–0.000002	0.47	0.001
	(2.06)*	(1.91)**	(–0.79)	(3.53)*	(1.70)**
$\Delta GDP(-2)$	0.001	0.0001	–	–	0.002
	(0.74)	(2.53)*			(1.79)**
$I(-1)$	1.55	0.17	0.30	–0.94	–1.74
	(16.33)*	(1.06)	(2.51)*	(–4.63)*	(–21.6)*
$I(-2)$	–0.58	0.28	0.30	0.82	–0.72
	(–5.85)*	(1.71)**	(2.45)*	(3.36)*	(–8.67)*
$I(-3)$	–	0.50	0.31	–	–
		(3.16)*	(2.57)*		
$I(-4)$	–	–	–	0.39	–
				(5.96)*	
ADJ–R^2	0.99	0.73	0.89	0.89	0.999
DW	2.002	–	–	–	1.89
D–H	–0.022	0.14	–0.47	0.52	0.80
F-statistic	6828	20.73	85.76	150	14259
Chow test	0.753	5.54*	–	2.23*	0.38

Notes: *, ** indicate parameter significance at 5% and 10% level.

is the real rate of interest and it has an inverse relationship with investment. In Singapore, with perfect capital mobility and a high savings rate mandated by law under the country's pension-cum-social policies (the central provident fund scheme) and government savings from unspent budget surplus from high government revenues, it is not surprising that there is no lack of funds to finance investments. This shows up in the insignificant coefficient of the credit supply variable. The results from Singapore suggest that in the long run, after liberalization has been completed,[6] credit supply no longer constrains investment and the real interest rate becomes significant in influencing it.

In South Korea, however, real credit and one period lag of change in GDP are significant determinants of investment. The most interesting results are obtained for Thailand, where all variables are statistically significant and have the expected signs. This indicates the strong effects of financial liberalization. All standard statistics are satisfactory. Using the Chow test, it is found that there is a possibility of a structural break in the investment function for the Philippines and South Korea. Again, the results in general are consistent with what the financial liberalization hypothesis would predict.

4.3   Estimates for the Economic Growth Equation

The results of estimating the economic growth function are presented in Table 16.3. One would expect growth of exports (xg) to be an important argument for growth in Malaysia. Surprisingly, the foreign savings to GDP ratio (Sfy) is statistically significant but negative in sign. That is, leakages in the form of foreign savings constrained growth to some extent.

Real interest rates are the only significant variable explaining economic growth. Export growth is important in explaining growth in Korea, Malaysia, Singapore and Thailand, but not in the Philippines. Indeed, many studies on the success of the East Asian economies have attributed rapid economic growth to export growth. The coefficient of government savings is positive and significant in Korea's growth model, suggesting the importance of the government in Korea's industrialization and development process. The only significant variable for growth in Thailand is lagged growth, though there is some weak evidence of a negative impact of export growth on GDP growth. Chow tests suggest a structural break in the growth equation for Malaysia. The results are consistent with the financial liberalization hypothesis with the exception of Thailand.

4.4   Estimates for the Money Demand Equation

Based on our discussion in Section 3, we estimated the open-economy money demand function for our sample countries (see the results in Table 16.4) Real income is the only significant determinant of money demand in Malaysia. This result is closer to a monetarist hypothesis, where interest rates have a negligible

Table 16.3   Parameter estimates of growth function

Variable	Malaysia 75Q4–96Q4	Philippines 83Q1–95Q2	Singapore 80Q2–95Q2	South Korea 71Q2–95Q2	Thailand 76Q1–96Q4
Constant	3.05	0.04	0.01	0.91	0.55
	(3.71)*	(0.85)	(0.96)	(0.51)	(0.68)
Real interest rate (R)	−6.75	0.28	−0.11	28.34	−3.36
	(−0.77)	(3.13)*	(−0.85)	(2.50)*	(−0.97)
Growth of exports (xg)	0.07	−0.04	0.67	4.49	−0.03
	(3.38)*	(−1.37)	(2.42)*	(2.28)*	(−1.86)**
Sgy	−144	0.000004	0.017	44.01	−496
	(−0.60)	(0.16)	(0.56)	(2.86)*	(−0.97)
Sfy	−921	−0.00007	0.04	−4.61	271
	(−2.77)*	(−0.42)	(1.04)	(−0.53)	(0.43)
$G(-1)$	0.73	0.26	0.78	0.26	0.91
	(6.51)*	(2.00)*	(9.78)*	(2.56)*	(8.04)*
$G(-2)$	−0.14	0.43	–	0.12	0.14
	(−1.40)	(3.64)*		(1.17)*	(1.06)
$G(-3)$	–	–	–	0.05	–
				(0.56)	
$G(-4)$	–	–	–	−0.19	–
				(−2.05)*	
ADJ–R^2	0.71	0.67	0.77	0.35	0.76
DW	2.01	–	–	–	1.93
D–H	0.037	−1.04	1.09	1.56	0.23
F-statistic	34.98	17.95	42.49	7.59	45.51
Chow test	2.84*	0.59	–	1.43	0.73

Notes: *, ** indicate parameter significance at 5% and 10% level.

role to play in individuals' decision-making process as regards money-holding. The results for the Philippines show that real income and foreign interest rates are important determinants of money demand.

In Singapore, coefficients of real income, the nominal foreign interest rate and the real exchange rate are all significant in the money demand function. Since Singapore is a small open economy, it is heavily trade-dependent since internationalization of its financial markets and the domestic nominal interest rate is not a significant variable. In Korea, it is seen that besides real income, only the domestic nominal rate of interest is significant in the money demand function. Finally, real income and foreign interest rates determine the money demand function in Thailand.

The above results for the Philippines, Singapore and Thailand are consistent with the financial liberalization hypothesis, while the hypothesis appears not to hold for Malaysia and South Korea. However, the Chow test does indicate a structural break for the money demand function in the case of South Korea.

Table 16.4   Parameter estimates of money demand function

Variable	Malaysia 76Q1–96Q4	Philippines 83Q1–95Q2	Singapore 80Q2–95Q2	South Korea 71Q2–95Q2	Thailand 76Q1–96Q4
Constant	−9.49	−2.62	5.35	0.039	−15.66
	(−23.2)	(−1.66)	(4.39)*	(0.42)	(−47.7)*
Real income (Y)	1.57	0.48	0.62	0.107	1.41
	(40.3)*	(3.15)*	(5.27)*	(5.30)*	(58.21)*
Domestic nominal	0.06	0.42	0.11	−0.39	−0.13
interest rate (i)	(0.14)	(0.90)	(0.27)	(−3.09)*	(−0.42)
Foreign nominal	0.18	−3.02	−1.29	−0.12	−1.93
interest rate (i^*)	(0.64)	(−1.81)**	(−2.26)*	(−0.52)	(−5.63)*
e	0.0009	−0.005	−0.164	−0.00003	0.003
	(0.26)	(−0.61)	(−2.07)*	(−0.56)	(1.25)
M2(−1)	–	0.46	–	0.92	–
		(3.79)*		(10.6)*	
M2(−2)	–	0.29	–	−0.23	–
		(2.11)*		(−1.75)**	
M2(−3)	–	–	–	0.203	–
				(2.20)*	
M2(−4)	–	–	–	–	–
ADJ–R^2	0.98	0.90	0.38	0.99	0.99
DW	–	–	–	–	–
D–H	0.41	−0.25	1.85	0.28	0.66
F-statistic	835	73.4	10.2	8343	3475
Chow test	–	3.80	–	3.35*	–

Notes: *, ** indicate parameter significance at 5% and 10% level.

5.   CONCLUSIONS

With the discovery of financial repression as a potent force working against economic growth, the Asian countries embarked on financial liberalization as part of their development strategy to secure sustainable economic development and, through that, social development. The main concern was to increase savings and improve resource mobilization for development purposes. In all countries included in our tests, the main motivation for adopting liberalization was to overcome the effects of the oil shocks of 1973 and 1978, which forced many policy-makers to realize the inflexibility of the regulations in financial markets. We used econometric tests to analyse the impacts of financial liberalization on savings, investment, economic growth and money demand.

Some important conclusions and policy implications we arrived at are summarized below. From the empirical estimation of savings function for sample countries, we find that financial liberalization is effective in mobilizing savings. On the investment side, we found that financial liberalization is important in reducing the credit constraint in the short run (the Philippines) and eliminating it in the long run (Singapore). In the case of Korea, credit remains a binding constraint even after liberalization because investment is growing at a much faster rate than credit supply: recall that Korea had double-digit growth and had experienced recession only once in 1980. This is not evidence against financial liberalization. Rather, this empirical result suggests that, without liberalization, there would be slower growth in investment as credit would not be forthcoming. Hence there is scope for policy-makers to improve the credit supply situation in Korea, even though liberalization has helped to increased credit supply domestically, and self-imposed regulation on foreign capital until 1996 reduced foreign capital inflows.

The empirical results of the growth model for Korea and the Philippines show that economic growth can be enhanced by financial liberalization. However, in the long run, after the eradication of financial repression, the positive effect of the real interest rate on growth would disappear. This is the case for Singapore.

Looking at the overall evidence for savings, investment and growth, there is strong support for the financial liberalization hypothesis, the central theme advanced in this book in each of the country analysis. A carefully considered and properly implemented programme of removing regulations that cause financial repression would increase the flow of financial savings and hence increase credit supply, both domestic and foreign. This would in turn stimulate investment and economic growth. In addition, there is evidence supporting the notion that financial liberalization opens up a virtuous circle of higher savings, credit growth, higher investments and enhanced economic growth because increases in real income induce higher savings. With regard to the open-economy money demand function foreign variables such as the foreign nominal interest rate, net exports, and so on are significant. An implication of these results is that the monetary authority should take into account the role of foreign variables in the money demand function after liberalization when choosing an instrument for monetary control and in the formulation of monetary policies. In short, financial liberalization is growth-promoting in the Asian context.

NOTES

1. Note that there is no *a priori* reason for the coefficient of real interest rate to be positive, as a change in real interest rate has a positive substitution effect but a negative income effect. Thus savings may be related positively, negatively or unrelatedly to the real interest rate.
2. It is recognized that other measurements or proxies for income can be used, depending on the theory of consumption that one is subscribing to. For the purpose of this analysis, the use of a

simple income variable is sufficient and this measurement is similar to the one used in WT (1994).

3. This method of obtaining the proxy for uncertainty associated with volatile inflation is derived from WT (1994).

4. This is consistent with the export-led-growth theory.

5. An interesting exercise would be to go one step further and identify the year of the structural break, then split the data into two groups, one pre-liberalization and the other post-liberalization, and compare the effects of financial liberalization. We believe that such an exercise would be beyond the scope of this book and we defer it for future research.

6. Singapore's interest rates were completely deregulated by 1975 and exchange control was completely removed by 1978.

17.   Lessons for developing and transitional economies

1.   WHAT YOU CHOOSE IS WHAT YOU GET

Even a casual visitor to Asia will get an overriding impression of progress in some countries and an abject lack of progress in others. Herein lies the lessons to be learned for development. Some countries, such as Korea, Malaysia, Taiwan and so on, appear to have created more visible creature comforts for their peoples than some other countries, such as Vietnam or Bangladesh or Sri Lanka. The key to the achievement or non-achievement of creature comforts appears to us to derive from one constant factor. That factor is the extent of liberal policies adopted or not adopted by the Asian nations (assuming a country is not at war). This finding is true even after considering the damage from economic and social shocks due to the Asian financial crisis during the closing three years of the twentieth century.

The policy mix adopted as liberalization is quite often based on a common-sense approach to managing an economy with the sole aim of creating better conditions for people in severely war-ravaged countries after World War II. The choices made by the bigger players such as China and India were based on a clear vision – so it seemed at that time – of the founding fathers of these newly freed nations. But for smaller countries, the choices to be made had to produce quick results because these nations were in dire conditions. Taiwan was reduced to a burdened island nation in 1949 after the Communists in China drove an opposing (Nationalist) government along with a lot of skilled people across the Straits to Taiwan. The Koreans were devastated by a 1954 war brought to their shores by superpower hegemony. The Malaysians were rudely awakened by a savage civil war, the root cause of which was inequity among different peoples making up that country. Indonesia almost broke up in a 1965 civil war that needed a quick fix to alleviate suffering. Singapore, an island of about 2.4 million people living in a space no larger than Manhattan Island, had been cut off from the more resource-rich Malaysia because of political policy differences and ethnic competition.

These latter nations, all much smaller than China or India, were more pragmatic and less doctrinaire, less vision-bound, but nevertheless more able to see what would work quickly. These nations chose the export-led industrial growth path through vigorous liberalization. Thus the economic policy choices made by a given nation of people were to some extent preconditioned by the individual experiences of these countries. Somewhat shocked people in war-torn or resource-poor countries were eager to follow schemes to make them successful, it appears.

Of course, the liberal policies these countries adopted, which later produced the most beneficial outcomes, as can be seen by any observer in Asia, have their roots elsewhere. The modern ideas about how to formulate and execute growth-promoting policies to harness growth to improve the well-being of peoples in nation-states with different resource endowments already existed. But there was no consensus back in the 1960s and 1970s about liberalization being the correct path, when in fact competing ideas of central planning or import substitution held sway. That liberalization is possibly the route to sustainable development was not well understood in those days. It took time to sweep across the world from a germ of an idea born in an Austrian economics school, which today is linked with the classical ideas of Ricardo and Marshall, and the later ideas of Friedman, Tobin, Bhagwati, Sen and others to form the neoclassical development paradigm so much in vogue today.

The first lesson of development is therefore a paradoxical one. The choice is among alternative paths to development. This holds the key to success or failure, since choices made at the start of the process appear to condition what follows in the ensuing period. It is like the choice the heroes in *Iliad* had to make! In this regard Asia can be said to have made choices from among conflicting ideas then prevailing some three to five decades ago: central planning on the Soviet model; import substitution for a closed model of development; and liberalization to ensure export-led industrial growth. It appears that the choices were made more on political grounds to suit the conditions prevailing in the postwar years than on any rational examination of what was an already well-argued path to development.

In any event, import substitution appeared then to be a rational path, based on the Keynesian idea that a government deficit is needed to bring unemployed resources – and Asia had plenty of them – to full use, as was being done soon after the Second World War in the more developed countries in the West. The natural attraction of this policy was not surprising. Even Taiwan followed this policy for about a decade in the 1960s, which led to the building up of a huge foreign ownership of the means of production. That of course led to the end of that path for Taiwan. Not so for India, which relentlessly created a rule-based bureaucracy in which most significant economic activities were abrogated to the public sector, which, over time, created the licence Raj syndrome from which India is still reluctantly extricating itself. (The 'licence Raj syndrome' refers to the practice of using the Indian bureaucratic rules and corrupt politics to obtain licences for production of economic goods.) Then there was the attraction of the Marxist–Leninist model of central planning. That choice led to disastrous economic outcomes from which Asia's Communist adherents are still trying to extricate themselves by returning to a market-economy model, a euphemism for adopting capitalism after a failed Communist policy. Finally, there is the open-economy model pursued quite happily by much smaller nations such as Hong Kong, Korea, Singapore and Taiwan on a path to development, which made them the first Asian tiger economies, later to become the newly industrializing economies (NIEs). These nations created per capita income growth twice as quickly as other nations on average. The result is that all of them have today become middle- and upper-income countries.

After a period of failure to secure the development needed to make the people better off, the wrong policies were reversed by China in 1979 and India in 1987 with the right policies slowly being put in place since then. This gave us the early reformers, all of whom managed to create higher levels of creature comforts, be it in Taipei or Seoul or Kuala Lumpur, while the hesitant reformers in Delhi or Dhaka and the transitional economies made short-term gains from their later adoption of liberalization as the route to growth. The early adopters of economic and social reforms managed to secure a far greater degree of improvements in the social well-being of their peoples, while even the late reformers are now beginning to achieve some success. That is what will impress an observer about Asia.

In this book, readers were in a sense conducted on a grand tour of the process of policy-making by governments and economic agents across several decades, as steps were taken to put through a series of connected ideas which became relevant for their changing circumstances. It is a careful analysis of the much-talked-about Asian experience, which in some cases secured and in others failed to secure social development. Financial and social statistics over a 30-year period have been presented to support the findings from which we now look for lessons for those within and outside Asia. What are the other lessons, apart from the choice of models for development?

In the next section, we identify two classes of lessons, one relating to the pre-conditions for liberal economic policies to work, and the other relating to the elements of the liberal policies themselves. In the following section, we examine the lessons from the Asian financial crisis. Financial fragility appears to be the source of the troubles, while the exchange rate peg is to some extent responsible for the overshoot of the currencies in 1997–98. Comparative statistics are given in Section 4. Section 5 discusses the important question of sequencing of the reform steps. Though no consensus among experts existed before the crisis, it is now widely accepted that some degree of current account control is needed to fend off sudden systemic shocks to an economy. The final section of this chapter gives a glimpse of the future prospects for the kind of reforms this book advocates for all those people who yearn to experience more rather than fewer creature comforts. This is attainable, is our optimistic message, provided the political process is in the hands of the peoples in Asia – we hope Asians will stop listening to demagogues promising quick fixes for their conditions – and provided that the right measures are then taken by their élites and rulers.

2. THE TEN COMMANDMENTS OF A FREE-MARKET ECONOMY

2.1 Preconditions

While the grand design of what one chooses appears to be preconditioned by history, it is much easier to document the elements that make up a good liberal policy mix. In our opinion, this task is less controversial. Good neighbourliness is a precondition for sustaining growth over time.[1] Failures of nations to create good neighbourliness have caused many countries with potentially fairly good prospects of growth to slide slowly into a malaise. Pakistan and Sri Lanka are apt examples. The Philippines had to clear the decks so to speak, to make peace with internal dissenters by signing agreements to give them their dues before the path to present growth was taken by Ramos[2] during the 1990s. Why is this not easy for Sri Lanka or Pakistan to understand as the critical building-block for progress? If a third party is willing to underwrite the costs of conducting war (United States in the case of North Korea vs South Korea), then of course, one can throw all the resources into making an economy grow. In fact a nation at war could order people to work harder and make sacrifices, as did Korea. Not many nations are so lucky as Korea, perhaps! Thus the first element in a growth-promoting policy mix appears to be an absence of resource allocation to war efforts, so that the famous Samuelson's choice can be made by a nation of peoples for more bread and butter instead of more guns and tanks.[3]

The second element is building a consensus for liberal policies. Lack of consensus, as in India and Vietnam, on adopting credible liberal policies will mean slowing down the growth process substantially. The consequence in India and in Vietnam has been a marked reduction in the speed with which growth-promoting policies can bring about favourable outcomes. We saw that the *doi moi* II in Vietnam is still in the process of being born, while India's weak coalition governments since 1994 are unable to go all the way in adopting the reforms that Rao's government put on the agenda. Deng Xiaoping of China and Mahathir of Malaysia of course are two famous cases of building coalitions for adopting liberal policies. This second element is a political lesson on economic development.

Leaders must be aware of the need to build a coalition of support among the people to want to make the reforms, and get a mandate to do so. Of course, there are rare examples of some men forcing through liberal economic policies without necessarily actively building coalitions. This happened in Korea when Park Chung-Hee unilaterally dismissed the elected government and initiated market-friendly policies, thus laying the groundwork in the period 1963–73 for Korea's road to prosperity. Let us not forget that this man had several attempts made on his life and that one was fatal. These two elements of development are more in the domain of political economy than the other elements to be discussed shortly. McIntaire (1998) shows clearly the dominant influence of political factors that precipitated, for example, the Asian crisis. So, do not belittle the political factors. Asia, take a lesson in democracy.

A third set of elements in the form of institution-building for development has been pointed out as essential for making the transition to an open-economy model. These require the development of sound laws that enshrine private ownership as the backbone of a developing process. Let us not forget that only when private initiatives were in place did the Communist economies respond to reforms. This also requires that an independent judiciary is developed to protect the rights of individuals to pursue private-gain activities consistent with ideas of fairness. Along with this are institutions such as good disclosure of information by economic agents (government, corporations and banks) and developed accounting standards, and not an undue tax burden, all of which are needed to give the assurance that there is sufficient prudent behaviour needed for development. The idea of State is invoked by authoritarians to retard this basic individualism, a precondition for development.

2.2   Elements of a Liberal Policy Mix

We refer to the three elements so far discussed as 'preconditioning factors', and proceed now to identify the economic–financial policy elements, the proper concerns of this book. Our discussion about these remaining elements is based on the experiences of the cases included here. First among them is the need for competition policy. Whatever a country does to put in place or manage existing producing units, an important precondition for success appears to be active promotion of competition among firms. Here the economic dictum, 'many buyers and many sellers', any one of whom is unlikely to influence the equilibrium prices, has to have real meaning in policy implementation. Disasters lay in wait several years after Communist China started one company that had the sole licence to produce cars for China; India licensed one company to produce its cars; Indonesia created cartels to manage its very profitable spice production, with disastrous results. The reader will find many cases of restrictive competition in the production process practised in Asia. Years after these decisions were put in place by well-meaning bureaucrats or politicians, the results were production of poor-quality goods and often the sole company producing the goods goes about shutting out any new entrants from making better-quality products.

On the other hand, when the Japanese decide to enter goods production, they start at least three companies – unlike the rest of Asia! When Japan decided to make cars, it had the Nissan, the Toyota and the Honda corporations all competing among themselves to produce better-quality cars. In electronics, the NEC, Hitachi, and National corporations competed fiercely to produce world-class electronic products. One does not have to learn this lesson in any business schools! At the appropriate stage of development, opening the domestic markets to international competition is also observed – Taiwan and Korea as two examples – after the infant-industry protection is removed by scaling down the tariff rates to more or less a single-digit level.[4] Financial corporations should also be subjected to competition. Thus domestic, real and financial sectors must have broad-based competition through reduced barriers to entry within the country in the early phases of development, when infant-industry protection is needed. But the kind of Indian or Chinese practices of licensing one company or cartels to produce goods should be avoided. Of course in these two countries, the firms were owned and controlled by civil servants, not by the private sector. Systematic feather-bedding practices in the state-owned enterprises led these firms to make shoddy products and yet the profits were not there to justify the high prices the public were paying for these shoddy goods, out of necessity.

The next element is progressively to expose the real sector to international competition by first reducing tariff rates steadily to a single digit, as did many successful economies. This is often done in two stages. In the first stage, while the tariff is being reduced, domestic firms are encouraged to seek joint ventures to bring in expertise that is efficiency-improving. India and China did this extensively, and are still practising it as a major strategy. At the later stage, foreign firms are given full entry, with 100 per cent ownership rights to produce and sell their goods. India moved to this stage in the 1990s while China is still keeping foreign firms in the economic zones. Needless to emphasize, those countries that had very few resources and were themselves small economies – Hong Kong, Singapore, Malaysia, and so on – adopted the two stages of opening to competition almost at the same time, by lifting restrictions on foreign entry at a very early stage of opening the economy. As a result, such economies have abundant multinational firms and financial institutions in the domestic sector while the tariff levels remained very low for a considerable period of time.

Real-sector openness is, then, an important reform that readers will have noticed in all 13 countries. While real-sector openness is taking place, decisions on two further elements are likely to be made. There is widespread debate, particularly after the 1997–98 crisis, as to the appropriate time for these steps to be taken. We refer to current account and capital account openness: these are the next elements. Restrictions maintained in the current and capital accounts in China, India and Taiwan, it appears, prevented speculative attacks on the currencies of these countries in 1997–98, while the same restrictions prevented the domestic firms and individuals from joining in the speculation on their own currencies, as happened in Indonesia and Malaysia. This appears to be a sound enough reason why *full* current and capital account openness may not be advised during the early stages of development. The consensus among experts (McKinnon, Cole and Frenkel, among others) is that current and capital account openness must not be undertaken until real-sector opening is advanced enough and even then only after government budgets are in balance. This will be discussed in a later section.

Capital account openness is needed for the producing units, the domestic and foreign firms, to seek capital resources outside the country and then to be able to pay for such services as dividends, royalties, management fees, and so on. To a lesser extent, individuals may not need the full freedom, provided that the ceiling on individuals to move capital is set at reasonable levels – as is now the case in India and Malaysia – not at levels injurious to the demands for foreign capital. There are good reasons, therefore, for a moderately high level of openness to be put in place early enough to obtain market-based rates for exchange rates and to permit the efficient flow of capital resources into an economy for all the real-sector participants under development. In a later section, our discussion will move to this issue of where to place these steps in an overall design of the policy mix.

The next element is fiscal reforms. The current idea of development within a non-inflationary economic environment requires that the government budget be balanced except when exceptional circumstances such as an economic recession requires temporary overspending. Our analysis of the 13 cases shows three dominant patterns in this regard. Budget surplus countries are Singapore and Taiwan. Budget-balanced countries are Thailand, Korea and Indonesia (ostensibly). Deficit countries are China, India, Pakistan, and so on, all of which had budget deficits over most periods. Budget surplus countries created huge external resources, in this regard also being able to obtain foreign currency reserves from trade and/or capital flows. This led to consistent appreciation of their currencies, as did non-traded goods: if you live in Taipei or Singapore, you know what it means to own non-traded assets such as a house.

Budget-balanced Thailand and Indonesia gained some degree of control on inflation during the period when the budget was in balance. Korean firms, given their huge demands for capital raised in a largely closed financial sector, bid up interest rates, and through this lost control on inflation. Indonesia had high demands for capital, often raised in the capital markets in Hong Kong and Singapore at high interest rates. It also had off-budget expenses under the control of the president; the impact of this on the budget is still not fully understood. The third group, the majority, appears to have muddled through long periods of inflationary experiences given the loss of control on monetary policy because of the need to balance the budget by printing more money or from over-borrowing or from raising too much domestic debt. The ill-effects were rampant inflation rates in these countries.

A balanced budget thus appears to be critical for managing an economy well, and the norm for achieving price stability. Appreciating currencies often require constant upgrading of the skill contents of the producing sector, which means that large doses of capital have to be made available periodically to make the adjustments to higher technology. This perhaps explains the high capital use of the Singapore economy, say, relative to others at a similar stage of growth. An appreciating currency makes the non-traded sector too expensive for domestic purchasers. In the cases of balanced budgets, noticeable improvements in price stability and exchange rates were achieved. This was the case for most East Asian economies in the 1990s, which gave the impression of good fundamentals. (The rot from bad investments sanctioned by very imprudent banks was revealed when the financial crisis hit in July 1997. This will be discussed in the next section.)

Much has been said about mismanaged fiscal budgets. This took two forms. In those cases with significant state firms in the producing sector (China, India, Malaysia until 1984, and Vietnam), budget support for the loss-making firms was squarely to be blamed for the loss of fiscal control. Even today, when the state sector is more inclined to make profits as their target, China and Vietnam are still supporting loss-making firms in order not to create unemployment, which will foster discontent with the government. China pursued the spectacular strategy of allowing private-sector growth over 1979–99 to smother the inefficiency of the state sector, but the rot is still there, to be removed under the brave reforms of the new Chinese administration in the new century. India has sold part of the loss-making firms, having decided to nurture about 150 of the central-government-owned firms to become efficient through restructuring and corporatizing.

Thus a significant problem of fiscal budget balance is tied to the next element of reforms, namely privatization of state-owned firms belonging to central, state, provincial and city governments. The need to return state firms to private-sector competition has been a theme of popular capitalism all around the world. But in Asia, not every country is enthusiastic about this. China has, rightly or wrongly, decided to nurture 1000 of its state firms to satisfy East Asia's liking for 'big-is-better', despite the failings of the big firms, *zaibatsus* and *chaebols*, and the success of small and medium-sized firms in Taiwan. The worldwide preference is to see the reduction of state firms accounting for less than 10 per cent of GDP in areas that are considered to be in the domain of public-goods production. This is a critical factor in many large countries even outside Asia.

Unless this element of the reform mix is achieved, a weakness may linger in the management of the economy even if all other elements are correctly managed.

Three final elements of the reform package relate to the financial sector. These are (a) need for sufficient competition among the financial-sector firms, (b) prudential supervision of the financial institutions and (c) central bank independence in conducting prudential supervision. We remarked very early in Chapter 1 that weakness in the financial sector – which was closely aligned with capital flows as well – precipitated the Asian financial crisis. Throughout Asia, the worst-managed corporations are the firms in the financial sector. Exceptions are the completely open economies of Hong Kong and Singapore; some writers (Delhaise, 1998) add the Sri Lankan and Filipino financial sectors as being better managed. Why the first two are efficient is easy to see. These two are international financial centres where the presence of international players has improved competition among the financial institutions and the governments cannot interfere, and if they tried, may not be able to control these firms without sacrificing their status as financial centres. There is an even balance created by the self-interest of the government and that of the international banks. The central banks in these countries, whether they have independence or not, are aware of this fine balance that creates efficiency.

As for the rest, the common problems are many. The critical ones may be summarized as severe lack of competition. In the transition economies of China and Vietnam, only now is private ownership of banks beginning. At current rates, it will take decades before the impact of private-sector banks can make a difference to this state of affairs. There is a fear of foreign banks. Domestic banks are state-owned. In the South Asian countries, Sri Lanka excepted, the banks have been nationalized and efficiency has gone down to pretty low levels. But the increasing presence of significant private-sector financial institutions in these countries is beginning to introduce competition to the public-sector banks, thus producing efficiency gains much faster than is the case with transition economies. In each country chapter, we have presented the impacts of financial structures on the performance of this sector.

Competition policy requires privatizing the state-owned financial-sector firms too, and then removing barriers to entry for domestic and foreign firms. This must be done speedily in order to improve the financial efficiency so essential for the real-sector firms to reduce their financing costs. Imagine the high costs of about 7 per cent for capital-raising in Jakarta or Vietnam compared with just 1.5 per cent in Kuala Lumpur or Singapore. Firms work so hard to earn a rate of return of about 10–15 per cent on capital, whereas the investment banks in less competitive situations can cream off 7–10 per cent of the capital raised as fees alone for fund-raising activities! Mutual fund managers return to fund contributors a rate less than half the average market return rate in these places! These are some stark results from lack of sufficient competition in financial 'firms', as well as lack of prudential rules such as self-listing rules or zero front-end-fee rules for funds to improve competition.

Next, prudential regulations must be carefully devised and implemented. Some commentators (Cole and Slade, 1999) have gone to the extent of suggesting separating the savings function from the transaction function of banks so that the damage to savings can be limited if inefficiency from payment systems is the main reason why banks are damaged. New approaches are being suggested in the light of the Asian financial crisis. Among them is a suggestion that the Basle standards on capital adequacy (8 per cent cap on equity capital and risk-weighted capital) are sorely inadequate to meet the needs of developing countries. No one can fault these suggestions given the mess the banking systems are in in 11 of the 13 countries included in this study.

Finally, a word about central banking independence. This is not taken kindly by all the governments of the countries included in this study. For a brief period following the financial crisis, the central banks gained some degree of independence when their minders, the World Bank and the IMF, were sought to help nurse their economies back to health. In some cases, such as Indonesia and Korea, laws have been passed to mandate the independence of central banks. Only time can tell if the new minders, the governments, will be generous enough to let independent central banks exist when the temptation to order quick remedies through interventions is the order of the day in Asian countries, at least going by past patterns.[5]

In some countries, Indonesia included, far-reaching changes to the management of the central bank and banking supervision are being put in place. Central banking independence is being enshrined in new legal and administrative structures. After a phasing-out period, the prudential supervision of financial institutions will be centralized in a new independent body in the way practised in Australia and the United Kingdom. The central bank retains the responsibility to manage the monetary policy and fiscal agency functions. Of course, the lawmakers have provided that central banking independence is attained. Again, only time will tell if these experiments will lead to signal success in Indonesia and Korea so that others will also want to put such reforms in place.

2.4 The Lessons in a Chart

Figure 17.1 is a schematic representation of the discussion on the lessons about the liberal policy mix needed for ensuring sustained economic growth. The reform steps are sequenced in an order often claimed by experts to be the desirable one. In actual practice, some countries may take a slightly different approach as, for example, in 1970, when Indonesia, flushed with cash from petroleum sales, opened the current account fully before lifting the high tariff in the real sector. This could well be the pattern followed by a financial centre

---

PRECONDITIONS

1   Development strategy choice among competing models.

2   Good neighbourliness or absence of war.

3   Institution-building to strengthen private-sector initiatives via property
    rights, independent judiciary and effective bankruptcy laws and low
    taxation. Software for development.

ELEMENTS OF LIBERAL POLICY MIXTURE

4   Competition policy
    Domestic real sector competition to improve efficiency; gradual tariff
    reduction under infant-industry protection; foreign firm entry relaxation
    after real-sector efficiency.

5   Capital account opening
    Capital account for domestic firms opened; individuals restricted later
    capital account for foreign firms opened.

6   Current account opening for real-sector firms
    Limited current account openness for individuals; fuller opening of current
    accounts to individuals later.

7   Fiscal prudence through balanced budgets
    Taxation reform and tax administration reforms; privatization programme
    to limit damage to fiscal sector; build civil service's administrative
    capacity for reforms.

8   Competition policy for financial institutions[a]
    Remove or relax entry barriers; modernization; training.

9   Prudential supervision of financial institutions
    Build capacity for transparent prudential capacity; emerging economies
    need higher capital adequacy norms.

10 Central banking independence
    Slowly restrict central banks to perform monetary functions.

---

[a] Opening the financial-sector firms to competition takes place at the same time as non-financial
firms, as noted in element number 4 in this figure. The numbering does not indicate any particular
sequencing of reform steps.

Figure 17.1   Elements of liberal policy mix needed for development

such as Singapore, which must open its current and capital accounts fully to achieve growth from the financial sector. This economy produces some three times more GDP from its financial sector compared to an economy with no financial centre status.

In summarizing the lessons from this study, it appears that a modernizing economy, to secure growth towards a sustainable path, needs to pay attention to the ten elements included in Figure 17.1. Three of them are in the domain of political decision-making and institution-building to serve the development process. These are very long-term in nature, and are today considered as necessary conditions to put an economy on a growth-seeking path. The seven economic elements, on which much evidence has been given in this book, are essentially to do with real- and financial-sector reforms within the context of competition, prudential management and opening to the rest of the world. The specifics may be different in each country; the broad thrust seems to be gradual openness and prudential discipline of matters financial.

3. THE RESULTS SPEAK VOLUMES

This book has provided analysis of data over several decades as to how reforms in some cases or failure to take reforms in other cases led to the outcomes described. We shall not belabour this point. Wherever reforms were in the direction of improving competition, greater openness and prudential discipline, the result was a stunning income growth, which led to great social improvements in several countries. When prudential discipline became a scarce commodity in the 1990s, countries such as Korea, Indonesia and Thailand experienced sudden loss of control that led to loss of several years' gains. Table 17.1 records some of the striking results just before the Asian financial crisis hit some of the economies.

While the early reformers achieved an average economic growth rate of 8.1 per cent per annum in the 1991–96 period, the hesitant reformers achieved about half that rate. The transition economies, which had only recently adopted liberal reforms, grew at an astonishing rate of 10.1 per cent, ahead of the early reformers simply because of the sudden release of pent-up energy leading to huge investment splurges in these economies. Look at their price management outcomes.

The Communists failed to control inflation in that period, with an average inflation rate of 23 per cent, which is six times the rate achieved by the early reformers with more appropriate management of the economy. The hesitant reformers had an average inflation of 9.4 per cent per annum. Thus, using the criterion of growth under price stability, only the early reformers achieved notable successes, while the slightly less rigid economies of the hesitant groups did moderately well. Of course, one needs to compare these outcomes with almost zero growth in many Asian countries not included in this study.

Table 17.1   Growth friendly policy outcomes in Asia, 1991–96

Economies	Growth (%)	Inflation (%)	Capital/GDP (%)	Trade/GDP* (%)	Income class
Early reformers	8.1	4.9	34.7	64.2	–
Indonesia	7.3	7.4	34.8	27.0	Low
Korea	7.4	7.2	36.9	38.0	Middle
Malaysia	8.7	4.2	37.8	96.0	Middle
Singapore	8.5	2.1	34.8	135.0	Upper
Taiwan	8.8	3.2	22.7	47.0	Upper
Thailand	8.1	5.0	41.2	42.0	Middle
Hesitant reformers	4.5	9.4	21.1	13.5	–
Bangladesh	4.4	3.9	15.4	4.3	Low
India	5.2	10.5	23.9	8.5	Low
Pakistan	5.0	11.4	19.1	9.5	Low
Philippines	2.8	11.2	22.5	38.0	Low
Sri Lanka	5.0	9.9	24.5	7.4	Low
Transitional economies	10.1	23.1	28.6	11.8	–
China	11.3	13.4	37.6	17.5	Low
Vietnam	8.9	32.8	19.5	5.0	Low

Note: * Trade value divided by twice the GDP.

Sources: See individual chapters for sources.

Looking at the ability to increase savings and or to attract foreign capital, the early reformers had almost twice the amount of investment as the others. The Communist market economies attracted large capital inflows and yet their capital formation is still at 28.6 per cent of GDP compared with the 34.7 per cent for the early reformers. One might also point out that the over-dependence on foreign capital in all these countries except Taiwan created conditions ripe for the financial crisis. That is certainly part of the story. The real reason why too much borrowing led to that crisis in the first place is the long-gestation investments using short-term capital to offset the economic slow-down from declining export earnings during 1994–97. The entry of more cost-effective economies such as China led to loss of competitiveness, and when China devalued its currency twice in the early 1990s to attract more investment, troubles started to arise for the early reformers. This theme will be taken up later in our discussion of the crisis. Finally, trade dependence, which is a measure of the openness of the economy to the rest of the world, is very high (five times higher) for the early reformers. These countries chose the pragmatic path of export-led growth through industrialization, and in that process also made themselves more subject to world demand for their goods, dictating their policy choices. That is not a surprising result for a quick and favourable route to prosperity. The others are still not very open economies, and are unlikely to perform that well for some years to come. The transition economies have in fact moved up by taking an export-led growth path: note that they have built up a high level of external exposure in a short period. The hesitant reformers (excepting the Philippines) who followed a closed policy naturally have the lowest trade dependence: their ratio is one-fifth that of the early reformers.

Finally, and more importantly, the social impacts of growth are very telling. The early reformers, all of whom were a notch lower in the income classification, moved up the income ladder. The exception is Indonesia, with its huge population absorbing all the benefits of its high growth without any effect on the class of income group to which that country still belongs. One of the boasts of Indonesia was that 30 years after development started under Suharto, the number of people in poverty was reduced from some 60 per cent of the population to just 10 per cent by the mid-1990s. Of course, the political and economic crisis in Indonesia, given the huge share of GDP going to a small group of people, has forced about one-third of the population below the poverty line during just three years of the crisis. If the incomes from all these years of good growth had been more evenly distributed, the impact of the crisis would have been very different indeed. The Nobel laureate Sen's argument appears to hold very well here. The trickle-down effect of growth has to be countered by good policy of income equality, so it appears to us, to forestall the kind of collapse Indonesia experienced by following a policy of very low wages. Low wages kept a large segment of the population just above the poverty line even though economic growth of the same order was taking place as in the other early-reforming countries with better income policy.

Thus the statistics presented in Table 17.1 can be used to show that the liberal policy mix followed by the 13 countries produced predictable results. The outcomes are welfare-improving for the peoples of these countries. Data from earlier periods can be used to show that the decent growth rates that the hesitant reformers and the transitional economies achieved in the 1990s are due to the liberal reforms they undertook. Otherwise, their 1990s growth would have been pitiable, had they continued their command-economy or import-substitution approaches to growth. The outcomes of liberalization are clear for all to see. Now we turn to the effects of the 1997–98 Asian financial crisis to draw additional lessons about how not to reverse the favourable results of liberalization.

4.   LIBERALIZATION AND THE ASIAN FINANCIAL CRISIS

It has taken a long period of trial and error to learn from mistakes in the making of development policies in all the countries. But the biggest of the mistakes made so far appear to have been (a) the benign neglect of banking reforms and (b) over-exposure to short-term foreign capital flows at exactly the wrong time, when the declining export sectors were weakening the currencies of Korea, Thailand, the Philippines and Indonesia. Understanding the major reason for the financial crisis will enable other countries to learn a lesson from this one episode which has sapped more energy from the world community than any before. The appendix to this chapter lists the sequence of events from June 1997 to June 1999 to provide a background reference to the Asian financial crisis. In this section, we will describe the sequence of events to derive lessons for others to learn.

The Asian financial crisis had its origin in two events that began several years before the onset of the crisis. The first is related to export growth. With the memory of the 1989 Tiananmen Square massacre beginning to fade, China resumed its attractiveness as the cheapest place to produce many things the world wanted to consume. The rise of China as an attractive place for cost-reducing production (more joined in as Vietnam, India and others removed restrictions on foreign investments in the closing years of the 1980s) meant that some day the early reformers would lose their competition; they started to lose it from 1994. Thailand was the first country where export growth started to decline. Export growth rates that hovered in excess of 20 per cent on a year-on-year basis began to come down from 1991 until in the fourth quarter in 1994 they became negative. It took a mere six quarters thereafter to reveal the bad shape these economies were in.

Meanwhile, China which had regained its momentum after the fallout from 4 June 1989, had lowered the exchange rates twice by 1994, which gave China a tremendous advantage over other countries. One by one exports declined in all the hitherto fast-growing countries. And pressure built up in these countries to maintain a high level of investment. Paul Krugman wrote an article in 1994 questioning the myth of the East Asian Miracle, claiming that without positive total factory productivity, the high growth was merely input-driven and not the result of efficiency. This led to a revaluation in the political closets of the Asian countries. Secret meetings were held behind closed doors in the capital cities since Krugman's preaching went directly against the claims of all the politicians that they were good at economic policy-making. Led by some cash-rich countries, a call was made, and a few conferences later a scheme was mooted to improve the infrastructures of the economies in Asia, with massive investment in such long-term projects as power plants, roads, airports, bridges, and so on to improve factor productivity. This is exactly the opposite of what these countries had been doing for 25 years. Caution in using demand-creating policies was the order of the previous 25 years. That caution was now relaxed. Soon the politician's major benefactors, the World Bank and the Asian Development Bank, produced documents to suggest that US$500 billion was needed to upgrade the infrastructures in Asia to gain efficiency and momentum for growth. It was the politician's answer to gaining factor productivity!

With permission granted in 1994 to borrow and lend in foreign currencies (in some countries), a great deal of short-term cash found its way into these countries, and became channelled through new financial institutions (the failed Bangkok Bank of Commerce, for example) to unproductive investments. The managed float of the currencies was made possible and was thought to be a permanent fixture as these countries had huge foreign reserves to throw at speculators to defend their currencies. This is exactly what had been happening since 1995 as the currencies were weakening and the ever-vigilant central banks were defending their pegs to the dollar or to a basket of currencies, as desired by their political masters. Meanwhile more and more money was being committed or planned to be committed to investments that would provide decent returns in the long run, but not in the short run.

This went on for almost a year and half, until the weak coalition government of businessman Barnharn in Thailand committed serious errors in managing the impending disasters arising from the connected lending problems in the Thai financial system. The rot set in after 1994 and the disease became full-blown by mid-1997. Weaknesses started to develop after the 1994 reforms in several countries to attract short-term capital. At one time, 91 Thai finance companies had as much as 25 per cent of the total credits, most of them to the overpriced property markets in Bangkok.[6] Property bubbles built up in all the countries except Indonesia. For example, in two years in the first half of the 1990s, the property index went up 120 per cent in Singapore. Once the free-wheeling economy of Thailand buckled, it was a matter of time before investors started to do some new arithmetic and started pulling out of their cash positions. On closer inspection lenders found that the money sent to these star emerging markets was probably being squandered on grandiose projects, though many of them were sound ones, and they began to pull out their cash from the region in a general rout as had never been experienced in Asia. As the currency tumbled, so did the stock markets (in foreign currency terms, the stock markets of the crisis-hit countries lost 75 per cent of their pre-crisis value).

The currency crisis (see Chapter 2) started on 2 July, and is often said to have ended only in May 1999. There were three distinct phases in the event. The first was from 2 July 1997 to September 1997. By September, the IMF was already in charge of some economies and there was much optimism that the crisis would soon pass. The strident explanation was that the fundamentals were right and that the speculative attack alone was to be blamed for the crisis in all countries, not only in Malaysia. No one at that time made any connection with the hollowing out of the free-market economies by the attraction of China (and other new entrants) as a major competitor, nor to the clever revaluations of renminbi that gave a severe jolt to the hitherto good-quality economies of East and Southeast Asia. It has still not dawned on the analysts that a fundamental shift is taking place. The currency realignment from this major crisis is a mere but large-scale revaluation of the values of these small economies in a more competitive world with the entry of the third-generation developing countries with much cheaper resources. One observer said that if the world opened the door for the skilled workers of China and India alone, there would be a total of several millions who would out-qualify for the jobs in the more successful economies.

From November to May 1998, the second phase of the currency crisis revealed itself as actual new policies were being put in place. Thailand's government had fallen and a new one was narrowly elected to office. The election in March of Suharto for a seventh term unleashed political fallout, which led to riots and then his resignation on 20 May 1998. Things started to get worse as the Asian crisis appeared to have spread worldwide between June 1998 and January 1999. Two episodes, one in Russia in the form of a currency collapse of 12 per cent in November 1998 and the other in the USA, when the First Capital Fund was threatened with a loss of some US$3000 billion, occurred that observers linked to the Asian crisis. Fortuitously, the timely intervention of the US Fed halted worldwide panic. By June 1999, the crisis seemed to have dissipated and several of the currencies except the fixed ringgit and the rupiah had recovered part of the losses on the back of healthy growth in foreign currency reserves from improved export growth due to regaining competitiveness and from aid disbursements.

A significant statistic to bear in mind in order to understand the crisis is the capital flow to these countries. In 1996 a total of US$96 000 million found its way to this part of the world: in 1997 and 1998, the net outflows were negative US$34 000 million and US$12 000 million respectively. These statistics speak volumes about what had happened to these economies. In 1999, cash inflow was positive US$91 000 million! Next, all the countries lost more than half their long-term growth rates in 1996, while 1998 saw a net economic decline of some 3 per cent. By all predictions, a modest growth was expected in 1999 for all but Indonesia. Indonesia elected a new parliament on 6 June 1999. The parliament was expected to elect a new president in an election in November, when the choices would be more between the bad and the worse than ever before in its history. Normalcy is expected to occur for Indonesia, the largest economy in Southeast Asia, in the year 2000. And the centre-left government of President Abdurahman Wahid is holding steady to reforms.

What lessons are there for others from this crisis? We agree with the assessment made by McKinnon (1998, p. 97).

For many years, diverse financial institutions in each of the five [crisis] countries had struggled with festering bad-loan problems from over-investment in real estate: lending to profitless real industry; government-sponsored mega projects; subsidized rural lending; and so on ... undermined the capital position of banks.

The straw that broke the camel's back appear to have come from the way banking business has been conducted, with no prudential concerns in almost all these countries. Even when the finance ministers or the central bankers pointed to the right decisions to make (recall what happened to the brave Thanong Bidaya, the Finance Minister of Thailand in June 1997 or Marse Mohammad of Indonesia) the system favoured quick fixes and moved on to doing the same thing again. In our opinion, banking fragility resulted from corporations taking on too much debt, as evidenced in Chapter 2, undertaking profitless investments, and so on. These activities gave rise to a general financial fragility, which appeared to be tolerated by the regulators as a necessity to address the urgent problem of lack of infrastructure, which, if not remedied, it was thought, might continue to make growth unsustainable. These politicians some of whom are paid huge salaries, could not have been more wrong at the worst times.

The origin of tolerance for financial fragility came from political decision-making, in particular to continue the high-growth path even when these countries were losing competitiveness to China, Vietnam and India, resulting in declining exports. Cole and Slade (1999) actually advocate setting lower growth targets under these changed circumstances. No country could afford this strategy of fine tuning by adding more infrastructure at this inappropriate time. Had exports been held at a level of 20 per cent or more, the pursuit of high growth coupled with some improvements in infrastructure would have gone on for several more years. Thus, in our opinion, financial-fragility-promoting policies – we mean, of course, that lack of prudential regulation stems from financial fragility – were the sources of the problem. The banking sector mirrored this condition, described by McKinnon as a festering bad-loan problem. The father of financial liberalization theory appears to have got it right.

Several other observers have attributed the origin of this crisis to political reasons (McIntaire, 1998); to excessive private debt amid asset bubbles (Ichimura et al., 1998, p. 3); to the wrong exchange rate policy based on some sort of pegging. Political reasons are certainly often powerful explanations of single events, but they fail to explain systematically across all countries. The exchange rate is perhaps a better explanation at least for the way the rupiah behaved during July to December 1997. Had the Indonesians moved to some form of free-floating long before, the market might not have deeply devalued the rupiah by some 27 per cent by December 1997, since all indicators for this country then suggested strong fundamentals (there was no public knowledge of the off-budget expenses of the president) and the government was always ready to act decisively, unlike the Thai government of Barnharn. If the more open economies had had some residual controls of the type Taiwan had on the current and capital accounts, at least domestic firms and individuals would not have lined up behind foreigners taking short-term money out of the country. But an exchange rate explanation as a source of the crisis can only explain over-shooting. A free float, tested and well in place, may still lead to depreciation but certainly not to the extent of overshooting experienced.

The reader will note, therefore, that the primary origin of the crisis is the gradual loss of competitiveness by the free-market economies when Communist China and later Communist Vietnam started to hollow out the free-market economies by their aggressive pursuit of capital flows into their economies. The captains of the free market economies are on record abetting this hollowing out. The currency peg in place was especially protected by the huge foreign reserves. This meant that politicians did not have to mandate or even punish central banks which permitted lending by banks to sustain unwise investment in what Nasution called land-based investments. Prudential oversights normally expected to come into force were relaxed when *un*profitable investments in whatever form were being encouraged by banks working in concert with big business and big government, using savings entrusted to them. The decisions of the network of powerful people undermined the safety of the bank savings of ordinary firms and individuals in many countries. The speculators exploited this weakness to make fortunes for themselves. That will happen again unless the reforms of the kind that Korea and Indonesia are making take real hold. As long as these reforms are implemented with the prudence required of the central banks in the new century, we may yet see another crisis of this kind.

Thus the lesson from the financial crisis appears to be consistent with what we suggested in an earlier section. That is, prudential oversight of the financial sector has to be done by independent central banks and regulators: see Figure 17.1. Needless to say, connected lending, where some form of implicit encour-agement is given by governments, must be avoided at all costs.[7] This practice, if ever tolerated in the new century, will again lead to sanctioning unprofitable investments if politicians use this loophole of bad investments to pay off the political support of interest groups (Thailand), or to ingratiate the children of first families (Indonesia, and others), to gain favours from presidents or prime ministers, related party lending (the *chaebols* of Korea), and so on.

5.   CORRECT SEQUENCING OF REFORMS

Economists have long debated the benefits of free markets and economic lib-eralization. However, the speed and sequence of financial-sector reforms have been found to be crucial to the success of liberalization policies. The literature on this issue is mixed and sadly suggests that there is no universal rule to be adopted by all countries. Before we discuss the optimal sequencing of the liberalization process, it seems important to look into the specific reasons why an economy may be undertaking liberalization. In general, the financial-sector reforms are intended to relax interest rate controls, develop money and interbank markets, tighten prudential regulation and the supervisory system, strengthen competition among banks while also liberalizing credit regulations, developing capital markets and payment systems, and restructuring foreign exchange markets. It is the structural linkage between these goals that provides a basis for debate on which policy action should be taken first, and which later. Research on sequencing is merely finding out what ought to be done first, and what later.

The handful of serious researchers on this subject appear to have two main concerns (Gibson and Tsakalotos, 1994). The first research question is 'Is there an optimal order for liberalizing the domestic real sector, the domestic financial sector, the external real sector and the external financial sector?' That is, find out the best order in which things should be liberalized as would be suggested by a given model of what outcomes may be expected. The second approach is based on McKinnon's work, where he seeks to ascertain if certain prerequisites exist before financial liberalization to enhance economic outcomes. Despite the simplicity of the issues involved, no consensus exists among the experts about an optimal sequencing path.

Most disagreement appears to be on the issue of whether the domestic financial sector should be liberalized before the trade sector. If a country liberalizes its domestic financial sector before the trade sector, credit could flow to the tradable sector, which may be kept profitable by the protection provided by the high tariff wall. In theory, this must be an inefficient allocation of credit because one sector, namely the traded sector, gets more ready credit lines than the non-traded sector. On the other hand, if the domestic financial sector is liberalized after the traded sector, that would hamper the ability of domestic industry to compete in the world market, at least in the initial stage of reforms.

Similarly, opening the capital account too early increases opportunities for currency substitution. That would lead to capital flight in search of higher returns. This will lead to an appreciation of the real exchange rate and incorrect allocation of resources between tradables and non-tradables. Liberalization of the capital account will also restrict the ability of the domestic banking industry to compete with foreign banks, given the strict regulatory system under which they often have to operate, with more stringent domestic regulations for domestic firms. At the same time, capital account liberalization and real appreciation of the exchange rate will increase the resource availability of an economy. On the prerequisites, McKinnon (1991b) therefore suggests that two conditions must exist before financial liberalization: fiscal discipline and prudential control over domestic banks.

The debate on sequencing was initiated by Shaw (1973) and McKinnon (1973), who advocated reforming the whole economy at one go. Initial financial liberalization based on the original recommendations led to severe adverse effects in some Latin American countries during the 1970s, when financial liberalization policies were first implemented. In the wake of such a bad experience, Edwards (1984a) and McKinnon (1982; 1989; 1991b) contributed a series of papers making some original contributions on sequencing. Many other economists joined in this search, including Edwards (1994), Levine (1997), Cole (1998), Fry (1997), Villanueva and Mirakhor (1990), Eichengreen (1998), among others. One point they all agree on is that the external sector should be liberalized after the domestic sector. In this chapter, we referred to these as element number 4 in Figure 17.1. The reader will note that the tariff reduction and entry relaxation for foreign firms are listed after the domestic firms have been subjected to more competition.

Earlier literature on sequencing dealt with this issue in a political economy framework and recommended a gradual liberalization. It was only in 1973 that McKinnon restated this question as an important economic policy issue, and the subject is now treated as such. As stated earlier, McKinnon changed his view in his later articles and concluded that complete liberalization should not be performed at one go; it is a gradual process.

The main message from his research to date is that the capital account should be the last to open. He argues that Chile performed better than Mexico because it first opened the trade sector and kept the capital account closed.[8] Argentina suffered severe currency depreciation and later high inflation because the capital account was opened before the trade sector had been subjected to tariff-reduction-induced competition. He argues that relaxing the capital account earlier would lead to capital inflow and hence make the real exchange rate appreciate. This is an unwelcome economic effect when the trade sector is liberalized because it would work against export competitiveness. It is also counter-productive, as such capital inflows can become unsustainable, exactly what happened in the Asian financial crisis, no doubt after a long period of capital flows.

McKinnon (1982) also suggested that trade liberalization should take place after fiscal deficit has been eliminated. He continued the same arguments in his later articles. Edwards (1987) supported this view by developing a theoretical model and testing it empirically on a group of developing countries, with favourable results. Frenkel (1982; 1983) believes that liberalization affects goods and asset markets at different speeds. While the asset market, because of its greater fungibility, may clear instantaneously, the goods market, with sticky prices and satiation of utility constraints, takes some time to clear. Therefore, he also suggests that the current account should be liberalized before the capital account. Krueger (1992) analysed the issue in a broader framework, involving other markets such as labour and agriculture markets. She does not specify an order of reforms, favouring abrupt simultaneous reforms in all sectors based on welfare and credibility considerations. Edwards (1984c), however, favours gradual rather than abrupt reforms. His findings are based on a general equilibrium model and he also advocates such a policy has welfare gains. In a later article, Edwards (1986) supports an argument in favour of gradual trade reforms as it would reduce unemployment dislocations, while deferring capital account opening to a later date.

Cole (1998) argues that the capital account should be the last major policy area to be liberalized. Liberalization of capital accounts before financial- and trade-sector reforms, he argues, would lead to less efficient capital allocation to investments and could lead to potential economic disruptions. Cole also notes, however, that opening of the capital account in the early phase of liberalization may help to maintain fiscal discipline because of the fear that unbalanced government expenditures, if sustained for too long, would bring in severe devaluations. Fry (1997), based on the findings of comprehensive empirical research, suggests that reforms in small economies compared with the large economies should be faster. He argues in favour of capital account liberalization soon *after* government budgets are balanced – so this is an argument for sequencing. Lal and Myint (1999) and Sell (1988) argued that the capital account should be opened before the current account. These are two too many important dissenting views on the order of sequencing. They believe that a free-floating exchange rate is crucial to a liberalized economy. If one examines the behaviour of the more open Asian economies, especially at the levels of high growth secured in Indonesia, Malaysia, Singapore and Thailand soon after they introduced current account liberalization, these views appear to make good sense. But this is no longer the case, since the very same condition made these economies ready for the huge output losses via the Asian financial crisis. Only the speculators laughed all the way to the banks.

Villanueva and Mirakhor (1990) took a different point of view and looked at appropriate sequencing of liberalization along with effective bank regulation.[9] They argue that eliminating credit controls abruptly, without adequate prudential supervision of bank lending, may increase the moral hazard problem. Once again, McKinnon's quote comes to mind. It is the absence of prudential oversight that led to financial fragility and then the collapse of economic growth in 1997–99. Villanueva and Mirakhor suggest that macroeconomic stabilization and stringent prudential regulations must exist *before* complete relaxation of interest rate controls. The paper refers to the experiences of three Latin American countries, namely, Chile, Argentina and Uruguay.

Some of the East Asian countries adopted this gradual approach in interest rate liberalization in their years of more prudent behaviour. Alas, the same countries later relaxed bank supervision. Indonesia permitted foreign loans to be freely available to domestic firms in foreign currencies. Government banks and one private bank were actually given permission to lend to domestic firms in foreign currencies! Indonesia is also an example of reverse sequencing, where the capital account was thrown completely open as early as 1970, but the country then had a huge capital inflow from its crude oil export. One may argue that Indonesia paid the price for such a policy in 1997. Thailand permitted credit creation at 68 per cent in some years in the 1990s, and most of that went to related party lending and to land-based investments. At the end of June 1997, just before the crisis erupted, lending to the property sector constituted 28 per cent of all bank lending, not counting the loans from the finance companies. Most listed firms in Malaysia went into the property development business in the 1990s when the trade sector was declining, and the banks joined in to provide easy credit. The same thing happened in Singapore. This was one of the main causes of the currency crisis in Thailand, Korea and Indonesia, when the post-1991 financial reforms were in total disregard of all prudential rules. Some observers in the financial press were aghast at the level of stupidity in such actions, when these countries were the paragon of proper economic behaviour before 1991. Wealth created in good years perhaps makes people less vigilant.

Theoretically, it is possible to identify an optimal sequence of reforms but in practice it is a daunting task. Most developing countries have a variety of distortions present in their economic systems – that is not exactly true of developed ones too – and any reform process would be meaningless without removing some such serious distortions at the same time as taking reform steps. The experience of the 1997–98 Asian financial crisis suggests that there is a need for proper sequencing and adequate – perhaps the reader would say more than adequate – prudential regulations if there is an optimal path to a uniform strategy.

The exact sequencing for a particular country may also depend on the political will to take hard decisions in the face of interest groups running the financial systems and the stage of economic development, the ability of the legal system to act impartially and fairly, the presence of institutional traditions, and so on. Cole and Slade (1999, p. 182) were rightly cautious about this when they wrote:

> these recent crises compel us to consider *whether it is possible* to create in few years the essential preconditions for a safe and sound, privately-owned financial system, operating in a free-wheeling globalized world, especially in developing countries that are still in the early stages of establishing effective, democratic political and legal systems.

Thus it appears that there is less likelihood of a distortion-free economy by relying on a simultaneous no-holds-barred liberalization in an imperfect world. Perhaps only in the sterilized world of model-building would such a world exist;

such big-bang approaches have not produced a single successful case so far. Just think of the pains in Poland, Hungary – even Russia. Oh, for the perfect world!

There is, however, an agreement that economic liberalization should not be delayed because some of the prerequisites do not exist or because it is difficult to implement the 'big bang'. The literature reviewed in this section draws some policy conclusions. The capitalist system creates its own distortions and hence freeing the market to do the watching through invisible hands is the first priority when reforms are initiated. Capital controls should not be relaxed completely (Chile, Taiwan and now Malaysia) before the complete liberalization of the domestic economy. The order of sequencing suggested and supported by most writers amounts to four simple lessons.

- The liberalization process should start with curtailing the budget deficits of governments followed by reforming the labour market (see the coverage of labour reforms in the Singapore chapter).
- The liberalization of the goods market should then take effect, followed by liberalization of the domestic financial markets, which must include greater competition within the banking sector.
- The capital account should be liberalized only after the above steps are completed successfully. As in Chile, some legal power should be retained even as controls are relaxed.
- A good dose of prudential regulations should be designed and implemented under transparent regulatory controls by well-trained, efficient regulators with independence to act prudentially, under the watchful eyes of a stable government. Only then should the financial-sector reforms be implemented.

What this section advocates, therefore, is not at all contrary to what we have stated in earlier sections in this chapter. There is thus a desirable sequencing in a world with distortions. Given that, any simultaneous big-bang opening, as in the Russian experiment, is at best risky. Experimental economic reforms of the Chinese type are less risky. Hesitancy to take the right steps towards reform could be misguided.

6. THE BRAVE NEW CENTURY FOR OPPORTUNITIES?

New beginnings are possible to make up for missed opportunities. Will this be the case for Asia? We think it will. It was not until the 1990s that the fruits of liberal policies began to be noticed more clearly as having made a big difference to all parties. Even after the ill-effects of the financial crisis had done their predictable damage to five of the 13 economies, the attraction of liberalization has not waned at all, though some aspects of liberal policies may not receive enthusiastic support after the lessons learned from the crisis years. In this concluding section, we make an educated guess about where Asia may be heading in some possible scenarios.

First and foremost, liberalization has gained a sufficient reputation as a correct choice for putting ailing economies back to work. This is especially true after the spectacular results from experiments with market-economy reforms, where once the command-economy model had led to spectacular failures around the world. So, it appears that liberalization will be a favourite fixture in the new century, offering greater attractions to many Asian economies which have not yet made the transition to the new way of managing their economic affairs. Here, we are anticipating the adoption of this policy by the majority of Central and West Asian economies long used to central guidance and unaccustomed to market signals. The first thing we are confident about is that the platform for liberal reforms may reach broad-based consensus in Asia very quickly as the new Century begins.

Next, globalization at its current rate of progress is likely to speed up the demands for visible economic growth in more countries than the 13 described in this book. Political developments in Asia appear to have moved away from colonial rule to self-rule; in some countries self-rule has been replaced by authoritarian regimes only to find that growth collapses, as happened under the military regimes in Myanmar (formerly Burma), Thailand in the 1970s and Pakistan in the 1980s and so on. More and more countries are experimenting, not of course with the Pukka English democracy, but are slowly evolving more democratic traditions as the days of the despotic rules of Mao or of Zia or of Marcos have given way to a more people-focused rule. That is good for preparing the ground for liberal policies to find more adherents.

But there are also rare exceptions when authoritarian rule was growth-consistent: two examples are the periods under Park Chung-Hee in Korea and Chiang Kai-shek in Taiwan. For a while some Asian countries squandered opportunities when they were trapped within the Soviet model, or under despots, who set the clock back in almost all cases. Faith in great helmsmen was waning as people become more educated and able to take collective responsibility for their own decisions. The second theme we predict, therefore, is more democratization of the political system, which is good for liberalization. Even in the worst case of Communism, China in this case, villagers are beginning to make democratic choices to flush out corrupt Communist cadres and prevent them from mismanaging their affairs. Suharto's error was not lack of development, but the mistake of not yielding to demands for more democratic institutions. This slow consensus that is building everywhere in Asia that some degree of free choice and ownership rights is needed for growth to occur augurs well, especially under a more democratic decision process.

If we assume that the entry of larger economies with cheaper resources are constantly going to rearrange the ranks of countries in a competition table, then changes in the fortunes of countries are ever more linked to their ability to undertake meaningful reforms. Necessarily a few of the countries, especially Hong Kong and Singapore, may emerge as the leading financiers of Asian countries. This is not any different from the role New York plays in the USA or London plays in the City for the world. Asians would increasingly resort to finance from Asia as more resources are found in Asia for Asia's development needs.

The group of nations now forming the NIEs will continue to resemble Japan; in the manner Japan helped to spread industrialization in Korea and Taiwan, so would these clones. In this, the new century may find Malaysia and Thailand becoming members of the NIEs not too far in the future. With pursuit of correct policies, the Vietnams of Asia may find themselves coming out of poverty by adopting liberal policies in the same way as others before them. The transitional economies with resources, Myanmar, Kazhakstan, Uzbekistan, and so on, may make fast gains as their resources are increasingly exploited by multinational capital and know-how brought in by reforms. If liberal policies take them along the same route as, for example, Thailand, then there is much hope for Asia to progress. That of course needs clear political choices for liberal policies in these countries.

A big unknown in all this prediction is the way the Communist countries will bring in their love of doctrine to play economic games with free-market economies. If the hollowing out of the free-market economies is possible, then why not do by stealth what the guerrilla wars of the 1960s and 1970s failed to achieve – the spread of control through doctrinaire uprising? If Communist countries use the economic clout from the cheap input cost advantages they have, then the free-market economies must move up the skill ladder just as Taiwan has done. This will create some degree of beggar-thy-neighbour policies, which may create tension in the years to come. Some economists are predicting that more instability will arise, not just from this gamesmanship but also from other larger economies constantly rearranging the game of competition through trading blocs. Happily, the remedy for such calls lies in more focused and dedicated pursuit of development policy to reach a higher economic stage of development. That again is a happy outcome, as has been demonstrated by Korea and Taiwan as they moved to become NIEs or attain the developed-country stage. Thanks to the rich menu of experiences of the 13 countries over the last 30 to 40 years, the rest of Asia can learn some tried lessons for their formulation of long-term policy to secure prosperity for their peoples. These tried lessons did not come from the rarefied rooms of a few famous prognosticators. In the predictions based on tried and tested policies, we are more confident.

NOTES

1. Mohamed Ariff is deeply indebted to John Dunning for his elucidation of this concept. John used it in his speech at the Melbourne Club in 1999. Of course, in his paradigm for development, good neighbourliness features prominently.
2. Ramos, trained by the Americans in psychological warfare, prepared the country for reforms, recognizing the need for domestic peace before economic development policies could work for the Philippines. Would his successor see this wisdom!
3. In his widely popular economics textbook in the 1960s and 1970s, Samuelson, the famous economist, proposed that a country has a choice between allocating more scarce resources to producing guns and tanks for making war or making bread and butter to increase prosperity. That adage is still apt, and we feel that those countries that chose to make more of the means of war-making in Asia did not make as much progress as the others.
4. It is observed that these two countries put in place invisible barriers to trade in the form of onerous health certification for food products, for example. We disregard this aspect in our analysis.
5. Imagine the Hong Kong government being told not to attempt a stock market rescue in August 1998. Or imagine the People's Bank of China cutting budget support to the 1000 firms that are being nurtured as firms of excellence to provide competition to the foreign and private-sector companies. In the week before the floating of the currency, Thai Prime Minister Banharn ordered a US$2.86 billion bailout of 16 finance companies declared closed by the central bank and the finance minister in July 1997. To expect the unthinkable – that the right things will happen – is to fool ourselves. Only time will tell. Marie Mohammed was sacked by Suharto for doing the right thing.
6. One crude index of property bubbles is the number of cranes you see as you drive past a city's airports. This index must have fallen by 95 percentage points between early June 1997 and May 1998. The authors were in Thailand on those dates on research trips, and were not surprised to find this, even as the Thai economy was brought to its lowest point by end-1998.
7. The US government gives implicit guarantees to borrowing by agencies and even some foreign governments. But such decisions are subject to the vote of the House and the Senate. The point is that this is an institutionalized way of borrowing, with full disclosure, compared with the behind-the-scenes deals promoted in the 1990s in the East Asian economies.
8. There has been a re-examination of this conclusion by none other than the IMF. The consensus as of 1999 was that there are other explanations as to why Chile did better. However, currency speculators have noted that capital controls that Chile had in law could be reimposed very easily if speculative attacks were to occur. The residual capital controls have not yet been removed from the law books in Chile.
9. Cole and Slade (1996) and Caprio (1997) also supported measures to ensure adequate bank and non-bank supervision before steps for financial-sector liberalization are taken.

APPENDIX: A DIARY OF EVENTS SURROUNDING THE ASIAN FINANCIAL CRISIS

Date	Country	Description of events
1997		
27 June	Thailand	The Thai finance minister orders 16 finance companies closed. The decision is reversed by prime minister with US$2.86 billion bailout.
2 July		After defending the weakening baht from above news, the Bank of Thailand announced free float of the baht. Baht loses 10% of its pre-float value on that day, and 17% in a week.
20 July	Philippines	IMF grants US$1000 million as emergency grant after peso falls outside a widened band to defend the basket peg. IMF warns Thailand to cut its spending, requests it to take a loan from the IMF.
July (undated)		The trade economist Bhagwati condemns free trade in money.
24 July	Malaysia	Malaysian ringgit comes under speculative attack. Mahathir's attack on speculations such as those of George Soros.
11 August	Thailand	IMF, led by Japan's pressure, pledges US$16 billion to Thailand as rescue package.
	Indonesia	Indonesia's rupiah under attack. Bank Indonesia's attempt to contain the troubles proves unsuccessful.
4 September	Asia	Asian stock markets plunge in unison: Manila 9.3%; 4.5% in Jakarta.
	Philippines	Philippine peso falls to the lowest level before central bank intervenes to maintain basket peg. Indonesian rupee recovers.
8 October	Malaysia	Malaysia spends US$20 billion to prop the share market.
27 October	Indonesia	Indonesia considers asking IMF for emergency bailout.
23–8 October	USA	New York share market loses 7.2% in value.
3 November	Hong Kong	Hong Kong share market declined by nearly 25% in value.
	Japan	Japan's Sanyo Securities files for bankruptcy.
8 November	Korea	South Korean won loses 7%, biggest one-day loss.
20 November		South Korea begins talks with IMF for tens of billions in emergency aid after Japan showed signs of reluctance
24 November		to finance rescue.
25 November	Japan	Japan's third financial house to apply for closure: the
3 December		seventh largest Yamaichi Securities goes under.
	Korea	Korean Stock Market plunges with a loss of 7.2%
	Japan	Tokyo City Bank, a regional bank, closes.

Date	Country	Description of events
22 December	Korea	Korea agrees to IMF conditions for restructuring $55 billion.
25 December	Malaysia	Malaysia imposes tough reforms including expenditure cuts.
1998		
12 January	Korea	Korean won plunges further with fresh problems of Hanban.
		IMF and lender nations move to finance US$10 billion loan to Korea.
17 January	Hong Kong	Peregrine of Hong Kong files for liquidation from share market loss.
21 May	Indonesia	Indonesian president fires the central bank governor.
		Indonesia's President Suharto resigns after a wave of bloody riots.
11–27August	World	Stock markets plunge around the world in expectation of interest rate rises in the USA. Hong Kong mounts an expensive support to prop up the stock market. Malaysia had done a similar rescue in Sept.
20 August	(Internet)	Paul Krugman goes public in support of temporary imposition of fixed exchange rate as the desperate Plan B for a troubled world.
7 August	Website	Paul Krugman writes a radical proposal to go back to fixed rate.
1 September	Malaysia	Malaysia announces going back to fixed (RM 3.8 = US$1) from November 1998. All free-market currency transaction outside the country is abolished and made illegal, thus cutting off outside origin of currency speculation.
27 September	Japan	A major leasing company in Japan files for bankruptcy.
2 October	USA	The Long Term Capital Fund is reported to have lost US$5 billion.
17 October		The Federal Reserve mounts a rescue by putting together a consortium to rescue the Long Term Capital Fund.
October–November	USA	The Fed announces interest rate cuts, and the share market rebounds.
		This averts world panic from spreading. Two more rate cuts follow by 20 November 1998. Russian ruble tumbles 12%.
December	Asia	Most currencies that had overshot (baht, rupiah, peso, ringgit and won) recovered about half-way from their worst declines. Rupiah gained the most from its low of some Rp 17 000 to Rp 7600 to US$.
1999		
16 January	Brazil	Speculative attack on Brazilian currency: 8%, then a 18% devaluation. Free-floated the currency. Capital outflow of US$40–80 bn.

Date	Country	Description of events
January	Europe	The euro starts phase one to replace 11 EU currencies by year 2002.
	China	About 240 mutual funds suffered loss: decision to close the second largest fund and notice given of further reduction of a total of 40 of them. It was later revealed in a Guangdong court that the total loss from GITIC would amount to about US$50 bn.
6 February	Malaysia	Capital controls replaced by graduated penalty for short-term withdrawals. Meanwhile, raised long-term loans domestically.
March	Japan	Japan announces far-reaching reforms, which pulls the stock market from its low of around 13 000 to somewhere close to 16 000.
May	London	George Soros announces that the currency crisis is over. No reactions in the markets. Reserves of several countries improve, one of which is Korea.
June	World	Interbank and discount rates and bond yields go up, signalling an expectation of interest rises in the future. Stock markets declining.
June	Europe	The euro, the third world currency, loses out, reaching parity with dollar.
		This prompts speculation that the British pound will not find its way into the euro since the expected euro's strength not revealed.
9 June	USA	The long-term bond yield goes up to 6% triggering dollar to depreciate, and the stock markets to begin losing value.

Sources: Internet publications of *Asian Economies Reports*, 1997–98; and *The Economist*.

Select bibliography

Adhikary, G.P. (1989), *Deregulation in the Financial System of the SEACEN Countries*, Kuala Lumpur: SEACEN Research and Training Center.

Aghevli, Bijan B., Mohsin Khan and Peter Montiel (1991), 'Exchange Rate Policy in Developing Countries: Some Analytical Issues', *IMF Occasional Paper No. 78*, Washington, DC: International Monetary Fund.

Agtmael, Antoine W. van (1994), 'Thailand: From Mini-Market to Leading Emerging Market', in Keith K.H. Park and Antoine W. van Agtmael (eds), *The World's Emerging Stock Markets: Structure, Developments, Regulations and Opportunities*, Singapore: Heinemann Asia, pp. 121–42.

Aijazuddin, F.S. (1996), 'The Investment Banking Industry in Pakistan', paper presented at the International Conference on Management and Business, Lahore University of Management Sciences, 3–5 June.

Ariff, M. (1995a), 'International Interest Rate Factors in India and Singapore: Fisher's Uncovered Parity Test over 1972–1992', in Banoji Rao and Yong Mun Chong (eds), *Singapore–India Relations*, Singapore: National University of Singapore pp. 225–31.

Ariff, M. (1995b), 'Indian Financial System Development Opportunities', in Banoji Rao and Yong Mun Chong (eds), *Singapore–India Relations*, Singapore: National University of Singapore, pp. 195–224.

Ariff, Mohamed (1996), 'Effects of Financial Liberalization on Four Southeast Asian Financial Markets, 1973–94', *ASEAN Economic Bulletin*, **12** (3), 325–38.

Ariff, M. (1997), 'Is it an Asian Miracle or Shared Growth or Simply Good Socio-Economic Governance?', *Southeast Asian Journal of Social Science*, **25** (2), 189–201.

Ariff, M. (1998a), 'A Fresh Approach to Understanding Financial Instability in ASEAN with Reference to Indonesia', paper presented to Bank Indonesia, September.

Ariff, M. (1998b), 'The Wallis Report and Australian Financial System', *Monash Mt. Eliza Business Review*, **2**, 19–21.

Ariff, M. (1998c), *APEC & Development Co-operation*, Singapore: Institute of Southeast Asian Studies.

Ariff, M. and Nicolas Groenewold (1998), 'The Effects of De-Regulation on Share-Market Efficiency in the Asia-Pacific', *International Economic Journal*, **12** (4), 23–47.

Ariff, M. and L.W. Johnson (1990), S*ecurities Markets and Stock Pricing Evidence from a Developing Asian Capital Market*, Singapore, London and Sydney: Longman.

Ariff, M., B. Kapur and A. Tyabji (1995), 'Money Markets in Singapore', in David C. Cole, Hal S. Scott and Philip A. Whellons (eds), *Asian Money Markets*, New York and Oxford: Oxford University Press, pp. 349–87.

Ariff, M., M. Shamsher and M.N. Annuar (1998), *Stock Pricing in Malaysia: Corporate Financial and Investment Management*, Serdang, Selangar: University Putra Malaysia, Press International Edition.

Arndt, H. and H. Hall (eds) (1999), *Southeast Asia's Economic Crisis: Origins, Lessons, and the Way Forward*, (Current Economic Affairs Series), Singapore: Institute of Southeast Asian Studies.

Asher, M. and C.D. Wadhra (1987) *ASEAN – South Asia economic relations*, Singapore: Institute of South East Asian Studies.

Asher, M.G., S. Rolt, M. Ariff and M.H. Khan (1992), *Fiscal Incentives and Economic Management in Indonesia*, Malaysia and Singapore: Asian-Pacific Tax and Investment Research Centre.

Asian Development Bank (1995), *Asian Development Outlook*, Manila: Asian Development Bank.

Asian Development Bank (1996a), *Asian Development Outlook*, Oxford: Oxford University Press.

Asian Development Bank (1996b), *Critical Issues in Asian Development – Theories Experiences, Policies*, Oxford: Oxford University Press.

Asian Development Bank (1997a), *Asian Development Outlook*, Oxford: Oxford University Press.

Asian Development Bank (1997b), *Key Indicators of Developing Asian and Pacific Countries*, Manila: Asian Development Bank.

Asian Development Bank (1997c), *Emerging Asia: Changes and Challenges*, Manila: Asian Development Bank.

Asian Development Bank (1997d), *Annual Report*, Manila: Asian Development Bank.

Asian Development Bank (1998a), *Asian Development Outlook*, Manila: Asian Development Bank.

Asian Development Bank (1998b), *Report of the Working Group on Strengthening International Financial Systems*, Manila: Asian Development Bank.

Asian Development Bank (1999), *Annual Report*, Manila: Asian Development Bank.

Asiaweek (1998–99), Hong Kong, various issues.

Athukorala, P. and S. Jayasuriya (1993), *Crises, Adjustment and Growth: Macroeconomic Policies in Post-Independence Sri Lanka*, New York: Oxford University Press for the World Bank.

Australian Government (1992), *Australia and the Multilateral Development Banks*, Canberra, Australia: Australian Government Publishing Service.

Bangko Sentral Ng Pilipinas (1996a), *1996 Year-End Report*, the Philippines: Bangko Sentral Ng Pilipinas.

Bangko Sentral Ng Pilipinas (1996b), *Report on Economic and Financial Development, Fourth Quarter 1996*, the Philippines: Bangko Sentral Ng Pilipinas.

Bangkok Bank Public Company Limited, *Monthly Review*, various issues.

Bank of International Settlements, *Annual Reports*, various years.

Bank of Korea, *Annual Reports*, various years.

Bank Negara Malaysia (1994a), *Money and Banking in Malaysia*, Kuala Lumpur: Government Printing Office.

Bank Negara Malaysia (1994b), *The Structure of Financial Institutions*, Kuala Lumpur: Government Printing Office.

Bank Negara Malaysia releases on the Internet (www.bnm.gov.my).

Bank of Thailand (1992), *50 Years of Bank of Thailand: 1942–1992*, Bangkok: Bank of Thailand.

Bank of Thailand (1995), *Financial Institutions and Market in Thailand*, Bangkok: Economic Research Department, Bank of Thailand.

Bank of Thailand, *Quarterly Review*, various issues.

BankWatch releases on the Internet (www.bankWatch.com).

Bell, Michael W., Hoe Ee Khor and Kalpana Kochhar (1993), 'China at the Threshold of a Market Economy', *IMF Occasional Paper No. 107*, Washington, DC: International Monetary Fund.

Bendix, P.J. (1987), *The United Kingdom's Development Cooperation Policy*, Berlin, Germany: German Development Institute.

Berg, R.J. and D.F. Gordon (eds) (1989), *Cooperation for International Development: The United States and the Third World in the 1990s*, Boulder, CO and London: Lynne Rienner Publishing.

Bergdtern, C.F. and M. Noland (eds) (1993) *Pacific Dynamism and the International Economic System*, Washington, DC: Institute of International Economics.

Berger, Allen N., W.C. Hunter and S.G. Timme (1993), 'The Efficiency of Financial Institutions', *Journal of Banking and Finance*, **17** (3), 222–49.

Berlage, L. and O. Stokke, (1992), *Evaluating Development Assistance: Approaches and Methods*, London: Frank Cass.

Bernanke, B. (1973), 'Non-Monetary Effects of the Banking Crisis in the Propagation of the Great Depression', *American Economic Review*, **73** (1), 57–276.

Bhagwati, J. and Richard Eckaus (1970), *Foreign Aid: Selected Readings*, Harmondsworth, UK: Penguin Books.

Bhagwati, J.N. (1970), Economic Criteria for Foreign Aid for Economic Development', in Bhagwati and Eckaus (1970).

Bhagwati, Jagdish (1998), 'The Capital Myth: The Difference Between Trade in Widgets and Dollars', *Foreign Affairs*, **77** (3), 7–12.

Bordo, Michael D. and Ehsan U. Choudhri (1982), 'Currency Substitution and the Demand for Money: Some Evidence for Canada', *Journal of Money, Credit and Banking*, **14**, 48–57.

Bordo, M. and Anna Schwartz (1998), 'Under What Circumstances, Past and Present, Have International Rescues of Countries in Financial Distress Been Successful?', *NBER Working Paper No. 6824*, December.

Bose, A. and P. Burnell (eds) (1991), *Britain's Overseas Aid Since 1979*, Manchester, UK: Manchester University Press.

Bowles, Paul and Gordon White (1993), *The Political Economy of China's Financial Reforms: Finance in Late Development*, Boulder, CO: Westview Press.

Boyce, James and Lyuba Zarsky (1988), 'Capital Flight from the Philippines, 1962–1986', *Journal of Philippine Development*, **15**, 191–222.

Brinkerhoff, D.W. (1991), *Improving Development Program Performance: Guidelines for Managers*, Boulder, CO: Lynne Rienner Publishers.

Campos, E.J. and H.L. Root (1996), *The Key to the Asian Miracle: Making Shared Growth Credible*, Washington, DC: Brookings Institution.

Caprio, A. (1997), *Repairing Financial System: Historical Implications for Policy*, Cambridge University Press.

Caprio, G. (1997), 'Safe and Sound Banking in Developing Countries: We're Not in Kansas Anymore', *Policy Research Working Paper 1739*, Washington, DC: World Bank.

Caprio, Gerard Jr and Dimitri Vittas (eds) (1997), *Reforming Financial Systems: Historical Implications for Policy*, Cambridge, New York and Melbourne: Cambridge University Press.

Cassen, R. (1994), *Does Aid Work?*, New York: Oxford University Press.

Central Bank of China, *Financial Statistics*, various years, Taiwan District, Republic of China, Taipei, Taiwan.

Central Bank of Sri Lanka (1998), *Annual Report*, Colombo: Government Publication Unit.

Centre for Policy Dialogue (1996), *Growth or Stagnation?*, Dhaka, Bangladesh: University Press.

Chai, Joseph C.H. (1994), 'Transition to Market Economy: The Chinese Experience', *Communist Economies and Economic Transformation*, **6** (2), 231–45.

Chan, Roger C.K. (1998), 'The Prospects of the Special Economic Zones Policy' in Joseph Y.S. Cheng (ed.), *China in Post-Deng Era*, Hong Kong: The Chinese University Press, pp. 425–51.

Chandavakar, A. (1977), 'Monetization of Developing Economies', *IMF Staff Papers*, **24** (3), 665–721.

Chawla, A.S., K.K. Uppal and Keshav Malhotra (1988), *Indian Banking Towards 21st Century*, New Delhi: Deep & Deep Publishing.

Chee, P.L. (1993), 'Flows of Private International Capital in the Asia and the Pacific Region', *Asian Development Review*, **11** (2), 104–39.

Cheng, F. (1984), 'The Structure of Banking Industry in Singapore', unpublished mimeo, Manchester: Centre for Business Research.

Cheng, Hang-Sheng (1986), 'Financial Policy and Reform in Taiwan, China', in Hang-Sheng Cheng (ed.), *Financial Policy and Reform in Pacific Basin Countries*, Lexington, MA: Lexington Books, pp. 143–59.

Chhipa, M.L. (1987), *Commercial Banking Development in India*, Delhi, India: Printwell Publishing.

China Statistical Yearbook, 1993, State Statistical Bureau of the People's Republic of China, Hong Kong.

Cho, Y.J. (1989), 'Finance and Development: The Korean Approach', *Oxford Review of Economic Policy*, **5** (4), 88–102.

Choksi, A.M. and D. Papageorgiou (eds) (1986), *Economic Liberalization in Developing Countries*, Oxford: Basil Blackwell.

Chow, Gregory C. (1987), *The Chinese Economy*, Singapore: World Scientific.

Chow, Kit Boey, Chew Moh Leen and Elizabeth Su (1989), *One Partnership in Development: UNDP and Singapore*, Singapore: United Nations Association of Singapore.

Christensen, Scott R., David Dollar, Ammar Siamwalla and Pakorn Vichyanond (1997), 'Thailand: The Institutional and Political Underpinnings of Growth', in Danny M. Leipziger (ed.), *Lessons from East Asia*, Ann Arbor: The University of Michigan Press, pp. 345–85.

Clarke, R. (1996), 'Equilibrium Interest Rates and Financial Liberalization in Developing Countries', *The Journal of Development Studies*, **32** (3), 391–413.

Coats, W.L. Jr and D.R. Khatkhate (1983), *Money and Monetary Policy in Less Developed Countries*, Oxford, UK: Pergamon Press.

Cole, David C. (1998), 'Financial Development in Asia: Asia Pacific', *Economic Literature*, **2** (2), 26–47.

Cole, David C. and Yung Chul Park (1983), *Financial Development in Korea, 1945–78*, Cambridge, MA: Harvard University Press.

Cole, David C. and Betty F. Slade (1995), 'Money Markets in Indonesia', in David C. Cole, Hal S. Scott and Philip A. Wellons (eds), *Asian Money Markets*, New York and Oxford: Oxford University Press.

Cole, David C. and Betty F. Slade (1996), *Building a Modern Financial System; The Indonesian Experience* (Trade and Development Series), Cambridge, New York and Melbourne: Cambridge University Press.

Cole, D. and B. Slade (1999), 'The Crisis and Financial Sector Reform', in H. Arndt and H. Hall (eds), *Southeast Asia's Economic Crisis: Origins, Lessons, and the Way Forward*, (Current Economic Affairs Series), Singapore: Institute of Southeast Asian Studies, p. 182.

Cole, David C., Hal S. Scott and Philip A. Wellons (eds) (1995), *Asian Money Markets*, New York and Oxford: Oxford University Press.

Collier, P. and C. Mayer (1980), 'The Assessment: Financial Liberalization, Financial Systems and Economic Growth, *Oxford Review of Economic Policy*, **5** (4), 1–12.

Cuddington, J.T. (1986), 'Capital Flight: Issues, Estimates and Explanations', *Princeton Studies in International Finance*, **58**, December, Princeton: Princeton University Press.

DBS Bank (1991), 'Financial Development in Thailand: Implications for Foreign Financial Institutions', *ASEAN Briefing No. 23*, Singapore: Economic Research Department, DBS Bank, November.

DBS Bank (1996), 'Outlook for the Thai Baht and Philippine Peso and their Economic Implications', *ASEAN/Singapore Briefing No. 16*, Singapore: Economic Research Department, DBS Bank, July.

Delhaise P.F. (1998), *Asia in Crisis: The Implosion of the Banking and Finance Systems*, Singapore: John Wiley & Sons (Asia) International.

de Melo, J. and J. Tybout (1986), 'The Effects of Financial Liberalization on Savings and Investment in Uruguay', *Economic Development and Cultural Change*, **34**, April, 561–87.

Demetriades, P.O. and K.A. Hussein (1996), 'Does Financial Development Cause Economic Growth? Time Series Evidence From 16 Countries', *Journal of Development Economics*, **51**, December, 387–411.

Department of Foreign Affairs, Australia (1998), *The Philippines: Beyond the Crisis, 1998*, Canberra: East Asia Analytical Unit, Ministry of Foreign Affairs and Trade.

Department of Statistics, *TRENDS Database, 1996*, Singapore.

Deyo, F. (1987), *The Political Economy of the New Asian Industrialism*, Ithaca, New York: Cornell University Press.

Dipchand, Cecil R., Zhang Yichun and Ma Mingjia (1994), *The Chinese Financial System*, Westport, CT: Greenwood Press.

Dodworth, John R., Erich Spitaller, Michael Braulke, Keon Hyok Lee, Kenneth Miranda, Chistian Mulder, Hisanobu Shishido and Krishna Srinivasan (1996), 'Vietnam: Transition to a Market Economy', *IMF Occasional Paper No. 135*, Washington, DC: International Monetary Fund.

Doner, R. (1992), 'The Limits of State Strength: Towards an Institutional View of Economic Development', *World Politics*, **44** (3), 398–431.

Easson, A.J. and Li Jinyan (1989), *Taxation of Foreign Investment in the People's Republic of China*, Netherlands: Kluwer Law and Taxation Publishers.

Economist Intelligence Unit (1995), 'China', *EIU Country Profile 1994–95*, pp. 11–47.

Economist Intelligence Unit, *Country Report* for various countries.

Edwards, S. (1984a), 'The Demand for International Reserves and Monetary Equilibrium: Some Evidence from Developing Countries', *Review of Economics and Statistics*, **66** (3), 495–500.

Edwards, S. (1984b), 'Financial System: the Structuralists, and Stabilisation Policy in Semi-Industrialised Economies', *Journal of Development Economics*, **14** (3), 35–53.

Edwards, S. (1984c), 'The Order of Liberalization of the Current and Capital Accounts of the Balance of Payments', NBER Working Paper No. 1507.

Edwards, S. (1986), 'Terms of Trade, Exchange Rates and Labor Markets Adjustment in Developing Countries', University of California at Los Angeles Department of Economics Working Paper No. 425, December, p. 49.

Edwards, S. (1987), 'Sequencing Economic Liberalization in Developing Countries', *Finance and Development*, **24** (1), 26–9.

Edwards, S. (1994), *The Order of Liberalization of the External Sector in Developing Countries. Essays in International Finance 156*, Princeton, NJ: Princeton University Press.

Edwards, M. and D. Hulme (eds) (1992), *Making a Difference: NGOs and Development in a Changing World*, London: Earthscan Publications.

Edwards, S. and M.S. Khan (1985), 'Interest Rate Determination in Developing Countries', *IMF Staff Paper*, Washington, DC: IMF, pp. 377–403.

Eichengreen, Barry (1998), *Globalizing Capital: A History of International Capital*, Princeton, NJ: Princeton University Press.

Eichengreen, Barry and Tamim Bayoumi (1997), 'Is Asia an Optimal Currency Area? Can it Become One? Regional and Historical Perspectives on Asian Monetary Relations', mimeo presented for the CEPII/AMUE/KDI conference on exchange arrangements for East Asian countries.

Eichengreen, B. and Andrew Rose (1997), 'Staying Afloat When the Wind Shifts: External Factors and Emerging-Market Banking Crises', paper presented at the ANU–Monash Asia Institute Conference, December 1998, Melbourne, Australia.

Emery, Robert F. (1970), *The Financial Institutions of Southeast Asia*, New York: Praeger.

Emery, Robert F. (1991), *The Money Markets of Developing East Asia*, New York: Praeger.

ESCAP (1995), 'Macroeconomic Reforms in the Economies in Transition', *United Nations Development Paper No. 18*, New York: UN.

Euromoney Books (1996), *Thailand: Reaping the Rewards of Growth*, London: Euromoney Publications.

Feinberg, R. and R. Avakov (1991), *From Confrontation to Co-operation*, Baltimore, MD: Transaction Publications.

Fforde, Adam and Stefan de Vylder (1996), *From Plan to Market: The Economic Transition in Vietnam*, Boulder, CO: Westview Press.

Fisher, I. (1930), *Theory of Interest*, New York: Macmillan.

'Financial turmoil hits Taiwan', *Lateline News*, 12 February 1999.

Folkerts-Landau, D. et al. (1997), 'Effect of Capital Flows on the Domestic Financial Sectors in APEC Developing Countries', in M. Khan and C. Reinhart (eds), *Capital Flows in the APEC Region, IMF Occasional Paper 122*, Washington, DC: International Monetary Fund.

Frenkel, J.A. (1982), 'Aspects of the Optimal Management of Exchange Rates', *Journal of International Economics*, **13** (31–4), 231–57.

Frenkel, J.A. (1983), 'Monetary Policy: Domestic and International Constraints', *The American Economic Review*, **73** (2), 48–54.

Friedman, M. (1958), 'Foreign Economic Aid: Means and Objectives', *Yale Review*, **47**, June, 500–517.

Friedman, J. (1980), *Oligopoly and the Theory of Games*, Amsterdam: North-Holland.

Fry, M.J. (1978), 'Money and Capital or Financial Deepening in Economic Development?', *Journal of Money, Credit and Banking*, **10** (4), 464–75.

Fry, M.J. (1980), 'Saving, Investment and Growth and the Cost of Financial Repression', *World Development*, **8** (4), 317–27.

Fry, M.J. (1988), *Money, Interest, and Banking in Economic Development*, Baltimore: Johns Hopkins University Press.

Fry, M.J. (1989), 'Financial Development: Theories and Recent Experience', *Oxford Review of Economic Policy*, **5** (4), 13–28.

Fry, M.J. (1995), *Money, Interest and Banking in Economic Development*, Baltimore, MD: Johns Hopkins University Press.

Fry, M.J. (1997), 'In Favour of Financial Liberalization', *The Economic Journal*, **107** (442), 754–71.

Fukasaku, Keiichiro (1995), *Regional Co-Operation and Integration in Asia*, Paris: OECD.

Fukusaka, K. and D. Wall (eds) (1994), 'China's Long March to an Open Economy', *OECD Development Centre Studies*, Paris: OECD.

Galang, Jose (1996), *Philippines: The Next Asian Tiger*, Los Angeles: Euromoney Publications.

Ganzoneri, M., W. Ethier and V. Grilli (eds) (1996), *The New Transatlantic Economy*, New York: Cambridge University Press.

Gibson, H.D. and E. Tsakalotos (1994), 'The Scope and Limits of Financial Liberalization in Developing Countries: A Critical Survey', *Journal of Development Studies*, **3** (3), 578–628.

Giovanni, A. (1983), 'The Interest Elasticity of Savings in Developing Countries: The Existing Evidence', *World Development*, **11** (7), 601–7.

Giovanni, A. (1985), 'Savings and the Real Interest Rate in LDCs', *Journal of Development Economics*, **18**, August, 197–217.

Goldie-Scott, Duncan (1995), 'China's Financial Markets', *Financial Times*, London: Financial Times Publishing.

Goldsmith, R.W. (1969), *Financial Structure and Development*, New Haven, CT: Yale University Press.

Goldsmith, R.W. (1978), *The Financial Development of India, 1860–1977*, New Haven, CT: Yale University Press.

Goldstein, M., D. Folkerts-Landau et al. (1992), 'International Capital Markets: Developments, Prospects and Policy Issues', *World Economic and Financial Surveys*, Washington, DC: International Monetary Fund.

Gonzales, A. and M. Gerado (1988), 'Interest Rates, Savings and Growth in Developing LDCs: An Assessment of Recent Empirical Research', *World Development*, **16** (5), 589–605.

Gonzalez, Joaquin L. (1996), 'An Analysis of the Relative Size and Magnitude of Foreign Development Assistance to Southeast Asia', *Pacific Focus*, **11** (2), 79–93.

Government Finance Statistics Yearbook, 1985–1996, Washington, DC: IMF.

Government of India (1991), *Report of the Committee on the Financial Systems*, New Delhi: Government Printing Office.

Government of Pakistan (1991), *Economic Reforms (November 1990–May 1991)*, Islamabad: Ministry of Finance and Economic Affairs.

Government of Pakistan, *Economic Survey*, Islamabad: Ministry of Planning, various issues.

Grenville, S.A. (1998), 'The Asia Crisis, Capital Flows and the International Financial Architecture', Reserve Bank of Australia, June (www.rba.gov.au).

Greenwood, John G. (1988), 'Monetary Policy in Thailand', in Hang-Sheng Cheng (ed.), *Monetary Policy in Pacific Basin Countries*, Boston, MA: Kluwer Academic Publishers, pp. 303–19.

Gupta, K.L. (1984), *Finance and Economic Growth in Developing Countries*, London: Croom Helm.

Hanna, D.P. (1994), 'Indonesian Experience with Financial Sector Reform', *World Bank Discussion Paper*, Washington, DC: World Bank.

Hanson, J.A. and Craig R. Neal (1986), 'Interest Policies in Selected Developing Countries, 1970–1982', *World Bank Staff Working Paper 753*, Washington, DC: World Bank.

Haq, Inam-ul (1990), 'The Role of Non-Bank Financial Institutions in Pakistan', in Anjum Nasim (ed.), *Financing Pakistan's Development in the 1990s*, Oxford: Oxford University Press, pp. 419–30.

Haque, Nadeem Ul and Shahid Kardar (1995), 'Development of the Financial Section in Pakistan', in Shahid N. Zahid (ed.), *Financial Sector Development in Asia*, Manila: Asian Development Bank.

Harding, Harry (1987), 'The Legacy of Mao Zedong', in *China's Second Revolution: Reform After Mao*, Washington, DC: Brookings Institution, pp. 11–39.

Hardy D. and C. Pazarbasiolu (1998), 'Leading Indicators of Banking Crises: Was Asia Different?', *IMF Working Papers*, Washington, DC: International Monetary Fund.

Hasan, M. Aynul, Ashfaque H. Khan and S. Sajid Ali (1996), 'Financial Sector Reform and its Impact on Investment and Economic Growth: An Econometric Approach', *The Pakistan Development Review*, **35** (4), 885–95.

Hatch, Walter and Koza Yamamura (1996), *Asia in Japan's Embrace*, New York: Cambridge University Press.

Hawes, Gary (1992), 'Marcos, His Cronies, and the Philippines' Failure to Develop', in John Ravenhill (ed.), *The Political Economy of East Asia 3: Singapore, Indonesia, Malaysia, the Philippines and Thailand Vol. II*, Aldershot, UK and Brookfield, US: Edward Elgar, pp. 275–93.

Hellmann, D.C. and K.B. Pyle (eds) (1997), *From APEC to Xanadu: Creating a Viable Community in the Post-Cold War Pacific*, New York: M.E. Sharpe.

Hinds, M. (1988), 'Economic Effects of Financial Crises', *Working Paper Series No. 104*, Washington, DC: World Bank.

Ho, Lok-Sang (1998), 'China's Road to Exchange Rate Liberalization' in Joseph Y.S. Cheng (ed.), *China in Post-Deng Era*, Hong Kong: The Chinese University Press, pp. 453–70.

Hu, Zuliu and Mohsin S. Khan (1997), 'Why China is Growing So Fast', *International Monetary Fund Economic Issues No. 8*, Washington, DC: International Monetary Fund.

Huang, Guobo (1998), 'Banking Reforms in China', in Joseph Y.S. Cheng (ed.), *China in Post-Deng Era*, Hong Kong: The Chinese University Press, pp. 328–61.

Hutchcroft, Paul D. (1991), 'Oligarch and Cronies in the Philippine State: The Politics of Patrimonial Plunder', in John Ravenhill (ed.), *The Political Economy of East Asia 3: Singapore, Indonesia, Malaysia, the Philippines and Thailand Vol. II*, Aldershot, UK and Brookfield, US: Edward Elgar, pp. 238–74.

Ichimura, Shinichi, W. James and E. Ramsetter (1998), 'The Financial Crisis in East Asia', *The Asia Pacific Journal of Economics and Business*, **2** (1), 3–33.

IFC Emerging Stock Markets Fact Book, Washington, DC: IFC and the World Bank (annual), various issues.

IMF, *Government Financial Statistics*, various issues, Washington, DC: IMF.

IMF, *Government Financial Statistics Yearbook, 1985–1998*, Washington, DC: IMF.

IMF, *International Financial Statistics (CD-ROM) 1996*, Washington, DC: IMF.

IMF, *International Financial Statistics*, various issues, Washington, DC: IMF.

Institute of International Trade under MOFTEC (1996), *Utilization of Japanese ODA: Present Situation and Risks, from Situation and Hot Spots (Essay Collection)*, Beijing: China Publishing House of Foreign Economic and Trade Relations.

Intal, Ponciano S. and Gilberto Llanto (1998), 'Improvement Management of the Financial Sector: A Case Study of the Philippines', paper presented at Seminar on Improved Management of the Financial Sector, organized by Economic and Social Commission for Asia and the Pacific (ESCAP), Bangkok, Thailand, May.

Islam, I. and A. Chowdhury (1997), *Asia-Pacific Economies: A Survey*, London and New York: Routledge.

Jansen, Karel (1990), *Finance, Growth and Stability: Financing Economic Development in Thailand, 1960–86*, Aldershot, UK: Avebury.

Jao, Y.C. (1976), 'Financial Deepening and Economic Growth: A Cross Section Analysis', *Malayan Economic Review*, **21** (1), 47–58.

Jayasuriya, S.K. (1987), 'The Politics of Economic Policy in the Philippines during the Marcos Era', in John Ravenhill (ed.), *The Political Economy of East Asia 3: Singapore, Indonesia, Malaysia, the Philippines and Thailand Vol. II*, Aldershot, UK and Brookfield, US: Edward Elgar, pp. 200–237.

Jayawardena, Lal, Anne Maasland and P.N. Radhakrishnan (1988), 'Sri Lanka', *Country Study No. 15, SAPP project*, Helsinki: WIDER.

Jitsuchon, Somchai and Chalangphob Sussangkarn (1993), 'Thailand', in Lance Taylor (ed.), *The Rocky Road to Reform: Adjustment, Income Distribution, and Growth in the Developing Countries*, Cambridge, MA: MIT Press, pp. 149–70.

Kahagalle, S. (1975), 'An Estimate of Savings and Its Determinants in the Sri Lanka Economy', *Staff Studies* [Central Bank of Ceylon], **5** (2), 34–76.

Kahler, M. (ed.) (1998), *Capital Flows and Financial Crisis*, Ithaca: Cornell University Press.

Kane, E. (ed.) (1999), 'Banking Crisis and Non-Performing Loans', mimeo presented at Monash University's Special Seminar at Caulfield, Victoria, in April 1999.

Karunaratne, S.A. and Carlos Fonseka (1993), 'Sri Lanka', in Lance Taylor (ed.), *Rocky Road to Reform: Adjustment, Income Distribution and Growth in the Developing Countries*, Cambridge, MA: MIT Press, pp. 193–212.

Kawagode, T. and Sueo Sekiguchi (1995), *East Asian Economies: Transformation and Challenges*, Centre for Asian and Pacific Studies, Seiko University, Singapore: Institute of Southeast Asian Studies.

Khalid, Ahmed M. (1994a), 'Monetary, Financial, and Fiscal Sector Developments in Vietnam', paper presented at the 3rd EMSE–CSTE workshop on Economic Management and Transition Towards a Market Economy, Singapore, 23–30 October.

Khalid, Ahmed M. (1994b), 'Investment Flows to Pakistan', *The Straits Times*, 4 March.

Khalid, Ahmed M. (1994c), 'Financial Programming for the Economy', The 20th SEANZA central banking course, Karachi, Pakistan, October–November, pp. 103–28.

Khalid, Ahmed M. (1999), 'Modelling Money Demand in Open Economies: The Case of Selected Asian Countries', *Applied Economics*, **31** (September), 1129–35.

Khalid, Ahmed M. and Habib Ahmed (1996), 'Anticipated, Unanticipated Money Growth and Aggregate Output: Evidence from Malaysia', *Malaysian Journal of Economic Studies*, **23** (2), 99–105.

Khalid, Ahmed M. and Tan Mui Ling (1997), 'Macroeconomic Effects of Financial Liberalization: Evidence from Selected Asian Economies', paper presented at 1997 conference of ESRC-sponsored Development Economics Study Group, University of Birmingham, UK, September.

Khalid, Ahmed M. and Inayat U. Mangla (1994), 'Monetary and Financial Sector Reforms During Transition Towards a Market Economy: The Vietnam Experience', in Anthony T.H. Chin and Ng Hock Guan (eds), *Economic Management and Transition Towards a Market Economy: An Asian Perspective*, Singapore: World Scientific, pp. 376–406.

Khan, M.S. and C.M. Reinhart (eds) (1995), 'Capital Flows in the APEC Region', *IMF Occasional Papers, 122*, Washington, DC: International Monetary Fund.

Khan, Mohammad Zubair (1996), 'Pakistan: Prospects for private capital flows and financial sector development', *The Pakistan Development Review*, **35** (4), 853–83.

Kharas, Homi J. (1997), 'The Philippines: Three Decades of Lost Opportunities', in Danny M. Leipziger (ed.), *Lessons from East Asia*, Ann Arbor: The University of Michigan Press, pp. 443–79.

Khatkhate, D.R. (1982), 'Anatomy of Financial Retardation in a LDC: The Case of Sri Lanka 1951–76', *World Development*, **10** (9), 829–40.

Khatkhate, D.R. (1988), 'Assessing The Impact of Interest Rates in Less Developed Countries', *World Development*, **16** (5), 577–88.

Kim, Eun Mee (1988), 'From Dominance to Symbiosis: State and Chaebol in Korea', *Pacific Focus*, **3** (2), 105–21.

Kim, Linsu (1997), 'The Dynamics of Samsung's Technological Learning in Semiconductors', *California Management Review*, **39** (3), 86–100.

Kindleberger, C. Manias (1996), *Panics and Crashes: A History of Financial Crisis*, New York: John Wiley and Sons, 3rd edn.

Kitagawa, H. (1995), 'Financial Liberalization in Asian Countries', in Toshi Hiko Kawagoe and Seeo Seki Guchi (eds), *East Asian Economies*, Singapore: Institute of South East Asian Studies, pp. 139–71.

Klein, Michael U. (1990), 'Commercial Banking in Pakistan', in Anjum Nasim (ed.), *Financing Pakistan's Development in the 1990s*, Oxford: Oxford University Press, pp. 387–413.

Kochhar, J. et al. (1996), 'Thailand: The Road to Sustained Growth', *IMF Occasional Paper No. 146*, Washington, DC: International Monetary Fund.

Korea Development Institute (1998), 'Structural Reforms and Economic Prospects', Seoul, Korea (www.mofe.go.kr).

Krause, L. (1998), *The Economics and Politics of the Asian Financial Crisis of 1997–8*, New York: Council of Foreign Relations.

Krueger, Anne O. (1992), 'Economic Policy Reforms in Developing Countries: The Kuznets Memorial Lectures at The Economic Growth Center', Yale University, Cambridge and Oxford: Blackwell, p. 184.

Krugman, P. (1979), 'A Model of Balance of Payments Crises', *Journal of Money, Credit and Banking*, **11** (3), 311–25.

Krugman, Paul (1994), 'The Myth of Asia's Miracle', *Foreign Affairs*, **73** (6), 3–12.

Krugman, Paul (1999), 'What Happened to Asia', in R. Sato, R.V. Ramachandran and K. Mino (eds), *Global Competition and Integration*, Boston, MA: Kluwer Academic Publishers, pp. 315–28.

Kuznets, Simon S. (1955), 'Economic Growth and Income Inequality', *American Economic Review*, **65**, 1–28.

Lal, Deepak (1992), 'In Praise of the Classics: The Relevance of Classical Political Economy for Development Policy and Research', University of California at Los Angeles Department of Economics Working Paper No. 679.

Lal, Deepak and H. Myint (1999), *The Political Economy, Poverty Equity and Growth: A Comparative Study*, Oxford: Clarendon Press, p. 458.

Lamberte, Mario B. (1993), 'Assessment of Financial Market Reforms in the Philippines, 1980–1992', *Journal of Philippine Development*, **20** (2), 231–59.

Lamberte, Mario B. (1995), 'Outlook for Philippines', paper presented at Workshop on Econometric Outlook for Singapore and the Region,

Econometric Studies Unit, National University of Singapore, Singapore, February.

Lamberte, Mario B. and Gilberto M. Lianto (1995), 'A Study of Financial Sector Policies: The Philippines Case', in S.N. Zahid (ed.), *Financial Sector Development in Asia*, Manila: Asian Development Bank, pp. 235–301.

Lauridsen, Laurids S. (1998), 'The Financial Crisis in Thailand: Causes, Conduct and Consequences', *World Development*, **26** (8), 1575–91.

Le Dang, Doanh and Adam McCarty (1995), 'Economic Reform in Vietnam: Achievements and Prospects', in Seiji Finch Naya and Joseph L.H. Tan (eds), *Asian Transitional Economies: Challenges and Prospects for Reform and Transformation*, Singapore: Institute of Southeast Asian Studies, pp. 99–153.

Lee, Sheng-Yi (1986), *The Monetary and Banking Development of Singapore and Malaysia*, Singapore: Singapore University Press, 2nd edn.

Lee, S.Y. and Y.C. Jao (1982), *Financial Structures and Monetary Policies in Southeast Asia*, New York: St Martin's Press.

Levine, R. (1996), 'Stock Markets: A Spur to Economic Growth', *Finance and Development*, **33** (1), 7–10.

Levine, R. (1997), 'Financial Development and Economic Growth', *Journal of Economic Literature*, **35** (2), 688–727.

Li, Lanqing (ed.) (1995), *Basic Knowledge on China's Utilization of Overseas Capital*, Beijing: China Publishing House of Foreign Economic and Trade Relations.

Lim, Joseph Y., Manuel F. Montes and Agnes R. Quisumbing (1992), 'The Philippines', in Lance Taylor (ed.), *The Rocky Road to Reform: Adjustment, Income Distribution, and Growth in the Developing Countries*, Cambridge, MA: MIT Press, pp. 245–66.

Lin, Cyril Zhiren (1989), 'Open-Ended Economic Reforms in China', in Victo Nee and David Stark (eds), *Remaking the Economic Institutions of Socialism: China and Eastern Europe*, Stanford, CA: Stanford University Press, pp. 95–136.

Lin, Zhaomu and Shao Ning (1995), *Trans-Century Development Thinking*, Beijing: China Planning Publishing House.

Lipworth, Gabrielle and Erich Spitaller (1993), 'Vietnam – Reform and Stabilization, 1986–92', *IMF Working Paper 93/46*, Washington, DC: International Monetary Fund.

MacCarthy, F.D. (1990), *Problems of Developing Countries in the 1990s*, Washington, DC: World Bank.

MacIntyre, A. (ed.) (1994), *Business and Government in Industrialising Asia*, Ithaca, NY: Cornell University Press.

Malaysia, Department of Statistics (1998), *Monthly Statistical Bulletin*.

Mangla, Inayat U. (1993), 'Market Oriented Financial Reforms and the Development of Money and Capital markets: The Case of the People's Republic of China', paper presented at the Second Annual International Conference on Comparative Economic Reform: China and Central/Eastern Europe, Shanghai, People's Republic of China, 24–9 May.

Martokoesoemo, S. (1994), 'Small Scale Finance: Lessons from Indonesia' in R. McLeod (ed.), *Indonesia Assessment 1994*, Canberra: Australian National University, pp. 292–313.

McIntaire, A. (1998), 'Political Institutions and the Economic Crisis in Thailand and Indonesia', in H. Arndt and H. Hall (eds), *Southeast Asia's Economic Crisis: Origins, Lessons, and the Way Forward*, (Current Economic Affairs Series), Singapore: Institute of Southeast Asian Studies.

McKinnon, R.I. (1973), *Money and Capital in Economic Development*, Washington, DC: Brookings Institution.

McKinnon, R.I. (1982), 'The Order of Economic Liberalization: Lessons from Chile and Argentina', in K. Brunner and A. Metzler (eds), *Economic Policy in a World of Change: Carnegie-Rochester Conference Series on Public Policy Vol. 17*, Amsterdam: North-Holland, pp. 159–86.

McKinnon, R.I. (1986), 'Issues and Perspectives: An Overview of Banking Regulation and Monetary Control', in A.H.H. Tan and B. Kapur (eds), *Pacific Growth and Financial Interdependence*, Sydney: Allen and Unwin Australia, pp. 319–36.

McKinnon, R.I. (1989), 'Financial Liberalization and Economic Development: A Reassessment of Interest-Rate Policies in Asia and Latin America', *Oxford Review of Economic Policy*, **5** (4), 29–54.

McKinnon, R.I. (1991a), 'Monetary Stabilization in LDCs', in Lawrence B. Krause and Kim Kihwan (eds), *Liberalization in the Process of Economic Development*, Berkeley and Los Angeles: University of California Press, pp. 366–400.

McKinnon, Ronald I. (1991b), *The Order of Economic Liberalization: Financial Control in the Transition to a Market Economy* (Johns Hopkins Studies in Development), Baltimore and London: John Hopkins University Press.

McKinnon, R.I. (1993), *The Order of Economic Liberalization: Financial Control in the Transition to a Market Economy*, Baltimore, MD: Johns Hopkins University Press, 2nd edn.

McKinnon, R.I. (1998), 'Exchange Rate Co-ordination for Surmounting the East Asian Currency Crisis', *The Asia Pacific Journal of Economics and Business*, **2** (1), 95–103.

McLeod, R. and R. Gamaut (eds) (1998), *East Asia in Crisis: From Being a Miracle to Needing One?*, London: Routledge.

McLindon, Michael P. (1996), *Privatization and Capital Market Development: Strategies to Promote Economic Growth*, Westport, CT and London: Praeger.

Meir, M.G. (1995), *Leading Issues in Economic Development*, New York: Oxford University Press, 6th edn.

Mijares, Roy (1995) 'The Financing of Infrastructure in Asia', *RIM: Pacific Business and Industries*, **1** (1), 27–39.

Milanovic, Branko (1989), *Liberalization and Entrepreneurship: Dynamics of Reform in Socialism and Capitalism*, Armonk, NY: M.E. Sharpe.

Mishkin, F. (1981) 'Monetary Policy and Long-term Interest Rates', *Journal of Monetary Economics*, **7** (1), 29–55.

Mohammed, Azizali F. (1992), 'Monetary Management in Pakistan', *The Pakistan Development Review*, 89–96.

Monetary Authority of Singapore, *Annual Reports*, various years.

Monetary Authority of Singapore, *Monthly Statistical Bulletin*, various issues.

Monetary Authority of Singapore (1989), *The Financial Structure of Singapore*.

Monetary Authority of Singapore, *Monthly Statistical Bulletin*, various years.

Monetary Authority of Singapore, website announcements on deregulations (www.mas.gov.sg).

Montes, Manuel F. (1996), 'Sustaining Growth in China and Vietnam: Macroeconomic Constraints', paper presented at the conference 'Financial Interdependence in East and Southeast Asia', Fifth East Asian Economic Association Meeting, Bangkok, 25–26 October.

Montes, M.F. (1998), *The Currency Crisis in Southeast Asia*, Singapore: Institute of Southeast Asian Studies.

Mosley, P. (1987), *Overseas Aid: Its Defence and Reform*, London: Wheatsheaf Books.

Nasution, Anwar (1983), *Financial Institutions and Policies in Indonesia*, Singapore: Institute of Southeast Asian Studies.

Newsweek, various articles on Asian financial crisis.

Ng, W.C. (1998), 'Monetary Management of Exchange Rates', speech to Association of Banks in Singapore and reported in the press.

Ng, B.K. (1995), 'Financial Reforms in the ASEAN Countries: Approach, Focus and Assessment', *Working Paper Series No. 10–95*, Singapore: Nanyang Technological University.

Nidhiprabha, Bhanupong (1997), 'Macroeconomic Policies and Thailand's Institutional Mechanism', in ESCAP, United Nations Special Issues on Institutional Structures, Policy Formulation and Implementation within Central Banks, Bangkok, Thailand.

OECD, *Development Co-operation Review*, Paris: OECD, various issues.

OECD (1988), *Principles for the Appraisal, Selection and Design of Development Projects as Agreed in the DAC of the OECD*, Paris: OECD.

Ohlin, G. (1956), 'The Evolution of Aid Doctrine', in *Foreign Aid Policies Reconsidered*, Paris: OECD.

Oi, Jean C. (1992), 'Fiscal Reform and the Economic Foundations of Local State Corporatism in China', *World Politics*, **45** (1), 99–126.

Pack, H. and J. Pack (1990), 'Is Foreign Aid Fungible? The Case of Indonesia', *The Economic Journal*, **100**, 188–99.

Panitchpakdi, Supachai (1985), *Financial Development in Thailand and Other Developing Countries*, Bangkok, Thailand: Marketing Media LP.

Park, Yoon S. (1983), 'Asian Money Markets', in Abraham M. George and Jan H. Giddy (eds), *International Finance Handbook*, New York: John Wiley and Sons, pp. 3–20.

People's Bank of China (1992), *Annual Report*.

People's Bank of China (1996), *China Financial Outlook*, China: China Financial Publishing House.

Phongpaichit, Pasuk (1992), 'The Open Economy and Its Friends: The "Development" of Thailand', in John Ravenhill (ed.), *The Political Economy of East Asia 3: Singapore, Indonesia, Malaysia, the Philippines and Thailand Vol. II*, Aldershot, UK and Brookfield, US: Edward Elgar, pp. 354–74.

Phongpaichit, Pasuk (1992), 'Technocrats, Businessmen, and Generals: Democracy and Economic Policy-Making in Thailand', in John Ravenhill (ed.), *The Political Economy of East Asia 3: Singapore, Indonesia, Malaysia, The Philippines and Thailand Vol. II*, Aldershot, UK and Brookfield, US: Edward Elgar, pp. 418–39.

Piggot, C. (1996), 'Emerging Markets Boost Ratings', *Euromoney*, March, 160–65.

Prybyla, Jan S. (1981), *The Chinese Economy: Problems and Policies*, Charlotesville, South Carolina: University of South Carolina Press.

Qureshi, Sarfraz Khan (1994), 'An overview of Pakistan's economy: Recent policy changes and future Prospects', 20th SEANZA central banking course, Karachi, Pakistan: State Bank of Pakistan.

Rachmann, G. (1991), 'Survey of Asian Finance: The Age of the Bond', *The Economist*, 12 November.

Radelet, S. and Jeffrey Sachs (1998), 'The East Asian Financial Crisis: Diagnostics, Remedies and Prospects', *Brookings Papers on Economic Activity*, **1**, 1–90.

Rajapatirana, S. (1988), 'Foreign Trade and Economic Development: Sri Lanka's Experience', *World Development*, **16** (10), 1143–57.

Rana, P. (1981), *ASEAN Exchange Rates: Policies and Trade Effects*, Singapore: Institute of Southeast Asian Studies.

Rao, B.V.V. (1995), 'Indian Economy: Past, Present and Future', in Banoji Rao and Yong Mun Chong (eds), *Singapore–India Relations: A Primer*, Singapore: Centre for Advanced Studies, National University of Singapore.

Reserve Bank of India, various publications.

Riedel, James (1993), 'Vietnam: On the Trail of the Tigers', *World Economy*, **16** (4), 401–22.

Rittenberg, L. (1991), 'Investment Spending and Interest Rate Policy: The Case of Financial Liberalization in Turkey', *Journal of Development Studies*, **27** (2), 151–67.

Robert, J. (1994), 'Vietnam: Open for Business', *Euro Asia Centre Research Series 32*, Fontainebleau: INSEAD Euro-Asia Centre.

Rodrigo, Francisco (1993), 'The Philippines', in Keith K.H. Park and Antoine van Agtmael (eds), *The World's Emerging Stock Markets: Structure, Developments, Regulations and Opportunities*, Singapore: Heinemann Asia, pp. 181–96.

Rondinelli, D.A. (1987), *Development Administration and the U.S. Foreign Aid Policy*, Boulder, CO: Lynne Rienner Publishing.

Root, H. (1996), *Small Countries Big Lesson: Governance and the Rise of East Asia*, Hong Kong: Oxford University Press.

Rose, Peter (1999), *Commercial Bank Management*, Chicago: Irwin–McGraw-Hill Books.

Rostow, W.W. (1960), *The Stages of Economic Growth: A Non-Communist Manifesto*, New York: Cambridge University Press.

Rowley, Anthony (1998), 'Lehman puts regional banks' problem loans at US$ 1.2t', *Business Times*, 19 October.

Rudner, Martin (1994), 'Canadian Development Cooperation with Asia', in Cranford Pratt (ed.), *Canadian International Development Assistance Policies: An Appraisal*, Montreal and Kingston: McGill-Queen's University Press, pp. 292–312.

Sachs, Jeffrey and Wing Thye Woo (1994), 'Experiences in the Transition to a Market Economy', *Journal of Comparative Economics*, **18**, pp. 271–75.

Sadoulet, E. and A. de Janvry (1995), *Quantitative Development Policy Analysis*, Baltimore, MD and London: Johns Hopkins University Press.

Sarkar, M.N. (1988), *Bank Nationalisation and Corporate Financing in India*, Delhi, India: Discovery Publishing House.

Sell, Friedrich L. (1988), '"True Exposure": The Analysis of Trade Liberalization in a General Equilibrium Framework', *Weltwirtschaftliches Archiv/Review of World Economics*, **124** (4), 635–52.

Shah, Salman (1990), 'Capital Market Development in Pakistan', in Anjum Nasim (ed.), *Pakistan in Financing Pakistan's Development in the 1990s*, Oxford: Oxford University Press, pp. 369–82.

Shanmuganathan, M. (1975), 'Incentives to Save: An Appraisal of their Effectiveness in Sri Lanka', *Economic Bulletin for Asia and the Pacific*, **26** (1), 153–69.

Shaw, E.S. (1973), *Financial Deepening in Economic Development*, New York: Oxford University Press.

Shea, Jia-Dong (1995), 'Financial Sector Development and Policies in Taipei, China', in Shahid N. Zahid (ed.), *Financial Sector Development in Asia*, Manila: Asian Development Bank, pp. 81–162.

Sheng, A. (1992), 'Bank Restructuring: Techniques and Experiences', mimeo, Washington, DC: World Bank.

Sheu, Y.D. (1998), 'Developing Taipei into a Regional Financial Centre', *Review of Pacific Basin Financial Markets and Policies*, **1** (1), 59–68.

Shirazi, Javad K. (1998), 'The East Asian Crisis: Origins, Policy Challenges and Prospects', paper to the East Asia in Crisis Conference, Seattle, 10 June.

Siew, Vincent C. (1998), 'Taiwan Weathers the Asian Financial Crisis', a paper to the 68th Conference of the International Law Association, Taipei, 29 May.

Skully, M. (ed.) (1984), *Financial Institutions and Markets in Southeast Asia*, London: Macmillan.

Sripana, Thanyathip (1992), 'Economic Development in Thailand and Indochinese Countries', in Tsutomu Murano and Ikuo Takeuchi (eds), *Indochina Economic Reconstruction and International Cooperation, Institute of Development Economics Symposium Proceedings No. 12*, Tokyo: Institute of Developing Economies. pp. 63–78.

State Bank of India, various publications.

State Bank of Pakistan, *Annual Report*, various issues.

State Bank of Vietnam, *Annual Report*, 1995.

State Planning Committee (1996), *Answers to 400 Questions on 9th 5-year Programme and 2010 long-term Target of National Economic and Social Development*, Beijing: Economy and Science Publishing House.

Stiglitz, J. (1989), 'Financial Markets and Development', *Oxford Review of Economic Policy*, **5** (4), 55–68.

Stokke, O. (ed.) (1991), *Evaluating Development Assistance: Policies and Performance*, London: Frank Cass.

Sundararajan, V. and T.J.T. Balino (1990), 'Issues in Recent Banking Crises in Developing Countries', *IMF Working Paper No. 19*, Washington, DC: International Monetary Fund.

Sundararajan, V. and R.J. Johnston (eds) (1988), *Sequencing Financial Sector Reform: Country Experiences and Issues*, IMF and the World Bank, Washington, DC.

Tang, Min (1996), 'Capital Flows to Developing Asia: Past Trends and Future Prospects', *Statistical Report Series*, Manila: Asian Development Bank.

Tan, Mya and Joseph L.H. Tan (eds) (1993), *Vietnam's Dilemmas and Options: The Challenges of Economic Transition in the 1990s*, Singapore: Institute of Southeast Asian Studies.

Thirwall, A.P. and N. Hussain (1982), 'The Balance of Payments Constraint, Capital Flows and Growth Rate Differences Between Developing Countries', *Oxford Economic Papers*, **34** (3), 498–510.

Thompson BankWatch (1997), 'Taiwan: asset quality of regional business banks', *Interdata Finance Asia Handbook 2*, p. 127.

Thornton, J. (1991), 'The Financial Repression Paradigm: A Survey of Empirical Research', *Savings and Development*, **15** (1), 5–17.

Thuyet, Pham van (1995), 'The Emerging Legal Framework for Private Sector Development in Vietnam's Transitional Economy', *Policy Research Working Paper No. 1486*, Washington, DC: Transition Economics Division, Policy Research Department, World Bank.

Thynne, I.S. and M. Ariff (eds) (1989), *Privatisation: Singapore's Experience in Perspective*, Singapore: Longman Professional Books.

Tisch, S.J. and M.B. Wallace (1994), *Dilemmas of Development Assistance*, Boulder, CO, San Francisco, CA and Oxford: Westview Press.

Tobin, J. (1965), 'Money and Economic Growth' *Econometrica*, **33**, 671–84.

Tseng, Wanda, Hoe Ee Khor, Kalpana Kochhr, Durbravko Mihalijek and David Burton (1994), 'Economic Reform in China: A New Phase', *IMF Occasional Paper No. 114*, Washington, DC: International Monetary Fund.

United Nations (1992), 'Thailand: Coping with the Strains of Success', *United Nations Industrial Development Organization, Industrial Development Review Series*, Oxford: Blackwell.

United Nations (1995), *World Development Report*, New York: United Nations.

United Nations (1996a) *Economic and Social Survey of Asia and the Pacific*, New York: United Nations.

United Nations (1996b), *World Development Report*, New York: United Nations.

United Nations (1997a), 'Financial Sector Reforms in Selected Asian Countries', *Economic and Social Commission for Asia and Pacific*, ESCAP/SPC Country Monograph series, Bangkok, Thailand.

United Nations (1997b), *Overcoming Institutional Constraints to Implementing Macroeconomic Policies*, New York: United Nations.

United Nations (1997c), *World Development Report*, New York: United Nations.

Vicente, B. and V.B. Valdepenas Jr (1994), *Structural Changes and Policy Issues in ASEAN Financial Markets*, Kuala Lumpur, Malaysia: Southeast Asian Central Banks Research and Training Centre.

Vicyanond, Pakorn (1995), 'Financial Sector Development in Thailand', in Shahid N. Zahid (ed.), *Financial Sector Development in Asia*, Hong Kong: Oxford University Press, pp. 303–70.

Villanueva, Delano and Abbas Mirakhor (1990), 'Strategies for Financial Reforms: Interest Rate, Policies, Stabilization, and Bank Supervision in Developing Countries', International Monetary Fund Staff Papers.

Wade, R. (1990), *Governing the Market, Economic Theory and the Role of the Government in East Asian Industrialisation*, Princeton, NJ: Princeton University Press.

Warman, F. and A.P. Thirwall (1994), 'Interest Rates, Saving, Investment and Growth in Mexico 1960–1990: Tests of the Financial Liberalization Hypothesis', *Journal of Development Studies*, **30** (3), 629–49.

Weijland, H.J.W. (1982), *Distributive Forces in Economic Development Process*, Amsterdam: VU Boekhandel/Uitgeverij.

White, L. (1995a), 'An Analytical Framework', in Shahid N. Zahid (ed.), *Financial Sector Development in Asia*, New York: Oxford University Press, pp. 3–35.

White, L. (1995b), 'Structure of Finance in Selected Asian Economies', in Shahid N. Zahid (ed.), *Financial Sector Development in Asia*, New York: Oxford University Press, pp. 37–122.

Wickramanayake, Jayasinghe (1995), 'Sri Lanka – Liberalised Economic Policy Regime: An Evaluation of the First Ten Years', Working Paper No. 95/3, Syme Department of Banking and Finance, Monash University.

Wong, Christine P.W. and Christopher Heady (1995), *Financial Management and Economic Reform in the People's Republic of China*, Oxford and New York: Oxford University Press and Asian Development Bank.

Woo, Tun-oy (1998), 'Foreign Trade and Investment Policies in the Post-Deng Era', in Joseph Y.S. Cheng (ed.), *China in the Post-Deng Era*, Hong Kong: The Chinese University Press, pp. 363–424.

Woo, Wing Pau (1996), 'Directed Credit and its Consequence in Indonesia', mimeo presented at the NUS seminar in Singapore.

World Bank (1989), *World Development Report*, Washington, DC: World Bank.

World Bank (1989), *India, An Industrialising Economy in Transition*, Washington, DC: World Bank.

World Bank (1990), *Financial Systems and Development*, Washington, DC: World Bank.

World Bank (1993), *The East Asian Miracle – Economic Growth and Public Policy*, Washington, DC: Oxford University Press.

World Bank (1993), *Vietnam: Transition to the Market*, Washington, DC: Country Operations Division, Department 1, East Asia and Pacific Region, World Bank.

World Bank (1995a), 'Vietnam: Poverty Assessment and Strategy', *Country Department I, East Asia and Pacific Region, Report No. 14645-VN*, Washington, DC: World Bank, January.

World Bank (1995b), 'Vietnam: Economic Report on Industrialization and Industrial Policy', *Country Department I, East Asia and Pacific Region, Report No. 14645-VN*, Washington, DC: World Bank, October.

World Bank (1995c), *The Emerging Asian Bond Market*, Washington, DC: World Bank.

World Bank (1995d), *Indonesia Country Report 1995*, Washington, DC: World Bank.

World Bank, *World Development Reports*, various years.

World Bank, *World Bank Databank*, Feb. 1997, May 1999.

World Bank (1998), *East Asia: the Road to Recovery*, Washington, DC: World Bank.

World Tables, 1994, Baltimore, MD: World Bank and Johns Hopkins University Press.

WTO (1995), *Regionalism and the World Trading System*, Geneva: World Trade Organization.

Yap, J. (1990), 'Central Bank Policies and the Behavior of the Money Market: The Case Study of the Philippines', *Working Paper Series 90–34*, the Philippines: Philippine Institute for Development Studies.

Zaidi, S. Akbar (1997), 'Debt retirement Programme: its Back-up Needs', *Dawn*, the Internet edition, 17 March.

Index